Praise for the First Edition

"What's significant about this book is that the examples are nontrivial. It's clear that much effort went into thinking out useful designs that both demonstrate the technologies and leave the reader with a practical starting point for professional development ... the book is full of pragmatic solutions ... the very kind you need to address in production and can't typically find answers for anywhere. I recommend this book to any serious Swing developer. If you're a Swing beginner, you'll get something out of this book, thanks to its frank, no-nonsense approach to teaching Swing development. What impressed me most was the focus on developing comprehensive examples... All in all, this is a real value for any Swing developer."

–Claude Duguay
JavaZone

"UI development is a very time consuming business. Even with such a powerful next generation API at your fingertips it can be still overwhelming. *Swing* is a wonderful book that lightens the burden. It presents a complex subject in smaller manageable portions for the programmer who has learnt the basics and wants to go much further. This excellent book is impossible to take in at the first reading, because of the scope and breadth of its subject matter. I think you will find that it hits its target audience and goals repeatedly. A massive quality and quantity win for the publisher, Manning."

–Peter Pilgrim
C Vu Journal

"How many times have you opened a book in search of a solution and found not only an answer, but also an elegant enhancement to your application? How many times have you ignored an O'Reilly book on the same subject lying on your table? The answer is Manning's new book *Swing* authored by Matthew Robinson and Pavel Vorobiev. And that is my final answer."

–Jayakrishnan
Slashdot

"An excellent resource for the developer of mid-level and advanced Swing applications. Many of the techniques I've had to investigate and develop over the last two years are described in this text. One of the few books to address the needs of serious Java 2 apps (e.g. printing, tables, trees, threads and Swing). Especially useful are the real-world NOTES and WARNINGs describing issues and anomalies."

–Christian Forster
Amazon

Swing

SECOND EDITION

MATTHEW ROBINSON
PAVEL VOROBIEV

UI Guidelines by David Anderson
Code Notes by David Karr

MANNING

Greenwich
(74° w. long.)

For online information and ordering of this and other Manning books, visit
http://www.manning.com. The publisher offers discounts on this book
when ordered in quantity. For more information, please contact:

Special Sales Department
Manning Publications Co.
209 Bruce Park Avenue   Fax: (203) 661-9018
Greenwich, CT 06830   email: orders@manning.com

Manning Publications Co.   Copyeditor: Elizabeth Martin
209 Bruce Park Avenue   Typesetter: Aleksandra Sikora
Greenwich, CT 06830   Cover designer: Leslie Haimes

ISBN 1930110-88-X
Printed in the United States of America
1 2 3 4 5 6 7 8 9 10 – VHG – 07 06 05 04 03

To Deirdre—
Matt

To my wife, Maria—
Pavel

brief contents

contents

foreword

It's been amazing to see the applications that have been built using Swing. It is an extraordinarily sophisticated user interface toolkit that gives great power to developers. This power leads to the biggest problem with Swing: the wide variety of facilities can be intimidating. One's first contact with the Swing APIs can be a little like sticking your head into the cockpit of a 747: a dizzying array of levers and dials that can be confusing. But there is a logic to it all. Once you know the territory, it's easy to get around and the available facilities will make your job much easier.

The authors of this book have done a great job mapping out the territory and explaining the standard patterns that make Swing great. I love the way they have gone beyond just laying out the APIs to covering issues about what makes a good user interface, and what makes an application easy to understand and use. They also go beyond the usual snippets of code to develop complete applications. This is a great way to inter-relate all of the parts of the Swing API.

JAMES GOSLING
Vice President and Fellow
Sun Microsystems

preface

This book is best described as a programmer's guide, serving both as a reference and a tutorial. Emphasis is placed on using Swing to solve a broad selection of realistic and creative problems. We assume an intermediate knowledge of Java, including the basics of putting together an AWT-based GUI, how the event model works, and familiarity with anonymous and explicit inner classes. Those who do not have this background can pick it up in any beginner book on AWT or Swing. However, the first edition of this book has proven to be most useful to those who come to it with an intermediate understanding of Swing. For this reason we do not recommend this book to Swing beginners. For beginners we suggest Manning's own *Up to Speed with Swing* by Steven Gutz.

Our goal was to produce a book that contains enough explanation and examples to satisfy the most demanding Swing developer. We feel we have accomplished this goal again with the updates in this edition, but please judge for yourself and we welcome all constructive feedback. Unlike the first edition, however, this version is not freely available on the publisher's web site. The first edition will remain available online at www.manning.com/sbe, but we hope that we have developed enough of a following to generate more sales with the second edition without giving it away for free. Let's hope this is true!

What's changed since the first edition?

Java 1.4 (aka Merlin) is the first major release of the Java platform that was planned through a Java Community Process (JCP), allowing participants outside of Sun to have an influence on the overall feature set. Each new feature, whether an addition or a change, had a dedicated expert group which handled the description of that functionality according to certain rules underlying Java Specification Requests (JSRs), which are the building blocks of any JCP. Similar to an open-source project, but with actual development still done by Sun engineers, this process allowed Java 1.4 to evolve for the first time in a democratic fashion. The result is a platform containing improvements that the Java community as a whole voted for, not just Sun.

This updated edition of *Swing* contains many new examples, revised text, and additional material to bring the book up to date with Java 1.4. This includes complete coverage of the new JSpinner and JFormattedTextField components, the new focus and keyboard architectures, scrollable tabbed panes, indeterminate progress bars, variable height JTable rows, and many other new features. Larger changes to the book include the addition of three new chapters: "Constructing an HTML Editor Applications," "Constructing an XML Editor," and "Drag and

Drop" with Swing. A new appendix on Java Web Start has also been added and all examples throughout the book have been enhanced to conform to the Java look and feel design guidelines.

Organization

In general, each chapter starts with class and interface explanations occasionally interspersed with small examples to demonstrate key features. The bulk of each chapter is then devoted to the construction of several larger examples, often building on top of previous examples, illustrating more complex aspects of the components under investigation.

Part I contains two chapters that introduce Swing and discuss the most significant mechanisms underlying it. The first chapter is a brief overview that we suggest for all Swing newcomers. More experienced developers will want to read straight through most of chapter 2, as it provides an understanding of Swing's most significant underlying behavior. This chapter is referenced throughout the book, and we expect all readers to refer to it often. At minimum we recommend that all readers skim this chapter to at least get a rough idea of what is covered.

Part II consists of twelve chapters covering all the basic Swing components with detailed descriptions and helpful examples of each. These chapters discuss the bread and butter of Swing-based GUIs, and each includes usage guidelines written by a usability and interface design expert.

Part III contains seven chapters dealing with the more advanced components. These chapters are significantly more complex than those in part II, and they require a thorough understanding of Swing's architecture, as well as the basic Swing components.

Part IV consists of three chapters on special topics with a focus on Swing, including printing, constructing an XML editor application, and implementing Drag and Drop.

Most examples are presented in three distinct parts:

The code: After a general introduction to the example, including one or more screenshots, the underlying code is listed. Annotations appear to the right of significant blocks of code to provide a brief summary of its purpose. Each annotation has a number which links it to the explanation of that code in the *Understanding the code* section.

Understanding the code: This section contains a detailed explanation of the code. Most paragraphs are accompanied by a number which links that text with the associated annotated code listed in the code section.

Running the code: After the code is explained, this brief section provides suggestions for testing the program. This section may also include references and suggestions for taking the example further.

Conventions

NOTE   Throughout the book we point out specific behaviors or functionality that either differs from what is expected or that can be achieved through alternate techniques. We also use this icon to denote various other types of notes, such as a reference or suggested background knowledge for the material being discussed.

JAVA 1.3   We use this mark wherever a new feature or update is introduced from Java 1.3.

JAVA 1.4   We use this mark wherever a new feature or update is introduced from Java 1.4.

BUG ALERT   Occasionally, incorrect or unexpected behavior is caused by known Swing bugs. We do not attempt to hide or gloss over these; rather, we explicitly discuss these bugs and explain possible workarounds or fixes where applicable.

UI GUIDELINE David Anderson, a usability and interface design expert, has provided detailed usage guidelines throughout the book. These guidelines do not represent hard-and-fast rules, but they are highly recommended for the development of consistent, user-friendly interfaces (see appendix B for David's references and recommended UI design readings).

All source code appears in Courier font. For example:

```
public void main( String args[] ) {
    Example myExample = new Example();
}
```

We prefix all instance variables with "m_," and capitalize all static variables with underscores separating compound words. For example:

```
protected int m_index;
protected static int INSTANCE_COUNT;
```

Many examples are built from examples presented earlier in the book. In these cases we have minimized the amount of repeated code by replacing all unchanged code with references to the sections that contain that code. All new and modified code of any class is highlighted in bold. When a completely new class is added, we do not highlight that class in bold (the only exceptions to this rule are anonymous inner classes).

Author Online

Purchase of *Swing Second Edition* includes free access to a private Internet forum where you can make comments about the book, ask technical questions, and receive help from the authors and from other Swing users. To access the forum, point your web browser to www.manning.com/robinson. There you will be able to subscribe to the forum. This site also provides information on how to access the forum once you are registered, what kind of help is available, and the rules of conduct on the forum.

Matt can be contacted directly at matt@mattrobinson.com.

Pavel can be contacted directly at pvorobiev@yahoo.com.

David Anderson, author of the UI Guidelines, can be contacted through www.uidesign.net.

Obtaining the source code

All source code for the examples presented in *Swing Second Edition* is available from www.-manning.com/sbe.

acknowledgments

First we'd like to thank James Gosling for writing the foreword to this edition. Java has changed our careers in many ways and it is an honor to have its creator introduce our book.

Thanks to the readers of the first edition, especially those who bought the book. Without you this edition would not exist. Thanks to the translators who have made our work available in languages accessible to other cultures and regions. Thanks to those professors and instructors at instututions around the globe who have used our book as a course reference.

Special thanks to our publisher, Marjan Bace, as well as Syd Brown, Leslie Haimes, Ted Kennedy, Elizabeth Martin, Mary Piergies, Aleksandra Sikora and the whole Manning team for transforming our manuscript updates and penciled-in margin notes into an organized, presentable form.

Last but not least we'd like to thank David Karr and Laurent Michalkovic for their many valuable suggestions and corrections that have improved the manuscript significantly.

about the cover illustration

The illustration on the cover of *Swing Second Edition* is taken from the 1805 edition of Sylvain Maréchal's four-volume compendium of regional dress customs. This book was first published in Paris in 1788, one year before the French Revolution. Each illustration is colored by hand. The caption for this illustration reads "Homme Salamanque," which means man from Salamanca, a province in Western Spain, on the border with Portugal. The region is known for its wild beauty, lush forests, ancient oak trees, rugged mountains, and historic old towns and villages.

The Homme Salamanque is just one of many figures in Maréchal's colorful collection. Their diversity speaks vividly of the uniqueness and individuality of the world's towns and regions just 200 years ago. This was a time when the dress codes of two regions separated by a few dozen miles identified people uniquely as belonging to one or the other. The collection brings to life a sense of the isolation and distance of that period and of every other historic period—except our own hyperkinetic present.

Dress codes have changed since then and the diversity by region, so rich at the time, has faded away. It is now often hard to tell the inhabitant of one continent from another. Perhaps, trying to view it optimistically, we have traded a cultural and visual diversity for a more varied personal life. Or a more varied and interesting intellectual and technical life.

We at Manning celebrate the inventiveness, the initiative, and the fun of the computer business with book covers based on the rich diversity of regional life of two centuries ago brought back to life by the pictures from this collection.

PART I

Foundations

Part I consists of two chapters that lay the foundation for a successful and productive journey through the JFC Swing class library. The first chapter begins with a brief overview of what Swing is and an introduction to its architecture. The second chapter contains a detailed discussion of the key mechanisms underlying Swing, and it shows you how to interact with them. There are several sections on topics that are fairly advanced, such as multithreading and painting. This material is central to many areas of Swing and by introducing it in chapter 2, your understanding of what is to come will be significantly enhanced. We expect that you will want to refer back to this chapter quite often, and we explicitly refer you to it throughout the text. At the very least, we recommend that you know what chapter 2 contains before moving on.

C H A P T E R   1

Swing overview

1.1   AWT

The Abstract Window Toolkit (AWT) is the part of Java designed for creating user interfaces and painting graphics and images. It is a set of classes intended to provide everything a developer needs to create a graphical interface for any Java applet or application. Most AWT components are derived from the `java.awt.Component` class, as figure 1.1 illustrates. (Note that AWT menu bars and menu bar items do not fit within the `Component` hierarchy.)

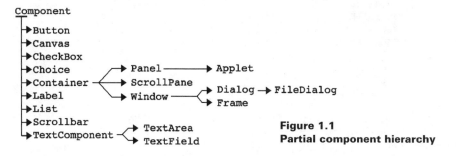

Figure 1.1
Partial component hierarchy

The Java Foundation Classes (JFC) consist of five major parts: AWT, Swing, Accessibility, Java 2D, and Drag and Drop. Java 2D has become an integral part of AWT, Swing is built on top of AWT, and Accessibility support is built into Swing. The five parts of JFC are certainly not mutually exclusive, and Swing is expected to merge more deeply with AWT in future versions of Java. Thus, AWT is at the core of JFC, which in turn makes it one of the most important libraries in Java 2.

1.2   SWING

Swing is a large set of components ranging from the very simple, such as labels, to the very complex, such as tables, trees, and styled text documents. Almost all Swing components are derived from a single parent called JComponent which extends the AWT Container class. For this reason, Swing is best described as a layer on top of AWT rather than a replacement for it. Figure 1.2 shows a partial JComponent hierarchy. If you compare this with the AWT Component hierarchy of figure 1.1, you will notice that each AWT component has a Swing equivalent that begins with the prefix "J." The only exception to this is the AWT Canvas class, for which JComponent, JLabel, or JPanel can be used as a replacement (we discuss this in detail in section 2.8). You will also notice many Swing classes that don't have AWT counterparts.

Figure 1.2 represents only a small fraction of the Swing library, but this fraction contains the classes you will be dealing with the most. The rest of Swing exists to provide extensive support and customization capabilities for the components these classes define.

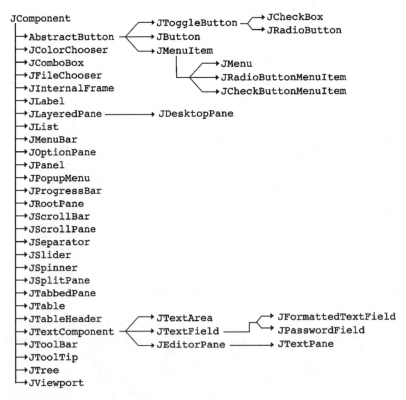

Figure 1.2   Partial JComponent hierarchy

1.2.1   Z-order

Swing components are referred to as *lightweight*s while AWT components are referred to as *heavyweight*s. One difference between lightweight and heavyweight components is *z-order*: the notion of depth or layering. Each heavyweight component occupies its own z-order layer. All lightweight components are contained inside heavyweight components, and they maintain their own layering scheme as defined by Swing. When you place a heavyweight inside another heavyweight container, it will, by definition, overlap all lightweights in that container.

What this ultimately means is that you should avoid using both heavyweight and lightweight components in the same container whenever possible. The most important rule to follow is that you should never place heavyweight components inside lightweight containers that commonly support overlapping children. Some examples of these containers are JInternal-Frame, JScrollPane, JLayeredPane, and JDesktopPane. Secondly, if you use a pop-up menu in a container holding a heavyweight component, you need to force that pop-up to be heavyweight. To control this for a specific JPopupMenu instance, you can use its setLight-WeightPopupEnabled() method.

> **NOTE**   For JMenus (which use JPopupMenus to display their contents) you first have to use the getPopupMenu() method to retrieve the associated pop-up menu. Once it is retrieved, you can then call setLightWeightPopupEnabled(false) on that pop-up to enforce heavyweight functionality. This needs to be done with each JMenu in your application, including menus contained within menus.

Alternatively, you can call JPopupMenu's static setDefaultLightWeightPopupEnabled() method, and pass it a value of false to force all popups in a Java session to be heavyweight. Note that this will only affect pop-up menus created *after* this call is made. It is therefore a good idea to call this method early within initialization.

1.2.2   Platform independence

The most remarkable thing about Swing components is that they are written in 100% Java and they do not directly rely on peer components, as most AWT components do. This means that a Swing button or text area can look and function identically on Macintosh, Solaris, Linux, and Windows platforms. This design reduces the need to test and debug applications on each target platform.

> **NOTE**   The only exceptions to this are four heavyweight Swing components that are direct subclasses of AWT classes that rely on platform-dependent peers: JApplet, JDialog, JFrame, and JWindow. See chapter 3 for more information.

1.2.3   Swing package overview

javax.swing

Contains the most basic Swing components, default component models and interfaces. (Most of the classes shown in figure 1.2 are contained in this package.)

javax.swing.border

Contains the classes and interfaces used to define specific border styles. Note that borders can be shared by any number of Swing components, as they are not components themselves.

`javax.swing.colorchooser`

Contains classes and interfaces that support the `JColorChooser` component, which is used for color selection. (This package also contains some interesting undocumented private classes.)

`javax.swing.event`

Contains all Swing-specific event types and listeners. Swing components also support events and listeners defined in `java.awt.event` and `java.beans`.

`javax.swing.filechooser`

Contains classes and interfaces supporting the `JFileChooser` component used for file selection.

`javax.swing.plaf`

Contains the pluggable look and feel API used to define custom UI delegates. Most of the classes in this package are abstract. They are subclassed and implemented by look and feel implementations such as Metal, Motif, and Basic. The classes in this package are intended for use only by developers who, for one reason or another, cannot build on top of an existing look and feel.

`javax.swing.plaf.basic`

This package is the Basic look and feel implementation on top of which all look and feels provided with Swing are built. We are normally expected to subclass the classes in this package if we want to create our own customized look and feel.

`javax.swing.plaf.metal`

Metal is the default look and feel of Swing components; it is also known as the Java look and feel. It is the only look and feel that ships with Swing which is not designed to be consistent with a specific platform.

`javax.swing.plaf.multi`

This package is the Multiplexing look and feel. This is not a regular look and feel implementation in that it does not define the actual look or feel of any components. Instead, it provides the ability to combine several look and feels for simultanteous use. A typical example might be using an audio-based look and feel in combination with metal or motif.

`javax.swing.table`

Contains classes and interfaces that support the `JTable` control. This component is used to manage tabular data in spreadsheet form. It supports a high degree of customization without requiring look and feel enhancements.

`javax.swing.text`

Contains classes and interfaces used by the text components, including support for plain and styled documents, the views of those documents, highlighting, caret control and customization, editor actions, and keyboard customization.

`javax.swing.text.html`

Contains support for parsing, creating, and viewing HTML documents.

`javax.swing.text.html.parser`

Contains support for parsing HTML.

`javax.swing.text.rtf`

Contains support for RTF (rich text format) documents.

`javax.swing.tree`

Contains classes and interfaces that support the `JTree` component. This component is used for the display and management of hierarchical data. It supports a high degree of customization without requiring look and feel enhancements.

`javax.swing.undo`

Contains support for implementing and managing undo/redo functionality.

1.3 MVC ARCHITECTURE

The Model-View-Controller architecture (MVC) is a well known object-oriented user interface design decomposition that dates back to the late 1970s. Components are broken down into three parts: a model, a view, and a controller. Each Swing component is based on a more modern version of this design. Before we discuss how MVC works in Swing, we need to understand how it was originally designed to work.

NOTE   The three-way separation described here, and illustrated in figure 1.3, is used today by only a small number of user interface frameworks, VisualWorks being the most notable.

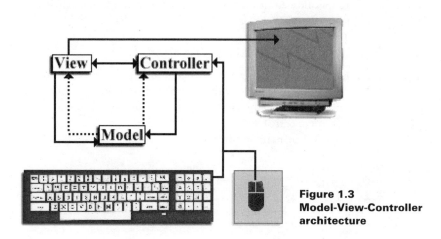

**Figure 1.3
Model-View-Controller
architecture**

1.3.1 Model

The model is responsible for maintaining all aspects of the component state. This includes, for example, such values as the pressed/unpressed state of a push button, and a text component's character data and information about how it is structured. A model may be responsible for *indirect* communication with the view and the controller. By indirect, we mean that the model does not "know" its view and controller—it does not maintain or retrieve references to them. Instead, the model will send out notifications or *broadcasts* (what we know as events). In figure 1.3 this indirect communication is represented by dashed lines.

1.3.2   View

The view determines the visual representation of the component's model. This is a component's "look." For example, the view displays the correct color of a component, whether the component appears raised or lowered (in the case of a button), and the rendering of a desired font. The view is responsible for keeping its on-screen representation updated, which it may do upon receiving indirect messages from the model or messages from the controller.

1.3.3   Controller

The controller is responsible for determining whether the component should react to any input events from input devices such as the keyboard or mouse. The controller is the "feel" of the component, and it determines what actions are performed when the component is used. The controller can receive messages from the view, and indirect messages from the model.

For example, suppose we have a checked (selected) check box in our interface. If the controller determines that the user has performed a mouse click, it may send a message to the view. If the view determines that the click occurred on the check box, it sends a message to the model. The model then updates itself and broadcasts a message, which will be received by the view, to tell it that it should update itself based on the new state of the model. In this way, a model is not bound to a specific view or controller; this allows us to have several views and controllers manipulating a single model.

1.3.4   Custom view and controller

One of the major advantages Swing's MVC architecture provides is the ability to customize the "look" and "feel" of a component without modifying the model. Figure 1.4 shows a group of components using two different user interfaces. The important point to know about this figure is that the components shown are actually the same, but they are shown using two different *look and feel* implementations (different views and controllers).

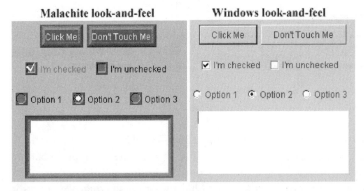

Figure 1.4   Malachite and Windows look and feels of the same components

Some Swing components also provide the ability to customize specific parts of a component without affecting the model. For example, some components allow us to define custom cell renderers and editors used to display and accept specific data, respectively. Figure 1.5 shows the columns of a table containing stock market data rendered with custom icons and colors. We will examine how to take advantage of this functionality in our study of Swing combo boxes, lists, spinners, tables, and trees.

Sun Microsystems	140 5/8	10.625	⇑ SUNW	130 15/16	10	17,734,600
Lucent Technology	64 5/8	9.65	⇑ LU	59 15/16	4 11/16	29,856,300
Dell Computers	46 3/16	6.24	⇑ DELL	44 1/2	1 11/16	47,310,000
Sony Corp.	96 3/16	1.18	⇑ SNE	95 5/8	1 1/8	330,600
Hitachi, Ltd.	78 1/2	1.12	⇑ HIT	77 5/8	7/8	49,400
Enamelon Inc.	4 7/8	0.0	⇓ ENML	5	-1/8	35,900
AT&T	65 3/16	-0.1	⇓ T	66	-13/16	554,000
Intl. Bus. Machines	183	-0.51	⇓ IBM	183 1/8	-1/8	4,371,400
Microsoft Corp.	94 1/16	-0.92	⇓ MSFT	95 3/16	-1 1/8	19,836,900
Egghead.com	17 1/4	-1.43	⇓ EGGS	17 7/16	-3/16	2,146,400
Sprint	104 9/16	-1.82	⇓ FON	106 3/8	-1 13/16	1,135,100
Hewlett-Packard	70	-2.01	⇓ HWP	71 1/16	-1 7/16	2,410,700
Compaq Computers	30 7/8	-2.18	⇓ CPQ	31 1/4	-3/8	11,853,900

Figure 1.5   Custom rendering

1.3.5   Custom models

Another major advantage of Swing's MVC architecture is the ability to customize and replace a component's data model. For example, we can construct our own text document model that enforces the entry of a date or phone number in a very specific form. We can also associate the same data model with more than one component. For instance, two JTextAreas can store their textual content in the same document model, while maintaining two different views of that information.

We will design and implement our own data models for JComboBox, JList, JSpinner, JTree, and JTable throughout our coverage of text components. We've listed some of Swing's model interface definitions along with a brief description of what data the implementations are designed to store and what components they are used with:

BoundedRangeModel

   Used by: JProgressBar, JScrollBar, JSlider.

   Stores: 4 integers: value, extent, min, max.

   The value and the extent must be between specified min and max values. The extent is always <= max and >=value. The value of extent is not necessarily larger than value. Also, the extent represents the length of the *thumb* in JScrollBar (see chapter 7).

ButtonModel

   Used by: All AbstractButton subclasses.

   Stores: A boolean representing whether the button is selected (armed) or unselected (disarmed).

ListModel

   Used by: JList.

   Stores: A collection of objects.

`ComboBoxModel`

> *Used by*: JComboBox.
>
> *Stores*: A collection of objects and a selected object.

`MutableComboBoxModel`

> *Used by*: JComboBox.
>
> *Stores*: A Vector (or another mutable collection) of objects and a selected object.

`ListSelectionModel`

> *Used by*: JList, TableColumnModel.
>
> *Stores*: One or more indices of selected list or table items. Allows single, single-interval, or multiple-interval selections.

`SpinnerModel`

> *Used by*: JSpinner.
>
> *Stores*: A sequenced collection that can be bounded or unbounded, and the currently selected element in that sequence.

`SingleSelectionModel`

> *Used by*: JMenuBar, JPopupMenu, JMenuItem, JTabbedPane.
>
> *Stores*: The index of the selected element in a collection of objects owned by the implementor.

`ColorSelectionModel`

> *Used by*: JColorChooser.
>
> *Stores*: A Color.

`TableModel`

> *Used by*: JTable.
>
> *Stores*: A two-dimensional array of objects.

`TableColumnModel`

> *Used by*: JTable.
>
> *Stores*: A collection of TableColumn objects, a set of listeners for table column model events, the width between columns, the total width of all columns, a selection model, and a column selection flag.

`TreeModel`

> *Used by*: JTree.
>
> *Stores*: Objects that can be displayed in a tree. Implementations must be able to distinguish between branch and leaf objects, and the objects must be organized hierarchically.

`TreeSelectionModel`

> *Used by*: JTree.
>
> *Stores*: Selected rows. Allows single, contiguous, and discontiguous selection.

`Document`

> *Used by*: All text components.
>
> *Stores*: Content. Normally this is text (character data). More complex implementations support styled text, images, and other forms of content (such as embedded components).

Not all Swing components have models. Those that act as containers, such as JApplet, JFrame, JLayeredPane, JDesktopPane, and JInternalFrame, do not have models. However, interactive components such as JButton, JTextField, and JTable *do* have models. In fact, some Swing components have more than one model (for example, JList uses one model to hold selection information and another model to store its data). The point is that MVC is not a hard-and-fast rule in Swing. Simple components, or complex components that don't store lots of information (such as JDesktopPane), do not need separate models. The view and controller of each component is, however, almost always separate for each component, as we will see in the next section.

So how does the component itself fit into the MVC picture? The component acts as a mediator between the model(s), the view, and the controller. It is neither the M, the V, nor the C, although it can take the place of any or all of these parts if we so design it. This will become more clear as we progress through this chapter, and throughout the rest of the book.

1.4 UI DELEGATES AND PLAF

Almost all modern user interface frameworks coalesce the view and the controller, whether they are based on Smalltalk, C++, or Java. Examples include MacApp, Smalltalk/V, Interviews, and the X/Motif widgets used in IBM Smalltalk. Swing is the newest addition to this crowd. Swing packages each component's view and controller into an object called a UI delegate. For this reason Swing's underlying architecture is more accurately referred to as model-delegate rather than model-view-controller. Ideally, communication between both the model and the UI delegate is indirect, allowing more than one model to be associated with one UI delegate, and vice versa. Figure 1.6 illustrates this principle.

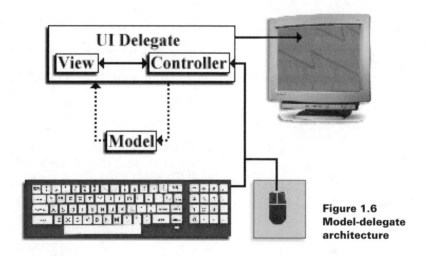

Figure 1.6
Model-delegate architecture

1.4.1 The ComponentUI class

Each UI delegate is derived from an abstract class called ComponentUI. ComponentUI methods describe the fundamentals of how a UI delegate and a component using it will communicate. Note that each method takes a JComponent as a parameter.

Here are the ComponentUI methods:

```
static ComponentUI createUI(JComponent c)
```
Returns an instance of the UI delegate defined by the defining `ComponentUI` sub-class itself, in its normal implementation. This instance is often shared among components of the same type (for example, all `JButton`s using the Metal look and feel share the same static UI delegate instance defined in `javax.swing.plaf.metal.MetalButtonUI` by default).

```
installUI(JComponent c)
```
Installs this `ComponentUI` on the specified component. This normally adds listeners to the component and/or its model(s), to notify the UI delegate when changes in state occur that require a view update.

```
uninstallUI(JComponent c)
```
Removes this `ComponentUI` and any listeners added in `installUI()` from the specified component and/or its model(s).

```
update(Graphics g, JComponent c)
```
If the component is opaque, this method paints its background and then calls `paint(Graphics g, JComponent c)`.

```
paint(Graphics g, JComponent c)
```
Gets all information it needs from the component and possibly its model(s) to render it correctly.

```
getPreferredSize(JComponent c)
```
Returns the preferred size for the specified component based on this `ComponentUI`.

```
getMinimumSize(JComponent c)
```
Returns the minimum size for the specified component based on this `ComponentUI`.

```
getMaximumSize(JComponent c)
```
Returns the maximum size for the specified component based on this `ComponentUI`.

To enforce the use of a specific UI delegate, we can call a component's `setUI()` method:

```
JButton m_button = new JButton();
m_button.setUI((MalachiteButtonUI)
  MalachiteButtonUI.createUI(m_button));
```

Most UI delegates are constructed so that they know about a component and its models only while performing painting and other view-controller tasks. Swing normally avoids associating UI delegates on a per-component basis by using a shared instance.

NOTE The `JComponent` class defines methods for assigning UI delegates because the method declarations required do not involve component-specific code. However, this is not possible with data models because there is no base interface that all models can be traced back to (for example, there is no base abstract class such as `ComponentUI` for Swing models). For this reason, methods to assign models are defined in subclasses of `JComponent` where necessary.

1.4.2   Pluggable look and feel

Swing includes several sets of UI delegates. Each set contains `ComponentUI` implementations for most Swing components; we call each of these sets a *look and feel* or a *pluggable look and feel* (PLAF) implementation. The `javax.swing.plaf` package consists of abstract classes derived from `ComponentUI`, and the classes in the `javax.swing.plaf.basic` package extend these abstract classes to implement the Basic look and feel. This is the set of UI delegates that all other look and feel classes are expected to use as a base for building from. (Note that the Basic look and feel cannot be used on its own, as `BasicLookAndFeel` is an abstract class.) There are three main pluggable look and feel implemenations derived from the Basic look and feel:

> Windows: `com.sun.java.swing.plaf.windows.WindowsLookAndFeel`
> CDE\Motif: `com.sun.java.swing.plaf.motif.MotifLookAndFeel`
> Metal (default): `javax.swing.plaf.metal.MetalLookAndFeel`

There is also a `MacLookAndFeel` for simulating Macintosh user interfaces, but this does not ship with Java 2—it must be downloaded separately. The Windows and Macintosh pluggable look and feel libraries are only supported on the corresponding platform.

The Multiplexing look and feel, `javax.swing.plaf.multi.MultiLookAndFeel`, extends all the abstract classes in `javax.swing.plaf`. It is designed to allow combinations of look and feels to be used simultaneously, and it is intended for, but not limited to, use with Accessibility look and feels. The job of each Multiplexing UI delegate is to manage each of its child UI delegates.

Each look and feel package contains a class derived from the abstract class `javax.swing. LookAndFeel`; these include `BasicLookAndFeel`, `MetalLookAndFeel`, and `WindowsLookAndFeel`. These are the central points of access to each look and feel package. We use them when changing the current look and feel, and the `UIManager` class (used to manage installed look and feels) uses them to access the current look and feel's `UIDefaults` table (which contains, among other things, UI delegate class names for that look and feel corresponding to each Swing component). To change the current look and feel of an application we can simply call the `UIManager`'s `setLookAndFeel()` method, passing it the fully qualified name of the `LookAndFeel` to use. The following code can be used to accomplish this at run-time:

```
try {
  UIManager.setLookAndFeel(
    "com.sun.java.swing.plaf.motif.MotifLookAndFeel");
  SwingUtilities.updateComponentTreeUI(myJFrame);
}
catch (Exception e) {
  System.err.println("Could not load LookAndFeel");
}
```

`SwingUtilities.updateComponentTreeUI()` informs all children of the specified component that the look and feel has changed and they need to discard their UI delegate in exchange for a different one of the new look and feel. Note that the call to `updateComponentTree()` is only necessary if the frame is already visible.

1.4.3   Where are the UI delegates?

We've discussed `ComponentUI` and the packages that `LookAndFeel` implementations reside in, but we haven't really mentioned anything about the specific UI delegate classes derived from `ComponentUI`. Each abstract class in the `javax.swing.plaf` package extends `ComponentUI` and corresponds to a specific Swing component. The name of each class follows the general

scheme of class name (without the "J" prefix) plus a "UI" suffix. For instance, `LabelUI`
extends `ComponentUI` and is the base delegate used for `JLabel`.

These classes are extended by concrete implementations such as those in the `basic` and
`multi` packages. The names of these subclasses follow the general scheme of the look and feel
name prefix added to the superclass name. For instance, `BasicLabelUI` and `MultiLabelUI`
both extend `LabelUI` and reside in the `basic` and `multi` packages respectively. Figure 1.7
illustrates the `LabelUI` hierarchy.

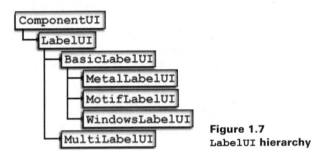

Figure 1.7
`LabelUI` **hierarchy**

Most look and feel implementations are expected to either extend the concrete classes defined
in the `basic` package, or use them directly. The Metal, Motif, and Windows UI delegates are
built on top of Basic versions. The Multi look and feel, however, is unique in that each implementation does not extend from Basic; each is merely a shell allowing an arbitrary number of
UI delegates to be installed on a given component.

Figure 1.7 should emphasize the fact that Swing supplies a very large number of UI delegate classes. If we were to create an entirely new pluggable look and feel implementation, some
serious time and effort would be required. In chapter 21 we will learn all about this process,
as well as how to modify and work with the existing look and feels.

NOTE   We do not detail the complete functionality and construction of any of the provided
UI delegate classes in this book.

C H A P T E R   2

Swing mechanics

2.1   JCOMPONENT PROPERTIES, SIZING, AND POSITIONING

All Swing components conform to the JavaBeans specification, which we'll discuss in detail in section 2.7. Among the five features a JavaBean is expected to support is a set of properties and associated accessor methods.

2.1.1   Properties

A *property* is a member variable, and its accessor methods are normally of the form `setPropertyname()`, `getPropertyname()`, or `isPropertyname()` where `Propertyname` is the name of the variable. There are five types of properties we refer to throughout this book: simple, bound, constrained, change, and client. We will discuss each of these in turn.

Many classes are designed to fire events when the value of a property changes. A property for which there is no event firing associated with a change in its value is called a *simple* property.

A *bound* property is one for which `PropertyChangeEvents` are fired after the property changes value. We can register `PropertyChangeListeners` to listen for `PropertyChangeEvents` through `JComponent`'s `addPropertyChangeListener()` method.

15

A *constrained* property is one for which `PropertyChangeEvents` are fired before the property changes value. We can register `VetoableChangeListeners` to listen for `PropertyChangeEvents` through `JComponent`'s `addVetoableChangeListener()` method. A change can be vetoed in the event handling code of a `VetoableChangeListener()` by throwing `PropertyVetoException`. (As of JDK1.4 `JInternalFrame` is the only Swing class with constrained properties.)

NOTE   Each of these event and listener classes is defined in the `java.beans` package.

`PropertyChangeEvents` carry three pieces of information with them: the name of the property, the old value, and the new value. Beans can use an instance of `java.beans.PropertyChangeSupport` to manage the dispatching, to each registered listener, of the `PropertyChangeEvents` corresponding to each bound property. Similarly, an instance of `VetoableChangeSupport` can be used to manage the dispatching of all `PropertyChangeEvents` corresponding to each constrained property.

JAVA1.4   Java 1.4 has added two APIs to allow access to the property change listeners of a `JComponent`.

```
PropertyChangeListener[] getPropertyChangeListeners()
PropertyChangeListener[] getPropertyChangeListeners(String pro-pertyName)
```

This change is part of an effort from Sun to offer a more complete solution to manage event listeners within AWT and Swing by providing getXXXListeners() methods in addition to the existing add/remove convention.

Swing includes an additional property support class called `SwingPropertyChangeSupport` (defined in `javax.swing.event`) which is a subclass of, and almost identical to, `PropertyChangeSupport`. The difference is that `SwingPropertyChangeSupport` has been built to be more efficient. It does this by sacrificing thread safety, which, as we will see later in this chapter, is not an issue in Swing if the multithreading guidelines are followed consistently (because all event processing should occur on only one thread—the event-dispatching thread). So if you are confident that your code has been constructed in a thread-safe manner, we encourage you to use this more efficient version, rather than `PropertyChangeSupport`.

NOTE   There is no Swing equivalent of `VetoableChangeSupport` because there are currently very few constrained properties defined in Swing.

Swing also introduces a new type of property which we will call a *change* property, for lack of a given name. We use `ChangeListeners` to listen for `ChangeEvents` that get fired when these properties change state. A `ChangeEvent` only carries one piece of information with it: the source of the event. For this reason, change properties are less powerful than bound or constrained properties, but they are more widely used throughout Swing. A `JButton`, for instance, sends change events whenever it is armed (pressed for the first time), pressed, and released (see chapter 5).

NOTE   You can always find out which properties have change events associated with them, as well as any other type of event, by referencing the Swing source code. Unless you are using Swing for building very simple GUIs, we strongly suggest getting used to referencing source code.

Another new property-like feature Swing introduces is the notion of *client properties*. These are basically key/value pairs stored in a `Hashtable` provided by each Swing component. (The client properties `Hashtable` is actually inherited from `JComponent`.) This feature allows properties to be added and removed at run-time.

WARNING   Client properties may seem like a great way to extend a component by essentially adding member variables. However, we are explicitly advised against this in the API documentation: "The `clientProperty` dictionary is not intended to support large scale extensions to `JComponent` nor should it be considered an alternative to subclassing when designing a new component." In other words, it is better to create a subclass with new properties rather than use client properties to add meaningful state. Client properties are best used for experimentation.

Client properties are also bound properties: when a client property changes, a `PropertyChange-Event` is dispatched to all registered `PropertyChangeListeners`. To add a property to a component's client properties you can do something like the following:

```
myComponent.putClientProperty("myname", myValue);
```

To retrieve a client property:

```
Object obj = myComponent.getClientProperty("myname");
```

To remove a client property you can provide a `null` value:

```
myComponent.putClientProperty("mykey", null);
```

Five Swing components have special client properties that only the Metal look and feel pays attention to. We've listed these property key names along with a brief description of their values.

NOTE   These property key names are actually the values of protected fields defined in the corresponding `MetalXXUI` delegates in the `javax.swing.plaf.metal` package. Unfortunately the only way to make use of them is to either hardcode them into your application or subclass the corresponding Metal UI delegates to make these fields available.

"JTree.lineStyle"

A `String` used to specify whether node relationships are displayed as angular connecting lines ("Angled"), horizontal lines defining cell boundaries ("Horizontal" (default)), or no lines at all ("None").

"JScrollBar.isFreeStanding"

A `Boolean` value used to specify whether all sides of a `JScrollbar` will have an etched border (`Boolean.FALSE` (default)) or only the top and left edges (`Boolean.TRUE`).

"JSlider.isFilled"

A `Boolean` value used to specify whether the lower portion of a slider should be filled (`Boolean.TRUE`) or not (`Boolean.FALSE` (default)).

"JToolBar.isRollover"

A `Boolean` value used to specify whether a toolbar button displays an etched border only when the mouse is within its bounds and no border if it is not (`Boolean.TRUE`), or whether to always use an etched border (`Boolean.FALSE` (default)).

"JInternalFrame.isPalette"
>A `Boolean` value used to specify whether a very thin border is used (`Boolean.TRUE`) or the regular border is used (`Boolean.FALSE` (default)).

NOTE There are also other non Metal-specific client properties used by various UI delegates such as `JTable.autoStartsEdit`. The best way to find out about more client properties is to look at the actual UI delegate source code. However, the use of client properties often changes from release to release and for this reason avoid them whenever possible.

2.1.2   Size and positioning

Because `JComponent` extends `java.awt.Container`, it inherits all the sizing and positioning functionality we are used to. We suggest you manage a component's preferred, minimum, and maximum sizes using the following methods:

`setPreferredSize()`, `getPreferredSize()`
>The most comfortable size of a component. Used by most layout managers to size each component.

`setMinimumSize()`, `getMinimumSize()`
>Used during layout to act as a lower bounds for a component's dimensions.

`setMaximumSize()`, `getMaximumSize()`
>Used during layout to act as an upper bounds for a component's dimensions.

Each `setXX()`/`getXX()` method accepts/returns a `Dimension` instance. We will learn more about what these sizes mean in terms of each layout manager in chapter 4. Whether a layout manager pays attention to these sizes is solely based on that layout manager's implementation. It is perfectly feasible to construct a layout manager that simply ignores all of them, or pays attention to only one. The sizing of components in a container is layout-manager specific.

   `JComponent`'s `setBounds()` method can be used to assign a component both a size and a position within its parent container. This overloaded method can take either a `Rectangle` parameter (`java.awt.Rectangle`) or four `int` parameters representing the x-coordinate, y-coordinate, width, and height. For example, the following two code segments are equivalent:

```
myComponent.setBounds(120,120,300,300);

Rectangle rec = new Rectangle(120,120,300,300);
myComponent.setBounds(rec);
```

Note that `setBounds()` will not override any layout policies in effect due to a parent container's layout manager. For this reason, a call to `setBounds()` may appear to have been ignored in some situations because it tried to do its job and was forced back to its original size by the layout manager (layout managers always have the first crack at setting the size of a component).

   `setBounds()` is commonly used to manage child components in containers with no layout manager (such as `JLayeredPane`, `JDesktopPane`, and `JComponent` itself). For instance, we normally use `setBounds()` when adding a `JInternalFrame` to a `JDesktopPane`.

A component's size can safely be queried in typical AWT style, such as this:

```
int height = myComponent.getHeight();
int width = myComponent.getWidth();
```

NOTE This information is only meaningful after the component has been realized.

Size can also be retrieved as a `Rectangle` or a `Dimension` instance:

```
Rectangle rec = myComponent.getBounds();
Dimension dim = myComponent.getSize();
```

`Rectangle` contains four publicly accessible properties describing its location and size:

```
int recX = rec.x;
int recY = rec.y;
int recWidth = rec.width;
int recHeight = rec.height;
```

`Dimension` contains two publicly accessible properties describing size:

```
int dimWidth = dim.width;
int dimHeight = dim.height;
```

The coordinates returned in the `Rectangle` instance using `getBounds()` represent a component's location within its parent. These coordinates can also be obtained using the `getX()` and `getY()` methods. Additionally, you can set a component's position within its container using the `setLocation(int x, int y)` method (but as with `setBounds()`, this method may or may not have any effect depending on the layout manager in use).

`JComponent` also maintains an alignment. Horizontal and vertical alignments can be specified by float values between 0.0 and 1.0: 0.5 means center, closer to 0.0 means left or top, and closer to 1.0 means right or bottom. The corresponding `JComponent` methods are:

```
setAlignmentX(float f)
setAlignmentY(float f)
```

Alignment values are used only in containers managed by `BoxLayout` and `OverlayLayout`.

2.2 *EVENT HANDLING AND DISPATCHING*

Events occur any time a key or mouse button is pressed. The way components receive and process events has not changed from JDK1.1. Swing components can generate many different types of events, including those in `java.awt.event` and even more in `javax.swing.event`. Many of the `java.Swing.event` event types are component-specific. Each event type is represented by an object that, at the very least, identifies the source of the event. Some events carry additional information such as an event type name and identifier, and information about the state of the source before and after the event was generated. Sources of events are most commonly components or models, but different kinds of objects can also generate events.

In order to receive notification of events we need to register listeners with the source object. A listener is an implementation of any of the `XXListener` interfaces (where XX is an event type) defined in the `java.awt.event`, `java.beans`, and `javax.swing.event` packages. There is always at least one method defined in each interface that takes a corresponding `XXEvent` as a parameter. Classes that support notification of `XXEvents` generally implement the `XXListener` interface, and have support for registering and unregistering those listeners through the use of the `addXXListener()` and `removeXXListener()` methods, respectively.

Most event sources allow any number of listeners to be registered with them. Similarly, any listener instance can be registered to receive events from any number of event sources.

Usually classes that support XXEvents provide protected fireXX() methods used for constructing event objects and sending them to event handlers for processing (see section 2.7.7 for an example of this). Application-defined events should use this same pattern.

JAVA 1.3   In Java 1.2 there was no way to access the listeners of a component without subclassing. For this reason the getlisteners() method was added to Component in Java 1.3. This method takes a listener Class instance as its argument and returns an array of EventListeners (EventListener is the interface all XXListeners extend). For example, to obtain all ActionListeners attached to a given component we can do the following:

```
ActionListener[] actionListeners = (ActionListener[])
        myComponent.getListeners(ActionListener.class);
```

JAVA 1.4   The getListeners() methods were stop gap measures created in the Java 1.3 to allow direct access to the list of EventListeners registered with a specific component, while keeping the changes to the AWT/Swing public API minimal. In version 1.4, the design team has opted for a more complete solution, more in line with the JavaBean convention. We've listed the additions here:

java.awt.Component

In Java 1.3:
```
getListeners()
addHierarchyListener()
removeHierarchyListener()
addHierarchyBoundsListener()
removeHierarchyBoundsListener()
```

Java 1.4 added the following:
```
getComponentListeners()
getFocusListeners()
getHierarchyListeners()
getHierarchyBoundsListeners()
getKeyListeners()
getMouseListeners()
getMouseMotionListeners()
addMouseWheelListener()
removeMouseWheelListener()
getMouseWheelListeners()
getInputMethodListeners()
getContainerListeners()
```

javax.swing.JComponent

In Java 1.3:
```
getListeners()
```

Java 1.4 added the following:
```
getAncestorListeners()
getVetoableChangeListeners()
getPropertyChangeListeners()
```

For purposes of completeness, in tables 2.1 and 2.2 below we summarize the event listeners in the `java.awt.event` and `javax.swing.event` packages (for more detail, please refer to the JavaDoc documentation).

Table 2.1 Event listener interfaces in `java.awt.events`

Event	Related to
ActionListener	Action events
AdjustmentListener	Adjustment events
AWTEventListener	Observe passively all events dispatched within AWT
ComponentListener	Component (move, size, hide, show) events
ContainerListener	Container (ad, remove component) events
FocusListener	Focus (gain, loss) events
HierarchyBoundsListener	Hierarchy (ancestor moved/resized) events
HierarchyListener	Hierarchy (visibility) events
InputMethodListener	Input method events (multilingual framework)
ItemListener	Item events
KeyListener	Keyboard events
MouseListener	Mouse buttons events
MouseMotionListener	Mouse motion events
MouseWheelListener	Mouse wheel events
TextListener	Text events
WindowFocusListener	Window focus events (new focus management framework)
WindowListener	Window events (non focus related)
WindowStateListener	Window state events

Table 2.2 Event listener interfaces in `javax.swing.event`

Event	Related to
AncestorListener	Changes to location and visible state of a JComponent or its parents
CaretListener	Text cursor movement events
CellEditorListener	Cell editor events
ChangeListener	Change events (see p. 16)
DocumentListener	Text document events
HyperlinkListener	Hyperlink events
InternalFrameListener	Internal frame events
ListDataListener	List data events
ListSelectionListener	List selection events
MenuDragMouseListener	Menu mouse movement events
MenuKeyListener	Menu keyboard events
MenuListener	Menu selection events
MouseInputListener	Aggregrated mouse and mouse motion events
PopupMenuListener	Popup meny events
TableColumnModelListener	Table column events
TableModelListener	Table model data events
TreeExpansionListener	Tree expand/collapse events
TreeModelListener	Tree model data events
TreeSelectionListener	Tree selection events
TreeWillExpandListener	Tree expand/collapse pending events
UndoableEditListener	Undo/Redo events

2.2.1　EventListenerList

class javax.swing.event.EventListenerList

EventListenerList is an array of XXEvent/XXListener pairs. JComponent and each of its descendants use an EventListenerList to maintain their listeners. All default models also maintain listeners and an EventListenerList. When a listener is added to a Swing component or model the associated event's Class instance (used to identify event type) is added to its EventListenerList array, followed by the listener instance itself. Since these pairs are stored in an array rather than a mutable collection (for efficiency purposes), a new array is created on each addition or removal using the System.arrayCopy() method. For thread safety the methods for adding and removing listeners from an EventListenerList synchronize access to the array when it is manipulated.

When events are received the array is traversed and events are sent to each listener with a matching type. Because the array is ordered in an XXEvent, XXListener, YYEvent, YYListener fashion, a listener corresponding to a given event type is always next in the array. This approach allows very efficient event-dispatching routines (see section 2.7.7 for an example).

JComponent defines its EventListenerList as a protected field called listenerList so that all subclasses inherit it. Swing components manage most of their listeners directly through listenerList.

2.2.2　Event-dispatching thread

class java.awt.EventDispatchThread [package private]

By default all AWT and Swing-based applications start off with two threads. One is the main application thread which handles execution of the main() method. The other, referred to as the *event-dispatching thread,* is responsible for handling events, painting, and layout. All events are processed by the listeners that receive them within the event-dispatching thread. For example, the code you write inside the body of an actionPerformed() method is executed within the event-dispatching thread automatically (you don't have to do anything special to make this happen). This is also the case with all other event-handling methods. All painting and component layout also occurs within this thread. For these reasons the event-dispatching thread is of primary importance to Swing and AWT, and plays a fundamental role in keeping updates to component state and display under control

Associated with the event-dispatching thread is a FIFO (first in first out) queue of events called the *system event queue* (an instance of java.awt.EventQueue). This gets filled up, as does any FIFO queue, in a serial fashion. Each request takes its turn executing event-handling code, whether it is updating component properties, layout, or painting. All events are processed serially to avoid such situations as a component's state being modified in the middle of a repaint. Knowing this, you must be careful not to dispatch events outside of the event-dispatching thread. For instance, calling a fireXX() method directly from within a separate (either the main application thread or one that you created yourself) is unsafe.

Since the event-dispatching thread executes all listener methods, painting and layout, it is important that event-handling, painting, and layout methods be executed quickly. Otherwise the whole system event queue will be blocked waiting for one event process, repaint, or layout to finish, and your application will appear to be frozen or locked up.

NOTE If you are ever in doubt whether or not event-handling code you have written is being handled in the right thread, the following static method comes in handy:

`SwingUtilities.isEventDispatchThread()`. This will return `true` or `false` indicating whether or not the method was called from within the event-dispatching thread.

To illustrate this point, let's say you have a Swing application running in front of you with a button and table of data. The button has an attached `ActionListener` and inside this listener's `actionPerformed()` method a database access occurs. After the data is retrieved it is then added to the table's model and the table updates its display accordingly. The problem with this is that if the connection to the database is slow or not working when we press the button, or if the amount of data retrieved is large and takes a while to send, the GUI will become unresponsive until the send finishes or an exception is thrown. To solve this problem and ensure that the `actionPerformed()` method gets executed quickly, you need to create and use your own separate thread for doing this time-consuming work.

2.3 *MULTITHREADING*

Multithreading is necessary when any time-consuming work occurs in a GUI application. The following code shows how to create and start a separate thread:

```
Thread workHard = new Thread() {
   public void run() {
     doToughWork(); // do some time-intensive work
  }
};
workHard.start(); {
```

However, designing multithreaded GUI applications is not just simply creating separate threads for time-consuming work (although this is a big part of it). There are several other things that need to be kept in mind when designing such applications. The first is that all updates to any component's state should be executed from within the event-dispatching thread only (see 2.2.2). For example, let's say you have created your own separate thread that starts when the user presses a button. This thread accesses a database to gather data for display in a table. When the data is retrieved the table model and display must be updated, but this update must occur in the event-dispatching thread, not within our separate thread. To accomplish this we need a way of wrapping up code and sending it to the system event queue for execution in the event-dispatching thread.

NOTE Use `invokeLater()` instead of `invokeAndWait()` whenever possible. If you must use `invokeAndWait()` make sure that there are no locks held by the calling thread that another thread might need during the operation.

Swing provides a very helpful class that, among other things, allows us to add `Runnable` objects to the system event queue. This class is called `SwingUtilities` and it contains two methods that we are interested in: `invokeLater()` and `invokeAndWait()`. The first method adds a `Runnable` to the system event queue and returns immediately. The second method adds a `Runnable` and waits for it to be dispatched, then returns after it finishes. The basic syntax of each follows:

```
Runnable trivialRunnable = new Runnable() {
 public void run() {
  doWork(); // do some work
 }
};
SwingUtilities.invokeLater(trivialRunnable);

try {
 Runnable trivialRunnable2 = new Runnable() {
  public void run() {
   doWork(); // do some work
  }
 };
 SwingUtilities.invokeAndWait(trivialRunnable2);
}
catch (InterruptedException ie) {
 System.out.println("...waiting thread interrupted!");
}
catch (InvocationTargetException ite) {
 System.out.println(
  "...uncaught exception within Runnable's run()");
}
```

So, putting this all together, the following code shows a typical way to build your own separate thread to do some time-intensive work while using `invokeLater()` or `invokeAndWait()` in order to safely update the state of any components in the event-dispatching thread:

```
Thread workHard = new Thread() {
 public void run() {
  doToughWork(); // do some time-intensive work
  SwingUtilities.invokeLater( new Runnable () {
   public void run() {
    updateComponents(); // do some work in event thread
   }
  });
 }
};
workHarder.start();
```

NOTE It is often necessary to explicitly lower the priority of a separate thread so that the event-dispatching thread will be given more processor time and thus allow the GUI to remain responsive. If you have created a separate thread for time-consuming work and you notice that the GUI is still slow or freezes often, try lowering the priority of your separate thread before starting it:

```
workHard.setPriority(Thread.MIN_PRIORITY);
```

This use of a separate thread solves the problem of responsiveness and it correctly dispatches component-related code to the event-dispatching thread. However, in an ideal solution the user should be able to interrupt the time-intensive procedure. If you are waiting to establish a network connection you certainly don't want to continue waiting indefinitely if the destination is not responding. So in most circumstances the user should have the ability to interrupt the thread. The following pseudocode shows a typical way to accomplish this, where the ActionListener attached to stopButton causes the thread to be interrupted, updating component state accordingly:

```
JButton stopButton = new JButton("Stop");
// Before starting the thread make sure
// the stop button is enabled.
stopButton.setEnabled(true);

Thread workHard = new Thread() {
  public void run() {
    doToughWork();
    SwingUtilities.invokeLater {new Runnable() {
      public void run() {
        updateComponents();
      }
    });
  }
};
workHard.start();

Public void doToughwork() {
  try {
    while(job is not finished) {
      // We must do at least one of the following:
      // 1. Periodically check Thread.interrupted()
      // 2. Periodically sleep or wait
      if (thread.interrupted()) {
        throw new InterruptedException();
      }
      Thread.wait(1000);
    }
  }
catch (InterruptedException e) {
    // Notify the application that the thread has
    // has been interrupted
  }
// No matter what happens, disable the
// stop button when finished
finally {
    stopButton.setEnabled(false);
  }
}

actionListener stopListener = new ActionListener() {
  public void actionPerformed(ActionEvent e) {
    workHard.interrupt();
  }
};
stopbutton.addActionListener(stopListener);
```

stopButton interrupts the workHard thread when it is pressed. There are two ways that do-ToughWork() will know whether workHard (the thread that doToughWork() is executed in) has been interrupted by stopButton. If the thread is currently sleeping or waiting, an InterruptedException will be thrown which you can catch and process accordingly. The only other way to detect interruption is to periodically check the interrupted state by calling Thread.interrupted(). Both cases are handled in the doToughWork() method.

This approach is often used for constructing and displaying complex dialogs, I/O processes that result in component state changes (such as loading a document into a text component), intensive class loading or calculations, waiting for messages, and to establish network or database connections.

> **REFERENCE** Members of the Swing team have written a few articles about using threads with Swing, and have provided a class called SwingWorker that makes managing the type of multithreading described here more convenient. See http://java.sun.com/ products/jfc/tsc.

Additionally, progress bars are often used to further enhance the user experience by visually displaying how much of a time-consuming process is complete. Chapter 13 covers this in detail.

2.3.1   Special cases

There are some special cases in which we do not *need* to delegate code affecting the state of components to the event-dispatching thread:

1.   Some methods in Swing, although few and far between, are marked as thread-safe in the API documentation and do not need special consideration. Some methods are thread-safe but are not marked as such: repaint(), revalidate(), and invalidate().

2.   A component can be constructed and manipulated in any fashion we like, without regard for threads, as long as it has not yet been *realized* (meaning it has been displayed or a repaint request has been queued). Top-level containers (JFrame, JDialog, JApplet) are realized after any of setVisible(true), show(), or pack() have been called on them. Also note that a component is considered realized as soon as it is added to a realized container.

3.   When dealing with Swing applets (JApplets), all components can be constructed and manipulated without regard for threads until the start() method has been called; this occurs after the init() method.

2.3.2   How do we build our own thread-safe methods?

Building our own thread-safe cases is quite easy. Here is a thread-safe method template we can use to guarantee that a method's code only executes in the event-dispatching thread:

```
public void doThreadSafeWork() {
  if (SwingUtilities.isEventDispatchThread()) {
   //
   // do all work here...
   //
  }
  else {
```

```
  Runnable callDoThreadSafeWork = new Runnable() {
    public void run() {
      doThreadSafeWork();
    }
  };
  SwingUtilities.invokeLater(callDoThreadSafeWork);
 }
}
```

2.4   TIMERS

class javax.swing.Timer

You can think of the `Timer` as a unique thread conveniently provided by Swing to fire `ActionEvents` at specified intervals (although this is not exactly how a `Timer` works internally, as you will see in section 2.6). `ActionListeners` can be registered to receive these events just as you register them on buttons and other components. To create a simple `Timer` that fires `ActionEvents` every second, you can do something like the following:

```
import java.awt.event.*;
import javax.swing.*;

class TimerTest
{
 public TimerTest() {
  ActionListener act = new ActionListener() {
   public void actionPerformed(ActionEvent e) {
    System.out.println("Swing is powerful!!");
   }
  };
  Timer tim = new Timer(1000, act);
  tim.start();

  while(true) {};
 }
 public static void main( String args[] ) {
  new TimerTest();
 }
}
```

First we set up an `ActionListener` to receive `ActionEvents`. Then we build a new `Timer` by passing the following parameters to the constructor: the time in milliseconds between events, (the delay time), and an `ActionListener` to send `Timer` events to. Finally, we call the `Timer`'s `start()` method to turn it on. Since a GUI isn't running for us, the program will immediately exit; therefore, we set up a loop to let the `Timer` continue to do its job indefinitely (we will explain why this is necessary in section 2.6).

When you run this code, you will see "Swing is powerful!!" sent to standard output every second. Note that the `Timer` does not fire an event right when it is started. This is because its *initial delay* time defaults to the delay time passed to the constructor. If you want the `Timer` to fire an event right when it is started, you need to set the initial delay time to 0 using the `setInitialDelay()` method.

At any point, you can call `stop()` to stop the `Timer` and `start()` to start it (`start()` does nothing if the `Timer` is already running). You can call `restart()` on a `Timer` to start the whole process over. The `restart()` method is just a shortcut way to call `stop()` and `start()` sequentially.

You can set a `Timer`'s delay using the `setDelay()` method and tell it whether to repeat using the `setRepeats()` method. Once a `Timer` has been set to non-repeating, it will fire only one action when started (or if it is currently running), and then it will stop.

The `setCoalesce()` method allows several `Timer` event postings to be combined (coalesced) into one. This can be useful under heavy loads when the `TimerQueue` thread (see 2.6) doesn't have enough processing time to handle all its `Timers`.

`Timers` are easy to use and can often be used as convenient replacements for building our own threads. However, there is a lot more going on behind the scenes that deserves to be revealed. Before we are ready to look at how `Timers` work under the hood, we'll take a look at how Swing's `AppContext` service class mapping works.

JAVA 1.3   A new `Timer` class, and an associated `TimerTask` class, have been added to the `java.util` package in Java 1.3. The `java.util.Timer` class differs from the `javax.swing.Timer` class in that it has an associated separate thread of execution. This thread can be specified as either a deamon or non-deamon thread. `TimerTasks`, which implement the `Runnable` interface, can be added to a `Timer` for execution once or at given intervals at a given future time. This combination adds yet another means for building multithreaded applications.

2.5   APPCONTEXT SERVICES

class sun.awt.AppContext [platform specific]

This section is of interest only to those seeking a low-level understanding of how service classes are shared throughout a Java session. Be aware that `AppContext` is not meant to be used by *any* developer, as it is not part of the Java 2 core API. We are discussing it here only to facilitate a more thorough understanding of how Swing service classes work behind the scenes.

`AppContext` is an application/applet (we'll say app for short) *service* table that is unique to each Java session. For applets, a separate `AppContext` exists for each `SecurityContext` which corresponds to an applet's codebase. For instance, if we have two applets on the same page, each using code from a different directory, both of those applets would have distinct `SecurityContexts` associated with them. If, however, they each were loaded from the same codebase, they would necessarily share a `SecurityContext`. Java applications do not have `SecurityContexts`. Rather, they run in namespaces which are distinguished by `ClassLoaders`. We will not go into the details of `SecurityContexts` or `ClassLoaders` here, but suffice it to say that they can be used by `SecurityManagers` to indicate security domains. The `AppContext` class is designed to take advantage of this by allowing only one instance of itself to exist per security domain. In this way, applets from different codebases cannot access each other's `AppContext`. So why is this significant?

A *shared instance* is an instance of a class that can normally be retrieved using a static method defined in that class. Each `AppContext` maintains a `Hashtable` of shared instances available to the associated security domain, and each instance is referred to as a *service*. When a service is requested for the first time, it registers its shared instance with the associated AppContext, meaning it creates a new instance of itself and adds it to the AppContext key/value mapping.

For example, here are PopupFactory's getSharedInstanceKey() and setShared-Instance() methods:

```
private static final Object SharedInstanceKey =
  new StringBuffer(PopupFactory.SharedInstanceKey");

public static void setSharedInstance(PopupFactory factory) {
  If (factor == null) {
    throw new IllegalArgumentException(
      "PopupFactor can not be null");
  }
  SwingUtilities.appContextPut(SharedInstance() {
}

public static PopupFactory getSharedInstance() {
  PopupFactory factory =
    (PopupFactory) Swingtilities.appContextGet (
    SharedInstanceKey);
  if (factory == null) {
  factory = new PopupFactory();
  setSharedInstance(factory);
  }
  return factory;
}
```

One reason these shared instances are registered with an AppContext, instead of being implemented as normal static instances directly retrievable by the service class, is for security purposes. Services registered with an AppContext can only be accessed by trusted apps, whereas classes directly providing static instances of themselves allow these instances to be used on a global basis (therefore requiring us to implement our own security mechanism if we want to limit access to them). Another reason is robustness. According to Tom Ball of Sun Microsystems, the less applets interact with each other in undocumented ways, the more robust they can be.

For example, suppose an app tries to access all of the key events on the system EventQueue (where all events get queued for processing in the event-dispatching thread) to try to steal passwords. By using distinct EventQueues in each AppContext, the only key events that the app would have access to are its own. (There is, in fact, only one EventQueue per AppContext.)

So how do you access AppContext to add, remove, and retrieve services? AppContext is not meant to be accessed by developers. But you *can* if you really need to, though it would guarantee that your code would never be certified as 100% pure, because AppContext is not part of the core API. Nevertheless, here's what is involved: The static AppContext.getApp-Context() method determines the correct AppContext to use, depending on whether you are running an applet or an application. You can then use the returned AppletContext's put(), get(), and remove() methods to manage shared instances. In order to do this, you would need to implement your own methods, such as the following:

```
  private static Object appContextGet(Object key) {
    return sun.awt.AppContext.getAppContext().get(key);
  }
```

```
private static void appContextPut(Object key, Object value) {
  sun.awt.AppContext.getAppContext().put(key, value);
}

private static void appContextRemove(Object key) {
  sun.awt.AppContext.getAppContext().remove(key);
}
```

In Swing, this functionality is implemented as three `SwingUtilities` static methods (refer to `SwingUtilities.java` source code):

```
static void appContextPut(Object key, Object value)
static void appContextRemove(Object key, Object value)
static Object appContextGet(Object key)
```

However, you cannot access these methods because they are package private. They are used by Swing's service classes. Some of the Swing service classes that register shared instances with `AppContext` include `PopupFactory`, `TimerQueue`, `RepaintManager`, and `UIManager.LAFState` (all of which we will discuss at some point in this book). Interestingly, `SwingUtilities` secretly provides an invisible `Frame` instance registered with `AppContext` to act as the parent to all `JDialogs` and `JWindows` with `null` owners.

2.6 INSIDE TIMERS AND THE TIMERQUEUE

class javax.swing.TimerQueue [package private]

A `Timer` is an object containing a small `Runnable` capable of dispatching `ActionEvents` to a list of `ActionListeners` (which are stored in an `EventListenerList`). Each `Timer` instance is managed by the shared `TimerQueue` instance (which is registered with `AppContext`).

A `TimerQueue` is a service class whose job it is to manage all `Timer` instances in a Java session. The `TimerQueue` class provides the static `sharedInstance()` method to retrieve the `TimerQueue` service from `AppContext`. Whenever a new `Timer` is created and started it is added to the shared `TimerQueue`, which maintains a singly linked list of `Timers` sorted by the order in which they will expire (which is equal to the amount of time before a `Timer` will fire the next event).

The `TimerQueue` is a daemon thread which is started immediately upon instantiation. This occurs when `TimerQueue.sharedInstance()` is called for the first time (such as when the first `Timer` in a Java session is started). It continuously waits for the `Timer` with the nearest expiration time to expire. Once this occurs, it signals that `Timer` to post `ActionEvents` to all its listeners, it assigns a new `Timer` as the head of the list, and finally, it removes the expired `Timer`. If the expired `Timer`'s repeat mode is set to `true`, it is added back into the list at the appropriate place based on its delay time.

NOTE The real reason why the `Timer` example from section 2.4 would exit immediately if we didn't build a loop is because the `TimerQueue` is a *daemon* thread. Daemon threads are service threads. When the Java virtual machine has only daemon threads running, it will exit because it assumes that no real work is being done. Normally, this behavior is desirable.

A `Timer`'s events are always posted in a thread-safe manner to the event-dispatching thread by sending its `Runnable` object to `SwingUtilities.invokeLater()`.

2.7   JAVABEANS ARCHITECTURE

Since we are concerned with creating Swing applications in this book, we need to understand and appreciate the fact that every component in Swing is a JavaBean.

If you are familiar with the JavaBeans component model, you may want to skip to section 2.8.

2.7.1   The JavaBeans component model

The JavaBeans specification identifies five features that each bean is expected to provide. We will review these features here, along with the classes and mechanisms that make them possible. We'll construct a simple component such as a label, and apply what we discuss in this section to that component. We will also assume that you have a basic knowledge of the Java reflection API (the following list comes directly from the API documentation):

- Instances of `Class` represent classes and interfaces in a running Java application.
- A `Method` provides information about, and access to, a single method of a class or an interface.
- A `Field` provides information about, and dynamic access to, a single field of a class or an interface.

2.7.2   Introspection

Introspection is the ability to discover the methods, properties, and events information of a bean. This is accomplished through use of the `java.beans.Introspector` class. `Introspector` provides static methods to generate a `BeanInfo` object containing all discoverable information about a specific bean. This includes information from each of a bean's superclasses, unless we specify at which superclass introspection should stop (for example, you can specify the "depth" of an introspection). The following code retrieves all discoverable information of a bean:

```
BeanInfo myJavaBeanInfo =
  Introspector.getBeanInfo(myJavaBean);
```

A `BeanInfo` object partitions all of a bean's information into several groups. Here are a few:

- A `BeanDescriptor`: Provides general descriptive information such as a display name.
- An array of `EventSetDescriptors`: Provides information about a set of events a bean fires. These can be used to retrieve that bean's event-listener-related methods as `Method` instances, among other things.
- An array of `MethodDescriptors`: Provides information about the methods of a bean that are externally accessible (this would include, for instance, all public methods). This information is used to construct a `Method` instance for each method.
- An array of `PropertyDescriptors`: Provides information about each property that a bean maintains which can be accessed through `get`, `set`, and/or `is` methods. These objects can be used to construct `Method` and `Class` instances corresponding to that property's accessor methods and class type respectively.

2.7.3 Properties

As we discussed in section 2.1.1, beans support different types of properties. *Simple* properties are variables that, when modified, mean a bean will do nothing. *Bound* and *constrained* properties are variables that, when modified, instruct a bean to send notification events to any listeners. This notification takes the form of an event object which contains the property name, the old property value, and the new property value. Whenever a bound property changes, the bean should send out a `PropertyChangeEvent`. Whenever a constrained property is about to change, the bean should send out a `PropertyChangeEvent` *before* the change occurs, allowing the change to possibly be vetoed. Other objects can listen for these events and process them accordingly; this leads to *communication* (see 2.7.5).

Associated with properties are a bean's `setXX()`, `getXX()`, and `isXX()` methods. If a `setXX()` method is available, the associated property is said to be *writeable*. If a `getXX()` or `isXX()` method is available, the associated property is said to be *readable*. An `isXX()` method normally corresponds to retrieval of a boolean property (occasionally, `getXX()` methods are used for this as well).

2.7.4 Customization

A bean's properties are exposed through its `setXX()`, `getXX()`, and `isXX()` methods, and they can be modified at run-time (or design-time). JavaBeans are commonly used in interface development environments where property sheets can be displayed for each bean, thereby allowing read/write (depending on the available accessors) property functionality.

2.7.5 Communication

Beans are designed to send events that notify all event listeners registered with that bean whenever a bound or constrained property changes value. Apps are constructed by registering listeners from bean to bean. Since you can use introspection to determine event listener information about any bean, design tools can take advantage of this knowledge to allow more powerful, design-time customization. Communication is the basic glue that holds an interactive GUI together.

2.7.6 Persistency

All JavaBeans must implement the `Serializable` interface, either directly or indirectly, to allow serialization of their state into persistent storage (storage that exists beyond program termination). All objects are saved except those declared `transient`. (Note that `JComponent` directly implements this interface.)

Classes which need special processing during serialization need to implement the following private methods:

```
private void writeObject(java.io.ObjectOutputStream out)
private void readObject(java.io.ObjectInputStream in )
```

These methods are called to write or read an instance of this class to a stream. The default serialization mechanism will be invoked to serialize all subclasses because these are private methods. (Refer to the API documentation or Java tutorial for more information about serialization.)

Standard serialization of Swing-based classes has not been recommended since the earliest versions of Swing, and according to the API documentation, it is still not ready. However, as of Java 1.4. all JavaBeans (and thus all Swing components) are serializable into XML form using the java.beans.XMLEncoder class:

"*Warning:* Serialized objects of this class will not be compatible with future Swing releases. The current serialization support is appropriate for short term storage or RMI between applications running the same version of Swing. As of 1.4, support for long-term storage of all JavaBeans^{TM} has been added to the java.beans package. Please see XMLEncoder."

To serialize a component to an XML file you can write code similar to the following:

```
XMLEncoder encoder = new XMLEncoder(
  new BufferedOutputStream(
    new FileOutputStream("myTextField.xml")));
encoder.writeObject (myTextField);
encoder.close();
```

Similarly, to recreate an object serialized using XMLEncoder, the java.beans.XML-Decoder class can be used:

```
XMLDecoder decoder = new XMLDecoder(
  new BufferedInputStream(
    new FileInputStream("myTextField.xml")));
myTextField = (JTextField) decoder.readObject();
decoder.close();
```

Classes that intend to take complete control of their serialization and deserialization should, instead, implement the Externalizable interface.

Two methods are defined in the Externalizable interface:

```
public void writeExternal(ObjectOutput out)
public void readExternal(ObjectInput in)
```

These methods will be invoked when writeObject() and readObject() (discussed above) are invoked to handle any serialization/deserialization.

2.7.7   A simple Swing-based JavaBean

Example 2.1 demonstrates how to build a serializable Swing-based JavaBean with simple, bound, constrained, and change properties.

Example 2.1

BakedBean.java

see \Chapter2\1

```
import javax.swing.*;
import javax.swing.event.*;
import java.beans.*;
```

```java
import java.awt.*;
import java.io.*;

public class BakedBean extends JComponent implements Externalizable
{
  // Property names (only needed for bound or constrained properties)
  public static final String BEAN_VALUE = "Value";
  public static final String BEAN_COLOR = "Color";

  // Properties
  private Font m_beanFont;           // simple
  private Dimension m_beanDimension; // simple
  private int m_beanValue;           // bound
  private Color m_beanColor;         // constrained
  private String m_beanString;       // change

  // Manages all PropertyChangeListeners
  protected SwingPropertyChangeSupport m_supporter =
   new SwingPropertyChangeSupport(this);

  // Manages all VetoableChangeListeners
  protected VetoableChangeSupport m_vetoer =
   new VetoableChangeSupport(this);

  // Only one ChangeEvent is needed since the event's only
  // state is the source property. The source of events generated
  // is always "this". You'll see this in lots of Swing source.
  protected transient ChangeEvent m_changeEvent = null;

  // This can manage all types of listeners, as long as we set
  // up the fireXX methods to correctly look through this list.
  // This makes you appreciate the XXSupport classes.
  protected EventListenerList m_listenerList =
   new EventListenerList();

  public BakedBean() {
   m_beanFont = new Font("SansSerif", Font.BOLD | Font.ITALIC, 12);
   m_beanDimension = new Dimension(150,100);
   m_beanValue = 0;
   m_beanColor = Color.black;
   m_beanString = "BakedBean #";
  }

  public void paintComponent(Graphics g) {
   super.paintComponent(g);
   g.setColor(m_beanColor);
   g.setFont(m_beanFont);
   g.drawString(m_beanString + m_beanValue,30,30);
  }

  public void setBeanFont(Font font) {
   m_beanFont = font;
  }

  public Font getBeanFont() {
   return m_beanFont;
  }
```

```java
public void setBeanValue(int newValue) {
 int oldValue = m_beanValue;
 m_beanValue = newValue;

 // Notify all PropertyChangeListeners
 m_supporter.firePropertyChange(BEAN_VALUE,
  new Integer(oldValue), new Integer(newValue));
}

public int getBeanValue() {
 return m_beanValue;
}

public void setBeanColor(Color newColor)
 throws PropertyVetoException {
 Color oldColor = m_beanColor;

 // Notify all VetoableChangeListeners before making change
 // ...an exception will be thrown here if there is a veto
 // ...if not, continue on and make the change
 m_vetoer.fireVetoableChange(BEAN_COLOR, oldColor, newColor);

 m_beanColor = newColor;
 m_supporter.firePropertyChange(BEAN_COLOR, oldColor, newColor);
}

public Color getBeanColor() {
 return m_beanColor;
}

public void setBeanString(String newString) {
 m_beanString = newString;

 // Notify all ChangeListeners
 fireStateChanged();
}

public String getBeanString() {
 return m_beanString;
}

public void setPreferredSize(Dimension dim) {
 m_beanDimension = dim;
}

public Dimension getPreferredSize() {
 return m_beanDimension;
}

public void setMinimumSize(Dimension dim) {
 m_beanDimension = dim;
}

public Dimension getMinimumSize() {
 return m_beanDimension;
}

public void addPropertyChangeListener(
  PropertyChangeListener l) {
```

```java
  m_supporter.addPropertyChangeListener(1);
}

public void removePropertyChangeListener(
 PropertyChangeListener l) {
 m_supporter.removePropertyChangeListener(l);
}

public void addVetoableChangeListener(
 VetoableChangeListener l) {
 m_vetoer.addVetoableChangeListener(l);
}

public void removeVetoableChangeListener(
 VetoableChangeListener l) {
 m_vetoer.removeVetoableChangeListener(l);
}

// Remember that EventListenerList is an array of
// key/value pairs:
//   key = XXListener class reference
//   value = XXListener instance
public void addChangeListener(ChangeListener l) {
 m_listenerList.add(ChangeListener.class, l);
}

public void removeChangeListener(ChangeListener l) {
 m_listenerList.remove(ChangeListener.class, l);
}

// This is typical EventListenerList dispatching code.
// You'll see this in lots of Swing source.
protected void fireStateChanged() {
 Object[] listeners = m_listenerList.getListenerList();
 // Process the listeners last to first, notifying
 // those that are interested in this event
 for (int i = listeners.length-2; i>=0; i-=2) {
  if (listeners[i]==ChangeListener.class) {
   if (m_changeEvent == null)
    m_changeEvent = new ChangeEvent(this);
    ((ChangeListener)listeners[i+1]).stateChanged(m_changeEvent);
  }
 }
}

public void writeExternal(ObjectOutput out) throws IOException {
 out.writeObject(m_beanFont);
 out.writeObject(m_beanDimension);
 out.writeInt(m_beanValue);
 out.writeObject(m_beanColor);
 out.writeObject(m_beanString);
}

public void readExternal(ObjectInput in)
 throws IOException, ClassNotFoundException {
 setBeanFont((Font)in.readObject());
 setPreferredSize((Dimension)in.readObject());
```

```
 // Use preferred size for minimum size
 setMinimumSize(getPreferredSize());
 setBeanValue(in.readInt());
 try {
  setBeanColor((Color)in.readObject());
 }
 catch (PropertyVetoException pve) {
  System.out.println("Color change vetoed.");
 }
 setBeanString((String)in.readObject());
 }

public static void main(String[] args) {
 JFrame frame = new JFrame("BakedBean");
 frame.getContentPane().add(new BakedBean());
 frame.setDefaultCloseOperation(JFrame.EXIT_ON_CLOSE);
 frame.setVisible(true);
 frame.pack();
 }
}
```

BakedBean has a visual representation (this is not a requirement for a bean). It has *properties*: m_beanValue, m_beanColor, m_beanFont, m_beanDimension, and m_beanString. It supports *persistency* by implementing the Externalizable interface and implementing the writeExternal() and readExternal() methods to control its own serialization (note that the orders in which data is written and read match). BakedBean supports *customization* through its setXX() and getXX() methods, and it supports *communication* by allowing the registration of PropertyChangeListeners, VetoableChangeListeners, and ChangeListeners. And, without having to do anything special, it supports *introspection*.

Attaching a main method to display BakedBean in a frame does not get in the way of any JavaBeans functionality. Figure 2.1 shows BakedBean when it is executed as an application.

Figure 2.1
BakedBean in our custom
JavaBeans property editor

In chapter 18, section 18.9, we will construct a full-featured JavaBeans property editing environment. Figure 2.2 shows a BakedBean instance in this environment. The BakedBean shown has had its m_beanDimension, m_beanColor, and m_beanValue properties modified with our property editor, and it was then serialized to disk. What figure 2.2 really shows is an instance of that BakedBean after it had been deserialized (loaded from disk). Any Swing component can be created, modified, serialized, and deserialized using this environment because every component is JavaBeans compliant.

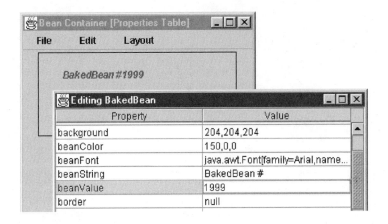

Figure 2.2 **BakedBean in our custom JavaBeans property editor**

2.8 FONTS, COLORS, GRAPHICS, AND TEXT

Now to begin our look at how to render fonts, colors, and text using graphics objects.

2.8.1 Fonts

class java.awt.Font, abstract class java.awt.GraphicsEnvironment

As we saw in the BakedBean example, fonts are quite easy to create:

```
m_beanFont = new Font("SansSerif", Font.BOLD | Font.ITALIC, 12);
```

In this code, SansSerif is the font *name*, Font.BOLD | Font.ITALIC is the font *style* (which in this case is both bold and italic), and 12 is the font *size*. The Font class defines three static int constants to denote font style: Font.BOLD, Font.ITALIC, and Font.PLAIN. You can specify font size as any int in the Font constructor. Using Java 2, we ask the local GraphicsEnvironment for a list of available font names at run-time.

```
GraphicsEnvironment ge = GraphicsEnvironment.
 getLocalGraphicsEnvironment();
String[] fontNames = ge.getAvailableFontFamilyNames();
```

NOTE   Java 2 introduces a new, powerful mechanism for communicating with devices that can render graphics, such as screens, printers, or image buffers. These devices are represented as instances of the GraphicsDevice class. Interestingly, a GraphicsDevice might reside on the local machine, or it might reside on a remote machine. Each GraphicsDevice has a set of GraphicsConfiguration objects associated with it. A GraphicsConfiguration describes specific characteristics of the associated device. Usually each GraphicsConfiguration of a GraphicsDevice represents a different mode of operation (for instance, resolution and the number of colors).

NOTE In JDK1.1 code, getting a list of font *name*s often looked like this:

```
String[] fontnames = Toolkit.getDefaultToolkit().getFontList();
```

The `getFontList()` method has been deprecated in Java 2, and this code should be updated.

`GraphicsEnvironment` is an abstract class that describes a collection of `GraphicsDevices`. Subclasses of `GraphicsEnvironment` must provide three methods for retrieving arrays of `Fonts` and `Font` information:

`Font[] getAllFonts()`: Retrieves all available `Fonts` in one-point size.

`String[] getAvailableFontFamilyNames()`: Retrieves the names of all available font families.

`String[] getAvailableFontFamilyNames(Locale l)`: Retrieves the names of all available font families using the specific `Locale` (internationalization support).

`GraphicsEnvironment` also provides static methods for retrieving `GraphicsDevices` and the local `GraphicsEnvironment` instance. In order to find out what `Fonts` are available to the system on which your program is running, you must refer to this local `GraphicsEnvironment` instance, as shown above. It is much more efficient and convenient to retrieve the available names and use them to construct `Fonts` than it is to retrieve an actual array of `Font` objects (no less, in one-point size).

You might think that, given a `Font` object, you can use typical `getXX()/setXX()` accessors to alter its name, style, and size. Well, you would be half right. You *can* use `getXX()` methods to retrieve this information from a `Font`:

```
String getName()
int getSize()
float getSize2D()
int getStyle()
```

However, you *cannot* use typical `setXX()` methods. Instead, you must use one of the following `Font` instance methods to derive a new `Font`:

```
deriveFont(float size)
deriveFont(int style)
deriveFont(int style, float size)
deriveFont(Map attributes)
deriveFont(AffineTransform trans)
deriveFont(int style, AffineTransform trans)
```

Normally, you will only be interested in the first three methods.

NOTE `AffineTransforms` are used in the world of Java 2D to perform things such as translations, scales, flips, rotations, and shears. A `Map` is an object that maps keys to values (it does not contain the objects involved), and the *attributes* referred to here are key/value pairs as described in the API documents for `java.text.TextAttribute`.

2.8.2 Colors

class java.awt. Color

The `Color` class provides several static `Color` instances to be used for convenience (`Color.blue`, `Color.yellow`, etc.). You can also construct a `Color` using the following constructors, among others:

```
Color(float r, float g, float b)
Color(int r, int g, int b)
Color(float r, float g, float b, float a)
Color(int r, int g, int b, int a)
```

Normally you use the first two methods, and if you are familiar with JDK1.1, you will probably recognize them. The first method allows red, green, and blue values to be specified as `floats` from 0.0 to 1.0. The second method takes these values as `ints` from 0 to 255.

The second two methods are new to Java 2. They each contain a fourth parameter which represents the `Color`'s *alpha* value. The alpha value directly controls transparency. It defaults to 1.0 or 255, which means completely opaque. 0.0 or 0 means completely transparent.

As with `Fonts`, there are plenty of `getXX()` accessors but no `setXX()` accessors. Instead of modifying a `Color` object, we are normally expected to create a new one.

> **NOTE**   The `Color` class does have static `brighter()` and `darker()` methods that return a `Color` brighter or darker than the `Color` specified, but their behavior is unpredictable due to internal rounding errors. We suggest staying away from these methods for most practical purposes.

By specifying an alpha value, you can use the resulting `Color` as a component's background to make it transparent. This will work for any lightweight component provided by Swing such as labels, text components, and internal frames. (Of course, there will be component-specific issues involved, such as making the borders and title bar of an internal frame transparent.) The next section demonstrates a simple Swing canvas example that uses the alpha value to paint some transparent shapes.

> **NOTE**   A Swing component's opaque property, controlled using `setOpaque()`, is not directly related to `Color` transparency. For instance, if you have an opaque `JLabel` whose background has been set to a transparent green (`Color(0,255,0,150)`) the label's bounds will be completely filled with this color only because it is opaque. You will be able to see through it only because the color is transparent. If you then turned off opacity, the background of the label would not be rendered. Both need to be used together to create transparent components, but they are not directly related.

2.8.3 Graphics and text

abstract class java.awt. Graphics, abstract class java.awt.FontMetrics

Painting is different in Swing than it is in AWT. In AWT you typically override `Component`'s `paint()` method to do rendering, and you override the `update()` method for things like implementing our own double-buffering or filling the background before `paint()` is called.

With Swing, component rendering is much more complex. Though `JComponent` is a subclass of `Component`, it uses the `update()` and `paint()` methods for different reasons. In fact, the `update()` method is never invoked at all. There are also five additional stages of painting that normally occur from within the `paint()` method. We will discuss this process in section 2.11, but suffice it to say here that any `JComponent` subclass that wants to take control of its own rendering should override the `paintComponent()` method and not the `paint()` method. Additionally, it should always begin its `paintComponent()` method with a call to `super.paintComponent()`.

Knowing this, it is quite easy to build a `JComponent` that acts as your own *lightweight canvas*. All you have to do is subclass it and override the `paintComponent()` method. You can do all of your painting inside this method. This is how to take control of the rendering of simple custom components. However, do not attempt this with normal Swing components because UI delegates are in charge of their rendering (we will show you how to customize UI delegate rendering at the end of chapter 6 and throughout chapter 21).

NOTE   The AWT `Canvas` class can be replaced by a simple subclass of `JComponent`. See example 2.2.

Inside the `paintComponent()` method, you have access to that component's `Graphics` object (often referred to as a component's *graphics context*) which you can use to paint shapes and draw lines and text. The `Graphics` class defines many methods used for these purposes; refer to the API docs for more information on these methods. Example 2.2 shows how to construct a `JComponent` subclass that paints an `ImageIcon` and some shapes and text using various `Fonts` and `Colors`, some completely opaque and some partially transparent (we saw similar but less interesting functionality in `BakedBean`). Figure 2.3 illustrates the output of example 2.2.

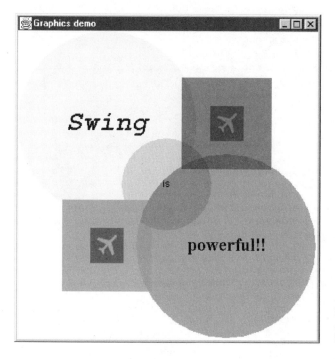

**Figure 2.3
A Graphics demo
in a lightweight canvas**

Example 2.2

see \Chapter2\2

```java
import java.awt.*;
import javax.swing.*;

class TestFrame extends JFrame
{
 public TestFrame() {
  super( "Graphics demo" );
  getContentPane().add(new JCanvas());
 }

 public static void main( String args[] ) {
  TestFrame mainFrame = new TestFrame();
  mainFrame.pack();
  mainFrame.setDefaultCloseOperation(JFrame.EXIT_ON_CLOSE);
  mainFrame.setVisible( true );
 }
}

class JCanvas extends JComponent {
 private static Color m_tRed = new Color(255,0,0,150);
 private static Color m_tGreen = new Color(0,255,0,150);
 private static Color m_tBlue = new Color(0,0,255,150);

 private static Font m_biFont =
  new Font("Monospaced", Font.BOLD | Font.ITALIC, 36);
 private static Font m_pFont =
  new Font("SansSerif", Font.PLAIN, 12);
 private static Font m_bFont = new Font("Serif", Font.BOLD, 24);

 private static ImageIcon m_flight = new ImageIcon("flight.gif");

 public JCanvas() {
  setDoubleBuffered(true);
  setOpaque(true);
 }

 public void paintComponent(Graphics g) {
  super.paintComponent(g);

  // Fill the entire component with white
  g.setColor(Color.white);
  g.fillRect(0,0,getWidth(),getHeight());

  // Filled yellow circle
  g.setColor(Color.yellow);
  g.fillOval(0,0,240,240);

  // Filled magenta circle
  g.setColor(Color.magenta);
  g.fillOval(160,160,240,240);

  // Paint the icon below the blue square
```

```java
        int w = m_flight.getIconWidth();
        int h = m_flight.getIconHeight();
        m_flight.paintIcon(this,g,280-(w/2),120-(h/2));

        // Paint the icon below the red square
        m_flight.paintIcon(this,g,120-(w/2),280-(h/2));

        // Filled transparent red square
        g.setColor(m_tRed);
        g.fillRect(60,220,120,120);

        // Filled transparent green circle
        g.setColor(m_tGreen);
        g.fillOval(140,140,120,120);

        // Filled transparent blue square
        g.setColor(m_tBlue);
        g.fillRect(220,60,120,120);

        g.setColor(Color.black);

        // Bold, Italic, 36-point "Swing"
        g.setFont(m_biFont);
        FontMetrics fm = g.getFontMetrics();
        w = fm.stringWidth("Swing");
        h = fm.getAscent();
        g.drawString("Swing",120-(w/2),120+(h/4));

        // Plain, 12-point "is"
        g.setFont(m_pFont);
        fm = g.getFontMetrics();
        w = fm.stringWidth("is");
        h = fm.getAscent();
        g.drawString("is",200-(w/2),200+(h/4));

        // Bold, 24-point "powerful!!"
        g.setFont(m_bFont);
        fm = g.getFontMetrics();
        w = fm.stringWidth("powerful!!");
        h = fm.getAscent();
        g.drawString("powerful!!",280-(w/2),280+(h/4));
    }

    // Most layout managers need this information
    public Dimension getPreferredSize() {
     return new Dimension(400,400);
    }

    public Dimension getMinimumSize() {
     return getPreferredSize();
    }

    public Dimension getMaximumSize() {
     return getPreferredSize();
    }
 }
```

Note that we overrode JComponent's getPreferredSize(), getMinimumSize(), and getMaximumSize() methods so most layout managers can intelligently size this component (otherwise, some layout managers will set its size to 0x0). It is always a good practice to override these methods when implementing custom components.

The Graphics class uses what is called the *clipping area*. Inside a component's paint() method, this is the region of that component's view that is being repainted (we often say that the clipping area represents the *damaged* or *dirtied* region of the component's view). Only painting done within the clipping area's bounds will actually be rendered. You can get the size and position of these bounds by calling getClipBounds(), which will give you back a Rectangle instance describing it. A clipping area is used for efficiency purposes: there is no reason to paint undamaged or invisible regions when we don't have to. We will show you how to extend this example to work with the clipping area for maximum efficiency in the next section.

NOTE   All Swing components are double buffered by default. If you are building your own lightweight canvas, you do not have to worry about double-buffering. This is not the case with an AWT Canvas.

As we mentioned earlier, Fonts and Font manipulation are very complex under the hood. We are certainly glossing over their structure, but one thing we should discuss is how to obtain useful information about fonts and the text rendered using them. This involves the use of the FontMetrics class. In our example, FontMetrics allowed us to determine the width and height of three Strings, rendered in the current Font associated with the Graphics object, so that we could draw them centered in the circles.

Figure 2.4 illustrates some of the most common information that can be retrieved from a FontMetrics object. The meaning of *baseline*, *ascent*, *descent*, and *height* should be clear from the diagram. The ascent is supposed to be the distance from the baseline to the top of most characters in that font. Notice that when we use g.drawString() to render text, the coordinates specified represent the position in which to place the baseline of the first character.

FontMetrics provides several methods for retrieving this and more detailed information, such as the width of a String rendered in the associated Font.

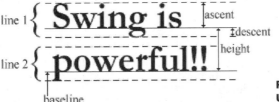

Figure 2.4
Using FontMetrics

In order to get a FontMetrics instance, you first tell your Graphics object to use the Font you are interested in examining using the setFont() method. Then you create the FontMetrics instance by calling getFontMetrics() on your Graphics object:

```
g.setFont(m_biFont);
FontMetrics fm = g.getFontMetrics();
```

CHAPTER 2   SWING MECHANICS

A typical operation when rendering text is to center it on a given point. Suppose you want to center the text "Swing" on 200,200. Here is the code you would use (assuming you have retrieved the `FontMetrics` object, fm):

```
int w = fm.stringWidth("Swing");
int h = fm.getAscent();
g.drawString("Swing",200-(w/2),200+(h/4));
```

You get the width of "Swing" in the current font, divide it by two, and subtract it from 200 to center the text horizontally. To center it vertically, you get the ascent of the current font, divide it by four, and add 200. The reason you divide the ascent by four is probably NOT so clear but we'll explain it in the following example.

It is now time to address a common mistake that has arisen with Java 2. Figure 2.4 is not an entirely accurate way to document `FontMetrics`. This is the way we have seen things documented in the Java tutorial and just about everywhere else that we have referenced. However, there appear to be a few problems with `FontMetrics` that existed in Java 1.2, and still appear to exist in Java 1.3 and 1.4. Example 2.3 is a simple program that demonstrates these problems. Our program draws the text "Swing" in a 36-point bold, monospaced font. We draw lines where its ascent, ascent/2, ascent/4, baseline, and descent lie. Figure 2.5 illustrates this.

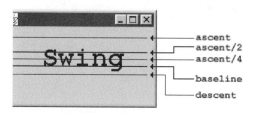

Figure 2.5
The real deal with
FontMetrics in Java 2

Example 2.3

TestFrame.java

See \Chapter2\3\fontmetrics

```
import java.awt.*;
import javax.swing.*;

class TestFrame extends JFrame
{
 public TestFrame() {
  super( "Let's get it straight!" );
  getContentPane().add(new JCanvas());
 }

 public static void main( String args[] ) {
  TestFrame mainFrame = new TestFrame();
  mainFrame.pack();
  mainFrame.setDefaultCloseOperation(JFrame.EXIT_ON_CLOSE);
  mainFrame.setVisible( true );
 }
}
```

```
class JCanvas extends JComponent
{
 private static Font m_biFont = new Font("Monospaced", Font.BOLD, 36);

 public void paintComponent(Graphics g) {
  g.setColor(Color.black);

  // Bold, 36-point "Swing"
  g.setFont(m_biFont);
  FontMetrics fm = g.getFontMetrics();
  int h = fm.getAscent();

  g.drawString("Swing",50,50); // Try these as well: Ñ Ö Ü ^

  // Draw ascent line
  g.drawLine(10,50-h,190,50-h);

  // Draw ascent/2 line
  g.drawLine(10,50-(h/2),190,50-(h/2));

  // Draw ascent/4 line
  g.drawLine(10,50-(h/4),190,50-(h/4));

  // Draw baseline line
  g.drawLine(10,50,190,50);

  // Draw descent line
  g.drawLine(10,50+fm.getDescent(),190,50+fm.getDescent());
 }
 public Dimension getPreferredSize() {
  return new Dimension(200,100);
 }
}
```

We encourage you to try this demo program with various fonts, font sizes, and even characters with diacritical marks such as Ñ, Ö, or Ü. You may find that the ascent is always much higher than it is typically documented to be, and the descent is always lower. The most reliable means of vertically centering text we found turned out to be baseline + ascent/4. However, baseline + descent might also be used, and, depending on the font being used, it may provide more accurate centering.

The point is that there is no correct way to perform this task because of the current state of FontMetrics. You may experience very different results if you're using a different platform or font. It is a good idea to run the sample program we just gave you and verify whether results similar to those shown in figure 2.5 are produced on your system. If they're not, you may want to use a different centering mechanism for your text (depending on the platform used by your target users); it should be fairly simple to determine through experimentation with this application.

NOTE   In JDK1.1 code, getting a FontMetrics instance often looked like this:

FontMetrics fm = Toolkit.getDefaultToolkit().getFontMetrics(myfont);

The getFontMetrics() method has been deprecated in Java 2 and this code should be updated to use the Graphics class's getFontMetrics method.

2.9   USING THE GRAPHICS CLIPPING AREA

You can use the clipping area to optimize component rendering. This may not noticeably improve rendering speed for simple components such as JCanvas, but it is important to understand how to implement such functionality, as Swing's whole painting system is based on this concept (you will find out more about this in the next section).

In example 2.4, we'll modify JCanvas so that each of our shapes, strings, and images is only painted if the clipping area intersects its bounding rectangular region. (These intersections are fairly simple to compute, and it may be helpful for you to work through and verify each one.) Additionally, we'll maintain a local counter that is incremented each time one of our items is painted. At the end of the paintComponent() method, we'll display the total number of items that were painted. Our optimized JCanvas paintComponent() method (with counter) follows.

Example 2.4

JCanvas.java

see \Chapter2\3

```
public void paintComponent(Graphics g) {
  super.paintComponent(g);

  // Counter
  int c = 0;

  // For use below
  int w = 0;
  int h = 0;
  int d = 0;

  // Get damaged region
  Rectangle r = g.getClipBounds();
  int clipx = r.x;
  int clipy = r.y;
  int clipw = r.width;
  int cliph = r.height;

  // Fill damaged region only
  g.setColor(Color.white);
  g.fillRect(clipx,clipy,clipw,cliph);

  // Draw filled yellow circle if bounding region has been damaged
  if (clipx <= 240 && clipy <= 240) {
   g.setColor(Color.yellow);
   g.fillOval(0,0,240,240); c++;
  }

  // Draw filled magenta circle if bounding region has been damaged
  if (clipx + clipw >= 160 && clipx <= 400
    && clipy + cliph >= 160 && clipy <= 400) {
   g.setColor(Color.magenta);
   g.fillOval(160,160,240,240); c++;
  }
```

```
w = m_flight.getIconWidth();
h = m_flight.getIconHeight();
// Paint the icon below blue square if bounding region is damaged
if (clipx + clipw >= 280-(w/2) && clipx <= (280+(w/2))
   && clipy + cliph >= 120-(h/2) && clipy <= (120+(h/2))) {
 m_flight.paintIcon(this,g,280-(w/2),120-(h/2)); c++;
}

// Paint the icon below red square if bounding region is damaged
if (clipx + clipw >= 120-(w/2) && clipx <= (120+(w/2))
   && clipy + cliph >= 280-(h/2) && clipy <= (280+(h/2))) {
 m_flight.paintIcon(this,g,120-(w/2),280-(h/2)); c++;
}

// Draw filled transparent red square if bounding region is damaged
if (clipx + clipw >= 60 && clipx <= 180
   && clipy + cliph >= 220 && clipy <= 340) {
 g.setColor(m_tRed);
 g.fillRect(60,220,120,120); c++;
}

// Draw filled transparent green circle if bounding region is damaged
if (clipx + clipw > 140 && clipx < 260
   && clipy + cliph > 140 && clipy < 260) {
 g.setColor(m_tGreen);
 g.fillOval(140,140,120,120); c++;
}

// Draw filled transparent blue square if bounding region is damaged
if (clipx + clipw > 220 && clipx < 380
   && clipy + cliph > 60 && clipy < 180) {
 g.setColor(m_tBlue);
 g.fillRect(220,60,120,120); c++;
}

g.setColor(Color.black);

g.setFont(m_biFont);
FontMetrics fm = g.getFontMetrics();
w = fm.stringWidth("Swing");
h = fm.getAscent();
d = fm.getDescent();
// Bold, Italic, 36-point "Swing" if bounding region is damaged
if (clipx + clipw > 120-(w/2) && clipx < (120+(w/2))
   && clipy + cliph > (120+(h/4))-h && clipy < (120+(h/4))+d)
{
 g.drawString("Swing",120-(w/2),120+(h/4)); c++;
}

g.setFont(m_pFont);
fm = g.getFontMetrics();
w = fm.stringWidth("is");
h = fm.getAscent();
d = fm.getDescent();
// Plain, 12-point "is" if bounding region is damaged
if (clipx + clipw > 200-(w/2) && clipx < (200+(w/2))
```

```
       && clipy + cliph > (200+(h/4))-h && clipy < (200+(h/4))+d)
   {
     g.drawString("is",200-(w/2),200+(h/4)); c++;
   }

   g.setFont(m_bFont);
   fm = g.getFontMetrics();
   w = fm.stringWidth("powerful!!");
   h = fm.getAscent();
   d = fm.getDescent();
   // Bold, 24-point "powerful!!" if bounding region is damaged
   if (clipx + clipw > 280-(w/2) && clipx < (280+(w/2))
       && clipy + cliph > (280+(h/4))-h && clipy < (280+(h/4))+d)
   {
     g.drawString("powerful!!",280-(w/2),280+(h/4)); c++;
   }

   System.out.println("# items repainted = " + c + "/10");
 }
```

Try running this example and dragging another window in your desktop over parts of the
JCanvas. Keep your console in view so that you can monitor how many items are painted
during each repaint. Your output should be displayed something like the following (of course,
you'll probably see different numbers):

```
# items repainted = 4/10
# items repainted = 0/10
# items repainted = 2/10
# items repainted = 2/10
# items repainted = 1/10
# items repainted = 2/10
# items repainted = 10/10
# items repainted = 10/10
# items repainted = 8/10
# items repainted = 4/10
```

Optimizing this canvas wasn't that bad, but imagine how tough it would be to optimize a
container with a variable number of children, possibly overlapping, with double-buffering
options and transparency. This is what JComponent does, and it does it quite efficiently. We
will learn a little more about how this is done in section 2.11. But first we'll finish our high-
level overview of graphics by introducing a very powerful and well-met feature new to Swing:
graphics debugging.

2.10   GRAPHICS DEBUGGING

Graphics debugging provides the ability to observe each painting operation that occurs during
the rendering of a component and all of its children. This is done in slow motion, using distinct flashes to indicate the region being painted. It is intended to help find problems with
rendering, layouts, and container hierarchies—just about any display-related problems. If graphics debugging is enabled, the Graphics object used in painting is actually an instance of
DebugGraphics (a subclass of Graphics). JComponent, and thus all Swing components,
supports graphics debugging and it can be turned on or off with JComponent's setDebug-

Graphics-Options() method. This method takes an int parameter which is normally one of four static values defined in DebugGraphics (or it's a bitmask combination using the bitwise | operator).

2.10.1 Graphics debugging options

There are four graphics debugging options: DebugGraphics.FLASH_OPTION, DebugGraphics.LOG_OPTION, DebugGraphics.BUFFERED_OPTION, and DebugGraphics.NONE_ OPTION. They will all be discussed in this section.

With the DebugGraphics.FLASH_OPTION, each paint operation flashes a specified number of times, in a specified flash color, with a specified flash interval. The default flash interval is 250ms, the default flash number is 4, and the default flash color is red. These values can be set with the following DebugGraphics static methods:

```
setFlashTime(int flashTime)
setFlashCount(int flashCount)
setFlashColor(Color flashColor)
```

If you don't disable double-buffering in the RepaintManager (which is discussed in the next section), you will not see the painting as it occurs:

```
RepaintManager.currentManager(null).
  setDoubleBufferingEnabled(false);
```

NOTE   Turning off buffering in the RepaintManager has the effect of ignoring *every* component's doubleBuffered property.

The DebugGraphics.LOG_OPTION sends messages describing each paint operation as it occurs. By default, these messages are directed to standard output (the console: System.out). However, we can change the log destination with DebugGraphics' static setLogStream() method. This method takes a PrintStream parameter. To send output to a file, you would do something like the following:

```
PrintStream debugStream = null;
try {
 debugStream = new PrintStream(
  new FileOutputStream("JCDebug.txt"));
}
catch (Exception e) {
 System.out.println("can't open JCDebug.txt..");
}
DebugGraphics.setLogStream(debugStream);
```

If at some point you need to change the log stream back to standard output, you can do this:

```
DebugGraphics.setLogStream(System.out);
```

You can insert any string into the log by retrieving it with DebugGraphics' static logStream() method, and then printing into it:

```
PrintStream ps = DebugGraphics.logStream();
ps.println("\n===> paintComponent ENTERED <===");
```

WARNING   Writing a log to a file will overwrite that file each time you reset the stream.

Each operation is printed with the following syntax:

```
"Graphics" + (isDrawingBuffer() ? "<B>" : "") +
"(" + graphicsID + "-" +  debugOptions + ")"
```

Each line starts with "Graphics." The isDrawingBuffer() method tells you whether buffering is enabled. If it is, a "<B>" is appended. The graphicsID and debugOptions values are then placed in parentheses, and separated by a "-." The graphicsID value represents the number of DebugGraphics instances that have been created during the application's lifetime (it's a static int counter). The debugOptions value represents the current debugging mode:

```
LOG_OPTION = 1
LOG_OPTION and FLASH_OPTION = 3
LOG_OPTION and BUFFERED_OPTION = 5
LOG_OPTION, FLASH_OPTION, and BUFFERED_OPTION = 7
```

For example, with logging and flashing enabled, you see output similar to the following for each operation:

```
Graphics(1-3) Setting color: java.awt.Color[r=0,g=255,b=0]
```

Calls to each Graphics method will get logged when this option is enabled. The code example line was generated when a call to setColor() was made.

The DebugGraphics.BUFFERED_OPTION is supposed to pop up a frame showing rendering as it occurs in the offscreen buffer if double-buffering is enabled. As of the Java 1.4, this option is not still functional.

The DebugGraphics.NONE_OPTION nullifies graphics debugging settings and shuts off graphics debugging altogether.

2.10.2   Graphics debugging caveats

There are two issues to be aware of when using graphics debugging. First, graphics debugging will not work for any component whose UI is null. Thus, if you have created a direct JComponent subclass without a UI delegate, as we did with JCanvas above, graphics debugging will simply do nothing. The simplest way to work around this is to define a trivial (empty) UI delegate. We'll show you how to do this in the example below.

Second, DebugGraphics does not properly clean up after itself. By default, a solid red flash color is used. When a region is flashed, that region is filled in with the red flash color and it does not get erased—it just gets painted over. This presents a problem because transparent rendering will not show up as transparent. Instead, it will be alpha-blended with the red below (or whatever the flash color happens to be set to). This is not necessarily a design flaw, because there is nothing stopping us from using a completely transparent flash color. With an alpha value of 0, the flash color will never be seen. The only downside is that we don't see any flashing. However, in most cases it is easy to follow what is being drawn if we set the flashTime and flashCount to wait long enough between operations.

2.10.3   Using graphics debugging

We'll now enable graphics debugging in our JCanvas example from the last two sections. Because we must have a non-null UI delegate, we define a trivial extension of ComponentUI and implement its createUI() method to return a static instance of itself:

```
class EmptyUI extends ComponentUI
{
 private static final EmptyUI sharedInstance = new EmptyUI();

 public static ComponentUI createUI(JComponent c) {
  return sharedInstance;
 }
}
```

In order to properly associate this UI delegate with JCanvas, we simply call super.setUI(EmptyUI.createUI(this)) from the JCanvas constructor. We also set up a PrintStream variable in JCanvas and use it to add a few of our own lines to the log stream during the paintComponent() method in order to log when the method starts and finishes. Other than this, no changes have been made to the JCanvas's paintComponent() code.

In our test application, TestFrame (example 2.5), we create an instance of JCanvas and enable graphics debugging with the LOG_OPTION and FLASH_OPTION options. We disable buffering in the RepaintManager, set the flash time to 100ms, set the flash count to 2, and use a completely transparent flash color.

Example 2.5

TestFrame.java

see \Chapter2\5

```
import java.awt.*;
import javax.swing.*;
import javax.swing.plaf.*;
import java.io.*;

class TestFrame extends JFrame
{
 public TestFrame() {
  super( "Graphics demo" );
  JCanvas jc = new JCanvas();
  RepaintManager.currentManager(jc).
   setDoubleBufferingEnabled(false);
  jc.setDebugGraphicsOptions(DebugGraphics.LOG_OPTION |
   DebugGraphics.FLASH_OPTION);
  DebugGraphics.setFlashTime( 100 );
  DebugGraphics.setFlashCount( 2 );
  DebugGraphics.setFlashColor(new Color(0,0,0,0));
  getContentPane().add(jc);
 }

 public static void main( String args[] ) {
  TestFrame mainFrame = new TestFrame();
  mainFrame.pack();
  mainFrame.setDefaultCloseOperation(JFrame.EXIT_ON_CLOSE);
  mainFrame.setVisible( true );
 }
}
```

```
class JCanvas extends JComponent
{
 // Unchanged code from example 2.4

 private PrintStream ps;

 public JCanvas() {
  super.setUI(EmptyUI.createUI(this));
 }

 public void paintComponent(Graphics g) {
  super.paintComponent(g);

  ps = DebugGraphics.logStream();
  ps.println("\n===> paintComponent ENTERED <===");

  // All painting code unchanged

  ps.println("\n# items repainted = " + c + "/10");
  ps.println("===> paintComponent FINISHED <===\n");
 }

 // Unchanged code from example 2.4
}

class EmptyUI extends ComponentUI
{
 private static final EmptyUI sharedInstance = new EmptyUI();
 public static ComponentUI createUI(JComponent c) {
  return sharedInstance;
 }
}
```

By setting the LOG_OPTION, graphics debugging provides us with a more informative way of checking how well our clipping area optimization we discussed in the last section works. When this example is run, you should see the following output in your console, assuming you don't obscure JCanvas's visible region as it is painted for the first time:

```
Graphics(0-3) Enabling debug
Graphics(0-3) Setting color:
  javax.swing.plaf.ColorUIResource[r=0,g=0,b=0]
Graphics(0-3) Setting font:
  javax.swing.plaf.FontUIResource[family=dialog,name=Dialog,
  style=plain,size=12]

===> paintComponent ENTERED <===
Graphics(1-3) Setting color: java.awt.Color[r=255,g=255,b=255]
Graphics(1-3) Filling rect: java.awt.Rectangle[x=0,y=0,
  width=400,height=400]
Graphics(1-3) Setting color: java.awt.Color[r=255,g=255,b=0]
Graphics(1-3) Filling oval: java.awt.Rectangle[x=0,y=0,
  width=240,height=240]
Graphics(1-3) Setting color: java.awt.Color[r=255,g=0,b=255]
Graphics(1-3) Filling oval:
  java.awt.Rectangle[x=160,y=160,width=240,height=240]
Graphics(1-3) Drawing image: sun.awt.windows.WImage@32a5625a at:
```

```
   java.awt.Point[x=258,y=97]
Graphics(1-3) Drawing image: sun.awt.windows.WImage@32a5625a at:
   java.awt.Point[x=98,y=257]
Graphics(1-3) Setting color: java.awt.Color[r=255,g=0,b=0]
Graphics(1-3) Filling rect:
   java.awt.Rectangle[x=60,y=220,width=120,height=120]
Graphics(1-3) Setting color: java.awt.Color[r=0,g=255,b=0]
Graphics(1-3) Filling oval:
   java.awt.Rectangle[x=140,y=140,width=120,height=120]
Graphics(1-3) Setting color: java.awt.Color[r=0,g=0,b=255]
Graphics(1-3) Filling rect:
   java.awt.Rectangle[x=220,y=60,width=120,height=120]
Graphics(1-3) Setting color: java.awt.Color[r=0,g=0,b=0]
Graphics(1-3) Setting font:
   java.awt.Font[family=monospaced.bolditalic,name=Mono
   spaced,style=bolditalic,size=36]
Graphics(1-3) Drawing string: "Swing" at:
   java.awt.Point[x=65,y=129]
Graphics(1-3) Setting font:
   java.awt.Font[family=Arial,name=SansSerif,style=plain,size=12]
Graphics(1-3) Drawing string: "is" at:
   java.awt.Point[x=195,y=203]
Graphics(1-3) Setting font:
   java.awt.Font[family=serif.bold,name=Serif,style=bold,size=24]
Graphics(1-3) Drawing string: "powerful!!" at:
   java.awt.Point[x=228,y=286]

# items repainted = 10/10
===> paintComponent FINISHED <===
```

2.11 PAINTING AND VALIDATION

At the heart of JComponent's painting and validation mechanism lies a service class called RepaintManager. The RepaintManager is responsible for sending painting and validation requests to the system event queue for dispatching. To summarize, it does this by intercepting repaint() and revalidate() requests, coalescing any requests where possible, wrapping them in Runnable objects, and sending them to invokeLater(). A few issues we have encountered in this chapter deserve more attention here before we actually discuss details of the painting and validation processes.

NOTE   This section contains a relatively exhaustive explanation of the most complex mechanism underlying Swing. If you are relatively new to Java or Swing, we encourage you to skim this section now and come back at a later time for a more complete reading. If you are just looking for information on how to override and use your own painting methods, see section 2.8. For customizing UI delegate rendering, see chapter 21.

REFERENCE   For a higher-level summary of the painting process, see the Swing Connection article "Painting in AWT and Swing" at http://java.sun.com/products/jfc/tsc/special_ report/Painting/painting.html.

2.11.1 Double-buffering

We've mentioned double-buffering, but you may be wondering how to disable it in the RepaintManager and how to specify the double-buffering of individual components with JComponent's setDoubleBuffered() method. In this section, we'll explain how it works.

Double-buffering is the technique of painting into an off-screen image rather than painting directly to a visible component. In the end, the resulting image is painted to the screen relatively quickly. Using AWT components, developers were required to implement their own double-buffering to reduce flashing. It was clear that double-buffering should be a built-in feature because of its widespread use. Thus, it is not much of a surprise to find this feature in Swing.

Behind the scenes, double-buffering consists of creating an Image (actually a Volatile-Image) and retrieving its Graphics object for use in all painting methods. If the component being repainted has children, this Graphics object will be passed down to them to use for painting, and so on. So if you are using double-buffering for a component, all its children will also be using double-buffering (regardless of whether they have double-buffering enabled) because they will be rendering into the same Graphics object. There is only one off-screen image per RepaintManager, and there is normally only one RepaintManager instance per applet or application (RepaintManager is a service class that registers a shared instance of itself with AppContext; see section 2.5 for details).

JAVA 1.4   The Java2D team has implemented a new class called VolatileImage which allows Java to take advantage of available graphics acceleration hardware. RepaintManager has a new getVolatileOffscreenBuffer() method used to obtain a VolatileImage for use in double-buffering.

As we will discuss in chapter 3, JRootPane is the top-level Swing component in any window, including JInternalFrame (which isn't really a window). By enabling double-buffering on JRootPane, all of its children will also be painted using double-buffering. As we saw in the last section, RepaintManager also provides global control over all component double-buffering. So another way to guarantee that all components will use double-buffering is to call

```
RepaintManager.currentManager(null).setDoubleBufferingEnabled(true);
```

2.11.2 Optimized drawing

We haven't yet really discussed the fact that components can overlap each other in Swing, but they can. JLayeredPane, for example, is a container that allows any number of components to overlap each other. Repainting such a container is much more complex than repainting a container we know does not allow overlapping, mainly because of the ability for components to be transparent.

What does it mean for a component to be transparent? Technically, this means its isOpaque() method returns false. We can set this property by calling setOpaque(). Opacity means, in this context, that a component will paint every pixel within its bounds. If the opaque property is set to false, we are not guaranteed that this will happen. When it is set to false, it increases the workload of the whole painting mechanism.

JComponent's isOptimizedDrawingEnabled() method is overridden to return true for almost all JComponent subclasses except JLayeredPane, JViewport, and JDesktopPane (which is a subclass of JLayeredPane). Basically, calling this method is equivalent to asking a component whether it is possible that any of its child components can overlap each other. If it is possible, then much more repainting work must be done to take into account the fact that any number of components, from virtually anywhere in our container hierarchy, can overlap each other. Since components can be transparent, components layered completely behind others may still show through. Such components are not necessarily siblings (meaning in the same container) because we could conceivably have several non-opaque containers layered one on top of another. In situations like this, we must do a whole lot of "tree walking" to figure out which components need to be refreshed. If isOptimizedDrawingEnabled() is overridden to return true, then we assume we do not have to consider any situations like this. Thus, painting becomes more efficient, or optimized.

2.11.3   Root validation

A revalidate() request is generated when a component needs to be laid out again. When a request is received from a certain component, there must be some way of determining whether laying that component out will affect anything else. JComponent's isValidateRoot() method returns false for most components. Calling this method is equivalent to asking it the question: If I lay your contents out again, can you guarantee that none of your parents or siblings will be adversely affected—meaning will they need to be laid out again? By default, only JRootPane, JScrollPane, and JTextField return true. This seems surprising at first, but it is true that these components are the only Swing components whose contents can be successfully laid out in any situation without affecting parents or siblings. No matter how big we make anything *inside* a JRootPane, JScrollPane, or JTextField, the container will not change size or location unless some *outside* influence comes into play, such as a sibling or parent. To help convince you of this, try adding a multiline text component (such as a JTextArea) to a container *without* placing it in a scroll pane. You may notice that creating new lines will change its size, depending on the layout. The point is not that it rarely happens or that it can be prevented, but that it *can* happen. This is the type of incident that isValidateRoot() is supposed to warn us about. So where is this method used?

A component or its parent is normally revalidated when a property value changes and that component's size, location, or internal layout has been affected. By recursively calling isValidateRoot() on a Swing component's parent until you obtain true, you will end with the closest ancestor of that component that guarantees us its validation will not affect its siblings or parents. We will see that RepaintManager relies on this method for dispatching validation requests.

NOTE   When we say siblings, we mean components in the same container. When we say parents, we mean parent containers.

Cell renderers used in components such as JList, JTree, and JTable are special in that they are wrapped in instances of CellRendererPane and all validation and repainting requests do not propogate up through containment hierarchy. See chapter 17 for more information about CellRendererPane and why this behavior exists. We'll simply say here that cell renderers do not follow the painting and validation scheme discussed in this section.

2.11.4 RepaintManager

class javax.swing.RepaintManager

There is usually only one instance of a service class in use per applet or application. So unless we specifically create our own instance of `RepaintManager`, which we will almost never need to do, all repainting is managed by the shared instance which is registered with `AppContext`. We normally retrieve it using `RepaintManager`'s static `currentManager()` method:

```
myRepaintManager = RepaintManager.currentManager(null);
```

This method takes a `Component` as its parameter. However, it doesn't matter what we pass it. In fact, the component passed to this method is not used anywhere inside the method at all (see the RepaintManager.java source code), so a value of `null` can safely be used here. (This definition exists for subclasses to use if they want to work with more than one `RepaintManager`, possibly on a per-component basis.)

`RepaintManager` exists for two purposes: to provide efficient revalidation and repainting by coalescing the paint/validation requests for all the components of a specific component tree. It intercepts all `repaint()` and `revalidate()` requests. This class also handles all double-buffering in Swing and maintains a single `Image` used for this purpose. This `Image`'s maximum size is, by default, the size of the screen. However, we can set its size manually using `RepaintManager`'s `setDoubleBufferMaximumSize()` method. (All other `RepaintManager` functionality will be discussed throughout this section where applicable.)

2.11.5 Revalidation

`RepaintManager` maintains a `Vector` of components that need to be validated. Whenever a `revalidate()` request is intercepted, the source component is sent to the `addInvalidComponent()` method and its `validateRoot` property is checked using `isValidateRoot()`. This occurs recursively on that component's parent until `isValidateRoot()` returns `true`. The resulting component, if any, is then checked for visibility. If any one of its parent containers is not visible, there is no reason to validate it. Otherwise, if no parent container returns true for `isValidateRoot()`, `RepaintManager` "walks down the component's tree" until it reaches the root component, which will be a `Window` or an `Applet`. `RepaintManager` then checks the invalid components `Vector`, and if the component isn't already there, it is added. After being successfully added, `RepaintManager` then passes the root container to the `SystemEventQueueUtilities`' `queueComponentWorkRequest()` method (we saw this class in section 2.3). This method checks to see if there is a `ComponentWorkRequest` (this is a private static class in `SystemEventQueueUtilities` that implements `Runnable`) corresponding to that root already stored in the work requests table. If there isn't one, a new one is created. If one already exists, a reference to it is obtained. Then the `queueComponent-WorkRequest()` method synchronizes access to that `ComponentWorkRequest`, places it in the work requests table if it is a new one, and checks if it is pending (meaning it has been added to the system event queue). If it isn't pending, this method sends it to `Swing-Utilities.invokeLater()`. It is then marked as pending and the synchronized block is finished. When the `ComponentWorkRequest` is finally run from the event-dispatching thread, it notifies `RepaintManager` to execute `validateInvalidComponents()`, followed by `paintDirtyRegions()`.

The `validateInvalidComponents()` method checks `RepaintManager`'s `Vector` that contains the components which are in need of validation, and it calls `validate()` on each one. (This method is actually a bit more careful than we describe here, as it synchronizes access to prevent the addition of invalid components while executing).

NOTE The `validateInvalidComponents()` should only be called from within the event-dispatching thread. Never call this method from any other thread. The same rules apply for `paintDirtyRegions()`.

The `paintDirtyRegions()` method is much more complicated, and we'll discuss *some* of its details in this chapter. For now, all you need to know is that this method paints all the damaged regions of each component maintained by `RepaintManager`.

2.11.6 Repainting

`JComponent` defines two `repaint()` methods, and the no-argument version of `repaint()` is inherited from `java.awt.Container`:

```
public void repaint(long tm, int x, int y, int width, int height)
public void repaint(Rectangle r)
public void repaint() // Inherited from java.awt.Container
```

If you call the no-argument version, the whole component is repainted. For small, simple components, this is fine. But for larger, more complex components, this is often not efficient. The other two methods take the bounding region to be repainted (the *dirtied* region) as parameters. The first method's `int` parameters correspond to the x-coordinate, y-coordinate, width, and height of that region. The second method takes the same information encapsulated in a `Rectange` instance. The second `repaint()` method shown above just sends its traffic to the first. The first method sends the dirtied region's parameters to `RepaintManager`'s `addDirtyRegion()` method.

NOTE The `long` parameter in the first `repaint()` method represents absolutely nothing and is not used at all. It does not matter what value you use for this. The only reason it is here is to override the correct `repaint()` method from `java.awt.Component`.

`RepaintManager` maintains a `Hashtable` of dirty regions. Each component will have, at most, one dirty region in this table at any time. When a dirty region is added using `addDirtyRegion()`, the size of the region and the component are checked. If either item has a width or height <= 0, the method returns and nothing happens. If a measurement is bigger than 0x0, the source component's visibility is then tested, along with each of its ancestors. If they are all visible, its root component, a `Window` or `Applet`, is located by "walking down its tree," similar to what occurs in `addInvalidateComponent()`. The dirty regions `Hashtable` is then asked if it already has a dirty region of our component stored. If it does, it returns its value (a `Rectangle`) and the handy `SwingUtilities.computeUnion()` method is used to combine the new dirty region with the old one. Finally, `RepaintManager` passes the root to the `SystemEventQueueUtilities`' `queueComponentWorkRequest()` method. What happens from here on is identical to what we saw earlier for revalidation.

Now we can talk a bit about the `paintDirtyRegions()` method we summarized earlier. (Remember that this should only be called from within the event-dispatching thread.) This method starts out by creating a local reference to `RepaintManger`'s dirty regions `Hashtable` and redirecting RepaintManager's dirty regions Hashtable reference to a different, empty one. This is all done in a critical section so that no dirty regions can be added while the swap occurs. The remainder of this method is fairly long and complicated, so we'll conclude with a summary of the most significant code (see the RepaintManager.java source code for details).

The paintDirtyRegions() method continues by iterating through an Enumeration of the dirty components, calling RepaintManager's collectDirtyComponents() method for each one. This method looks at all the ancestors of the specified dirty component and checks each one for any overlap with its dirty region using the SwingUtilities.computeIntersection() method. In this way, each dirty region's bounds are minimized so that only its visible region remains. (Note that collectDirtyComponents() *does* take transparency into account.) Once this has been done for each dirty component, the paintDirtyRegions() method enters a loop which computes the final intersection of each dirty component and its dirty region. At the end of each iteration, paintImmediately() is called on the associated dirty component, which actually paints each minimized dirty region in its correct location (we'll discuss this later). This completes the paintDirtyRegions() method, but we still have the most significant feature of the whole process left to discuss: painting.

2.11.7   Painting

JComponent includes an update() method which simply calls paint(). The update() method is never actually used by any Swing components; it is provided only for backward compatibility. The JComponent paint() method, unlike typical AWT paint() implementations, does not handle all of a component's painting. In fact, it very rarely handles *any* of it directly. The only rendering work JComponent's paint() method is really responsible for is working with clipping areas, translations, and painting pieces of the Image used by RepaintManager for double-buffering. The rest of the work is delegated to several other methods. We will briefly discuss each of these methods and the order in which painting operations occur. But first we need to discuss how paint() is actually invoked.

As you know from our discussion of the repainting process above, RepaintManager is responsible for invoking a method called paintImmediately() on each component to paint its dirty region (remember, there is always just one dirty region per component because they are intelligently coalesced by RepaintManager). This method, together with the private ones it calls, makes an intelligently crafted repainting process even more impressive. It first checks to see if the target component is visible, as it could have been moved, hidden, or disposed since the original request was made. Then it recursively searches the component's non-opaque parents (using isOpaque()) and it increases the bounds of the region to repaint accordingly until it reaches an opaque parent. It then has two options.

1   If the parent reached is a JComponent subclass, the private _paintImmediately() method is called and the newly computed region is passed to it. This method queries the isOptimizedDrawing() method, checks whether double-buffering is enabled (if so, it uses the off-screen Graphics object associated with RepaintManager's buffered Image), and continues working with isOpaque() to determine the final parent component and bounds to invoke paint() on.

A   If double-buffering is *not* enabled, a single call to paint() is made on the parent.

B   If double-buffering *is* enabled, it calls `paintWithBuffer()`, which is another private method. This method works with the off-screen `Graphics` object and its clipping area to generate many calls to the parent's `paint()` method, passing it the off-screen `Graphics` object using a specific clipping area each time. After each call to `paint()`, it uses the off-screen `Graphics` object to draw directly to the visible component.

2   If the parent is not a `JComponent` subclass, the region's bounds are sent to that parent's `repaint()` method, which will normally invoke the `java.awt.Component paint()` method. This method will then forward traffic to each of its lightweight children's `paint()` methods. However, before doing this, it makes sure that each lightweight child it notifies is not completely covered by the current clipping area of the `Graphics` object that was passed in.

In all cases, we have *finally* reached `JComponent`'s `paint()` method!

Inside `JComponent`'s `paint()` method, if graphics debugging is enabled, a `DebugGraphics` instance will be used for all rendering.

NOTE   Interestingly, a quick look at `JComponent`'s painting code shows heavy use of a class called `SwingGraphics`. (This isn't in the API docs because it's package private). It appears to be a very slick class for handling custom translations, clipping area management, and a `Stack` of `Graphics` objects used for caching, recyclability, and undo-type operations. `SwingGraphics` actually acts as a wrapper for all `Graphics` instances used during the painting process. It can only be instantiated by passing it an existing `Graphics` object. This functionality is made even more explicit by the fact that it implements an interface called `GraphicsWrapper`, which is also package private.

The `paint()` method checks whether double-buffering is enabled and whether it was called by `paintWithBuffer()` (see above). There are two possible scenarios.

1   If `paint()` was called from `paintWithBuffer()` or if double-buffering is not enabled, `paint()` checks whether the clipping area of the current `Graphics` object is completely obscured by any child components. If it isn't, `paintComponent()`, `paintBorder()`, and `paintChildren()` are called in that order. If it is completely obscured, then only `paintChildren()` needs to be called. (We will see what these three methods do shortly.)

2   If double-buffering is enabled and this method was not called from `paintWith-Buffer()`, it will use the off-screen `Graphics` object associated with `RepaintMan-ager`'s buffered `Image` throughout the remainder of this method. Then it will check whether the clipping area of the current `Graphics` object is completely obscured by any child components. If it isn't, `paintComponent()`, `paintBorder()`, and `paintChil-dren()` will be called in that order. If it is completely obscured, only `paintChildren()` needs to be called.

A   The `paintComponent()` method checks to see if the component has a UI delegate installed. If it doesn't, the method just exits. If it does, it simply calls `update()` on that UI delegate and then exits. The `update()` method of a UI delegate is normally responsible for painting a component's background if it is opaque, and then calling `paint()`. A UI delegate's `paint()` method is what actually paints the corresponding component's content. (We will see how to customize UI delegates throughout this text.)

B The `paintBorder()` method simply paints the component's border, if it has one.

C The `paintChildren()` method is a bit more involved. To summarize, it searches through all child components and determines whether `paint()` should be invoked on them using the current `Graphics` clipping area, the `isOpaque()` method, and the `isOptimizedDrawingEnabled()` method. The `paint()` method called on each child will essentially start that child's painting process from part 2 above, and this process will repeat until either no more children exist or none need to be painted.

2.11.8 Custom painting

When building or extending lightweight Swing components, it is normally expected that if you want to do any painting within the component itself (instead of in the UI delegate where it normally should be done), you will override the `paintComponent()` method and immediately call `super.paintComponent()`. In this way, the UI delegate will be given a chance to render the component first. Overriding the `paint()` method, or any of the other methods mentioned earlier, should rarely be necessary, and it is always good practice to avoid doing so.

2.12 FOCUS MANAGEMENT

With Java 1.4 comes a completely revised focus subsystem. The primary concepts underlying this subsystem consist of the following.

Focus Owner: A focus owner is the component which currently has the focus and is the ultimate target of all keyboard input (except key combinations that indicate a focus change; detailed here).

Permanent Focus Owner: A permanent focus owner is the same as the current focus owner unless there is temporary focus change in effect (for example, using a drop–down menu while editing a text component document).

Focus Cycle: A focus cycle is the sequence in which components within a container receive focus. It is referred to as a cycle because it acts as a loop—each component in the cycle will receive the focus once if the cycle is completely traversed from the first component in the cycle to the last.

Focus Traversal: Focus traversal is the ability to move the focus from one component to the next within a focus cycle. This can be accomplished through use of key combinations to move the focus forward or backward.

Focus Cycle Root: A focus cycle root is the uppermost parent container of the components in a focus cycle. Every `Window` is a focus cycle by default (this includes `JInternal-Frame` even though it is technically not a `Window`). Normal focus traversal within a focus cycle cannot extend above or below the focus cycle root with respect to its containment hierarchy. Distinct traversal options called *up cycle* and *down cycle* are used to change the focus cycle root

In example 2.6, shown in figure 2.6, we construct a container with four focus cycle roots. We will walk you through using this example to illustrate the above focus management concepts.

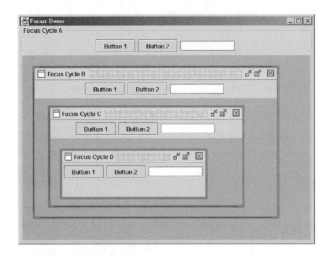

Figure 2.6
Focus Cycle Demo

Example 2.6

FocusTest.java

see \Chapter2\6

```java
import java.awt.*;
import javax.swing.*;
import javax.swing.border.*;

public class FocusDemo extends JFrame {

  public FocusDemo() {
    super("Focus Demo");

    JPanel contentPane = (JPanel) getContentPane();
    contentPane.setBorder(new TitledBorder("Focus Cycle A"));
    contentPane.add(createComponentPanel(), BorderLayout.NORTH);
    JDesktopPane desktop1 = new JDesktopPane();
    contentPane.add(desktop1, BorderLayout.CENTER);

    JInternalFrame internalFrame1 =
      new JInternalFrame("Focus Cycle B", true, true, true, true);
    contentPane = (JPanel) internalFrame1.getContentPane();
    contentPane.add(createComponentPanel(), BorderLayout.NORTH;
    JDesktopPane desktop2 = new JDesktopPane();
    contentPane.add(desktop2, BorderLayout.CENTER);
    desktop1.add(internalFrame1);
    internalFrame1.setBounds(20,20,500,300);
    internalFrame1.show();

    JInternalFrame internalFrame2 =
      new JInternalFrame("Focus Cycle C", true, true, true, true);
    contentPane = (JPanel) internalFrame2.getContentPane();
    contentPane.add(createComponentPanel(), BorderLayout.NORTH;
    JDesktopPane desktop3 = new JDesktopPane();
```

```
        contentPane.add(desktop3, BorderLayout.CENTER);
        desktop2.add(internalFrame2);
        internalFrame2.setBounds(20,20,400,200);
        internalFrame2.show();

        JInternalFrame internalFrame3 =
          new JInternalFrame("Focus Cycle D", false, true, true, true);
        contentPane = (JPanel) internalFrame3.getContentPane();
        contentPane.add(createComponentPanel(), BorderLayout.NORTH);
        desktop3.add(internalFrame3);
        internalFrame3.setBounds(20,20,300,100);
        internalFrame3.show();
    }
    public static void main(String[] args) {
      FocusDemo frame = new FocusDemo();
      frame.setDefaultCloseOperation(JFrame.EXIT_ON_CLOSE);
      frame.setBounds(0,0,600,450);
      frame.setVisible(true);
    }

    protected JPanel createComponentPanel() {
      JPanel panel = new JPanel();
      panel.add(new JButton("Button 1"));
      panel.add(new Jbutton("Button 2"));
      Panel.add(new JTextField(10));
      return panel;
    }
}
```

When you first run this example don't use your mouse. Notice that the first component with the focus, the *focus owner*, is "Button 1" in Focus Cycle A. This is evident by the blue selection box drawn around that button's text. Press TAB to move the focus forward to the next component in the cycle. When you move the focus forward from the last component in the cycle (the text field), notice that the focus moves down a cycle rather than continuing from the beginning of the current cycle.

Press SHIFT+TAB to move the focus backward through the cycle. When you move the focus backward the focus stays within the current focus cycle endlessly.

Now try moving the focus forward until you reach Focus Cycle D. At this point there are no more focus cycle roots to traverse through and cycle D loops endlessly, whether you move the focus forward or backward. If you minimize the "Focus Cycle D" internal frame, the "Focus Cycle C" internal frame then becomes the lowest focus cycle root and focus traversal will loop endlessly there. If you restore the "Focus Cycle D" internal frame then it becomes the lowest focus cycle root once again.

By default there is no direct way to use the keyboard to move to a higher focus cycle. The only way to move down a focus cycle with the keyboard is to traverse the focus cycle hierarchy manually. There is no default way to move up the hierarchy using only the keyboard without removing cycle roots (in the earlier example minimizing an internal frame accomplishes this temporarily). However, you can easily use the mouse to jump to any focus cycle. Simply click on a focusable component and the focus will be transferred to the cycle containing that component.

Now try typing some text into one of the text fields. Then use your mouse to click on the Java cup frame icon in the upper left-hand corner of the JFrame. A popup menu appears but notice that the cursor still remains blinking in the text area. This is an example of a temporary focus change–focus is temporarily transferred to the popup menu. Once the popup menu is dismissed you can continue typing in the text field as if a focus change never happened. In this scenario the text field is a *permanent focus owner* with respect to the popup menu.

2.12.1   KeyboardFocusManager

abstract class java.awt.KeyboardFocusManager

Central to the focus management system is a new class called keyboardFocusManager (an AppContext-registered service class–see section 2.5), the default implementation of which is DefaultKeyboardFocusManager. To obtain a reference to the current Keyboard-FocusManager in use, the static getCurrentKeyboardFocusManager() method is used. Once you've obtained this you can programmatically inquire about the current focus state, change the focus state, and add to or replace focus change event handling functionality.

> **NOTE**   We recommend programmatically changing focus through the keyboardFocus-Manager rather than calling methods such as requestFocus() on components directly.

VetoableChangeListeners (see section 2.1.1) can be added to KeyboardFocusManager for the opportunity to veto a component focus or window activation change by throwing a PropertyVetoException. In the event that a veto occurs, all VetoableChangeListeners that may have previously approved the change will be notified and will revert any changes to their original state.

2.12.2   Key events and focus management

abstract class java.awt.KeyEventDispatcher

Implementations of this class can be registered with the current KeyboardFocusManager to receive key events before they are sent to the currently focused component. In this way key events can be redirected to a different target component, consumed, or changed in some other way.

KeyboardFocusManager is actually a subclass of KeyEventDispatcher and by default acts as the last KeyEventDispatcher to receive key events. This abstract class defines one method, dispatchKeyEvent(), which returns a boolean value. If any KeyEventDispatcher registered with the KeyboardFocusManager returns true for this method, indicating that it dispatched the key event, then no further dispatching of that event will take place. In this way we can define our own KeyEventDispatcher to alter the behavior of Keyboard-FocusManager.

2.12.3   Focus and Window events

java.awt.event.FocusEvent and java.awt.event.WindowEvent

FocusEvent and WindowEvent define several event types that are central to the operation of the focus management subsystem. They generally occur in the following order during focus traversal and can be intercepted by attaching `WindowListeners` and `FocusListeners` respectively:

- `WindowEvent.WINDOW_ACTIVATED`: event sent to a `Frame` or `Dialog` when it becomes active.
- `WindowEvent.WINDOW_GAINED_FOCUS`: event sent to a `Window` when it becomes focused.
- `windowEvent.WINDOW_LOST_FOCUS`: event sent to a `Window` when it loses focus.
- `windowevent.WINDOW_DEACTIVATED`: event sent to a `Frame` or `Dialog` when it is no longer the active window.
- `FocusEvent.FOCUS_GAINED`: event sent to a `Component` when it becomes the focus owner.
- `FocusEvent.FOCUS_LOST`: event sent to a `Component` when it loses focus ownership, whether temporary or permanent.

2.12.4 Focusability and traversal policies

abstract class java.awt.FocusTraversalPolicy

You can easily change whether or not specific components act as part of a focus cycle. Each `Component` can toggle its traversability with the `setFocusable()` method. Similarly each `Window` can do the same with the `setFocusableWindow()` method.

However, if we need to customize focus traversal in a more creative way, the `FocusTraversalPolicy` class provides a way to accomplish this. This abstract class defines several methods used during focus traversal to determine which component is next, previous, first, last, and so forth. within a given `Container`'s focus cycle. Once a defined a traversal policy can be applied to any `Container` with the `setTraversalPolicy()` method.

`ContainerOrderFocusTraversalPolicy` (and its `DefaultFocusTraversalPolicy` subclass) is the default policy of most containers. `Component`s are traversed based on their order of appearance, from left to right and top to bottom, within the container–corresponding to the ordering of the array returned by the `Container.getComponents()` method. By default this policy traverses down to lower focus cycles whenever a new focus cycle root is reached. This behavior can be toggled with the `setImplicitDownCycleTraversal()` method.

`InternalFrameFocusTraversalPolicy` is a policy meant for use by `JInternalFrame` to provide a way for determining the initial focus owner when the internal frame is selected for the first time. `SortingFocusTraversalPolicy` is a subclass of `InternalFrameFocusTraversalPolicy` that determines traversal order by comparing child components using a given `Comparator` implementation. A subclass of this, `LayoutFocusTraversalPolicy`, is used to determine traversal order based on size, position, and orientation. Used in conjunction with a component's `ComponentOrientation` (the language-sensitive orientation that determines whether text or components should appear from left to right, top to bottom, etc.), `LayoutFocusTraversalPolicy` can adjust focus traversal based on the orientation required by, for instance, the current language in use.

REFERENCE   For a more detailed description of focus management in Java 1.4 see "the AWT Focus Subsystem for Merlin" at http://java.sun.com/j2se/1.4/docs/api/java/awt/doc-files/FocusSpec.html.

2.13 KEYBOARD INPUT

In this section, we discuss the mechanisms underlying keyboard input and how to intercept key events.

2.13.1 Listening for keyboard input

KeyEvents are fired by a component whenever that component has the current focus and the user presses a key. To listen for these events on a particular component, we can attach KeyListeners using the addKeyListener() method. We can devour these events using the consume() method before they are handled further by key bindings or other listeners. We'll discuss in this section exactly who gets notification of keyboard input, and in what order this occurs.

There are three KeyEvent event types, each of which normally occurs at least once per keyboard activation (such as a press and release of a single keyboard key):

- KEY_PRESSED: This type of key event is generated whenever a keyboard key is pressed. The key that is pressed is specified by the keyCode property and a *virtual key code* representing it can be retrieved with KeyEvent's getKeyCode() method. A virtual key code is used to report the exact keyboard key that caused the event, such as KeyEvent.VK_ENTER. KeyEvent defines numerous static int constants that each start with the prefix "VK," meaning *Virtual Key* (see the KeyEvent API docs for a complete list). For example, if CTRL-C is typed, two KEY_PRESSED events will be fired. The int returned by getKeyCode() corresponding to pressing CTRL will be a value matching KeyEvent.VK_CTRL. Similarly, the int returned by getKeyCode() corresponding to pressing the C key will be a value matching KeyEvent.VK_C. (Note that the order in which these are fired depends on the order in which they are pressed.) KeyEvent also maintains a keyChar property which specifies the Unicode representation of the character that was pressed (if there is no Unicode representation, KeyEvent.CHAR_UNDEFINED is used—for example, the function keys on a typical PC keyboard). We can retrieve the keyChar character corresponding to any KeyEvent using the getKeyChar() method. For example, the character returned by getKeyChar() corresponding to pressing the C key will be c. If SHIFT was pressed and held while the C key was pressed, the character returned by getKeyChar() corresponding to the C key press would be C. (Note that distinct keyChars are returned for upper- and lower-case characters, whereas the same keyCode is used in both situations—for example, the value of VK_C will be returned by getKeyCode() regardless of whether SHIFT is held down when the C key is pressed. Also note that there is no keyChar associated with keys such as CTRL, and getKeyChar() will simply return an empty char in this case.)
- KEY_RELEASED: This type of key event is generated whenever a keyboard key is released. Other than this difference, KEY_RELEASED events are identical to KEY_PRESSED events; however, as we will discuss below, they occur much less frequently.
- KEY_TYPED: This type of event is fired somewhere between a KEY_PRESSED and KEY_RELEASED event. It never carries a keyCode property corresponding to the actual key pressed, and 0 will be returned whenever getKeyCode() is called on an event of this type. For keys with no Unicode representation (such as PAGE UP and PRINT SCREEN), no KEY_TYPED event will be generated at all.

JAVA 1.4   As of Java 1.4 there are several new `InputEvent` modifiers linked to keyboard events: `SHIFT_DOWN_MASK`, `CTRL_DOWN_MASK`, `META_DOWN_MASK`, `ALT_DOWN_MASK`, `ALT_GRAPH_DOWN_MASK`. There are also two new APIs to retrieve the extended modifiers: `getModifiersEx()` and `getModifiersEx-Text()`, making it possible to handle cases in which multiple keys are down simultaneously.

Most keys with Unicode representations, when held down for longer than a few moments, repeatedly generate `KEY_PRESSED` and `KEY_TYPED` events, in this order. The set of keys that exhibit this behavior, and the rate at which they do so, cannot be controlled and is platform-specific.

Each `KeyEvent` maintains a set of modifiers which specifies the state of the SHIFT, CTRL, ALT, and META keys. This is an `int` value that is the result of the bitwise OR of `InputEvent.SHIFT_MASK`, `InputEvent.CTRL_MASK`, `InputEvent.ALT_MASK`, and `InputEvent.META_MASK`, depending on which keys are pressed at the time of the event. We can retrieve this value with `getModifiers()`, and we can query specifically whether any of these keys was pressed at the time the event was fired using `isShiftDown()`, `isControlDown()`, `isAltDown()`, and `isMetaDown()`.

`KeyEvent` also maintains the boolean `actionKey` property which specifies whether the invoking keyboard key corresponds to an action that should be performed by that app (`true`) versus data that is normally used for such things as addition to a text component's document content (`false`). We can use `KeyEvent`'s `isActionKey()` method to retrieve the value of this property.

2.13.2   KeyStrokes

Using `KeyListeners` to handle all keyboard input on a component-by-component basis was required prior to Java 2. Because of this, a significant and often tedious amount of time was spent planning and debugging keyboard operations. The Swing team recognized this, and thankfully included functionality for key event interception regardless of which component currently has the focus. This functionality is implemented by binding instances of the `javax.swing.KeyStroke` class with instances of `javax.swing.Action` (discussed next).

NOTE   Registered keyboard actions are also commonly referred to as keyboard accelerators.

Each `KeyStroke` instance encapsulates a `KeyEvent` keyCode, a `modifiers` value (analogous to that of `KeyEvent`), and a boolean property specifying whether it should be activated on a key press (`false`, which is the default) or on a key release (`true`). The `KeyStroke` class provides five static methods for creating `KeyStroke` objects. Note that all `KeyStrokes` are cached, and it is not necessarily the case that these methods will return a brand-new instance. (Actually `KeyStroke` provides six static methods for creating `KeyStrokes`, but `getKeyStroke(char keyChar, boolean onKeyRelease)` has been deprecated.)

- `getKeyStroke(char keyChar)`
- `getKeyStroke(int keyCode, int modifiers)`
- `getKeyStroke(int keyCode, int modifiers, boolean onKeyRelease)`
- `getKeyStroke(String representation)`
- `getKeyStroke(KeyEvent anEvent)`
- `getKeyStroke(Character Keychar, int modifiers)`

The last method will return a `KeyStroke` with properties corresponding to the given `KeyEvent`'s attributes. The `keyCode`, `keyChar`, and `modifiers` properties are taken from the `KeyEvent` and the `onKeyRelease` property is set to `true` if the event is of type `KEY_RELEASED`; otherwise, it returns `false`.

2.13.3 Scopes

There are three scopes defined by `JComponent` used to determine the conditions under which a `KeyStroke` falls:

- `JComponent.WHEN_FOCUSED`: the corresponding `Action` will only be invoked if the component this `KeyStroke` is associated with has the current focus.
- `JComponent.WHEN_ANCESTOR_OF_FOCUSED_COMPONENT`: the corresponding `Action` will only be invoked if the component this `KeyStroke` is associated with is the ancestor of (i.e., it contains) the component with the current focus. Typically this is used to define `Actions` associated with mnemonics.
- `JComponent.WHEN_IN_FOCUSED_WINDOW`: the corresponding `Action` will be invoked if the component this `KeyStroke` is associated with is anywhere within the peer-level window (i.e., `JFrame`, `JDialog`, `JWindow`, `JApplet`, or any other heavyweight component) that has the current focus.

2.13.4 Actions

interface javax.swing.Action

An `Action` is an `ActionListener` implementation that encapsulates a `Hashtable` of bound properties similar to `JComponent`'s client properties. In the context of keyboard bindings each `KeyStroke` is associated with at most one `Action` (this relationship is not one-to-one, however, as one `Action` can be associated with an arbitrary number of `KeyStrokes`). When a key event is detected that matches a `KeyStroke` under a certain scope, the appropriate `Action` is invoked. In chapter 12 we will work with `Actions` in detail; but it suffices to say here that `Actions` are used for, among other things, handling all component key events in Swing.

2.13.5 InputMaps and ActionMaps

javax.swing.InputMap and javax.swing.ActionMap

Before Java 1.3 there were two different mechanisms for mapping `KeyStrokes` to `Actions`. For `JTextComponents` the `KeyMap` class was used to store a list of `Action`/`Keystroke` pairs. For all other `JComponents` a `Hashtable` was maintained by the component itself containing `KeyStroke`/`ActionListener` pairs.

In Java 1.3 these mechanisms were unified so that all components can be treated the same with regard to keyboard bindings. To accomplish this two new classes have been added: `InputMap` and `ActionMap`. Each component has one `ActionMap` and three `InputMaps` associated with it (one `InputMap` for each scope: `WHEN_FOCUSED`, `WHEN_IN_FOCUSED_WINDOW`, `WHEN_ANCESTOR_OF_FOCUSED_COMPONENT`).

Each `InputMap` associates a `KeyStroke` with an `Object` (usually a `String` representing the name of the corresponding action that should be invoked), and the `ActionMap` associates an `Object` (also usually a `String` representing the name of an action) with an `Action`. In this way `KeyStrokes` are mapped to `Actions` based on the current scope.

Each component's main `ActionMap` and `InputMaps` are created by its UI Delegate. For most intents and purposes you will not need to directly access these maps because `JComponent` provides methods to easily add and remove `Keystrokes` and `Actions`. For example, to bind the F1 key to the "HOME" action in a `JList` you would write the following code:

```
myJList.getInputMap().put(
  KeyStroke.getKeyStroke(F1"), "HOME");
```

To disable an existing key combination, for instance the "F1" key in the previous code, you would write the following:

```
myJList.getInputMap().put(
  KeyStroke.getKeyStroke(F1"), "none");
```

Similarly you can create an `Action` or override an existing `Action` as follows:

```
Action homeAction = new AbstractAction("HOME") {
  public void actionPerformed() {
   // place custom event-handling code here
  }
};
myList.getActionMap().put(
homeAction.get(Action.NAME), homeAction);
```

Note that the `getInputMap()` method used here with no parameters returns the `InputMap` associated with the WHEN_FOCUSED scope. To get the `InputMap` corresponding to a different scope you can use the `getInputMap()` method which takes the scope as parameter: `get-InputMap(int condition)` where `condition` is one of `JComponent.WHEN_FOCUSED`, `JComponent.WHEN_ANCESTOR_OF_FOCUSED_COMPONENT`, `JComponent.WHEN_IN_FOCUS-ED_WINDOW`.

In the case of text components, the code will work the same. Under the hood there is an `InputMap` wrapped around the text component's main `KeyMap` so that text components still internally use `KeyMaps` while conforming to the new keyboard bindings infrastructure.

2.13.6   The flow of keyboard input

Each `KeyEvent` is first dispatched to the `KeyboardFocusManager` (see 2.12). If the `KeyboardFocusManager` does not consume the event it is sent to the focused component. The event is received in the component's `processKeyEvent()` method. Note that this method will only be invoked if `KeyEvents` have been enabled (which is true whenever there is an `InputMap` in use and whenever `KeyEvents` are enabled on the component using the `enableEvents()` method—true by default for most Swing components) or if there is a `Key-Listener` registered with the component.

Next any registered `KeyListeners` get a chance to handle the event. If it is not consumed by a `KeyListener` then the event is sent to the component's `processComponent-KeyEvent()` method which allows for any `JComponent` subclasses to handle key events in specific ways (`JComponent` itself has an empty implementation of this method).

If the event has not been consumed the WHEN_FOCUSED InputMap is consulted. If there is a match the corresponding action is performed and the event is consumed. If not the container hierarchy is traversed upward from the focused component to the focus cycle root where the WHEN_ANCESTOR_OF_FOCUSED_COMPONENT InputMap is consulted. If the event is not consumed there it is sent to KeyboardManager, a package private service class (note that unlike most service classes in Swing, KeyboardManager does not register its shared instance with AppContext, see section 2.5).

KeyboardManager looks for components with registered KeyStrokes with the WHEN_IN_FOCUSED_WINDOW condition and sends the event to them. If none of these are found then KeyboardManager passes the event to any JMenuBars in the current window and lets their accelerators have a crack at it. If the event is still not handled a check is performed to determine if the current focus resides in a JInternalFrame (because it is the only focus cycle root that can be contained inside another lightweight Swing component). If this is the case, the event is handed to the JInternalFrame's parent. This process continues until either the event is consumed or the top-level window is reached.

PART II

The basics

Part II consists of twelve chapters containing discussion and examples of the basic Swing components.

Chapter 3 introduces frames, panels, and borders, including an example showing how to create a custom rounded-edge border.

Chapter 4 is devoted to layout managers with a comparison of the most commonly used layouts, a contributed section on the use of `GridBagLayout`, the construction of several custom layouts, and the beginnings of a JavaBeans property editing environment with the ability to change the layout manager dynamically.

Chapter 5 covers labels and buttons, and presents the construction of a custom transparent polygonal button designed for use in applets, as well as a custom tooltip manager to provide proper tooltip functionality for these polygonal buttons.

Chapter 6 is about using tabbed panes.

Chapter 7 discusses scroll panes and how to customize scrolling functionality. Examples show how to use the row and column headers for tracking scroll position, how to change the speed of scrolling through implementation of the `Scrollable` interface, how to implement grab-and-drag scrolling, and how to programmatically invoke scrolling.

Chapter 8 takes a brief look at split panes with an example showing how to synchronize two dividers.

Chapter 9 covers combo boxes with examples showing how to build custom combo box models and cell renderers, add functionlity to the default combo box editor, and serialize a combo box model for later use.

Chapter 10 is about list boxes and spinners with examples of building a custom tab-based cell renderer, adding keyboard search functionality for quick item selection, and constructing a custom check box cell renderer.

Chapter 11 introduces the text components and undo/redo functionality with basic examples and discussions of each (text package coverage continues in chapters 19 and 20).

Chapter 12 is devoted to menu bars, menus, menu items, toolbars and actions. Examples include the construction of a basic text editor with floatable toolbar, custom toolbar buttons, and a custom color chooser menu item.

Chapter 13 discusses progress bars, sliders and scroll bars, including a custom scroll pane, a slider-based date chooser, a JPEG image quality editor, and an FTP client application.

Chapter 14 covers dialogs, option panes, and file and color choosers. Examples demonstrate the basics of custom dialog creation and the use of `JOptionPane`, as well as how to add a custom component to `JColorChooser`, and how to customize `JFileChooser` to allow multiple file selection and the addition of a custom component (a ZIP/JAR archive creation, extraction and preview tool).

CHAPTER 3

Frames, panels, and borders

3.1 FRAMES AND PANELS OVERVIEW

Swing applications are built from basic framework components.

3.1.1 JFrame

class javax.swing.JFrame

The main container for a Swing-based application is JFrame. All objects associated with a JFrame are managed by its only child, an instance of JRootPane. JRootPane is a simple container for several child panes. When we add components to a JFrame, we don't directly add them to the JFrame as we did with an AWT Frame. Instead we have to specify into exactly which pane of the JFrame's JRootPane we want the component to be placed. In most cases components are added to the contentPane by calling:

```
getContentPane().add(myComponent);
```

Similarly, when setting a layout for a JFrame's contents, we usually just want to set the layout for the contentPane:

```
getContentPane().setLayout(new FlowLayout());
```

Each `JFrame` contains a `JRootPane`, which is accessible though the `getRootPane()` method. Figure 3.1 illustrates the hierarchy of a `JFrame` and its `JRootPane`. The lines in this diagram extend downward representing the "has a" relationship of each container.

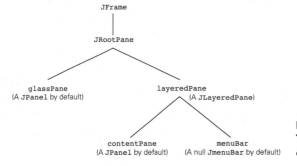

Figure 3.1
The default `JFrame` and
`JRootPane` "has a" relationship

3.1.2 JRootPane

class javax.swing.JRootPane

Each `JRootPane` contains several components referred to here by variable name: `glassPane` (a `JPanel` by default), `layeredPane` (a `JLayeredPane`), `contentPane` (a `JPanel` by default), and `menuBar` (a `JMenuBar`).

NOTE   `glassPane` and `contentPane` are just variable names used by `JRootPane`. They are not unique Swing classes, as some explanations might lead you to believe.

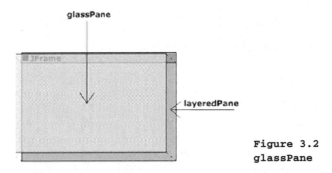

Figure 3.2
glassPane

The `glassPane` is initialized as a non-opaque `JPanel` that sits on top of the `JLayeredPane` as illustrated in figure 3.2. This component is very useful in situations where we need to intercept mouse events to display a certain cursor over the whole frame or to redirect the current application focus. The `glassPane` can be any component, but it is a `JPanel` by default. To change the `glassPane` from a `JPanel` to another component, a call to the `setGlass-Pane()` method must be made:

```
setGlassPane(myComponent);
```

Though the `glassPane` does sit on top of the `layeredPane`, it is, by default, not visible. It can be set visible (show itself) by calling:

```
getGlassPane().setVisible(true);
```

The `glassPane` allows you to display components in front of an existing `JFrame`'s contents.

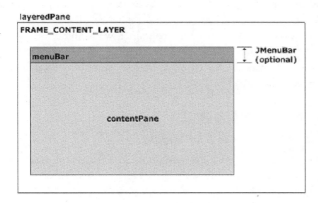

**Figure 3.3
Default `JFrame` contents
of the `JLayeredPane`
`FRAME_CONTENT_LAYER`**

The `contentPane` and optional `menuBar` are contained within `JRootPane`'s `layeredPane` at the `FRAME_CONTENT_LAYER` (this is layer –30000; see chapter 15). The `menuBar` does not exist by default, but it can be set by calling the `setJMenuBar()` method:

```
JMenuBar menu = new JMenuBar();
setJMenuBar(menu);
```

When the `JMenuBar` is set, it is automatically positioned at the top of the `FRAME_CONTENT _LAYER`. The rest of the layer is occupied by the `contentPane` as illustrated in figure 3.3.

The `contentPane` is, by default, an opaque `JPanel`. It can be set to any other component by calling:

```
setContentPane(myComponent);
```

NOTE   The default layout for the `contentPane` is `BorderLayout`. The default layout for any other `JPanel` is `FlowLayout`. Be careful not to set the layout of a `JFrame` directly. This will generate an exception. You should also avoid setting the layout of the `rootPane`, because every `JRootPane` uses its own custom layout manager called `RootLayout`. We will discuss layout managers further in chapter 4.

3.1.3   RootLayout

class javax.swing.JRootPane.RootLayout

`RootLayout` is a layout manager built specifically to manage `JRootPane`'s `layeredPane`, `glassPane`, and `menuBar`. If it is replaced by another layout manager, that manager must be able to handle the positioning of these components. `RootLayout` is an inner class defined within `JRootPane` and as such, it is not intended to have any use outside of this class. Thus it is not discussed in this text.

3.1.4 The RootPaneContainer interface

abstract interface javax.swing.RootPaneContainer

The purpose of the RootPaneContainer interface is to organize a group of methods that should be used to access a container's JRootPane and its different panes (refer to the API docs for more information). Because JFrame's main container is a JRootPane, it implements this interface (as do also JApplet, JInternalFrame, JDialog, and JWindow). If we were to build a new component which uses a JRootPane as its main container, we would most likely implement the RootPaneContainer interface. (Note that this interface exists for convenience, consistency, and organizational purposes. We are encouraged, but certainly not required, to use it in our own container implementations.)

3.1.5 The WindowConstants interface

abstract interface javax.swing.WindowConstants

We can specify how a JFrame, JInternalFrame, or JDialog act in response to a close using the setDefaultCloseOperation() method. There are four possible settings, as defined by WindowConstants interface fields:

```
WindowConstants.DISPOSE_ON_CLOSE
WindowConstants.DO_NOTHING_ON_CLOSE
WindowConstants.HIDE_ON_CLOSE
WindowConstants.EXIT_ON_CLOSE
```

The names are self-explanatory. DISPOSE_ON_CLOSE disposes of the container and its contents, DO_NOTHING_ON_CLOSE causes the window frame's Close button to not automatically do anything when pressed, and HIDE_ON_CLOSE removes the container from view. HIDE_ON_CLOSE may be useful if we need the container, or something it contains, at a later time but do not want it to be visible until then. DO_NOTHING_ON_CLOSE can be very useful, as you will see below. EXIT_ON_CLOSE will close the frame and terminate program execution (we use this close operation in all of the example applications throughout the book).

3.1.6 The WindowListener interface

abstract interface java.awt.event.WindowListener

Classes that want explicit notification of window events (such as window closing or iconification) need to implement this interface. Normally, the WindowAdapter class is extended instead. "When the window's status changes by virtue of being opened, closed, activated or deactivated, iconified or deiconified, the relevant method in the listener object is invoked, and the WindowEvent is passed to it." (API documentation)

The methods any implementation of this interface must define are these:
- void windowActivated(WindowEvent e)
- void windowClosed(WindowEvent e)
- void windowClosing(WindowEvent e)
- void windowDeactivated(WindowEvent e)
- void windowDeiconified(WindowEvent e)

- void windowIconified(WindowEvent e)
- void windowOpened(WindowEvent e)

3.1.7 WindowEvent

class java.awt.event.WindowEvent

This is the type of event used to indicate that a window has changed state. This event is passed to every WindowListener or WindowAdapter object which is registered on the source window to receive such events. The method getWindow() returns the window that generated the event. The method paramString() retrieves a String describing the event type and its source, among other things.

Six types of WindowEvents can be generated; each is represented by the following static WindowEvent fields: WINDOW_ACTIVATED, WINDOW_CLOSED, WINDOW_CLOSING, WINDOW_ DEACTIVATED, WINDOW_DEICONIFIED, WINDOW_ICONIFIED, and WINDOW_OPENED.

3.1.8 WindowAdapter

abstract class java.awt.event.WindowAdapter

This is an abstract implementation of the WindowListener interface. It is normally more convenient to extend this class than to implement WindowListener directly, as it is likely that most WindowEvent handlers will not care about all seven event types.

A useful idea for real-world applications is to combine WindowAdapter, values from the WindowConstants interface, and JOptionPane, to present the user with an exit confirmation dialog as follows:

```
myJFrame.setDefaultCloseOperation(
  WindowConstants.DO_NOTHING_ON_CLOSE);
WindowListener l = new WindowAdapter() {
  public void windowClosing(WindowEvent e) {
    int confirm = JOptionPane.showOptionDialog(myJFrame,
      "Really Exit?", "Exit Confirmation",
      JOptionPane.YES_NO_OPTION,
      JOptionPane.QUESTION_MESSAGE,
      null, null, null);
    if (confirm == 0) {
      myJFrame.dispose();
      System.exit(0);
    }
  }
};
myJFrame.addWindowListener(l);
```

NOTE This can also be done for JDialog.

Inserting this code into your application will always display the dialog shown in figure 3.4 when the JFrame Close button is clicked.

REFERENCE Dialogs and JOptionPane are discussed in chapter 14.

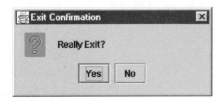

Figure 3.4
An application exit
confirmation dialog

3.1.9 Custom frame icons

We might want to use a custom icon to replace the default coffee cup icon. Because JFrame is a subclass of java.awt.Frame, we can set its icon using the setIconImage() method.

GUIDELINE

Brand identity   Use the frame icon to establish and reinforce your brand identity. Pick a simple image which can be both effective in the small space and reused throughout the application and any accompanying material. Figure 3.4 shows the Sun Coffee Cup which was used as a brand mark for Java.

```
ImageIcon image = new ImageIcon("spiral.gif");
myFrame.setIconImage(image.getImage());
```

There is no limit to the size of the icon that can be used. A JFrame will resize any image passed to setIconImage() to fit the bound it needs. Figure 3.5 shows the top of a JFrame with a custom icon.

Figure 3.5
JFrame custom icon

3.1.10 Centering a frame on the screen

By default, a JFrame displays itself in the upper left-hand corner of the screen, but we often want to place it in the center of the screen. Using the getToolkit() method of the Window class (of which JFrame is a second-level subclass), we can communicate with the operating system and query the size of the screen. (The Toolkit methods make up the bridge between Java components and their native, operating-system-specific, peer components.)

The getScreenSize() method gives us the information we need:

```
Dimension dim = getToolkit().getScreenSize();
```

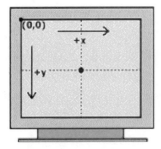

Figure 3.6
Screen coordinates

When setting the location of the JFrame, the upper left-hand corner of the frame is the relevant coordinate. So to center a JFrame on the screen, we need to subtract half its width and half its height from the center-of-screen coordinate:

```
myJFrame.setLocation(dim.width/2 - myJFrame.getWidth()/2,
  dim.height/2 - myJFrame.getHeight()/2);
```

Figure 3.6 illustrates how the screen coordinates work.

3.1.11 Headless frames and extended frame states

New to Java 1.4 are features that provide us with the ability to create frames without title bars and programmatically maximize, both of which were not possible in previous versions of Java.

To create an AWT Frame or a Swing JFrame without a title bar, once you have instantiated the frame call setUndecorated(false) on it. Note that once you make a frame visible you can no longer change the decorated setting (an IllegalComponentStateException will be thrown if you try). Make sure to use the setUndecorated() method only when a frame is not visible.

To programmatically maximize a frame you can use the setExtendedState() method. This method takes a bit mask of states. The available states are:

Frame.NORMAL: Non–iconified, non–maximized state
Frame.ICONIFIED: Iconified state
Frame.MAXIMIZED_HORIZ: maximized horizontally
Frame.MAXIMIZED_VERT: maximized vertically
Frame.MAZIMIZED_BOTH: Maximized both horizontally and vertically

Normally you will only need to use one of the above states at any given time. However, if you want to do something like iconify a frame while keeping it maximized in the vertical direction only, you can combine the flags as follows:

```
myFrame.setExtendedState(
  Frame.ICONIFIED | Frame.MAXIMIZED_VERT);
```

To clear all bits you can use the Frame.NORMAL flag by itself.

3.1.12 Look and feel window decorations

New to Java 1.4 is the ability to create JFrames and JDialogs with window decorations (i.e., title bar, icons, borders, etc.) in the style of the currently installed look and feel. To enable this for all JFrames and JDialogs we use the following new static methods:

```
JFrame.setDefaultLookAndFeelDecorated(true);
JDialog.setDefaultLookAndFeelDecorated(true);
```

After these methods are called all newly instantiated JFrames and JDialogs will have frame decorations in the style of the current look and feel. All those existing before the methods were called will not be affected.

To enable this on a single JFrame or JDialog instance we can do the following;

```
myJFrame.setUndecorated(true);
myJFrame.getRootPane().setWindowDecorationStyle(JRootPane.FRAME);
```

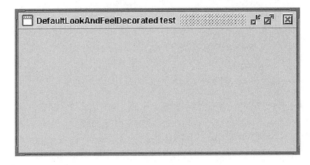

Figure 3.7
**A JFrame created with
defaultLookAndFeel-
Decorated set to true**

Figure 3.7 shows an empty JFrame created with defaultLookAndFeelDecorated set to true (looks jut like a JInternalFrame).

3.1.13 JApplet

class javax.swing.JApplet

JApplet is the Swing equivalent of the AWT Applet class. Like JFrame, JApplet's main child component is a JRootPane and its structure is the same. JApplet acts just like Applet, so we won't go into detail about how applets work.

    REFERENCE   We suggest that readers unfamiliar with applets refer to the Java tutorial to learn more: http://java.sun.com/docs/books/tutorial/.

Several examples in later chapters are constructed as Swing applets, so we will see JApplet in action soon enough.

3.1.14 JWindow

class javax.swing.JWindow

JWindow is very similar to JFrame except that it has no title bar and it is not resizable, minimizable, maximizable, or closable. Thus it cannot be dragged without writing custom code to do so in the same way that JToolBar's UI delegate provides this functionality for docking and undocking (see chapter 12). We normally use JWindow to display a temporary message or splash screen logo. Since JWindow is a RootPaneContainer, we can treat it just like JFrame or JApplet when manipulating its contents.

3.1.15 JPanel

class javax.swing.JPanel

This is the simple container component commonly used to organize a group or groups of child components. JPanel is an integral part of JRootPane, as we discussed, and it is used in each example throughout this book. Each JPanel's child components are managed by a layout manager. A layout manager controls the size and location of each child in a container. JPanel's default layout manager is FlowLayout (we will discuss this further in chapter 4). The only exception to this is JRootPane's contentPane, which is managed by a BorderLayout by default.

3.2 BORDERS

package javax.swing.border

The `border` package provides us with the following border classes; they can be applied to any Swing component.

`BevelBorder`
> A 3-D border with a raised or lowered appearance.

`CompoundBorder`
> A combination of two borders: an inside border and an outside border.

`EmptyBorder`
> A transparent border used to define empty space (often referred to as *white space*) around a component.

`EtchedBorder`
> A border with an etched line appearance.

`LineBorder`
> A flat border with a specified thickness and color. As of Java 1.3 there is an additional `LineBorder` constructor allowing you to specify whether or not the `LineBorder`'s corners should be slightly rounded.

`MatteBorder`
> A border consisting of either a flat color or a tiled image.

`SoftBevelBorder`
> A 3-D border with a raised or lowered appearance, and slightly rounded edges.

`TitledBorder`
> A border which allows a `String` title in a specific location and position. We can set the title font, color, and justification, and the position of the title text using `Title-Border` methods and constants where necessary (refer to the API docs).

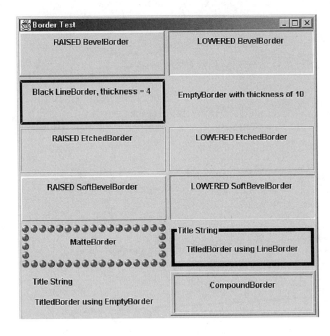

**Figure 3.8
A simple borders
demonstration**

To set the border of a Swing component, we simply call JComponent's setBorder() method. There is also a convenience class called BorderFactory, contained in the javax.swing package (not the javax.swing.border package as you might think), which contains a group of static methods used for constructing borders quickly. For example, to create an EtchedBorder, we can use BorderFactory as follows:

```
myComponent.setBorder(BorderFactory.createEtchedBorder());
```

The border classes do not provide methods for setting preferences such as dimensions and colors. Instead of modifying an existing border, we are normally expected to create a new instance to replace the old one.

Example 3.1 creates a JFrame containing twelve JPanels using borders of all types. The output is shown in figure 3.7.

Example 3.1

BorderTest.java

see \Chapter3\1

```
import java.awt.*;
import javax.swing.*;
import javax.swing.border.*;

class BorderTest extends JFrame {
  public BorderTest() {
    setTitle("Border Test");
    setSize(455, 450);

    JPanel content = (JPanel) getContentPane();
    content.setLayout(new GridLayout(6, 2, 5, 5));

    JPanel p = new JPanel();
    p.setBorder(new BevelBorder (BevelBorder.RAISED));
    p.add(new JLabel("RAISED BevelBorder"));
    content.add(p);

    p = new JPanel();
    p.setBorder(new BevelBorder (BevelBorder.LOWERED));
    p.add(new JLabel("LOWERED BevelBorder"));
    content.add(p);

    p = new JPanel();
    p.setBorder(new LineBorder (Color.black, 4, true));
    p.add(new JLabel("Black LineBorder, thickness = 4"));
    content.add(p);

    p = new JPanel();
    p.setBorder(new EmptyBorder (10,10,10,10));
    p.add(new JLabel("EmptyBorder with thickness of 10"));
    content.add(p);

    p = new JPanel();
    p.setBorder(new EtchedBorder (EtchedBorder.RAISED));
    p.add(new JLabel("RAISED EtchedBorder"));
```

```java
        content.add(p);

        p = new JPanel();
        p.setBorder(new EtchedBorder (EtchedBorder.LOWERED));
        p.add(new JLabel("LOWERED EtchedBorder"));
        content.add(p);

        p = new JPanel();
        p.setBorder(new SoftBevelBorder (SoftBevelBorder.RAISED));
        p.add(new JLabel("RAISED SoftBevelBorder"));
        content.add(p);

        p = new JPanel();
        p.setBorder(new SoftBevelBorder (SoftBevelBorder.LOWERED));
        p.add(new JLabel("LOWERED SoftBevelBorder"));
        content.add(p);

        p = new JPanel();
        p.setBorder(new MatteBorder (new ImageIcon("ball.gif")));
        p.add(new JLabel("MatteBorder"));
        content.add(p);

        p = new JPanel();
        p.setBorder(new TitledBorder (
          new LineBorder (Color.black, 5),
          "Title String"));
        p.add(new JLabel("TitledBorder using LineBorder"));
        content.add(p);

        p = new JPanel();
        p.setBorder(new TitledBorder (
          new EmptyBorder (Color.black, 5),
          "Title String"));
        p.add(new JLabel("TitledBorder using LineBorder"));
        content.add(p);

        Color c1 = new color(86, 86, 86);
        Color c2 = new Color(192, 192, 192); (
        Color c3 = new color(204, 204, 204);
        Border b1 = new BevelBorder(EtchedBorder.RAISED, c3, c1);
        Border b2 = new MatteBroder(3,3,3,3,c2);
        Border b3 = new BevelBorder (EtchedBorder.LOWERED, c3, c1);

        p = new JPanel();
        P.setBorder(new CompoundBorder(new CompoundBorder(b1, b2), b3));
        p.add(new JLabel("CompoundBorder"));
        content.add(p);
    }
    public static void main(String args[]) {
      BorderTest frame = new BorderTest();
      frame.setDefaultCloseOperation(JFrame.EXIT_ON_CLOSE);
      frame.setVisible(true);
    }
  }
```

Borders for visual layering   Use borders to create a visual association between components in a view. Beveled borders are graphically very striking and can be used to strongly associate items. The Windows look and feel does this. For example, buttons use a raised `BevelBorder` and data fields use a lowered `Bevel-Border`. If you want to visually associate components or draw attention to a component, then you can create a *visual layer* by careful use of `BevelBorder`. If you want to draw attention to a particular button or group of buttons, you might consider thickening the RAISED bevel using `BorderInsets` as discussed in section 3.2.1

Borders for visual grouping   Use borders to create group boxes. `Etched-Border` and `LineBorder` are particularly effective for this, as they are graphically weaker then `BevelBorder`. `EmptyBorder` is also very useful for grouping. It uses the power of negative (white) space to visually associate the contained components and draw the viewer's eye to the group.

You may wish to create a visual grouping of attributes or simply signify the bounds of a set of choices. Grouping related radio buttons and check boxes is particularly useful.

Achieving visual integration and balance using negative space   Use a compound border including an `EmptyBorder` to increase the negative (white) space around a component or panel. Visually, a border sets what is known as a ground (or area) for a figure. The figure is what is contained within the border. It is important to keep the figure and the ground in balance by providing adequate white space around the figure. The stronger the border, the more white space will be required; for example, a `BevelBorder` will require more white space than an `EtchedBorder`.

Border for visual grouping with layering   Doubly compounded borders can be used to group information and communicate hierarchy using visual layering. Consider the following implementation which is shown in figure 3.8. Here we are indicating a common container for the attributes within the border. They are both attributes of Customer. Because we have indicated the label Customer (top left-hand side of the box) in the border title, we do not need to repeat the label for each field. We are further communicating the type of the Customer with the VIP label (bottom right-hand side of the box).

Visual layering of the hierachy involved is achieved by position and font.

- Position: In western cultures, the eye is trained to scan from top left to bottom right. Thus, something located top left has a visual higher rank than something located bottom right.

- Font: By bolding the term Customer, we are clearly communicating it as the highest ranking detail.

What we are displaying is a Customer of type VIP, not a VIP of type Customer. The positioning and heavier font reinforcement clearly communicate this message.

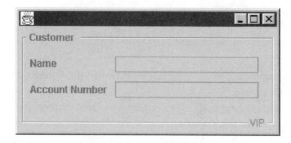

Figure 3.9
Visual grouping
with layering

3.2.1 Inside borders

It is important to understand that borders are not components. In fact, `AbstractBorder`, the abstract class all border classes are derived from, directly extends `Object`. Therefore, we cannot attach action and mouse listeners to borders, set tooltips, etc.

NOTE   The fact that borders are not components has certain side effects, one of which is that borders are much less efficient in painting themselves. There is no optimization support like there is in `JComponent`. We *can* do interesting things like using a very thick `MatteBorder` to tile a panel with an image, but this is an inefficient and unreliable solution. In general, don't use really large borders for anything. If you need an extremely large border, consider simulating one using `JLabels` and a container managed by `BorderLayout`.

One major benefit of `Borders` not being components is that we can use a single `Border` instance with an arbitrary number of components. In large-scale applications, this can reduce a significant amount of overhead.

When a Swing component is assigned a border, its `Insets` are defined by that border's width and height settings. When layout managers lay out `JComponents`, as we will see in the next chapter, they take into account their `Insets`; they normally use `JComponent`'s `getInsets()` method to obtain this information. Inside the `getInsets()` method, the current border is asked to provide its `Insets` using the `getBorderInsets()` method.

The `Insets` class consists of four publicly accessible `int` values: `bottom`, `left`, `right`, and `top`. `TitledBorder` must compute its `Insets` based on its current font and text position since these variables could potentially affect the size of any of the `Insets` values. In the case of `CompoundBorder`, both its outer and inner `Insets` are retrieved through calls to `getBorderInsets()`, and then they are added up. A `MatteBorder`'s `Insets` are determined by the width and height of its image. `BevelBorder` and `EtchedBorder` have `Insets` values: 2, 2, 2, 2. `SoftBevelBorder` has `Insets` values: 3, 3, 3, 3. `EmptyBorder`'s `Insets` are simply the values that were passed in to the constructor. Each of `LineBorder`'s `Insets` values equal the thickness that was specified in the constructor (or 1 as the default).

`Borders` get painted late in the `JComponent` rendering pipeline to ensure that they always appear on top of each associated component. `AbstractBorder` defines several `getInteriorRectangle()` methods to get a `Rectangle` representing the interior region of the component a border is attached to: `getInteriorRectangle()`. Any `JComponent` subclass implementing its own painting methods may be interested in this area. Combined with the `Graphics` clipping area, components may use this information to minimize their rendering work (refer back to chapter 2 for more information).

3.3 CREATING A CUSTOM BORDER

To create a custom border, we can implement the `javax.swing.Border` interface and define the following three methods:

- `void paintBorder(Component c, Graphics g)`: Performs the border rendering; only paint within the `Insets` region.
- `Insets getBorderInsets(Component c)`: Returns an `Insets` instance representing the top, bottom, left, and right thicknesses.
- `boolean isBorderOpaque()`: Returns whether or not the border is opaque or transparent.

The following class, shown in example 3.2, is a simple implementation of a custom rounded-rectangle border which we call `OvalBorder`.

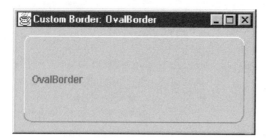

**Figure 3.10
A custom rounded-corner
border implementation**

Example 3.2

OvalBorder.java

see \Chapter3\2

```
import java.awt.*;

import javax.swing.*;
import javax.swing.border.*;

public class OvalBorder implements Border
{
  protected int m_w=6;
  protected int m_h=6;
  protected Color m_topColor = Color.white;
  protected Color m_bottomColor = Color.gray;

  public OvalBorder() {
    m_w=6;
    m_h=6;
  }

  public OvalBorder(int w, int h) {
    m_w=w;
    m_h=h;
  }
```

```
public OvalBorder(int w, int h, Color topColor,
 Color bottomColor) {
  m_w=w;
  m_h=h;
  m_topColor = topColor;
  m_bottomColor = bottomColor;
}

public Insets getBorderInsets(Component c) {
  return new Insets(m_h, m_w, m_h, m_w);
}

public  boolean isBorderOpaque() { return true; }

public void paintBorder(Component c, Graphics g,
 int x, int y, int w, int h) {
  w--;
  h--;
  g.setColor(m_topColor);
  g.drawLine(x, y+h-m_h, x, y+m_h);
  g.drawArc(x, y, 2*m_w, 2*m_h, 180, -90);
  g.drawLine(x+m_w, y, x+w-m_w, y);
  g.drawArc(x+w-2*m_w, y, 2*m_w, 2*m_h, 90, -90);

  g.setColor(m_bottomColor);
  g.drawLine(x+w, y+m_h, x+w, y+h-m_h);
  g.drawArc(x+w-2*m_w, y+h-2*m_h, 2*m_w, 2*m_h, 0, -90);
  g.drawLine(x+m_w, y+h, x+w-m_w, y+h);
  g.drawArc(x, y+h-2*m_h, 2*m_w, 2*m_h, -90, -90);
}

public static void main(String[] args) {
  JFrame frame = new JFrame("Custom Border: OvalBorder");
  JLabel label = new JLabel("OvalBorder");
  ((JPanel) frame.getContentPane()).setBorder(new CompoundBorder(
    new EmptyBorder(10,10,10,10), new OvalBorder(10,10)));
  frame.getContentPane().add(label);
  frame.setBounds(0,0,300,150);
  frame.setDefaultCloseOperation(JFrame.EXIT_ON_CLOSE);
  frame.setVisible(true);
}
}
```

3.3.1 Understanding the code

This border consists of a raised shadowed rectangle with rounded corners. Instance variables:

Table 3.1   OvalBorder.java instance variables

Variables	Description
int m_w	Left and right inset value.
int m_h	Top and bottom inset value.
Color m_topColor	Non-shadow color.
Color m_bottomColor	Shadow color.

Three constructors are provided to allow optional specification of the width and height of the left/right and top/bottom inset values respectively. We can also specify the shadow color (bottom color) and non-shadow color (top color). The inset values default to 6, the top color defaults to white, and the shadow color defaults to gray.

The `isBorderOpaque()` method always returns `true` to signify that this border's region will be completely filled. `getBorderInsets()` simply returns an `Insets` instance made up of the left/right and top/bottom inset values.

The `paintBorder()` method is responsible for rendering our border, and it simply paints a sequence of four lines and arcs in the appropriate colors. By reversing the use of `bottomColor` and `topColor`, we can switch from a raised look to a lowered look (a more flexible implementation might include a raised/lowered flag and an additional constructor parameter used to specify this).

The `main()` method creates a `JFrame` with a content pane surrounded by a `Compound-Border`. The outer border is an `EmptyBorder` to provide white space, and the inner border is an instance of our `OvalBorder` class with width and height values of 10.

3.3.2 Running the code

Figure 3.9 illustrates the output of example 3.2. Try running this class and resizing the parent frame. Notice that with a very small width or height, the border does not render itself perfectly. A more professional implementation will take this into account in the `paintBorder()` routine.

C H A P T E R 4

Layout managers

4.1   LAYOUTS OVERVIEW

In this chapter, we'll present several examples that show how to use various layouts to satisfy specific goals, and we'll also show how to create two custom layout managers that simplify the construction of many common interfaces. You'll also learn how to construct a basic container for JavaBeans which must be able to manage a dynamic number of components. But before we present these examples, it will help you to understand the big picture of layouts, which classes use their own custom layouts, and exactly what it means to be a layout manager.

All layout managers implement one of two interfaces defined in the `java.awt` package: `LayoutManager` or its subclass, `LayoutManager2`. `LayoutManager` declares a set of methods that are intended to provide a straightforward, organized means of managing component positions and sizes in a container. Each implementation of `LayoutManager` defines these methods in different ways according to its specific needs. `LayoutManager2` enhances this by adding methods intended to aid in managing component positions and sizes using *constraints-based* objects. Constraints-based objects usually store position and sizing information about one component, and implementations of `LayoutManager2` normally store one constraints-based object per component. For instance, `GridBagLayout` uses a `Hashtable` to map each `Component` it manages to its own `GridBagConstraints` object.

Figure 4.1 shows all the classes that implement `LayoutManager` and `LayoutManager2`. Notice that there are several UI classes that implement these interfaces to provide custom layout functionality for themselves. The other classes—the classes with which we are most familiar and concerned—are built solely to provide help in laying out the containers they are assigned to.

Each container should be assigned one layout manager, and no layout manager should be used to manage more than one container.

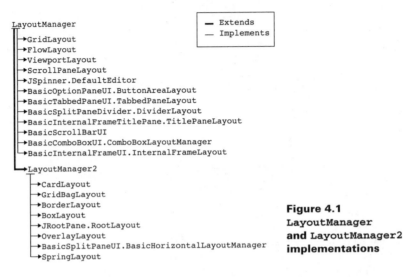

Figure 4.1
LayoutManager
and LayoutManager2
implementations

NOTE   We have purposely omitted the discussion of several layout managers in this chapter (such as `ViewportLayout`, `ScrollPaneLayout`, and `JRootPane.RootPane-Layout`) because they are rarely used by developers and are more appropriately discussed in terms of the components that rely on them. For instance, we discuss `ViewportLayout` and `ScrollPaneLayout` in chapter 7.

4.1.1   LayoutManager

abstract interface java.awt.LayoutManager

This interface must be implemented by any layout manager. Two methods are especially noteworthy:

- `layoutContainer(Container parent)`: Calculates and sets the bounds for all components in the given container.
- `preferredLayoutSize(Container parent)`: Calculates the preferred size requirements to lay out components in the given container and returns a `Dimension` instance representing this size.

4.1.2   LayoutManager2

abstract interface java.awt.LayoutManager2

This interface extends `LayoutManager` to provide a framework for those layout managers that use constraints-based layouts. The method `addLayoutComponent(Component comp, Object` constraints) adds a new component associated with a constraints-based object which carries information about how to lay out this component.

A typical implementation is BorderLayout, which requires a direction (such as north or east) to position a component. In this case, the constraint objects used are static Strings such as BorderLayout.NORTH and BorderLayout.EAST. We are normally blind to the fact that BorderLayout is constraints-based because we are never required to manipulate the constraint objects at all. This is not the case with layouts such as GridBagLayout, where we must work directly with the constraint objects (which are instances of GridBagConstraints).

4.1.3   BoxLayout

class javax.swing.BoxLayout

BoxLayout organizes the components it manages along either the x-axis or y-axis of the owner panel. The only constructor, BoxLayout(Container target, int axis), takes a reference to the Container component it will manage and a direction (BoxLayout.X_AXIS or BoxLayout.Y_AXIS). Components are laid out according to their preferred sizes and they are not wrapped, even if the container does not provide enough space.

4.1.4   Box

class javax.swing.Box

To make using the BoxLayout manager easier, Swing also provides a class named Box which is a container with an automatically assigned BoxLayout manager. To create an instance of this container, we simply pass the desired alignment to its constructor. The Box class also supports the insertion of invisible blocks (instances of Box.Filler—see below) which allow regions of unused space to be specified. These blocks are basically lightweight components with bounds (position and size) but no view.

4.1.5   Filler

static class javax.swing.Box.Filler

This static inner class defines invisible components that affect a container's layout. The Box class provides convenient static methods for the creation of three different variations: glue, struts, and rigid areas.

- createHorizontalGlue(), createVerticalGlue(): Returns a component which fills the space between its neighboring components, pushing them aside to occupy all available space (this functionality is more analogous to a spring than it is to glue).
- createHorizontalStrut(int width), createVerticalStrut(int height): Returns a fixed-width (height) component which provides a fixed gap between its neighbors.
- createRigidArea(Dimension d): Returns an invisible component of fixed width and height.

   NOTE   All relevant Box methods are static and, as such, they can be applied to any container managed by a BoxLayout, not just instances of Box. Box should be thought of as a utilities class as much as it is a container.

4.1.6 FlowLayout

class java.awt.FlowLayout

This is a simple layout which places components from left to right in a row using the preferred component sizes (the size returned by getPreferredSize()), until no space in the container is available. When no space is available a new row is started. Because this placement depends on the current size of the container, we cannot always guarantee in advance in which row a component will be placed.

FlowLayout is too simple to rely on in serious applications where we want to be sure, for instance, that a set of buttons will reside at the bottom of a dialog and not on its right side. However, it can be useful as a pad for a single component to ensure that this component will be placed in the center of a container. Note that FlowLayout is the default layout for all JPanels (the only exception is the content pane of a JRootPane which is always initialized with a BorderLayout).

4.1.7 GridLayout

class java.awt.GridLayout

This layout places components in a rectangular grid. There are three constructors:

- GridLayout(): Creates a layout with one column per component. Only one row is used.
- GridLayout(int rows, int cols): Creates a layout with the given number of rows and columns.
- GridLayout(int rows, int cols, int hgap, int vgap): Creates a layout with the given number of rows and columns, and the given size of horizontal and vertical gaps between each row and column.

GridLayout places components from left to right and from top to bottom, assigning the same size to each. It forces the occupation of all available container space and it shares this space evenly between components. When it is not used carefully, this can lead to undesirable component sizing, such as text boxes three times higher than expected.

4.1.8 GridBagLayout

class java.awt.GridBagLayout, class java.awt.GridBagConstraints

This layout extends the capabilities of GridLayout to become constraints-based. It breaks the container's space into equal rectangular pieces (like bricks in a wall) and places each component in one or more of these pieces. You need to create and fill a GridBagConstraints object for each component to inform GridBagLayout how to place and size that component.

GridBagLayout can be effectively used for placement of components if no special behavior is required on resizing. However, due to its complexity, it usually requires some helper methods or classes to handle all the necessary constraints information. James Tan, a usability expert and GridBagLayout extraordinaire, gives a comprehensive overview of this manager in section 4.3. He also presents a helper class to ease the burden of dealing with GridBagConstraints.

4.1.9 BorderLayout

class java.awt.BorderLayout

This layout divides a container into five regions: center, north, south, east, and west. To specify the region in which to place a component, we use Strings of the form "Center," "North," and so on, or the static String fields defined in BorderLayout, which include BorderLayout.CENTER, BorderLayout.NORTH, etc. During the layout process, components in the north and south regions will first be allotted their preferred height (if possible) and the width of the container. Once north and south components have been assigned sizes, components in the east and west regions will attempt to occupy their preferred width as well as any remaining height between the north and south components. A component in the center region will occupy all remaining available space. BorderLayout is very useful, especially in conjunction with other layouts, as we will see in this and future chapters.

4.1.10 CardLayout

class java.awt.CardLayout

CardLayout treats all components as similar to cards of equal size overlapping one another. Only one card component is visible at any given time (see figure 4.2). The methods first(), last(), next(), previous(), and show() can be called to switch between components in the parent Container.

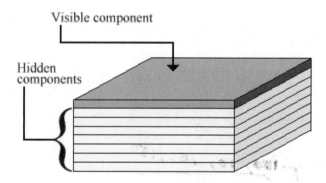

Figure 4.2
CardLayout

In a stack of several cards, only the top–most card is visible.

4.1.11 SpringLayout

class javax.swing.SpringLayout

This layout, new to Java 1.4, organizes its children according to a set of constraints (four for each child), each represented by a javax.swing.Spring object. An instance of Spring-Layout.Constraints is used as the overall constraint object when adding a child to container managed by a SpringLayout, for example:

```
container.setLayout(new SpringLayout());
container.add(new JButton("Button"),
   new SpringLayout.Constraints(
      Spring.constant(10),
```

```
        Spring.constant(10),
        Spring.constant(120),
        Spring.constant(70)));
```

`SpringLayout.Constraints`' four parameters are `Spring` objects, in this case created with the static `constant()` method to represent a minimum, maximum, and preferred value for each constraint. The first parameter represents the *x* location of the component, the second represents the *y* location, the third represents the component's width, and the fourth represents the component's height.

NOTE   The code illustrates one of the simplest uses of `SpringLayout`. See the API Java-docs for explanations of more detailed functionality such as using constraints to link the edges of two components in a container.

WARNING   `SpringLayout` does not automatically set the location of child components. If you do not set constraints on child components in a `SpringLayout`, each child will be placed at 0,0 in the container, each overlapping the next.

4.1.12   JPanel

class javax.swing.JPanel

This class represents a generic lightweight container. It works in close cooperation with layout managers. The default constructor creates a `JPanel` with a `FlowLayout`, but different layouts can be specified in a constructor or assigned using the `setLayout()` method.

NOTE   The content pane of a `JRootPane` container is a `JPanel`, which, by default, is assigned a `BorderLayout`, not a `FlowLayout`.

4.2   COMPARING COMMON LAYOUT MANAGERS

Example 4.1 demonstrates the most commonly used AWT and Swing layout managers. It shows a set of `JInternalFrames` that contain identical sets of components, each using a different layout. The purpose of this example is to allow direct simultaneous layout manager comparisons using resizable containers.

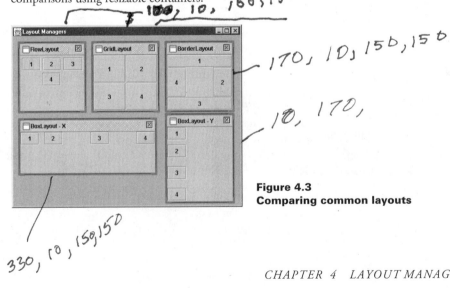

Figure 4.3
Comparing common layouts

CHAPTER 4   LAYOUT MANAGERS

Example 4.1

CommonLayouts.java

see \Chapter4\1

```java
import java.awt.*;
import java.awt.event.*;
import java.util.*;

import javax.swing.*;
import javax.swing.border.*;
import javax.swing.event.*;

public class CommonLayouts extends JFrame {
    public Integer LAYOUT_FRAME_LAYER = new Integer(1);

  public CommonLayouts() {
    super("Common Layout Managers");
    setSize(500, 460);

    JDesktopPane desktop = new JDesktopPane();
    getContentPane().add(desktop);

    JInternalFrame fr1 =
      new JInternalFrame("FlowLayout", true, true);
    fr1.setBounds(10, 10, 150, 150);
    Container c = fr1.getContentPane();
    c.setLayout(new FlowLayout());
    c.add(new JButton("1"));
    c.add(new JButton("2"));
    c.add(new JButton("3"));
    c.add(new JButton("4"));
    desktop.add(fr1, 0);
    fr1.show();

    JInternalFrame fr2 =
      new JInternalFrame("GridLayout", true, true);
    fr2.setBounds(170, 10, 150, 150);
    c = fr2.getContentPane();
    c.setLayout(new GridLayout(2, 2));
    c.add(new JButton("1"));
    c.add(new JButton("2"));
    c.add(new JButton("3"));
    c.add(new JButton("4"));
    desktop.add(fr2, 0);
    fr2.show();

    JInternalFrame fr3 =
      new JInternalFrame("BorderLayout", true, true);
    fr3.setBounds(330, 10, 150, 150);
    c = fr3.getContentPane();
    c.add(new JButton("1"), BorderLayout.NORTH);
    c.add(new JButton("2"), BorderLayout.EAST);
    c.add(new JButton("3"), BorderLayout.SOUTH);
    c.add(new JButton("4"), BorderLayout.WEST);
```

```
desktop.add(fr3, 0);
fr3.show();

JInternalFrame fr4 = new JInternalFrame("BoxLayout - X",
  true, true);
fr4.setBounds(10, 170, 250, 80);
c = fr4.getContentPane();
c.setLayout(new BoxLayout(c, BoxLayout.X_AXIS));
c.add(new JButton("1"));
c.add(Box.createHorizontalStrut(12));
c.add(new JButton("2"));
c.add(Box.createGlue());
c.add(new JButton("3"));
c.add(Box.createHorizontalGlue());
c.add(new JButton("4"));
desktop.add(fr4, 0);
fr4.show();

JInternalFrame fr5 = new JInternalFrame("BoxLayout - Y",
  true, true);
fr5.setBounds(330, 170, 150, 200);
c = fr5.getContentPane();
c.setLayout(new BoxLayout(c, BoxLayout.Y_AXIS));
c.add(new JButton("1"));
c.add(Box.createVerticalStrut(10));
c.add(new JButton("2"));
c.add(Box.createGlue());
c.add(new JButton("3"));
c.add(Box.createVerticalGlue());
c.add(new JButton("4"));
desktop.add(fr5, 0);
fr5.show();

JInternalFrame fr6 =
  new JInternal Frame("SpringLayout", true, true);
fr6.setBounds(10, 260, 250, 170);
c = fr6.getContentPane();
c.setLayout(new SpringLayout());
c.add(new JButton("1"), new SpringLayout.Constraints(
  Spring.constant(10),
  Spring.constant(10),
  Spring.constant(120),
  Spring.constant(70)));
c.add(new JButton("2"), new SpringLayout.Constraints(
  Spring.constant(160),
  Spring.constant(10),
  Spring.constant(70),
  Spring.constant(30)));
c.add(new JButton("3"), new SpringLayout.Constraints(
  Spring.constant(160),
  Spring.constant(50),
  Spring.constant(70),
  Spring.constant(30)));
```

```
    c.add(new JButton("4"), new SpringLayout.Constraints(
      Spring.constant(10),
      Spring.constant(90),
      Spring.constant(50),
      Spring.constant(40)));
    c.add(new JButton("5"), new SpringLayout.Constraints(
      Spring.constant(120),
      Spring.constant(90),
      Spring.constant(50),
      Spring.constant(40)));
    desktop.add(fr6, 0);
    fr6.show();

    desktop.setSelectedFrame(fr6);
  }

  public static void main(String argv[]) {
    CommonLayouts frame = new CommonLayouts();
    frame.setDefaultCloseOperation(JFrame.EXIT_ON_CLOSE);
    frame.setVisible(true);
  }
}
```

4.2.1   Understanding the code

Class CommonLayouts

The CommonLayouts constructor creates six JInternalFrames and places them in a JDesktopPane. Each of these frames contains several JButtons. Each frame is assigned a unique layout manager: a FlowLayout, a 2x2 GridLayout, a BorderLayout, an *x*-oriented BoxLayout, a *y*-oriented BoxLayout, and a SpringLayout. Notice that the internal frames using BoxLayout also use strut and glue filler components to demonstrate their behavior.

4.2.2   Running the code

Figure 4.3 shows CommonLayouts in action. Notice the differences in each frame's content as it changes size.

- FlowLayout places components in one or more rows depending on the width of the container.
- GridLayout assigns an equal size to all components and fills all container space.
- BorderLayout places components along the sides of the container, or in the center.
- *x*-oriented BoxLayout always places components in a row. The distance between the first and second components is 12 pixels (determined by the horizontal strut component). Distances between the second, third, and fourth components are equalized and take up all remaining width (determined by the two glue filler components).
- *y*-oriented BoxLayout always places components in a column. The distance between the first and second components is 10 pixels (determined by the vertical strut component). Distances between the second, third, and fourth components are equalized and take up all available height (determined by the two glue filler components).
- SpringLayout places components at preassigned coordinates with preassigned dimensions.

4.3 USING GRIDBAGLAYOUT

This section was written by James Tan, a systems analyst with
United Overseas Bank Singapore (jtan@coruscant.per.sg).

Of all the layouts included with Swing and AWT, GridBagLayout is by far the most complex. In this section, we will walk through the various constraints attributes it relies on, along with several short examples showing how to use them. We'll follow up this discussion with a comprehensive input dialog example which puts all these attributes together. We'll then conclude this section with the construction and demonstration of a helper class designed to make using GridBagLayout more convenient.

4.3.1 Default behavior of GridBagLayout

By simply setting a container's layout to a GridBagLayout and adding Components to it, the result will be a row of components, each set to their preferred size, tightly packed and placed in the center of the container. Unlike FlowLayout, GridBagLayout will allow components to be clipped by the edge of the managing container, and it will not move child components down into a new row. The following code demonstrates this, and figure 4.4 shows the result:

```
JInternalFrame fr1 = new JInternalFrame(
   "Example 1", true, true );
fr1.setBounds( 5, 5, 270, 100 );
cn = fr1.getContentPane();
cn.setLayout( new GridBagLayout() );
cn.add( new JButton( "Wonderful" ) );
cn.add( new JButton( "World" ) );
cn.add( new JButton( "Of" ) );
cn.add( new JButton( "Swing !!!" ) );
desktop.add( fr1, 0 );
fr1.show();
```

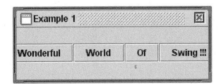

Figure 4.4
Default GridBagLayout behavior

4.3.2 Introducing GridBagConstraints

When a component is added to a container which has been assigned a GridBagLayout, the layout manager uses a default GridBagConstraints object to place the component accordingly, as shown in the above example. By creating and setting the attributes of a GridBagConstraints object and passing it in as an additional parameter in the add() method, we can flexibly manage the placement of our components.

Listed next are the various attributes we can set in a GridBagConstraints object along with their default values. The behavior of these attributes will be explained in the examples that follow.

```
public int gridx = GridBagConstraints.RELATIVE;
public int gridy = GridBagConstraints.RELATIVE;
public int gridwidth = 1;
public int gridheight = 1;
public double weightx = 0.0;
public double weighty = 0.0;
public int anchor = GridBagConstraints.CENTER;
public int fill = GridBagConstraints.NONE;
public Insets insets = new Insets( 0, 0, 0, 0 );
public int ipadx = 0;
public int ipady = 0;
```

4.3.3   Using the gridx, gridy, insets, ipadx, and ipady constraints

The gridx and gridy constraints (or column and row constraints) are used to specify the exact grid cell location where we want our component to be placed. Component placement starts from the upper left-hand corner of the container, and gridx and gridy begin with values of 0. Specifying negative values for either of these attributes is equivalent to setting them to GridBagConstraints.RELATIVE, which means that the next component added will be placed directly after the previous gridx or gridy location.

The insets constraint adds an invisible exterior padding around the associated component. Negative values can be used which will force the component to be sized larger than the cell it is contained in.

The ipadx and ipady constraints add an interior padding which increases the preferred size of the associated component. Specifically, the padding adds ipadx * 2 pixels to the preferred width and ipady * 2 pixels to the preferred height (* 2 because this padding applies to both sides of the component).

In this example, we place the "Wonderful" and "World" buttons in the first row and the other two buttons in the second row. We also associate insets with each button so that they don't look too cluttered, and they vary in both height and width.

```
JInternalFrame fr2 = new JInternalFrame("Example 2", true, true );
fr2.setBounds( 5, 110, 270, 140 );
cn = fr2.getContentPane();
cn.setLayout( new GridBagLayout() );

c = new GridBagConstraints();
c.insets = new Insets( 2, 2, 2, 2 );
c.gridx = 0;    // Column 0
c.gridy = 0;    // Row 0
c.ipadx = 5;    // Increases component width by 10 pixels
c.ipady = 5;    // Increases component height by 10 pixels
cn.add( new JButton( "Wonderful" ), c );

c.gridx = 1;    // Column 1
c.ipadx = 0;    // Reset the padding to 0
c.ipady = 0;
cn.add( new JButton( "World" ), c );

c.gridx = 0;    // Column 0
c.gridy = 1;    // Row 1
cn.add( new JButton( "Of" ), c );
```

```
c.gridx = 1;    // Column 1
cn.add( new JButton( "Swing !!!" ), c );

desktop.add( fr2, 0 );
fr2.show();
```

We begin by creating a `GridBagConstraints` object to set the constraints for the first button component. We pass it in together with the button in the `add()` method. We reuse this same constraints object by changing the relevant attributes and passing in again for each remaining component. This conserves memory, and it also relieves us of having to reassign a whole new group of attributes. Figure 4.5 shows the result.

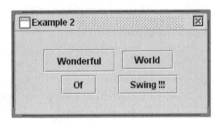

Figure 4.5
Using the `gridx`, `gridy`, `insets`,
`ipadx`, and `ipady` constraints

4.3.4   Using the weightx and weighty constraints

When the container in the example above is resized, the components respect the constraints we have assigned, but the whole group remains in the center of the container. Why don't the buttons grow to occupy a proportional amount of the increased space surrounding them? The answer lies in the use of the `weightx` and `weighty` constraints, which both default to zero when `GridBagConstraints` is instantiated.

These two constraints specify how any extra space in a container should be distributed among each component's cells. The `weightx` attribute specifies the fraction of extra horizontal space to occupy. Similarly, `weighty` specifies the fraction of extra vertical space to occupy. Both constraints can be assigned values ranging from `0.0` to `1.0`.

For example, let's say we have two buttons, A and B, placed in columns 0 and 1 of row 0 respectively. If we specify `weightx = 1.0` for the first button and `weightx = 0` for the second button, when we resize the container, all extra space will be distributed to the first button's cell—50% on the left of the button and 50% on the right. The other button will be pushed to the right of the container as far as possible. Figure 4.6 illustrates this concept.

Figure 4.6
Using `weightx` and `weighty` constraints

Getting back to our "Wonderful World Of Swing !!!" example, we now modify all button cells to share any extra container space equally as the container is resized. Specifying `weightx = 1.0` and `weighty = 1.0`, and keeping these attributes constant as each component is added, will tell GridBagLayout to use all available space for each cell. Figure 4.7 illustrates these changes.

```
JInternalFrame fr3 = new JInternalFrame("Example 3", true, true );
fr3.setBounds( 5, 255, 270, 140 );
cn = fr3.getContentPane();
cn.setLayout( new GridBagLayout() );

c = new GridBagConstraints();
c.insets = new Insets( 2, 2, 2, 2 );
c.weighty = 1.0;
c.weightx = 1.0;
c.gridx = 0;
c.gridy = 0;
cn.add( new JButton( "Wonderful" ), c );

c.gridx = 1;
cn.add( new JButton( "World" ), c );

c.gridx = 0;
c.gridy = 1;
cn.add( new JButton( "Of" ), c );

c.gridx = 1;
cn.add( new JButton( "Swing !!!" ), c );

desktop.add( fr3, 0 );
fr3.show();
```

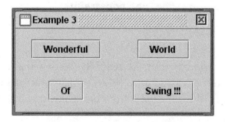

Figure 4.7
Using weightx and weighty constraints

4.3.5 Using the gridwidth and gridheight constraints

GridBagLayout also allows us to span components across multiple cells using the gridwidth and gridheight constraints. To demonstrate, we'll modify our example to force the "Wonderful" button to occupy two rows and the "World" button to occupy two columns. Figure 4.8 illustrates this. Notice that occupying more cells forces more rows and/or columns to be created based on the current container size.

```
JInternalFrame fr4 = new JInternalFrame("Example 4", true, true );
fr4.setBounds( 280, 5, 270, 140 );
cn = fr4.getContentPane();
cn.setLayout( new GridBagLayout() );

c = new GridBagConstraints();
c.insets = new Insets( 2, 2, 2, 2 );
c.weighty = 1.0;
```

```
c.weightx = 1.0;
c.gridx = 0;
c.gridy = 0;
c.gridheight = 2; // Span across 2 rows
cn.add( new JButton( "Wonderful" ), c );

c.gridx = 1;
c.gridheight = 1; // Remember to set back to 1 row
c.gridwidth = 2; // Span across 2 columns
cn.add( new JButton( "World" ), c );

c.gridy = 1;
c.gridwidth = 1; // Remember to set back to 1 column
cn.add( new JButton( "Of" ), c );

c.gridx = 2;
cn.add( new JButton( "Swing !!!" ), c );

desktop.add( fr4, 0 );
fr4.show();
```

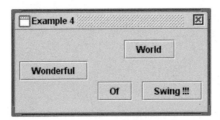

Figure 4.8
**Using gridwidth and
gridheight constraints**

4.3.6   Using anchor constraints

We can control how a component is aligned within its cell(s) by setting the anchor constraint. By default this is set to GridBagConstraints.CENTER, which forces the component to be centered within its occupied cell(s). We can choose from the following anchor settings:

```
GridBagConstraints.NORTH
GridBagConstraints.SOUTH
GridBagConstraints.EAST
GridBagConstraints.WEST
GridBagConstraints.NORTHEAST
GridBagConstraints.NORTHWEST
GridBagConstraints.SOUTHEAST
GridBagConstraints.SOUTHWEST
GridBagConstraints.CENTER
```

In the code below, we've modified our example to anchor the "Wonderful" button NORTH and the "World" button SOUTHWEST. The "Of" and "Swing !!!" buttons are anchored in the CENTER of their cells. Figure 4.9 illustrates.

```
JInternalFrame fr5 = new JInternalFrame("Example 5", true, true );
fr5.setBounds( 280, 150, 270, 140 );
cn = fr5.getContentPane();
```

```
cn.setLayout( new GridBagLayout() );

c = new GridBagConstraints();
c.insets = new Insets( 2, 2, 2, 2 );
c.weighty = 1.0;
c.weightx = 1.0;
c.gridx = 0;
c.gridy = 0;
c.gridheight = 2;
c.anchor = GridBagConstraints.NORTH;
cn.add( new JButton( "Wonderful" ), c );

c.gridx = 1;
c.gridheight = 1;
c.gridwidth = 2;
c.anchor = GridBagConstraints.SOUTHWEST;
cn.add( new JButton( "World" ), c );

c.gridy = 1;
c.gridwidth = 1;
c.anchor = GridBagConstraints.CENTER;
cn.add( new JButton( "Of" ), c );

c.gridx = 2;
cn.add( new JButton( "Swing !!!" ), c );

desktop.add( fr5, 0 );
fr5.show();
```

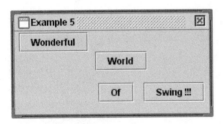

Figure 4.9
**Using `gridwidth` and
`gridheight` constraints**

4.3.7   Using fill constraints

The most common reason for spanning multiple cells is that we want the component contained in that cell to occupy the enlarged space. To do this we use the `gridheight`/`gridwidth` constraints as described above, as well as the `fill` constraint. The `fill` constraint can be assigned any of the following values:

```
GridBagConstraints.NONE
GridBagConstraints.HORIZONTAL
GridBagConstraints.VERTICAL
GridBagConstraints.BOTH
```

NOTE   Using `fill` without using `weight{x,y}` will have no effect

In the next code, we modify our example to force the "Wonderful" button to occupy all available cell space, both vertically and horizontally. The "World" button now occupies all available horizontal cell space, but it continues to use its preferred vertical size. The "Of" button does not make use of the fill constraint; it simply uses its preferred size. The "Swing !!!" button occupies all available vertical cell space, but it uses its preferred horizontal size. Figure 4.10 illustrates.

```
JInternalFrame fr6 = new JInternalFrame("Example 6", true, true );
fr6.setBounds( 280, 295, 270, 140 );
cn = fr6.getContentPane();
cn.setLayout( new GridBagLayout() );

c = new GridBagConstraints();
c.insets = new Insets( 2, 2, 2, 2 );
c.weighty = 1.0;
c.weightx = 1.0;
c.gridx = 0;
c.gridy = 0;
c.gridheight = 2;
c.fill = GridBagConstraints.BOTH;
cn.add( new JButton( "Wonderful" ), c );

c.gridx = 1;
c.gridheight = 1;
c.gridwidth = 2;
c.fill = GridBagConstraints.HORIZONTAL;
cn.add( new JButton( "World" ), c );

c.gridy = 1;
c.gridwidth = 1;
c.fill = GridBagConstraints.NONE;
cn.add( new JButton( "Of" ), c );

c.gridx = 2;
c.fill = GridBagConstraints.VERTICAL;
cn.add( new JButton( "Swing !!!" ), c );

desktop.add( fr6, 0 );
fr6.show();
```

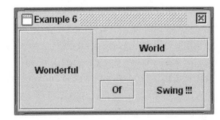

Figure 4.10
Using fill constraints

4.3.8   Putting it all together: constructing a complaints dialog

Figure 4.11 shows a sketch of a generic complaints dialog that can be used for various forms of user feedback. This sketch clearly shows how we plan to lay out the various components, and the columns and rows in which they will be placed. In order to set the constraints correctly so that the components will be laid out as shown, we must do the following:

- For the "Short Description" text field, we set the `gridwidth` constraint to 3 and the `fill` constraint to `GridBagConstraints.HORIZONTAL`. In order to make this field occupy all the horizontal space available, we also need to set the `weightx` constraints to `1.0`.
- For the "Description" text area, we set the `gridwidth` constraint to 3, the `gridheight` to 2, and the `fill` constraint to `GridBagConstraint.BOTH`. In order to make this field occupy all the available horizontal and vertical space, we set the `weightx` and `weighty` constraints to `1.0`.
- For the "Severity," "Priority," "Name," "Telephone," "Sex," and "ID Number" input fields, we want each to use their preferred width. Since the widths each exceed the width of one cell, we set `gridwidth`, and `weightx` so that they have enough space to fit, but they will not use any additional available horizontal space.
- For the Help button, we set the `anchor` constraint to `GridBagConstraint.NORTH` so that it will stick together with the upper two buttons, "Submit" and "Cancel." The `fill` constraint is set to `HORIZONTAL` to force each of these buttons to occupy all available horizontal cell space.
- All labels use their preferred sizes, and each component in this dialog is anchored `WEST`.

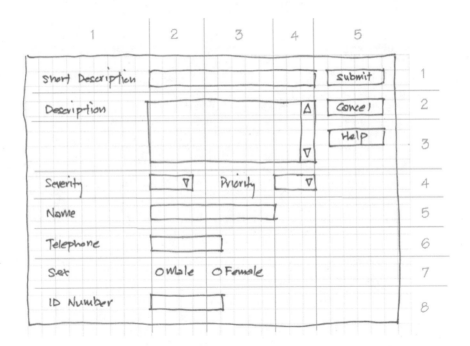

Figure 4.11   A sketch of a generic complaints dialog

Our implementation follows in example 4.2, and figure 4.12 shows the resulting dialog.

Example 4.2

ComplaintsDialog.java

see \Chapter4\Tan

```java
import javax.swing.*;
import javax.swing.border.*;
import java.awt.*;
import java.awt.event.*;

public class ComplaintsDialog extends JDialog
{
  public ComplaintsDialog( JFrame frame ) {
    super( frame, true );
    setTitle( "Simple Complaints Dialog" );
    setSize( 500, 300 );

    // Creates a panel to hold all components
    JPanel panel = new JPanel( new BorderLayout() );
    panel.setLayout( new GridBagLayout() );

    // Give the panel a border gap of 5 pixels
    panel.setBorder( new EmptyBorder( new Insets( 5, 5, 5, 5 ) ) );
    getContentPane().add( BorderLayout.CENTER, panel );

    GridBagConstraints c = new GridBagConstraints();

    // Define preferred sizes for input fields
    Dimension shortField = new Dimension( 40, 20 );
    Dimension mediumField = new Dimension( 120, 20 );
    Dimension longField = new Dimension( 240, 20 );
    Dimension hugeField = new Dimension( 240, 80 );

    // Spacing between label and field
    EmptyBorder border = new EmptyBorder( new Insets( 0, 0, 0, 10 ) );
    EmptyBorder border1 = new EmptyBorder( new Insets( 0, 20, 0, 10 ) );

    // Add space around all components to avoid clutter
    c.insets = new Insets( 2, 2, 2, 2 );

    // Anchor all components WEST
    c.anchor = GridBagConstraints.WEST;

    JLabel lbl1 = new JLabel( "Short Description" );
    lbl1.setBorder( border ); // Add some space to the right
    panel.add( lbl1, c );
    JTextField txt1 = new JTextField();
    txt1.setPreferredSize( longField );
    c.gridx = 1;
    c.weightx = 1.0; // Use all available horizontal space
    c.gridwidth = 3; // Spans across 3 columns
    c.fill = GridBagConstraints.HORIZONTAL; // Fills the 3 columns
    panel.add( txt1, c );

    JLabel lbl2 = new JLabel( "Description" );
    lbl2.setBorder( border );
```

```
c.gridwidth = 1;
c.gridx = 0;
c.gridy = 1;;
c.weightx = 0.0; // Do not use any extra horizontal space
panel.add( lbl2, c );
JTextArea area1 = new JTextArea();
JScrollPane scroll = new JScrollPane( area1 );
scroll.setPreferredSize( hugeField );
c.gridx = 1;
c.weightx = 1.0; // Use all available horizontal space
c.weighty = 1.0; // Use all available vertical space
c.gridwidth = 3; // Span across 3 columns
c.gridheight = 2; // Span across 2 rows
c.fill = GridBagConstraints.BOTH; // Fills the columns and rows
panel.add( scroll, c );

JLabel lbl3 = new JLabel( "Severity" );
lbl3.setBorder( border );
c.gridx = 0;
c.gridy = 3;
c.gridwidth = 1;
c.gridheight = 1;
c.weightx = 0.0;
c.weighty = 0.0;
c.fill = GridBagConstraints.NONE;
panel.add( lbl3, c );
JComboBox combo3 = new JComboBox();
combo3.addItem( "A" );
combo3.addItem( "B" );
combo3.addItem( "C" );
combo3.addItem( "D" );
combo3.addItem( "E" );
combo3.setPreferredSize( shortField );
c.gridx = 1;
panel.add( combo3, c );

JLabel lbl4 = new JLabel( "Priority" );
lbl4.setBorder( border1 );
c.gridx = 2;
panel.add( lbl4, c );
JComboBox combo4 = new JComboBox();
combo4.addItem( "1" );
combo4.addItem( "2" );
combo4.addItem( "3" );
combo4.addItem( "4" );
combo4.addItem( "5" );
combo4.setPreferredSize( shortField );
c.gridx = 3;
panel.add( combo4, c );

JLabel lbl5 = new JLabel( "Name" );
lbl5.setBorder( border );
c.gridx = 0;
```

```
c.gridy = 4;
panel.add( lbl5, c );
JTextField txt5 = new JTextField();
txt5.setPreferredSize( longField );
c.gridx = 1;
c.gridwidth = 3;
panel.add( txt5, c );

JLabel lbl6 = new JLabel( "Telephone" );
lbl6.setBorder( border );
c.gridx = 0;
c.gridy = 5;
panel.add( lbl6, c );
JTextField txt6 = new JTextField();
txt6.setPreferredSize( mediumField );
c.gridx = 1;
c.gridwidth = 3;
panel.add( txt6, c );

JLabel lbl7 = new JLabel( "Sex" );
lbl7.setBorder( border );
c.gridx = 0;
c.gridy = 6;
panel.add( lbl7, c );
JPanel radioPanel = new JPanel();

// Create a FlowLayout JPanel with 5 pixel horizontal gaps
// and no vertical gaps
radioPanel.setLayout( new FlowLayout( FlowLayout.LEFT, 5, 0 ) );
ButtonGroup group = new ButtonGroup();
JRadioButton radio1 = new JRadioButton( "Male" );
radio1.setSelected( true );
group.add( radio1 );
JRadioButton radio2 = new JRadioButton( "Female" );
group.add( radio2 );
radioPanel.add( radio1 );
radioPanel.add( radio2 );
c.gridx = 1;
c.gridwidth = 3;
panel.add( radioPanel, c);

JLabel lbl8 = new JLabel( "ID Number" );
lbl8.setBorder( border );
c.gridx = 0;
c.gridy = 7;
c.gridwidth = 1;
panel.add( lbl8, c );
JTextField txt8 = new JTextField();
txt8.setPreferredSize( mediumField );
c.gridx = 1;
c.gridwidth = 3;
panel.add( txt8, c );

JButton submitBtn = new JButton( "Submit" );
```

Figure 4.12
The Complaints Dialog

```java
      c.gridx = 4;
      c.gridy = 0;
      c.gridwidth = 1;
      c.fill = GridBagConstraints.HORIZONTAL;
      panel.add( submitBtn, c );

      JButton cancelBtn = new JButton( "Cancel" );
      c.gridy = 1;
      panel.add( cancelBtn, c );

      JButton helpBtn = new JButton( "Help" );
      c.gridy = 2;
      c.anchor = GridBagConstraints.NORTH; // Anchor north
      panel.add( helpBtn, c )

      setDefaultCloseOperation(JFrame.EXIT_ON_CLOSE);
       setVisible( true );
   }
  public static void main( String[] args ) {
    new ComplaintsDialog( new JFrame() );
  }
}
```

4.3.9   A simple helper class example

As we can see from example 4.2, constructing dialogs with more than a few components becomes a very tedious task and reduces source code legibility as well as organization. One way to make the use of GridBagLayout cleaner and easier is to create a helper class that manages all the constraints for us, and provides self-explanatory method names and pre-defined parameters.

The source code of a simple helper class we have constructed for this purpose is shown below in example 4.3. The method names used are easier to understand and laying out our components using row and column parameters is more intuitive than gridx and gridy. The methods implemented in this class are each a variation of one of the following:

- addComponent: Used to add a component that needs to adhere to its preferred size.
- addAnchoredComponent: Used to add a component that needs to be anchored.
- addFilledComponent: Used to add a component that will fill the entire cell space allocated to it.

Example 4.3

GriddedPanel.java

see \Chapter4\Tan

```java
import javax.swing.*;
import java.awt.*;

public class GriddedPanel extends JPanel
{
  private GridBagConstraints constraints;

  // Default constraints value definitions
  private static final int C_HORZ = GridBagConstraints.HORIZONTAL;
  private static final int C_NONE = GridBagConstraints.NONE;
  private static final int C_WEST = GridBagConstraints.WEST;
  private static final int C_WIDTH = 1;
  private static final int C_HEIGHT = 1;

  // Create a GridBagLayout panel using a default insets constraint
  public GriddedPanel() {
    this(new Insets(2, 2, 2, 2));
  }

  // Create a GridBagLayout panel using the specified insets
  // constraint
  public GriddedPanel(Insets insets) {
    super(new GridBagLayout());
    constraints = new GridBagConstraints();
    constraints.anchor = GridBagConstraints.WEST;
    constraints.insets = insets;
  }

  // Add a component to the specified row and column
  public void addComponent(JComponent component, int row, int col) {
    addComponent(component, row, col, C_WIDTH,
      C_HEIGHT, C_WEST, C_NONE);
  }

  // Add a component to the specified row and column, spanning across
  // a specified number of columns and rows
  public void addComponent(JComponent component, int row, int col,
   int width, int height ) {
    addComponent(component, row, col, width,
      height, C_WEST, C_NONE);
  }

  // Add a component to the specified row and column, using a specified
  // anchor constraint
  public void addAnchoredComponent(JComponent component, int row,
   int col, int anchor ) {
    addComponent(component, row, col, C_WIDTH,
      C_HEIGHT, anchor, C_NONE);
  }

  // Add a component to the specified row and column, spanning across
```

```java
// a specified number of columns and rows, using a specified
// anchor constraint
public void addAnchoredComponent(JComponent component,
 int row, int col, int width, int height, int anchor) {
    addComponent(component, row, col, width,
      height, anchor, C_NONE);
}

// Add a component to the specified row and column,
// filling the column horizontally
public void addFilledComponent(JComponent component,
 int row, int col) {
  addComponent(component, row, col, C_WIDTH,
    C_HEIGHT, C_WEST, C_HORZ);
}

// Add a component to the specified row and column
// with the specified fill constraint
public void addFilledComponent(JComponent component,
 int row, int col, int fill) {
  addComponent(component, row, col, C_WIDTH,
    C_HEIGHT, C_WEST, fill);
}

// Add a component to the specified row and column,
// spanning a specified number of columns and rows,
// with the specified fill constraint
public void addFilledComponent(JComponent component,
 int row, int col, int width, int height, int fill) {
  addComponent(component, row, col, width, height, C_WEST, fill);
}

// Add a component to the specified row and column,
// spanning the specified number of columns and rows, with
// the specified fill and anchor constraints
public void addComponent(JComponent component,
 int row, int col, int width, int height, int anchor, int fill) {
  constraints.gridx = col;
  constraints.gridy = row;
  constraints.gridwidth = width;
  constraints.gridheight = height;
  constraints.anchor = anchor;
  double weightx = 0.0;
  double weighty = 0.0;

  // Only use extra horizontal or vertical space if a component
  // spans more than one column and/or row
  if(width > 1)
    weightx = 1.0;
  if(height > 1)
    weighty = 1.0;

  switch(fill)
  {
    case GridBagConstraints.HORIZONTAL:
```

```
        constraints.weightx = weightx;
        constraints.weighty = 0.0;
        break;
      case GridBagConstraints.VERTICAL:
        constraints.weighty = weighty;
        constraints.weightx = 0.0;
        break;
      case GridBagConstraints.BOTH:
        constraints.weightx = weightx;
        constraints.weighty = weighty;
        break;
      case GridBagConstraints.NONE:
        constraints.weightx = 0.0;
        constraints.weighty = 0.0;
        break;
      default:
        break;
    }
    constraints.fill = fill;
    add(component, constraints);
  }
}
```

Example 4.4 is the source code used to construct the same complaints dialog as in example 4.2, using our helper class methods instead of manipulating the constraints directly. Notice that the length of the code has been reduced and the readability has been improved. Also note that we add components starting at row 1 and column 1, rather than row 0 and column 0 (see figure 4.11).

Example 4.4

ComplaintsDialog2.java

see \Chapter4\Tan

```
import javax.swing.*;
import javax.swing.border.*;
import java.awt.*;
import java.awt.event.*;

public class ComplaintsDialog2 extends JDialog
{
  public ComplaintsDialog2( JFrame frame ) {
    super( frame, true );
    setTitle( "Simple Complaints Dialog" );
    setSize( 500, 300 );

    GriddedPanel panel = new GriddedPanel();
    panel.setBorder(new EmptyBorder(new Insets(5, 5, 5, 5)));
    getContentPane().add(BorderLayout.CENTER, panel);

    // Input field dimensions
    Dimension shortField = new Dimension( 40, 20 );
```

```java
Dimension mediumField = new Dimension( 120, 20 );
Dimension longField = new Dimension( 240, 20 );
Dimension hugeField = new Dimension( 240, 80 );

// Spacing between labels and fields
EmptyBorder border = new EmptyBorder(
  new Insets( 0, 0, 0, 10 ));
EmptyBorder border1 = new EmptyBorder(
  new Insets( 0, 20, 0, 10 ));

JLabel lbl1 = new JLabel( "Short Description" );
lbl1.setBorder( border );
panel.addComponent( lbl1, 1, 1 );
JTextField txt1 = new JTextField();
txt1.setPreferredSize( longField );
panel.addFilledComponent( txt1, 1, 2, 3, 1,
  GridBagConstraints.HORIZONTAL );

JLabel lbl2 = new JLabel( "Description" );
lbl2.setBorder( border );
panel.addComponent( lbl2, 2, 1 );
JTextArea area1 = new JTextArea();
JScrollPane scroll = new JScrollPane( area1 );
scroll.setPreferredSize( hugeField );
panel.addFilledComponent( scroll, 2, 2, 3, 2,
  GridBagConstraints.BOTH );

JLabel lbl3 = new JLabel( "Severity" );
lbl3.setBorder( border );
panel.addComponent( lbl3, 4, 1 );
JComboBox combo3 = new JComboBox();
combo3.addItem( "A" );
combo3.addItem( "B" );
combo3.addItem( "C" );
combo3.addItem( "D" );
combo3.addItem( "E" );
combo3.setPreferredSize( shortField );
panel.addComponent( combo3, 4, 2 );

JLabel lbl4 = new JLabel( "Priority" );
lbl4.setBorder( border1 );
panel.addComponent( lbl4, 4, 3 );
JComboBox combo4 = new JComboBox();
combo4.addItem( "1" );
combo4.addItem( "2" );
combo4.addItem( "3" );
combo4.addItem( "4" );
combo4.addItem( "5" );
combo4.setPreferredSize( shortField );
panel.addComponent( combo4, 4, 4 );

JLabel lbl5 = new JLabel( "Name" );
lbl5.setBorder( border );
panel.addComponent( lbl5, 5, 1 );
JTextField txt5 = new JTextField();
```

```
    txt5.setPreferredSize( longField );
    panel.addComponent( txt5, 5, 2, 3, 1 );

    JLabel lbl6 = new JLabel( "Telephone" );
    lbl6.setBorder( border );
    panel.addComponent( lbl6, 6, 1 );
    JTextField txt6 = new JTextField();
    txt6.setPreferredSize( mediumField );
    panel.addComponent( txt6, 6, 2, 3, 1 );

    JLabel lbl7 = new JLabel( "Sex" );
    lbl7.setBorder( border );
    panel.addComponent( lbl7, 7, 1 );
    JPanel radioPanel = new JPanel();
    radioPanel.setLayout(new FlowLayout(FlowLayout.LEFT, 5, 0));
    ButtonGroup group = new ButtonGroup();
    JRadioButton radio1 = new JRadioButton( "Male" );
    radio1.setSelected( true );
    group.add( radio1 );
    JRadioButton radio2 = new JRadioButton( "Female" );
    group.add( radio2 );
    radioPanel.add( radio1 );
    radioPanel.add( radio2 );
    panel.addComponent( radioPanel, 7, 2, 3, 1 );

    JLabel lbl8 = new JLabel( "ID Number" );
    lbl8.setBorder( border );
    panel.addComponent( lbl8, 8, 1 );
    JTextField txt8 = new JTextField();
    txt8.setPreferredSize( mediumField );
    panel.addComponent( txt8, 8, 2, 3, 1 );

    JButton submitBtn = new JButton( "Submit" );
    panel.addFilledComponent( submitBtn, 1, 5 );

    JButton cancelBtn = new JButton( "Cancel" );
    panel.addFilledComponent( cancelBtn, 2, 5 );

    JButton helpBtn = new JButton( "Help" );
    panel.addComponent(helpBtn, 3, 5, 1, 1,
      GridBagConstraints.NORTH, GridBagConstraints.HORIZONTAL);

    setDefaultCloseOperation(JFrame.EXIT_ON_CLOSE);
     setVisible( true );
  }

  public static void main( String[] args ) {
    new ComplaintsDialog2( new JFrame() );
  }
}
```

4.4   CHOOSING THE RIGHT LAYOUT

In this section we'll show how to choose the right combination of layouts and intermediate containers to satisfy a predefined program specification. Consider a sample application which makes airplane ticket reservations. The following specification describes which components should be included and how they should be placed in the application frame:

1   A text field labeled "Date:," a combo box labeled "From:," and a combo box labeled "To:" must reside at the top of the frame. Labels must be placed to the left side of their corresponding component. The text fields and combo boxes must be of equal size, reside in a column, and occupy all available width.

2   A group of radio buttons entitled "Options" must reside in the top right corner of the frame. This group must include "First class," "Business," and "Coach" radio buttons.

3   A list component entitled "Available Flights" must occupy the central part of the frame and it should grow or shrink when the size of the frame changes.

4   Three buttons entitled "Search," "Purchase," and "Exit" must reside at the bottom of the frame. They must form a row, have equal sizes, and be center-aligned.

Our `FlightReservation` example demonstrates how to fulfill these requirements. We do not process any input from these controls and we do not attempt to put them to work; we just display them on the screen in the correct position and size. (Three variants are shown to accomplish the layout of the text fields, combo boxes, and their associated labels. Two are commented out, and a discussion of each is given below.)

NOTE   A similar control placement assignment is part of Sun's Java Developer certification exam.

Figure 4.13 `FlightReservation` **layout: variant 1**

Figure 4.14 `FlightReservation` **layout: variant 2**

Figure 4.15 `FlightReservation` **layout: variant 3**

Example 4.5

see \Chapter4\3

```java
import java.awt.*;
import java.awt.event.*;

import javax.swing.*;
import javax.swing.border.*;
import javax.swing.event.*;

public class FlightReservation extends JFrame
{
  public FlightReservation() {
    super("Flight Reservation Dialog");
    setSize(400, 300);

    JPanel p1 = new JPanel();
    p1.setLayout(new BoxLayout(p1, BoxLayout.X_AXIS));

    JPanel p1r = new JPanel();
    p1r.setBorder(new EmptyBorder(10, 10, 10, 10));

    // Variant 1
    p1r.setLayout(new GridLayout(3, 2, 5, 5));

    p1r.add(new JLabel("Date:"));
    p1r.add(new JTextField());

    p1r.add(new JLabel("From:"));
    JComboBox cb1 = new JComboBox();
    cb1.addItem("New York");
    p1r.add(cb1);

    p1r.add(new JLabel("To:"));
    JComboBox cb2 = new JComboBox();
    cb2.addItem("London");
    p1r.add(cb2);

    p1.add(p1r);

    ///////////////
    // Variant 2 //
    ///////////////
    // p11.setLayout(new BoxLayout(p11, BoxLayout.Y_AXIS));
    //
    // JPanel p12 = new JPanel();
    // p12.setLayout(new BoxLayout(p12, BoxLayout.Y_AXIS));
    //
    // p11.add(new JLabel("Date:"));
    // p12.add(new JTextField());
    //
    // p11.add(new JLabel("From:"));
    // JComboBox cb1 = new JComboBox();
    // cb1.addItem("New York");
```

1 Constructor positions all necessary GUI components

5 North panel with EmptyBorder for spacing

6 3 by 2 grid

2 Put 3 labeled components in grid (labels too wide)

7 Second variant, using two vertical BoxLayouts (labels and components not aligned)

```
//  p12.add(cb1);
//
//  p11.add(new JLabel("To:"));
//  JComboBox cb2 = new JComboBox();
//  cb2.addItem("London");
//  p12.add(cb2);
//
//  p1.add(p11);
//  p1.add(Box.createHorizontalStrut(10));
//  p1.add(p12);

///////////////
// Variant 3 //
///////////////
//  JPanel p11 = new JPanel();
//  p11.setLayout(new GridLayout(3, 1, 5, 5));
//
//  JPanel p12 = new JPanel();
//  p12.setLayout(new GridLayout(3, 1, 5, 5));
//
//  p11.add(new JLabel("Date:"));
//  p12.add(new JTextField());
//
//  p11.add(new JLabel("From:"));
//  JComboBox cb1 = new JComboBox();
//  cb1.addItem("New York");
//  p12.add(cb1);
//
//  p11.add(new JLabel("To:"));
//  JComboBox cb2 = new JComboBox();
//  cb2.addItem("London");
//  p12.add(cb2);
//
//  p1r.setLayout(new BorderLayout());
//  p1r.add(p11, BorderLayout.WEST);
//  p1r.add(p12, BorderLayout.CENTER);
//  p1.add(p1r);

JPanel p3 = new JPanel();
p3.setLayout(new BoxLayout(p3, BoxLayout.Y_AXIS));
p3.setBorder(new TitledBorder(new EtchedBorder(),
  "Options"));

ButtonGroup group = new ButtonGroup();
JRadioButton r1 = new JRadioButton("First class");
group.add(r1);
p3.add(r1);

JRadioButton r2 = new JRadioButton("Business");
group.add(r2);
p3.add(r2);
```

8 Third variant, using two 3 by I grids (arranged correctly, but complex)

9 Vertical BoxLayout for radio buttons, on East side of frame

```
        JRadioButton r3 = new JRadioButton("Coach");
        group.add(r3);
        p3.add(r3);

        p1.add(p3);

        getContentPane().add(p1, BorderLayout.NORTH);

        JPanel p2 = new JPanel(new BorderLayout());
        p2.setBorder(new TitledBorder(new EtchedBorder(),
          "Available Flights"));
        JList list = new JList();
        JScrollPane ps = new JScrollPane(list);
        p2.add(ps, BorderLayout.CENTER);
        getContentPane().add(p2, BorderLayout.CENTER);

        JPanel p4 = new JPanel();
        JPanel p4c = new JPanel();
        p4c.setLayout(new GridLayout(1, 3, 5, 5));

        JButton b1 = new JButton("Search");
        p4c.add(b1);

        JButton b2 = new JButton("Purchase");
        p4c.add(b2);

        JButton b3 = new JButton("Exit");
        p4c.add(b3);

        p4.add(p4c);
        getContentPane().add(p4, BorderLayout.SOUTH);

        setDefaultCloseOperation(EXIT_ON_CLOSE);
          setVisible(true);
    }

  public static void main(String argv[]) {
    new FlightReservation();
    }
}
```

⑨ Vertical BoxLayout for radio buttons, on East side of frame

② Place grid with labeled components in North side of frame

⑩ Scrollable list in titled panel

④ Place list in center of frame

⑪ Implicitly FlowLayout

③ Place row of push buttons in South of frame

4.4.1   Understanding the code

Class FlightReservation

❶ The constructor of the FlightReservation class creates and positions all necessary GUI components. We will explain step by step how we've chosen intermediate containers and their layouts to fulfill the requirements listed at the beginning of this section.

❷ The frame (more specifically, its contentPane) is managed by a BorderLayout by default.
A text field, the combo boxes, and associated labels are added in a separate container to the
❸ north along with the radio buttons; push buttons are placed in the south; and the list compo-
❹ nent is placed in the center. This guarantees that the top and bottom (north and south) containers will receive their natural height, and that the central component (the list) will occupy
all the remaining space.

⑤ The intermediate container, JPanel p1r, holds the text field, combo boxes, and their associated labels; it is placed in panel p1 which is managed by a horizontally aligned BoxLayout. The p1r panel is surrounded by an EmptyBorder to provide typical surrounding whitespace.

⑥ This example offers three variants of managing p1r and its six child components. The first variant uses a 3x2 GridLayout. This places labels and boxes in two columns opposite one another. Since this panel resides in the north region of the BorderLayout, it receives its natural (preferable) height. In the horizontal direction this layout works satisfactorily: it resizes boxes and labels to occupy all available space. The only remaining problem is that GridLayout assigns too much space to the labels (see figure 4.13). We do not need to make labels equal in size to their corresponding input boxes—we need only allow them to occupy their preferred width.

⑦ The second variant uses two vertical BoxLayouts so that one can hold labels and the other can hold the corresponding text field and combo boxes. If you try recompiling and running the code with this variant, you'll find that the labels now occupy only their necessary width, and the boxes occupy all the remaining space. This is good, but another problem arises: now the labels are not aligned exactly opposite with their corresponding components. Instead, they are shifted in the vertical direction (see figure 4.14).

⑧ The third variant offers the best solution. It places the labels and their corresponding components in two columns, but it uses 3x1 GridLayouts instead of BoxLayouts. This places all components evenly in the vertical direction. To provide only the minimum width to the labels (the first column) and assign all remaining space to the boxes (the second column), we place these two containers into another intermediate container managed by a BorderLayout: labels in the west, and corresponding components in the center. This solves our problem (see figure 4.15). The only downside to this solution is that it requires the construction of three intermediate containers with different layouts. In the next section we'll show how to build a custom layout manager that simplifies this relatively common layout task.

⑨ Now let's return to the remaining components. A group of JRadioButtons seems to be the simplest part of our design. They're placed into an intermediate container, JPanel p3, with a TitledBorder containing the required title: "Options". A vertical BoxLayout is used to place these components in a column and a ButtonGroup is used to coordinate their selection. This container is then added to panel p1 (managed by a horizontal BoxLayout) to sit on the eastern side of panel p1r.

⑩ The JList component is added to a JScrollPane to provide scrolling capabilities. It is then placed in an intermediate container, JPanel p2, with a TitledBorder containing the required title "Available Flights."

> **NOTE** We do not want to assign a TitledBorder to the JScrollPane itself because this would substitute its natural border, resulting in quite an awkward scroll pane view. So we nest the JScrollPane in its own JPanel with a TitledBorder.

Since the list should grow and shrink when the frame is resized and the group of radio buttons (residing to the right of the list) must occupy only the necessary width, it only makes sense to place the list in the center of the BorderLayout. We can then use the south region for the three remaining buttons.

❸ Since all three buttons must be equal in size, they're added to a `JPanel`, p4c, with a 1x3

⓫ `GridLayout`. However, this `GridLayout` will occupy all available width (fortunately, it's limited in the vertical direction by the parent container's `BorderLayout`). This is not exactly the behavior we are looking for. To resolve this problem, we use another intermediate container, `JPanel` p4, with a `FlowLayout`. This sizes the only added component, p4c, based on its preferred size, and centers it both vertically and horizontally.

4.4.2   Running the code

Figures 4.13, 4.14, and 4.15 show the resulting placement of our components in the parent frame using the first and the third variants described above. Note that the placement of variant 3 satisfies our specification—components are resized as expected when the frame container is resized.

When the frame is stretched in the horizontal direction, the text field, combo boxes, and list component consume additional space, and the buttons at the bottom are shifted to the center. When the frame is stretched in the vertical direction, the list component and the panel containing the radio buttons consume all additional space and all other components remain unchanged.

GUIDELINE

Harnessing the power of java layouts   Layout managers are powerful but awkward to use. In order to maximize the effectiveness of the visual communication, we must make extra effort with the code. Making a bad choice of layout or making sloppy use of default settings may lead to designs which look poorly or communicate badly.

In this example, we have shown three alternative designs for the same basic specification. Each exhibits pros and cons and highlights the design trade-offs which can be made.

A sense of balance   This occurs when sufficient white space is used to balance the size of the components. An unbalanced panel can be fixed by bordering the components with a compound border that includes an empty border.

A sense of scale   Balance can be further affected by the extraordinary size of some components such as the combo boxes shown in figure 4.14. The combo boxes are bit too big for the intended purpose. This affects the sense of scale as well as the balance of the design. It's important to size combo boxes appropriately. Layout managers have a tendency to stretch components to be larger than might be desirable.

4.5   *CUSTOM LAYOUT MANAGER, PART I: LABEL/FIELD PAIRS*

This section and its accompanying example are intended to familiarize you with developing custom layouts. You may find this information useful in cases where the traditional layouts are not satisfactory or are too complex. In developing large-scale applications, it is often more convenient to build custom layouts, such as the one we develop here, to help with specific tasks. This often provides increased consistency, and may save a significant amount of coding in the long run.

Example 4.5 in the previous section highlighted a problem: what is the best way to lay out input field components (such as text fields and combo boxes) and their corresponding labels? We have seen that it can be done using a combination of several intermediate containers and layouts. This section shows how we can simplify the process using a custom-built layout manager. The goal is to construct a layout manager that knows how to lay out labels and their associated input fields in two columns, allocating the minimum required space to the column containing the labels, and using the remainder for the column containing the input fields.

We first need to clearly state our design goals for this layout manager, which we will appropriately call `DialogLayout`. It is always a good idea to reserve plenty of time for thinking about your design. Well-defined design specifications can save you tremendous amounts of time in the long run, and can help pinpoint flaws and oversights before they arise in the code. (We strongly recommend that a design-specification stage becomes part of your development regimen.)

`DialogLayout` specification:

1 This layout manager will be applied to a container that has all the necessary components added to it in the following order: `label1`, `field1`, `label2`, `field2`, etc. (Note that when components are added to a container, they are tracked in a list. If no index is specified when a component is added to a container, it will be added to the end of the list using the next available index. As usual, this indexing starts from 0. A component can be retrieved by index using the `getComponent(int index)` method.) If the labels and fields are added correctly, all even-numbered components in the container will correspond to labels, and all odd-numbered components will correspond to input fields.

2 The components must be placed in pairs that form two vertical columns.

3 Components that make up each pair must be placed opposite one another, for example, `label1` and `field1`. Each pair's label and field must receive the same preferable height, which should be the preferred height of the field.

4 Each left component (labels) must receive the same width. This width should be the maximum preferable width of all left components.

5 Each right component (input fields) must also receive the same width. This width should occupy all the remaining space left over from that taken by the left component's column.

Example 4.6, found below, introduces our custom `DialogLayout` class which satisfies the above design specification. This class is placed in its own package named `dl`. The code used to construct the GUI is almost identical to that of the previous example. However, we will now revert back to variant 1 and use an instance of `DialogLayout` instead of a `GridLayout` to manage the `p1r JPanel`.

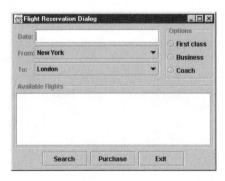

Figure 4.16
Using `DialogLayout`:
custom layout manager

Example 4.6

see \Chapter4\4

```java
import java.awt.*;
import java.awt.event.*;

import javax.swing.*;
import javax.swing.border.*;
import javax.swing.event.*;

import dl.*;

public class FlightReservation extends JFrame
{
  public FlightReservation() {
    super("Flight Reservation Dialog [Custom Layout]");

    // Unchanged code from example 4.5

    JPanel p1r = new JPanel();
    p1r.setBorder(new EmptyBorder(10, 10, 10, 10));
    p1r.setLayout(new DialogLayout(20, 5));

    p1r.add(new JLabel("Date:"));
    p1r.add(new JTextField());

    p1r.add(new JLabel("From:"));
    JComboBox cb1 = new JComboBox();
    cb1.addItem("New York");
    p1r.add(cb1);

    p1r.add(new JLabel("To:"));
    JComboBox cb2 = new JComboBox();
    cb2.addItem("London");
    p1r.add(cb2);

    p1.add(p1r);
    getContentPane().add(p1, BorderLayout.NORTH);

// All remaining code is unchanged from example 4.5
```

① Import for DialogLayout class

① Import class

see \Chapter4\4\dl

```java
package dl;

import java.awt.*;
import java.util.*;

public class DialogLayout implements LayoutManager
{
```

② Means DialogLayout can be used anywhere a LayoutManager is used

```
      protected int m_divider = -1;                    ② Width and
      protected int m_hGap = 10;                           gap values
      protected int m_vGap = 5;

      public DialogLayout() {}                          ③ Constructor which
                                                            uses default gaps
      public DialogLayout(int hGap, int vGap) {
        m_hGap = hGap;                                      From base interface, ④
        m_vGap = vGap;          Constructor to  ③      not managing internal
      }                         set gap values            components list

      public void addLayoutComponent(String name, Component comp) {}
                                                        Returns preferred
      public void removeLayoutComponent(Component comp) {}  size to lay out all
                                                        managed  ⑤
      public Dimension preferredLayoutSize(Container parent) {  components
        int divider = getDivider(parent);

        int w = 0;
        int h = 0;                                      Determine width  ⑥
        for (int k=1 ; k<parent.getComponentCount(); k+=2) {  of labels column
          Component comp = parent.getComponent(k);
          Dimension d = comp.getPreferredSize();        Determine maximum
          w = Math.max(w, d.width);                  ⑧ input field width and
          h += d.height + m_vGap;                         accumulate height
        }
        h -= m_vGap;

        Insets insets = parent.getInsets();            ⑨  Calculate
        return new Dimension(divider+w+insets.left+insets.right,  total pre-
          h+insets.top+insets.bottom);                     ferred size
      }

      public Dimension minimumLayoutSize(Container parent) {
        return preferredLayoutSize(parent);       ⑩ Minimum size will be the
      }                                               same as the preferred size

      public void layoutContainer(Container parent) { ⑪ Most important method,
        int divider = getDivider(parent);                calculates position and size
                                                         of each managed component
        Insets insets = parent.getInsets();
        int w = parent.getWidth() - insets.left    ⑫ Determine divider
          - insets.right - divider;                      size and width of
        int x = insets.left;                             all input fields
        int y = insets.top;

        for (int k=1 ; k<parent.getComponentCount(); k+=2) {
          Component comp1 = parent.getComponent(k-1);
          Component comp2 = parent.getComponent(k);
          Dimension d = comp2.getPreferredSize();

          comp1.setBounds(x, y, divider-m_hGap, d.height);
          comp2.setBounds(x+divider, y, w, d.height);
          y += d.height + m_vGap;
        }
      }                                   Set each label and  ⑬
                                            input field to
      public int getHGap() { return m_hGap; }  calculated bounds
```

```
public int getVGap() { return m_vGap; }

public void setDivider(int divider) {
   if (divider > 0)
      m_divider = divider;
}

public int getDivider() { return m_divider; }

protected int getDivider(Container parent) {
   if (m_divider > 0)
      return m_divider;

   int divider = 0;
   for (int k=0 ; k<parent.getComponentCount(); k+=2) {
      Component comp = parent.getComponent(k);
      Dimension d = comp.getPreferredSize();
      divider = Math.max(divider, d.width);
   }
   divider += m_hGap;
   return divider;
}

public String toString() {
   return getClass().getName() + "[hgap=" + m_hGap + ",vgap="
      + m_vGap + ",divider=" + m_divider + "]";
}
}
```

14 Minimum size will be the same as the preferred size

7 If no divider set yet

7 Determine maximum label size plus gap

15 Useful debugging information

4.5.1 Understanding the code

Class FlightReservation

1 This class now imports the dl package and uses the DialogLayout layout manager for JPanel p1r, which contains the labels and input fields. The dl package contains our custom layout, DialogLayout.

Class DialogLayout

2 This class implements the LayoutManager interface to serve as our custom layout manager. Three instance variables are needed:

- int m_divider: Width of the left components. This can be calculated or set to some mandatory value. ·
- int m_hGap: Horizontal gap between components.
- int m_vGap: Vertical gap between components.

3 Two constructors are available to create a DialogLayout: a no-argument default constructor and a constructor which takes horizontal and vertical gap sizes as parameters. The rest of the code implements methods from the LayoutManager interface.

4 The addLayoutComponent() and removeLayoutComponent() methods are not used in this class, and they receive empty implementations. We do not support an internal collection of the components to be managed. Rather, we refer to these components directly from the container which is being managed.

⑤
⑥ The purpose of the `preferredLayoutSize()` method is to return the preferable container size required to lay out the components in the given container according to the rules used in this layout. In our implementation, we first determine the `divider` size (the width of the first column plus the horizontal gap, m_hGap) by calling our `getDivider()` method.

```
int divider = getDivider(parent);
```

⑦ If no positive divider size has been specified using our `setDivider()` method (see below), the `getDivider()` method looks at each even-indexed component in the container (this should be all the labels if the components were added to the container in the correct order) and returns the largest preferred width found plus the horizontal gap value, m_hGap (which defaults to 10 if the default constructor is used):

```
if (m_divider > 0)
  return m_divider;

int divider = 0;
for (int k=0 ; k<parent.getComponentCount(); k+=2) {
  Component comp = parent.getComponent(k);
  Dimension d = comp.getPreferredSize();
  divider = Math.max(divider, d.width);
}
divider += m_hGap;
return divider;
```

⑧ Now, let's go back to the `preferredLayoutSize()` method. Once `getDivider()` returns, we then examine all the components in the container with odd indices (this should be all the input fields) and determine the maximum width, w. This is found by checking the preferred width of each input field. While we are determining this maximum width, we are also continuing to accumulate the height, h, of the whole input fields column by summing each field's preferred height (not forgetting to add the vertical gap size, m_vGap, each time; notice that m_vGap is subtracted from the height at the end because there is no vertical gap for the last field. Also remember that m_vGap defaults to 5 if the the default constructor is used.)

```
int w = 0;
int h = 0;
for (int k=1 ; k<parent.getComponentCount(); k+=2) {
  Component comp = parent.getComponent(k);
  Dimension d = comp.getPreferredSize();
  w = Math.max(w, d.width);
  h += d.height + m_vGap;
}
h -= m_vGap;
```

⑨ So at this point we have determined the width of the labels column (including the space between columns), `divider`, and the preferred height, h, and width, w, of the input fields column. So `divider+w` gives us the preferred width of the container, and h gives us the total preferred height. Not forgetting to take into account any `Insets` that might have been applied to the container, we can now return the correct preferred size:

```
Insets insets = parent.getInsets();
return new Dimension(divider+w+insets.left+insets.right,
  h+insets.top+insets.bottom);
```

10 The purpose of the `minimumLayoutSize()` method is to return the minimum size required to lay out the components in the given container according to the rules used in this layout. We return `preferredLayoutSize()` in this method, because we choose not to make a distinction between minimum and preferred sizes (to avoid over-complication).

11 `layoutContainer()` is the most important method in any layout manager. This method is responsible for actually assigning the bounds (position and size) for the components in the

12 container being managed. First it determines the size of the `divider` (as discussed above), which represents the width of the labels column plus an additional `m_hGap`. From this, it determines the width, `w`, of the fields column by subtracting the container's left and right insets and `divider` from the width of the whole container:

```
int divider = getDivider(parent);

Insets insets = parent.getInsets();
int w = parent.getWidth() - insets.left
  - insets.right - divider;
int x = insets.left;
int y = insets.top;
```

13 Then all pairs of components are examined in turn. Each left component receives a width equal to `divider-m_hGap`, and all right components receive a width of `w`. Both left and right components receive the preferred height of the right component (which should be an input field).

Coordinates of the left components are assigned starting with the container's `Insets`, `x` and `y`. Notice that `y` is continually incremented based on the preferred height of each right component plus the vertical gap, `m_vGap`. The right components are assigned a y-coordinate identical to their left component counterpart, and an x-coordinate of `x+divider` (remember that `divider` includes the horizontal gap, `m_hGap`):

```
for (int k=1 ; k<parent.getComponentCount(); k+=2) {
  Component comp1 = parent.getComponent(k-1);
  Component comp2 = parent.getComponent(k);
  Dimension d = comp2.getPreferredSize();

  comp1.setBounds(x, y, divider-m_hGap, d.height);
  comp2.setBounds(x+divider, y, w, d.height);
  y += d.height + m_vGap;
}
```

14 The `setDivider()` method allows us to manually set the size of the left column. The `int` value, which is passed as a parameter, gets stored in the `m_divider` instance variable. Whenever `m_divider` is greater than 0, the calculations of `divider` size are overridden in the `getDivider()` method and this value is returned instead.

15 The `toString()` method provides typical class name and instance variable information. (It is always a good idea to implement informative `toString()` methods for each class. Although we don't consistently do so throughout this text, we feel that production code should often include this functionality.)

4.5.2 Running the code

Figure 4.16 shows the sample interface introduced in the previous section now using Dia-logLayout to manage the layout of the input fields (the text field and two combo boxes) and their corresponding labels. Note that the labels occupy only their preferred space and they do not resize when the frame resizes. The width of the left column can be managed easily by manually setting the divider size with the setDivider() method, as discussed above. The input fields form the right column and occupy all the remaining space.

Using DialogLayout, all that is required is to add the labels and input fields in the correct order. We can now use this layout manager each time we encounter label/input field pairs without worrying about intermediate containers. In the next section, we will build upon DialogLayout to create an even more general layout manager that can be used to create complete dialog GUIs very easily.

UI GUIDELINE

Alignment across controls as well as within It is a common mistake in UI design to achieve good alignment with a control or component but fail to achieve this across a whole screen, panel, or dialog. Unfortunately, the architecture of Swing lends itself to this problem. For example, say you have four custom components which inherit from a JPanel, each has its own layout manager and each is functional in its own right. You might want to build a composite component which requires all four. So you create a new component with a Grid-Layout, for example, then add each of your four components in turn.

The result can be very messy. The fields within each component will align—three radio buttons, for example—but those radio buttons will not align with the three text fields in the next component. Why not? The answer is simple. With Swing, there is no way for the layout manager within each component to negotiate with the others, so alignment cannot be achieved across the components. The answer to this problem is that you must flatten out the design into a single panel, as DialogLayout achieves.

4.6 CUSTOM LAYOUT MANAGER, PART II: COMMON INTERFACES

In section 4.4 we saw how to choose both intermediate containers and appropriate layouts for placing components according to a given specification. This required the use of several intermediate containers, and several variants were developed in a search for the best solution. This raises a question: can we somehow just add components one after another to a container which is intelligent enough to lay them out as we would typically expect? The answer is yes, to a certain extent.

In practice, the contents of many Java frames and dialogs are constructed using a scheme similar to the following (we realize that this is a big generalization, but you will see these situations arise in other examples later in this text):

1 Groups (or panels) of controls are laid out in the vertical direction.

2 Labels and their corresponding input fields form two-column structures as described in the previous section.

3 Large components (such as lists, tables, text areas, and trees) are usually placed in scroll panes and they occupy all space in the horizontal direction.

4 Groups of buttons, including check boxes and radio buttons, are centered in an intermediate container and laid out in the horizontal direction. (In this example we purposefully avoid the vertical placement of buttons for simplicity.)

Example 4.7, found below, shows how to build a layout manager that places components according to this specification. Its purpose is to further demonstrate that layout managers can be built to define template-like pluggable containers. By adhering to intelligently designed specifications, such templates can be developed to help maximize code reuse and increase productivity. Additionally, in the case of large-scale applications, several different interface designers may consider sharing customized layout managers to enforce consistency.

Example 4.7 introduces our new custom layout manager, `DialogLayout2`, which builds upon `DialogLayout`. To provide boundaries between control groupings, we construct a new component, `DialogSeparator`, which is simply a label containing text and a horizontal bar that is drawn across the container. Both `DialogLayout2` and `DialogSeparator` are added to our `dl` package. The `FlightReservation` class now shows how to construct the sample airline ticket reservation interface we have been working with since section 4.4 using `Dialog-Layout2` and `DialogSeparator`. In order to comply with our new layout scheme, we are forced to place the radio buttons in a row above the list component. The main things to note are that the code involved to build this interface is done with little regard for the existence of a layout manager, and that absolutely no intermediate containers need to be created.

NOTE Constructing custom layout managers for use in a single application is not recommended. Only build them when you know that they will be reused again and again to perform common layout tasks. In general, custom layout manager classes belong within custom packages or they should be embedded as inner classes in custom components.

Figure 4.17
Using the `DialogLayout2` custom layout manager

Example 4.7

FlightReservation.java

see \Chapter4\5

```java
import java.awt.*;
import java.awt.event.*;

import javax.swing.*;
import javax.swing.border.*;
import javax.swing.event.*;

import dl.*;

public class FlightReservation extends JFrame
{
  public FlightReservation() {
    super("Flight Reservation Dialog [Custom Layout - 2]");

    Container c = getContentPane();
    c.setLayout(new DialogLayout2(20, 5));

    c.add(new JLabel("Date:"));
    c.add(new JTextField());

    c.add(new JLabel("From:"));
    JComboBox cb1 = new JComboBox();
    cb1.addItem("New York");
    c.add(cb1);

    c.add(new JLabel("To:"));
    JComboBox cb2 = new JComboBox();
    cb2.addItem("London");
    c.add(cb2);

    c.add(new DialogSeparator("Available Flights"));
    JList list = new JList();
    JScrollPane ps = new JScrollPane(list);
    c.add(ps);

    c.add(new DialogSeparator("Options"));

    ButtonGroup group = new ButtonGroup();
    JRadioButton r1 = new JRadioButton("First class");
    group.add(r1);
    c.add(r1);

    JRadioButton r2 = new JRadioButton("Business");
    group.add(r2);
    c.add(r2);

    JRadioButton r3 = new JRadioButton("Coach");
    group.add(r3);
    c.add(r3);

    c.add(new DialogSeparator());

    JButton b1 = new JButton("Search");
```

1 All components added directly to the content pane and managed by the new layout

2 Separates groups of components

2 Separates groups of components

```
    c.add(b1);

    JButton b2 = new JButton("Purchase");
    c.add(b2);

    JButton b3 = new JButton("Exit");
    c.add(b3);

    setDefaultCloseOperation(EXIT_ON_CLOSE);
    pack();
    setVisible(true);
  }

  public static void main(String argv[]) {
    new FlightReservation();
  }
}
```

1 All components added directly to the content pane and managed by the new layout

DialogLayout2.java

see \Chapter4\5\dl

```
package dl;

import java.awt.*;
import java.util.*;

import javax.swing.*;

public class DialogLayout2 implements LayoutManager
{
  protected static final int COMP_TWO_COL = 0;
  protected static final int COMP_BIG = 1;
  protected static final int COMP_BUTTON = 2;

  protected int m_divider = -1;
  protected int m_hGap = 10;
  protected int m_vGap = 5;
  protected Vector m_v = new Vector();

  public DialogLayout2() {}

  public DialogLayout2(int hGap, int vGap) {
    m_hGap = hGap;
    m_vGap = vGap;
  }

  public void addLayoutComponent(String name, Component comp) {}

  public void removeLayoutComponent(Component comp) {}

  public Dimension preferredLayoutSize(Container parent) {
    m_v.removeAllElements();
    int w = 0;
    int h = 0;

    int type = -1;
    for (int k=0 ; k<parent.getComponentCount(); k++) {
      Component comp = parent.getComponent(k);
```

3 Implements LayoutManager to be a custom LayoutManager

4 Constants to specify how to manage specific component types

5 Width and gap values and components list

6 Steps through parent's components totalling preferred layout size

```
    int newType = getLayoutType(comp);
    if (k == 0)
      type = newType;

    if (type != newType) {
      Dimension d = preferredLayoutSize(m_v, type);
      w = Math.max(w, d.width);
      h += d.height + m_vGap;
      m_v.removeAllElements();
      type = newType;
    }

    m_v.addElement(comp);
  }

  Dimension d = preferredLayoutSize(m_v, type);
  w = Math.max(w, d.width);
  h += d.height + m_vGap;

  h -= m_vGap;

  Insets insets = parent.getInsets();
  return new Dimension(w+insets.left+insets.right,
    h+insets.top+insets.bottom);
}

protected Dimension preferredLayoutSize(Vector v, int type) {
  int w = 0;
  int h = 0;
  switch (type)
  {
    case COMP_TWO_COL:
      int divider = getDivider(v);
      for (int k=1 ; k<v.size(); k+=2) {
        Component comp = (Component)v.elementAt(k);
        Dimension d = comp.getPreferredSize();
        w = Math.max(w, d.width);
        h += d.height + m_vGap;
      }
      h -= m_vGap;
      return new Dimension(divider+w, h);
    case COMP_BIG:
      for (int k=0 ; k<v.size(); k++) {
        Component comp = (Component)v.elementAt(k);
        Dimension d = comp.getPreferredSize();
        w = Math.max(w, d.width);
        h += d.height + m_vGap;
      }
      h -= m_vGap;
      return new Dimension(w, h);
    case COMP_BUTTON:
      Dimension d = getMaxDimension(v);
      w = d.width + m_hGap;
      h = d.height;
      return new Dimension(w*v.size()-m_hGap, h);
```

7 Found break in sequence of component types

8 Process last block of same-typed components

9 Compute final preferred size

10 Steps through a components list of a specific type, totalling preferred layout size

11 Assumes two-column arrangement, computes preferred size

12 Assumes components take up entire width, computes preferred size

13 Assumes centered row of equal width components, computes preferred size

```
        }
      throw new IllegalArgumentException("Illegal type "+type);
    }

    public Dimension minimumLayoutSize(Container parent) {
      return preferredLayoutSize(parent);
    }

    public void layoutContainer(Container parent) {
      m_v.removeAllElements();
      int type = -1;
      Insets insets = parent.getInsets();
      int w = parent.getWidth() - insets.left - insets.right;
      int x = insets.left;
      int y = insets.top;
      for (int k=0 ; k<parent.getComponentCount(); k++) {
        Component comp = parent.getComponent(k);
        int newType = getLayoutType(comp);
        if (k == 0)
          type = newType;
        if (type != newType) {
          y = layoutComponents(m_v, type, x, y, w);
          m_v.removeAllElements();
          type = newType;
        }
        m_v.addElement(comp);
      }
      y = layoutComponents(m_v, type, x, y, w);
      m_v.removeAllElements();
    }

    protected int layoutComponents(Vector v, int type,
      int x, int y, int w)
    {
      switch (type)
      {
        case COMP_TWO_COL:
          int divider = getDivider(v);
          for (int k=1 ; k<v.size(); k+=2) {
            Component comp1 = (Component)v.elementAt(k-1);
            Component comp2 = (Component)v.elementAt(k);
            Dimension d = comp2.getPreferredSize();
            comp1.setBounds(x, y, divider-m_hGap, d.height);
            comp2.setBounds(x+divider, y, w-divider, d.height);
            y += d.height + m_vGap;
          }
          return y;
        case COMP_BIG:
          for (int k=0 ; k<v.size(); k++) {
            Component comp = (Component)v.elementAt(k);
            Dimension d = comp.getPreferredSize();
            comp.setBounds(x, y, w, d.height);
```

14 Lays out container, treating blocks of same-typed components in the same way

15 Lays out block of same-typed components, checking for component type

Assumes two-column arrangement, lays out each pair in that fashion **16**

17 Assumes components take up entire width, one component per row

```
              y += d.height + m_vGap;
          }
          return y;
       case COMP_BUTTON:
          Dimension d = getMaxDimension(v);
          int ww = d.width*v.size() + m_hGap*(v.size()-1);
          int xx = x + Math.max(0, (w - ww)/2);
          for (int k=0 ; k<v.size(); k++) {
            Component comp = (Component)v.elementAt(k);
            comp.setBounds(xx, y, d.width, d.height);
            xx += d.width + m_hGap;
          }
          return y + d.height;
       }
       throw new IllegalArgumentException("Illegal type "+type);
  }

  public int getHGap() { return m_hGap; }

  public int getVGap() { return m_vGap; }

  public void setDivider(int divider) {
     if (divider > 0)
       m_divider = divider;
  }

  public int getDivider() { return m_divider; }

  protected int getDivider(Vector v) {
     if (m_divider > 0)
       return m_divider;
     int divider = 0;
     for (int k=0 ; k<v.size(); k+=2) {
       Component comp = (Component)v.elementAt(k);
       Dimension d = comp.getPreferredSize();
       divider = Math.max(divider, d.width);
     }
     divider += m_hGap;
     return divider;
  }

  protected Dimension getMaxDimension(Vector v) {
     int w = 0;
     int h = 0;
     for (int k=0 ; k<v.size(); k++) {
       Component comp = (Component)v.elementAt(k);
       Dimension d = comp.getPreferredSize();
       w = Math.max(w, d.width);
       h = Math.max(h, d.height);
     }
     return new Dimension(w, h);
  }

  protected int getLayoutType(Component comp) {
     if (comp instanceof AbstractButton)
```

Assumes components take up entire width, one component per row ⑰

⑱ **Assumes centered row of equal width components, lays them out in that fashion**

```
      return COMP_BUTTON;
    else if (comp instanceof JPanel ||
     comp instanceof JScrollPane ||
     comp instanceof DialogSeparator)
      return COMP_BIG;
    else
      return COMP_TWO_COL;
  }

  public String toString() {
    return getClass().getName() + "[hgap=" + m_hGap + ",vgap="
      + m_vGap + ",divider=" + m_divider + "]";
  }
}
```

DialogSeparator.java

see \Chapter4\5\dl

```
package dl;

import java.awt.*;

import javax.swing.*;

public class DialogSeparator extends JLabel
{
  public static final int OFFSET = 15;

  public DialogSeparator() {}

  public DialogSeparator(String text) { super(text); }

  public Dimension getPreferredSize() {
    return new Dimension(getParent().getWidth(), 20);
  }
  public Dimension getMinimumSize() { return getPreferredSize(); }
  public Dimension getMaximumSize() { return getPreferredSize(); }

  public void paintComponent(Graphics g) {
    super.paintComponent(g);
    g.setColor(getBackground());
    g.fillRect(0, 0, getWidth(), getHeight());

    Dimension d = getSize();
    int y = (d.height-3)/2;
    g.setColor(Color.white);
    g.drawLine(1, y, d.width-1, y);
    y++;
    g.drawLine(0, y, 1, y);
    g.setColor(Color.gray);
    g.drawLine(d.width-1, y, d.width, y);
    y++;
    g.drawLine(1, y, d.width-1, y);

    String text = getText();
    if (text.length()==0)
```

19 Implements horizontal separator between vertically-spaced components

20 Returns shallow area with a small fixed height and variable width

21 Draws separating bar with raised appearance

```
      return;

    g.setFont(getFont());
    FontMetrics fm = g.getFontMetrics();
    y = (d.height + fm.getAscent())/2;
    int l = fm.stringWidth(text);

    g.setColor(getBackground());
    g.fillRect(OFFSET-5, 0, OFFSET+1, d.height);

    g.setColor(getForeground());
    g.drawString(text, OFFSET, y);
  }
}
```

4.6.1 Understanding the code

Class FlightReservation

1 This variant of our airplane ticket reservation sample application uses an instance of DialogLayout2 as a layout for the whole content pane. No other JPanels are used, and no other layouts are involved. All components are added directly to the content pane and managed by the new layout. This incredibly simplifies the creation of the user interface. Note, however, that we still need to add the label/input field pairs in the correct order because DialogLayout2 manages these pairs the same way that DialogLayout does.

2 Instances of our DialogSeparator class are used to provide borders between groups of components.

Class DialogLayout2

3 This class implements the LayoutManager interface to serve as a custom layout manager. It builds on features from DialogLayout to manage all components in its associated container. Three constants declared at the top of the class correspond to the three types of components which are recognized by this layout:

4 • int COMP_TWO_COL: Text fields, combo boxes, and their associated labels which must be laid out in two columns using a DialogLayout.

• int COMP_BIG: Wide components (instances of JPanel, JScrollPane, or Dialog-Separator) which must occupy the maximum horizontal container space wherever they are placed.

• int COMP_BUTTON: Button components (instances of AbstractButton) which must all be given an equal size, laid out in a single row, and centered in the container.

5 The instance variables used in DialogLayout2 are the same as those used in DialogLayout with one addition: we declare Vector m_v to be used as a temporary collection of components.

To lay out components in a given container we need to determine, for each component, which category it falls under with regard to our DialogLayout2.COMP_XX constants. All components of the same type which are added in a contiguous sequence must be processed according to the specific rules described above.

6 The preferredLayoutSize() method steps through the list of components in a given container, determines their type with our custom getLayoutType() method (see below), and stores it in the `newType` local variable. The local variable `type` holds the type of the *previous* component in the sequence. For the first component in the container, `type` receives the same value as `newType`.

```
public Dimension preferredLayoutSize(Container parent) {
  m_v.removeAllElements();
  int w = 0;
  int h = 0;

  int type = -1;
  for (int k=0 ; k<parent.getComponentCount(); k++) {
    Component comp = parent.getComponent(k);
    int newType = getLayoutType(comp);
    if (k == 0)
      type = newType;
```

7 A break in the sequence of types triggers a call to the overloaded `preferredLayoutSize(Vector v, int type)` method (discussed below) which determines the preferred size for a temporary collection of the components stored in the `Vector m_v`. Then `w` and `h` local variables, which are accumulating the total preferred width and height for this layout, are adjusted, and the temporary collection, `m_v`, is cleared. The newly processed component is then added to `m_v`.

```
    if (type != newType) {
      Dimension d = preferredLayoutSize(m_v, type);
      w = Math.max(w, d.width);
      h += d.height + m_vGap;
      m_v.removeAllElements();
      type = newType;
    }

    m_v.addElement(comp);
  }
```

8 Once our loop finishes, we make the unconditional call to `preferredLayoutSize()` to take into account the last (unprocessed) sequence of components and update `h` and `w` accordingly (just as we did in the loop). We then subtract the vertical gap value, `m_vGap`, from `h` because we know that we have just processed the last set of components and therefore no vertical gap **9** is necessary. Taking into account any `Insets` set on the container, we can now return the computed preferred size as a `Dimension` instance:

```
    Dimension d = preferredLayoutSize(m_v, type);
    w = Math.max(w, d.width);
    h += d.height + m_vGap;

    h -= m_vGap;

    Insets insets = parent.getInsets();
    return new Dimension(w+insets.left+insets.right,
      h+insets.top+insets.bottom);
  }
```

10 The overloaded method `preferredLayoutSize(Vector v, int type)` computes the preferred size to lay out a collection of components of a given type. This size is accumulated in **11** `w` and `h` local variables. For a collection of type `COMP_TWO_COL`, this method invokes a mechanism that should be familiar (see section 4.5). For a collection of type COMP_BIG, this method adjusts the preferable width and increments the height for each component, since these components will be placed in a column:

```
case COMP_BIG:
  for (int k=0 ; k<v.size(); k++) {
    Component comp = (Component)v.elementAt(k);
    Dimension d = comp.getPreferredSize();
    w = Math.max(w, d.width);
    h += d.height + m_vGap;
  }
  h -= m_vGap;
  return new Dimension(w, h);
```

For a collection of type COMP_BUTTON, this method invokes our getMaxDimension() method (see below) to calculate the desired size of a single component. Since all components of this type will have an equal size and be contained in one single row, the resulting width for this collection is calculated through multiplication by the number of components, v.size():

```
case COMP_BUTTON:
  Dimension d = getMaxDimension(v);
  w = d.width + m_hGap;
  h = d.height;
  return new Dimension(w*v.size()-m_hGap, h);
```

The layoutContainer(Container parent) method assigns bounds to the components in the given container. (Remember that this is the method that actually performs the layout of its associated container.) It processes an array of components similar to the preferredLayout-Size() method. It steps through the components in the given container, forms a temporary collection from contiguous components of the same type, and calls our overloaded layout-Components(Vector v, int type, int x, int y, int w) method to lay out that collection.

The layoutContainer(Vector v, int type, int x, int y, int w) method lays out components from the temporary collection of a given type, starting from the given coordinates x and y, and using the specified width, w, of the container. It returns an adjusted y-coordinate which may be used to lay out a new set of components.

For a collection of type COMP_TWO_COL, this method lays out components in two columns identical to the way DialogLayout did this (see section 4.5). For a collection of type COMP_BIG, the method assigns all available width to each component:

```
case COMP_BIG:
  for (int k=0 ; k<v.size(); k++) {
    Component comp = (Component)v.elementAt(k);
    Dimension d = comp.getPreferredSize();
    comp.setBounds(x, y, w, d.height);
    y += d.height + m_vGap;
  }
  return y;
```

For a collection of type COMP_BUTTON, this method assigns an equal size to each component and places the components in the center, arranged horizontally:

```
case COMP_BUTTON:
  Dimension d = getMaxDimension(v);
  int ww = d.width*v.size() + m_hGap*(v.size()-1);
  int xx = x + Math.max(0, (w - ww)/2);
  for (int k=0 ; k<v.size(); k++) {
    Component comp = (Component)v.elementAt(k);
    comp.setBounds(xx, y, d.width, d.height);
    xx += d.width + m_hGap;
  }
  return y + d.height;
```

NOTE   A more sophisticated implementation might split a sequence of buttons into several rows if not enough space is available. To avoid over-complication, we do not do that here. This might be an interesting exercise to give you more practice at customizing layout managers.

The remainder of the `DialogLayout2` class contains methods which were either explained already, or which are simple enough to be considered self-explanatory.

Class DialogSeparator

19 This class implements a component that is used to separate two groups of components placed in a column. It extends `JLabel` to inherit all its default characteristics such as font and foreground. Two available constructors allow the creation of a `DialogSeparator` with or without a text label.

20 The `getPreferredSize()` method returns a fixed height, and a width equal to the width of the container. The methods `getMinimumSize()` and `getMaximumSize()` simply delegate calls to the `getPreferredSize()` method.

21 The `paintComponent()` method draws a separating bar with a raised appearance across the available component space, and it draws the title text (if any) at the left-most side, taking into account a pre-defined offset, 15.

4.6.2   Running the code

Figure 4.17 shows our sample application which now uses `DialogLayout2` to manage the layout of *all* components. You can see that we have the same set of components placed and sized in accordance with our general layout scheme presented in the beginning of this section. The most important thing to note is that we did not have to use any intermediate containers or layouts to achieve this: all components are added directly to the frame's content pane, which is intelligently managed by `DialogLayout2`.

GUIDELINE

Button placement consistency   It is important to be consistent with the placement of buttons in dialogs and option panes. In the example shown here, a symmetrical approach to button placement has been adopted. This is a good safe choice and it ensures balance. With data entry dialogs, it is also common to use an asymmetrical layout such as the bottom right-hand side of the dialog.

In addition to achieving balance with the layout, by being consistent with your placement you allow the user to rely on directional memory to find a specific button location. Directional memory is strong. Once the user learns where you have placed buttons, he will quickly be able to locate the correct button in many dialog and option situations. It is therefore vital that you place buttons in a consistent order—for example, always use OK, Cancel, never Cancel, OK. As a general rule, always use a symmetrical layout with option dialogs and be consistent with whatever you decide to use for data entry dialogs.

It makes sense to develop custom components such as JOKCancelButtons and JYesNoButtons. You can then reuse these components every time you need such a set of buttons. This encapsulates the placement and ensures consistency.

4.7   DYNAMIC LAYOUT IN A JAVABEANS CONTAINER

In this section we will use different layouts to manage JavaBeans in a simple container application. This will help us to further understand the role of layouts in dynamically managing containers with a variable number of components. Example 4.8 also sets up the framework for a powerful bean editor environment that we will develop in chapter 18 using JTables. By allowing modification of component properties, we can use this environment to experiment with preferred, maximum, and minimum sizes, and we can observe the behavior that different layout managers exibit in various situations. This provides us with the ability to learn much more about each layout manager, and allows us to prototype simple interfaces without actually implementing them.

Example 4.8 consists of a frame container that allows the creation, loading, and saving of JavaBeans using serialization. Beans can be added and removed from this container, and we implement a focus mechanism to visually identify the currently selected bean. Most importantly, the layout manager of this container can be changed at run-time. (You may want to review the JavaBeans material in chapter 2 before attempting to work through this example.) Figures 4.18 through 4.23 show BeanContainer using five different layout managers to arrange four Clock beans. These figures and figure 4.24 are explained in more detail in section 4.7.2.

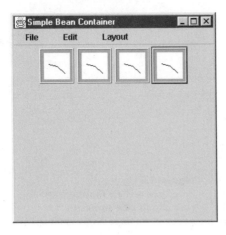

Figure 4.18
BeanContainer displaying
four clock components
using a FlowLayout

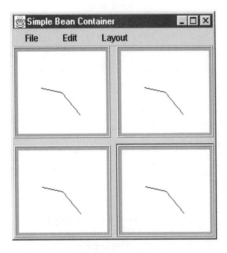

Figure 4.19
BeanContainer displaying
four clock components
using a GridLayout

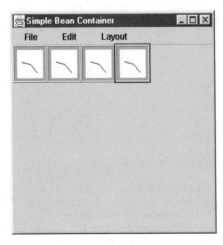

Figure 4.20
BeanContainer displaying
four clock components
using a horizontal BoxLayout

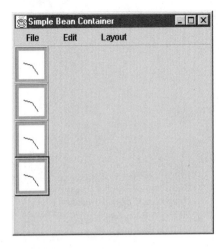

Figure 4.21
BeanContainer displaying
four clock components
using a vertical `BoxLayout`

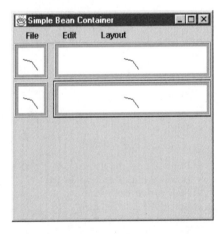

Figure 4.22
BeanContainer displaying
four clock components
using a `DialogLayout`

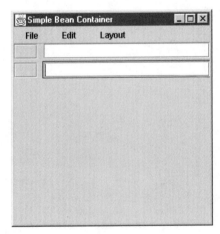

Figure 4.23
BeanContainer displaying
button/input field pairs
using `DialogLayout`

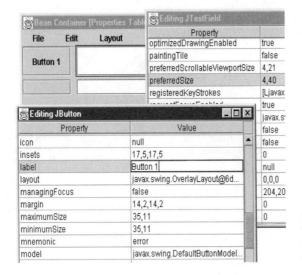

Figure 4.24
The `BeanContainer` **property editor environment as it is continued in chapter 18**

Example 4.8

BeanContainer.java

see \Chapter4\6

```java
import java.awt.*;
import java.awt.event.*;
import java.io.*;
import java.beans.*;
import java.lang.reflect.*;

import javax.swing.*;

import dl.*;

public class BeanContainer extends JFrame implements FocusListener
{
  protected File m_currentDir = new File(".");
  protected Component m_activeBean;
  protected String m_className = "clock.Clock";
  protected JFileChooser m_chooser = new JFileChooser();

  public BeanContainer() {
    super("Simple Bean Container");
    getContentPane().setLayout(new FlowLayout());

    setSize(300, 300);

    JPopupMenu.setDefaultLightWeightPopupEnabled(false);

    JMenuBar menuBar = createMenuBar();
    setJMenuBar(menuBar);
```

Provides frame for application and listens for focus transfer between beans in container **1**

```
      try {
        m_currentDir = (newFile(".")).getCanonicalFile();
          getCanonicalFile();
      }
      catch(IOException ex){}
      setDefaultCloseOperation(EXIT_ON_CLOSE);
      setVisible(true);

}

protected JMenuBar createMenuBar() {
  JMenuBar menuBar = new JMenuBar();

  JMenu mFile = new JMenu("File");

  JMenuItem mItem = new JMenuItem("New...");
  ActionListener lst = new ActionListener() {
    public void actionPerformed(ActionEvent e) {
      Thread newthread = new Thread() {
        public void run() {
          String result = (String)JOptionPane.showInputDialog(
            BeanContainer.this,
            "Please enter class name to create a new bean",
            "Input", JOptionPane.INFORMATION_MESSAGE, null,
            null, m_className);
          repaint();
          if (result==null)
            return;
          try {
            m_className = result;
            Class cls = Class.forName(result);
            Object obj = cls.newInstance();
            if (obj instanceof Component) {
              m_activeBean = (Component)obj;
              m_activeBean.addFocusListener(
                BeanContainer.this);
              m_activeBean.requestFocus();
              getContentPane().add(m_activeBean);
            }
            validate();
          }
          catch (Exception ex) {
            ex.printStackTrace();
            JOptionPane.showMessageDialog(
              BeanContainer.this, "Error: "+ex.toString(),
              "Warning", JOptionPane.WARNING_MESSAGE);
          }
        }
      };
      newthread.start();
    }
  };
  mItem.addActionListener(lst);
  mFile.add(mItem);
```

2 Creates menu bar, menu items, and action listeners

3 Load class, instantiate it, and add it to container

4 Request focus and set up FocusListener

```
mItem = new JMenuItem("Load...");
lst = new ActionListener() {
  public void actionPerformed(ActionEvent e) {
    Thread newthread = new Thread() {
      public void run() {
        m_chooser.setCurrentDirectory(m_currentDir);
        m_chooser.setDialogTitle(
          "Please select file with serialized bean");
        int result = m_chooser.showOpenDialog(
          BeanContainer.this);
        repaint();
        if (result != JFileChooser.APPROVE_OPTION)
          return;
        m_currentDir = m_chooser.getCurrentDirectory();
        File fChoosen = m_chooser.getSelectedFile();
        try {
          FileInputStream fStream =
            new FileInputStream(fChoosen);
          ObjectInput  stream  =
            new ObjectInputStream(fStream);
          Object obj = stream.readObject();
          if (obj instanceof Component) {
            m_activeBean = (Component)obj;
            m_activeBean.addFocusListener(
              BeanContainer.this);
            m_activeBean.requestFocus();
            getContentPane().add(m_activeBean);
          }
          stream.close();
          fStream.close();
          validate();
        }
        catch (Exception ex) {
          ex.printStackTrace();
          JOptionPane.showMessageDialog(
            BeanContainer.this, "Error: "+ex.toString(),
            "Warning", JOptionPane.WARNING_MESSAGE);
        }
        repaint();
      }
    };
    newthread.start();
  }
};
mItem.addActionListener(lst);
mFile.add(mItem);

mItem = new JMenuItem("Save...");
lst = new ActionListener() {
  public void actionPerformed(ActionEvent e) {
    Thread newthread = new Thread() {
      public void run() {
```

5 Select a file containing a serialized bean

6 Open a stream, read the object, and add it to the container, if it is a Component

```
         if (m_activeBean == null)
           return;
         m_chooser.setDialogTitle(
           "Please choose file to serialize bean");
         m_chooser.setCurrentDirectory(m_currentDir);
         int result = m_chooser.showSaveDialog(
           BeanContainer.this);
         repaint();
         if (result != JFileChooser.APPROVE_OPTION)
           return;
         m_currentDir = m_chooser.getCurrentDirectory();
         File fChoosen = m_chooser.getSelectedFile();
         try {
           FileOutputStream fStream =
             new FileOutputStream(fChoosen);
           ObjectOutput stream  =
             new ObjectOutputStream(fStream);
           stream.writeObject(m_activeBean);
           stream.close();
           fStream.close();
         }
         catch (Exception ex) {
           ex.printStackTrace();
         JOptionPane.showMessageDialog(
           BeanContainer.this, "Error: "+ex.toString(),
           "Warning", JOptionPane.WARNING_MESSAGE);
         }
       }
     };
     newthread.start();
   }
};
mItem.addActionListener(lst);
mFile.add(mItem);

mFile.addSeparator();

mItem = new JMenuItem("Exit");
lst = new ActionListener() {
  public void actionPerformed(ActionEvent e) {
    System.exit(0);
  }
};
mItem.addActionListener(lst);
mFile.add(mItem);
menuBar.add(mFile);

JMenu mEdit = new JMenu("Edit");

mItem = new JMenuItem("Delete");
lst = new ActionListener() {
  public void actionPerformed(ActionEvent e) {
    if (m_activeBean == null)
      return;
```

7 Serialize component to stream and write it to file

8 Item and action to exit application

9 Delete will remove the currently active component from the container

```
      getContentPane().remove(m_activeBean);
      m_activeBean = null;
      validate();
      repaint();
    }
};
mItem.addActionListener(lst);
mEdit.add(mItem);
menuBar.add(mEdit);

JMenu mLayout = new JMenu("Layout");
ButtonGroup group = new ButtonGroup();

mItem = new JRadioButtonMenuItem("FlowLayout");
mItem.setSelected(true);
lst = new ActionListener() {
  public void actionPerformed(ActionEvent e){
    getContentPane().setLayout(new FlowLayout());
    validate();
    repaint();
  }
};
mItem.addActionListener(lst);
group.add(mItem);
mLayout.add(mItem);

mItem = new JRadioButtonMenuItem("GridLayout");
lst = new ActionListener() {
  public void actionPerformed(ActionEvent e){
    int col = 3;
    int row = (int)Math.ceil(getContentPane().
      getComponentCount()/(double)col);
    getContentPane().setLayout(new GridLayout(row, col, 10, 10));
    validate();
    repaint();
  }
};
mItem.addActionListener(lst);
group.add(mItem);
mLayout.add(mItem);

mItem = new JRadioButtonMenuItem("BoxLayout - X");
lst = new ActionListener() {
  public void actionPerformed(ActionEvent e) {
    getContentPane().setLayout(new BoxLayout(
      getContentPane(), BoxLayout.X_AXIS));
    validate();
    repaint();
  }
};
mItem.addActionListener(lst);
group.add(mItem);
mLayout.add(mItem);

mItem = new JRadioButtonMenuItem("BoxLayout - Y");
```

9 Delete will remove the currently active component from the container

10 Relayout with FlowLayout configuration

Relayout with GridLayout configuration **10**

10 Relayout with vertical BoxLayout configuration

```
      lst = new ActionListener() {
        public void actionPerformed(ActionEvent e) {
          getContentPane().setLayout(new BoxLayout(
            getContentPane(), BoxLayout.Y_AXIS));
          validate();
          repaint();
        }
      };
      mItem.addActionListener(lst);
      group.add(mItem);
      mLayout.add(mItem);

      mItem = new JRadioButtonMenuItem("DialogLayout");
      lst = new ActionListener() {
        public void actionPerformed(ActionEvent e) {
          getContentPane().setLayout(new DialogLayout());
          validate();
          repaint();
        }
      };
      mItem.addActionListener(lst);
      group.add(mItem);
      mLayout.add(mItem);

      menuBar.add(mLayout);

      return menuBar;
    }
    public void focusGained(FocusEvent e) {
      m_activeBean = e.getComponent();
      repaint();
    }

    public void focusLost(FocusEvent e) {}

    // This is a heavyweight component so we override paint
    // instead of paintComponent. super.paint(g) will
    // paint all child components first, and then we
    // simply draw over top of them.
    public void paint(Graphics g) {
      super.paint(g);

      if (m_activeBean == null)
        return;

      Point pt = getLocationOnScreen();
      Point pt1 = m_activeBean.getLocationOnScreen();
      int x = pt1.x - pt.x - 2;
      int y = pt1.y - pt.y - 2;
      int w = m_activeBean.getWidth() + 2;
      int h = m_activeBean.getHeight() + 2;

      g.setColor(Color.black);
      g.drawRect(x, y, w, h);
    }
```

⑪ On focus change, stores currently active component and redisplays

⑫ Redraw container with box around currently active component

```
  public static void main(String argv[]) {
    new BeanContainer();
  }
}
```

Clock.java

see \Chapter4\6\clock

```
package clock;

import java.applet.*;
import java.awt.*;
import java.awt.event.*;
import java.beans.*;
import java.io.*;
import java.util.*;

import javax.swing.*;
import javax.swing.border.*;

public class Clock extends JButton
 implements Customizer, Externalizable, Runnable
{
  protected PropertyChangeSupport m_helper;
  protected boolean   m_digital = false;
  protected Calendar m_calendar;
  protected Dimension m_preffSize;

  public Clock() {
   m_calendar = Calendar.getInstance();
   m_helper = new PropertyChangeSupport(this);

   Border br1 = new EtchedBorder(EtchedBorder.RAISED,
    Color.white, new Color(128, 0, 0));
   Border br2 = new MatteBorder(4, 4, 4, 4, Color.red);
    setBorder(new CompoundBorder(br1, br2));

   setBackground(Color.white);
   setForeground(Color.black);

   (new Thread(this)).start();
  }

  public void writeExternal(ObjectOutput out)
   throws IOException {
    out.writeBoolean(m_digital);
    out.writeObject(getBackground());
    out.writeObject(getForeground());
    out.writeObject(getPreferredSize());
  }

  public void readExternal(ObjectInput in)
   throws IOException, ClassNotFoundException {
    setDigital(in.readBoolean());
    setBackground((Color)in.readObject());
    setForeground((Color)in.readObject());
```

⑬ Clock bean on button which can listen for property changes, manage its own serialization, and run on a separate thread

⑭ Constructor creates helper objects, puts "clock-like" border on, and starts a new thread to run on

⑮ Managed serialization, writing out each field and reading it back in the same order

```java
    setPreferredSize((Dimension)in.readObject());
  }

  public Dimension getPreferredSize() {
    if (m_preffSize != null)
      return m_preffSize;
    else
      return new Dimension(50, 50);
  }

  public void setPreferredSize(Dimension preffSize) {
    m_preffSize = preffSize;
  }

  public Dimension getMinimumSize() {
    return getPreferredSize();
  }

  public Dimension getMaximumSize() {
    return getPreferredSize();
  }

  public void setDigital(boolean digital) {
    m_helper.firePropertyChange("digital",
      new Boolean(m_digital),
      new Boolean(digital));
    m_digital = digital;
    repaint();
  }

  public boolean getDigital() {
    return m_digital;
  }

  public void addPropertyChangeListener(
   PropertyChangeListener lst) {
    if (m_helper != null)
      m_helper.addPropertyChangeListener(lst);
  }

  public void removePropertyChangeListener(
   PropertyChangeListener lst) {
    if (m_helper != null)
      m_helper.removePropertyChangeListener(lst);
  }

  public void setObject(Object bean) {}

  public void paintComponent(Graphics g) {
    super.paintComponent(g);

    g.setColor(getBackground());
    g.fillRect(0, 0, getWidth(), getHeight());
    getBorder().paintBorder(this, g, 0, 0, getWidth(), getHeight());

    m_calendar.setTime(new Date()); // Get current time
    int hrs = m_calendar.get(Calendar.HOUR_OF_DAY);
    int min = m_calendar.get(Calendar.MINUTE);
```

16 Displays clock value in either digital or analog form

```
    g.setColor(getForeground());
    if (m_digital) {
      String time = ""+hrs+":"+min;
      g.setFont(getFont());
      FontMetrics fm = g.getFontMetrics();
      int y = (getHeight() + fm.getAscent())/2;
      int x = (getWidth() - fm.stringWidth(time))/2;
      g.drawString(time, x, y);
    }
    else {
      int x = getWidth()/2;
      int y = getHeight()/2;
      int rh = getHeight()/4;
      int rm = getHeight()/3;

      double ah = ((double)hrs+min/60.0)/6.0*Math.PI;
      double am = min/30.0*Math.PI;

      g.drawLine(x, y, (int)(x+rh*Math.sin(ah)),
        (int)(y-rh*Math.cos(ah)));
      g.drawLine(x, y, (int)(x+rm*Math.sin(am)),
        (int)(y-rm*Math.cos(am)));
    }
  }

  public void run() {
    while (true) {
      repaint();
      try {
        Thread.sleep(30*1000);
      }
      catch(InterruptedException ex) { break; }
    }
  }
}
```

4.7.1   Understanding the code

Class BeanContainer

❶ This class extends JFrame to provide the frame for this application. It also implements the FocusListener interface to manage focus transfer between beans in the container. Four instance variables are declared:

- File m_currentDir: The most recent directory used to load and save beans.
- Component m_activeBean: A bean component which currently has the focus.
- String m_className: The fully qualified class name of our custom Clock bean.
- JFileChooser m_chooser: Used for saving and loading beans.

❷ The only GUI provided by the container itself is the menu bar. The createMenuBar() method creates the menu bar, its items, and their corresponding action listeners. Three menus are added to the menu bar: File, Edit, and Layout.

All code corresponding to New, Load, and Save in the File menu is wrapped in a separate thread to avoid an unnecessary load on the event-dispatching thread. See chapter 2 for more information about multithreading.

3 The New… menu item in the File menu displays an input dialog (using the JOption-Pane.showInputDialog() method) to enter the class name of a new bean to be added to the container. Once a name has been entered, the program attempts to load that class, create a **4** new class instance using a default constructor, and add that new object to the container. The newly created component requests the focus and receives a this reference to BeanContainer as a FocusListener. Any exceptions caught will be displayed in a message box.

5 The Load… menu item from the File menu displays a JFileChooser dialog to select a file **6** containing a previously serialized bean component. If this succeeds, the program opens an input stream on this file and reads the first stored object. If this object is derived from the java.awt.Component class, it is added to the container. The loaded component requests the focus and receives a this reference to BeanContainer as a FocusListener. Any exceptions caught will be displayed in a message box.

7 The Save… menu item from the File menu displays a JFileChooser dialog to select a file destination for serializing the bean component which currently has the focus. If this succeeds, the program opens an output stream on that file and writes the currently active component to that stream. Any exceptions caught will be displayed in a message box.

8 The Exit menu item simply quits and closes the application with System.exit(0).

9 The Edit menu contains a single item entitled Delete, which removes the currently active bean from the container:

```
getContentPane().remove(m_activeBean);
m_activeBean = null;
validate();
repaint();
```

10 The Layout menu contains several JRadioButtonMenuItems managed by a ButtonGroup group. These items are entitled "FlowLayout," "GridLayout," "BoxLayout – X," "BoxLayout – Y," and "DialogLayout." Each item receives an ActionListener which sets the corresponding layout manager of the application frame's content pane, calls validate() to lay out the container again, and then repaints it. For example:

```
getContentPane().setLayout(new DialogLayout());
validate();
repaint();
```

11 The focusGained() method stores a reference to the component which currently has the **12** focus as instance variable m_activebean. The paint() method is implemented to draw a rectangle around the component which currently has the focus. It is important to note here the static JPopupMenu method called in the BeanContainer constructor:

```
JPopupMenu.setDefaultLightWeightPopupEnabled(false);
```

This method forces all pop-up menus (which menu bars use to display their contents) to use heavyweight popups rather than lightweight popups. (By default, pop-up menus are lightweight unless they cannot fit within their parent container's bounds.) The reason we disable this is because our paint() method will render the bean selection rectangle over the top of the lightweight popups otherwise.

Class Clock

13 This class is a simple bean clock component which can be used in a container just as any other bean. This class extends the JButton component to inherit its focus-grabbing functionality. This class also implements three interfaces: Customizer to handle property listeners, Externalizable to completely manage its own serialization, and Runnable to be run by a thread. Four instance variables are declared:

- PropertyChangeSupport m_helper: An object to manage PropertyChangeListeners.
- boolean m_digital: A custom property for this component which manages the display state of the clock (digital or arrow-based).
- Calendar m_calendar: A helper object to handle Java's time objects (instances of Date).
- Dimension m_preffSize: A preferred size for this component which may be assigned using the setPreferredSize() method.

14 The constructor of the Clock class creates the helper objects and sets the border for this component as a CompoundBorder that contains an EtchedBorder and a MatteBorder. It then sets the background and foreground colors and starts a new Thread to run the clock.

15 The writeExternal() method writes the current state of a Clock object into an ObjectOutput stream. Four properties are written: m_digital, background, foreground, and preferredSize. The readExternal() method reads the previously saved state of a Clock object from an ObjectInput stream. It reads these four properties and applies them to the object previously created with the default constructor. These methods are called from the Save and Load menu bar action listener code in BeanContainer. Specifically, they are called when writeObject() and readObject() are invoked.

> **NOTE** The serialization mechanism in Swing has not yet fully matured. You can readily discover that both lightweight and heavyweight components throw exceptions during the process of serialization. For this reason, we implement the Externalizable interface to take complete control over the serialization of the Clock bean. Another reason is that the default serialization mechanism tends to serialize a substantial amount of unnecessary information, whereas our custom implementation stores only the necessities.

16 The rest of this class need not be explained here, as it does not relate directly to the topic of this chapter and it represents a simple example of a bean component. If you're interested, take note of the paintComponent() method which, depending on whether the clock is in digital mode (determined by m_digital), either computes the current position of the clock's arrows and draws them, or renders the time as a digital String.

4.7.2 Running the code

This application provides a framework for experimenting with any available JavaBeans; both lightweight (Swing) and heavyweight (AWT) components: we can create, serialize, delete, and restore them.

We can apply several layouts to manage these components dynamically. Figures 4.18 through 4.22 show BeanContainer using five different layout managers to arrange four Clock beans. To create a bean, choose New from the File menu and type the fully qualified name of the class. For instance, to create a Clock you need to type "clock.Clock" in the input dialog.

Once you've experimented with Clock beans, try loading some Swing JavaBeans. Figure 4.23 shows BeanDialog with two JButtons and two JTextFields. They were created in the following order (and thus have corresponding container indices): JButton, JTextField, JButton, and JTextField. Try doing this: remember that you need to specify fully qualified class names such as javax.swing.JButton when you add a new bean. This ordering adheres to our DialogLayout label/input field pairs scheme, except that here we are using buttons in place of labels. That way, when we set BeanContainer's layout to DialogLayout, we know what to expect.

NOTE   You will notice selection problems with components such as JComboBox, JSplit-Pane, and JLabel (which has no selection mechanism). A more complete version of BeanContainer would take this into account and implement more robust focus-requesting behavior.

Later in this book, after a discussion of tables, we will add powerful functionality to this example to allow bean property manipulation. We highly suggest that you skip ahead for a moment and run example 18.8.

Start the chapter 18 example and create JButton and JTextField beans exactly as described above. Select DialogLayout from the Layout menu and then click on the top-most JButton to give it the focus. Now select Properties from the Edit menu. A separate frame will pop up with a JTable that contains all of the JButton's properties. Navigate to the label property and change it to "Button 1" (by double-clicking on its Value field). Now select the corresponding top-most JTextField and change its preferredSize property to "4,40." Figure 4.24 illustrates what you should see.

By changing the preferred, maximum, and minimum sizes, as well as other component properties, we can directly examine the behavior that different layout managers impose on our container. Experimenting with this example is a very convenient way to learn more about how the layout managers behave. It also forms the foundation for an interface development environment (IDE), which many developers use to simplify interface design.

C H A P T E R   5

Labels and buttons

5.1 LABELS AND BUTTONS OVERVIEW

We start with the basics, the concepts needed to work with Swing labels, buttons, and tooltips. Once we understand the basics, we build on them to create customized versions.

5.1.1 JLabel

class javax.swing.JLabel

JLabel is one of the simplest Swing components, and it is most often used to identify other components. JLabel can display text, an icon, or both in any combination of positions (note that text will always overlap the icon). The code in example 5.1 creates four different JLabels and places them in a GridLayout as shown in figure 5.1.

Figure 5.1 JLabel demo

155

Example 5.1

LabelDemo.java

see \Chapter5\1

```java
import java.awt.*;
import javax.swing.*;

class LabelDemo extends JFrame
{
  public LabelDemo() {
    super("JLabel Demo");
    setSize(600, 100);

    JPanel content = (JPanel) getContentPane();
    content.setLayout(new GridLayout(1, 4, 4, 4));

    JLabel label = new JLabel();
    label.setText("JLabel");
    label.setBackground(Color.white);
    content.add(label);

    label = new JLabel("JLabel",
      SwingConstants.CENTER);
    label.setOpaque(true);
    label.setBackground(Color.white);
    content.add(label);

    label = new JLabel("JLabel");
    label.setFont(new Font("Helvetica", Font.BOLD, 18));
    label.setOpaque(true);
    label.setBackground(Color.white);
    content.add(label);

    ImageIcon image = new ImageIcon("flight.gif");
    label = new JLabel("JLabel", image,
      SwingConstants.RIGHT);
    label.setVerticalTextPosition(SwingConstants.TOP);
    label.setOpaque(true);
    label.setBackground(Color.white);
    content.add(label);

    setDefaultCloseOperation(JFrame.EXIT_ON_CLOSE);
    setVisible(true);

  }

  public static void main(String args[]) {
     new LabelDemo();
  }
}
```

The first label is created with the default constructor and its text is set using the setText() method. We then set its background to white, but when we run this program the background of the label shows up as light gray. This happens because we didn't force the label to be opaque. In chapter 2 we learned that Swing components support transparency, which means that a component does not have to paint every pixel within its bounds. So when a component is not opaque, it will not fill its background. A `JLabel` (as with most components) is non-opaque by default.

We can also set the font and foreground color of a `JLabel` using `JComponent`'s `setFont()` and `setForeground()` methods. Refer back to chapter 2 for information about working with the `Font` and `Color` classes.

The default horizontal alignment of `JLabel` is `LEFT` if only text is used, and `CENTER` if an image or an image and text are used. An image will appear to the left of the text by default, and every `JLabel` is initialized with a centered vertical alignment. Each of these default behaviors can easily be adjusted, as we will see below.

5.1.2 Text alignment

To specify alignment or position in many Swing components, we use the `javax.swing.SwingConstants` interface. This defines several constant strings, five of which are applicable to `JLabel`'s text alignment settings:

```
SwingConstants.LEFT
SwingConstants.CENTER
SwingConstants.RIGHT
SwingConstants.TOP
SwingConstants.BOTTOM
```

Alignment of both a label's text and icon can be specified either in the constructor or through the `setHorizontalAlignment()` and `setVerticalAlignment()` methods. The text can be aligned both vertically or horizontally, independent of the icon (text will overlap the icon when necessary) using the `setHorizontalTextAlignment()` and `setVerticalTextAlignment()` methods. Figure 5.2 shows where a `JLabel`'s text will be placed, corresponding to each possible combination of vertical and horizontal text alignment settings.

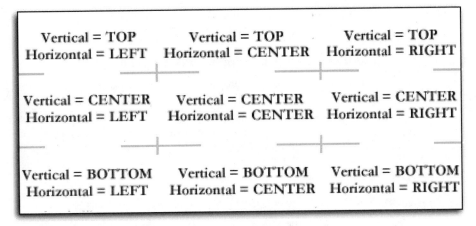

Figure 5.2 `JLabel` **text alignment**

5.1.3 Icons and icon alignment

The simple example in figure 5.1 included a label with an image of an airplane. This was done by reading a GIF file in as an `ImageIcon` and passing it to a `JLabel` constructor:

```
ImageIcon image = new ImageIcon("flight.gif");
label = new JLabel("JLabel", image,
  SwingConstants.RIGHT);
```

An image can also be set or replaced at any time using the `setIcon()` method (passing `null` will remove the current icon, if any). `JLabel` also supports a disabled icon to be used when a label is in the disabled state. To assign a disabled icon, we use the `setDisabled-Icon()` method.

NOTE   Animated GIFs can be used with `ImageIcons` and labels just as any static GIF can be, and they don't require any additional code. `ImageIcon` also supports JPGs.

5.1.4 GrayFilter

class javax.swing.GrayFilter

The static `createDisabledImage()` method of the `GrayFilter` class can be used to create "disabled" images.

```
ImageIcon disabledImage = new ImageIcon(
  GrayFilter.createDisabledImage(image.getImage()));
```

Figure 5.3 shows the fourth label in `LabelDemo` now using a disabled icon generated by `GrayFilter`. `JLabel` only displays the disabled icon when it has been disabled using `JComponent`'s `setEnabled()` method.

Figure 5.3
Demonstrating a disabled icon
using `GrayFilter`

5.1.5 The labelFor and the displayedMnemonic properties

`JLabel` maintains a `labelFor` property and a `displayedMnemonic` property. The displayed mnemonic is a character that, when pressed in synchronization with ALT (for example, ALT+R), will call `JComponent`'s `requestFocus()` method on the component referenced by the `labelFor` property. The first instance of the displayed mnemonic character (if any) in a label's text will be underlined. We can access these properties using typical get/set accessors.

5.1.6 AbstractButton

abstract class javax.swing.AbstractButton

`AbstractButton` is the template class from which all buttons are defined. This includes push buttons, toggle buttons, check boxes, radio buttons, menu items, and menus themselves.

Its direct subclasses are JButton, JToggleButton, and JMenuItem. There are no subclasses of JButton in Swing. JToggleButton has two subclasses: JCheckBox and JRadioButton. JMenuItem has three subclasses: JCheckBoxMenuItem, JRadioButtonMenuItem, and JMenu. The remainder of this chapter will focus on JButton and the JToggleButton family. Refer to chapter 12 for more information about menus and menu items.

JAVA 1.4   In Java 1.4 a new setDisplayedMnemonicIndex() method was added to JLabel and AbstractButton. This allows you to specify the index of the character you want underlined. For instance, in a menu item with the text "Save As" if you want the second 'A' to be underlined you would use the following code:

```
myMenuItem.setMnemonic('A');
myMenuItem.setDisplayedMnemonicIndex(5);
```

Also new to Java 1.4 are the new setIconGap() and getIconGap() methods allowing specification of the size of the space to appear between button text and icon.

5.1.7   The ButtonModel interface

abstract interface javax.swing.ButtonModel

Each button class uses a model to store its state. We can access any button's model with AbstractButton's getModel() and setModel() methods. The ButtonModel interface is the template interface from which all button models are defined. JButton uses the DefaultButtonModel implementation. JToggleButton defines an inner class extension of DefaultButtonModel; this extension is JToggleButton.ToggleButtonModel, which is used by JToggleButton and both JToggleButton subclasses.

The following boolean property values represent the state of a button, and they have associated isXX() and setXX() accessors in DefaultButtonModel:

- selected: Switches state on each click (only relevant for JToggleButtons).
- pressed: Returns true when the button is held down with the mouse.
- rollover: Returns true when the mouse is hovering over the button.
- armed: Stops events from being fired when we press a button with the mouse and then release the mouse when the cursor is outside that button's bounds.
- enabled: Returns true when the button is active. None of the other properties can normally be changed when this is false.

A button's keyboard mnemonic is also stored in its model, as is the ButtonGroup it belongs to, if any. (We'll discuss the ButtonGroup class when we discuss JToggleButtons, as it only applies to this family of buttons.)

JAVA 1.3   In Java 1.3 a new getGroup() method was added to DefaultButtonModel allowing access to the ButtonGroup a button belongs to.

5.1.8   JButton

class javax.swing.JButton

JButton is a basic push button, which is one of the simplest Swing components. Almost everything we know about JLabel also applies to JButton. We can add images, specify text and image alignment, set foreground and background colors (remember to call setOpaque(true)),

and set fonts, among other tasks. Additionally, we can add `ActionListeners`, `ChangeLis-`
`teners`, and `ItemListeners` to receive `ActionEvents`, `ChangeEvents`, and `ItemEvents`
respectively when any properties in its model change value.

In most application dialogs, we might expect to find a button which initially has the focus
and will capture an Enter key press, regardless of the current keyboard focus, unless focus is
within a multi-line text component. This is referred to as the *default button*. Any `JRootPane`
container can define a default button using `JRootPane`'s `setDefaultButton()` method
(passing `null` will disable this feature). For instance, to make a button, the default button for
a `JFrame`, we would do the following:

```
myJFrame.getRootPane().setDefaultButton(myButton);
```

The `isDefaultButton()` method returns a boolean value indicating whether the button
instance it was called on is a default button for a `JRootPane`.

We most often register an `ActionListener` with a button to receive `ActionEvents`
from that button whenever it is clicked (if a button has the focus, pressing the Space bar will
also fire an `ActionEvent`). `ActionEvents` carry with them information about the event that
occurred, including, most importantly, which component they came from.

To create an `ActionListener`, we need to create a class that implements the `Action-`
`Listener` interface, which requires the definition of its `actionPerformed()` method.
Once we have built an `ActionListener` we can register it with a button using `JCompo-`
`nent`'s `addActionListener()` method. The following code segment is a typical inner class
implementation. When an `ActionEvent` is intercepted, "Swing is powerful!!" is printed to
standard output.

```
JButton myButton = new JButton();
ActionListener act = new ActionListener() {
  public void actionPerformed(ActionEvent e) {
    System.out.println("Swing is powerful!!");
  }
};
myButton.addActionListener(act);
```

We primarily use this method throughout this book to attach listeners to components. However,
some developers prefer to implement the `ActionListener` interface in the class that owns the
button instance. With classes that have several registered components, this is not as efficient as
using a separate listener class, and it can require writing common code in several places.

JAVA 1.3   In Java 1.3 all buttons have a new constructor that takes an `Action` instance as a
parameter. `Actions` are covered in detail in Chapter 12, but it suffices to say here
that they are `ActionListener` implementations that encapsulate all needed information to provide an icon, displayed text, enabled state, and event handling code.

An icon can be assigned to a `JButton` instance via the constructor or the `setIcon()`
method. We can optionally assign individual icons for the normal, selected, pressed, rollover,
and disabled states. See the API documentation for more detail on the following methods:

```
setDisabledSelectedIcon()
setPressedIcon()
setRolloverIcon()
```

```
setRolloverSelectedIcon()
setSelectedIcon()
```

A button can also be disabled and enabled the same way as a JLabel, using setEnabled(). As we would expect, a disabled button will not respond to any user actions.

A button's keyboard mnemonic provides an alternative means of activation. To add a keyboard mnemonic to a button, we use the setMnemonic() method:

```
button.setMnemonic('R');
```

We can then activate a button (equivalent to clicking it) by pressing ALT and its mnemonic key simultaneously (for example, ALT+R). The first appearance of the assigned mnemonic character, if any, in the button text will be underlined to indicate which key activates it. In Java 1.3 the setDisplayedMnemonicIndex() method was added to allow control over this. No dis-tinction is made between upper- and lower-case characters. Avoid duplicating mnemonics for components that share a common ancestor.

5.1.9   JToggleButton

class javax.swing.JToggleButton

JToggleButton provides a selected state mechanism which extends to its children, JCheckBox and JRadioButton, and corresponds to the selected property we discussed in section 5.1.7. We can test whether a toggle button is selected using AbstractButton's isSelected() method, and we can set this property with its setSelected() method.

5.1.10   ButtonGroup

class javax.swing.ButtonGroup

JToggleButtons are often used in ButtonGroups. A ButtonGroup manages a set of buttons by guaranteeing that only one button within that group can be selected at any given time. Thus, only JToggleButton and its subclasses are useful in a ButtonGroup because a JButton does not maintain a selected state. Example 5.2 constructs four JToggleButtons and places them in a single ButtonGroup.

Figure 5.4
JToggleButtons in a **ButtonGroup**
Newtocome

Example 5.2

ToggleButtonDemo.java

see \Chapter5\2

```
import java.awt.*;
import java.awt.event.*;
import javax.swing.*;
```

```
class ToggleButtonDemo extends JFrame {
  public ToggleButtonDemo () {
    super("ToggleButton Demo");
    getContentPane().setLayout(new FlowLayout());

    ButtonGroup buttonGroup = new ButtonGroup();
    char ch = (char) ('1'+ k);
    for (int k=0; k<4; k++) {
      JToggleButton button = new JToggleButton("Button "+ch, k==0);
      button.setMnemonic(ch);
      button.setEnabled(k<3);
      button.setToolTipText("This is button " + ch);

      button.setIcon(new ImageIcon("ball_bw.gif"));
      button.setSelectedIcon(new ImageIcon("ball_red.gif"));
      button.setRolloverIcon(new ImageIcon("ball_blue.gif"));
      button.setRolloverSelectedIcon(new ImageIcon("ball_blue.gif"));

      getContentPane().add(button);
      buttonGroup.add(button);
    }

    pack();
  }

  public static void main(String args[] {
    ToggleButtonDemo frame = new ToggleButtonDemo();
    frame.setDefaultCloseOperation(JFrame.EXIT_ON_CLOSE);
    frame.setVisible(true);
  }
}
```

5.1.11   JCheckBox and JRadioButton

class javax.swing.JCheckBox, class javax.swing.JRadioButton

JCheckBox and JRadioButton both inherit all JToggleButton functionality. In fact, the only significant differences between all three components is their UI delegates (how they are rendered). Both button types are normally used to select the mode of a particular application function. Figures 5.5 and 5.6 show the previous example running with JCheckBoxes and JRadioButtons as replacements for the JToggleButtons.

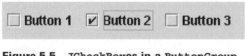

Figure 5.5   JCheckBoxes in a ButtonGroup

Figure 5.6   JRadioButtons in a ButtonGroup

5.1.12   JToolTip and ToolTipManager

class javax.swing.JToolTip, class javax.swing.ToolTipManager

A `JToolTip` is a small pop-up window designed to contain informative text about a component when the mouse moves over it. We don't generally create instances of these components ourselves. Rather, we call `setToolTipText()` on any `JComponent` subclass and pass it a descriptive `String`. This `String` is then stored as a client property within that component's client properties `Hashtable`, and that component is then registered with the `ToolTipManager` using `ToolTipManager`'s `registerComponent()` method. The `ToolTipManager` adds a `MouseListener` to each component that registers with it.

To unregister a component, we can pass `null` to that component's `setToolTipText()` method. This invokes `ToolTipManager`'s `unregisterComponent()` method, which removes its `MouseListener` from that component. Figure 5.7 shows a `JToggleButton` with simple tooltip text.

**Figure 5.7
JToggleButton
with tooltip text**

The `ToolTipManager` is a service class that maintains a shared instance of itself. We can access the `ToolTipManager` directly by calling its static `sharedInstance()` method:

```
ToolTipManager toolTipManager = ToolTipManager.sharedInstance();
```

Internally this class uses three non-repeating `Timers` with delay times defaulting to 750, 500, and 4000. `ToolTipManager` uses these `Timers` in coordination with mouse listeners to determine if and when to display a `JToolTip` with a component's specified tooltip text. When the mouse enters a component's bounds, `ToolTipManager` will detect this and wait 750ms before displaying a `JToolTip` for that component. This is referred to as the *initial delay time*. A `JToolTip` will stay visible for 4000ms or until we move the mouse outside of that component's bounds, whichever comes first. This is referred to as the *dismiss delay time*. The 500ms `Timer` represents the *reshow delay time*, which specifies how soon the `JToolTip` we have just seen will appear again when this component is re-entered. These delay times can be set using `ToolTipManager`'s `setDismissDelay()`, `setInitialDelay()`, and `setReshowDelay()` methods.

`ToolTipManager` is a very nice service, but it does have significant limitations. When we construct our polygonal buttons in section 5.6 below, we will find that it is not robust enough to support non-rectangular components.

5.1.13   Labels and buttons with HTML text

JDK1.2.2 offers a particularly interesting new feature. Now we can use HTML text in `JButton` and `JLabel` components as well as for tooltip text. We don't have to learn any new methods to use this functionality, and the UI delegate handles the HTML rendering for us. If a button/label's text starts with `<HTML>`, Swing knows to render the text in HTML format. We can use normal paragraph tags (`<P>` and `</P>`), line break tags (`<BR>`), and other HTML tags. For instance, we can assign a multiple-line tooltip to any component like this:

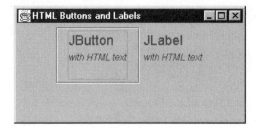

Figure 5.8
A `JButton` **and** `JLabel`
with HTML text

```
myComponent.setToolTipText("<html>Multi-line tooltips<br>" +
    "are easy!");
```

The <br> tag specifies a line break. Example 5.3 demonstrates this functionality.

Example 5.3

HtmlButtons.java

see \Chapter5\3

```java
import java.awt.*;
import java.awt.event.*;
import javax.swing.*;

public class HtmlButtons extends JFrame
{
  public HtmlButtons() {
    super("HTML Buttons and Labels");
    setSize(400, 300);

    getContentPane().setLayout(new FlowLayout());

    String htmlText =
      "<html><p><font color=\"#800080\" "+
      "size=\"4\" face=\"Verdana\">JButton</font> </p>"+
      "<address><font size=\"2\"><em>"+
      "with HTML text</em></font>"+
      "</address>";
    JButton btn = new JButton(htmlText);
    getContentPane().add(btn);

    htmlText =
      "<html><p><font color=\"#800080\" "+
      "size=\"4\" face=\"Verdana\">JLabel</font> </p>"+
      "<address><font size=\"2\"><em>"+
      "with HTML text</em></font>"+
      "</address>";
    JLabel lbl = new JLabel(htmlText);
    getContentPane().add(lbl);

    setDefaultCloseOperation(JFrame.EXIT_ON_CLOSE);
    setVisible(true);
  }
```

```
public static void main(String args[]) {
    new HtmlButtons();
  }
}
```

5.2   CUSTOM BUTTONS, PART I: TRANSPARENT BUTTONS

Buttons in Swing can adopt almost any presentation we can think of. Of course, some presentations are tougher to implement than others. In the remainder of this chapter we will deal directly with these issues. Example 5.4 in this section shows how to construct invisible buttons which only appear when the user moves the mouse cursor over them. Specifically, a border will be painted, and tooltip text will be activated in the default manner.

Buttons such as these can be useful in applets for predefined hyperlink navigation, and we will design our invisible button class with this in mind. Thus, we will show how to create an applet that reads a set of parameters from the HTML page in which it is embedded and loads a corresponding set of invisible buttons. For each button, the designer of the HTML page must provide three parameters: the desired hyperlink URL, the button's bounds (positions and size), and the button's tooltip text. Additionally, our sample applet in example 5.4 will require a background image parameter. Our button's bounds are intended to directly correspond to an "active" region of this background image, much like the venerable HTML image mapping functionality.

**Figure 5.9
Transparent
rectangular
buttons
in an applet**

Example 5.4

ButtonApplet.java

see \Chapter5\4

```
import java.applet.*;
import java.awt.*;
import java.awt.event.*;
```

```java
import java.net.*;
import java.util.*;

import javax.swing.*;
import javax.swing.border.*;
import javax.swing.event.*;

public class ButtonApplet extends JApplet
{
  public ButtonApplet() {}

  public synchronized void init() {
    String imageName = getParameter("image");
    if (imageName == null) {
      System.err.println("Need \"image\" parameter");
      return;
    }
    URL imageUrl = null;
    try {
      imageUrl = new URL(getDocumentBase(), imageName);
    }
    catch (MalformedURLException ex) {
      ex.printStackTrace();
      return;
    }
    ImageIcon bigImage = new ImageIcon(imageUrl);
    JLabel bigLabel = new JLabel(bigImage);
    bigLabel.setLayout(null);

    int index = 1;
    int[] q = new int[4];
    while(true) {
      String paramSize = getParameter("button"+index);
      String paramName = getParameter("name"+index);
      String paramUrl = getParameter("url"+index);
      if (paramSize==null || paramName==null || paramUrl==null)
        break;

      try {
        StringTokenizer tokenizer = new StringTokenizer(
          paramSize, ",");
        for (int k=0; k<4; k++) {
          String str = tokenizer.nextToken().trim();
          q[k] = Integer.parseInt(str);
        }
      }
      catch (Exception ex) { break; }

      NavigateButton btn = new NavigateButton(this,
        paramName, paramUrl);
      bigLabel.add(btn);
      btn.setBounds(q[0], q[1], q[2], q[3]);

      index++;
    }
```

1 Applet instead of Frame, so it can run on a web page

2 Reads "image" parameter to set background image on label

3 Sets up one transparent button for each iteration

4 Creates the button and adds it to the container

```
      getContentPane().setLayout(null);
      getContentPane().add(bigLabel);
      bigLabel.setBounds(0, 0, bigImage.getIconWidth(),
        bigImage.getIconHeight());
  }

  public String getAppletInfo() {
    return "Sample applet with NavigateButtons";
  }

  public String[][] getParameterInfo() {
    String pinfo[][] = {
      {"image",  "string",   "base image file name"},
      {"buttonX","x,y,w,h",  "button's bounds"},
      {"nameX",  "string",   "tooltip text"},
      {"urlX",   "url",      "link URL"} };
    return pinfo;
  }
}

class NavigateButton extends JButton implements ActionListener
{
  protected Border m_activeBorder;
  protected Border m_inactiveBorder;

  protected Applet m_parent;
  protected String m_text;
  protected String m_sUrl;
  protected URL    m_url;

  public NavigateButton(Applet parent, String text, String sUrl) {
    m_parent = parent;
    setText(text);
    m_sUrl = sUrl;
    try {
      m_url = new URL(sUrl);
    }
    catch(Exception ex) { m_url = null; }

    setOpaque(false);
    enableEvents(AWTEvent.MOUSE_EVENT_MASK);

    m_activeBorder = new MatteBorder(1, 1, 1, 1, Color.yellow);
    m_inactiveBorder = new EmptyBorder(1, 1, 1, 1);
    setBorder(m_inactiveBorder);

    addActionListener(this);
  }

  public void setText(String text) {
    m_text = text;
    setToolTipText(text);
  }

  public String getText() {
    return m_text;
  }
```

5 Useful information for applets, but not required

6 Implementation of invisible button

7 Borders shown when button has and does not have focus

8 Sets URL for button

9 Sets up to process its own mouse events

10 Overrides methods from JButton, but to manage tooltip text, not label text

```
     protected void processMouseEvent(MouseEvent evt) {
       switch (evt.getID()) {
         case MouseEvent.MOUSE_ENTERED:
           setBorder(m_activeBorder);
           setCursor(Cursor.getPredefinedCursor(
             Cursor.HAND_CURSOR));
           m_parent.showStatus(m_sUrl);
           break;
         case MouseEvent.MOUSE_EXITED:
           setBorder(m_inactiveBorder);
           setCursor(Cursor.getPredefinedCursor(
             Cursor.DEFAULT_CURSOR));
           m_parent.showStatus("");
           break;
       }
       super.processMouseEvent(evt);
     }

     public void actionPerformed(ActionEvent e) {
       if (m_url != null) {
         AppletContext context = m_parent.getAppletContext();
         if (context != null)
           context.showDocument(m_url);
       }
     }

     public void paintComponent(Graphics g) {
       paintBorder(g);
     }
   }
```

⑪ Gets all mouse events, but only handles mouse enter and exit events, to change the border and cursor

Called when user presses button with mouse or keyboard

5.2.1   Understanding the code

Class ButtonApplet

①
② This class extends JApplet to provide web page functionality. The init() method creates and initializes all GUI components. It starts by reading the applet's image parameter, which is then used along with the applet's codebase to construct a URL:

```
        imageUrl = new URL(getDocumentBase(), imageName);
```

This URL points to the image file which is used to create our bigLabel label, which is used as the applet's background image.

③ The applet can be configured to hold several invisible buttons for navigating to predefined URLs. For each button, three applet parameters must be provided:

- buttonN: Holds four comma-delimited numbers for the x, y, width, and height of button N.
- nameN: Tooltip text for button N.
- urlN: URL to redirect the browser to when the user clicks the mouse over button N.

④ As soon as these parameters are parsed for a given N, a new button is created and added to bigLabel:

```
        NavigateButton btn = new NavigateButton(this,
```

```
            paramName, paramUrl);
        bigLabel.add(btn);
        btn.setBounds(q[0], q[1], q[2], q[3]);
```

Finally, the `bigLabel` component is added to the applet's content pane. It receives a fixed size to avoid any repositioning if the label's parent is somehow resized.

5 The `getAppletInfo()` method returns a `String` description of this applet. The `getParameterInfo()` method returns a two-dimensional `String` array that describes the parameters accepted by this applet. Both are strongly recommended constituents of any applet, but they are not required for raw functionality.

Class NavigateButton

6 This class extends `JButton` to provide our custom implementation of an invisible button. It implements the `ActionListener` interface, eliminating the need to add an external listener, and it shows how we can enable mouse events without implementing the `MouseListener` interface.

7 Several parameters are declared in this class:

- `Border m_activeBorder`: The border which will be used when the button is active (when the mouse cursor is moved over the button).
- `Border m_inactiveBorder`: The border which will be used when the button is inactive (when no mouse cursor is over the button). This will not usually be visible.
- `Applet m_parent`: A reference to the parent applet.
- `String m_text`: The tooltip text for this button.
- `String m_sUrl`: A string representation of the URL (for display in the browser's status bar).
- `URL m_url`: The actual URL to redirect the browser to when a mouse click occurs.

8 The constructor of the `NavigateButton` class takes three parameters: a reference to the parent applet, the tooltip text, and a `String` representation of a URL. It assigns all instance variables and creates a URL from the given `String`. If the URL address cannot be resolved, it is set to `null` (this will disable navigation). The `opaque` property is set to `false` because this component **9** is supposed to be transparent. Notice that this component processes its own `MouseEvents`, which is enabled with the `enableEvents()` method. This button will also receive `Action-Events` by way of implementing `ActionListener` and adding itself as a listener.

10 The `setText()` and `getText()` methods manage the `m_text` (tooltip text) property. They also override the corresponding methods inherited from the `JButton` class.

11 The `processMouseEvent()` method will be called for notification about mouse events on this component. We want to process only two kinds of events: `MOUSE_ENTERED` and `MOUSE_EXITED`. When the mouse enters the button's bounds, we set the border to `m_activeBorder`, change the mouse cursor to the hand cursor, and display the `String` description of the URL in the browser's status bar. When the mouse exits the button's bounds, we perform the opposite actions: set the border to `m_inactiveBorder`, set the mouse cursor to the default cursor, and clear the browser's status bar.

12 The `actionPerformed()` method will be called when the user presses this button (note that we use the inherited `JButton` processing for both mouse *clicks* and the keyboard mnemonic). If both the URL and `AppletContext` instances are not `null`, the `showDocument()` method is called to redirect the browser to the button's URL.

NOTE Do not confuse `AppletContext` with the `AppContext` class we discussed in section 2.5. `AppletContext` is an interface for describing an applet's environment, including information about the document in which it is contained, as well as information about other applets that might also be contained in that document.

The `paintComponent()` method used for this button has a very simple implementation. We just draw the button's border by calling `paintBorder()`. Since this component is not designed to have a UI delegate, we do not need to call `super.paintComponent()` from this method.

5.2.2 Running the code

To run example 5.4 in a web browser, we have constructed the following HTML file:

```
<html>

<head>
<title></title>
</head>

<body>

<OBJECT classid="clsid:8AD9C840-044E-11D1-B3E9-00805F499D93"
WIDTH = 563 HEIGHT = 275  codebase="http://java.sun.com/products/plugin/
1.2/jinstall-12-win32.cab#Version=1,2,0,0">
<PARAM NAME = "CODE" VALUE = "ButtonApplet.class" >
<PARAM NAME = "type" VALUE ="application/x-java-applet;version=1.2">
  <param name="button1" value="49, 134, 161, 22">
  <param name="button2" value="49, 156, 161, 22">
  <param name="button3" value="16, 178, 194, 22">
  <param name="button4" value="85, 200, 125, 22">
  <param name="button5" value="85, 222, 125, 22">
  <param name="image" value="nasa.gif">
  <param name="name1" value="What is Earth Science?">
  <param name="name2" value="Earth Science Missions">
  <param name="name3" value="Science of the Earth System">
  <param name="name4" value="Image Gallery">
  <param name="name5" value="For Kids Only">
  <param name="url1"
   value="http://www.earth.nasa.gov/whatis/index.html">
  <param name="url2"
   value="http://www.earth.nasa.gov/missions/index.html">
  <param name="url3"
   value="http://www.earth.nasa.gov/science/index.html">
  <param name="url4"
   value="http://www.earth.nasa.gov/gallery/index.html">
  <param name="url5"
   value="http://kids.mtpe.hq.nasa.gov/">

<COMMENT>
<EMBED type="application/x-java-applet;version=1.2" CODE = "ButtonAp-
plet.class"
  WIDTH = "563" HEIGHT = "275"
  codebase="./"
```

```
            button1="49, 134, 161, 22"
            button2="49, 156, 161, 22"
            button3="16, 178, 194, 22"
            button4="85, 200, 125, 22"
            button5="85, 222, 125, 22"
            image="nasa.gif"
            name1="What is Earth Science?"
            name2="Earth Science Missions"
            name3="Science of the Earth System"
            name4="Image Gallery"
            name5="For Kids Only"
            url1="http://www.earth.nasa.gov/whatis/index.html"
            url2="http://www.earth.nasa.gov/missions/index.html"
            url3="http://www.earth.nasa.gov/science/index.html"
            url4="http://www.earth.nasa.gov/gallery/index.html"
            url5="http://kids.mtpe.hq.nasa.gov/"
            pluginspage=
               "http://java.sun.com/products/plugin/1.2/plugin-install.html">
<NOEMBED>
</COMMENT>
alt="Your browser understands the &lt;APPLET&gt; tag but isn't
running the applet, for some reason."
Your browser is completely ignoring the &lt;APPLET&gt; tag!
</NOEMBED>
</EMBED>
</OBJECT>
</p>

<p> </p>
</body>
</html>
```

NOTE   The HTML file above works with appletviewer, Netscape Navigator 6.0, and Micro-soft Internet Explorer 5.5. This compatibility is achieved thanks to Java plug-in technology. See http://www.javasoft.com/products/plugin for details on how to write plug-in-compatible HTML files. The downside to this file is that we need to include all applet parameters two times for each web browser.

REFERENCE   For additional information about the Java plug-in and the plug-in HTML converter (a convenient utility to generate plug-in-compliant HTML), see: http://java.sun.com/products/plugin/1.3/features.html.

Figure 5.9 shows `ButtonApplet` running in Netscape Navigator 4.05 using the Java plug-in. Notice how invisible buttons react when the mouse cursor moves over them. Click a button and navigate to one of the NASA sites.

5.3   *CUSTOM BUTTONS, PART II: POLYGONAL BUTTONS*

The approach described in the previous section assumes that all navigational buttons have a rectangular shape. This can be too restrictive for the complex active regions that are needed in the navigation of images such as geographical maps. In example 5.5, we will show how to extend the idea of transparent buttons, developed in the previous example, to transparent non-rectangular buttons.

The `java.awt.Polygon` class is extremely helpful for this purpose, especially the two related methods which follow (see the API documentation for more information):

- `Polygon.contains(int x, int y)`: Returns `true` if a point with the given coordinates is contained inside the `Polygon`.
- `Graphics.drawPolygon(Polygon polygon)`: Draws an outline of a `Polygon` using the given `Graphics` object.

The first method is used in this example to verify that the mouse cursor is located inside a given polygon. The second method will be used to actually draw a polygon representing the bounds of a non-rectangular button.

This seems fairly basic, but there is one significant complication. All Swing components are encapsulated in rectangular bounds; nothing can be done about this. If some component receives a mouse event which occurs in its rectangular bounds, the overlapped underlying components do not have a chance to receive this event. Figure 5.10 illustrates two non-rectangular buttons. The part of Button B that lies under the rectangle of Button A will never receive mouse events and cannot be clicked.

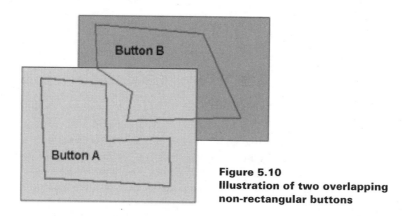

**Figure 5.10
Illustration of two overlapping
non-rectangular buttons**

To resolve this situation, we can skip any mouse event processing in our non-rectangular components. Instead, all mouse events can be directed to the parent container. All buttons can then register themselves as `MouseListeners` and `MouseMotionListeners` with that container. In this way, mouse events can be received without worrying about overlapping and all buttons will receive notification of all events without any preliminary filtering. To minimize the resulting impact on the system's performance, we need to provide a quick discard of events lying outside a button's bounding rectangle.

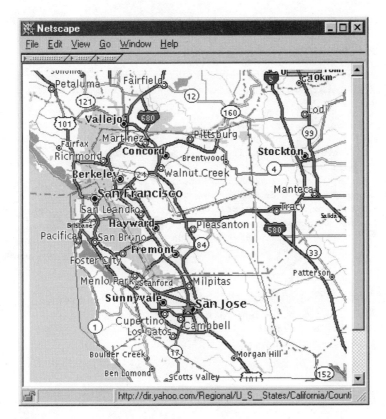

Figure 5.11   Polygonal buttons in an applet

Example 5.5

ButtonApplet2.java

see \Chapter5\5

```java
import java.applet.*;
import java.awt.*;
import java.awt.event.*;
import java.net.*;
import java.util.*;

import javax.swing.*;
import javax.swing.border.*;
import javax.swing.event.*;

public class ButtonApplet2 extends JApplet
{
  public ButtonApplet2() {}

  public synchronized void init() {
    // Unchanged code from example 5.4
```

❶ Like ButtonApplet, but buttons are polygons, instead of just rectangles

```
            int index = 1;
            while(true) {
              String paramSize = getParameter("button"+index);
              String paramName = getParameter("name"+index);
              String paramUrl = getParameter("url"+index);
              if (paramSize==null || paramName==null || paramUrl==null)
                break;

              Polygon p = new Polygon();
              try {
                StringTokenizer tokenizer = new StringTokenizer(
                  paramSize, ",");
                while (tokenizer.hasMoreTokens()) {
                  String str = tokenizer.nextToken().trim();
                  int x = Integer.parseInt(str);
                  str = tokenizer.nextToken().trim();
                  int y = Integer.parseInt(str);
                  p.addPoint(x, y);
                }
              }
              catch (Exception ex) { break; }

              PolygonButton btn = new PolygonButton(this, p,
                paramName, paramUrl);
              bigLabel.add(btn);

              index++;
            }

            getContentPane().setLayout(null);
            getContentPane().add(bigLabel);
            bigLabel.setBounds(0, 0, bigImage.getIconWidth(),
            bigImage.getIconHeight());
          }

          public String getAppletInfo() {
            return "Sample applet with PolygonButtons";
          }

          public String[][] getParameterInfo() {
            String pinfo[][] = {
              {"image",   "string",   "base image file name"},
              {"buttonX","x1,y1, x2,y2, ...", "button's bounds"},
              {"nameX",   "string",   "tooltip text"},
              {"urlX",    "url",      "link URL"} };
            return pinfo;
          }
        }

class PolygonButton extends JComponent
 implements MouseListener, MouseMotionListener
{
  static public Color ACTIVE_COLOR = Color.red;
  static public Color INACTIVE_COLOR = Color. darkGray;

  protected JApplet m_parent;
```

1 Form polygon from unspecified number of integer coordinates

1 Format of polygon coordinates

2 Replaces NavigateButton from previous example, but gets all mouse events from parent to check against polygon

```
protected String m_text;
protected String m_sUrl;
protected URL     m_url;

protected Polygon m_polygon;
protected Rectangle m_rc;
protected boolean m_active;

protected static PolygonButton m_currentButton;

public PolygonButton(JApplet parent, Polygon p,
 String text, String sUrl)
{
  m_parent = parent;
  m_polygon = p;
  setText(text);
  m_sUrl = sUrl;
  try {
    m_url = new URL(sUrl);
  }
  catch(Exception ex) { m_url = null; }

  setOpaque(false);

  m_parent.addMouseListener(this);
  m_parent.addMouseMotionListener(this);

  m_rc = new Rectangle(m_polygon.getBounds()); // Bug alert!
  m_rc.grow(1, 1);

  setBounds(m_rc);
  m_polygon.translate(-m_rc.x, -m_rc.y);
}
public void setText(String text) { m_text = text; }

public String getText() { return m_text; }

public void mouseMoved(MouseEvent e) {
    if (!m_rc.contains(e.getX(), e.getY()) || e.isConsumed()) {
      if (m_active)
        setState(false);
      return; // Quickly return, if outside our rectangle
    }
    int x = e.getX() - m_rc.x;
    int y = e.getY() - m_rc.y;
    boolean active = m_polygon.contains(x, y);

    if (m_active != active)
      setState(active);
    if (m_active)
      e.consume();
}
public void mouseDragged(MouseEvent e) {}

protected void setState(boolean active) {
  m_active = active;
  repaint();
```

3 This component listens to parent's events

4 Create bounding rectangle

5 Compare against polygon; fix activation state

6 Translate event coordinates to button coordinates and set state accordingly

7 Resets active button; redraws component, cursor, and URL

```
        if (m_active) {
          if (m_currentButton != null)
            m_currentButton.setState(false);
          m_currentButton = this;
          m_parent.setCursor(Cursor.getPredefinedCursor(
            Cursor.HAND_CURSOR));
          m_parent.showStatus(m_sUrl);
        }
        else {
          m_currentButton = null;
          m_parent.setCursor(Cursor.getPredefinedCursor(
            Cursor.DEFAULT_CURSOR));
          m_parent.showStatus("");
        }
      }

      public void mouseClicked(MouseEvent e) {
        if (m_active && m_url != null && !e.isConsumed()) {
          AppletContext context = m_parent.getAppletContext();
          if (context != null)
            context.showDocument(m_url);
          e.consume();
        }
      }
      public void mousePressed(MouseEvent e) {}
      public void mouseReleased(MouseEvent e) {}
      public void mouseExited(MouseEvent e) { mouseMoved(e); }
      public void mouseEntered(MouseEvent e) { mouseMoved(e); }

      public void paintComponent(Graphics g) {
        g.setColor(m_active ? ACTIVE_COLOR : INACTIVE_COLOR);
        g.drawPolygon(m_polygon);
      }
    }
}
```

❽ If mouse click is for this button, then show the URL document

❾ Draws Red if active, Grey if inactive

5.3.1 Understanding the code

Class ButtonApplet2

❶ This class is a slightly modified version of the ButtonApplet class in the previous section; it accommodates polygonal button sizes rather than rectangles (the parser has been modified to read in an arbitrary number of points). Now it creates a Polygon instance and parses a data string, which is assumed to contain pairs of comma-separated coordinates, adding each coordinate to the Polygon using the the addPoint() method. The resulting Polygon instance is used to create a new PolygonButton component.

Class PolygonButton

❷ This class serves as a replacement for the NavigateButton class in the previous example. Notice that it extends JComponent directly. This is necessary to disassociate any mouse handling inherent in buttons (the mouse handling is actually built into the button UI delegates). Remember, we want to handle mouse events ourselves, but we want them each to be sent from within the parent's bounds to each `PolygonButton`, not from each `PolygonButton` to the parent.

> **NOTE**   This is the opposite way of working with mouse listeners than we are used to. The idea may take a few moments to sink in because directing events from child to parent is so much more common that we generally don't think of things the other way around.

So, to be notified of mouse events from the parent, we'll need to implement the `MouseListener` and `MouseMotionListener` interfaces.

Four new instance variables are declared:

- `Polygon m_polygon`: The polygonal region representing this button's bounds.
- `Rectangle m_rc`: This button's bounding rectangle as seen in the coordinate space of the *parent*.
- `boolean m_active`: The flag indicating that this button is active.
- `PolygonButton m_currentButton`: A static reference to the instance of this class which is currently active.

③ The constructor of the `PolygonButton` class takes four parameters: a reference to the parent applet, the `Polygon` instance representing this component's bounds, the tooltip text, and a `String` representation of a URL. It assigns all instance variables and instantiates a URL using the associated `String` parameter (similar to what we saw in the last example). This component adds itself to the parent applet as a `MouseListener` and a `MouseMotionListener`:

```
m_parent.addMouseListener(this);
m_parent.addMouseMotionListener(this);
```

④ The bounding rectangle `m_rc` is computed with the `Polygon.getBounds()` method. This method does not create a new instance of the `Rectangle` class, but it does return a reference to an internal `Polygon` instance variable which is subject to change. This is not safe, so we must explicitly create a new `Rectangle` instance from the supplied reference. This `Rectangle`'s bounds are expanded (using its `grow()` method) to take border width into account. Finally, the `Rectangle m_rc` is set as the button's bounding region, and the `Polygon` is translated into the component's local coordinates by shifting its origin using its `translate()` method.

⑤ The `mouseMoved()` method is invoked when mouse events occur in the parent container. We first quickly check whether the event lies inside our bounding rectangle and if it has not yet been consumed by another component. If both conditions are met, we continue processing this event; otherwise, our method returns. Before we return, however, we first must check whether this button is still active for some reason—this can happen if the mouse cursor moves too fast out of this button's bounds, and the given component did not receive a `MOUSE_EXITED` MouseEvent to deactivate itself. If this is the case, we deactivate the button and then exit the `mouseMoved()` method.

⑥ We next manually translate the coordinates of the event into our button's local system (remember that this is an event from the parent container) and check whether the point lies within our polygon. This gives us a boolean result which should indicate whether this component is currently active or inactive. If our button's current activation state (`m_active`) is not equal to this value, we call the `setState()` method to change it so that it is. Finally, if this component is active, we consume the given `MouseEvent` to avoid activation of two components simultaneously.

7 The `setState()` method is called, as described above, to set a new activation state of this component. It takes a boolean value as a parameter and stores it in the `m_active` instance variable. Then it repaints the component to reflect a change in state, if any. Depending on the state of the `m_active` flag in the `setState()` method, one of the following will happen:

- If the `m_active` flag is set to `true`, this method checks the static reference to the currently active button stored in the `m_currentButton` static variable. In the case where this reference still points to some other component (again, it potentially can happen if the mouse cursor moves too quickly out of a component's rectangular bounds), we force that component to be inactive. Then we store a `this` reference as the `m_currentButton` static variable, letting all the other buttons know that this button is now the currently active one. We then change the mouse cursor to the hand cursor (as in the previous example) and display our URL in the browser's status bar.

- If the `m_active` flag is set to `false`, this method sets the `m_currentButton` static variable to `null`, changes the mouse cursor to the default cursor, and clears the browser's status bar.

8 The `mouseClicked()` method checks whether this component is active (this implies that the mouse cursor is located within our polygon, and not just within the bounding rectangle), the URL is resolved, and the mouse event is not consumed. If all three checks are satisfied, this method redirects the browser to the component's associated URL and consumes the mouse event to avoid processing by any other components.

The rest of this class's methods, implemented due to the `MouseListener` and `MouseMotionListener` interfaces, receive empty bodies, except for `mouseExited()` and `mouseEntered()`. Both of these methods send all their traffic to the `mouseMoved()` method to notify the component that the cursor has left or has entered the container, respectively.

9 The `paintComponent()` method simply draws the component's `Polygon` in gray if it's inactive, and in red if it's active.

> **NOTE** We've purposefully avoided including tooltip text for these non-rectangular buttons because the underlying Swing `ToolTipManager` essentially relies on the rectangular shape of the components it manages. Somehow, invoking the Swing tooltip API destroys our model of processing mouse events. In order to allow tooltips, we have to develop our own version of a tooltip manager—this is the subject of the next example.

5.3.2 Running the code

To run this code in a web browser, we have constructed the following HTML file (see the Java plug-in and Java plug-in HTML converter notes in the previous example):

```
<html>
<head>
<title></title>
</head>
<body>
```

```
<OBJECT classid="clsid:8AD9C840-044E-11D1-B3E9-00805F499D93"
WIDTH = 400 HEIGHT = 380  codebase="http://java.sun.com/products/plugin/
1.2/jinstall-12-win32.cab#Version=1,2,0,0">
<PARAM NAME = "CODE" VALUE = "ButtonApplet2.class" >
<PARAM NAME = "type"
       VALUE ="application/x-java-applet;version=1.2">
<param name="image" value="bay_area.gif">

<param name="button1"
       value="112,122, 159,131, 184,177, 284,148, 288,248, 158,250,
100,152">
<param name="name1" value="Alameda County">
<param name="url1"
       value="http://dir.yahoo.com/Regional/U_S__States/
California/Counties_and_Regions/Alameda_County/">

<param name="button2"
       value="84,136, 107,177, 76,182, 52,181, 51,150">
<param name="name2" value="San Francisco County">
<param name="url2"
       value="http://dir.yahoo.com/Regional/U_S__States/
California/Counties_and_Regions/San_Francisco_County/">

<param name="button3"
       value="156,250, 129,267, 142,318, 235,374, 361,376, 360,347, 311,324,
291,250">
<param name="name3" value="Santa Clara County">
<param name="url3"
       value="http://dir.yahoo.com/Regional/U_S__States/
California/Counties_and_Regions/Santa_Clara_County/">

<param name="button4"
       value="54,187, 111,180, 150,246, 130,265, 143,318, 99,346, 63,314">
<param name="name4" value="San Mateo County">
<param name="url4"
       value="http://dir.yahoo.com/Regional/U_S__States/
California/Counties_and_Regions/San_Mateo_County/">

<param name="button5"
       value="91,71, 225,79, 275,62, 282,147, 185,174, 160,129, 95,116,
79,97">
<param name="name5" value="Contra Costa County">
<param name="url5"
       value="http://dir.yahoo.com/Regional/U_S__States/
California/Counties_and_Regions/Contra_Costa_County/">

<COMMENT>
<EMBED type="application/x-java-applet;version=1.2" CODE =
"ButtonApplet2.class"
  WIDTH = "400" HEIGHT = "380"
  codebase="./"
  image="bay_area.gif"
  button1="112,122, 159,131, 184,177, 284,148, 288,248, 158,250, 100,152"
  name1="Alameda County"
```

```
    url1="http://dir.yahoo.com/Regional/U_S__States/California/
Counties_and_Regions/Alameda_County/"
    button2="84,136, 107,177, 76,182, 52,181, 51,150"
    name2="San Francisco County"
    url2="http://dir.yahoo.com/Regional/U_S__States/California/
Counties_and_Regions/San_Francisco_County/"
    button3="156,250, 129,267, 142,318, 235,374, 361,376, 360,347, 311,324,
291,250"
    name3="Santa Clara County"
    url3="http://dir.yahoo.com/Regional/U_S__States/California/
Counties_and_Regions/Santa_Clara_County/"
    button4="54,187, 111,180, 150,246, 130,265, 143,318, 99,346, 63,314"
    name4="San Mateo County"
    url4="http://dir.yahoo.com/Regional/U_S__States/California/
Counties_and_Regions/San_Mateo_County/"
    button5="91,71, 225,79, 275,62, 282,147, 185,174, 160,129, 95,116, 79,97"
    name5="Contra Costa County"
    url5="http://dir.yahoo.com/Regional/U_S__States/California/
Counties_and_Regions/Contra_Costa_County/"
    pluginspage="http://java.sun.com/products/plugin/1.2/plugin-
install.html">
<NOEMBED></COMMENT>
alt="Your browser understands the &lt;APPLET&gt; tag but isn't running the
applet, for some reason."
        Your browser is completely ignoring the &lt;APPLET&gt; tag!
</NOEMBED>
</EMBED>
</OBJECT>
</p>

<p> </p>
</body>
</html>
```

Figure 5.10 shows the ButtonApplet2 example running in Netscape 4.05 with the Java plug-in. Our HTML file has been constructed to display an active map of the San Francisco bay area. Five non-rectangular buttons correspond to this area's five counties. Watch how the non-rectangular buttons react when the mouse cursor moves in and out of their boundaries. Verify that they behave correctly even if a part of a given button lies under the bounding rectangle of another button (a good place to check is the sharp border between Alameda and Contra Costa counties). Click over the button and notice the navigation to one of the Yahoo sites containing information about the selected county.

It is clear that tooltip displays would help to dispel any confusion as to which county is which. The next example shows how to implement this feature.

5.4   CUSTOM BUTTONS, PART III: TOOLTIP MANAGEMENT

In this section we'll discuss how to implement custom management of tooltips in a Swing application. If you're completely satisfied with the default ToolTipManager provided with

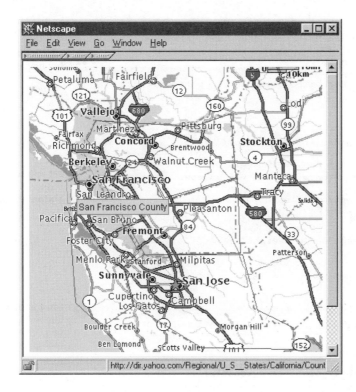

**Figure 5.12
Polygonal buttons
with a custom
tooltip manager**

Swing, you can skip this section. But there may be situations when this default implementation is not satisfactory, as in our example above using non-rectangular components.

In example 5.6, we will construct our own version of a tooltip manager to display a tooltip window if the mouse cursor rests over some point inside a button's polygonal area longer than a specified time interval. It will be displayed for a specified amount of time; then, to avoid annoying the user, we will hide the tooltip window until the mouse cursor moves to a new position. In designing our tooltip manager, we will take a different approach than that taken by Swing's default `ToolTipManager` (see 5.1.12). Instead of using three different `Timers`, we will use just one. This involves tracking more information, but it is slightly more efficient because it avoids the handling of multiple `ActionEvents`.

Example 5.6

ButtonApplet3.java

see \Chapter5\6

```
import java.applet.*;
import java.awt.*;
import java.awt.event.*;
import java.net.*;
import java.util.*;

import javax.swing.*;
```

```
import javax.swing.border.*;
import javax.swing.event.*;

public class ButtonApplet3 extends JApplet
{
    protected CustomToolTipManager m_manager;

    public ButtonApplet3() {}

    public synchronized void init() {
        // Unchanged code from example 5.5

        m_manager = new CustomToolTipManager(this);
        PolygonButton.m_toolTip = m_manager.m_toolTip;

        getContentPane().setLayout(null);
        getContentPane().add(bigLabel);
        bigLabel.setBounds(0, 0, bigImage.getIconWidth(),
            bigImage.getIconHeight());
    }

    // Unchanged code from example 5.5
}

class PolygonButton extends JComponent
 implements MouseListener, MouseMotionListener
{
    // Unchanged code from example 5.5

    public static JToolTip m_toolTip;

    protected void setState(boolean active) {
        m_active = active;
        repaint();
        if (active) {
            if (m_currentButton != null)
                m_currentButton.setState(false);
            m_parent.setCursor(Cursor.getPredefinedCursor(
                Cursor.HAND_CURSOR));
            m_parent.showStatus(m_sUrl);
            if (m_toolTip != null)
                m_toolTip.setTipText(m_text);
        }
        else {
            m_currentButton = null;
            m_parent.setCursor(Cursor.getPredefinedCursor(
                Cursor.DEFAULT_CURSOR));
            m_parent.showStatus("");
            if (m_toolTip != null)
                m_toolTip.setTipText(null);
        }
    }
}

class CustomToolTipManager extends MouseMotionAdapter
 implements ActionListener
{
```

1 Like ButtonApplet2, but manages tooltips

2 Set sole tooltip instance for all buttons in applet

3 Same as in ButtonApplet2, but sets "global" tooltip to tooltip for this button

4 TooltipManager that doesn't assume rectangular components

```
      protected Timer m_timer;
      protected int m_lastX = -1;
      protected int m_lastY = -1;
      protected boolean m_moved = false;
      protected int m_counter = 0;

      public JToolTip m_toolTip = new JToolTip();

      CustomToolTipManager(JApplet parent) {
          parent.addMouseMotionListener(this);
          m_toolTip.setTipText(null);
          parent.getContentPane().add(m_toolTip);
          m_toolTip.setVisible(false);
          m_timer = new Timer(1000, this);
          m_timer.start();
      }

      public void mouseMoved(MouseEvent e) {
          m_moved = true;
          m_counter = -1;
          m_lastX = e.getX();
          m_lastY = e.getY();
          if (m_toolTip.isVisible()) {
            m_toolTip.setVisible(false);
            m_toolTip.getParent().repaint();
          }
      }

      public void actionPerformed(ActionEvent e) {
          if (m_moved || m_counter==0 || m_toolTip.getTipText()==null) {
              if (m_toolTip.isVisible())
                m_toolTip.setVisible(false);
              m_moved = false;
              return;
          }

          if (m_counter < 0) {
            m_counter = 4;
            m_toolTip.setVisible(true);
            Dimension d = m_toolTip.getPreferredSize();
            m_toolTip.setBounds(m_lastX, m_lastY+20,
            d.width, d.height);
          }
          m_counter--;
      }
  }
}
```

⑤ Listens for mouse events on parent; installs tooltip in parent; installs timer to check and control tooltip state

⑥ Mouse has moved, so reset tooltip state

⑦ Called for Timer events; hides or displays tooltip

⑧ If ready to display tooltip, set it up to display for about 4 seconds, over the last mouse position

5.4.1   Understanding the code

Class ButtonApplet3

❶ This class requires very few modifications from ButtonApplet2 in the last section. It declares and creates CustomToolTipManager m_manager and passes a this reference to it:

```
m_manager = new MyToolTipManager(this);
```

As you will see below, our `CustomToolTipManager` class manages a publicly accessible `JToolTip`, `m_toolTip`. `CustomToolTipManager` itself is not intended to provide any meaningful content to this tooltip. Rather, this is to be done by other components—in our case, by `PolygonButtons`. Thus, our `PolygonButton` class declares a `static` reference to a `JToolTip` component. Whenever a button becomes active, this `JToolTip`'s text will be assigned to that of the active button. So, when we create our instance of `CustomToolTipManager`, we assign its publicly accessible `JToolTip` as our `Polygon` class's static `JToolTip` (which is also publicly accessible):

<code>PolygonButton.m_toolTip = m_manager.m_toolTip;</code>

Thus, only one `JToolTip` instance will exist for the lifetime of this applet, and both `CustomToolTipManager` and our `PolygonButtons` have control over it.

Class PolygonButton

❸ As we've mentioned earlier, this class now declares the static variable `JToolTip m_toolTip`. The `PolygonButton` class does not initialize this reference. However, this reference is checked during `PolygonButton` activation in the `setState()` method. If `m_toolTip` is not `null` (set to point to a valid tooltip window by some outer class, which, in our example, is done in the `ButtonApplet3` `init()` method shown above), the `setTipText()` method is invoked to set the proper text while the mouse cursor hovers over the button.

Class CustomToolTipManager

❹ This class represents a custom tooltip manager which is free from assumption of the rectangularity of its child components. It extends the `MouseMotionAdapter` class and implements the `ActionListener` interface to work as both a `MouseMotionListener` and an `ActionListener`. Six instance variables are declared:

- `Timer m_timer`: Our managing timer.
- `int m_lastX, m_lastY`: The last coordinates of the mouse cursor, these two variables are reassigned each time the mouse is moved.
- `boolean m_moved`: A flag indicating that the mouse cursor has moved.
- `int m_counter`: The time ticks counter that is used to manage the tooltip's time to live (see below).
- `JToolTip m_toolTip`: The tooltip component to be displayed.

❺ The constructor of the `CustomToolTipManager` class takes a reference to the parenting `JApplet` as a parameter and registers itself as a `MouseMotionListener` on this component. Then it creates the `JToolTip m_toolTip` component and adds it to the applet's content pane. `m_toolTip` is set invisible, using `setVisible(false)`; it can then be used by any interested class by repositioning it and calling `setVisible(true)`. Finally, a `Timer` with a 1000ms delay time is created and started.

❻ The `mouseMoved()` method will be invoked when the mouse cursor moves over the applet. It sets the `m_moved` flag to `true`, `m_counter` to `-1`, and stores the coordinates of the mouse cursor. Then this method hides the tooltip component if it's visible.

⑦ The `actionPerformed()` method is called when the `Timer` fires events (see section 2.6 for details). It implements the logic of displaying/hiding the tooltip window based on two instance variables: m_moved and m_counter:

```
if (m_moved || m_counter==0 || m_toolTip.getTipText()==null) {
  if (m_toolTip.isVisible())
    m_toolTip.setVisible(false);
  m_moved = false;
  return;
}
```

The block of code above is invoked when any one of the following statements are true:

1. The mouse cursor has been moved since the last time tick.
2. The counter has reached zero.
3. No tooltip text is set.

In any of these cases, the tooltip component is hidden (if it was previously visible), and the m_moved flag is set to `false`. The m_counter variable remains unchanged.

```
if (m_counter < 0) {
  m_counter = 4;
  m_toolTip.setVisible(true);
  Dimension d = m_toolTip.getPreferredSize();
  m_toolTip.setBounds(m_lastX, m_lastY+20,
  d.width, d.height);
}
```

⑧ The above block of code is responsible for displaying the tooltip component. It will be executed only when m_counter is equal to –1 (set by `mouseMoved()`), and when the m_moved flag is `false` (cleared by the previous code fragment). m_counter is set to 4, which determines the amount of time the tooltip will be displayed (4000ms in this example). Then we make the tooltip component visible and place it at the current mouse location with a vertical offset approximately equal to the mouse cursor's height. This construction provides an arbitrary delay between the time when mouse motion stops and the tooltip is displayed.

The last line of code in the `actionPerformed()` method is m_counter--, which decrements the counter each time tick until it reaches 0. As we saw above, once it reaches 0 the tooltip will be hidden.

> **NOTE** The actual delay time may vary from 1000ms to 2000ms since the mouse movements and time ticks are not synchronized. A more accurate and complex implementation could start a new timer after each mouse movement, as is done in Swing's `ToolTipManager`.

The following table illustrates how the m_counter and m_moved variables control this behavior.

Table 5.1 `m_counter` and `m_moved` variables

Timer tick	m_moved flag	m_counter before	m_counter after	Comment
0	false	0	0	
1	true	−1	−1	Mouse moved between 0th and 1st ticks.
2	false	−1	4	Tooltip is displayed.
3	false	4	3	
4	false	3	2	
5	false	2	1	
6	false	1	0	
7	false	0	0	Tooltip is hidden.
8	false	0	0	Waiting for the next mouse move.

5.4.2   Running the code

Figure 5.12 shows `ButtonApplet3` running in Netscape Navigator 4.05 with the Java plug-in. You can use the same HTML file that was presented in the previous section. Move the mouse cursor over some non-rectangular component and note how it displays the proper tooltip message. This tooltip disappears after a certain amount of time or when the mouse is moved to a new location.

C H A P T E R   6

Tabbed panes

6.1   JTABBEDPANE

class javax.swing.JTabbedPane

JTabbedPane is simply a stack of components in selectable layers. Each layer can contain one component which is normally a container. Tab extensions are used to move a given layer to the front of the tabbed pane view. These tab extensions are similar to labels in that they can have assigned text, an icon (as well as a disabled icon), background and foreground colors, and a tooltip.

To add a component to a tabbed pane, you use one of its overloaded add() methods. This creates a new selectable tab and reorganizes the other tab extensions, if necessary, so the new one will fit. You can also use the addTab() and insertTab() methods to create new selectable layers. The remove() method takes a component as a parameter and removes the tab associated with that component, if there is one.

Tab extensions can reside to the north, south, east, or west of the tabbed pane's content. The location is specified using its setTabPlacement() method and passing one of the corresponding SwingConstants fields as a parameter.

Vertical or horizontal tabs?   When is it best to choose between vertical or horizontal tabs?

Three possible rules of thumb help make the decision whether to place tabs horizontally or vertically. First, consider the nature of the data to be displayed. Is vertical or horizontal space at a premium within the available display space? If, for example, you have a list with a single column but 200 entries, then clearly vertical space is at a premium. If you have a table with only 10 entries but 15 columns, then horizontal space is at a premium. Simply place the tabs where space is cheaper to obtain. In the first example with the long list, place the tabs vertically so they use horizontal space which is available. In the second example, place the tabs horizontally so you use vertical space which is available while horizontal space is completely taken by the table columns.

The second rule concerns the number and size of the tabs. If you need to display 12 tabs, for example, each with a long label, then it is unlikely that these will fit across the screen horizontally. In this case you are more likely to fit them by placing them vertically. Using space in these ways when introducing a tabbed pane should minimize the introduction of scroll panes and maximize ease of use. Finally, the third rule of thumb is to consider the layout and mouse movements required for operating the software. If, for example, your application uses a toolbar, then it may make sense to align the tabs close to the toolbar, thus minimizing mouse movements between the toolbar buttons and the tabs. If you have a horizontal toolbar across the top of the screen, then choose a horizontal set of tabs across the top (to the north).

JAVA 1.4   As of Java 1.4 you can choose whether tabs should wrap to form rows of tabs, or whether they should always form one scrollable row of column. When in the latter form two buttons appear for scrolling through the existing tabs.

The tab layout policy can be assigned with the new `setTabLayoutPolicy()` method. This method takes either of the following as a parameter:

```
JTabbedPane.WRAP_TAB_LAYOUT
JTabbedPane.SCROLL_TAB_LAYOUT
```

Example 6.1, along with the corresponding figures, illustrates this new feature.

You can get and set the selected tab index at any given time using its `getSelectedIndex()` and `setSelectedIndex()` methods respectively. You can get/set the component associated with the selected tab similarly, using the `getSelectedComponent()` and `setSelectedComponent()` methods.

One or more `ChangeListeners` can be added to a `JTabbedPane`, which gets registered with its model (an instance of `DefaultSingleSelectionModel` by default—see chapter 12 for more information about `SingleSelectionModel` and `DefaultSingleSelectionModel`). When a new tab is selected, the model will send out `ChangeEvents` to all registered `ChangeListeners`. The `stateChanged()` method of each listener is invoked, so you can capture and perform any desired actions when the user selects any tab. `JTabbed-`

Pane also fires `PropertyChangeEvents` whenever its model or tab placement properties change state.

GUIDELINE

Transaction boundaries and tabbed panes   If you're using a tabbed pane within a dialog, the transaction boundary is normally clear—it will be an OK or Cancel button on the dialog. In this case, it is obvious that the OK and Cancel buttons would lie outside the tabbed pane and in the dialog itself. This is an important point. Place action buttons which terminate a transaction outside the tabbed panes. If, for example, you had a tabbed pane which contained a Save and Cancel button within the first tab, would it be clear that the Save and Cancel buttons work across all tabs or only on the first? Actually, it can be very ambiguous. To clearly define the transaction, define the buttons outside the tabbed pane so it is clear to the user that any changes made to any tab will be accepted or saved when OK or Save is pressed or discarded when Cancel is pressed. The action buttons will then apply across the complete set of tabs.

6.2   A DYNAMICALLY CHANGEABLE TABBED PANE

We will now turn to a `JTabbedPane` example applet that demonstrates a dynamically reconfigurable tab layout as well as the addition and removal of any number of tabs. A `Change-Listener` is attached to the tabbed pane to listen for tab selection events and to display the currently selected tab index in a status bar. For enhanced feedback, audio clips are played when the tab layout changes and whenever a tab is added and removed. Example 6.1 contains the code.

Example 6.1

TabbedPaneDemo.java

see \Chapter6\1

```java
import java.awt.*;
import java.applet.*;
import java.awt.event.*;
import javax.swing.*;
import javax.swing.event.*;
import javax.swing.border.*;

public class TabbedPaneDemo extends JApplet
  implements ActionListener {

    private ImageIcon m_tabimage;
    private ImageIcon m_utsguy;
    private ImageIcon m_jfcgirl;
    private ImageIcon m_sbeguy;
    private ImageIcon m_tiger;
    private JTabbedPane m_tabbedPane;
```

❶ Images for tab extensions and container

```
   private JRadioButton m_topButton;
   private JRadioButton m_bottomButton;
   private JRadioButton m_leftButton;
   private JRadioButton m_rightButton;
   private JRadioButton m_wrapButton;
   private JRadioButton m_scrollButton;
   private JButton m_addButton;
   private JButton m_removeButton;
   private JLabel m_status;
   private JLabel m_loading;
   private AudioClip m_layoutsound;
   private AudioClip m_tabsound;

   public void init() {
     m_loading = new JLabel("Initializing applet...",
       SwingConstants.CENTER);
     getContentPane().add(m_loading);

     Thread initialize = new Thread() {
       public void run() {
         try {
           m_tabimage = new
             ImageIcon(getClass().getResource("ball.gif"));
           m_utsguy = new
             ImageIcon(getClass().getResource("utsguy.gif"));
           m_jfcgirl = new
             ImageIcon(getClass().getResource("jfcgirl.gif"));
```

① Buttons to
control tab
alignment

① Buttons to
control tab
layout

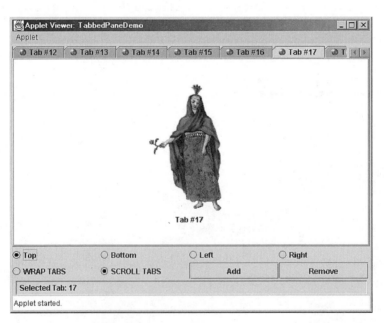

Figure 6.1 `TabbedPaneDemo` **showing** `SCROLL_TAB_LAYOUT` **policy
with TOP alignment**

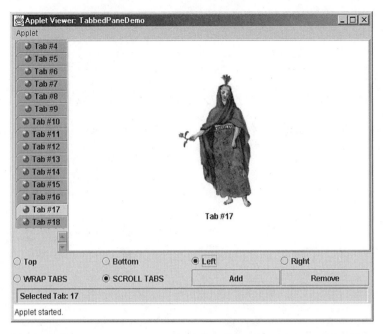

Figure 6.2 `TabbedPaneDemo` showing `SCROLL_TAB_LAYOUT` policy
with **LEFT alignment**

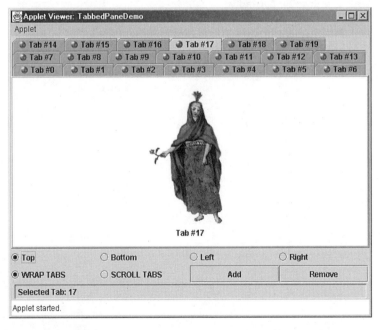

Figure 6.3 `TabbedPaneDemo` showing `WRAP_TAB_LAYOUT` policy
with **TOP alignment**

```
m_sbeguy = new
    ImageIcon(getClass().getResource("sbeguy.gif"));
m_tiger = new
    ImageIcon(getClass().getResource("tiger.gif"));
m_tabbedPane = newJTabbedPane(SwingConstants.TOP);

m_topButton = new JRadioButton("TOP");
m_bottomButton = new JRadioButton("BOTTOM");
m_leftButton = new JRadioButton("LEFT");
m_rightButton = new JRadioButton("RIGHT");
m_addButton = new JButton("Add");
m_removeButton = new JButton("Remove");

m_wrapButton = new JRadioButton("WRAP TABS");
m_scrollButton = new JRadioButton("SCROLL TABS");

m_topButton.setSelected(true);
buttonGroup bgAlignment = new ButtonGroup();
bgAlignment.add(m_topButton);
bgAlignment.add(m_botomButton);
bgAlignment.add(m_leftButton);
bgAlignment.add(m_rightBtton);

m_wrapButton.setSelected(true);
ButtonGroup bgScrollMode = new ButtonGroup();
bgScrollMode.add(m_wrapButton);
bgScrollMode.add(m_scrollButton);

m_topButton.addActionListener(TabbedPaneDemo.this);
m_bottomButton.addActionListener(TabbedPaneDemo.this);
m_leftButton.addActionListener(TabbedPaneDemo.this);
m_rightButton.addActionListener(TabbedPaneDemo.this);
m_addButton.addActionListener(TabbedPaneDemo.this);
m_removeButton.addActionListener(TabbedPaneDemo.this);
m_wrapButton.addActionListener(TabbedPaneDemo.this);
m_scrollButton.addActionListener(TabbedPaneDemo.this);

JPanel buttonPanel.new JPanel();
buttonPanel.setLayout(new GridLayout(2,4));
buttonPanel.add(m_topButton);
buttonPanel.add(m_bottomButton);
buttonPanel.add(m_leftButton);
buttonPanel.add(m_rightButton);
buttonPanel.add(m_wraptButton);
buttonPanel.add(m_scrolltButton);
buttonPanel.add(m_addButton);
buttonPanel.add(m_removeButton);

m_status = new JLabel();
m_status.setForeground(Color.black);
m_status.setBorder(new CompoundBorder(
new EmptyBorder(2, 5, 2, 5),
new SoftBevelBorder(SoftBevelBorder.LOWERED)));

JPanel lowerPanel = new JPanel();
lowerPanel.setLayout(new BorderLayout());
```

2 **Buttons in GridLayout**

```
      lowerPanel.add(buttonPanel, BorderLayout.CENTER);
      lowerPanel.add(m_status, Borderlayout.SOUTH);

      for (int i=0; i<20; i++) {
        createTab();
      }

      getContentPane().removeAll();
      getContentPane().setLayout(new BorderLayout());
      getcontentPane(). add(m_tabbedPane, BorderLayout.CENTER);
      getContentPane().add(lowerPanel, BorderLayout.SOUTH);

      m_tabbedPane.addChangeListener(new TabChangeListener());
      m_layoutsound = getAudioClip(getCodeBase(), "switch.wav");
      m_tabsound = getAudioClip(getCodeBase(), "tab.wav");

      getContentPane().remove(m_loading);
      getRootPane().revalidate();
      getRootPane().repaint();
    }
    catch (Exception ex) {
      ex.printStackTrace();
    }
  }
};
    initialize.start();
}

public void createTab() {
  JLabel label = null;
  switch (m_tabbedPane.getTabCount()%4) {
    case 0:
      label = new JLabel("Tab #" + m_tabbedPane.getTabCount(),
        m_utsguy, SwingConstants.CENTER);
      break;
    case 1:
      label = new JLabel("Tab #" + m_tabbedPane.getTabCount(),
        m_jfcgirl, SwingConstants.CENTER);
      break;
    case 2:
      label = new JLabel("Tab #" + m_tabbedPane.getTabCount(),
        m_sbeguy, SwingConstants.CENTER);
      break;
    case 3:
      label = new JLabel("Tab #" + m_tabbedPane.getTabCount(),
        m_tiger, SwingConstants.CENTER);
      break;
  }
  label.setVerticalTextPosition(SwingConstants.BOTTOM);
  label.setHorizontalTextPosition(SwingConstants.CENTER);
  label.setOpaque(true);
  label.setBackground(Color.white);
  m_tabbedPane.addTab("Tab #" + m_tabbedPane.getTabCount(),
    m_tabimage, label);
```

❸ Creates a tab with image icon

```java
    m_tabbedPane.setSelectedIndex(m_tabbedPane.getTabCount()-1);
    setStatus(m_tabbedPane.getSelectedIndex());
}

public void killTab() {
  if (m_tabbedPane.getTabCount() > 0) {
    m_tabbedPane.removeTabAt(m_tabbedPane.getTabCount()-1);
    setStatus(m_tabbedPane.getSelectedIndex());
  }
  else
    setStatus(-1);
}

public void setStatus(int index) {
  if (index > -1)
    m_status.setText(" Selected Tab: " + index);
  else
    m_status.setText(" No Tab Selected");
}

public void actionPerformed(ActionEvent e) {
  if (e.getSource() == m_topButton) {
    m_tabbedPane.setTabPlacement(SwingConstants.TOP);
    m_layoutsound.play();
  }
  else if(e.getSource() == m_bottomButton) {
    m_tabbedPane.setTabPlacement(SwingConstants.BOTTOM);
    m_layoutsound.play();
  }
  else if(e.getSource() == m_leftButton) {
    m_tabbedPane.setTabPlacement(SwingConstants.LEFT);
    m_layoutsound.play();
  }
  else if(e.getSource() == m_rightButton) {
    m_tabbedPane.setTabPlacement(SwingConstants.RIGHT);
    m_layoutsound.play();
  }
  else if(e.getSource() == m_wrapButton) {
    m_tabbedPane.setTabLayoutPolicy(
      JTabbedPane.WRAP_TAB_LAYOUT);
    m_layoutsound.play();
  }

  else if(e.getSource() == m_scrollButton) {
    m_tabbedPane.setTabLayoutPolicy(
      JTabbedPane.SROLL_TAB_LAYOUT);
    m_layoutsound.play();
  }

  else if(e.getSource() == m_addButton)
    createTab();
  else if(e.getSource() == m_removeButton)
    killTab();
  m_tabbedPane.revalidate();
```

4 Removes tab with the highest index

5 Update status label with selected tab index

6 Called when one of the buttons is clicked; changes tab orientation or adds/removes tab

```
        m_tabbedPane.repaint();
    }

    class TabChangeListener implements ChangeListener {
        public void stateChanged(ChangeEvent e) {
            setStatus(
                ((JTabbedPane) e.getSource()).getSelectedIndex());
            m_tabsound.play();
        }
    }
}
```

(7) **Plays sound when tab set**

6.2.1   Understanding the code

Class TabbedPaneDemo

TabbedPaneDemo extends JApplet and implements ActionListener to listen for button events. Several instance variables are used:

(1)
- ImageIcon m_tabimage: The image used in each tab extension.
- ImageIcon m_utsguy, m_jfcgirl, m_sbeguy, m_tiger: The images used in the tab containers.
- JTabbedPane m_tabbedPane: The main tabbed pane.
- JRadioButton m_topButton: The top tab alignment button.
- JRadioButton m_bottomButton: The bottom tab alignment button.
- JRadioButton m_leftButton: The left tab alignment button.
- JRadioButton m_rightButton: The right tab alignment button.
- JButton m_addButton: The add tab button.
- JButton m_removeButton: The remove tab button.
- JRadioButton m_wrapButton: the WRAP_TAB_LAYOUT layout policy button.
- JRadioButton m_scrollButton: the SCROLL_TAB_LAYOUT layout policy button.
- JLabel m_status: The status bar label.

Our JTabbedPane, m_tabbedPane, is created with TOP tab alignment. (Note that TOP is actually the default, so this is really not necessary here. The default JTabbedPane constructor would do the same thing.)

(2) The init() method organizes the buttons inside a JPanel using GridLayout, and it associates ActionListeners with each one. We wrap all instantiation and GUI initialization processes in a separate thread and start the thread in this method. (Loading can take several seconds and it is best to allow the interface to be as responsive as possible during this time.) We also provide an explicit visual cue to the user that the application is loading by placing an "Initializing applet..." label in the content pane where the tabbed pane will be placed once it is initialized. In this initialization, our createTab() method is called four times. We then add both the panel containing the tabbed pane controller buttons and our tabbed pane to the content pane. Finally, an instance of MyChangeListener is attached to our tabbed pane to listen for tab selection changes.

(3) The createTab() method is called whenever m_addButton is clicked. Based on the current tab count, this method chooses between four ImageIcons, creates a JLabel containing the

chosen icon, and adds a new tab containing that label. The `killTab()` method is called
4 whenever `m_removeButton` is clicked to remove the tab with the highest index.

5 The `setStatus()` method is called each time a different tab is selected. The `m_status`
`JLabel` is updated to reflect which tab is selected at all times.

6 The `actionPerformed()` method is called whenever any of the buttons are clicked. Clicking
`m_topButton`, `m_bottomButton`, `m_leftButton`, or `m_rightButton` causes the tab layout of the `JTabbedPane` to change accordingly, using the `setTabPlacement()` method.
Clicking `m_wrapButton` or `m_scrollButton` changes the tab layout policy to
`WRAP_TAB_LAYOUT` or `SCROLL_TAB_LAYOUT` respectively. Each time one of these tab layout
buttons is clicked, a WAV file is played. Similarly, when a tab selection change occurs, a different WAV file is invoked. These sounds, `m_tabsound` and `m_layoutsound`, are loaded at the
end of the `init()` method:

```
m_layoutsound = getAudioClip(getCodeBase(), "switch.wav");
m_tabsound = getAudioClip(getCodeBase(), "tab.wav");
```

Before the `actionPerformed()` method exits, it revalidates the `JTabbedPane`. (If this revalidation were to be omitted, we would see that a layout change caused by clicking one of our
tab layout buttons will result in incorrect tabbed pane rendering.)

Class TabbedPaneDemo.MyChangeListener

7 `MyChangeListener` implements the `ChangeListener` interface. Only one method must be
defined when implementing this interface: `stateChanged()`. This method can process
`ChangeEvents` corresponding to when a tabbed pane's selected state changes. In our `state-
Changed()` method, we update the status bar in `TabbedPaneDemo` and play an appropriate
tab switching sound:

```
public void stateChanged(ChangeEvent e) {
  setStatus(
    ((JTabbedPane) e.getSource()).getSelectedIndex());
  m_tabsound.play();
}
```

6.2.2 Running the code

Figure 6.1, 6.2, and 6.3 show `TabbedPaneDemo` in action. To deploy this applet, the following simple HTML file is used (this is not Java plug-in compliant):

```
<HTML> <BODY>
<applet code=TabbedPaneDemo width=570 height=400> </applet>
</BODY> </HTML>
```

Add and remove some tabs, and play with the tab layout to get a feel for how it works in different situations. You can use your arrow keys to move from tab to tab (if the focus is currently
on a tab), and remember to turn your speakers on for the sound effects.

NOTE   You may have problems with this applet if your system does not support WAV files.
If so, comment out the audio-specific code and recompile the applet.

6.2.3 Interesting JTabbedPane characteristics

In cases where there is more than one row or column of tabs, most of us are used to the situation where selecting a tab that is not already in the frontmost row or column moves that row or column to the front. This does not occur in a JTabbedPane using the default Metal look and feel, as you can see in the TabbedPaneDemo example above. However, this does occur when using the Windows, Motif, and Basic look and feel tabbed pane UI delegates. This feature was purposefully disabled in the Metal look and feel (as can be verified in the MetalTabbedPaneUI source code).

**UI
GUIDELINE**

Avoid multiple rows of tabs   As a general rule, you should seek to design for no more than a single row or column of tabs.

There are three key reasons for this. The first is a cognitive reason: the user has trouble discerning what will happen with the multiple rows of tabs. With the Windows look and feel for example, the behavior somewhat mimics the behavior of a Rolodex filing card system. For some users this mental model is clear and the behavior is natural; for others it is simply confusing.

The second reason is a human factors/usability problem. When a rear set of tabs comes to the front, as with the Windows look and feel, the positions of all the other tabs change. Therefore the user has to discern the new position of a tab before visually selecting it and moving the mouse toward it. This makes it harder for the user to learn the positions of the tabs. Directional memory is a strong attribute and is highly productive for usability. Thus it is always better to keep the tabs in the same position. This was the reason why Sun and Apple designers chose to implement multiple tabs in this fashion.

The final reason is a design problem. When a second or subsequent row or column of tabs is introduced, the tabbed pane must be resized. Although the layout manager will cope with this, it may not look visually satisfactory when completed. The size of the tabbed pane becomes dependent on the ability to render the tabs in a given space. Those who remember the OS2 Warp UI will recall that the designers avoided this problem by allowing only a single row of tabs and the ability to scroll them if they didn't fit into the given space. As of Java 1.4 this design is available by setting JTabbedPane's tab layout policy to SCROLL_TAB_LAYOUT respectively.

6.3   *TAB VALIDATION*

In example 6.2 we show how to programmatically invoke or deny a tab switch. The first tab contains a hypothetical list of employees. The second tab contains input fields displaying, and allowing modification to, a specific employee's personal data. When the application starts the first tab is selected. If no employee is selected from the list the second tab cannot be selected. If an employee is selected from the list the second tab is selectable (either by clicking the tab or double-clicking the employee name in the list). A ChangeListener is responsible for controlling this behavior.

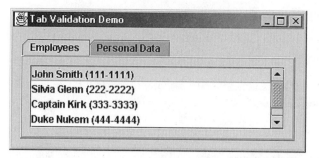

Figure 6.4
Tab validation demo–
first tab

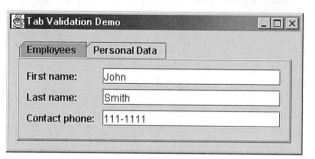

Figure 6.5
Tab validation demo–
second tab

Example 6.2

TabDemo.java

see \Chapter6\2

```java
import java.awt.*;
import java.awt.event.*;

import javax.swing.*;
import javax.swing.border.*;
import javax.swing.eent.*;

import dl.*;

public class TabDemo extends JFrame {
  public static final int LIST_TAB = 0;
  public static final int DATA_TAB = 1;

  protected Person[] m_employee = {
    new Person("John", "Smith", "111-1111"),
    new Person("Silvia", "Glenn", "222-2222"),
    new Person("Captain", "Kirk", "333-3333"),
    new Person("Duke", "Nukem", "444-4444"),
    new Person("James", "Bond", "000-7777")
  }

  protected JList m_list;
  protected JTextField m_firstTxt;
  protected JTextField m_lastTxt;
```

① Array of Person instances representing employees

```java
  protected JTextField m_phoneTxt;
  protected JTabbedPane m_tab;

public TabDemo() {
  super("Tab Validation Demo");

  JPanel p1 = new JPanel(new BorderLayout());
  p1.setBorder(new EmptyBorder(10, 10, 10, 10));
  m_list = new JList(m_employees);
  m_list.setVisibleRowCount(4);
  JscrollPane sp = newJScrollPane(m_list);
  p1.add(sp, borderLayout.CENTER);

  MouseListener mlst = new MouseAdapter() {
    public void mouseClicked(MouseEvent evt) {
      if (evt.getClickCount() == 2)
        m_tab.setSelectedIndex(DATA_TAB);
    }
  };
  m_list.addMouseListener(mlst);

  JPanel p2 = new JPanel(new dialogLayout());
  p2.setBorder(new emptyBorder(10, 10, 10, 10));
  p2.add(new JLabel("First name:"));
  m_firstTxt = new JTextfield(20);
  p2.add(m_firstTxt);
  p2.add(new JLabel("Last name:"));
  m_lastTxt = new JTextfield(20);
  p2.add(m_lastTxt);
  p2.add(new JLabel("Contact phone:"));
  m_phonetTxt = new JTextfield(20);;
  p2.add(m_pnoneTxt);

  m_tab = new JTabbedPane();
  m_tab.addTab("Employees", p1);
  m-tab.addTab("Personal Data", p2);
  m-tab.addchangeListener(new TabChangelistener());

  JPanel p = new JPanel();
  p.add(m_tab);
  p.setBorder(new EmptyBorder(5, 5, 5, 5));
  getContentPane().add(p);
  pack();
}

public Person getSelectedPerson() {
  return (Person)m_list.getSelectedValue();
}

public static void main(String[] args) {
  Jframe frame = new Tabdemo();
  frame.setDefaultCloseOperation(JFrame.EXIT_ON_CLOSE);
  frame.setVisible(true);
}
```

❷ MouseListener used to change the tab when a list item is double-clicked

```
class TabChangeListener implements ChangeListener {
  public void stateChanged(ChangeEvent e) {
    Person sp = getSelectedPerson();
    switch(m_tab.getSelectedIndex())
    {
      case DATA_TAB:
        if (sp == null) {
          m_tab.setSelectedIndex(LIST_TAB);
          return;
        }
        m_firstTxt.setText(sp.m_firstname);
        m_lastTxt.setText(sp.m_lastName);
        m_phoneTxt.setText(sp.m_phone);
        break;

      case LIST_TAB:
        if (sp != null) {
          sp.m_firstName = m_firstTxt.getText();
          sp.m_lastName = m_lastTxt.getText();
          sp.m_phone = m_phoneTxt.getText()
          m_list.repaint();
        }

      break;
    }
  }
}

class Person{
  public String m_firstName;
  public String m_lastName;
  public String m_phone;

  public Person(String firstName, String lastName, String phone) {
    m_firstName = firstName;
    m_lastName = lastName;
    m_phone =phone;
  }

  public String toString() {
    String str = m_firstName+" "+m_lastName;
    if (m_phone.lengh() > 0)
      str +=" ("+m_phone+")";
    return str.trim();
  }
 }
}
```

❸ ChangeListener to control tab switching behavior

❹ Class representing a Person (employee)

6.3.1   Understanding the code

Class TabDemo

Two class variables and six instance variables are defined. Class variables:

- int LIST_TAB: Index of the tab containing the employee list
- int DATA_TAB: Index of the tab containing the selected employee's data

Instance variables:

❶
- `Person[] m_employees`: Array of `Person` instances representing the employees.
- `JTextfield m_firstTxt`: Text field containing employee's first name.
- `JTextfield m_lastTxt`: Text field containing employee's last name.
- `JTextfield m_phoneTxt`: Text field containing employee's phone number.
- `JTabbedPane m_tab`: The main tabbed pane.

A `JList` is created by passing the array of `Person` instances, `m_employees`, to the `JList` constructor. As we will discuss soon, the `Person` class contains a `toString()` method responsible for displaying the information for each employee seen in the list. A **❷** `MouseListener` is added to this `JList` which is responsible for switching the selected tab to the personal data tab when an employee is double-clicked.

❸ *Class TabChangeListener*

An instance of this class is registered with our `m_tab` tabbed pane to control tab selection behavior. If a tab change is detected this `ChangeListener` checks which tab the user is trying to select and reacts accordingly.

If the second tab, (the `DATA_TAB`) is selected, we check whether there is a selected person item in the list using our custom `getSelectedPerson()` method. If there isn't a selected `Person` we switch tab selection back to the first tab. If there is a `Person` selected we set the data in the text fields to match the data corresponding to the selected `Person` in the list.

If the first tab (the `LIST_TAB`) is selected, we update the selected `Person` instance's data to reflect any changes that may have been made in the data tab.

❹ *Class Person*

This class represents an employee and contains three `String` instance variables to hold first name, last name and phone number data. The `toString()` method is overridden to return a `String` appropriate for display in a `JList`.

CHAPTER 7

Scrolling panes

7.1   JSCROLLPANE

class javax.swing.JScrollPane

Using JScrollPane is normally very simple. Any component or container can be placed in a JScrollPane and scrolled. You can easily create a JScrollPane by passing its constructor the component you'd like to scroll:

```
JScrollPane jsp = new JScrollPane(myLabel);
```

Normally, our use of JScrollPane will not need to be much more extensive than the one line of code shown above. Example 7.1 is a simple JScrollPane demo application. Figure 7.1 illustrates the output.

Figure 7.1
JScrollPane demo

Example 7.1

see \Chapter7\1

```java
import java.awt.*;
import javax.swing.*;

public class ScrollPaneDemo extends JFrame
{
  public ScrollPaneDemo() {
    super("JScrollPane Demo");
    ImageIcon ii = new ImageIcon("earth.jpg");
    JScrollPane jsp = new JScrollPane(new JLabel(ii));
    getContentPane().add(jsp);
    setSize(300,250);
    setVisible(true);
  }

  public static void main(String[] args) {
    new ScrollPaneDemo();
  }
}
```

When you run this example, try scrolling by pressing or holding down any of the scroll bar buttons. You will find this unacceptably slow because the scrolling occurs one pixel at a time. We will see how to control this shortly.

Many components use a JScrollPane internally to display their contents, such as JComboBox and JList. On the other hand, we are normally expected to place all multi-line text components inside scroll panes, as this is not default behavior.

GUIDELINE

Using scroll panes   For many applications, it is best to avoid introducing a scroll pane; instead, concentrate on placing the required data on the screen so that scrolling is unnecessary. As you have probably found, however, this is not always possible. When you do need to introduce scrolling, put some thought into the type of data and application you have. If possible, try to introduce scrolling in only one direction. For example, with text documents, western culture has been used to scrolling vertically since Egyptian times. Usability studies for world wide web pages have shown that readers can find data quickly when they are vertically scrolling. Scrolling horizontally, on the other hand, is laborious and difficult with text. Try to avoid it. With visual information, such as tables of information, horizontal scrolling may be more appropriate, but try to avoid both horizontal and vertical scrolling if at all possible.

We can access a JScrollPane's scroll bars directly with its getXXScrollBar() and setXX-ScrollBar() methods, where XX is either HORIZONTAL or VERTICAL.

REFERENCE   In chapter 13 we'll talk more about JScrollBars.

As of Java 1.4 mouse wheel support has been added and is activated by default in JScrollPane. The MouseWheelListener and MouseWheelEvent classes have been added to the java.awt.event package and a new addMouseWheelListener() method has been added to java.awt.Component.

To disable or re-enable mouse wheel scrolling for a particular JScrollPane the new setWheelScrollingEnabled() method can be used. There is no need to create your own MouseWheelListener for use in a JScrollPane unless you'd like to customize wheel scrolling behavior.

7.1.1 The ScrollPaneConstants interface

abstract interface javax.swing.ScrollPaneConstants

We can specify policies for when and when not to display a JScrollPane's horizontal and vertical scroll bars. We simply use its setVerticalScrollBarPolicy() and setHorizontalScrollBarPolicy() methods, providing one of three constants for each that are defined in the ScrollPaneConstants interface:

```
HORIZONTAL_SCROLLBAR_AS_NEEDED
HORIZONTAL_SCROLLBAR_NEVER
HORIZONTAL_SCROLLBAR_ALWAYS
VERTICAL_SCROLLBAR_AS_NEEDED
VERTICAL_SCROLLBAR_NEVER
VERTICAL_SCROLLBAR_ALWAYS
```

For example, to enforce the display of the vertical scroll bar at all times and always keep the horizontal scroll bar hidden, we could do the following where jsp is a JScrollPane:

```
jsp.setHorizontalScrollBarPolicy(
   ScrollPaneConstants.HORIZONTAL_SCROLLBAR_NEVER);

jsp.setVerticalScrollBarPolicy(
   ScrollPaneConstants.VERTICAL_SCROLLBAR_ALWAYS);
```

7.1.2 JViewport

class javax.swing.JViewport

The JViewport class is the container that is really responsible for displaying a specific visible region of the component in a JScrollPane. We can set/get a viewport's *view* (the component it contains) using its setView() and getView() methods. We can control how much of this component JViewport displays by setting its *extent* size to a specified Dimension using its setExtentSize() method. We can also specify where the origin (upper left corner) of a JViewport should begin displaying its contained component by providing specific coordinates (as a Point) of the contained component to the setViewPosition() method. In fact, when we scroll a component in a JScrollPane, this view position is constantly being changed by the scroll bars.

NOTE   JViewport enforces a view position that lies within the view component only. We cannot set negative or extremely large view positions (as of JDK1.2.2 we can assign negative view positions). However, since the view position is the upper right hand corner of the viewport, we are still allowed to set the view position such that only part of the viewport is filled by the view component. We will show how to watch for this, and how to stop it from happening, in some of the examples below.

Whenever a change is made to the position or size of the visible portion of the view, JViewport fires ChangeEvents. We can register ChangeListeners to capture these events using JViewport's addChangeListener() method. These are the only events that are associated with JScrollPane by default. For instance, whenever we scroll using JScrollPane's scroll bars, its main viewport, as well as its row and column header viewports (see below), will each fire ChangeEvents.

The visible region of JViewport's view can be retrieved as a Rectangle or Dimension instance using the getViewRect() and getViewSize() methods respectively. This will give us the current view position as well as the extent width and height. The view position alone can be retrieved with getViewPosition(), which returns a Point instance. To remove a component from JViewport we use its remove() method.

We can translate specific JViewport coordinates to the coordinates of its contained component by passing a Point instance to its toViewCoordinates() method. We can do the same for a region by passing a Dimension instance to toViewCoordinates(). We can also manually specify the visible region of the *view* component by passing a Dimension instance to JViewport's scrollRectToVisible() method.

We can retrieve JScrollPane's main JViewport by calling its getViewport() method, or assign it a new one using setViewport(). We can replace the component in this viewport through JScrollPane's setViewportView() method, but there is no getViewportView() counterpart. Instead, we must first access its JScrollPane's JViewport by calling getViewport(), and then call getView() on that (as discussed above). Typically, to access a JScrollPane's main child component, we would do the following:

```
Component myComponent = jsp.getViewport().getView();
```

JAVA 1.3   As of Java 1.3 JViewport supports three distinct scrolling modes which can be assigned with its setScrollMode() method:

JViewport.BLIT_SCROLL_MODE: This mode uses the Grahics.copyArea() method to repaint the visible area that was visible before the most recent scroll (instead of redrawing it). In general this is the most efficient scroll mode.

JViewport.BACKINGSTORE_SCROLL_MODE: This mode renders the viewport contents in an offscreen image which is then painted to screen. It requires more memory than BLIT_SCROLL_MODE but, in our experience, this mode is more reliable.

JViewport.SIMPLE_SCROLL_MODE: This mode, while being the most reliable, is the slowest performer, as it redraws the entire contents of the viewport view each time a scroll occurs.

The default mode is BLIT_SCROLL_MODE. Occasionally you may find that this causes rendering problems with tables, images, and so forth. This can usually be solved by switching to BACKINGSTORE_SCROLL_MODE. If this doesn't work SIMPLE_SCROLL_MODE will usually do the trick, although some performance benefits will be sacrificed by doing this.

7.1.3 ScrollPaneLayout

class javax.swing.ScrollPaneLayout

By default, JScrollPane's layout is managed by an instance of ScrollPaneLayout. JScrollPane can contain up to nine components and it is ScrollPaneLayout's job to make sure that they are positioned correctly. These components are listed here:

- A JViewport that contains the main component to be scrolled.
- A JViewport that is used as the row header. This viewport's view position changes vertically in sync with the main viewport.
- A JViewport that is used as the column header. This viewport's view position changes horizontally in sync with the main viewport.
- Four components for placement in each corner of the scroll pane.
- Two JScrollBars for vertical and horizontal scrolling.

The corner components will only be visible if the scroll bars and headers surrounding them are also visible. To assign a component to a corner position, we call JScrollPane's setCorner() method. This method takes both a String and a component as parameters. The String is used to identify in which corner this component is to be placed, and it is recognized by ScrollPaneLayout. In fact, ScrollPaneLayout identifies each JScrollPane component with a unique String. Figure 7.2 illustrates this concept.

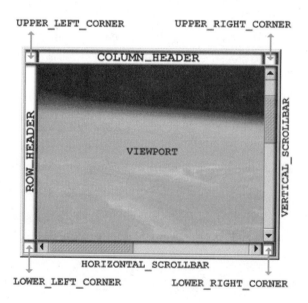

Figure 7.2
JScrollPane **components as identified by** Scroll-PaneLayout

To assign `JViewports` as the row and column headers, we use `JScrollPane`'s `setRow-Header()` and `setColumnHeader()` methods respectively. We can also avoid having to create a `JViewport` ourselves by passing the component to be placed in the row or column viewport to `JScrollPane`'s `setRowHeaderView()` or `setColumnHeaderView()` methods.

Because `JScrollPane` is often used to scroll images, an obvious use for the row and column headers is to function as some sort of ruler. In example 7.2, we present a basic example showing how to populate each corner with a label and create simple rulers for the row and column headers that display ticks every 30 pixels and render themselves based on their current viewport position. Figure 7.3 illustrates the result.

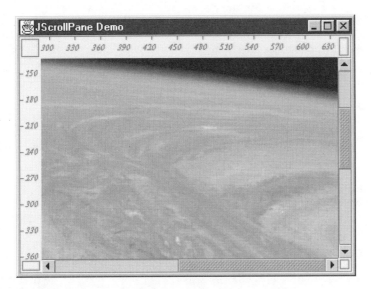

Figure 7.3 A `JScrollPane` demo with four corners, a row header, and a column header

Example 7.2

HeaderDemo.java

see \Chapter7\2

```
import java.awt.*;
import javax.swing.*;

public class HeaderDemo extends JFrame
{
  public HeaderDemo() {
    super("JScrollPane Demo");
    ImageIcon ii = new ImageIcon("earth.jpg");
    JScrollPane jsp = new JScrollPane(new JLabel(ii));

    JLabel[] corners = new JLabel[4];
```

```
for(int i=0;i<4;i++) {
  corners[i] = new JLabel();
  corners[i].setBackground(Color.yellow);
  corners[i].setOpaque(true);
  corners[i].setBorder(BorderFactory.createCompoundBorder(
    BorderFactory.createEmptyBorder(2,2,2,2),
    BorderFactory.createLineBorder(Color.red, 1)));
}

JLabel rowheader = new JLabel() {
  Font f = new Font("Serif",Font.ITALIC | Font.BOLD,10);
  public void paintComponent(Graphics g) {
    super.paintComponent(g);
    Rectangle r = g.getClipBounds();
    g.setFont(f);
    g.setColor(Color.red);
    for (int i = 30-(r.y % 30);i<r.height;i+=30) {
      g.drawLine(0, r.y + i, 3, r.y + i);
      g.drawString("" + (r.y + i), 6, r.y + i + 3);
    }
  }
  public Dimension getPreferredSize() {
    return new Dimension(25,label.getPreferredSize().getHeight());
  }
};
rowheader.setBackground(Color.yellow);
rowheader.setOpaque(true);

JLabel columnheader = new JLabel() {
  Font f = new Font("Serif",Font.ITALIC | Font.BOLD,10);
  public void paintComponent(Graphics g) {
    super.paintComponent(g);
    Rectangle r = g.getClipBounds();
    g.setFont(f);
    g.setColor(Color.red);
    for (int i = 30-(r.x % 30);i<r.width;i+=30) {
      g.drawLine(r.x + i, 0, r.x + i, 3);
      g.drawString("" + (r.x + i), r.x + i - 10, 16);
    }
  }
  public Dimension getPreferredSize() {
    return new Dimension(label.getPreferredSize().getWidth(),25);
  }
};
columnheader.setBackground(Color.yellow);
columnheader.setOpaque(true);

jsp.setRowHeaderView(rowheader);
jsp.setColumnHeaderView(columnheader);
jsp.setCorner(JScrollPane.LOWER_LEFT_CORNER, corners[0]);
jsp.setCorner(JScrollPane.LOWER_RIGHT_CORNER, corners[1]);
jsp.setCorner(JScrollPane.UPPER_LEFT_CORNER, corners[2]);
jsp.setCorner(JScrollPane.UPPER_RIGHT_CORNER, corners[3]);
```

1 Each row header uses clipping for speed

2 Thin and very tall

1 Clipping for speed

2 Short and very wide

```
    getContentPane().add(jsp);
    setSize(400,300);
    setDefaultCloseOperation(JFrame.EXIT_ON_CLOSE);
    setVisible(true);     .
  }

  public static void main(String[] args) {
    new HeaderDemo();
  }
}
```

❶
❷ Notice that the row and column headers use the graphics clipping area in their `paintCompo-`
`nent()` routine for optimal efficiency. We also override the `getPreferredSize()` method
so that the proper width (for the row header) and height (for the column header) will be used
by `ScrollPaneLayout`. The other dimensions are obtained by simply grabbing the label's
preferred size, as they are completely controlled by `ScrollPaneLayout`.

Note that we are certainly not limited to labels for corners, row headers, or the main viewport
itself. As we mentioned in the beginning of this chapter, any component can be placed in a
`JViewport`.

7.1.4   The Scrollable interface

abstract interface javax.swing.Scrollable

The `Scrollable` interface describes five methods that allow us to customize how `JScrollPane`
scrolls its contents. Specifically, by implementing this interface we can specify how many pixels are scrolled when a scroll bar button or scroll bar *paging area* (the empty region between
the scroll bar *thumb* and the buttons) is pressed. (The thumb is the part of the scroll bar that
you drag.) Two methods control this functionality: `getScrollableBlockIncrement()` and
`getScrollableUnitIncrement()`. The former is used to return the amount to scroll when
a scroll bar paging area is pressed, and the latter is used when the button is pressed.

> **NOTE**   In text components, these two methods are implemented so that scrolling will
> move one line of text at a time. (`JTextComponent` implements the `Scrollable`
> interface.)

The other three methods of this interface involve `JScrollPane`'s communication with the
main viewport. The `getScrollableTracksViewportWidth()` and `getScrollable-`
`TracksHeight()` methods can return `true` to disable scrolling in the horizontal or vertical
direction respectively. Normally these just return `false`. The `getPreferredSize()`
method is supposed to return the preferred size of the viewport that will contain this component (the component implementing the `Scrollable` interface). Normally we just return the
preferred size of the component.

Example 7.3 shows how to implement the `Scrollable` interface to create a custom `JLabel`
whose *unit* and *block* increments will be 10 pixels. As we saw in example 7.1, scrolling one pixel
at a time is tedious at best. Increasing this to a 10-pixel increment provides a more natural feel.

Example 7.3

ScrollableDemo.java

see \Chapter7\3

```java
import java.awt.*;
import javax.swing.*;

public class ScrollableDemo extends JFrame
{
  public ScrollableDemo() {
    super("JScrollPane Demo");
    ImageIcon ii = new ImageIcon("earth.jpg");
    JScrollPane jsp = new JScrollPane(new MyScrollableLabel(ii));
    getContentPane().add(jsp);
    setSize(300,250);
    setDefaultCloseOperation(JFrame.EXIT_ON_CLOSE);
    setVisible(true);
  }

  public static void main(String[] args) {
    new ScrollableDemo();
  }
}

class MyScrollableLabel extends JLabel implements Scrollable
{
  public MyScrollableLabel(ImageIcon i){
    super(i);
  }

  public Dimension getPreferredScrollableViewportSize() {
    return getPreferredSize();
  }

  public int getScrollableBlockIncrement(Rectangle r,
    int orientation, int direction) {
      return 10;
  }

  public boolean getScrollableTracksViewportHeight() {
    return false;
  }

  public boolean getScrollableTracksViewportWidth() {
    return false;
  }

  public int getScrollableUnitIncrement(Rectangle r,

    int orientation, int direction) {
      return 10;
  }
}
```

7.2 GRAB-AND-DRAG SCROLLING

Many paint programs and document readers (such as Adobe Acrobat) support grab-and-drag scrolling, which is the ability to click on an image and drag it in any direction with the mouse. It is fairly simple to implement; however, we must take care to make the operation smooth without allowing users to scroll past the view's extremities. JViewport takes care of the negative direction for us, as it does not allow the view position coordinates to be less than 0. But it *will* allow us to change the view position to very large values, which can result in the viewport displaying a portion of the view smaller than the viewport itself.

Example 7.4 demonstrates how to support grab-and-drag scrolling.

Example 7.4

GrabAndDragDemo.java

see \Chapter7\4

```java
import java.awt.*;
import java.awt.event.*;
import javax.swing.*;
import javax.swing.event.*;
public class GrabAndDragDemo extends JFrame
{
  public GrabAndDragDemo() {
    super("Grab-and-drag Demo");
    ImageIcon ii = new ImageIcon("earth.jpg");
    JScrollPane jsp = new JScrollPane(new GrabAndScrollLabel(ii));
    getContentPane().add(jsp);
    setSize(300,250);
    setDefaultCloseOperation(JFrame.EXIT_ON_CLOSE);
    setVisible(true);

  }

  public static void main(String[] args) {
    new GrabAndDragDemo();
  }
}

class GrabAndScrollLabel extends JLabel
{
  public GrabAndScrollLabel(ImageIcon i){
    super(i);
    MouseInputAdapter mia = new MouseInputAdapter() {
      int m_XDifference, m_YDifference;
      Container c;

      public void mouseDragged(MouseEvent e) {
        c = GrabAndScrollLabel.this.getParent();
        if (c instanceof JViewport) {
          JViewport jv = (JViewport) c;
          Point p = jv.getViewPosition();
```

1 JLabel which can scroll by dragging the mouse

3 Scroll the Viewport the label is contained in

```
                int newX = p.x - (e.getX()-m_XDifference);
                int newY = p.y - (e.getY()-m_YDifference);

                int maxX = GrabAndScrollLabel.this.getWidth()
                   - jv.getWidth();
                int maxY = GrabAndScrollLabel.this.getHeight()
                   - jv.getHeight();
                if (newX < 0)
                  newX = 0;
                if (newX > maxX)
                  newX = maxY;
                if (newY < 0)
                   newY = 0;
                if (newY > maxY)
                   newY = maxY;

                  jv.setViewPosition(new Point(maxX, maxY));
            }
          }

        public void mousePressed(MouseEvent e) {
          setCursor(Cursor.getPredefinedCursor(
          Cursor.MOVE_CURSOR));
          m_XDifference = e.getX();
          m_YDifference = e.getY();
        }

        public void mouseReleased(MouseEvent e) {
          setCursor(Cursor.getPredefinedCursor(
            Cursor.DEFAULT_CURSOR));
        }
      };
      addMouseMotionListener(mia);
      addMouseListener(mia);
    }
  }
```

④ Only scroll to maximum coordinates

② Start dragging, saving start location

7.2.1 Understanding the code

Class GrabAndScrollLabel

① This class extends JLabel and overrides the JLabel(Imageicon ii) constructor. The Grab-AndScrollLabel constructor starts by calling the superclass version and then it proceeds to set up a MouseInputAdapter. This adapter is the heart of the GrabAndScrollLabel class.

The adapter uses three variables:

- int m_XDifference: The x-coordinate which has been saved on a mouse press event and used for dragging horizontally.
- int m_YDifference: The y-coordinate which has been saved on a mouse press event and used for dragging vertically.
- Container c: Used to hold a local reference to the parent container in the mouse-Dragged() method.

② The `mousePressed()` method changes the cursor to `MOVE_CURSOR` and stores the event coordinates in the variables `m_XDifference` and `m_YDifference`, so they can be used in `mouseDragged()`.

③ The `mouseDragged()` method first grabs a reference to the parent, then it checks to see if it is a `JViewport`. If it isn't, we do nothing. If it is, we store the current view position and calculate the new view position the drag will bring us into:

```
Point p = jv.getViewPosition();
int newX = p.x - (e.getX()-m_XDifference);
int newY = p.y - (e.getY()-m_YDifference);
```

④ When dragging components, this would normally be enough (as we will see in future chapters); however, we must make sure that we do not move the label in such a way that it does not fill the viewport. So we calculate the maximum allowable x- and y-coordinates by subtracting the viewport dimensions from the size of this label (since the view position coordinates start from the upper-left hand corner):

```
int maxX = GrabAndScrollLabel.this.getWidth()
   - jv.getWidth();
int maxY = GrabAndScrollLabel.this.getHeight()
   - jv.getHeight();
```

The remainder of this method compares the `newX` and `newY` values with the `maxX` and `maxY` values, and adjusts the view position accordingly. If `newX` or `newY` is ever greater than the `maxX` or `maxY` values respectively, we use the max values instead. If `newX` or `newY` is ever less than 0, we use 0 instead. This is necessary to allow smooth scrolling in all situations.

7.3 SCROLLING PROGRAMMATICALLY

We are certainly not required to use a `JScrollPane` for scrolling. We can place a component in a `JViewport` and control the scrolling ourselves if we want to. This is what `JViewport` was designed for; it just happens to be used by `JScrollPane` as well. We've constructed this example to show how to implement our own scrolling in a `JViewport`. Four buttons are used for scrolling. We enable and disable these buttons based on whether the view component is at any of its extremities. These buttons are assigned keyboard mnemonics which we can use as an alternative to clicking.

This example also shows how to use a `ChangeListener` to capture `ChangeEvents` that are fired when the `JViewport` changes state. We need to capture these events so that when our viewport is resized to be bigger than its view component child, the scrolling buttons will become disabled. If these buttons are disabled and the viewport is then resized so that it is no longer bigger than its child view component, the buttons should then become enabled. It is quite simple to capture and process these events, as we will see in example 7.5. (As with most of the examples we have presented, it may help if you run this example before stepping through the code.)

Figure 7.4 Programmatic scrolling with JViewport

Example 7.5

ButtonScroll.java

see \Chapter7\5

```
import java.awt.*;
import java.awt.event.*;

import javax.swing.*;
import javax.swing.event.*;

public class ButtonScroll extends JFrame
{
  protected JViewport m_viewport;
  protected JButton m_up;
  protected JButton m_down;
  protected JButton m_left;
  protected JButton m_right;

  protected int m_pgVert;
  protected int m_pgHorz;

  public ButtonScroll() {
    super("Scrolling Programmatically");
    setSize(400, 400);
    getContentPane().setLayout(new BorderLayout());
```

❶ **Viewport, scroll buttons, and scrolling distances**

❷ **Constructor places label with image along with scroll buttons**

```
ImageIcon shuttle = new ImageIcon("shuttle.gif");
m_pgVert = shuttle.getIconHeight()/5;
m_pgHorz = shuttle.getIconWidth()/5;
JLabel lbl = new JLabel(shuttle);
```

Listen for size changes on Viewport and reconfigure scroll buttons ❸

```
m_viewport = new JViewport();
m_viewport.setView(lbl);
m_viewport.addChangeListener(new ChangeListener() {
  public void stateChanged(ChangeEvent e) {
    enableButtons(
      ButtonScroll.this.m_viewport.getViewPosition());
  }
});
getContentPane().add(m_viewport, BorderLayout.CENTER);

JPanel pv = new JPanel(new BorderLayout());
m_up = createButton("up", 'u');
ActionListener lst = new ActionListener() {
  public void actionPerformed(ActionEvent e) {
    movePanel(0, -1);
  }
};
m_up.addActionListener(lst);
pv.add(m_up, BorderLayout.NORTH);
```

❹ Create buttons to scroll image up and down

```
m_down = createButton("down", 'd');
lst = new ActionListener() {
  public void actionPerformed(ActionEvent e) {
    movePanel(0, 1);
  }
};
m_down.addActionListener(lst);
pv.add(m_down, BorderLayout.SOUTH);
getContentPane().add(pv, BorderLayout.EAST);

JPanel ph = new JPanel(new BorderLayout());
m_left = createButton("left", 'l');
lst = new ActionListener() {
  public void actionPerformed(ActionEvent e) {
    movePanel(-1, 0);
  }
};
m_left.addActionListener(lst);
ph.add(m_left, BorderLayout.WEST);
```

❹ Create buttons to scroll image left and right

```
m_right = createButton("right", 'r');
lst = new ActionListener() {
  public void actionPerformed(ActionEvent e) {
    movePanel(1, 0);
  }
};
m_right.addActionListener(lst);
ph.add(m_right, BorderLayout.EAST);
getContentPane().add(ph, BorderLayout.SOUTH);
```

SCROLLING PROGRAMMATICALLY

215

```
      setDefaultCloseOperation (JFrame.EXIT_ON_CLOSE);
      setVisible(true);
      movePanel(0, 0);
    }

  protected JButton createButton(String name, char mnemonics) {
      JButton btn = new JButton(new ImageIcon(name+"1.gif"));
      btn.setPressedIcon(new ImageIcon(name+"2.gif"));
      btn.setDisabledIcon(new ImageIcon(name+"3.gif"));
      btn.setToolTipText("Move "+name);
      btn.setBorderPainted(false);
      btn.setMargin(new Insets(0, 0, 0, 0));
      btn.setContentAreaFilled(false);
      btn.setMnemonic(mnemonics);
      return btn;
    }

  protected void movePanel(int xmove, int ymove) {
      Point pt = m_viewport.getViewPosition();
      pt.x += m_pgHorz*xmove;
      pt.y += m_pgVert*ymove;

      pt.x = Math.max(0, pt.x);
      pt.x = Math.min(getMaxXExtent(), pt.x);
      pt.y = Math.max(0, pt.y);
      pt.y = Math.min(getMaxYExtent(), pt.y);

      m_viewport.setViewPosition(pt);
      enableButtons(pt);
    }

  protected void enableButtons(Point pt) {
      if (pt.x == 0)
        enableComponent(m_left, false);

      else enableComponent(m_left, true);
      if (pt.x >= getMaxXExtent())
        enableComponent(m_right, false);
      else enableComponent(m_right, true);

      if (pt.y == 0)
        enableComponent(m_up, false);
      else enableComponent(m_up, true);

      if (pt.y >= getMaxYExtent())
        enableComponent(m_down, false);
      else enableComponent(m_down, true);
    }

  protected void enableComponent(JComponent c, boolean b) {
      if (c.isEnabled() != b)
        c.setEnabled(b);
    }

  protected int getMaxXExtent() {
      return m_viewport.getView().getWidth()-m_viewport.getWidth();
    }
```

⑤ Create scroll button with direction string and mnemonic

⑥ Move the image panel in the specified direction, from which scroll button was pressed

⑦ Enable or disable scroll buttons based on whether the image is already scrolled to edge of range

⑧ Get maximum scrolling dimensions

```
    protected int getMaxYExtent() {
        return m_viewport.getView().getHeight()-m_viewport.getHeight();
    }
    public static void main(String argv[])  {
        new ButtonScroll();
    }
}
```

**Get maximum
scrolling dimensions** **8**

7.3.1 Understanding the code

Class ButtonScroll

1 Several instance variables are declared:

- `JViewport m_viewport`: The viewport used to display a large image.
- `JButton m_up`: The button to scroll up programmatically.
- `JButton m_down`: The button to scroll down programmatically.
- `JButton m_left`: The button to scroll left programmatically.
- `JButton m_right`: The button to scroll right programmatically.
- `int m_pgVert`: The number of pixels for a vertical scroll.
- `int m_pgHorz`: The number of pixels for a horizontal scroll.

2 The constructor of the `ButtonScroll` class creates and initializes the GUI components for this example. A `BorderLayout` is used to manage the components in this frame's content pane. `JLabel lbl` which stores a large image, is placed in the viewport, `m_viewport`, to provide programmatic viewing capabilities. This `JViewport` is added to the center of our frame.

3 As we mentioned above, we need to capture the `ChangeEvents` that are fired when our `JViewport` changes size so that we can enable and disable our buttons accordingly. We do this by attaching a `ChangeListener` to our viewport and calling our `enableButtons()` method (see below) from `stateChanged()`:

```
m_viewport.addChangeListener(new ChangeListener() {
    public void stateChanged(ChangeEvent e) {
        enableButtons(
            ButtonScroll.this.m_viewport.getViewPosition());
    }
});
```

4 Two buttons, `m_up` and `m_down`, are created for scrolling in the vertical direction. The `createButton()` method is used to create a new `JButton` component and set a group of properties for it (see below). Each of the new buttons receives an `ActionListener` which calls the `movePanel()` method in response to a mouse click. These two buttons are added to the intermediate container, `JPanel pv`, which is added to the east side of our frame's content pane. Similarly, two buttons, `m_left` and `m_right`, are created for scrolling in the horizontal direction and are added to the south region of the content pane.

5 The `createButton()` method creates a new `JButton` component. It takes two parameters: the name of the scrolling direction as a `String` and the button's mnemonic as a `char`. This method assumes that three image files are prepared:

- name1.gif: The default icon.

- name2.gif: The pressed icon.
- name3.gif: The disabled icon.

These images are loaded as `ImageIcons` and attached to the button with the associated `setXX()` method:

```
JButton btn = new JButton(new ImageIcon(name+"1.gif"));
btn.setPressedIcon(new ImageIcon(name+"2.gif"));
btn.setDisabledIcon(new ImageIcon(name+"3.gif"));
btn.setToolTipText("Move "+name);
btn.setBorderPainted(false);
btn.setMargin(new Insets(0, 0, 0, 0));
btn.setContentAreaFilled(false);
btn.setMnemonic(mnemonic);
return btn;
```

Then we remove any border or content area rendering, so the presentation of our button is completely determined by our icons. Finally, we set the tooltip text and mnemonic and return that component instance.

6 The `movePanel()` method programmatically scrolls the image in the viewport in the direction determined by the `xmove` and `ymove` parameters. These parameters can have the value −1, 0, or 1. To determine the actual amount of scrolling, we multiply these parameters by `m_pgHorz` (`m_pgVert`). The local variable `Point pt` determines a new viewport position. It is limited so the resulting view will not display any empty space (space not belonging to the displayed image), similar to how we enforce the viewport view position in the grab-and-drag scrolling example above. Finally, the `setViewPosition()` method is called to scroll to the new position, and `enableButtons()` enables/disables buttons according to the new position:

```
Point pt = m_viewport.getViewPosition();
pt.x += m_pgHorz*xmove;
pt.y += m_pgVert*ymove;

pt.x = Math.max(0, pt.x);
pt.x = Math.min(getMaxXExtent(), pt.x);
pt.y = Math.max(0, pt.y);
pt.y = Math.min(getMaxYExtent(), pt.y);

m_viewport.setViewPosition(pt);
enableButtons(pt);
```

7 The `enableButtons()` method disables a button if scrolling in the corresponding direction is not possible; otherwise, it enables the button. For example, if the viewport position's x-coordinate is 0, we can disable the scroll left button (remember that the view position will never be negative, as enforced by `JViewport`):

```
if (pt.x <= 0)
  enableComponent(m_left, false);
else enableComponent(m_left, true);
```

Similarly, if the viewport position's x-coordinate is greater than or equal to our maximum allowable x-position (determined by `getMaxXExtent()`), we disable the scroll right button:

```
if (pt.x >= getMaxXExtent())
```

```
        enableComponent(m_right, false);
  else enableComponent(m_right, true);
```

8 The methods `getMaxXExtent()` and `getMaxYExtent()` return the maximum coordinates available for scrolling in the horizontal and vertical directions, respectively, by subtracting the appropriate viewport dimension from the appropriate dimension of the child component.

7.3.2   Running the code

NOTE   The shuttle image for this example was found at http://shuttle.nasa.gov/sts-95/images/esc/.

Press the buttons and watch how the image is scrolled programmatically. Use the keyboard mnemonic as an alternative way to pressing buttons, and notice how this mnemonic is displayed in the tooltip text. Also note how a button is disabled when scrolling in the corresponding direction is no longer available, and how it is enabled otherwise. Now try resizing the frame and see how the buttons will change state depending on whether the viewport is bigger or smaller than its child component.

C H A P T E R   8

Split panes

8.1 JSPLITPANE

class javax.swing.JSplitPane

Split panes allow the user to dynamically change the size of two or more components that are displayed side by side (either within a window or another panel). A divider can be dragged with the mouse to increase space for one component and decrease the display space for another; however, the total display area does not change. A familiar example is the combination of a tree and a table separated by a horizontal divider (such as in file explorer-like applications). The Swing framework for split panes consists only of JSplitPane.

JSplitPane can hold two components that are separated by a horizontal or vertical divider. The components on either side of a JSplitPane can be added either in one of the constructors, or with the proper setXXComponent() methods (where XX is substituted by Left, Right, Top, or Bottom). We can also set the orientation to vertical split or horizontal split at run-time using its setOrientation() method.

The divider between the components is the only visible part of JSplitPane. Its size can be managed with the setDividerSize() method, and its position can be managed by the two overloaded setDividerLocation() methods (which take an absolute location in pixels or a proportional location as a double). The divider location methods have no effect until a JSplitPane is displayed. JSplitPane also maintains a oneTouchExpandable property which, when true, places two small arrows inside the divider that will move the divider to its extremities when clicked.

Resizable paneled display   Split panes are useful when your design has paneled the display for ease of use but you (as designer) have no control over the actual window size. The Netscape email reader is a good example of this; a split pane is introduced to let the user vary the size of the message header panel against the size of the message text panel.

An interesting feature of the JSplitPane component is that you can specify whether to repaint side components *during* the divider's motion using the setContinuousLayout() method. If you can repaint components fast enough, resizing will have a more natural view with this setting. Otherwise, this flag should be set to false, in which case side components will be repainted only when the divider's new location is chosen. In this latter case, a divider line will be shown as the divider location is dragged to illustrate the new position.

JSplitPane will not size any of its constituent components smaller than their minimum sizes. If the minimum size of each component is larger than the size of the split pane, the divider will be effectively disabled (unmovable). We can call its resetToPreferredSize() method to resize its children to their preferred sizes, if possible.

JAVA 1.3   As of Java 1.3 you can specify how JSplitPane distributes space when its size changes. This is controlled with the setResizeWeight() method and can range from 0 to 1. The default is 0 which means the right/bottom component will be allocated all the extra/negative space and the left/top component's size will remain the same. 1 means just the opposite. This works according to the following formula:

right/bottom change in size=(resize weight* size change)
left/bottom change in size=((1-resize weight)* size change)

For example, setting the resize weight to 0.5 will have the effect of distributing extra space, or taking it away if the split pane is made smaller, equally for both components.

Using split panes in conjunction with scroll panes   It's important to use a scroll pane on the panels which are being split with the split pane. Scroll bars will then appear automatically as required when data is obscured as the split pane is dragged back and forth. With the introduction of the scroll pane, the viewer has a clear indication that there is hidden data. They can then choose to scroll with the scroll bar or uncover the data using the split pane.

8.2   *BASIC SPLIT PANE EXAMPLE*

Example 8.1 shows JSplitPane at work in a basic, introductory demo. We can manipulate the size of four custom panels placed in three JSplitPanes:

Example 8.1

SplitSample.java

see \Chapter8\1

```java
import java.awt.*;
import java.awt.event.*;

import javax.swing.*;

public class SplitSample extends JFrame
{

  public SplitSample() {
    super("Simple SplitSample Example");
    setSize(400, 400);

    Component c11 = new SimplePanel();
    Component c12 = new SimplePanel();
    JSplitPane spLeft = new JSplitPane(
      JSplitPane.VERTICAL_SPLIT, c11, c12);
    spLeft.setDividerSize(8);
    spLeft.setDividerLocation(150);

    spLeft.setContinuousLayout(true);

    Component c21 = new SimplePanel();
    Component c22 = new SimplePanel();
    JSplitPane spRight = new JSplitPane(
      JSplitPane.VERTICAL_SPLIT, c21, c22);
    spRight.setDividerSize(8);
    spRight.setDividerLocation(150);
    spRight.setContinuousLayout(true);

    JSplitPane sp = new JSplitPane(
      JSplitPane.HORIZONTAL_SPLIT, spLeft, spRight);
    sp.setDividerSize(8);
    sp.setDividerLocation(200);
    sp.setResizeWeight(0.5);
    sp.setContinuousLayout(false);
    sp.setOneTouchExpandable(true);

    getContentPane().add(sp, BorderLayout.CENTER);

    setDefaultCloseOperation(JFrame.EXIT_ON_CLOSE);
    setVisible(true);

  }

  public static void main(String argv[]) {
    new SplitSample();
  }
}

class SimplePanel extends JPanel
{
  public Dimension getPreferredSize() {
```

❶ Constructor composes 4 SimplePanels into 2 JSplitPanes, 2 panels in each

❶ Two SimplePanels in left pane

❶ Two SimplePanels in right pane

❶ One JSplitPane to hold the other two

❷ Simple component to take up space in halves of JSplitPane

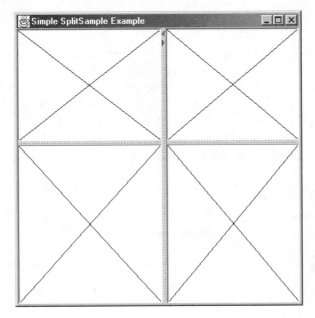

Figure 8.1
A split pane example displaying simple custom panels

```
      return new Dimension(200, 200);
   }
   public Dimension getMinimumSize() {
      return new Dimension(40, 40);
   }
   public void paintComponent(Graphics g) {
      super.paintComponent(g);
      g.setColor(Color.black);
      Dimension sz = getSize();
      g.drawLine(0, 0, sz.width, sz.height);
      g.drawLine(sz.width, 0, 0, sz.height);
   }
}
```

8.2.1   Understanding the code

Class SplitSample

1 Four instances of SimplePanel are used to fill a 2x2 structure. The two left components (c11 and c12) are placed in the spLeft vertically split JSplitPane. The two right components (c21 and c22) are placed in the spRight vertically split JSplitPane. The spLeft and spRight panels are placed in the sp horizontally split JSplitPane. The continuous-Layout property is set to true for spLeft and spRight, and false for sp. So as the divider moves inside the left and right panels, child components are repainted continuously, producing immediate results. However, as the vertical divider is moved, it is denoted by a black line until a new position is chosen (when the mouse is released). Only then are its child components validated and repainted. The first kind of behavior is recommended for simple components that can be rendered quickly, while the second is recommended for components whose repainting can take a significant amount of time.

The oneTouchExpandable property is set to true for the vertical JSplitPane sp. This places small arrow widgets on the divider. By pressing these arrows with the mouse, we can instantly move the divider to the left-most or right-most position. When the slider is in the left-most or right-most positions, pressing these arrows will then move the divider to its most recent location, which is maintained by the lastDividerLocation property.

The resizeWeight property is set to 0.5 for the vertical JSplitPane sp. This tells the split pane to increase/decrease the size of the left and right components equally when it is resized.

Class SimplePanel

2 SimplePanel represents a simple Swing component whose paintComponent() method draws two diagonal lines across its area. The overridden getMinimumSize() method defines the minimum space required for this component. JSplitPane will prohibit the user from moving the divider if the resulting child size will become less than its minimum size.

NOTE   The arrow widgets associated with the oneTouchExpandable property will move the divider to the extreme location without regard to minimum sizes of child components.

8.2.2   Running the code

Notice how child components can be resized with dividers. Also notice the difference between resizing with continuous layout (side panes) and without it (center pane). Play with the "one touch expandable" widgets for quick expansion and collapse. Resize the frame and note how the left and right components share the space proportionately.

8.3   *SYNCHRONIZED SPLIT PANE DIVIDERS*

In this section example 8.2 shows how to synchronize the left and right split pane dividers from example 8.1 so that whenever the left divider is moved the right divider moves to an identical location and vice versa.

Example 8.2

SplitSample.java

see\Chapter8\2

```
import java.awt.*;
import java.awt.event.*;
import javax.swing.*;

public class SplitSample
  extends JFrame {

  private boolean m_resizing = false;

  public SplitSample() {
```

1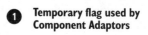
Temporary flag used by Component Adaptors

```java
      super("SplitSample With Synchronization");
      setSize(400, 400);
      getContentPane().setLayout(new BorderLayout());

      Component c11 = new SimplePanel()
      Component c12 = new Simple Panel();
      final JSplitPane spLeft = new JSplitPane(
        JSplitPane.VERTICAL_SPLIT, c11, c12);
      spLeft.setDividerSize(8);
      spLeft.setDividerLocation(150);
      spLeft.setContinuousLayout(true);

      Component c21 = new SimplePanel()
      Component c22 = new Simple Panel();
      final JSplitPane spRight = new JSplitPane(
        JSplitPane.VERTICAL_SPLIT, c21, c22);
      spRight.setDividerSize(8);
      spRight.setDividerLocation(150);
      spRight.setContinuousLayout(true);
```
2 Split pane made final so they can be referenced by anonymous inner classes

```java
ComponentListener caLeft = new ComponentAdapter() {
 public void componentResized(ComponentEvent e) {
   if (!m_resizing) {
    m_resizing = true;
    spRight.setDividerLocation(spLeft.getDividerLocation());
      m_resizing=false
  }
 }
};
c11.addComponentListener(caLeft);

ComponentListener caRight = new ComponentAdapter() {

 public void componentResized(ComponentEvent e) {
   if (!m_resizing) {
    m_resizing = true;
    spLeft.setDividerLocation(spRight.getDividerLocation());
      m_resizing=false
   }
 }
};
c21.addComponentListener(caRight);
```
3 ComponentListeners responsible for keeping split panes synchronized

```java
      JSplitPane sp = new JSplitPane(JSplitPane.HORIZONTAL_SPLIT,
        spLeft, spRight);
      sp.setDividerSize(8);
      sp.setDividerLocation(200);
      sp.setResizeWeight(0.5);
      sp.setContinuousLayout(false);
      sp.setOneTouchExpandable(true);

      getContentPane().add(sp, borderLayout.CENTER);
    }

    public static void main(String argv[]) {
```

```
        SplitSample frame = new SplitSample();
        frame.setDefaultCloseOperation(JFrame.EXIT_ON_CLOSE);
        frame.setVisible(true);
    }
}

//class SimplePanel unchanged from example 8.1
```

8.3.1 Understanding the code

❶ The m_resizing flag is added to this example for temporary use by the Component-Listeners.

❷ The spLeft and spRight split panes are made final so that they can be referenced from within the ComponentListener anonymous inner classes.

❸ In order to synchronize the dividers of spLeft and spRight, a ComponentListener, caLeft and caRight respectively, is added to the top/right component of each (c11 for spLeft and c21 for spRight). Whenever the divider moves in spLeft or spRight, the componentResized() method will be invoked in the respective ComponentListener. This method first checks m_resizing. If m_resizing is true this means another Component-Listener is handling the synchronization, so the method exits (this stops any potential race conditions). If m_resizing is false it is first set true, then the opposite divider is set to its new synchronized location, and finally m_resizing is set to false again.

8.3.2 Running the code

This example looks just like example 8.1. But try moving the left or right horizontal dividers and notice that they always sit in the same location no matter which one we move, and no matter how we resize the frame. Such synchronization produces a cleaner visual design.

C H A P T E R   9

Combo boxes

9.1   JCOMBOBOX

class javax.swing.JComboBox

This class represents a basic GUI component which consists of two parts:

- A pop-up menu (an implementation of `javax.swing.plaf.basic.ComboPopup`). By default, this is a `JPopupMenu` subclass (`javax.swing.plaf.basic.BasicCombo-Popup`) that contains a `JList` in a `JScrollPane`.
- A button that acts as a container for an editor or renderer component, and an arrow button that is used to display the pop-up menu.

The `JList` uses a `ListSelectionModel` (see chapter 10) that allows `SINGLE_SELECTION` only. Apart from this, `JComboBox` directly uses only one model, a `ComboBoxModel`, which manages data in its `JList`.

A number of constructors are available to build a `JComboBox`. The default constructor can be used to create a combo box with an empty list, or we can pass data to a constructor as a one-dimensional array, a `Vector`, or an implementation of the `ComboBoxModel` interface (this will be explained later). The last variant allows maximum control over the properties and appearance of a `JComboBox`, as we will see.

As do other complex Swing components, JComboBox allows a customizable renderer for displaying each item in its drop-down list (by default, this is a JLabel subclass implementation of ListCellRenderer), and it allows a customizable editor to be used as the combo box's data entry component (by default, this is an instance of ComboBoxEditor which uses a JText-Field). We can use the existing default implementations of ListCellRenderer and ComboBoxEditor, or we can create our own according to our particular needs (as we will see later in this chapter). Unless we use a custom renderer, the default renderer will display each element as a String defined by that object's toString() method; the only exceptions to this are Icon implementations which will be rendered as they would be in any JLabel. Take note that a renderer returns a Component, but that component is not interactive and it is only used for display purposes (meaning it acts as a "rubber stamp," according to the API documentation). For instance, if a JCheckBox is used as a renderer, we will not be able to check and uncheck it. Editors, however, are fully interactive.

JAVA 1.4   As of Java 1.4 JComboBox supports a prototype display value. Without a prototype display value JComboBox would configure a renderer for each cell. This can be a performance bottleneck when there is a large number of items. If a prototype display value is used, only one renderer is configured and it is used for each cell. The prototype display value is configured by passing an Object to JComboBox's setPrototype-DisplayValue() method.

For example, if you want your JComboBox's cells to be no wider than what is required to display 10 'X' characters, you can do the following:

```
mJComboBox.setPrototypeDisplayValue(
new String ("XXXXXXXXXX"));
```

Similar to JList, which is discussed in the next chapter, this class uses ListDataEvents to deliver information about changes in the state of its drop-down list's model. ItemEvents and ActionEvents are fired from any source when the current selection changes—the source can be programmatic or input from the user. Correspondingly, we can attach ItemListeners and ActionListeners to receive these events.

The drop-down list of a JComboBox is a pop-up menu that contains a JList (this is actually defined in the UI delegate, not the component itself) and it can be programmatically displayed/hidden using the showPopup() and hidePopup() methods. As with any other Swing pop-up menu (which we will discuss in chapter 12), it can be displayed as either heavyweight or lightweight. JComboBox provides the setLightWeightPopupEnabled() method, which allows us to choose between these modes.

JAVA 1.4   As of Java 1.4 you can add a PopupMenuListener to JComboBox to listen for PopupMenuEvents; these occur whenever the popup is made visible, invisible, or canceled. JComboBox has the following new public methods to support usage of this new listener type: addPopupMenuListener(), removePopupMenuListener(), and getPopupMenuListeners(). See sections 12.1.18 and 12.1.19 for more on PopupMenuListener and PopupMenuEvent.

JComboBox also defines an inner interface called KeySelectionManager that declares one method, selectionForKey(char aKey, ComboBoxModel aModel), which we can define to return the index of the list element that should be selected when the list is visible (meaning the pop-up is showing) and the given keyboard character is pressed.

The JComboBox UI delegate represents JComboBox graphically using a container with a button. This button contains both an arrow button and either a renderer displaying the currently selected item or an editor that allows changes to be made to the currently selected item. The arrow button is displayed on the right of the renderer/editor and it will show the pop-up menu that contains the drop-down list when it is clicked.

NOTE   Because of the JComboBox UI delegate construction, setting the border of a JComboBox does not have the expected effect. Try this and you will see that the container containing the main JComboBox button gets the assigned border, when in fact we want that button to receive the border. There is no easy way to set the border of this button without customizing the UI delegate. We hope to see this limitation disappear in a future version.

When a JComboBox is editable (which it is not by default) the editor component will allow modification of the currently selected item. The default editor will appear as a JTextField that accepts input. This text field has an ActionListener attached that will accept an edit and change the selected item accordingly when/if the ENTER key is pressed. If the focus changes while editing, all editing will be cancelled and a change will not be made to the selected item.

JComboBox can be made editable with its setEditable() method, and we can specify a custom ComboBoxEditor with JComboBox's setEditor() method. Setting the editable property to true causes the UI delegate to replace the renderer in the button with the assigned editor. Similarly, setting this property to false causes the editor in the button to be replaced by a renderer.

The cell renderer used for a JComboBox can be assigned and retrieved with the setRenderer() and getRenderer() methods, respectively. Calls to these methods actually get passed to the JList contained in the combo box's pop-up menu.

UI
GUIDELINE

Advice on usage and design

Usage   Combo boxes and list boxes are very similar to each other. In fact, a combo box is an entry field with a drop-down list box. Deciding when to use one or the other can be difficult. Our advice is to think about reader output rather than data input. When the reader only needs to see a single item, then a combo box is the best choice. Use a combo box where a single selection is made from a collection and users only need to see a single item, such as "Currency USD." You'll learn about using list boxes in the next chapter.

Design   There are a number of things affect the usability of a combo box. If it contains more than a few items, it becomes unusable unless the data is sorted in some logical fashion, such as in alphabetical or numerical order. When a list gets longer, usability is affected in yet another way. Once a list gets beyond a couple of hundred items, even when sorted, locating a specific item in the list becomes a very slow process for the user. Some implementations have solved this by offering the ability to type in partial text, and the list "jumps" to the best match or a partial match item; for example, type in "ch" and the combo box will jump to "Chevrolet" in example 9.1. You may want to consider such an enhancement to a JComboBox to improve the usability of longer lists.

There are a number of graphical considerations, also. Like all other data entry fields, combo boxes should be aligned to fit attractively into a panel. However, this is not always easy. Avoid making a combo box which is simply too big for the list items it contains. For example, a combo box for a currency code only needs to be 3 characters long (USD is the code for U.S. dollars), so don't make it big enough to take 50 characters. It will look unbalanced. Another problem concerns the nature of the list items. If you have 50 items in a list where most items are around 20 characters long but one item is 50 characters long, should you make the combo box big enough to display the longer one? Possibly, but for most occasions your display will be unbalanced again. It is probably best to optimize for the more common length, providing the longer one still has meaning when read in its truncated form. One solution to display the whole length of a truncated item is to use the tooltip facility. When the user places the mouse over an item, a tooltip appears that contains the full text.

One thing you must never do is dynamically resize the combo box to fit a varying length item selection. This will incur alignment problems and it may also add a usability problem because the pull-down button may become a moving target, which then makes it harder for the user to learn its position through directional memory.

9.1.1 The ComboBoxModel interface

abstract interface javax.swing.ComboBoxModel

This interface extends the `ListModel` interface which handles the combo box drop-down list's data. This model separately handles its selected item with two methods, `setSelectedItem()` and `getSelectedItem()`.

9.1.2 The MutableComboBoxModel interface

abstract interface javax.swing.MutableComboBoxModel

This interface extends `ComboBoxModel` and adds four methods to modify the model's contents dynamically: `addElement()`, `insertElementAt()`, `removeElement()`, and `removeElementAt()`.

9.1.3 DefaultComboBoxModel

class javax.swing.DefaultComboBoxModel

This class represents the default model used by `JComboBox`, and it implements `MutableComboBoxModel`. To programmatically select an item, we can call its `setSelectedItem()` method. Calling this method, as well as any of the `MutableComboBoxModel` methods mentioned above, will cause a `ListDataEvent` to be fired. To capture these events we can attach `ListDataListeners` with `DefaultComboBoxModel`'s `addListDataListener()` method. We can also remove these listeners with its `removeListDataListener()` method.

9.1.4　The ListCellRenderer interface

abstract interface javax.swing.ListCellRenderer

This is a simple interface used to define the component to be used as a renderer for the JCombo-Box drop-down list. It declares one method, getListCellRendererComponent(JList list, Object value, int Index, boolean isSelected, boolean cellHasFocus), which is called to return the component used to represent a given combo box element visually. The component returned by this method is not at all interactive, and it is used for display purposes only (it's referred to as a "rubber stamp" in the API documentations).

When a JComboBox is in noneditable mode, –1 will be passed to this method to return the component used to represent the selected item in the main JComboBox button. Normally, this component is the same as the component used to display that same element in the drop-down list.

9.1.5　DefaultListCellRenderer

class javax.swing.DefaultListCellRenderer

This is the concrete implementation of the ListCellRenderer interface that is used by JList by default (and thus by JComboBox's drop-down JList). This class extends JLabel and its getListCellRenderer() method returns a this reference. It also renders the given value by setting its text to the String returned by the value's toString() method (unless the value is an instance of Icon, in which case it will be rendered as it would be in any JLabel), and it uses JList foreground and background colors, depending on whether the given item is selected.

> **NOTE**　Unfortunately, there is no easy way to access JComboBox's drop-down JList, which prevents us from assigning new foreground and background colors. Ideally, JComboBox would provide this communication with its JList. We hope to see this functionality in a future version.

A single static EmptyBorder instance is used for all cells that do not have the current focus. This border has top, bottom, left, and right spacing of 1, and unfortunately, it cannot be reassigned.

9.1.6　The ComboBoxEditor interface

abstract interface javax.swing.ComboBoxEditor

This interface describes the JComboBox editor. The default editor is provided by the only implementing class, javax.swing.plaf.basic.BasicComboBoxEditor, but we are certainly not limited to this. The purpose of this interface is to allow us to implement our own custom editor. The getEditorComponent() method should be overridden to return the editor component to use. BasicComboBoxEditor's getEditorComponent() method returns a JTextField that will be used for the currently selected combo box item. Unlike cell renderers, components returned by the getEditorComponent() method are fully interactive.

The setItem() method is intended to tell the editor which element to edit (this is called when an item is selected from the drop-down list). The getItem() method is used to return the object being edited (which is a String using the default editor).

`ComboBoxEditor` also declares functionality for attaching and removing `ActionLis-`
`teners` which are notified when an edit is accepted. In the default editor this occurs when
ENTER is pressed while the text field has the focus.

NOTE   Unfortunately, Swing does not provide an easily reusable `ComboBoxEditor`
implementation, forcing custom implementations to manage all `ActionListener`
and item selection/modification functionality from scratch. We hope to see this
limitation accounted for in a future Swing release.

9.2   BASIC JCOMBOBOX EXAMPLE

Example 9.1 displays information about popular cars in two symmetrical panels to provide a
natural means of comparison. To be realistic, we need to take into account the fact that any car
model can come in several trim lines which actually determine the car's characteristics and
price. Numerous characteristics of cars are available on the web. For this simple example, we've
selected the following two-level data structure:

CAR

Name	Type	Description
Name	`String`	Model's name
Manufacturer	`String`	Company manufacturer
Image	`Icon`	Model's photograph
Trims	`Vector`	A collection of the model's trims

TRIM

Name	Type	Description
Name	`String`	Trim's name
MSRP	`int`	Manufacturer's suggested retail price
Invoice	`int`	Invoice price
Engine	`String`	Engine description

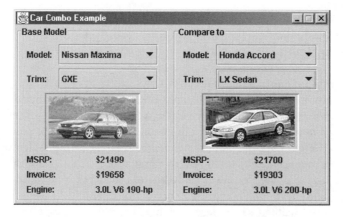

**Figure 9.1   Dynamically changeable `JComboBoxes`
that allow comparison of car model and trim information**

Example 9.1

`ComboBox1.java`

see \Chapter9\1

```java
import java.awt.*;
import java.awt.event.*;
import java.util.*;

import javax.swing.*;
import javax.swing.border.*;
import javax.swing.event.*;

public class ComboBox1 extends JFrame
{
  public ComboBox1() {
    super("ComboBoxes [Compare Cars]");
    getContentPane().setLayout(new BorderLayout());

    Vector cars = new Vector();
    Car maxima = new Car("Maxima", "Nissan", new ImageIcon(
      "maxima.gif"));
    maxima.addTrim("GXE", 21499, 19658, "3.0L V6 190-hp");
    maxima.addTrim("SE",  23499, 21118, "3.0L V6 190-hp");
    maxima.addTrim("GLE", 26899, 24174, "3.0L V6 190-hp");
    cars.addElement(maxima);

    Car accord = new Car("Accord", "Honda", new ImageIcon(
      "accord.gif"));
    accord.addTrim("LX Sedan", 21700, 19303, "3.0L V6 200-hp");
    accord.addTrim("EX Sedan", 24300, 21614, "3.0L V6 200-hp");
    cars.addElement(accord);

    Car camry = new Car("Camry", "Toyota", new ImageIcon(
      "camry.gif"));
    camry.addTrim("LE V6", 21888, 19163, "3.0L V6 194-hp");
    camry.addTrim("XLE V6", 24998, 21884, "3.0L V6 194-hp");
    cars.addElement(camry);

    Car lumina = new Car("Lumina", "Chevrolet", new ImageIcon(
      "lumina.gif"));
    lumina.addTrim("LS", 19920, 18227, "3.1L V6 160-hp");
    lumina.addTrim("LTZ", 20360, 18629, "3.8L V6 200-hp");
    cars.addElement(lumina);

    Car taurus = new Car("Taurus", "Ford", new ImageIcon(
      "taurus.gif"));
    taurus.addTrim("LS", 17445, 16110, "3.0L V6 145-hp");
    taurus.addTrim("SE", 18445, 16826, "3.0L V6 145-hp");
    taurus.addTrim("SHO", 29000, 26220, "3.4L V8 235-hp");
    cars.addElement(taurus);

    Car passat = new Car("Passat", "Volkswagen", new ImageIcon(
      "passat.gif"));
    passat.addTrim("GLS V6", 23190, 20855, "2.8L V6 190-hp");
```

One of several Cars with Trims in car list ①

```
      passat.addTrim("GLX", 26250, 23589, "2.8L V6 190-hp");
      cars.addElement(passat);

      getContentPane().setLayout(new GridLayout(1, 2, 5, 3));
      CarPanel pl = new CarPanel("Base Model", cars);
      getContentPane().add(pl);
      CarPanel pr = new CarPanel("Compare to", cars);
      getContentPane().add(pr);

      setDefaultCloseOperation(JFrame.EXIT_ON_CLOSE);
      pl.selectCar(maxima);
      pr.selectCar(accord);
      setResizable(false);
      pack();
      setVisible(true);
   }

   public static void main(String argv[]) {
      new ComboBox1();
   }
}

class Car
{
   protected String m_name;
   protected String m_manufacturer;
   protected Icon   m_img;
   protected Vector m_trims;

   public Car(String name, String manufacturer, Icon img) {
      m_name = name;
      m_manufacturer = manufacturer;
      m_img = img;
      m_trims = new Vector();
   }

   public void addTrim(String name, int MSRP, int invoice,
    String engine) {
      Trim trim = new Trim(this, name, MSRP, invoice, engine);
      m_trims.addElement(trim);
   }

   public String getName() { return m_name; }

   public String getManufacturer() { return m_manufacturer; }

   public Icon getIcon() { return m_img; }

   public Vector getTrims() { return m_trims; }

   public String toString() { return m_manufacturer+" "+m_name; }
}

class Trim
{
   protected Car      m_parent;
   protected String m_name;
   protected int      m_MSRP;
```

2 Simple data object with basic car model information, including list of trims

3 Creates new Trim and adds it to Trims list

4 Simple data object with Trim information, including link to owning Car object

CHAPTER 9 COMBO BOXES

```java
  protected int    m_invoice;
  protected String m_engine;

  public Trim(Car parent, String name, int MSRP, int invoice,
   String engine) {
    m_parent = parent;
    m_name = name;
    m_MSRP = MSRP;
    m_invoice = invoice;
    m_engine = engine;
  }

  public Car getCar() { return m_parent; }

  public String getName() { return m_name; }

  public int getMSRP() { return m_MSRP; }

  public int getInvoice() { return m_invoice; }

  public String getEngine() { return m_engine; }

  public String toString() { return m_name; }
}

class CarPanel extends JPanel
{
  protected JComboBox m_cbCars;
  protected JComboBox m_cbTrims;
  protected JLabel m_lblImg;
  protected JLabel m_lblMSRP;
  protected JLabel m_lblInvoice;
  protected JLabel m_lblEngine;

  public CarPanel(String title, Vector cars) {
    super();
    setLayout(new BoxLayout(this, BoxLayout.Y_AXIS));
    setBorder(new TitledBorder(new EtchedBorder(), title));

    JPanel p = new JPanel();
    p.add(new JLabel("Model:"));
    m_cbCars = new JComboBox(cars);
    ActionListener lst = new ActionListener() {
      public void actionPerformed(ActionEvent e) {
        Car car = (Car)m_cbCars.getSelectedItem();
        if (car != null)
          showCar(car);
      }
    };
    m_cbCars.addActionListener(lst);
    p.add(m_cbCars);
    add(p);

    p = new JPanel();
    p.add(new JLabel("Trim:"));
    m_cbTrims = new JComboBox();
    lst = new ActionListener() {
```

5 GUI components to display Car information

7 Vertical BoxLayout for major components

7 FlowLayout for labels and input fields

6 Combo box to select Car models

7 FlowLayout for labels and input fields

```
        public void actionPerformed(ActionEvent e) {
          Trim trim = (Trim)m_cbTrims.getSelectedItem();
          if (trim != null)
            showTrim(trim);
        }
      };
      m_cbTrims.addActionListener(lst);
      p.add(m_cbTrims);
      add(p);
      p = new JPanel();
      m_lblImg = new JLabel();
      m_lblImg.setHorizontalAlignment(JLabel.CENTER);
      m_lblImg.setPreferredSize(new Dimension(140, 80));
      m_lblImg.setBorder(new BevelBorder(BevelBorder.LOWERED));
      p.add(m_lblImg);
      add(p);

      p = new JPanel();
      p.setLayout(new GridLayout(3, 2, 10, 5));
      p.add(new JLabel("MSRP:"));
      m_lblMSRP = new JLabel();
      p.add(m_lblMSRP);

      p.add(new JLabel("Invoice:"));
      m_lblInvoice = new JLabel();
      p.add(m_lblInvoice);

      p.add(new JLabel("Engine:"));
      m_lblEngine = new JLabel();
      p.add(m_lblEngine);
      add(p);
    }

    public void selectCar(Car car) { m_cbCars.setSelectedItem(car); }

    public void showCar(Car car) {
      m_lblImg.setIcon(car.getIcon());
      if (m_cbTrims.getItemCount() > 0)
        m_cbTrims.removeAllItems();
      Vector v = car.getTrims();
      for (int k=0; k<v.size(); k++)
        m_cbTrims.addItem(v.elementAt(k));
      m_cbTrims.grabFocus();
    }

    public void showTrim(Trim trim) {
      m_lblMSRP.setText("$"+trim.getMSRP());
      m_lblInvoice.setText("$"+trim.getInvoice());
      m_lblEngine.setText(trim.getEngine());
    }
  }
```

8 Labels and values in GridLayout

9 Used by client of this class to select a particular Car

10 For selected Car, updates image and available Trims

11 Bad to remove items from empty combo box

12 Updates value labels for selected Car and Trim

9.2.1 Understanding the code

Class ComboBox1

1 The ComboBox1 class extends JFrame to implement the frame container for this example. It has no instance variables. The constructor creates a data collection with the car information as listed above. A collection of cars is stored in Vector cars, and each car, in turn, receives one or more Trim instances. Other than this, the ComboBox1 constructor doesn't do much. It creates two instances of CarPanel (see below) and arranges them in a GridLayout. These panels are used to select and display car information. Finally, two cars are initially selected in both panels.

Class Car

2 The Car class is a typical data object that encapsulates three data fields which are listed at the beginning of this section: car name, manufacturer, and image. In addition, it holds the m_trims vector that stores a collection of Trim instances.

3 The addTrim() method creates a new Trim instance and adds it to the m_trims vector. The rest of this class implements typical getXX() methods to allow access to the protected data fields.

Class Trim

4 The Trim class encapsulates four data fields, which are listed at the beginning of this section: trim name, suggested retail price, invoice price, and engine type. In addition, it holds a reference to the parent Car instance. The rest of this class implements typical getXX() methods to allow access to the protected data fields.

Class CarPanel

The CarPanel class extends JPanel to provide the GUI framework for displaying car information. Six components are declared as instance variables:

5
- JComboBox m_cbCars: Used to select a car model.
- JComboBox m_cbTrims: Used to select a car trim of the selected model.
- JLabel m_lblImg: Used to display the model's image.
- JLabel m_lblMSRP: Used to display the MSRP.
- JLabel m_lblInvoice: Used to display the invoice price.
- JLabel m_lblEngine: Used to display the engine description.

6 Two combo boxes are used to select cars and trims respectively. Note that Car and Trim data objects are used to populate these combo boxes, so the actual displayed text is determined by their toString() methods. Both combo boxes receive ActionListeners to handle item selection. When a Car item is selected, this triggers a call to the showCar() method described below. Similarly, selecting a Trim item triggers a call to the showTrim() method.

7 The rest of the CarPanel constructor builds JLabels to display a car's image and trim data. Notice how layouts are used in this example. A y-oriented BoxLayout creates a vertical axis used to align and position all components. The combo boxes and supplementary labels are encapsulated in horizontal JPanels. JLabel m_lblImg receives a custom preferred size to

8 reserve enough space for the photo image. This label is encapsulated in a panel (with its default

FlowLayout) to ensure that this component will be centered over the parent container's space. The rest of CarPanel is occupied by six labels, which are hosted by a 3x2 GridLayout.

⑨ The selectCar() method allows us to select a car programmatically from outside this class. It invokes the setSelectedItem() method on the m_cbCars combo box. This call will trigger an ActionEvent which will be captured by the proper listener, resulting in a showCar() call.

⑩ The showCar() method updates the car image, and it updates the m_cbTrims combo box to
⑪ display the corresponding trims of the selected model. The (getItemCount() > 0) condition is necessary because Swing throws an exception if removeAllItems() is invoked on an empty JComboBox. Finally, focus is transferred to the m_cbTrims component.

⑫ The showTrim() method updates the contents of the labels that display trim information: MSRP, invoice price, and engine type.

9.2.2 Running the code

Figure 9.1 shows the ComboBox1 application that displays two cars simultaneously for comparison. All the initial information is displayed correctly. Try experimenting with various selections and notice how the combo box contents change dynamically.

GUIDELINE

Symmetrical layout   In example 9.1, the design avoids the problem of having to align the different length combo boxes by using a symmetrical layout. Overall, the window has a good balance and it uses white space well; so do each of the bordered panes used for individual car selections.

9.3   CUSTOM MODEL AND RENDERER

Ambitious Swing developers may want to provide custom rendering in combo boxes to display structured data in the drop-down list. Different levels of structure can be identified by differing left margins and icons; this is also how it's done in trees, which we will study in chapter 17. Such complex combo boxes can enhance functionality and provide a more sophisticated appearance.

In this section we will show how to merge the model and trim combo boxes from the previous section into a single combo box. To differentiate between model and trim items in the drop-down list, we can use different left margins and different icons for each. Our list should look something like this:

```
Nissan Maxima
   GXE
   SE
   GLE
```

We also need to prevent the user from selecting models (such as "Nissan Maxima" above), since they do not provide complete information about a specific car, and they only serve as separators between sets of trims.

NOTE   The hierarchical list organization shown here can easily be extended for use in a JList, and it can handle an arbitrary number of levels. We only use two levels in example 9.2, but the design does not limit us to this.

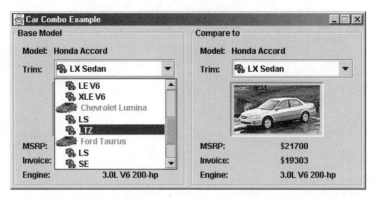

Figure 9.2 A `JComboBox` with a custom model and a custom hierarchical rendering scheme

Example 9.2

ComboBox2.java

see \Chapter9\2

```java
// Unchanged code from example 9.1
class CarPanel extends JPanel
{
  protected JComboBox m_cbCars;
  protected JLabel m_txtModel;
  protected JLabel m_lblImg;
  protected JLabel m_lblMSRP;
  protected JLabel m_lblInvoice;
  protected JLabel m_lblEngine;

  public CarPanel(String title, Vector cars) {
    super();
    setLayout(new BoxLayout(this, BoxLayout.Y_AXIS));
    setBorder(new TitledBorder(new EtchedBorder(), title));

    JPanel p = new JPanel();
    m_txtModel = new JLabel("");
    m_txtModel.setForeground(Color.black);
    p.add(m_txtModel);
    add(p);

    p = new JPanel();
    p.add(new JLabel("Car:"));
    CarComboBoxModel model = new CarComboBoxModel(cars);
    m_cbCars = new JComboBox(model);
    m_cbCars.setRenderer(new IconComboRenderer());
    ActionListener lst = new ActionListener() {
      public void actionPerformed(ActionEvent e) {
        ListData data = (ListData)m_cbCars.getSelectedItem();
```

❶ Label to show Car model name

❷ Variable length label will always be centered

❸ m_cbCars will show model names along with icons

```
              Object obj = data.getObject();
              if (obj instanceof Trim)
                showTrim((Trim)obj);
          }
        };
        m_cbCars.addActionListener(lst);
        p.add(m_cbCars);
        add(p);

        //Unchanged code from example 9.1
    }

    public synchronized void selectCar(Car car) {
        for (int k=0; k < m_cbCars.getItemCount(); k++) {
            ListData obj = (ListData)m_cbCars.getItemAt(k);
            if (obj.getObject() == car) {
                m_cbCars.setSelectedItem(obj);
                break;
            }
        }
    }

    public synchronized void showTrim(Trim trim) {
        Car car = trim.getCar();
        m_txtModel.setText(car.toString());
        m_lblImg.setIcon(car.getIcon());
        m_lblMSRP.setText("$" + trim.getMSRP());
        m_lblInvoice.setText("$" + trim.getInvoice());
        m_lblEngine.setText(trim.getEngine());
    }
}

class ListData
{
    protected Icon      m_icon;
    protected int       m_index;
    protected boolean m_selectable;
    protected Object    m_data;

    public ListData(Icon icon, int index, boolean selectable,
     Object data) {
        m_icon = icon;
        m_index = index;
        m_selectable = selectable;
        m_data = data;
    }

    public Icon getIcon() { return m_icon; }

    public int getIndex() { return m_index; }

    public boolean isSelectable() { return m_selectable; }

    public Object getObject() { return m_data; }

    public String toString() { return m_data.toString(); }
}
```

4 Both Car and Trim instances, although only Trims can

5 Finds ListData object in combo box whose Car object is equal to the parameter, and selects that one

6 Now displays Model name in addition to Trim name

7 Encapsulates combo box data and rendering information

```java
class CarComboBoxModel extends DefaultComboBoxModel
{
  public static final ImageIcon ICON_CAR =
    new ImageIcon("car.gif");
  public static final ImageIcon ICON_TRIM =
    new ImageIcon("trim.gif");

  public CarComboBoxModel(Vector cars) {
    for (int k=0; k<cars.size(); k++) {
      Car car = (Car)cars.elementAt(k);
      addElement(new ListData(ICON_CAR, 0, false, car));

      Vector v = car.getTrims();
      for (int i=0; i < v.size(); i++) {
        Trim trim = (Trim)v.elementAt(i);
        addElement(new ListData(ICON_TRIM, 1, true, trim));
      }
    }
  }

  // This method only allows trims to be selected
  public void setSelectedItem(Object item) {
    if (item instanceof ListData) {
      ListData ldata = (ListData)item;
      if (!ldata.isSelectable()) {
        Object newItem = null;
        int index = getIndexOf(item);
        for (int k = index + 1; k < getSize(); k++) {
          Object item1 = getElementAt(k);
          if (item1 instanceof ListData) {
            ListData ldata1 = (ListData)item1;
            if (!ldata1.isSelectable())
              continue;
          }
          newItem = item1;
          break;
        }
        if (newItem==null)
          return;          // Selection failed
        item = newItem;
      }
    }
    super.setSelectedItem(item);
  }
}

class IconComboRenderer extends JLabel implements ListCellRenderer
{
  public static final int OFFSET = 16;

  protected Color m_textSelectionColor = Color.white;
  protected Color m_textNonSelectionColor = Color.black;
  protected Color m_textNonselectableColor = Color.gray;
  protected Color m_bkSelectionColor = new Color(0, 0, 128);
  protected Color m_bkNonSelectionColor = Color.white;
```

8 Data model for combo box; holds icons for Car and Trim

8 Data model for combo box; holds icons for Car and Trim

8 Adds list element for Trim; selectable

9 If not selectable, try to move selection to next selectable item (a Trim object)

10 Acts as custom combo box list item renderer; shows text with icon

```
protected Color m_borderSelectionColor = Color.yellow;

protected Color  m_textColor;
protected Color  m_bkColor;

protected boolean m_hasFocus;
protected Border[] m_borders;

public IconComboRenderer() {
  super();
  m_textColor = m_textNonSelectionColor;
  m_bkColor = m_bkNonSelectionColor;
  m_borders = new Border[20];
  for (int k=0; k < m_borders.length; k++)
    m_borders[k] = new EmptyBorder(0, OFFSET * k, 0, 0);
  setOpaque(false);
}

public Component getListCellRendererComponent(JList list,
 Object obj, int row, boolean sel, boolean hasFocus) {
  if (obj == null)
    return this;
  setText(obj.toString());
  boolean selectable = true;
  if (obj instanceof ListData) {
    ListData ldata = (ListData)obj;
    selectable = ldata.isSelectable();
    setIcon(ldata.getIcon());
    int index = 0;
    if (row >= 0)    // No offset for editor (row=-1)
      index = ldata.getIndex();
    Border b = (index < m_borders.length ? m_borders[index] :
      new EmptyBorder(0, OFFSET * index, 0, 0));
    setBorder(b);
  }
  else
    setIcon(null);

  setFont(list.getFont());
  m_textColor = (sel ? m_textSelectionColor :
    (selectable ? m_textNonSelectionColor :
    m_textNonselectableColor));
  m_bkColor = (sel ? m_bkSelectionColor :
    m_bkNonSelectionColor);
  m_hasFocus = hasFocus;
  return this;
}

public void paint (Graphics g) {
  Icon icon = getIcon();
  Border b = getBorder();

  g.setColor(m_bkNonSelectionColor);
  g.fillRect(0, 0, getWidth(), getHeight());

  g.setColor(m_bkColor);
  int offset = 0;
```

11 Creates set of stepped EmptyBorders to provide "indents" for list items

12 Use matching EmptyBorder from list

13 Draws background excluding icon, and draws focus highlight

```
    if(icon != null && getText() != null) {
      Insets ins = getInsets();
      offset = ins.left + icon.getIconWidth() + getIconTextGap();
    }
    g.fillRect(offset, 0, getWidth() - 1 - offset,
      getHeight() - 1);

    if (m_hasFocus) {
      g.setColor(m_borderSelectionColor);
      g.drawRect(offset, 0, getWidth()-1-offset, getHeight()-1);
    }

    setForeground(m_textColor);
    setBackground(m_bkColor);
    super.paint(g);
  }
}
```

9.3.1   Understanding the code

Class CarPanel

1 The ComboBox2 (formerly ComboBox1), Car, and Trim classes remain unchanged in this example, so we'll start from the CarPanel class. Compared to example 9.1, we've removed combo box m_cbTrims and added JLabel m_txtModel, which is used to display the current model's name. When the combo box pop-up is hidden, the user can see only the selected trim, so we need to display the corresponding model name separately. Curiously, the constructor of the CarPanel class places this label component in its own JPanel (using its default FlowLayout) to ensure its location in the center of the base panel.

2   **NOTE**   The reason for this is that JLabel m_txtModel has a variable length, and the Box-Layout which manages CarPanel cannot dynamically center this component correctly. Placing this label in a FlowLayout panel will make sure it's always centered.

3 The single combo box, m_cbCars, has a bit in common with the component of the same name in example 9.1. First, it receives a custom model, an instance of the CarComboBoxModel class, which will be described below. It also receives a custom renderer, an instance of the IconCombo-Renderer class, which is also described below.

4 The combo box is populated by both Car and Trim instances encapsulated in ListData objects (see below). This requires some changes in the actionPerformed() method which handles combo box selection. We first extract the data object from the selected ListData instance by calling the getObject() method. If this call returns a Trim object (as it should, since Cars cannot be selected), we call the showTrim() method to display the selected data.

5 The selectCar() method has been modified. As we mentioned above, our combo box now holds ListData objects, so we cannot pass a Car object as a parameter to the setSelected-Item() method. Instead, we have to examine, in turn, all items in the combo box, cast them to ListData objects, and verify that the encapsulated data object is equal to the given Car instance.

6 The showTrim() method now displays the model data as well as the trim data. To do this we obtain a parent Car instance for a given Trim and display the model's name and icon.

Class ListData

7 The `ListData` class encapsulates the data object to be rendered in the combo box and adds new attributes for our rendering needs.

These are the instance variables:

- `Icon m_icon`: The icon associated with the data object.
- `int m_index`: The item's index which determines the left margin (the hierarchical level, for example).
- `boolean m_selectable`: The flag indicating that this item can be selected.
- `Object m_data`: The encapsulated data object.

All variables are assigned parameters that have been passed to the constructor. The rest of the `ListData` class contains four `getXX()` methods and a `toString()` method, which all delegate calls to the `m_data` object.

Class CarComboBoxModel

8 This class extends `DefaultComboBoxModel` to serve as a data model for our combo box . It first creates two static `ImageIcon`s to represent the model and the trim. The constructor takes a `Vector` of `Car` instances and converts them and their trims into a linear sequence of `ListData` objects. Each `Car` object is encapsulated in a `ListData` instance with an `ICON_CAR` icon, the index set to 0, and the `m_selectable` flag set to `false`. Each `Trim` object is encapsulated in a `ListData` instance with an `ICON_TRIM` icon, the index set to 1, and the `m_selectable` flag set to `true`.

9 These manipulations could have been done without implementing a custom `ComboBoxModel`, of course. The real reason we implement a custom model here is to override the `setSelectedItem()` method to control item selection in the combo box. As we learned above, only `ListData` instances with the `m_selectable` flag set to `true` should be selectable. To achieve this goal, the overridden `setSelectedItem()` method casts the selected object to a `ListData` instance and examines its selection property using `isSelectable()`.

If `isSelectable()` returns `false`, a special action needs to be handled to move the selection to the first item following this item for which `isSelectable()` returns `true`. If no such item is found, our `setSelectedItem()` method returns and the selection in the combo box remains unchanged. Otherwise, the `item` variable receives a new value which is finally passed to the `setSelectedItem()` implementation of the superclass `DefaultComboBoxModel`.

> **NOTE** You may notice that the `selectCar()` method discussed above selects a `Car` instance which cannot be selected. This internally triggers a call to `setSelectedItem()` of the combo box model, which shifts the selection to the first available `Trim` item. You can verify this when running the example.

Class IconComboRenderer

10 This class extends `JLabel` and implements the `ListCellRenderer` interface to serve as a custom combo box renderer.

Class variable:

- `int OFFSET`: The offset, in pixels, to use for the left trim margin.

Here are the instance variables:

- `Color m_textColor`: The current text color.
- `Color m_bkColor`: The current background color.
- `boolean m_hasFocus`: The flag that indicates whether this item has the focus.
- `Border[] m_borders`: An array of borders used for this component.

⑪ The constructor of the `IconComboRenderer` class initializes these variables. `EmptyBorders` are used to provide left margins while rendering components of the drop-down list. To avoid generating numerous temporary objects, an array of 20 `Borders` is prepared with increasing left offsets corresponding to the array index (incremented by `OFFSET`). This provides us with a set of different borders to use for white space in representing data at 20 distinct hierarchical levels.

> **NOTE** Even though we only use two levels in this example, `IconComboRenderer` has been designed for maximum reusability. We've designed `getListCellRenderer-Component()` (see below) to create a new `EmptyBorder` in the event that more than 20 levels are used.

⑫ The `getListCellRendererComponent()` method is called prior to the painting of each cell in the drop-down list. We first set this component's text to that of the given object (which is passed as a parameter). Then, if the object is an instance of `ListData`, we set the icon and left margin by using the appropriate `EmptyBorder` from the previously prepared array (which is based on the given `ListData`'s `m_index` property). A call to this method with `row=-1` will be invoked prior to the rendering of the combo box button, which is the part of the combo box that is always visible (see section 9.1). In this case we don't need to use any border offset. Offset only makes sense when there are hierarchical differences between items in the list, not when an item is rendered alone.

The rest of the `getListCellRendererComponent()` method determines the background and foreground colors to use, based on whether an item is selected and selectable, and stores them in instance variables to be used within the `paint()` method. Non-selectable items receive their own foreground to distinguish them from selectable items.

⑬ The `paint()` method performs a bit of rendering before invoking the superclass implementation. It fills the background with the stored `m_bkColor`, excluding the icon's area (the left margin is already taken into account by the component's `Border`). It also draws a border-like rectangle if the component currently has the focus. This method then ends with a call to its superclass's `paint()` method, which takes responsibility for painting the label text and icon.

9.3.2 Running the code

Figure 9.2 shows our hierarchical drop-down list in action. Note that models and trim lines can be easily differentiated because of the varying icons and offsets. In addition, models have a gray foreground to imply that they cannot be selected.

This implementation is more user-friendly than example 9.1 because it displays all available data in a single drop-down list. Try selecting different trims and notice how this changes data for both the model and trim information labels. Try selecting a model and notice that it will result in the first trim of that model being selected instead.

Improved usability   From a usability perspective, the solution in figure 9.2 is an improvement over the one presented in figure 9.1. By using a combo box with a hierarchical data model, the designer has reduced the data entry to a single selection and has presented the information in an accessible and logical manner which also produces a visually cleaner result.

Further improvements could be made here by sorting the hierarchical data. In this example, it would seem appropriate to sort in a two-tiered fashion: alphabetically by manufacturer, and alphabetically by model. Thus Toyota would come after Ford and Toyota Corolla would come after Toyota Camry.

This is an excellent example of how a programmer can improve UI design and usability to make the program easier for the user to use.

9.4   COMBO BOXES WITH MEMORY

In some situations, you may want to use editable combo boxes which keep a historical list of choices for future reuse. This conveniently allows the user to select a previous choice rather than typing the same text over and over. A typical example of an editable combo box with memory is found in Find/Replace dialogs in many modern applications. Another example, familiar to almost every modern computer user, is provided in many Internet browsers which use an editable URL combo-box-with-history mechanism. These combo boxes accumulate typed addresses so the user can easily return to any previously visited site by selecting it from the drop-down list instead of manually typing it in again.

Example 9.3 shows how to create a simple browser application using an editable combo box with memory. It uses the serialization mechanism to save data between program sessions, and the `JEditorPane` component (which is described in more detail in chapters 11 and 19) to display non-editable HTMLfiles.

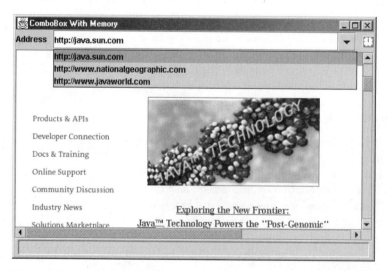

Figure 9.3   A `JComboBox` **with memory of previously visited URLs**

Example 9.3

see \Chapter9\3

```java
import java.awt.*;
import java.awt.event.*;
import java.io.*;
import java.net.*;

import javax.swing.*;
import javax.swing.event.*;
import javax.swing.text.*;
import javax.swing.text.html.*;

public class Browser extends JFrame
{
  protected JEditorPane m_browser;
  protected MemComboBox m_locator;
  protected AnimatedLabel m_runner;

  public Browser() {
    super("HTML Browser [ComboBox with Memory]");
    setSize(500, 300);

    JPanel p = new JPanel();
    p.setLayout(new BoxLayout(p, BoxLayout.X_AXIS));
    p.add(new JLabel("Address"));
    p.add(Box.createRigidArea(new Dimension(10, 1)));

    m_locator = new MemComboBox();
    m_locator.load("addresses.dat");
    BrowserListener lst = new BrowserListener();
    m_locator.addActionListener(lst);

    p.add(m_locator);
    p.add(Box.createRigidArea(new Dimension(10, 1)));

    m_runner = new AnimatedLabel("clock", 8);
    p.add(m_runner);
    getContentPane().add(p, BorderLayout.NORTH);

    m_browser = new JEditorPane();
    m_browser.setEditable(false);
    m_browser.addHyperlinkListener(lst);

    JScrollPane sp = new JScrollPane();
    sp.getViewport().add(m_browser);
    getContentPane().add(sp, BorderLayout.CENTER);

    WindowListener wndCloser = new WindowAdapter() {
      public void windowClosing(WindowEvent e) {
        m_locator.save("addresses.dat");
        System.exit(0);
      }
    };
    addWindowListener(wndCloser);
```

1 Creates custom combo box and loads it with some history

2 Saves history list

```
        setVisible(true);
        m_locator.grabFocus();
    }

    class BrowserListener implements ActionListener, HyperlinkListener
    {
        public void actionPerformed(ActionEvent evt) {
            String sUrl = (String)m_locator.getSelectedItem();
            if (sUrl == null || sUrl.length() == 0 ||
              m_runner.getRunning())
                return;
            BrowserLoader loader = new BrowserLoader(sUrl);
            loader.start();
        }

        public void hyperlinkUpdate(HyperlinkEvent e) {
            URL url = e.getURL();
            if (url == null || m_runner.getRunning())
                return;
            BrowserLoader loader = new BrowserLoader(url.toString());
            loader.start();
        }
    }

    class BrowserLoader extends Thread
    {
        protected String m_sUrl;

        public BrowserLoader(String sUrl) { m_sUrl = sUrl; }

        public void run() {
            setCursor(Cursor.getPredefinedCursor(Cursor.WAIT_CURSOR));
            m_runner.setRunning(true);

            try {
                URL source = new URL(m_sUrl);
                m_browser.setPage(source);
                m_locator.add(m_sUrl);
            }
            catch (Exception e) {
                JOptionPane.showMessageDialog(Browser.this,
                    "Error: "+e.toString(),
                    "Warning", JOptionPane.WARNING_MESSAGE);
            }
            m_runner.setRunning(false);
            setCursor(Cursor.getPredefinedCursor(Cursor.DEFAULT_CURSOR));
        }
    }

    public static void main(String argv[]) { new Browser(); }
}

class MemComboBox extends JComboBox
{
    public static final int MAX_MEM_LEN = 30;

    public MemComboBox() {
        super();
```

3 Listens for selected URLs, either from the combo box or from a hyperlink

4 Background thread to load documents from URLs into the browser

5 Retrieves, parses, and renders web page

6 JComboBox subclass which provides history mechanism

```
      setEditable(true);
   }
   public void add(String item) {                    ❼  Add to history list
      removeItem(item);
      insertItemAt(item, 0);
      setSelectedItem(item);
      if (getItemCount() > MAX_MEM_LEN)
        removeItemAt(getItemCount()-1);
   }
   public void load(String fName) {                  ❽  Loads history list
      try {                                              from file, using
        if (getItemCount() > 0)                          object serialization
          removeAllItems();
        File f = new File(fName);
        if (!f.exists())
          return;
        FileInputStream fStream =
          new FileInputStream(f);
        ObjectInput  stream  =
          new  ObjectInputStream(fStream);
        Object obj = stream.readObject();
        if (obj instanceof ComboBoxModel)
          setModel((ComboBoxModel)obj);
        stream.close();
        fStream.close();
      }
      catch (Exception e) {
        e.printStackTrace();
        System.err.println("Serialization error: "+e.toString());
      }
   }
   public void save(String fName) {                  ❽  Stores history list
      try {                                              to file, reverse of
        FileOutputStream fStream =                       load() method
          new FileOutputStream(fName);
        ObjectOutput  stream  =
          new  ObjectOutputStream(fStream);
        stream.writeObject(getModel());
        stream.flush();
        stream.close();
        fStream.close();
      }
      catch (Exception e) {
        e.printStackTrace();
        System.err.println("Serialization error: "+e.toString());
      }                                              Implements label
   }                                                 which presents
}                                                    a "slide show"
                                                     of several icons
class AnimatedLabel extends JLabel implements Runnable  ❾  in sequence
{
```

```
protected Icon[] m_icons;
protected int m_index = 0;
protected boolean m_isRunning;

public AnimatedLabel(String gifName, int numGifs) {
  m_icons = new Icon[numGifs];
  for (int k=0; k<numGifs; k++)
    m_icons[k] = new ImageIcon(gifName+k+".gif");
  setIcon(m_icons[0]);

  Thread tr = new Thread(this);
  tr.setPriority(Thread.MAX_PRIORITY);
  tr.start();
}

public void setRunning(boolean isRunning) {
  m_isRunning = isRunning;
}

public boolean getRunning() { return m_isRunning; }

public void run() {
  while(true) {
    if (m_isRunning) {
      m_index++;
      if (m_index >= m_icons.length)
        m_index = 0;
      setIcon(m_icons[m_index]);
      Graphics g = getGraphics();
      m_icons[m_index].paintIcon(this, g, 0, 0);
    }
    else {
      if (m_index > 0) {
        m_index = 0;
        setIcon(m_icons[0]);
      }
    }
    try { Thread.sleep(500); } catch(Exception ex) {}
  }
}
}
```

⑩ In background thread, displays each icon in sequence, sleeping between each one

9.4.1   Understanding the code

Class Browser

This class extends JFrame to implement the frame container for our browser. Here are the instance variables:

- JEditorPane m_browser: The text component to parse and render HTML files.
- MemComboBox m_locator: The combo box to enter/select a URL address.
- AnimatedLabel m_runner: The label that contains an icon which becomes animated when the browser requests a URL.

① The constructor creates the custom combo box, m_locator, and an associated label. Then it creates the m_runner icon and places all three components in the northern region of our frame's content pane. `JEditorPane m_browser` is created and placed in a `JScrollPane` to provide scrolling capabilities. This is then added to the center of the content pane.

② A `WindowListener`, which has been used in many previous examples to close the frame and terminate execution, receives an additional function: it invokes our custom `save()` method (see below) on our combo box component before destroying the frame. This saves the list of visited URLs that have been entered as a file called **addresses.dat** in the current running directory.

Class Browser.BrowserListener

③ This inner class implements both the `ActionListener` and `HyperlinkListener` interfaces to manage navigation to HTML pages. The `actionPerformed()` method is invoked when the user selects a new item in the combo box. It verifies that the selection is valid and that the browser is not currently busy (requesting a URL, for example). If these checks are passed, it then creates and starts a new `BrowserLoader` instance (see below) for the specified address.

The `hyperlinkUpdate()` method is invoked when the user clicks a hyperlink in the currently loaded web page. This method also determines the selected URL address and starts a new `BrowserLoader` to load it.

Class Browser.BrowserLoader

④ This inner class extends `Thread` to load web pages into our `JEditorPane` component. It takes a URL address parameter in the constructor and stores it in an instance variable. The `run()` method sets the mouse cursor to an hourglass (`Cursor.WAIT_CURSOR`) and starts the animated icon to indicate that the browser is busy.

The core functionality of this thread is enclosed in its `try/catch` block. If an exception occurs during the processing of the requested URL, it is displayed in a simple `JOptionPane` dialog message box (we will discuss `JOptionPane` in chapter 14).

⑤ The actual job of retrieving, parsing, and rendering the web page is hidden in a single call to the `setPage()` method. So why do we need to create this separate thread instead of making that simple call in `BrowserListener`, for example? As we discussed in chapter 2, by creating separate threads to do potentially time-consuming operations, we avoid clogging up the event-dispatching thread.

Class MemComboBox

⑥ This class extends `JComboBox` to add a history mechanism. The constructor simply sets its `editable` property to `true`.

⑦ The `add()` method adds a new text string to the beginning of the list. If this item is already present in the list, it is removed from the old position. If the resulting list is longer than the predefined maximum length, the last item in the list is truncated.

⑧ The `load()` method loads a previously stored `ComboBoxModel` from the **addresses.dat** file using the serialization mechanism. The significant portion of this method reads an object from an `ObjectInputStream` and sets it as the `ComboBoxModel`. Any possible exceptions are printed to the standard output.

Similarly, the `save()` method serializes our combo box's `ComboBoxModel`. Any possible exceptions are, again, printed to standard output.

Class AnimatedLabel

❾ Surprisingly, Swing does not provide any special support for animated components, so we have to create our own component for this purpose. This provides us with an interesting example of using threads in Java.

NOTE   Animated GIFs are fully supported by `ImageIcon` (see chapter 5) but we want complete control over each animated frame in this example.

`AnimatedLabel` extends `JLabel` and implements the `Runnable` interface. Here are the instance variables:

- `Icon[] m_icons`: An array of images to be used for animation.
- `int m_index`: The index of the current image.
- `boolean m_isRunning`: The flag that indicates whether the animation is running.

The constructor takes a common name of a series of GIF files that contain images for animation, and the number of those files. These images are loaded and stored in an array. When all images are loaded, a thread with maximum priority is created and started to run this `Runnable` instance.

The `setRunning()` and `getRunning()` methods simply manage the `m_isRunning` flag.

❿ In the `run()` method, we cyclically increment the `m_index` variable and draw an image from the `m_icons` array with the corresponding index, exactly as one would expect from an animated image. This is done only when the `m_isRunning` flag is set to `true`. Otherwise, the image with index 0 is displayed. After an image is painted, `AnimatedLabel` yields control to other threads and sleeps for 500 ms.

The interesting thing about this component is that it runs parallel with other threads which do not necessarily yield control explicitly. In our case, the concurrent `BrowserLoader` thread spends the main part of its time inside the `setPage()` method, and our animated icon runs in a separate thread that signals to the user that something is going on. This is made possible because this animated component is running in the thread with the maximum priority. Of course, we should use such thread priority with caution. In our case it is appropriate since our thread consumes only a small amount of the processor's time and it *does* yield control to the lesser-priority threads when it sleeps.

NOTE   As a good exercise, try using threads with normal priority or Swing's `Timer` component in this example. You will find that this doesn't work as expected: the animated icon does not show any animation while the browser is running.

9.4.2   Running the code

Figure 9.3 shows the `Browser` application displaying a web page. The animated icon comes to life when the browser requests a URL. Notice how the combo box is populated with URL addresses as we navigate to different web pages. Now quit the application and restart it. Notice that our addresses have been saved and restored by serializing the combo box model, as we discussed above.

HTML rendering functionality is not yet matured. Do not be surprised if your favorite web page looks significantly different in our Swing-based browser. As a matter of fact, even the JavaSoft home page throws several exceptions while being displayed in this Swing component. (These exceptions occur outside our code, during the `JEditorPane` rendering—this is why they are not caught and handled by our code.)

GUIDELINE

Memory combo box usage   The example given here is a good place to use a combo box with memory. However, a memory combo box will not always be appropriate. Remember the advice that the usability of an unsorted combo box tends to degrade rapidly as the number of items grows. Therefore, it is sensible to use this technique where the likelihood of more than 20 entries (to pick a good number) is very small.

If you have a domain problem which is likely to need a larger number of memory items, but you still want to use a memory combo box, consider adding a sorting algorithm. Rather than sorting the most recent item first, you sort into a more meaningful index, such as alphabetical order. Usability will improve and you could easily populate the list with up to 200 or 300 items.

9.5   *CUSTOM EDITING*

In this section, we will discuss a custom editing feature to make example 9.3 even more convenient and similar to modern browser applications. We will attach a key event listener to our combo box's editor and search for previously visited URLs with matching beginning strings. If a match occurs, the remainder of that URL is displayed in the editor, and we can accept the suggestion by pressing ENTER. Most modern browsers also provide this functionality.

In example 9.4, the caret position will remain unchanged, as will the text on the left side of the caret (this is the text the user typed). The text on the right side of the caret represents the browser's suggestion, which may or may not correspond to the user's intentions. To avoid distracting the user, this portion of the text is highlighted, so any newly typed character will replace that suggested text.

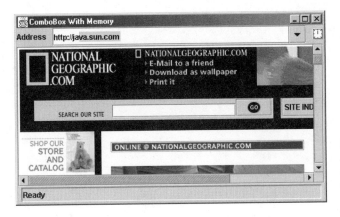

Figure 9.4
A `JComboBox` with a custom editor that suggests previously visited URLs

Example 9.4

Browser.java

see\Chapter9\4

```
public class Browser extends JFrame
{
  // Unchanged code from example 9.3

  public Browser() {
    super("HTML Browser [Advanced Editor]");

    // Unchanged code from example 9.3

    MemComboAgent agent = new MemComboAgent(m_locator);

    // Unchanged code from example 9.3
  }
  // Unchanged code from example 9.3
}

class MemComboAgent extends KeyAdapter
{
  protected JComboBox   m_comboBox;
  protected JTextField  m_editor;

  public MemComboAgent(JComboBox comboBox) {
    m_comboBox = comboBox;
    m_editor = (JTextField)comboBox.getEditor().
      getEditorComponent();
    m_editor.addKeyListener(this);
  }

  public void keyReleased(KeyEvent e) {
    char ch = e.getKeyChar();
    if (ch == KeyEvent.CHAR_UNDEFINED || Character.isISOControl(ch))
      return;
    int pos = m_editor.getCaretPosition();
    String str = m_editor.getText();
    if (str.length() == 0)
      return;

    for (int k=0; k<m_comboBox.getItemCount(); k++) {
      String item = m_comboBox.getItemAt(k).toString();
      if (item.startsWith(str)) {
        m_editor.setText(item);
        m_editor.setCaretPosition(item.length());
        m_editor.moveCaretPosition(pos);
        break;
      }
    }
  }
}
```

1 Creates KeyAdapter which attaches itself to combo box

2 Find list item that text begins with

9.5.1 Understanding the code

Class Browser

1 This class has only one change in comparison with the previous example: it creates an instance of our custom `MemComboAgent` class and passes it a reference to our `m_locator` combo box.

Class MemComboAgent

This class extends `KeyAdapter` to listen for keyboard activity. It takes a reference to a `JComboBox` component and stores it in an instance variable along with the `JTextField` component that is used as that combo box's editor. Finally, a `MemComboAgent` object adds itself to that editor as a `KeyListener` to be notified of all keyboard input that is passed to the editor component.

2 The `keyReleased()` method is the only method we implement. This method first retrieves the pressed characters and verifies that they are not control characters. We also retrieve the contents of the text field and check that it is not empty to avoid annoying the user with suggestions in an empty field. Note that when this method is invoked, the pressed key will already have been included in this text.

This method then walks through the list of combo box items and searches for an item starting with the combo box editor text. If such an item is found, it is set as the combo box editor's text. Then we place the caret at the end of that string using `setCaretPosition()`, and move it back to its initial position, going backward, using the `moveCaretPosition()` method. This method places the caret in its original position and highlights all the text to its right.

> **NOTE** A more sophisticated realization of this idea may include the separate processing of the URL protocol and host, as well as using threads for smooth execution.

9.5.2 Running the code

Figure 9.4 shows our custom combo box's editor displaying a portion of a URL address taken from its list. Try entering some new addresses and browsing to them. After some experimentation, try typing in an address that you have already visited with this application. Notice that the enhanced combo box suggests the remainder of this address from its pull-down list. Press ENTER as soon as an address matches your intended selection to avoid typing the complete URL.

CHAPTER 10

List boxes and Spinners

10.1   *JLIST*

class javax.swing.JList

This class represents a basic GUI component that allows the selection of one or more items
from a list of choices. JList has two models: ListModel, which handles data in the list, and
ListSelectionModel, which handles item selection (three different selection modes are
supported; we will discuss them below). JList also supports custom rendering, as we learned
in the last chapter, through the implementation of the ListCellRenderer interface. We can
use the existing default implementation of ListCellRenderer (DefaultListCellRenderer) or create our own according to our particular needs, as we will see later in this chapter.
Unless we use a custom renderer, the default renderer will display each element as a String
defined by that object's toString() method. The only exceptions to this are Icon implementations which will be rendered as they would be in any JLabel. Keep in mind that a
ListCellRenderer returns a Component, but that component is not interactive and is only
used for display purposes (it acts as a "rubber stamp"). For instance, if a JCheckBox is used as

a renderer, we will not be able to check and uncheck it. Unlike JComboBox, however, JList does not support editing of any sort.

A number of constructors are available to create a JList component. We can use the default constructor or pass list data to a constructor as a one-dimensional array, as a Vector, or as an implementation of the ListModel interface. The last variant provides maximum control over a list's properties and appearance. We can also assign data to a JList using either the setModel() method or one of the overloaded setListData() methods.

JList does not provide direct access to its elements, and we must access its ListModel to gain access to this data. JList does, however, provide direct access to its selection data by implementing all ListSelectionModel methods and delegating their traffic to the actual ListSelectionModel instance. To avoid repetition, we will discuss selection functionality in our overview of ListSelectionModel.

JAVA 1.4   In Java 1.4 JList has the added getNextMatch() method which returns the index of the next element in the list which starts with a given String prefix. The method also takes an index to start the search at and a direction to perform the search in (either Position.Bias.Forward or Position.Bias.Backward).

JList maintains selection foreground and background colors (which are assigned by its UI delegate when installed), and the default cell renderer, DefaultListCellRenderer, will use these colors to render selected cells. These colors can be assigned with setSelectedForeground() and setSelectedBackground(). Nonselected cells will be rendered with the component foreground and background colors that are assigned to JList with setForeground() and setBackground().

JList implements the Scrollable interface (see chapter 7) to provide vertical unit incremental scrolling corresponding to the list cell height, and vertical block incremental scrolling corresponding to the number of visible cells. Horizontal unit increment scrolling corresponds to the size of the list's font (1 if the font is null), and horizontal block unit increment scrolling corresponds to the current width of the list. Thus JList does not directly support scrolling, and it is intended to be placed in a JScrollPane.

The visibleRowCount property specifies how many cells should be visible when a JList is placed in a scroll pane. This defaults to 8, and it can be set with the setVisibleRowCount() method. Another interesting method provided by JList is ensureIndexIsVisible(), which forces the list to scroll itself so that the element corresponding to the given index becomes visible. JList also supports autoscrolling; for example, it will scroll element by element every 100ms if the mouse is dragged below or above its bounds.

By default, the width of each cell is the width of the widest item, and the height of each cell corresponds to the height of the tallest item. We can overpower this behavior and specify our own fixed cell width and height of each list cell using the setFixedCellWidth() and setFixedCellHeight() methods.

Another way to control the width and height of each cell is through the setPrototypeCellValue() method. This method takes an Object parameter and uses it to automatically determine the fixedCellWidth and fixedCellHeight. A typical use of this method would be to give it a String. This forces the list to use a fixed cell width and height equal to the width and height of that string when it is rendered in the Font currently assigned to the JList.

JAVA 1.4   As of Java 1.4 `JList` supports two new layouts, for a total of three:

VERTICAL: The default layout mode—one column of cells.
VERTICAL_WRAP: Cells flow in columns—the list becomes horizontally scrollable.
HORIZONTAL_WRAP: Cells flow in rows—the list becomes vertically scrollable.

The layout mode can be set with the new `setLayoutOrientation()` method.

`JList` also provides a method called `locationToIndex()` which will return the index of a cell at the given `Point` (in coordinate space of the list). -1 will be returned if the given point does not fall on a list cell. Unfortunately, `JList` does not provide support for double-clicking, but this method comes in very handy in implementing our own support for notification of double clicks. The following pseudocode shows how we can use a `MouseAdapter`, a `MouseEvent`, and the `locationToIndex()` method to determine which `JList` cell a double-click occurs on:

```
myJist.addMouseListener(new MouseAdapter() {
  public void mouseClicked(MouseEvent e) {
    if (e.getClickCount() == 2) {
      int cellIndex = myJList.locationToIndex(e.getPoint());
      // We now have the index of the double-clicked cell.
    }
  }
});
```

GUIDELINE

Advice on usage and design

Usage   Much of the UI Guideline advice for list boxes is similar to that given for combo boxes. Clearly the two components are different and they are intended for different purposes. Deciding when to use one or another can be difficult. Again, our advice is to think about reader output rather than data input. When the reader needs to see a collection of items, a list box is the correct choice. Use a list box where there is a collection of data which may grow dynamically, and when, for reading purposes, it is useful to see the whole collection or as much of the collection as can reasonably fit in the available space.

Design   Like combo boxes, a number of things affect the usability of a list box. Beyond more than a few items, it becomes unusable unless the data is sorted in some logical fashion, such as alphabetical or numerical. List boxes are designed to be used with scroll panes because lists are often too long to display each item in the available screen space at once. Using a sensible sorted order for the list allows the user to predict how much he needs to scroll to find what he is looking for.

When a list gets longer, usability is affected yet again. Once a list gets beyond a couple of hundred items, even when sorted, it becomes very slow for the user to locate a specific item in the list. When a list becomes that long, you may want to consider either providing a search facility or grouping the data inside the list using a tree-like organization.

Graphical considerations for list boxes are much like those for combo boxes. List boxes should be aligned to fit attractively into a panel. However, you must avoid making a list box which is simply too big for the list items contained. For example, a list box showing supported file formats such as ".gif" need only be a few characters long—don't make it big enough to handle 50 characters, as it will look unbalanced.

The nature of the list items must also be considered. If you have 50 items in a list where most items are around 20 characters but one item is 50 characters long, then should you make the list box big enough to display the longest item? Maybe, but for most occasions your display will be imbalanced again. It is probably best to optimize for the more common length, providing the longer one still has meaning when read in its truncated form. One solution to displaying the whole length of a truncated item is to use the tooltip facility. When the user places the mouse over an item, a tooltip appears with the full-length data text.

10.1.1 The ListModel interface

abstract interface javax.swing.ListModel

This interface describes a data model that holds a list of items. The `getElementAt()` method retrieves the item at the given position as an `Object` instance. The `getSize()` method returns the number of items in the list. `ListModel` also contains two methods that allow `ListData-Listeners` (see below) to be registered and notified of any additions, removals, and changes that occur to this model. This interface leaves the job of specifying how we store and structure the data, as well as how we add, remove, or change an item, completely up to its implementations.

10.1.2 AbstractListModel

abstract class javax.swing.AbstractListModel

This class represents a partial implementation of the `ListModel` interface. It defines the default event-handling functionality, and it implements the add/remove `ListDataListener` methods, as well as methods to fire `ListDataEvents` (see below) when additions, removals, and changes occur. The remainder of `ListModel`, the methods `getElementAt()` and `getSize()`, must be implemented in any concrete subclass.

10.1.3 DefaultListModel

class javax.swing.DefaultListModel

This class represents the concrete default implementation of the `ListModel` interface. It extends `AbstractListModel` and uses a `java.util.Vector` to store its data. Almost all of the methods of this class correspond directly to `Vector` methods; we will not discuss them here. Familiarity with `Vectors` implies familiarity with how `DefaultListModel` works (refer to the API documentation if you need further information).

10.1.4 The ListSelectionModel interface

abstract interface javax.swing.ListSelectionModel

This interface describes the model used for selecting list items. It defines three modes of selection: single selection, single contiguous interval selection, and multiple contiguous interval selection. A selection is defined as an indexed range, or set of ranges, of list elements.

The beginning of a selected range (where it originates) is referred to as the *anchor,* while the last item is referred to as the *lead* (the anchor can be greater than, less than, or equal to the lead). The lowest selected index is referred to as the *minimum,* and the highest selected index is referred to as the *maximum,* regardless of the order in which selection takes place. Each of these indices represents a `ListSelectionModel` property. The minimum and maximum properties should be –1 when no selection exists, and the anchor and lead maintain their most recent value until a new selection occurs.

To change the selection mode we use the `setSelectionMode()` method, passing it one of the following constants: `MULTIPLE_INTERVAL_SELECTION`, `SINGLE_INTERVAL_SELEC-TION`, or `SINGLE_SELECTION`. In `SINGLE_SELECTION` mode, only one item can be selected. In `SINGLE_INTERVAL_SELECTION` mode, a contiguous group of items can be selected by selecting an anchor item, holding down the SHIFT key, and choosing a lead item (which can be at a higher or lower index than the anchor). In `MULTIPLE_INTERVAL_SELECTION` mode, any number of items can be selected regardless of their location by holding down the CTRL key and clicking. Multiple selection mode also allows you to use SHIFT to select a contiguous interval; however, this clears the current selection.

`ListSelectionModel` provides several methods for adding, removing, and manipulating ranges of selections. Methods for registering/removing `ListSelectionListeners` are provided as well (see below). Each of these methods is explained clearly in the API documentation, so we will not describe them in detail here.

JAVA 1.4   In Java 1.4 `JList` has the added `getListSelectionListeners()` method which returns an array containing all registered `ListSelectionListener` instances.

`JList` defines all the methods declared in this interface and it delegates all traffic to its `List-SelectionModel` instance, thereby allowing access to selection data without the need to explicitly communicate with the selection model.

10.1.5   DefaultListSelectionModel

class javax.swing.DefaultListSelectionModel

This class represents the concrete default implementation of the `ListSelectionModel` interface. It defines methods to fire `ListSelectionEvents` when a selection range changes.

10.1.6   The ListCellRenderer interface

abstract interface javax.swing.ListCellRenderer

This interface describes a component that is used for rendering a list item. We discussed this interface, as well as its default concrete implementation, `DefaultListCellRenderer`, in the last chapter (see sections 9.1.4 and 9.1.5). We will show how to construct several custom renderers in the examples that follow.

10.1.7 The ListDataListener interface

abstract interface javax.swing.event.ListDataListener

This interface defines three methods for dispatching `ListDataEvents` when list elements are added, removed, or changed in the `ListModel`: `intervalAdded()`, `intervalRemoved()`, and `contentsChanged()`.

10.1.8 ListDataEvent

class javax.swing.event.ListDataEvent

This class represents the event that is delivered when changes occur in a list's `ListModel`. It includes the source of the event as well as the indexes of the lowest and highest indexed elements affected by the change. It also includes the type of event that occurred. Three `ListDataEvent` types are defined as static `int`s: `CONTENTS_CHANGED`, `INTERVAL_ADDED`, and `INTERVAL_REMOVED`. We can use the `getType()` method to discover the type of any `ListDataEvent`.

10.1.9 The ListSelectionListener interface

abstract interface javax.swing.event.ListSelectionListener

This interface describes a listener which listens for changes in a list's `ListSelectionModel`. It declares the `valueChanged()` method, which accepts a `ListSelectionEvent`.

10.1.10 ListSelectionEvent

class javax.swing.event.ListSelectionEvent

This class represents an event that is delivered by `ListSelectionModel` when changes occur in its selection. It is almost identical to `ListDataEvent`, except that the indices specified signify where there has been a change in the selection model, rather than in the data model.

10.2 BASIC JLIST EXAMPLE

Example 10.1 displays a list of the states in the United States using an array of `Strings` in the following format:

- 2-character abbreviation<*tab character*>full state name<*tab character*>state capital

The states are listed alphabetically by their 2-letter abbreviation.

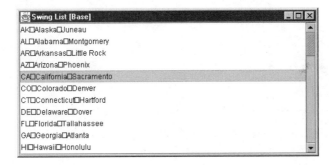

**Figure 10.1
A JList that displays
a list of strings containing
tab characters**

Example 10.1

see \Chapter10\1

```java
import java.awt.*;
import java.awt.event.*;
import java.util.*;

import javax.swing.*;
import javax.swing.border.*;
import javax.swing.event.*;

public class StatesList extends JFrame
{
  protected JList m_statesList;

  public StatesList() {
    super("Swing List [Base]");
    setSize(500, 240);

    String [] states = {
      "AK\tAlaska\tJuneau",
      "AL\tAlabama\tMontgomery",
      "AR\tArkansas\tLittle Rock",
      "AZ\tArizona\tPhoenix",
      "CA\tCalifornia\tSacramento",
      "CO\tColorado\tDenver",
      "CT\tConnecticut\tHartford",
      "DE\tDelaware\tDover",
      "FL\tFlorida\tTallahassee",
      "GA\tGeorgia\tAtlanta",
      "HI\tHawaii\tHonolulu",
      "IA\tIowa\tDes Moines",
      "ID\tIdaho\tBoise",
      "IL\tIllinois\tSpringfield",
      "IN\tIndiana\tIndianapolis",
      "KS\tKansas\tTopeka",
      "KY\tKentucky\tFrankfort",
      "LA\tLouisiana\tBaton Rouge",
      "MA\tMassachusetts\tBoston",
      "MD\tMaryland\tAnnapolis",
      "ME\tMaine\tAugusta",
      "MI\tMichigan\tLansing",
      "MN\tMinnesota\tSt.Paul",
      "MO\tMissouri\tJefferson City",
      "MS\tMississippi\tJackson",
      "MT\tMontana\tHelena",
      "NC\tNorth Carolina\tRaleigh",
      "ND\tNorth Dakota\tBismarck",
      "NE\tNebraska\tLincoln",
      "NH\tNew Hampshire\tConcord",
      "NJ\tNew Jersey\tTrenton",
```

```
         "NM\tNew Mexico\tSantaFe",
         "NV\tNevada\tCarson City",
         "NY\tNew York\tAlbany",
         "OH\tOhio\tColumbus",
         "OK\tOklahoma\tOklahoma City",
         "OR\tOregon\tSalem",
         "PA\tPennsylvania\tHarrisburg",
         "RI\tRhode Island\tProvidence",
         "SC\tSouth Carolina\tColumbia",
         "SD\tSouth Dakota\tPierre",
         "TN\tTennessee\tNashville",
         "TX\tTexas\tAustin",
         "UT\tUtah\tSalt Lake City",
         "VA\tVirginia\tRichmond",
         "VT\tVermont\tMontpelier",
         "WA\tWashington\tOlympia",
         "WV\tWest Virginia\tCharleston",
         "WI\tWisconsin\tMadison",
         "WY\tWyoming\tCheyenne"
      };

      m_statesList = new JList(states);

      JScrollPane ps = new JScrollPane();
      ps.getViewport().add(m_statesList);
      getContentPane().add(ps, BorderLayout.CENTER);

      seDefaultCloseOperation(JFrame.EXIT_ON_CLOSE);
      setVisible(true);
   }

   public static void main(String argv[]) {
      new StatesList();
   }
}
```

10.2.1   Understanding the code

Class StatesList

The StatesList class extends JFrame to implement the frame container for this example. One instance variable, JList m_statesList, is used to store an array of state Strings. This list is created by passing the states String array to the JList constructor. The list is then added to a JScrollPane instance to provide scrolling capabilities.

10.2.2   Running the code

Figure 10.1 shows StatesList in action displaying the list of states and their capitals. The separating tab character is displayed as an unpleasant square symbol, but we'll fix this in the next example.

GUIDELINE

Unbalanced layout   In this example, the design is unbalanced because the tab character is not displayed correctly. The box is ugly, and the spacing is also wrong. The large white space area to the right ought to be avoided. The next example corrects these problems.

10.3   CUSTOM RENDERING

In this section we'll add the ability to align `Strings` containing tab separators into a table-like arrangement. We want each tab character to shift all text to its right, to a specified location instead of being rendered as the square symbol we saw earlier. These locations should be determined uniformly for all elements of the list to form columns that line up correctly.

Note that this example works well with proportional fonts as well as with fixed width fonts (i.e., it doesn't matter what font we use because alignment is not designed to be font-dependent). This makes `JList` a powerful but simple component, which can be used in place of `JTable` in simple cases such as the example presented here (where the involvement of `JTable` would create unnecessary overhead).

To accomplish the desired rendering we construct a custom rendered, `TabListCell-Renderer`, which exposes accessor methods to specify and retrieve tab positions based on the index of a tab character in a `String` being rendered:

- `getDefaultTab()`/`setDefaultTab(int)`: manages the default tab size (defaults to 50). In case a position is not specified for a given tab index, we use a default size to determine how far to offset a portion of text.
- `getTabs()`/`setTabs(int[])`: manages an array of positions based on the index of a tab character in a `String` being rendered. These positions are used in rendering each element in the list to provide consistent alignment.

This example also demonstrates the use of the `LayoutOrientation` property new to J2SE 1.4. By using two different list models (one with short abbreviations and the original model from example 10.1), and allowing dynamic selection between both models as well as the three different list cell layout modes, this example illustrates how each layout mode behaves and in which situation each is most useful.

States List			_ □ ×
● VERTICAL	○ VERTICAL_WRAP	○ HORIZONTAL_WRAP	
● Long Model	○ Short Model		

AK	Alaska	Juneau
AL	Alabama	Montgomery
AR	Arkansas	Little Rock
AZ	Arizona	Phoenix
CA	California	Sacramento
CO	Colorado	Denver
CT	Connecticut	Hartford
DE	Delaware	Dover
FL	Florida	Tallahassee
GA	Georgia	Atlanta

Figure 10.2 States List example with custom rendering, Long model and default [VERTICAL] cell layout

Figure 10.3
Long model and
`VERTICAL_WRAP`
cell layout

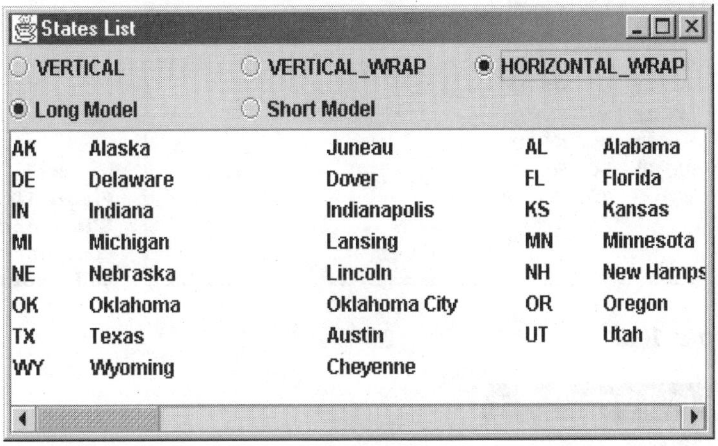

Figure 10.4
Long model and
`HORIZONTAL_WRAP`
cell layout

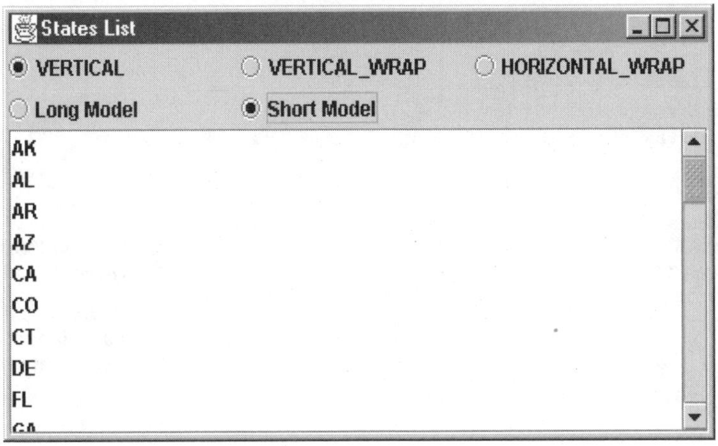

Figure 10.5
Short model
and default
[VERTICAL]
cell layout

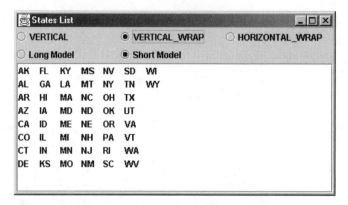

Figure 10.6
Short model and
`VERTICAL_WRAP`
cell layout

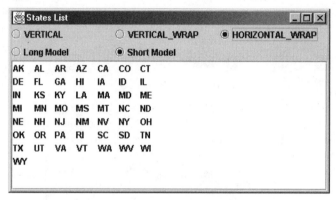

Figure 10.7
Short model and
`HORIZONTAL_WRAP`
cell layout

Example 10.2

StatesList.java

see \Chapter10\2

```java
import java.awt.*;
import java.awt.event.*;
import java.util.*;

import javax.swing.*;
import javax.swing.border.*;
import javax.swing.event.*;

public class StatesList extends JFrame {

    protected JList m_statesList;

    protected JRadioButton m_verticalRb;
    protected JRadioButton m_verticalWrapRb;
    protected JRadioButton m_horizontalWrapRb;

    protected JRadioButton mlongRb;
    protected JRadioButton m_shortRb;
```

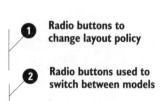

**❶ Radio buttons to
change layout policy**

**❷ Radio buttons used to
switch between models**

```
public static ArrayModel LONG_MODEL =
new ArrayModel(new String[] {
"AK\tAlaska\tJuneau",
"AL\tAlabama\tMontgomery",
"AR\tArkansas\tLittle Rock",
"AZ\tArizona\tPhoenix",
"CA\tCalifornia\tSacramento",
"CO\tColorado\tDenver",
"CT\tConnecticut\tHartford",
"DE\tDelaware\tDover",
"FL\tFlorida\tTallahassee",
"GA\tGeorgia\tAtlanta",
"HI\tHawaii\tHonolulu",
"IA\tIowa\tDes Moines",
"ID\tIdaho\tBoise",
"IL\tIllinois\tSpringfield",
"IN\tIndiana\tIndianapolis",
"KS\tKansas\tTopeka",
"KY\tKentucky\tFrankfort",
"LA\tLouisiana\tBaton Rouge",
"MA\tMassachusetts\tBoston",
"MD\tMaryland\tAnnapolis",
"ME\tMaine\tAugusta",
"MI\tMichigan\tLansing",
"MN\tMinnesota\tSt. Paul",
"MO\tMissouri\tJefferson City",
"MS\tMississippi\tJackson",
"MT\tMontana\tHelena",
"NC\tNorth Carolina\tRaleigh",
"ND\tNorth Dakota\tBismark",
"NE\tNebraska\tLincoln",
"NH\tNew Hampshire\tConcord",
"NJ\tNew Jersey\tTrenton",
"NM\tNew Mexico\tSanta Fe",
"NV\tNevada\tCarson City",
"NY\tNew York\tAlbany",
"OH\tOhio\tColumbus",
"OK\tOklahoma\tOklahoma City",
"OR\tOregon\tSalem",
"PA\tPennsylvania\tHarrisburg",
"RI\tRhode Island\tProvidence",
"SC\tSouth Carolina\tColumbia",
"SD\tSouth Dakota\tPierre",
"TN\tTennessee\tNashville",
"TX\tTexas\tAustin",
"UT\tUtah\tSalt Lake City",
"VA\tVirginia\tRichmond",
"VT\tVermont\tMontpelier",
"WA\tWashington\tOlympia",
"WV\tWest Virginia\tCharleston",
"WI\tWisconsin\tMadison",
"WY\tWyoming\tCheyenne",
```

```
});
  public static arrayModel SHORT_MODEL =
  new ArrayModel(new String[] {
  "AK", "AL", "AR", "AZ", "CA",
  "CO", "CT", "DE", "FL", "GA",
  "HI", "IA", "ID", "IL", "IN",
  "KS", "KY", "LA", "MA", "MD",
  "ME", "MI", "MN", "MO", "MS",
  "MT", "NC", "ND", "NE", "NH",
  "NJ", "NM", "NV", "NY", "OH",
  "OK", "OR", "PA", "RI", "SC",
  "SD", "TN", "TX", "UT", "VA",
  "VT", "WA", "WV", "WI", "WY"
});

  public StatesList() {
  super("States List");
  setSize(450, 250);

  m_statesList = new JList();
  m_statesList.setModel(LONG_MODEL);

  TabListCellRenderer renderer = new TabListCellRenderer();
  renderer.setTabs(new int[] {50, 200, 300});
  m_statesList.setCellRenderer(renderer;

  JScrollpane ps = new JScrollPane();
  ps.getViewport().add(m_statesList);
  getcontentPane().add(ps, BorderLayout.CENTER);

  JPanel pp = new JPanel(new GridLayout(2,3));

  ButtonGroup bg1 = new buttonGroup();
  m_verticalRb = new JRadioButton("VERTICAL", true);
  pp.add(m_verticalRb);
  bg1.add(m_verticalRb);
  m_verticalWrapRb = new JRadioButton("VERTICAL_WRAP");
  pp.add(m_verticalWrapRb);
  bg1.add(m_verticalWrapRb);
  m_horizontalWrapRb = new JRadioButton("HORIZONTAL_WRAP");
  pp.add(m_horizontalWrapRb);
  bg1.add(m_horizontalWrapRb);

  ButtonGroup bg2 = new ButtonGroup();
  m_longRb = new JRadioButton("Long Model", true);
  pp.add(m_longRb);
  bg2.add(m_longRb);
  m_shortRb = new JRadioButton("Short Model");
  pp.add(m_shortRb);
  bg2.add(m_shortRb);

  getContentPane().add(pp, BorderLayout.NORTH);

  ActionListener modelListener = new ActionListener() {
    public void actionPerformed(ActionEvent evt) {
      if (m_longRb.isSelected()) {
```

❸ ActionListener to change prototype cell value when model changes

```
      m_statesList.setPrototypeCellValue(
        "xxxxxxxxxxxxxxxxxxxxxxxxxxxxxxxxxxxxxxxxxxxxxxxx");
      m_statesList.setModel(LONG_MODEL);
    }
  }
};
m_longRb.addActionListener(modelListener);
m_shortRb.addActionListener(modelListener);

ActionListener layoutListener = new ActionListener() {
  public void actionPerformed(ActionEvent evt) {
    if (m_verticalRb.isSelected()) {
      m_statesList.setLaoutOrientation(JList.VERTICAL);
    }
    else if (m_verticalWrapRb.isSelected()) {
      m_statesList.setLayoutOrientation(JList.VERTICAL_WRAP);
    }
  }
};
m_verticalRb.addActionListener(layoutListener);
m_verticalWrapRb.addactionListener(layoutListener);
m_horizontalWrapRb.addActionListener(layoutListener);
}

public static void main(String argv[]) {
  Stateslist frame = new StatesList();
  frame.setDefaultcloseOperation(jFrame.EXIT_ON_CLOSE);
  frame.setvisible(true);
}
}

class TabListCellRenderer extends JLabel
  implements ListCellRenderer {

  protected static Border m_noFocusBorder;

  protected FontMetrics m_fm = null;
  protected Insets m_insets = new Insets(0, 0, 0, 0);
  protected int m_defaultTab = 50;
  protected int[]m_tabs = null;

  public TabListCellRenderer() {
    m_noFocusBorder = new EmptyBorder(1, 1, 1, 1);
    setOpaque(true);
    setBorder(m_nofocusborder);
  }

  public component getListCellRendererComponentJList list,
    Object value, int index, boolean isSelected, boolean cellHasFocus
  {
    setText(value.toString());

    setBackground(isSelected ? list.getSelectionBackground()
      : list.getBackground());
    setForeground(isSelected ? list.getSelectionForeground()
      : list.getForeground());
```

❸ **ActionListener to change prototype cell value when model changes**

❹ **Custom cell renderer used to align strings that contain tab characters into visual columns**

```
  set Font(list.etFont());
  setBorder((cellHasFocus) ?
    UIManager.getBorder("List.focusCellHighlightBorder")
      : m_nofocusBorder);

  return this;
}

public void setDefaultTab(int defaultTab) {
  m_defaultTab = defaultTab;
}

public int getDefaultTab() {
  return m_defaultTab;
}

public void setTabs(int[] tabs) {
  m_tabs = tabs;
}

public int[] getTabs() {
  return m_tabs;
}

public int getTab(int index) {
  if (m_tabs == null)
    return m_defaultTab*index;

  int len = m_tabs.length;
  if (index>=0 && index<len)
    return m_tabs[index];

  return m_tabs[len-1] +m_defaultTab*(index-len+1);
}

public void paintComponent(Graphics g) {
  super.paintComponent(g);
  Color colorRetainer = g.getColor();
  m_fm =g.getFontMetrics();

  g.setColor(getBackground());
  g.fillRect(0, 0, getWidth(), getHeight());
  getBorder().paintBorder(this, g,0, 0, getWidth(), getHeight());

  g.setColor(getForeground());
  g.setFont(getfont());
  m_insets = getInsets();
  int x = m_insets.left;
  int y = m_insets.top + m_fm.getAscent();

  StringTokenizer st = new StringTokenizer(getText(), "\t");
  while (st.hasMoreTokens()) {
    String sNext = st.nextToken();
    g.drawString(sNext, x,y);
    x += m_fm.stringWidth(sNext);

    if (!st.hasMoreTokens())
     break;
```

5 Method to calculate the distance to use corresponding to a given tab index

6 Method responsible for rendering each cell; the getTab() method is used to retrieve the number of pixels corresponding to a given tab index

```
    in index = 0;
    while (x >= getTab(index))
      index++;
    x = getTab(index);
  }

  g.setColor(colorRetainer);
  }
}

class ArrayModel extends AbstractListModel {
  Object[] m_data;

  public ArrayModel(Object[] data) {
    m_data = data;
  }

  public int getSize() {
    return m_data.length;
  }

  public Object getElementAt(int index) {
    if (index < 0 || index >= getSize())
      return null;
    return m_data[index];
  }
}
```

❼ **Custom list model to hold an array of objects**

10.3.1 Understanding the code

Class StatesList

In this enhanced version of StatesList we create an instance of our custom TabListCell-Renderer, pass it an array of positions and set it as the renderer for our JList component.
❶ Three radio buttons, m_verticalRb, m_verticalWrapRb, and m_horizontalWrapRb are
❷ used to change the list's LayoutOrientation property. Two more radio buttons are m_longRB and m_shortRB. When switching between these list models we change our list's prototype cell value to increase/decrease the width of the cells accordingly.

❸ *Class TabListCellRenderer*

The TabListCellRenderer class extends JLabel and implements the ListCellRenderer interface for use as our custom renderer.

Class variable:

- Border m_noFocusBorder: border to be used when a list item has no focus.

Instance variables:

- FontMetrics m_fm: used in calculating text positioning when drawing.
- Insets m_insets: insets of the cell being rendered.
- int m_defaultTab: default tab size.
- int[] m_tabs: an array of positions based on tab index in a String being rendered.

The constructor creates, assigns text, sets its opaque property to true (to render the component's area with the specified background), and sets the border to m_noFocusBorder.

The getListCellRendererComponent() method is required when implementing List-CellRenderer, and is called each time a cell is about to be rendered. It takes five parameters:

- JList list: reference to the list instance.
- Object value: data object to be painted by the renderer.
- int index: index of the item in the list.
- boolean isSelected: true if the cell is currently selected.
- boolean cellHasFocus: true if the cell currently has the focus.

Our implementation of this method assigns new text, sets the background and foreground (depending on whether or not the cell is selected), sets the font to that taken from the parent list component, and sets the border according to whether or not the cell has input focus.

4 Four additional methods provide set/get support for the m_defaultTab and m_tabs variables, and do not require detailed explanation beyond the code listing. Now let's take a close look at the getTab() method which calculates and returns the position for a given tab index. If no tab array, m_tabs, is set, this method returns the m_defaultTab distance (defaults to 50) multiplied by the given tab index. If the m_tabs array is not null and the tab index is less than its length, the proper value from that array is returned. Otherwise, if the tab index is greater than the array's length, we have no choice but to use the default tab size again, offset from the last value in the m_tabs array.

5 Since the JLabel component does not render tab characters properly, we do not benefit a lot from its inheritance and implement the paintComponent() method to draw tabbed Strings ourselves. First, our paintComponent() method requests a reference to the Font-Metrics instance for the given Graphics. Then we fill the component's rectangle with the background color (which is set in the getListCellRendererComponent() method depending on whether or not the cell is selected), and paint the component's border.

> **NOTE**   Alternatively, we could use the drawTabbedText() method from the javax.swing.text.Utilities class to draw tabbed text. However, this requires us to implement the TabExpander interface. In our case it's easier to draw text directly without using that utility. As an interesting exercise you can modify the code from this example to use drawTabbedText() method.

6 In the next step, we prepare to draw the tabbed String. We set the foreground color and font, and determine the initial x and y positions for drawing the text, taking into account the component's insets.

> **REMINDER**   To draw text in Java you need to use a baseline y-coordinate. This is why the get-Ascent() value is added to the y position. The getAscent() method returns the distance from the font's baseline to the top of most alphanumeric characters. See chapter 2 for more information on drawing text and Java 1.2 FontMetrics caveats.

We then use a StringTokenizer to parse the String and extract the portions separated by tabs. Each portion is drawn with the drawString() method, and the x-coordinate is adjusted to the length of the text. We cycle through this process, positioning each portion of text by calling the getTab() method, until no more tabs are found.

Class ArrayModel

7 This class extends `AbstractListModel` and is a simple, non-mutable (i.e., read-only) list model used to hold an array of `Objects`. This is the minimal `ListModel` implementation required for this example to function.

10.3.2 Running the code

Figure 10.2 shows `StatesList` displaying an array of tab-separated `Strings`. Notice that the tab symbols are not drawn directly, but form consistently aligned columns inside the list. Figures 10.3 through 10.7 show `StatesList` in all other permutations of short and long model, and cell layout mode. Note the order in which the items are listed in `VERTICAL_WRAP` and `HORIZONTAL_WRAP` modes. As these figures show, you can choose which wrap mode to use based on whether you want the user to read the list from top to bottom or from left to right.

GUIDELINE

Improved balance   With the tab character being displayed correctly, the list box has much better balance. The available area for the capital city is still very large, and as the designer you may want to consider reducing it, thus reducing the excessive white space on the right-hand side. Such a decision would normally be made after the list box is seen as it will appear and the necessary alignment and overall panel balance is taken into consideration.

10.4 PROCESSING KEYBOARD INPUT AND SEARCHING

In this section we will continue to enhance our `JList` states example by adding the ability to select an element whose text starts with a character corresponding to a key press. We will also show how to extend this functionality to search for an element whose text starts with a *sequence* of typed key characters.

To do this, we must use a `KeyListener` to listen for keyboard input, and we need to accumulate this input in a `String`. Each time a key is pressed, the listener must search through the list and select the first element whose text matches the `String` we have accumulated. If the time interval between two key presses exceeds a certain pre-defined value, the accumulated `String` must be cleared before appending a new character to avoid overflow.

States List		
● VERTICAL	○ VERTICAL_WRAP	○ HORIZONTAL_WRAP
● Long Model	○ Short Model	
MI	Michigan	Lansing
MN	Minnesota	St.Paul
MO	Missouri	Jefferson City
MS	Mississippi	Jackson
MT	Montana	Helena
NC	North Carolina	Raleigh
ND	North Dakota	Bismarck
NE	Nebraska	Lincoln
NH	New Hampshire	Concord
NJ	New Jersey	Trenton

**Figure 10.8
A `JList` that allows
accumulated keyboard
input to search for
a matching item**

Example 10.3

StatesList.java

see \Chapter10\3

```java
import java.awt.*;
import java.awt.event.*;
import java.util.*;

import javax.swing.*;
import javax.swing.border.*;
import javax.swing.event.*;

public class StatesList extends JFrame
{
  protected JList m_statesList;

  public StatesList() {
    // Unchanged code from example 10.2

    m_statesList = new JList(states);
    TabListCellRenderer renderer = new TabListCellRenderer();
    renderer.setTabs(new int[] {50, 200, 300});
    m_statesList.setCellRenderer(renderer);
    m_statesList.addKeyListener(new ListSearcher(m_statesList));

    // Unchanged code from example 10.2
  }
}

// Unchanged code from example 10.2

class ListSearcher extends KeyAdapter
{
  protected JList m_list;
  protected ListModel m_model;
  protected String m_key = "";
  protected long m_time = 0;

  public static int CHAR_DELTA = 1000;

  public ListSearcher(JList list) {
    m_list = list;
    m_model = m_list.getModel();
  }

  public void keyTyped(KeyEvent e) {
    char ch = e.getKeyChar();
    if (!Character.isLetterOrDigit(ch))
      return;
    if (m_time+CHAR_DELTA < System.currentTimeMillis())
      m_key = "";
    m_time = System.currentTimeMillis();

    m_key += Character.toLowerCase(ch);
    for (int k=0; k<m_model.getSize(); k++) {
      String str = ((String)m_model.getElementAt(k)).toLowerCase();
```

1 Add ListSearcher KeyListener to JList

2 If key is letter/digit, and event occurred shortly after last key, append it to search string and look for list item with that prefix

```
        if (str.startsWith(m_key)){
          m_list.setSelectedIndex(k);
          m_list.ensureIndexIsVisible(k);
          break;
        }
      }
    }
  }
```

10.4.1   Understanding the code

Class StatesList

1 An instance of `ListSearcher` is added to the `m_statesList` component as a `KeyListener`. This is the only change made to this class with respect to example 10.2.

Class ListSearcher

The `ListSearcher` class extends the `KeyAdapter` class and defines one class variable:

- `int CHAR_DELTA`: A static variable to hold the maximum time interval in ms between two subsequent key presses before clearing the search key character `String`.

Instance variables:

- `JList m_list`: The list component to search and change the selection based on keyboard input.
- `ListModel m_model`: The list model of `m_list`.
- `String m_key`: The key character `String` that is used to search for a match.
- `long m_time`: The time in ms of the last key press.

The `ListSearcher` constructor simply takes a reference to a `JList` component and stores it in instance variable `m_list`; its model is stored in `m_model`.

2 The `keyTyped()` method is called each time a new character is typed. Our implementation first obtains the typed character and returns if that character is not a letter or a digit. `keyTyped()` then checks the time interval between now and the time when the previous key type event occurred. If this interval exceeds `CHAR_DELTA`, the `m_key` `String` is cleared. Finally, this method walks through the list and performs a case-insensitive comparison of the list `Strings` and the searching `String` (`m_key`). If an element's text starts with `m_key`, this element is selected and it is forced to appear within our current `JList` view using the `ensureIndexIsVisible()` method.

GUIDELINE

Extending usability and list size   This technique of allowing accumulated keyboard input to sift and select a list item improves usability by making the task of searching and locating an item in the list easier. This extends the number of items you can put in a list and still have a usable design. A technique like this can easily improve the usefulness of the list for up to several thousand entries.

This is another good example of the improved usability that is possible when the developer takes extra time to provide additional code to make the user's task easier.

10.4.2 Running the code

Try out the search functionality. Figure 10.8 shows our list's selection after pressing "n" immediately followed by "j." As expected, New Jersey is selected.

10.5 LIST OF CHECK BOXES

Lists can certainly be used for more than just Strings. We can easily imagine a list of Swing components. A list of check boxes is actually common in software packages when users are prompted to select optional constituents during installation. In Swing, such a list can be constructed by implementing a custom renderer that uses the JCheckBox component. The catch is that mouse and keyboard events must be handled manually to check/uncheck these boxes.

Example 10.4 shows how to create a list of check boxes that represent imaginary optional program constituents. Associated with each component is an instance of our custom Install-Data class with the following fields:

Field	Type	Description
m_name	String	Option name.
m_size	int	Size in KB.
m_selected	boolean	Returns true if the option is selected.

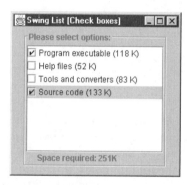

Figure 10.9
A JList with JCheckBox renderers

Example 10.4

CheckBoxList.java

see \Chapter 10\4

```java
import java.awt.*;
import java.awt.event.*;
import java.util.*;

import javax.swing.*;
import javax.swing.border.*;
import javax.swing.event.*;

public class CheckBoxList extends JFrame
{
```

```java
protected JList  m_list;
protected JLabel m_total;

public CheckBoxList() {
   super("Swing List [Check boxes]");
   setSize(280, 250);
   getContentPane().setLayout(new FlowLayout());

   InstallData[] options = {
     new InstallData("Program executable", 118),
     new InstallData("Help files", 52),
     new InstallData("Tools and converters", 83),
     new InstallData("Source code", 133)
   };

   m_list = new JList(options);
   CheckListCellRenderer renderer = new CheckListCellRenderer();
   m_list.setCellRenderer(renderer);
   m_list.setSelectionMode(ListSelectionModel.SINGLE_SELECTION);

   CheckListener lst = new CheckListener(this);
   m_list.addMouseListener(lst);
   m_list.addKeyListener(lst);

   JScrollPane ps = new JScrollPane();
   ps.getViewport().add(m_list);

   m_total = new JLabel("Space required: 0K");

   JPanel p = new JPanel();
   p.setLayout(new BorderLayout());
   p.add(ps, BorderLayout.CENTER);
   p.add(m_total, BorderLayout.SOUTH);
   p.setBorder(new TitledBorder(new EtchedBorder(),
     "Please select options:"));
   getContentPane().add(p);

   setDefaultCloseOperation(JFrame.EXIT_ON_CLOSE);
   setVisible(true);

   recalcTotal();
}
public void recalcTotal() {
   ListModel model = m_list.getModel();
   int total = 0;
   for (int k=0; k<model.getSize(); k++) {
     InstallData data = (InstallData)model.getElementAt(k);
     if (data.isSelected())
       total += data.getSize();
   }
   m_total.setText("Space required: "+total+"K");
}
public static void main(String argv[]) {
   new CheckBoxList();
}
```

1 List items for JList

2 "total" field below list, which is below the title label

3 Adds up "size" field of checked items and sets that in "total" field

```
}
class CheckListCellRenderer extends JCheckBox
 implements ListCellRenderer
{
  protected static Border m_noFocusBorder =
    new EmptyBorder(1, 1, 1, 1);

  public CheckListCellRenderer() {
    super();
    setOpaque(true);
    setBorder(m_noFocusBorder);
  }

  public Component getListCellRendererComponent(JList list,
   Object value, int index, boolean isSelected, boolean cellHasFocus)
  {
    setText(value.toString());

    setBackground(isSelected ? list.getSelectionBackground() :
      list.getBackground());
    setForeground(isSelected ? list.getSelectionForeground() :
      list.getForeground());

    InstallData data = (InstallData)value;
      setSelected(data.isSelected());

    setFont(list.getFont());
    setBorder((cellHasFocus) ?
    UIManager.getBorder("List.focusCellHighlightBorder")
      : m_noFocusBorder);

    return this;
  }
}

class CheckListener implements MouseListener, KeyListener
{
  protected CheckBoxList m_parent;
  protected JList m_list;

  public CheckListener(CheckBoxList parent) {
    m_parent = parent;
    m_list = parent.m_list;
  }

  public void mouseClicked(MouseEvent e) {
    if (e.getX() < 20)
    doCheck();
  }

  public void mousePressed(MouseEvent e) {}
  public void mouseReleased(MouseEvent e) {}
  public void mouseEntered(MouseEvent e) {}
  public void mouseExited(MouseEvent e) {}
```

Renderer shows a check box with label ❹

Processes mouse and key input to change check box states ❺

If mouse click is less than 20 pixels from left edge, consider it a click on check box ❺

```
    public void keyPressed(KeyEvent e) {
      if (e.getKeyChar() == ' ')
        doCheck();
    }
```

5 Space key does the same as the check box mouse click

```
    public void keyTyped(KeyEvent e) {}
    public void keyReleased(KeyEvent e) {}

    protected void doCheck() {
      int index = m_list.getSelectedIndex();
      if (index < 0)
        return;
      InstallData data = (InstallData)m_list.getModel().
        getElementAt(index);
      data.invertSelected();
      m_list.repaint();
      m_parent.recalcTotal();
    }
  }

class InstallData
{
  protected String m_name;
  protected int m_size;
  protected boolean m_selected;

  public InstallData(String name, int size) {
    m_name = name;
    m_size = size;
    m_selected = false;
  }

  public String getName() { return m_name; }

  public int getSize() { return m_size; }

  public void setSelected(boolean selected) {
    m_selected = selected;
  }

  public void invertSelected() { m_selected = !m_selected; }

  public boolean isSelected() { return m_selected; }

  public String toString() { return m_name+" ("+m_size+" K)"; }
}
```

6 Toggles InstallData "selected" flag and recalculates total

7 Data object to represent install item, including size and "selected" flag

10.5.1 Understanding the code

Class CheckBoxList

The CheckBoxList class extends JFrame to provide the basic frame for this example. Here are the instance variables:

- JList m_list: The list to display program constituents.
- JLabel m_total: The label to display the total space required for installation based on the selected constituents.

1 An array of four `InstallData` objects is passed to the constructor of our `JList` component (note that we use a `DefaultListModel`, which is sufficient for our purposes here). `SINGLE_SELECTION` is used as our list's selection mode. An instance of our custom `CheckListCellRenderer` is created and set as the cell renderer for our list. An instance of our custom `CheckListener` is then registered as both a mouse and a key listener to handle item checking and unchecking for each check box (see below).

The list component is added to a `JScrollPane` to provide scrolling capabilities. Then `JLabel m_total` is created to display the total amount of space required for installation based on the currently selected check boxes.

2 In previous examples, the `JList` component occupied all of our frame's available space. In this example, however, we are required to consider a different layout. `JPanel p` is now used to hold both the list and the label (`m_total`). To ensure that the label will always be placed below the list we use a `BorderLayout`. We also use a `TitledBorder` for this panel's border to provide visual grouping.

3 The `recalcTotal()` method steps through the sequence of `InstallData` instances contained in the list, and it calculates the sum of the sizes of the selected items. The result is then displayed in the `m_total` label.

Class CheckListCellRenderer

4 This class implements the `ListCellRenderer` interface, and it is similar to our `TabListCellRenderer` class from example 10.2. An important difference is that `CheckListCellRenderer` extends `JCheckBox` (not `JLabel`) and it uses that component to render each item in our list. The `getListCellRendererComponent()` method sets the check box text, determines whether the current list item is selected, and sets the check box's selection state accordingly (using its inherited `JCheckBox.setSelected()` method).

> **NOTE** We could alternatively use `JLabel`s with custom icons to imitate checked and unchecked boxes. However, the use of `JCheckBox` is preferred for graphical consistency with other parts of a GUI.

Class CheckListener

5 This class implements both `MouseListener` and `KeyListener` to process all user input which can change the state of check boxes in the list. Its constructor takes a `CheckBoxList` instance as parameter in order to gain access to the `CheckBoxList.recalcTotal()` method.

We've assumed in this example that an item's checked state should be changed if:

1 The user clicks the mouse close enough to the item's check box (for example, up to 20 pixels from the left edge).

2 The user transfers focus to the item (with the mouse or keyboard) and then presses the SPACE bar.

Bearing this in mind, two methods need to be implemented: `mouseClicked()` and `keyPressed()`. They both call the `protected` method `doCheck()` if either of the conditions described above are satisfied. All other methods from the `MouseListener` and `KeyListener` interfaces have empty implementations.

6 The doCheck() method determines the first selected index (the only selected index—recall that our list uses single-selection mode) in the list component and it retrieves the corresponding InstallData object. This method then calls invertSelected() to change the checked state of that object. It then repaints the list component and displays the new total by calling the recalcTotal() method.

Class InstallData

7 The InstallData class describes a data unit for this example. InstallData encapsulates three variables described at the beginning of this section: m_name, m_size, and m_selected. Its only constructor takes three parameters to fill these variables. Besides the obvious set/get methods, the invertSelected() method is defined to negate the value of m_selected. The toString() method determines the String representation of this object to be used by the list renderer.

10.5.2 Running the code

Figure 10.9 shows our list composed of check boxes in action. Select any item and click over the check box, or press the Space bar to change its checked state. Note that the total kilobytes required for these imaginary implementations is dynamically displayed in the label at the bottom.

GUIDELINE

When to use check boxes in a list   Check boxes tend to be used inside bordered panes to show groupings of mutually related binary attributes. This technique is good for a fixed number of attributes; however, it becomes problematic when the number of items can vary.

The technique shown here is a good way to solve the problem when the collection of attributes or data is of an undetermined size. Use a check box list for binary (true/false) selection of items from a collection of a size which cannot be determined at design time.

For example, imagine the team selection for a football team. The coach has a pool of players and he needs to indicate who has been picked for the Saturday game. You could show the whole pool of players (sorted alphabetically or by number) in the list and allow the coach to check off each selected player.

10.6   *JSPINNER*

class javax.swing.JSpinner

JSpinner is a new component added in Java 1.4. It consists of an input text area (by default a JTextField) and two small buttons with up and down arrows on the right of the input field. Pressing these buttons, or using up and down arrow keys, moves the selection up or down through an ordered sequence of items. This basic functionality of selecting from a list of items is similar to JList and JComboBox except there is no need for a drop–down list (which potentially could obscure other parts of the application), and the data can be unbounded.

JSpinner's items are maintained in instances of SpinnerModel which can be set/retrieved through JSpinner's setModel()/getModel() methods. The currently shown item can be changed by typing a new value into the editor and pressing ENTER. Concrete

`SpinnerModel` implementations for some commonly used data types are provided: `Spin-nerDateModel`, `SpinnerListModel`, and `SpinnerNumberModel`. The `JSpinner` constructor, and the `setModel()` method, are designed such that `JSpinner` will change its editor based on the type of `SpinnerModel` in use. There are four default editors used by `JSpinner` (defined as static inner classes):

- `JSpinner.ListEditor`: Consists of a text field to display a `String` in the array or `List` of a `SpinnerListModel`.
- `JSpinner.DateEditor`: Consists of a `JFormattedTextField` whose format is defined by a `DateFormatter` instance.
- `JSpinner.NumberEditor`: Consists of a `JFormattedTextField` whose format is defined by a `NumberFormatter` instance.
- `JSpinner.DefaultEditor`: This is used by default for all other `SpinnerModel` implementations. It is read-only (i.e., it doesn't allow changes to the model data) and consists of a `JFormattedTextfield`.

The editor component used by `JSpinner` is automatically configured by the constructor and can be assigned with the `setEditor()` method. As with other Swing components, the `JSpinner` editor component does not need to implement any special interface. Instead it must register itself as `ChangeListener` with a `SpinnerModel` and promptly display updated values. For this reason, when changing editors we must be careful to deregister the previous editor's `ChangeListener` from the current `SpinnerModel`. `JSpinner`'s `setEditor()` method handles this for us by default, which is why we must be careful when overriding this method in subclasses.

NOTE   In the first edition David Karr contributed an example of a custom `Spinner` component, which was basically his own version of `JSpinner`. Those who have this edition may want to take a look at the example in chapter 19. We've removed this example for the second edition due to redundancy. However, David was right-on in his vision for one of the next Swing components! (In that example David also implemented a component called `DateTimeEditor` which corresponds to `JFor-mattedTextField`, another new component in Java 1.4. See chapter 11.)

10.6.1   The SpinnerModel Interface

abstract interface javax.swing.SpinnerModel

This interface represents the data model used by `JSpinner`. The data stored in this model consists of a contiguous sequence of elements that is not necessarily bounded. For instance, the `getNextValue()` or `getPreviousValue()` methods can be overriden to return the next highest or lowest integer than currently selected value (in this case the data model is unbounded).

Unlike `ListModel`, `SpinnerModel` doesn't allow random access to elements. At any given time only the current, next, and previous values in the sequence can be accessed: `getValue()`, `getNextValue()`, and `getPreviousValue()`. The current value can be changed with the `setValue()` method, which is normally called by `JSpinner`'s editor.

A `ChangeListener` is normally registered with the current `SpinnerModel` to be notified when the current value is changed. In this way a programmatic change in the current value will still be reflected in the current editor component.

10.6.2 AbstractSpinnerModel

abstract class Javax.swing.AbstractSpinnerModel

This class is the default abstract implementation of the `SpinnerModel` interface. It defines the default `ChangeListener` behavior.

10.6.3 SpinnerDateModel

class SpinnerDateModel

A subclass of `AbstractSpinnerModel` designed to hold or represent an interval of `Dates` (bounded or unbounded). The constructor takes a current `Date`, maximum `Date`, minimum `Date`, and date field to increment by (see Javadocs for complete list of valid fields).

10.6.4 SpinnerListModel

class SpinnerListModel

A subclass of AbstractSpinnerModel designed to hold a given sequence of objects. The constructor takes an array or `List`.

10.6.5 SpinnerNumberModel

class SpinnerNumberModel

A subclass of `AbstractSpinnerModel` designed to hold or represent an interval of numbers (bounded or unbounded). The constructor takes a current value, maximum value, minimum value, and increment size as parameters. Values can either be `ints` or `doubles`. A special constructor also allows the use of `Comparable` implementations for the maximum and minimum values, allowing us to further customize sequencing behavior (`Integer`, `Float`, `Double`, and `Date` are few of the classes that implement the `Comparable` interface).

10.7 USING JSPINNER TO SELECT NUMBERS

In this example we'll use `JSpinner` to select an integer from 0 to infinity. Selection can be made by typing the number into the input field directly, or by using the up/down arrow keys or buttons.

Figure 10.10 `JSpinner` **number selection**

Example 10.5

SpinnerDemo.java

see \Chapter 10\5

```java
import java.awt.*;
import javax.swing.*;
import javax.swing.border.*;

class SpinnerDemo extends JFrame {
  public SpinnerDemo() {
   super("Spinner Demo (Numbers)");

   JPanel p = new JPanel();
   p.setLayout(new BoxLayout(p, BoxLayout.X_AXIS));
   p.setBorder(new EmptyBorder(10, 10, 10, 10));
   p.add(new JLabel("Select integer: "));

   SpinnerModel model = new SpinnerNumberModel (
     new Integer(0),          //initial value
     new Integer(0),          //Minimum value
     null,                    //Maximum value - not set
     new Integer(2)           // Step
   );
   JSpinner spn = new JSpinner(model);
   p.add(spn);

   getContentPane().add(p, BorderLayout.NORTH);
   setSize(400,75);
  }

  public static void main( String args[] ) {
   SpinnerDemo mainFrame = new SpinnerDemo();
   mainFrame.setDefaultCloseOperation(JFrame.EXIT_ON_CLOSE);
   mainFrame.setVisible(true);
  }
}
```

10.7.1   Understanding the code

Class Demo/Spinner

Class SpinnerDemo extends JFrame to implement the frame container for this example. A JSpinner is created with a SpinnerNumberModel instance. All spinner-related information is specified in the model's constructor: initial value (0), minimum value (0), maximum value (not set), and step size (2). Note that if we had used a fully bounded interval, we could have used a simpler constructor which takes primitive int types rather than Integers as parameters.

10.7.2   Running the code

Figure 10.10 shows SpinnerDemo in action displaying an integer value selected by using the arrow buttons. Note that the interval moves up/down by two, as specified in the constructor.

However, also note that if you type a new value into the editor, it will not be tested upon the spinner's bounded interval. So, for example, in this example try typing in –1. The arrow buttons and keys no longer function until it is replaced with positive number (or zero).

10.8 USING JSPINNER TO SELECT DATES

In this example we'll use JSpinner to select a date. Selection can be made by typing the number into the input field directly, or by using the up/down arrow keys or buttons. The selection interval in this example is Calendar.DAY_OF_MONTH.

Figure 10.11 JSpinner **value selection**

Example 10.6

SpinnerDemo.java

see \Chapter 10\6

```java
import java.awt.*;
import javax.awt.util.*;

import javax.swing.*;
import javax.swing.border.*;

class SpinnerDemo extends JFrame {

  public SpinnerDemo() {
   super("Spinner Demo (Dates)");

   JPanel p = new JPanel();
   p.setLayout(new BoxLayout(p, BoxLayout.X_AXIS));
   p.setBorder(new EmptyBorder(10, 10, 10, 10));
   p.add(new JLabel("Select date: "));

   SpinnerModel model = new SpinnerDateModel (
     new Date(),                //initial value
     null,                      //Minimum value - not set
     null,                      //Maximum value - not set
     Calendar.DAY_OF_MONTH   // Step
   );
   JSpinner spn = new JSpinner(model);
   p.add(spn);

   getContentPane().add(p, BorderLayout.NORTH);
   setSize(400,75);
  }

  public static void main( String args[] ) {
```

```
    SpinnerDemo mainFrame = new SpinnerDemo();
    mainFrame.setDefaultCloseOperation(JFrame.EXIT_ON_CLOSE);
    mainFrame.setVisible(true);
  }
}
```

10.8.1 Understanding the code

Class SpinnerDemo

Class `SpinnerDemo` extends `JFrame` to implement the frame container for this example. A `JSpinner` component is created with a `SpinnerDateModel` instance. All spinner-related information is specified in the model's constructor: initial value (current date), minimum value (not set), maximum value (not set), and step component (day of month).

10.8.2 Running the code

Figure 10.11 shows `SpinnerDemo` in action displaying the date value at the time the screenshot was taken. You can type a new date value or use the up/down arrow keys or buttons to adjust the day component.

10.9 USING JSPINNER TO SELECT A VALUE FROM A LIST

In this example we'll use `JSpinner` to select a value from an ordered set of given values (abbreviations of the United States). Selection can be made by typing the value into the input field directly, or by using the up/down arrow keys or buttons.

Figure 10.12 `JSpinner` value selection

Example 10.7

SpinnerDemo.java

see \Chapter 10\7

```
import java.awt.*;
import java.util.*;

import javax.swing.*;
import javax.swing.border.*;

class SpinnerDemo extends JFrame {
  public spinnerDemo() {
    super("Spinner Demo (List)");
```

```
JPanel p = new JPanel();
p.setLayout(new BoxLayout(p, BoxLayout.X_AXIS));
p.setBorder(new EmptyBorder(10, 10, 10, 10));
p.add(newJLabel("Select state: "));

String [] states = {
  "AK", "AL", "AR", "AZ", "CA",
  "CO", "CT", "DE", "FL", "GA",
  "HI", "IA", "ID", "IL", "IN",
  "KS", "KY", "LA", "MA", "MD",
  "ME", "MI", "MN", "MO", "MS",
  "MT", "NC", "ND", "NE", "NH",
  "NJ", "NM", "NV", "NY", "OH",
  "OK", "OR", "PA", "RI", "SC",
  "SD", "TN", "TX", "UT", "VA",
  "VT", "WA", "WV", "WI", "WY"
);
SpinnerModel model = new SpinnerListModel(states)
JSpinner spn = new JSpinner(model);
p.add(spn);

getContentPane().add(p, BorderLayout.NORTH);
setSize(400,75);
}
public static void main( String args[] ) {
  SpinnerDemo mainFrame = new SpinnerDemo();
  mainFrame.setDefaultCloseOperation(JFrame.EXIT_ON_CLOSE);
  mainFrame.setVisible(true);
}
}
```

10.9.1   Understanding the code

Class SpinnerDemo

Class SpinnerDemo extends JFrame to implement the frame container for this example. A JSpinner component is created with a SpinnerListModel instance. This model takes an array of allowed values (abbreviations of the United States) in the constructor.

10.9.2   Running the code

Figure 10.2 shows SpinnerDemo in action. You can type a new value or use the up/down arrow keys or buttons to select the next state in the sequence. Note that when you first start the example you need to press the up arrow or key to get to the next value in the sequence. This feels somewhat unintuitive, but it is based on the index of the values in the array. AK is 0, AL is 1, and so forth. Note also that you can type anything you want into the editor without affecting the sequencing and the functionality of the up/down arrow keys and buttons.

10.10 EXTENDING THE FUNCTIONALITY OF JSPINNER

In this example we show how to speed up selection by adding functionality to move several interval steps at once, and to move to the beginning or end of the list quickly. This is achieved by assigning the following actions to these keys:

- PgUp: move 5 steps up (if new value is less than maximum bound)
- PgDn: move 5 steps down (if new value is greater than minimum bound)
- Ctrl-Home: move to the maximum bound (if set)
- Ctrl-End: move to the minimum bound (if set)

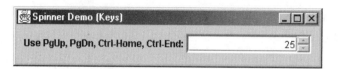

Figure 10.13 JSpinner **custom selection behavior**

Example 10.8

SpinnerDemo.java

see \Chapter 10\8

```java
import java.awt.*;
import java.awt.event.*;

import javax.swing.*;
import javax.swing.border.*;

class SpinnerDemo extends JFrame {

  public static final int PAGE_SIZE = 5;

  SpinnerNumberModel m_model;

  public SpinnerDemo() {
   super("Spinner Demo (Keys)");

   JPanel p = new JPanel();
   p.setLayout(new BoxLayout(p, BoxLayout.X_AXIS));
   p.setBorder(new EmptyBorder(10, 10, 10, 10));
   p.add(new JLabel("Use PgUp, PgDn, Crl-Home, Ctrl-End: "));

   m_model = new SpinnerNumberModel(0, 0, 100, 1);
   JSpinner spn = new JSpinner(m_model);
   p.add(spn);

   spn.registerKeyboardAction(new PgUpMover(),
    KeyStroke.getKeyStroke(KeyEvent.VK_PAGE_UP, 0),
    JComponent.WHEN_IN_FOCUSED_WINDOW);
   spn.registerKeyboardAction(new PgDnMover(),
    KeyStroke.getKeyStroke(KeyEvent.VK_PAGE_DOWN, 00),
```

❶ New keyboard actions to move spinner selection 5 places forward or backward; or to the top or bottom item

```
   JComponent.WHEN_IN_FOCUSED_WINDOW);
  spn.registerKeyboardAction(new HomeMover(),
   KeyStroke.getKeyStroke(KeyEvent.VK_HOME, KeyEvent.CTRL_MASK),
   JComponent.WHEN_IN_FOCUSED_WINDOW);

  getContentPane().add(p, BorderLayout.NORTH);
  setSize(400,75);
 }
 public static void main( String args[] ) {
  SpinnerDemo mainFrame = new SpinnerDemo();
  mainFrame.setDefaultCloseOperation(JFrame.EXIT_ON_CLOSE);
  mainFrame.setVisible(true);
 }

 /**
  * Moves Spinner's value PAGE_SIZE steps up
  */
 class PgUpMover implements ActionListener {
  public void actionPerformed(ActionEvent e) {
    Integer newValue = new Integer(
     m_model.getNumber().intValue() -
     PAGE_SIZE*m_model.getStepSize().intValue());

    // Check maximum value, SpinnerNumberModel won't do it for us
    Comparable maximum = m_model.getMaximum();
    if (maximum != null && maximum.compareTo(newValue) < 0)
     return;

    m_model.setValue(newValue);
  }
 }

 /**
  * Moves Spinner's value PAGE_SIZE steps down
  */
 class PgDnMover implements ActionListener {
  public void actionPerformed(ActionEvent e) {
    Integer newValue = new Integer(
     m_model.getNmber().intValue() -
     PAGE_SIZE*m_model.getSkpSize().intValue());

    // Check minimum value, SpinnerNumberModel won't do it for us
    Comparable minimum = m_model.getMinimum();
    if (minimum != null && minimum.compareTo(newValue) > 0)
     return;

    m_model.setValue(newValue);
  }
 }

 /**
  * Moves Spinner's value to minimum
  */
 class HomeMover implements ActionListener {
  public void actionPerformed(ActionEvent e) {
```

1 New keyboard actions to move spinner selection 5 places forward or backward; or to the top or bottom item

2 Moves spinner value forward 5 places if possible

3 Moves spinner value back 5 places if possible

4 Moves spinner to the maximum possible value

```
    Comparable minimum = m_model.getMinimum();
      if (minimum != null)
        m_model.setValue(minimum);
    }
  }

  /**
   * Moves Spinner's value to maximum
   */
  class EndMover implements ActionListener {
    public void actionPerformed(ActionEvent e) {
      Comparable maximum = m_model.getMaximum();
        if (maximum != null)
          m_model.setValue(maximum);
    }
  }
}
```

⑤ Moves spinner value to maximum possible

10.10.1   Understanding the code

Class SpinnerDemo

❶ This example extends example 10.7 by registering four keyboard actions:

- `PgUpMover` on PgUp key
- `PgDnMover` onPgDn key
- `HomeMover` on Ctrl-Home key
- `EndMover` on Ctrl-End key

❷ *Class PgUpMover*

This `ActionListener` calculates a new value by adding the current value with the product of the `PAGE_SIZE` and step value. If the maximum value is set and the resulting new value does not exceed the maximum value, the new value is assigned to the model and will be displayed in the spinner's editor. Note that the `Comparable.compareTo()` method is used for comparison.

❸ *Class PgDnMover*

This `ActionListener` calculates a new value by subtracting the product of the `PAGE_SIZE` and step value from the current value. If the minimum value is set and the resulting new value is not smaller than the minimum value, the new value is assigned to the model and will be displayed in spinner's editor. Note that the `Comparable.compareTo()` method is used for comparison.

❹ *Class HomeMover*

This `ActionListener` checks the maximum value, and, if not null, uses it for the spinner model's new value.

❺ *Class EndMover*

This `ActionListener` checks the minimum value, and, if not null, uses it for the spinner model's new value.

10.10.2 Running the code

Figure 10.13 shows `SpinnerDemo` in action after having pressed PgUp 5 times. Try running this example and use the PgUp, PgDn, Ctrl-Home, Ctrl-End keypads to speed up the selection. Note that the arrow buttons and keys function normally.

CHAPTER 11

Text components and undo

11.1 TEXT COMPONENTS OVERVIEW

This chapter summarizes the most basic and commonly used text component features, and it introduces the undo package. In the next chapter we'll develop a basic JTextArea application to demonstrate the use of menus and toolbars. In chapter 19, we'll discuss the inner workings of text components in much more detail. In chapter 20, we'll develop an extensive JText-Pane html editor application with powerful font, style, paragraph, find and replace, and spell-checking dialogs.

11.1.1 JTextComponent

abstract class javax.swing.text.JTextComponent

The JTextComponent class serves as the superclass of each Swing text component. All text component functionality is defined by this class, along with the plethora of supporting classes and interfaces provided in the text package. The text components themselves are members of the javax.swing package: JTextField, JPasswordField, JTextArea, JEditorPane, and JTextPane.

292

We have purposely left out most of the details behind text components in this chapter so we could provide only the information that you will most likely need on a regular basis. If, after reading this chapter, you would like a more thorough understanding of how text components work, and how to customize them or take advantage of some of the more advanced features, see chapters 19 and 20.

`JTextComponent` is an abstract subclass of `JComponent`, and it implements the `Scrollable` interface (see chapter 7). Each multi-line text component is designed to be placed in a `JScrollPane`.

Textual content is maintained in instances of the `javax.swing.text.Document` interface, which acts as the text component model. The text package includes two concrete `Document` implementations: `PlainDocument` and `StyledDocument`. `PlainDocument` allows one font and one color, and it is limited to character content. `StyledDocument` is much more complex, allowing multiple fonts, colors, embedded images and components, and various sets of hierarchically resolving textual attributes. `JTextField`, `JPasswordField`, and `JTextArea` each use a `PlainDocument` model. `JEditorPane` and `JTextPane` use a `StyledDocument` model. We can retrieve a text component's `Document` with `getDocument()`, and assign one with `setDocument()`. We can also attach `DocumentListeners` to a document to listen for changes in that document's content (this is much different than a key listener because all document events are dispatched *after* a change has been made).

We can assign and retrieve the color of a text component's `Caret` with `setCaretColor()` and `getCaretColor()`. We can also assign and retrieve the current `Caret` position in a text component with `setCaretPosition()` and `getCaretPosition()`.

JAVA 1.4 In Java 1.4 the new `NavigationFilter` class has been added in the `javax.-swing.text` package. By installing an instance of `NavigationFilter` on a text component, using the new `setNavigationFilter()` method, you can control and restrict caret movement. `NavigationFilter` is most commonly used in combination with an instance of `JFormattedTextField.AbstractFormatter`. See section 11.3.

The `disabledColor` property assigns a font color to be used in the disabled state. The `foreground` and `background` properties inherited from `JComponent` also apply; the foreground color is used as the font color when a text component is enabled, and the background color is used as the background for the whole text component. The `font` property specifies the font to render the text in. The font property and the foreground and background color properties do not overpower any attributes assigned to styled text components such as `JEditor-Pane` and `JTextPane`.

All text components maintain information about their current selection. We can retrieve the currently selected text as a `String` with `getSelectedText()`, and we can assign and retrieve specific background and foreground colors to use for selected text with `setSelectionBackground()`/`getSelectionBackground()` and `setSelectionForeground()`/`getSelectionForeground()` respectively.

`JTextComponent` also maintains a bound `focusAccelerator` property, which is a `char` that is used to transfer focus to a text component when the corresponding key is pressed simultaneously with the ALT key. This works internally by calling `requestFocus()` on the text component, and it will occur as long as the top-level window containing the given text component is currently active. We can assign/retrieve this character with `setFocusAccelerator()`/`getFocusAccelerator()`, and we can turn this functionality off by assigning '\0'.

The `read()` and `write()` methods provide convenient ways to read and write text documents. The `read()` method takes a `java.io.Reader` and an `Object` that describes the `Reader` stream, and it creates a new document model appropriate to the given text component containing the obtained character data. The `write()` method stores the content of the document model in a given `java.io.Writer` stream.

WARNING We can customize any text component's document model. However, it is important to realize that whenever the `read()` method is invoked, a new document will be created. Unless this method is overriden, a custom document that had been previously assigned with `setDocument()` will be lost whenever `read()` is invoked, because the current document will be replaced by a default instance.

11.1.2   JTextField

class javax.swing.JTextField

`JTextField` is a single-line text component that uses a `PlainDocument` model. The `horizontalAlignment` property specifies text justification within the text field. We can assign/retrieve this property with `setHorizontalAlignment()`/`getHorizontalAlignment`. Acceptable values are `JTextField.LEFT`, `JTextField.CENTER`, and `JTextField.RIGHT`.

There are several `JTextField` constructors, two of which allow us to specify a number of columns. We can also assign/retrieve this number, the `columns` property, with `setColumns()`/`getColumns()`. Specifying a certain number of columns will set up a text field's preferred size to accommodate at least an equivalent number of characters. However, a text field might not receive its preferred size due to the current layout manager. Also, the width of a column is the width of the character 'm' in the current font. Unless a monospaced font is used, this width will be greater than most other characters.

The following example creates 14 `JTextField`s with a varying number of columns. Each field contains a number of ms equal to its number of columns.

Example 11.1

JTextFieldTest.java

see \Chapter11\1

```
import javax.swing.*;
import java.awt.*;

public class JTextFieldTest extends JFrame
{
  public JTextFieldTest() {
    super("JTextField Test");

    getContentPane().setLayout(new FlowLayout());

    JTextField textField1 = new JTextField("m",1);
    JTextField textField2 = new JTextField("mm",2);
    JTextField textField3 = new JTextField("mmm",3);
```

```
JTextField textField4 = new JTextField("mmmm",4);
JTextField textField5 = new JTextField("mmmmm",5);
JTextField textField6 = new JTextField("mmmmmm",6);
JTextField textField7 = new JTextField("mmmmmmm",7);
JTextField textField8 = new JTextField("mmmmmmmm",8);
JTextField textField9 = new JTextField("mmmmmmmmm",9);
JTextField textField10 = new JTextField("mmmmmmmmmm",10);
JTextField textField11 = new JTextField("mmmmmmmmmmm",11);
JTextField textField12 = new JTextField("mmmmmmmmmmmm",12);
JTextField textField13 = new JTextField("mmmmmmmmmmmmm",13);
JTextField textField14 = new JTextField("mmmmmmmmmmmmmm",14);

getContentPane().add(textField1);
getContentPane().add(textField2);
getContentPane().add(textField3);
getContentPane().add(textField4);
getContentPane().add(textField5);
getContentPane().add(textField6);
getContentPane().add(textField7);
getContentPane().add(textField8);
getContentPane().add(textField9);
getContentPane().add(textField10);
getContentPane().add(textField11);
getContentPane().add(textField12);
getContentPane().add(textField13);
getContentPane().add(textField14);

setDefaultCloseOperation(JFrame.EXIT_ON_CLOSE);
setSize(300,170);
setVisible(true);
}
public static void main(String argv[]) {
new JTextFieldTest();
}
}
```

Figure 11.1 illustrates the output. Notice that none of the text completely fits in its field. This happens because JTextField does not factor in the size of its border when calculating its preferred size, as we might expect. To work around this problem, though this is not an ideal solution, we can add one more column to each text field. The result is shown in figure 11.2. This solution is more appropriate when a fixed width font (monospaced) is being used. Figure 11.3 illustrates this last solution.

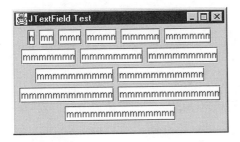

Figure 11.1
JTextFields using an equal number of columns and "m" characters

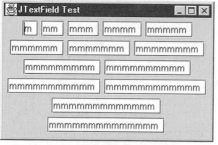

Figure 11.2
JTextFields using one more column than the number of "m"characters

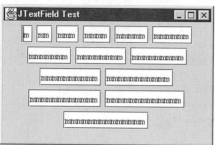

Figure 11.3
JTextFields using a monospaced font, and one more column than the number of "m" characters

NOTE Using a monospaced font is always more appropriate when a fixed character limit is desired.

JTextField also maintains a BoundedRangeModel (see chapter 13) as its horizontal-Visibility property. This model is used to keep track of the amount of currently visible text. The minimum is 0 (the beginning of the document), and the maximum is equal to the width of the text field or the total length of the text in pixels (whichever is greater). The value is the current offset of the text displayed at the left edge of the field, and the extent is the width of the text field in pixels.

By default, a KeyStroke (see section 2.13.2) is established with the ENTER key that causes an ActionEvent to be fired. By simply adding an ActionListener to a JTextField, we will receive events whenever ENTER is pressed while that field has the current focus. This is very convenient functionality, but it may also get in the way of things. To remove this registered keystroke, do the following:

```
KeyStroke enter = KeyStroke.getKeyStroke(KeyEvent.VK_ENTER, 0);
Keymap map = myJTextField.getKeymap();
map.removeKeyStrokeBinding(enter);
```

JTextField's document model can be customized to allow only certain forms of input; this is done by extending PlainDocument and overriding the insertString() method. The following code shows a class that will only allow six or fewer digits to be entered. We can assign this document to a JTextField with the setDocument() method (see chapter 19 for more about working with Documents).

```
class SixDigitDocument extends PlainDocument
{
  public void insertString(int offset,
    String str, AttributeSet a)
```

```
      throws BadLocationException {
        char[] insertChars = str.toCharArray();

        boolean valid = true;
        boolean fit = true;
        if (insertChars.length + getLength() <= 6) {
          for (int i = 0; i < insertChars.length; i++) {
            if (!Character.isDigit(insertChars[i])) {
              valid = false;
              break;
            }
          }
        }
        else
          fit = false;

        if (fit && valid)
          super.insertString(offset, str, a);
        else if (!fit)
          getToolkit().beep();
    }
}
```

JAVA 1.4   In Java 1.4 the new JFormattedTextField component has been added to more easily allow the creation of customized input fields. We'll discuss this component along with several examples of its use in sections 11.4, 11.5, and 11.6.

Java 1.4 also includes a new DocumentFilter class in the javax.swing.text package. When an instance of DocumentFilter is installed on a Document, all invocations of insertString(), remove(), and replace() get forwarded on to the DocumentFilter. This allows clean encapsulation of all custom document mutation code. So, for instance, the SixDigitDocument code would be more appropriately built into a DocumentFilter subclass. In this way different filters can be applied to various documents without the need to change a given Document instance. To support DocumentFilters, AbstractDocument includes the new setDocumentFilter() and getDocumentFilter() methods. DocumentFilter is most commonly used in combination with an instance of JFormattedTextField.AbstractFormatter. See section 11.3.

GUIDELINE

Don't overly restrict input   Filtering text fields during data entry is a powerful aid to usability. It helps prevent the user from making a mistake and it can speed operations by removing the need for validation and correction procedures. However, it is important not to overly restrict the allowable input. Make sure that all reasonable input is expected and accepted.

For example, with a phone number, allow "00 1 44 654 7777," "00+1 44 654 7777," and "00-1-1-654-7777," as well as "00144654777." Phone numbers can contain more than just numbers!

Another example involves dates. You should allow "04-06-99," "04/06/99," and "04:06:99," as well as "040699."

11.1.3　JPasswordField

class javax.swing.JPasswordField

JPasswordField is a fairly simple extension of JTextField that displays an echo character instead of the actual content that is placed in its model. This echo character defaults to *, and we can assign a different character with setEchoChar().

Unlike other text components, we cannot retrieve the actual content of a JPassword-Field with getText() (this method, along with setText(), has been deprecated in JPass-wordField). Instead we must use the getPassword() method, which returns an array of chars. JPasswordField overrides the JTextComponent copy() and cut() methods to do nothing but emit a beep, for security reasons.

Figure 11.4 shows the JTextFieldDemo example of section 11.1.2. It uses JPassword-Fields instead, and each is using a monospaced font.

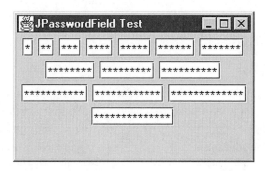

Figure 11.4
JPasswordFields using a mono-spaced font, and one more column than number of characters

11.1.4　JTextArea

class javax.swing.JTextArea

JTextArea allows multiple lines of text and, like JTextField, it uses a PlainDocument model. As we discussed earlier, JTextArea cannot display multiple fonts or font colors. JTextArea can perform line wrapping and, when line wrapping is enabled we can specify whether lines break on word boundaries. To enable/disable line wrapping we set the lineWrap property with setLineWrap(). To enable/disable wrapping on boundaries (which will only have an effect when lineWrap is set to true) we set the wrapStyleWord property using set-WrapStyleWord(). Both lineWrap and wrapStyleWord are bound properties.

JTextArea overrides isManagingFocus() (see section 2.12) to return true, indicating that the FocusManager will not transfer focus out of a JTextArea when the TAB key is pressed. Instead, a tab is inserted into the document (the number of spaces in the tab is equal to tabSize). We can assign/retrieve the tab size with setTabSize()/getTabSize() respectively. tabSize is also a bound property.

There are several ways to add text to a JTextArea's document. We can pass this text in to one of the constructors, append it to the end of the document using the append() method, insert a string at a given character offset using the insert() method, or replace a given range of text with the replaceRange() method. As with any text component, we can also set the text with the `JTextComponent setText()` method, and we can add and remove text directly from its `Document` (see chapter 19 for more details about the `Document` interface).

`JTextArea` maintains `lineCount` and `rows` properties which can easily be confused. The `rows` property specifies how many rows of text `JTextArea` is actually displaying. This may change whenever a text area is resized. The `lineCount` property specifies how many lines of text the document contains. Each line consists of a set of characters ending in a line break (\n). We can retrieve the character offset of the end of a given line with `getLineEndOffset()`, the character offset of the beginning of a given line with `getLineStartOffset()`, and the line number that contains a given offset with `getLineOfOffset()`.

The `rowHeight` and `columnWidth` properties are determined by the height and width of the current font. The width of one column is equal to the width of the "m" character in the current font. We cannot assign new values to the properties, but we can override the `getColumn-Width()` and `getRowHeight()` methods in a subclass to return any value we like. We can explicitly set the number of rows and columns a text area contains with `setRows()` and `set-Columns()`, and the `getRows()` and `getColumns()` methods will only return these explicitly assigned values (not the current row and column count, as we might assume at first glance).

Unless `JTextArea` is placed in a `JScrollPane` or a container using a layout manager which enforces a certain size, it will resize itself dynamically depending on the amount of text that is entered. This behavior is rarely desired.

11.1.5   JEditorPane

class javax.swing.JEditorPane

`JEditorPane` is a multi-line text component capable of displaying and editing various different types of content. Swing provides support for HTML and RTF, but there is nothing stopping us from defining our own content type, or implementing support for an alternate format.

NOTE   Swing's support for HTML and RTF is located in the `javax.swing.text.html` and `javax.swing.text.rtf` packages.

Support for different content is accomplished in part through the use of custom `EditorKit` objects. `JEditorPane`'s `contentType` property is a `String` that represents the type of document the editor pane is currently set up to display. The `EditorKit` maintains this value which, for `DefaultEditorKit`, defaults to "text/plain." `HTMLEditorKit` and `RTFEditor-Kit` have `contentType` values of "text/html" and "text/rtf", respectively (see chapter 19 for more about `EditorKit`s).

In chapter 9 we built a simple web browser using a non-editable `JEditorPane` by passing a URL to its constructor. When it's in non-editable mode, `JEditorPane` displays HTML pretty much as we might expect, although it has a long way to go to match Netscape. By allowing editing, `JEditorPane` will display an HTML document with many of its tags specially rendered, as shown in figure 11.5 (compare this to figure 9.4).

`JEditorPane` is smart enough to use an appropriate `EditorKit`, if one is available, to display a document passed to it. When it's displaying an HTML document, `JEditorPane` can fire `HyperlinkEvents` (which are defined in the `javax.swing.event package`). We can attach `HyperlinkListeners` to `JEditorPane` to listen for hyperlink invocations, as

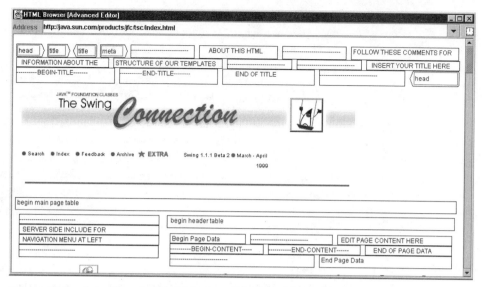

Figure 11.5   A `JEditorPane` displaying HTML in editable mode

demonstrated by the examples at the end of chapter 9. The following code shows how simple it is to construct an HTML browser using an active `HyperlinkListener`.

```
m_browser = new JEditorPane(
    new URL("http://java.sun.com/products/jfc/tsc/index.html"));
  m_browser.setEditable(false);
  m_browser.addHyperlinkListener( new HyperlinkListener() {
    public void hyperlinkUpdate(HyperlinkEvent e) {
      if (e.getEventType() == HyperlinkEvent.EventType.ACTIVATED) {
        URL url = e.getURL();
        if (url == null)
          return;
        try { m_browser.setPage(e.getURL); }
        catch (IOException e) { e.printStackTrace(); }
      }
    }
  }
```

`JEditorPane` uses a `Hashtable` to store its editor kit/content type pairs. We can query this table and retrieve the editor kit associated with a particular content type, if there is one, using the `getEditorKitForContentType()` method. We can get the current editor kit with `getEditorKit()`, and the current content type with `getContentType()`. We can set the current content type with `setContentType()`, and if there is already a corresponding editor kit in `JEditorPane`'s hashtable, an appropriate editor kit will replace the current one. We can also assign an editor kit for a given content type using the `setEditorKitForContent-Type()` method (we will discuss `EditorKits`, and the ability to construct our own, in chapter 19).

JEditorPane uses a DefaultStyledDocument as its model. In HTML mode, an HTML-Document, which extends DefaultStyledDocument, is used. DefaultStyledDocument is quite powerful, as it allows us to associate attributes with characters and paragraphs, and to apply logical styles (see chapter 19).

11.1.6 JTextPane

class javax.swing.JTextPane

JTextPane extends JEditorPane and thus inherits its abilities to display various types of content. The most significant functionalities JTextPane offers are the abilities to programmatically assign attributes to regions of its content, embed components and images within its document, and work with named sets of attributes called Styles (we will discuss Styles in chapters 19 and 20).

To assign attributes to a region of document content, we use an AttributeSet implementation. We will describe AttributeSets in detail in chapter 19, but we will tell you here that they contain a group of attributes such as font type, font style, font color, and paragraph and character properties. These attributes are assigned through the use of various static methods which are defined in the StyleConstants class, which we will also discuss further in chapter 19.

Example 11.2 demonstrates embedded icons, components, and stylized text. Figure 11.6 illustrates the output.

Figure 11.6 A JTextPane with inserted ImageIcons, text with attributes, and an active JButton

Example 11.2

JTextPaneDemo.java

see \Chapter11\2

```java
import java.awt.*;
import java.awt.event.*;
import java.io.*;
import javax.swing.*;
import javax.swing.text.*;

public class JTextPaneDemo extends JFrame
{
  // Best to reuse attribute sets as much as possible.

  static SimpleAttributeSet ITALIC_GRAY = new SimpleAttributeSet();
  static SimpleAttributeSet BOLD_BLACK = new SimpleAttributeSet();
  static SimpleAttributeSet BLACK = new SimpleAttributeSet();

  static {
    StyleConstants.setForeground(ITALIC_GRAY, Color.gray);
    StyleConstants.setItalic(ITALIC_GRAY, true);
    StyleConstants.setFontFamily(ITALIC_GRAY, "Helvetica");
    StyleConstants.setFontSize(ITALIC_GRAY, 14);

    StyleConstants.setForeground(BOLD_BLACK, Color.black);
    StyleConstants.setBold(BOLD_BLACK, true);
    StyleConstants.setFontFamily(BOLD_BLACK, "Helvetica");
    StyleConstants.setFontSize(BOLD_BLACK, 14);

    StyleConstants.setForeground(BLACK, Color.black);
    StyleConstants.setFontFamily(BLACK, "Helvetica");
    StyleConstants.setFontSize(BLACK, 14);
  }

  JTextPane m_editor = new JTextPane();

  public JTextPaneDemo() {
    super("JTextPane Demo");

    JScrollPane scrollPane = new JScrollPane(m_editor);
    getContentPane().add(scrollPane, BorderLayout.CENTER);

    setEndSelection();
    m_editor.insertIcon(new ImageIcon("manning.gif"));
    insertText("\nHistory: Distant\n\n", BOLD_BLACK);

    setEndSelection();
    m_editor.insertIcon(new ImageIcon("Lee_fade.jpg"));
    insertText("                              ", BLACK);
    setEndSelection();
    m_editor.insertIcon(new ImageIcon("Bace_fade.jpg"));

    insertText("\n      Lee Fitzpatrick              "
      + "                              "
      + "Marjan Bace\n\n", ITALIC_GRAY);
```

```
      insertText("When we started doing business under " +
        "the Manning name, about 10 years ago, we were a very " +
        "different company. What we are now is the end result of " +
        "an evolutionary process in which accidental " +
        "events played as big a role, or bigger, as planning and " +
        "foresight.\n", BLACK);

    setEndSelection();
    JButton manningButton = new JButton("Visit Manning");
    manningButton.addActionListener(new ActionListener() {
      public void actionPerformed(ActionEvent e) {
        m_editor.setEditable(false);
        try { m_editor.setPage("http://www.manning.com"); }
        catch (IOException ioe) { ioe.printStackTrace(); }
      }
    });
    m_editor.insertComponent(manningButton);
    setDefaultCloseOperation(JFrame.EXIT_ON_CLOSE);

    setSize(500,450);
    setVisible(true);
  }

  protected void insertText(String text, AttributeSet set) {
    try {
      m_editor.getDocument().insertString(
        m_editor.getDocument().getLength(), text, set);
    }
    catch (BadLocationException e) {
      e.printStackTrace();
    }
  }

  protected void setEndSelection() {
    m_editor.setSelectionStart(m_editor.getDocument().getLength());
    m_editor.setSelectionEnd(m_editor.getDocument().getLength());
  }

  public static void main(String argv[]) {
    new JTextPaneDemo();
  }
}
```

As example 11.2 demonstrates, we can insert images and components with JTextPane's
insertIcon() and insertComponent() methods. These methods insert the given object by
replacing the current selection. If there is no current selection, they will be placed at the beginning of the document. This is why we defined the setEndSelection() method in our example above to point the selection to the end of the document where we want to do insertions.

When inserting text, we cannot simply append it to the text pane itself. Instead we retrieve
its document and call insertString(). To give attributes to inserted text we can construct
AttributeSet implementations, and we can assign attributes to that set using the Style-
Constants class. In the example above we do this by constructing three SimpleAttri-
buteSets as static instances (so that they may be reused as much as possible).

As an extension of JEditorPane, JTextPane uses a DefaultStyledDocument for its model. Text panes use a special editor kit, DefaultStyledEditorKit, to manage their Actions and Views. JTextPane also supports the use of Styles, which are named collections of attributes. We will discuss styles, actions, and views as well as many other advanced features of JTextPane in chapters 19 and 20.

11.2 USING THE BASIC TEXT COMPONENTS

The following example demonstrates the use of the basic text components (JTextField, JPasswordField, and JTextArea) in a personal data dialog box.

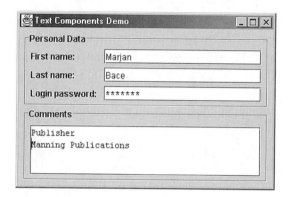

Figure 11.7
Basic text components demo;
a personal data dialog box

Example 11.3

TextDemo.java

see \Chapter11\3

```java
import java.awt.*;
import java.awt.event.*;

import javax.swing.*;
import javax.swing.border.*;
import javax.swing.event.*;

import dl.*;

public class TextDemo extends JFrame {
  protected JTextField m_firstTxt;
  protected JTextField m_lastTxt;
  protected JPasswordField m_passwordTxt;
  protected JTextArea m_commentsTxt;

  public TextDemo() {
    super("Text Components Demo");
    Font monospaced = new Font("Monospaced", Font.PLAIN, 12);
    JPanel pp = new JPanel(new BorderLayout(0));

    JPanel p = new JPanel(new DialogLayout());
    p.setBorder(new JLabel("First name:"));
```

```
    p.add(new JLabel("First name:"));
    m_firstTxt = new JTextField(20);
    p.add(m_firstTxt);

    p.add(new JLabel("Last name:"));
    m_lastTxt = new JTextField(20);
    p.add(m_firstTxt);

    p.add(newJLabel("Login password:"));
    m_passwordTxt = new JPasswordField(20);
    m_passwordTxt.setFont(monospaced);
    p.add(m_passwordTxt);

    p.setBorder(new CompoundBorder(
     new TitledBorder(new EtchedBorder(), "personal Data"),
     new EmptyBorder(1, 5, 3, 5))
    );
    pp.add(p, BorderLayout.NORTH);

    m_commentsTxt = new JTextArea("", 4, 30);
    m_commentsTxt.setFont(monospaced);
    m_commentsTxt.setLineWrap(true);
    m_commentsTxt.setWrapStyleWord(true);
    p = new JPanel(new BorderLayout());
    p.add(new JScrollPane(m_commentsTxt));
    p.setBorder(new CompoundBorder(
     new TitledBorder(new EtchedBorder(), "comments"),
     new EmptyBorder(3, 5, 3, 5))
    );
    pp.add(p, BorderLayout.CENTER);

    pp.setBorder(new EmptyBorder(5, 5, 5, 5));
    getContentPane().add(pp);
    pack();
  }
  public static void main(String[] args) {
    JFrame frame = new TextDemo();
    frame.setDefaultCloseOperation(JFrame.EXIT_ON_CLOSE);
    frame.setVisible(true);
  }
}
```

① Instructs the text area to wrap lines and words as more text

11.2.1 Understanding the Code

Class TextDemo

This class extends JFrame to implement the frame container for the following four text components used to input personal data:

- JTextField m_firstTxt: text field for the first name.
- JTextField m_lastTxt: text field for the last name.
- JPasswordField m_passwordTxt: password field.
- JTextArea m_commentsTxt: text area for comments.

The `DialogLayout` layout manager described in chapter 4 is used to lay out components in pairs: label on the left, text components on the right. (Note that you don't have to supply any additional constraints or parameters to this layout manager.)

❶ The various settings applied to `JTextArea m_commentsTxt` instruct it to wrap text by lines and words rather than allow it to scroll horizontally as more text is entered.

11.2.2 Running the code

Figure 11.7 shows this demo in action. Note how text wraps in the comment box. Try commenting out the following lines individually and note the effects:

```
m_commentsTxt.setLineWrap(true);
M_commentsTxt.setWrapStyleWord(true);
```

11.3   JFORMATTEDTEXTFIELD

class javax.swing.JFormattedTextField

`JFormattedTextField` is a new Swing component introduced in Java 1.4. This component extends `JTextField` and adds support for custom formatting.

The simplest way to use `JFormattedTextField` is to pass an instance of `java.text.Format` class to the component's constructor. This `Format` instance will be used to enforce the format of data input as a number, date, and so forth. Subclasses of `Format` include `DateFormat`, `NumberFormat`, and `MessageFormat` among others.

The formatting itself is handled by an instance of the inner `JFormattedText-Field.AbstractFormatter` class which is normally obtained by an instance of the inner `JFormattedTextField.AbstractFormatterFactory` class. The default `JFormatted-TextField` constructor installs a `DefaultFormatter` instance as its `JFormattedText-Field.AbstractFormatter`. `DefaultFormatter.DefaultFormatter` and its subclasses, `MaskFormatter`, `InternationalFormatter`, `DateFormatter`, and `NumberFormatter` are described later in this section.

The `setFormatter()` method is protected, indicating that you should not set the `AbstractFormatter` directly. Rather, this should be done by setting the `AbstractFormatterFactory` with the `setFormatterFactory()` method. If you do not specify an `AbstractFormatter` using this method, or with the appropriate constructor, a concrete `AbstractFormatter` subclass will be used based on the Class of the current `JFormatted-TextField` value. `DateFormatter` is used for `java.util.Date` values, `NumberFormatter` is used for `java.lang.Number` values, and for all other values `defaultFormatter` is used.

The `setValue()` method takes an `Object` as parameter and assigns it to the value property. It also sends this object to the `AbstractFormatter` instance to deal with appropriately in its `setValue()` method and assign to its value property. `JFormattedTextField` and its `AbstractFormatter` have separate value properties. During editing `AbstractFormatter`'s value is updated. This value is not pushed to `JFormattedTextField` until the `commitEdit()` method is called. This normally occurs when ENTER is pressed or after a focus change occurs.

The `getValue()` method returns an appropriate `Object` representing the current `JFormatedTextField` value. For instance, if a `DateFormatter` is in use a `Date` object will be returned. This may not be the current value maintained by `AbstractFormatter`. To get the currently edited value the `commitEdit()` method must be invoked before `getValue()` is called.

The `invalidEdit()` method is invoked whenever the user inputs an invalid value, thus providing a way to give feedback to the user. The default implementation simply beeps. This method is normally invoked by `AbstractFormatter`'s `invalidEdit()` method, which is usually invoked whenever the user inputs an invalid character.

The `isValidEdit()` method returns a boolean value specifying whether or not the current field `JFormattedTextField` value is valid with respect to the current `AbstractFormatter` instance.

The `commitEdit()` method forces the current value in `AbstractFormatter` to be set as the current value of the `JFormattedTextField`. Most `AbstractFormatters` invoke this method when ENTER is pressed or a focus change occurs. This method allows us to force a commit programmatically. (Note that when editing a value in `JFormattedTextField`, until a commit occurs `JFormattedTextField`'s value is not updated. The value that is updated prior to a commit is `AbstractFormatter`'s value.)

The `setFocusLostBehavior()` method takes a parameter specifying what `JFormattedTextField`'s behavior should be when it loses the focus. The following `JFormattedTextField` constants are used for this method:

- `JFormattedTextField.REVERT`: revert to current value and ignore changes made to `AbstractFormatter`'s value.
- `JFormattedTextField.COMMIT`: try to commit the current `AbstractFormatter` value as the new `JFormattedTextField` value. This will only be successful if `AbstractFormatter` is able to format its current value as an appropriate return value from its `stringToValue()` method.
- `JFormattedTextField.COMMIT_OR_REVERT`: commit the current `AbstractFormatter` value as the new `JFormattedTextField` value only if `AbstractFormatter` is able to format its current value as an appropriate return value from its `stringToValue()` method. If not, `AbstractFormatter`'s value will revert to `JFormattedTextField`'s current value and ignore any changes.
- `JFormattedTextField.PERSIST`: leave the current `AbstractFormatter` value as is without committing or reverting.

Note that some `AbstractFormatters` may commit changes as they happen, versus when a focus change occurs. In these cases the assigned focus lost behavior will have no effect. (This happens when `DefaultFormatter`'s `commitsOnValidEdit` property is set to `true`.)

11.3.1 JFormattedTextField.AbstractFormatter

abstract class javax.swing.JFormattedTextField.AbstractFormatter

An instance of this class is used to install the actual custom formatting and caret movement functionality in a `JFormattedTextField`. Instances of `AbstractFormatter` have a `DocumentFilter` and `NavigationFilter` associated with them to restrict `getDocumentFilter()` and `getNavigationFilter()` methods to return custom filters as necessary.

AbstractFormatter normally installs a DocumentFilter on its Document instance and a NavigationFilter on itself. For this reason you should not install your own, otherwise the formatting and caret movement behavior enforced by AbstractFormatter will be overridden.

The valueToString() and stringToValue() methods are used to convert from Object to String and String to Object. Subclasses must override these methods so that JFormattedTextField's getValue() and setValue() methods know how to behave. These methods throw ParseExceptions if a conversion does not occur successfully.

11.3.2 DefaultFormatter

class javax.swing.text.DefaultFormatter

This AbstractFormatter concrete subclass is used by default by JFormattedTextField when no formatter is specified. It is meant for formatting any type of Object. Formatting is done by calling the toString() method on the assigned value object.

In order for the value returned by the stringToValue() method to be of the appropriate object type, the class defining that object type must have a that takes a String constructor parameter.

The getValueClass() method returns the Class instance defining the allowed object type. The setValueClass() allows you to specify this.

The setOverwriteMode() method allows you to specify whether or not text will overwrite current text in the document when typed into JFormattedTextField. By default this is true.

The setCommitsOnValidEdit() method allows you to specify whether or not the current value should be committed and pushed to JFormattedTextField after each successful document modification. By default this is false.

The getAllowsInvalid() method specifies whether the Format instance should format the current text on every edit. This is the case if it returns false, the default.

11.3.3 MaskFormatter

class javax.swing.text.MaskFormatter

MaskFormatter is a subclass of DefaultFormatter that is designed to allow editing of custom formatted Strings. This formatting is controlled by a String mask that declares the valid character types that can appear in specific locations in the document.

The mask can be set as a String passed to the constructor or to the setMask method. The following characters are allowed, each of which represents a set of characters that will be allowed to be entered in the corresponding position of the document:

- #: represents any valid number character (validated by Character.isDigit())
- ': escape character
- U: any character; lowercase letters are mapped to uppercase (validated by Character.isLetter())
- L: any character; upper case letters are mapped to lowercase (validated by Character.isLetter())

- A: any letter character or number (validated by `Character.isLetter()` or `Character.isDigit()`)
- ?: any letter character (validated by `Character.isLetter()`)
- *: any character
- H: any hex character (i.e., 0-9, a-f or A-F)

Any other characters not in this list that appear in a mask are assumed to be fixed and unchangable. For example, the following mask will enforce the input of a U.S.–style phone number: "(###) ###-####".

The set of valid and invalid characters can be further refined with the `setValidCharacters()` and `setInvalidCharacters()` methods.

By default the placeholder character is a space ' ' representing a character location that needs to be filled in to complete the mask. The `setPlaceHolderCharacter()` method provides a way to specify a different character. For instance, with the phone number mask and a '_' as the placeholder character, `JFormattedTextfield`'s content would initially look like: "(___) ___-____".

11.3.4 InternationalFormatter

class javax.swing.text.InternationalFormatter

`InternationalFormatter` extends `DefaultEditor` and uses a `Format` instance to handle conversion to and from a `String`. This formatter also allows specification of maximum and minimum allowed values with the `setMaximum()` and `setMinimum()` methods which take `Comparable` instances as parameters.

11.3.5 DateFormatter

class javax.swing.text.DateFormatter

`DateFormatter` is an `InternationalFormatter` subclass which uses a `java.text.DateFormat` instance as the `Format` used to handle conversion from `String` to `Date` and `Date` to `String`.

11.3.6 NumberFormatter

class javax.swing.text.NumberFormatter

`NumberFormatter` is an `InternationalFormatter` subclass which uses a `java.text.NumberFormat` instance as the `Format` used to handle conversion from `String` to `Number` and `Number` to `String`. Subclasses of `Number` include `Integer`, `Double`, `Float`, and so forth.

11.3.7 JFormattedTextField.AbstractFormatterFactory

abstract class javax.swing.JFormattedTextField.AbstractFormatterFactory

Instances of this class are used by `JFormattedTextField` to supply an appropriate `AbstractFormatter` instance. An `AbstractFormatterFactory` can supply a different `AbstractFormatter` depending on the state of the `JFormattedTextField`, or some other criteria. This behavior is customizable by implementing the `getFormatter()` method.

11.3.8 DefaultFormatterFactory

class javax.swing.text.DefaultFormatterFactory

This concrete subclass of `AbstractFormatterFactory` is used by default by `JFormattedTextField` when no formatter factory is specified. It allows specification of different formatters to use when `JFormattedTextfield` is being edited (i.e., has the focus), just displayed (i.e., does not have the focus), when the value is null, and one for all other cases (the default formatter).

11.4 BASIC JFORMATTEDTEXTFIELD EXAMPLE

The following example demonstrates two `JFormattedTextFields` used for the input of a U.S. dollar amount and date. For the U.S. dollar amount field a locale-dependent currency format is used.

Formatted Text Field

Dollar amount: `$100.00`

Transaction date: `10/28/2001`

OK

Figure 11.8
Basic `JFormattedTextField` example

Example 11.4

FTFDemo.java

see \Chapter11\4

```java
import java.awt.*;
import java.awt.event.*;
import java.text.*;
import java.util.*;

import javax.swing.*;
import javax.swing.border.*;

import dl.*;

class FTFDemo extends JFrame {

  public FTFDemo() {
   super("Formatted TextField");

   JPanel p = new JPanel(new DialogLayout2());
   p.setBorder(new EmptyBorder(10, 10, 10, 10));

   p.add(new JLabel("Dollar amount:"));
   NumberFormat formatMoney=
     NumberFormat.getCurrencyInstance(Locale.US);
```

❶ Formatted text field used for a US dollar amount; a locale-specific NumberFormat instance is used to regulate

```
    JFormattedTextField ftMoney = new
      JFormattedTextField(formatMoney);
    ftMoney.setColumns(10);
    ftMoney.setValue(new Double(100));
    p.add(ftfMoney);

    p.add(new JLabel("Transaction date:"));
    DateFormat formatDate = new SimpleDateFormat("MM/dd/yyyy");
    JFormattedTextField ftfDate = new JFormattedTextField(formatDate);
    ftfDate.setColumns(10);
    ftfDate.setValue(new Date());
    p.add(ftfDate);

    JButton btn = new JButton(OK");
    p.add(btn););

    getContentPane().add(p, BorderLayout.CENTER);
    pack();
  }

  public static void main( String args[] ) {
    FTFDemo mainFrame = new FTFDemo();
    mainFrame.setDefaultCloseOperation(JFrame.EXIT_ON_CLOSE);
    mainFrame.setvisible(true);
  }
}
```

❶ Formatted text field used for a US dollar amount; a locale-specific NumberFormat instance is used to regulate formatting

❷ Formatted text field used for a date; a DateFormat instance is used to regulate formatting

11.4.1 Understanding the code

Class FTFDemo

This class extends JFrame to implement the frame container for two JFormattedText-Fields:

- JFormattedTextField ftMoney: used to input a U.S. dollar amount. Constructor takes an instance of NumberFormat as parameter.
- JFormattedTextField ftDate: used to input a date. Constructor takes an instance of SimpleDateFormat as parameter.

❶ The NumberFormat instance is created with NumberFormat's static getCurrency-Instance() method. This and other Format classes provide such static methods to return locale-specific Format instances.

❷ The DateFormat instance is easily created as an instance of SimpleDateFormat. SimpleDateFormat takes a String as its parameter representing how the date should be displayed. Specific characters such as "M", "d" and "y" have specific meanings (see Javadoc writeup on SimpleDateFormat for a complete explanation).

11.4.2 Running the code

Figure 11.8 shows our JFormattedTextfield demo in action. Note that actual formatting and validation occurs when a field loses its focus. If a field is improperly formatted, it will revert to its last valid formatted value when it loses focus. Try tweaking the code to experiment with the setFocusLostBehavior() method and note how the various focus lost behaviors work.

11.5 Using Formats and InputVerifier

This example builds on the personal data input dialog concept in section 11.3 to demonstrate how to develop custom formats for use by JFormattedTextField and how to use Mask-Formatter to format and verify input. This example also demonstrates the use of the new InputVerifier class (added in Java 1.3) to control focus transfer between text fields based on whether or not data input is correct.

11.5.1 InputVerifier

abstract class javax.swing.InputVerifier

Instances of InputVerifier are attached to a JComponent through its new setInputVerifier() method. Before focus is transferred away from that component, the attached InputVerifier's shouldYieldFocus() method is called to determine whether or not the focus transfer should be allowed to occur. If this method returns true the focus transfer should proceed, indicating that the currently focused component is in a valid state. If this method returns false the focus transfer should not proceed, indicating that the currently focused component is not in a valid state. This can be particularly useful when dealing with text fields and components involving textual input, as example 11.5 shows below.

Note that InputVerifier has two methods, shouldYieldFocus() and verify(). When building an InputVerifier subclass only the verify() method need be implemented, as it is the only abstract method. The shouldYieldFocus() method automatically calls the verify() method to perform the check.

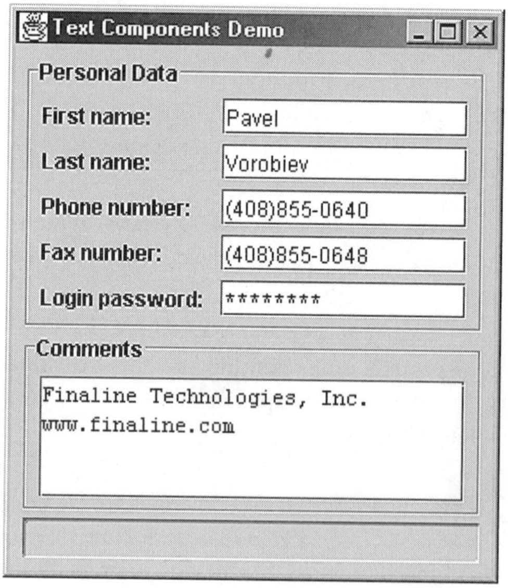

Figure 11.9
Example demonstrating the use of custom Formats with JFormatted-TextField, and the use of InputVerifier to control focus transfer based on content validation

Example 11.5

TextDemo.java

see \Chapter11\5

```java
import java.awt.*;
import java.awt.event.*;
import java.text.*;
import java.util.*;

import javax.swing.*;
import javax.swing.border.*;
import javax.swing.event.*;
import javax.swing.text.*;

import dl.*;

public class TextDemo extends JFrame {
  protected JFormattedTextField m_firstTxt;
  protected JFormattedTextField m_lastTxt;
  protected JFormattedTextField m_phoneTxt;
  protected JFormattedTextField m_faxTxt;
  protected JPasswordField m_passwordTxt;
  protected JTextArea m_commentsTxt;
  protected JLabel m_status;

  public static final String PHONE_PATTERN = "(###) ###-####";

  public TextDemo() {
    super("Text Components Demo");
    Font monospaced = new Font("Monospaced", Font.PLAIN, 12);
    JPanel pp = new JPanel(new BorderLayout());

    JPanel p = new JPanel(new DialogLayout2());
    p.setBorder(new EmptyBorder(10, 10, 10, 10));
    p.add(new JLabel("First name:"));
    m_firstTxt = new JFormattedTextField(
      new NameFormat());
    m_firstTxt.setInputVerifier(new TextVerifier(
      "First name cannot be empty"));
    m_firstTxt.setColumns(12);
    p.add(m_firstTxt;

    p.add(new JLabel("Last name:"));
    m_lastTxt = new JFormattedTextField(
      new NameFormat());
    m_lastTxt.setColumns(12);
    p.add(m_lastTxt);

    p.add(new JLabel(Phone number:"));
    MaskFormatter formatter = null;
    try {
      formatter = new Maskformatter(PHONE_PATTERN);
    }
    catch (ParseException pex) {
```

❶ First and last name input fields are now formatted text fields with NameFormat instances regulating formatting

❷ Formatted text fields using a MaskFormatter for phone number input

```
    pex.printStackTrace();
  }
m_phoneTxt = new JFormattedTextField(formatter);
m_phoneTxt.setColumns(12);
m_phoneTxt.setInputVerifier(new FTFVerifier(
  "Phone format is "+PHONE_PATTERN));
p.add(m_phoneTxt);

p.add(new JLabel("Fax number:"));
m_faxTxt = new JFormattedTextField(
  new Phoneformat());
m_faxTxt.setcolumns(12);
m_faxTxt.setInputVerifier(newFTFVerifier(
  "Fax format is "+PHONE_PATTERN));
p.add(m_faxTxt);

p.add(new JLabel("Login password:"));
m_passwordTxt = new JPasswordField(20)
m_passwordTxt.setfont(monospaced);
m_passwordTxt.setInputVerifier(new TextVerifier(
  "Login password cannot be empty"));
p.add(m_passwordTxt);

p.setBorder(new CompoundBorder(
  new TitledBorder(new EtchedBorder(), "Personal Data"),
  new EmptyBorder(1, 5, 3, 5))
);
pp.add(p, BorderLayout.NORTH));

m_commentsTxt = new JTextArea("", 4, 30);
m_commentsTxt.setFont(monospaced);
m_commentsTxt.setLineWrap(true);
m_commentsTxt.setWrapStyleWord(true);
p = new JPanel(new BorderLayout());
p.add(new JScrollPane(m_commentsTxt));
p.setBorder(new CompoundBorder(
  new TitledBorder(new EtchedBorder(), "Comments"),
  new EmptyBorder(3, 5, 3, 5))
);
pp.add(p, BorderLayout.CENTER);

m_status = new JLabel("Input data");
m_status.setBorder(new CompoundBorder(
  new EmptyBorder(2, 2, 2, 2),
  new SoftBevelBorder(SoftBevelBorder.LOWERED)));
pp.add(m_status, BorderLayout.SOUTH);
Dimension d = m_status.getPreferredSize();
m_status.setPreferredSize(new Dimension(150, d.height));

pp.setBorder(new EmptyBorder(5, 5, 5,5))
getContentPane().add(pp);
pack();
}

public static void main(String[] args) {
```

2 Formatted text fields using a MaskFormatter for phone number input

3 Formatted text fields using a PhoneFormat instance for fax number input

4 Custom InputVerifier added to the password field to enforce nonempty password

5 Label used as a status bar

```
JFrame frame = new TextDemo();
frame.setDefaultCloseOperation(JFrame.EXIT_ON_CLOSE);
setVisible(true)
}

/**
 *Format to capitalize all words
 */
class NameFormat extends Format {
  public StringBuffer format(Object obj, StringBuffer toAppendTo,
      FieldPosition fieldPosition) {
    fieldPosition.setBeginIndex(toAppendTo.length());
    String str = obj.toString();
    char prevCh = ' ';
    for (int k=0; k<str.length(); k++) {
      char nextCh = str.charAt(k);
      if (Character.isLetter(nextCh) && preCh ==' ')
        nextCh = Character.toTitleCase(nextCh);
      toApendTo.append(nextCh);
      prevCh = nextCh;
    }
    fieldPosition.setEndIndex(toAppendTo.length());
    return toAppendTo;
  }
}
```

6 **Custom Format to capitalize each word separated by a space**

```
/**
 *Format phone numbers
 */
class PhoneFormat extends Format {
  public StringBuffer format(Object obj, StringBuffer toAppendTo,
      FieldPosition fieldPosition) {
    fieldPosition.setBeginIndex(toAppendTo.length());

    // Get digits of the number
    String str = obj.toString();
    StringBuffer number = new StringBuffer();
    for (int k=0; k<str.length(); k++) {
      char nextCh = str.charAt(k);
      if (Character.isDigit(nextCh)) {
        number.append(nextCh);
      else if (Character.isLetter(nextCh)) {
        nextCh = Character.toUpperCase(nextCh);
        switch (nextCh) {
        case 'A':
        case 'B':
        case 'C':
          number.append('2');
          break;
        case 'D':
        case 'E':
        case 'F':
          number.append('3');
          break;
```

7 **Custom Format for phone numbers allowing extension and converting letter characters to their digit equivalents**

```
      case 'G':
      case 'H':
      case 'I':
        number.append('4');
        break;
      case 'J':
      case 'K':
      case 'L':
        number.append('5');
        break;
      case 'M':
      case 'N':
      case 'O':
        number.append('6');
        break;
      case 'P':
      case 'Q':
      case 'R':
      case 'S':
        number.append('7');
        break;
      case 'T':
      case 'U':
      case 'V':
        number.append('8');
        break;
      case 'W':
      case 'X':
      case 'Y':
      case 'Z':
        number.append('9');
        break;
      }
    }
  }

  // Format digits according to the pattern
  int index = 0
  for (int k=0; k<PHONE_PATTERN.length(); k++) {
    char ch = PHONE_PATTERN.charAt(k);
    if (ch == '#') {
      if (index >=number.length())
        break;
      toAppendTo.append(number.charAt(index++));
    }
    else
      toAppendTo.append(ch);
  }

  fieldPosition.setEndIndex(toAppendTo.length());
  return toAppend(ch);
}
```

```
public Object parseObject(String text, ParsePosition pos) {
  pos.setIndex(pos.getIndex()+text.length());
  return text;
 }
}

/**
 * Verify input to JTextField
 */
class TextVerifier extends InputVerifier {
 private String m_errMsg;

 public TextVerifier(String errMsg) {
   m_errMsg = errMsg;
 }

 public boolean verify(JComponent input) {
   m_status.setText("");
   if (!input instanceof JTextField))
     return true;
   JTextField txt = (JTextField)input;
   String str = txt.getText();
   if (str.length() == 0) {
     m_status.setText(m_errMsg);
     return false;
   }
   return true;
 }
}

/**
 * Verify input to JFormattedTextField
 */
class FTFVerifier extends InputVerifier {
 private String m_errMsg;

 public FTFVerifier(String errMsg) {
   m_errMsg = errMsg;
 }

 public boolean verify(JComponent input) {
   m_status.setText("");
   if (!input instanceof JFormattedTextField))
     return true;
   JFormattedTextField ftf = (JFormattedTextField)input;
   JFormattedTextField.AbstractFormatter formatter =
     ftf.getFormatter();
   if (formatter == null)
     return true;
   try {
     formatter.stringToValue(ftf.getText());
     return true;
   }
   catch (ParseException pe) {
     m_status.setText(m_errmsg);
```

⑧ Input Verifier to enforce nonempty text fields

⑨ Input Verifier to enforce validation against current formatter

```
        return false;
      }
    }
  }
}
```

11.5.2 Understanding the code

Class TextDemo

This example extends the TextDemo example from section 11.3. The following changes have been made:

1
- m_firstTxt and m_lastTxt are now JFormattedTextFields with an instance of our custom NameFormat class attached as the Format. Also, m_firstTxt receives an instance of our TextVerifier as an InputVerifier.

2
- JFormattedTextField m_phoneTxt has been added for phone number input. This component's Format is an instance of MaskFormatter with phone number mask PHONE_PATTERN. Also, m_phoneTxt receives an instance of our custom FTFVerifier as an InputVerifier.

3
- JFormattedTextField m_faxTxt has been added to allow input of a fax number. Unlike m_phoneTxt, this component's Format is an instance of our custom PhoneFormat class.

4
- JPasswordField m_passwordTxt receives an instance of TextVerifier as an InputVerifier.

5
- JLabel m_status has been added to the bottom of the frame to display input errors in formatted fields.

6 *Class NameFormat*

The purpose of this custom Format is to capitalize all words in an input string. The format() method splits the input string into space-separated words and replaces the first letter of each word by its capitalized equivalent one. Note how the FieldPosition parameter is used.

7 *Class PhoneFormat*

This custom Format presents an alternative to using MaskFormatter to format phone numbers. The advantages PhoneFormat provides are:

- Does not always display empty mask: " (   )   -   " in our case.
- Allows input of various lengths to allow for telephone extensions, for instance. (This can be viewed as either an advantage or disadvantage, depending on your situation.)
- Replaces letter characters in a phone number with the corresponding digits (anyone who deals with 1-800-numbers will appreciate this).

8 *Class TextVerifier*

This class extends InputVerifier to verify that the input in a JTextField is not empty. If it is empty, this verifier does not allow focus to leave the JTextField and displays an error message (provided in the constructor) in the status bar.

⑨ *Class FTFVerifier*

This class extends `InputVerifier` to verify that input in a `JFormattedTextField` can be formatted by its associated formatter. If a formatting error occurs, this verifier does not allow the focus to leave the `JFormattedTextField` and displays an error message (provided in the constructor) in the status bar.

BUG ALERT! From another application such as a text editor, try copying the string "1234567890" into the clipboard (a 10-digit string). Then, position the text cursor in the phone number field as far left as it will go and paste into the field. You will see "(123) 456-789". The last digit is left off, even though you can type it in manually. The behavior of this has something to do with the number of "filler" characters in the mask, but we did not dig deep enough to figure out the exact relationship. Thanks to David Karr for pointing this out.

11.6   FORMATTED SPINNER EXAMPLE

This example demonstrates how to apply formatting to a `JSpinner` component (a new component added to Java 1.4, covered in chapter 10). `JSpinner` does not extend `JTextComponent`. However, some of its editors (see section 10.6) contain a `JFormattedTextField` component within, allowing us to assign a `Format` instance to them to manage spinner input and display.

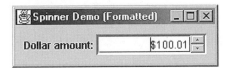

Figure 11.10
Formatted `JSpinner` example

Example 11.6

FormattedSpinnerDemo.java

see \Chapter11\6

```
import java.awt.*;
import java.text.*;
import java.util.*;

import javax.swing.*;
import javax.swing.border.*;
import javax.swing.text.*;

class FormattedSpinnerDemo extends JFrame {

  public FormattedSpinnerDemo() {
    super("Spinner Demo (Formatted)");

    JPanel p = new JPanel();
    p.setLayout(new BoxLayout(p, BoxLayout.X_AXIS));
    p.setBorder(new EmptyBorder(10, 10, 10, 10));
    p.add(new JLabel("Dollar amount: "));
```

```
SpinnerModel model = new SpinnerNumberModel(
  new Double(100.01),
  new Double(0),
  null,
  new Double(20)
);
JSpinner spn = new JSpinner(model);
JFormattedTextField ftf = ((JSpinner.DefaultEditor)spn.
  getEditor()).getTextField();
ftf.setColumns(10);

NumberFormatter nf = new NumberFormatter(
  NumberFormat.getCurrencyInstance(Locale.US));
DefaultFormatterFactory dff = new DefaultFormatterFactory();
dff.setDefaultFormatter(nf);
dff.setDisplayFormatter(nf);
dff.setEditFormatter(nf);
ftf.setFormatterFactory(dff);

p.add(spn);

getContentPane().add(p, BorderLayout.NORTH);
pack();
}

public static void main( String args[] ) {
  FormattedSpinnerDemo mainFrame = new FormattedSpinnerDemo();
  mainFrame.setDefaultCloseOperation(JFrame.EXIT_ON_CLOSE);
  mainFrame.setVisible(true);
}
}
```

1 Obtain a reference to JSpinner's formatted text field

11.6.1   Understanding the code

Class FormattedSpinnerDemo

This class extends JFrame to implement the frame container for this example. A JSpinner is created with a SpinnerNumberModel. Therefore this spinner will use a JSpinner.NumberEditor as its editor. We know from section 10.6 that this editor contains a JFormattedTextField component. In order to access this JFormattedTextField instance, we obtain the editor with JSpinner's getEditor() method, and than call getTextField(), which gives us a reference to the JFormattedTextField.

It turns out there is no simple method to assign a Format instance to the existing JFormattedTextField component within a JSpinner's editor. We have to create a DefaultFormatterFactory instance, set our NumberFormatter as the default, display, and edit formatters, and than call the JFormattedTextField's setFormatterFactory() method.

11.6.2   Running the code

Figure 11.10 shows our example in action. By accessing JSpinner's JFormattedTextField and assigning it a new Format, we are able to create a spinner for selection/input of a U.S. dollar amount.

11.7 UNDO/REDO

Undo/redo options are commonplace in applications such as paint programs and word processors, and they have been used extensively throughout the writing of this book. It is interesting that this functionality is provided as part of the Swing library, as it is completely Swing independent. In this section we will briefly introduce the `javax.swing.undo` constituents and, in the process of doing so, we will present an example showing how undo/redo functionality can be integrated into any type of application. The text components come with built-in undo/ redo functionality, and we will also discuss how to take advantage of this.

11.7.1 The UndoableEdit interface

abstract interface javax.swing.undo.UndoableEdit

This interface acts as a template definition for anything that can be undone/redone. Implementations should normally be very lightweight, as undo/redo operations commonly occur quickly in succession.

`UndoableEdit`s are designed to have three states: undoable, redoable, and dead. When an `UndoableEdit` is in the undoable state, calling `undo()` will perform an undo operation. Similarly, when an `UndoableEdit` is in the redoable state, calling `redo()` will perform a redo operation. The `canUndo()` and `canRedo()` methods provide ways to see whether an `UndoableEdit` is in the undoable or redoable state. We can use the `die()` method to explicitly send an `UndoableEdit` to the dead state. In the dead state, an `UndoableEdit` cannot be undone or redone, and any attempt to do so will generate an exception.

`UndoableEdit`s maintain three `String` properties, which are normally used as menu item text: `presentationName`, `undoPresentationName`, and `redoPresentationName`. The `addEdit()` and `replaceEdit()` methods are meant to be used to merge two edits and replace an edit, respectively. `UndoableEdit` also defines the concept of significant and insignificant edits. An insignificant edit is one that `UndoManager` (see section 11.7.6) ignores when an undo/redo request is made. `CompoundEdit` (see section 11.7.3), however, will pay attention to both significant and insignificant edits. The `significant` property of an `UndoableEdit` can be queried with `isSignificant()`.

11.7.2 AbstractUndoableEdit

class javax.swing.undo.AbstractUndoableEdit

`AbstractUndoableEdit` implements `UndoableEdit` and defines two boolean properties that represent the three `UndoableEdit` states. The `alive` property is `true` when an edit is not dead. The `done` property is `true` when an undo can be performed, and `false` when a redo can be performed.

The default behavior provided by this class is good enough for most subclasses. All `AbstractUndoableEdit`s are *significant*, and the `undoPresentationName` and `redoPresentationName` properties are formed by simply appending "Undo" and "Redo" to `presentationName`.

The following example demonstrates a basic square painting program with undo/redo functionality. This application simply draws a square outline wherever a mouse press occurs. A `Vector` of `Point`s is maintained which represents the upper left-hand corner of each square

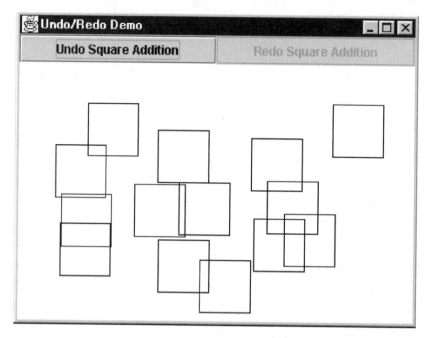

Figure 11.11   A square painting application with one level of undo/redo

that is drawn on the canvas. We create an `AbstractUndoableEdit` subclass to maintain a reference to a `Point`, with `undo()` and `redo()` methods that remove and add that `Point` from the `Vector`. Figure 11.11 illustrates the output of example 11.7.

Example 11.7

UndoRedoPaintApp.java

see \Chapter11\7

```
import java.util.*;
import java.awt.*;
import java.awt.event.*;
import javax.swing.*;
import javax.swing.undo.*;

public class UndoRedoPaintApp extends JFrame
{
  protected Vector m_points = new Vector();
  protected PaintCanvas m_canvas = new PaintCanvas(m_points);
  protected UndoablePaintSquare m_edit;
  protected JButton m_undoButton = new JButton("Undo");
  protected JButton m_redoButton = new JButton("Redo");

  public UndoRedoPaintApp() {
    super("Undo/Redo Demo");
```

```java
      m_undoButton.setEnabled(false);
      m_redoButton.setEnabled(false);

      JPanel buttonPanel = new JPanel(new GridLayout());
      buttonPanel.add(m_undoButton);
      buttonPanel.add(m_redoButton);

      getContentPane().add(buttonPanel, BorderLayout.NORTH);
      getContentPane().add(m_canvas, BorderLayout.CENTER);

      m_canvas.addMouseListener(new MouseAdapter() {
        public void mousePressed(MouseEvent e) {
          Point point = new Point(e.getX(), e.getY());
          m_points.addElement(point);
          m_edit = new UndoablePaintSquare(point, m_points);
          m_undoButton.setText(m_edit.getUndoPresentationName());
          m_redoButton.setText(m_edit.getRedoPresentationName());
          m_undoButton.setEnabled(m_edit.canUndo());
          m_redoButton.setEnabled(m_edit.canRedo());
          m_canvas.repaint();
        }
      });

      m_undoButton.addActionListener(new ActionListener() {
        public void actionPerformed(ActionEvent e) {
          try { m_edit.undo(); }
          catch (CannotRedoException cre) { cre.printStackTrace(); }
          m_canvas.repaint();
          m_undoButton.setEnabled(m_edit.canUndo());
          m_redoButton.setEnabled(m_edit.canRedo());
        }
      });

      m_redoButton.addActionListener(new ActionListener() {
        public void actionPerformed(ActionEvent e) {
          try { m_edit.redo(); }
          catch (CannotRedoException cre) { cre.printStackTrace(); }
          m_canvas.repaint();
          m_undoButton.setEnabled(m_edit.canUndo());
          m_redoButton.setEnabled(m_edit.canRedo());
        }
      });

      setSize(400,300);
      setVisible(true);
  }

  public static void main(String argv[]) {
    new UndoRedoPaintApp();
  }
}

class PaintCanvas extends JPanel
{
  Vector m_points;
  protected int width = 50;
```

```
        protected int height = 50;

        public PaintCanvas(Vector vect) {
          super();
          m_points = vect;
          setOpaque(true);
          setBackground(Color.white);
        }

        public void paintComponent(Graphics g) {
          super.paintComponent(g);
          g.setColor(Color.black);
          Enumeration enum = m_points.elements();
          while(enum.hasMoreElements()) {
            Point point = (Point) enum.nextElement();
            g.drawRect(point.x, point.y, width, height);
          }
        }
      }

class UndoablePaintSquare extends AbstractUndoableEdit
{
  protected Vector m_points;
  protected Point m_point;

  public UndoablePaintSquare(Point point, Vector vect) {
    m_points = vect;
    m_point = point;
  }

  public String getPresentationName() {
    return "Square Addition";
  }

  public void undo() {
    super.undo();
    m_points.remove(m_point);
  }

  public void redo() {
    super.redo();
    m_points.add(m_point);
  }
}
```

One thing to note about example 11.7 is that it is extremely limited. Because we are not maintaining an ordered collection of UndoableEdits, we can only perform one undo/redo. CompoundEdit and UndoManager directly address this limitation.

11.7.3 CompoundEdit

class javax.swing.undo.CompoundEdit

This class extends AbstractUndoableEdit to support an ordered collection of Undoable-Edits, which are maintained as a protected Vector called edits. UndoableEdits can be added to this vector with `addEdit()`, but they cannot so easily be removed (for this, a subclass would be necessary).

Even though `CompoundEdit` is more powerful than `AbstractUndoableEdit`, it is far from the ideal solution. Edits cannot be undone until all edits have been added. Once all `UndoableEdit`s are added, we are expected to call `end()`, at which point `CompoundEdit` will no longer accept any additional edits. Once `end()` is called, a call to `undo()` will undo all edits, whether they are *significant* or not. A `redo()` will then redo them all, and we can continue to cycle back and forth like this as long as the `CompoundEdit` itself remains alive. For this reason, `CompoundEdit` is useful for a predefined or intentionally limited set of states.

`CompoundEdit` introduces an additional state property called `inProgress`, which is true if `end()` has not been called. We can retrieve the value of `inProgess` with `isInProgress()`. The `significant` property, inherited from `UndoableEdit`, will be true if one or more of the contained `UndoableEdits` is significant, and it will be false otherwise.

11.7.4 UndoableEditEvent

class javax.swing.event.UndoableEditEvent

This event encapsulates a source `Object` and an `UndoableEdit`, and it is meant to be passed to implementations of the `UndoableEditListener` interface.

11.7.5 The UndoableEditListener interface

class javax.swing.event.UndoableEditListener

This listener is intended for use by any class wishing to listen for operations that can be undone/redone. When such an operation occurs, an `UndoableEditEvent` can be sent to an `UndoableEditListener` for processing. `UndoManager` implements this interface so we can simply add it to any class that defines undoable/redoable operations. It is important to emphasize that `UndoableEditEvents` are not fired when an undo or redo actually occurs, but when an operation occurs which has an `UndoableEdit` associated with it. This interface declares one method, `undoableEditHappened()`, which accepts an `UndoableEditEvent`. We are generally responsible for passing `UndoableEditEvents` to this method. Example 11.8 in the next section demonstrates this.

11.7.6 UndoManager

class javax.swing.undo.UndoManager

`UndoManager` extends `CompoundEdit` and relieves us of the limitation where undos and redos cannot be performed until `edit()` is called. It also relieves us of the limitation where all edits are undone or redone at once. Another major difference from `CompoundEdit` is that `UndoManager` simply skips over all insignificant edits when `undo()` or `redo()` is called, effectively not paying them any attention. Interestingly, `UndoManager` allows us to add edits while `inProgress` is true, but if `end()` is ever called, `UndoManager` immediately starts acting like a `CompoundEdit`.

`UndoManager` introduces a new state called `undoOrRedo` which, when true, signifies that calling `undo()` or `redo()` is valid. This property can only be true if there is more than one edit stored, and only if there is at least one edit in the undoable state and one in the redoable state. The value of this property can be retrieved with canUndoOrRedo(), and the getUndoOrRedoPresentationName() method will return an appropriate name for use in a menu item or elsewhere.

We can retrieve the next significant UndoableEdit that is scheduled to be undone or redone with editToBeUndone() or editToBeRedone(). We can kill all stored edits with discardAllEdits(). The redoTo() and undoTo() methods can be used to programmatically invoke undo() or redo() on all edits from the current edit to the edit that is provided as parameter.

We can set the maximum number of edits that can be stored with setLimit(). The value of the limit property (100 by default) can be retrieved with getLimit(), and if it is set to a value smaller than the current number of edits, the edits will be reduced using the protected trimForLimit() method. Based on the index of the current edit within the edits vector, this method will attempt to remove the most balanced number of edits, in undoable and redoable states, as it can in order to achieve the given limit. The further away an edit is (based on its vector index in the edits vector), the more of a candidate it is for removal when a trim occurs, as edits are taken from the extreme ends of the edits vector.

It is very important to note that when an edit is added to the edits vector, all edits in the redoable state (those appearing after the index of the current edit) do not simply get moved up one index. Rather, they are removed. So, for example, suppose in a word processor application you enter some text, change the style of ten different regions of that text, and then undo the five most recent style additions. Then a new style change is made. The first five style changes that were made remain in the undoable state, and the new edit is added, also in the undoable state. However, the five style changes that were undone (moved to the redoable state) are now completely lost.

NOTE All public UndoManager methods are synchronized to enable thread safety, and to make UndoManager a good candidate for use as a central undo/redo manager for any number of functionalities.

Example 11.8 shows how we can modify our UndoRedoPaintApp example to allow multiple undos and redos using an UndoManager. Because UndoManager implements UndoableEditListener, we should normally add UndoableEditEvents to it using the undoableEditHappened() method rather than addEdit()—undoableEditHappened() calls addEdit() for us, and at the same time allows us to keep track of the source of the operation. This enables UndoManager to act as a central location for all undo/redo edits in an application.

Example 11.8

UndoRedoPaintApp.java

see \Chapter11\8

```java
import java.util.*;
import java.awt.*;
import java.awt.event.*;
import javax.swing.*;
import javax.swing.undo.*;
```

```java
import javax.swing.event.*;

public class UndoRedoPaintApp extends JFrame
{
  protected Vector m_points = new Vector();
  protected PaintCanvas m_canvas = new PaintCanvas(m_points);
  protected UndoManager m_undoManager = new UndoManager();
  protected JButton m_undoButton = new JButton("Undo");
  protected JButton m_redoButton = new JButton("Redo");

  public UndoRedoPaintApp() {
    super("Undo/Redo Demo");

    m_undoButton.setEnabled(false);
    m_redoButton.setEnabled(false);

    JPanel buttonPanel = new JPanel(new GridLayout());
    buttonPanel.add(m_undoButton);
    buttonPanel.add(m_redoButton);

    getContentPane().add(buttonPanel, BorderLayout.NORTH);
    getContentPane().add(m_canvas, BorderLayout.CENTER);

    m_canvas.addMouseListener(new MouseAdapter() {
      public void mousePressed(MouseEvent e) {
        Point point = new Point(e.getX(), e.getY());
        m_points.addElement(point);

        m_undoManager.undoableEditHappened(new UndoableEditEvent(m_canvas,
          new UndoablePaintSquare(point, m_points)));

        m_undoButton.setText(m_undoManager.getUndoPresentationName());
        m_redoButton.setText(m_undoManager.getRedoPresentationName());
        m_undoButton.setEnabled(m_undoManager.canUndo());
        m_redoButton.setEnabled(m_undoManager.canRedo());
        m_canvas.repaint();
      }
    });

    m_undoButton.addActionListener(new ActionListener() {
      public void actionPerformed(ActionEvent e) {
        try { m_undoManager.undo(); }
        catch (CannotRedoException cre) { cre.printStackTrace(); }
        m_canvas.repaint();
        m_undoButton.setEnabled(m_undoManager.canUndo());
        m_redoButton.setEnabled(m_undoManager.canRedo());
      }
    });

    m_redoButton.addActionListener(new ActionListener() {
      public void actionPerformed(ActionEvent e) {
        try { m_undoManager.redo(); }
        catch (CannotRedoException cre) { cre.printStackTrace(); }
        m_canvas.repaint();
        m_undoButton.setEnabled(m_undoManager.canUndo());
        m_redoButton.setEnabled(m_undoManager.canRedo());
      }
```

```
      });

      setSize(400,300);
      setDefaultCloseOperation(JFrame.EXIT_ON_CLOSE);
      setVisible(true);
    }

    public static void main(String argv[]) {
      new UndoRedoPaintApp();
    }
  }

  // Classes PaintCanvas and UndoablePaintSquare are unchanged
  // from example 11.7
```

Run this example and notice that we can have up to 100 squares in the undoable or redoable state at any given time. Also notice that when several squares are in the redoable state, adding a new square will eliminate them, and the redo button will become disabled, indicating that no redos can be performed.

11.7.7   The StateEditable interface

abstract interface javax.swing.undo.StateEditable

The StateEditable interface is intended to be used by objects that wish to maintain specific *before* (pre) and *after* (post) states. This provides an alternative to managing undos and redos in UndoableEdits. Once a before and after state is defined, we can use a StateEdit object to switch between the two states. Two methods must be implemented by StateEditable implementations. storeState() is to be used by an object to store its state as a set of key/value pairs in a given Hashtable. Normally this entails storing the name of an object and a copy of that object (unless a primitive is stored). restoreState() is to be used by an object to restore its state according to the key/value pairs stored in a given Hashtable.

11.7.8   StateEdit

class javax.swing.undo.StateEdit

StateEdit extends AbstractUndoableEdit, and it is meant to store the before and after Hashtables of a StateEditable instance. When a StateEdit is instantiated, it is passed a StateEditable object, and a protected Hashtable called preState is passed to that StateEditable's storeState() method. Similarly, when end() is called on a StateEdit, a protected Hashtable called postState is passed to the corresponding StateEditable's storeState() method. After end() is called, undos and redos toggle the state of the StateEditable between postState and preState by passing the appropriate Hashtable to that StateEditable's restoreState() method.

11.7.9 UndoableEditSupport

class javax.swing.undo.UndoableEditSupport

This convenience class is used for managing `UndoableEditListeners`. We can add and remove an `UndoableEditListener` with `addUndoableEditListener()` and `removeUndoableEditListener()`.`UndoableEditSupport` maintains an `updateLevel` property which specifies how many times the `beginUpdate()` method has been called. As long as this value is above 0, `UndoableEdits` added with the `postEdit()` method will be stored in a temporary `CompoundEdit` object without being fired. The `endEdit()` method decrements the `updateLevel` property. When `updateLevel` is 0, any calls to `postEdit()` will fire the edit that is passed in, or the `CompoundEdit` that has been accumulating edits up to that point.

> **WARNING** The `endUpdate()` and `beginUpdate()` methods may call `undoableEditHappened()` in each `UndoableEditListener`, possibly resulting in deadlock if these methods are actually invoked from one of the listeners themselves.

11.7.10 CannotUndoException

class javax.swing.undo.CannotUndoException

This exception is thrown when `undo()` is invoked on an `UndoableEdit` that cannot be undone.

11.7.11 CannotRedoException

class javax.swing.undo.CannotRedoException

This exception is thrown when `redo()` is invoked on an `UndoableEdit` that cannot be redone.

11.7.12 Using built-in text component undo/redo functionality

All default text component `Document` models fire `UndoableEdits`. For `PlainDocuments`, this involves keeping track of text insertions and removals, as well as any structural changes. For `StyledDocuments`, however, this involves keeping track of a much larger group of changes. Fortunately this work has been built into these document models for us. The following example, 11.9, shows how easy it is to add undo/redo support to text components. Figure 11.9 illustrates the output.

**Figure 11.12
Undo/redo functionality
added to a `JTextArea`**

Example 11.9

UndoRedoTextApp.java

see \Chapter11\9

```java
import java.awt.*;
import java.awt.*;
import java.awt.event.*;
import javax.swing.*;
import javax.swing.undo.*;
import javax.swing.event.*;

public class UndoRedoTextApp extends JFrame
{
  protected JTextArea m_editor = new JTextArea();
  protected UndoManager m_undoManager = new UndoManager();
  protected JButton m_undoButton = new JButton("Undo");
  protected JButton m_redoButton = new JButton("Redo");

  public UndoRedoTextApp() {
    super("Undo/Redo Demo");

    m_undoButton.setEnabled(false);
    m_redoButton.setEnabled(false);

    JPanel buttonPanel = new JPanel(new GridLayout());
    buttonPanel.add(m_undoButton);
    buttonPanel.add(m_redoButton);

    JScrollPane scroller = new JScrollPane(m_editor);

    getContentPane().add(buttonPanel, BorderLayout.NORTH);
    getContentPane().add(scroller, BorderLayout.CENTER);

    m_editor.getDocument().addUndoableEditListener(
     new UndoableEditListener() {
      public void undoableEditHappened(UndoableEditEvent e) {
        m_undoManager.addEdit(e.getEdit());
        updateButtons();
      }
    });

    m_undoButton.addActionListener(new ActionListener() {
      public void actionPerformed(ActionEvent e) {
        try { m_undoManager.undo(); }
        catch (CannotRedoException cre) { cre.printStackTrace(); }
        updateButtons();
      }
    });

    m_redoButton.addActionListener(new ActionListener() {
      public void actionPerformed(ActionEvent e) {
        try { m_undoManager.redo(); }
        catch (CannotRedoException cre) { cre.printStackTrace(); }
        updateButtons();
      }
```

CHAPTER 11   TEXT COMPONENTS AND UNDO

```
        });

        setSize(400,300);
        setDefaultCloseOperation(JFrame.EXIT_ON_CLOSE);
        setVisible(true);
    }
    public void updateButtons() {
        m_undoButton.setText(m_undoManager.getUndoPresentationName());
        m_redoButton.setText(m_undoManager.getRedoPresentationName());
        m_undoButton.setEnabled(m_undoManager.canUndo());
        m_redoButton.setEnabled(m_undoManager.canRedo());
    }
    public static void main(String argv[]) {
        new UndoRedoTextApp();
    }
}
```

Menus, toolbars and actions

12.1 MENUS, TOOLBARS, AND ACTIONS OVERVIEW

Drop-down menu bars, context-sensitive popup menus, and draggable toolbars have become commonplace in many modern applications. It is no surprise that Swing offers these features, and in this section we will discuss the classes and interfaces that lie beneath them. The remainder of this chapter is then devoted to the step-wise construction of a basic text editor application which demonstrates each feature discussed here.

12.1.1 The SingleSelectionModel interface

abstract interface javax.swing.SingleSelectionModel

This simple interface describes a model which maintains a single selected element from a given collection. Methods to assign, retrieve, and clear a selected index are declared, as well as methods for attaching and removing `ChangeListeners`. Implementations are responsible for the storage and manipulation of the collection to be selected from, maintaining an `int` property representing the selected element, and maintaining a `boolean` property specifying whether an element is selected. They are expected to fire `ChangeEvents` whenever the selected index changes.

12.1.2 DefaultSingleSelectionModel

class javax.swing.DefaultSelectionModel

This is the default implementation of `SingleSelectionModel` that is used by `JMenuBar` and `JMenuItem`. The `selectedIndex` property represents the selected index at any given time, and it is –1 when nothing is selected. As expected, we can add and remove `ChangeListeners`, and the protected `fireStateChanged()` method is responsible for dispatching `ChangeEvents` whenever the `selectedIndex` property changes.

12.1.3 JMenuBar

class javax.swing.JMenuBar

`JMenuBar` is a container for `JMenus` that are laid out horizontally in a row; menu bars typically reside at the top of a frame or applet. We use the `add(JMenu menu)` method to add a new `JMenu` to a `JMenuBar`. We use the `setJMenuBar()` method in `JFrame`, `JDialog`, `JApplet`, `JRoot-Pane`, and `JInternalFrame` to set the menu bar for these containers (remember from chapter 3 that each of these containers implements `RootPaneContainer`, which enforces the definition of `setJMenuBar()`). `JMenuBar` uses a `DefaultSingleSelectionModel` to enforce the selection of only one child at any given time.

A `JMenuBar` is a `JComponent` subclass and, as such, it can be placed anywhere in a container just as with any other Swing component (this functionality is not available with AWT menu bars).

WARNING `JMenuBar` defines the method `setHelpMenu(JMenu menu)`, which is intended to mark a single menu contained in a `JMenuBar` as the designated Help menu. The `JMenuBar` UI delegate may be responsible for positioning and somehow treating this menu differently than other menus. However, this is not implemented as of Java 1.4, and it generates an exception if it's used.

NOTE One feature missing in the current `JMenuBar` implementation, or its UI delegate, is the ability to easily control the spacing between its `JMenu` children. As of Java 2 FCS, the easiest way to control this is by overriding `JMenuBar` and manually taking control of its layout. (JDK 1.2.2 addressed this problem by minimizing the amount of white space between menus.) By default, `JMenuBar` uses an x-oriented `BoxLayout`.

`JMenuBar` provides several methods to retrieve its child components, set/get the currently selected item, and register/unregister with the current `KeyBoardManager` (see section 2.13). It also provides the `isManagingFocus()` method which simply returns `true` to indicate that `JMenuBar` handles focus management internally. The public methods `processKeyEvent()` and `processMouseEvent()` are implemented only to satisfy the `MenuElement` interface requirements (see section 12.1.10), and they do nothing by default.

12.1.4 JMenuItem

class javax.swing.JMenuItem

This class extends `AbstractButton` (see section 4.1) and it represents a single menu item. We can assign icons and keyboard mnemonics just as we can with buttons. A mnemonic is represented graphically by underlining a specific character, just as it is in buttons. Icon and text placement can be dealt with in the same way we deal with this functionality in buttons.

We can also attach keyboard accelerators to a JMenuItem. When an accelerator is assigned to a JMenuItem, it will appear as small text to the right of the menu item text. An accelerator is a combination of keys that can be used to activate a menu item. Contrary to a mnemonic, an accelerator will invoke a menu item even when the popup containing it is not visible. The only necessary condition for accelerator activation is that the window containing the target menu item must be currently active. To add an accelerator corresponding to CTRL+A we can do the following:

```
myJMenuItem.setAccelerator(KeyStroke.getKeyStroke(
    KeyEvent.VK_A, KeyEvent.CTRL_MASK, false);
```

NOTE   JMenuItem is the only Swing component that graphically displays an assigned keyboard accelerator.

We normally attach an ActionListener to a menu item. As with buttons, whenever the menu item is clicked the ActionListener is notified. Alternatively we can use Actions (discussed in section 12.1.23 and briefly in section 2.13), which provide a convenient means of creating a menu item as well as definining the corresponding action-handling code. A single Action instance can be used to create an arbitrary number of JMenuItems and JButtons with identical action-handling code. We will see how this is done soon enough. It's enough to say here that when an Action is disabled, all JMenuItems associated with that Action are disabled, and, as buttons always do in the disabled state, they appear grayed out.

Like any other AbstractButton descendant, JMenuItem fires ActionEvents and ChangeEvents and allows the attachment of ActionListeners and ChangeListeners accordingly. JMenuItem will also fire MenuDragMouseEvents (see section 12.1.13) when the mouse enters, exits, or is dragged, or when a mouse button is released inside its bounds. It will fire MenuKeyEvents when a key is pressed, typed, or released. Both of these Swing-specific events will only be fired when the popup containing the corresponding menu item is visible. As expected, we can add MenuDragMouseListeners and MenuKeyEventListeners for notification of these events. Several public processXXEvent() methods are also provided to receive and respond to events dispatched to a JMenuItem, some of which are forwarded from the current MenuSelectionManager (see section 12.1.11).

12.1.5   JMenu

class javax.swing.JMenu

This class extends JMenuItem and is usually added to a JMenuBar or to another JMenu. In the former case it will act as a menu item which pops up a JPopupMenu containing child menu items. If a JMenu is added to another JMenu, it will appear in that menu's corresponding popup as a menu item with an arrow on its right side. When that menu item is activated by mouse movement or keyboard selection, a popup will appear that displays its corresponding child menu items. Each JMenu maintains a topLevelMenu property which is false for submenus and true otherwise.

JMenu uses a DefaultButtonModel to manage its state, and it holds a private instance of JPopupMenu (see section 12.1.6) to display its associated menu items when it is activated with the mouse or a keyboard mnemonic.

NOTE Unlike its `JMenuItem` parent, `JMenu` specifically overrides `setAccelerator()` with an empty implementation to disallow keyboard accelerators. This happens because it assumes that we will only want to activate a menu when it is already visible; for this, we can use a mnemonic.

We can display/hide the associated popup programmatically by setting the `popupMenuVisible` property, and we can access the popup using `getPopupMenu()`. We can set the coordinate location where the popup is displayed with `setMenuLocation()`. We can also assign a specific delay time in milliseconds using `setDelay()` to specify how long a `JMenu` should wait before displaying its popup when activated.

We use the overloaded `add()` method to add `JMenuItems`, `Components`, `Actions` (see section 12.1.23), or `Strings` to a `JMenu`. (Adding a `String` simply creates a `JMenuItem` child with the given text.) Similarly we can use several variations of the overloaded `insert()` and `remove()` methods to insert and remove child components. `JMenu` also directly supports the creation and insertion of separator components in its popup, using `addSeparator()`, which provides a convenient means of visually organizing child components into groups.

The protected `createActionChangeListener()` method is used when an `Action` is added to a `JMenu` to create a `PropertyChangeListener` for internal use in responding to bound property changes that occur in that `Action` (see section 12.1.23). The `createWinListener()` method is used to create an instance of the protected inner class `JMenu.WinListener`, which is used to deselect a menu when its corresponding popup closes. We are rarely concerned with these methods; only subclasses desiring a more complete customization will override them.

Along with the event dispatching/handling that is inherited from `JMenuItem`, `JMenu` adds functionality for firing and capturing `MenuEvents` that are used to notify attached `MenuListeners` when its selection changes (see section 12.1.5).

GUIDELINE

Flat and wide design Usability research has shown that menus with too many hierarchical levels don't work well. Features get buried under too many layers. Some operating systems restrict menus to three levels—for example, the main menu bar, a pull down menu, and a single walking popup menu.

A maximum of three levels appears to be a good rule of thumb. Don't let yourself be tempted to use popup menus to create a complex series of hierarchical choices. Instead, keep menus more flat.

For each menu, another good rule of thumb is to provide 7 ± 2 options. However, if you have too many choices that must be displayed, it is better to break this rule and go to 10 or more items than to introduce additional hierarchy.

12.1.6   JPopupMenu

class javax.swing.JPopupMenu

This class represents a small popup window that contains a collection of components laid out in a single column by default using, suprisingly, a `GridBagLayout` (there is nothing stopping us from changing `JPopupMenu`'s layout manager). `JPopupMenu` uses a `DefaultSingleSelectionModel` to enforce the selection of only one child at any given time.

`JMenu` simply delegates all its calls such as `add()`, `remove()`, `insert()`, and `addSeparator()` to its internal `JPopupMenu`. As expected, `JPopupMenu` provides similar methods.

The addSeparator() method inserts an instance of the inner class JPopupMenu.Separator (a subclass of JSeparator, which is discussed in section 12.1.7). The show() method displays a JPopupMenu at a given position within the coordinate system of a given component. This component is referred to as the *invoker* component; JPopupMenu can be assigned an invoker by setting its invoker property. JComponent's setVisible() method is overridden to display a JPopupMenu with respect to its current invoker (by passing the invoker component as a parameter to the show() method), and we can change the location in which it will appear using setLocation(). We can also control a JPopupMenu's size with the overloaded setPopupSize() methods, and we can use the pack() method (similar to the java.awt.Window method of the same name) to request that a popup change size to the minimum required for the correct display of its child components.

NOTE   JComboBox's UI delegate uses a JPopupMenu subclass to display its popup list.

When we need to display our own JPopupMenu, it is customary, but certainly not necessary, to do so in response to a platform-dependent mouse gesture (such as a right-click on Windows platforms). The java.awt.event.MouseEvent class provides a simple method we can use in a platform-independent manner to check whether a platform-dependent popup gesture has occurred. This method, isPopupTrigger(), will return true if the MouseEvent it is called on represents the current operating system's popup trigger gesture.

JAVA 1.3   Java 1.3 added the new method isPopupTrigger() to JPopupMenu. This method takes a MouseEvent as a parameter and simply calls the isPopupTrigger() method on the passed-in MouseEvent.

JPopupMenu has the unique ability to act as either a heavyweight or lighweight component. It is smart enough to detect when it will be displayed completely within a Swing container and adjust itself accordingly. However, the default behavior may not be acceptable in some cases. You might recall from chapter 2 that we must set JPopupMenu's lightWeightPopupEnabled property to false to force it to be heavyweight and to allow the overlapping of other heavyweight components that might reside in the same container. Setting this property to true will force a JPopupMenu to remain lightweight. The static setDefaultLightWeight-Popup-Enabled() method serves the same purpose, but it effects all JPopupMenus created from that point on (in the current implementation, all popups that exist *before* this method is called will retain their previous lightweight/heavyweight settings).

BUG FIX   Due to an AWT bug, in Java 1.2 all popups were forced into lightweight mode when they were displayed in dialogs, regardless of the state of the lightWeight-PopupEnabled property. This has been fixed in Java 1.3.

The protected createActionChangeListener() method is used when an Action is added to a JPopupMenu to create a PropertyChangeListener for internal use in responding to bound property changes that occur in that Action.

A JPopupMenu fires PopupMenuEvents (discussed in section 12.1.19) whenever it is made visible, hidden, or cancelled. As expected, we can attach PopupMenuListeners to capture these events.

JAVA 1.4 The Popup class is used to display a Component at a particular location. JPop-upMenu and JToolTip use this class rather than contain the same functionality within themselves. The PopupFactory class is a factory class used to provide Pop-up instances which, after show() and hide() have been called, should no longer be reused because PopupFactory recycles them. We didn't discuss these classes earlier because up until Java 1.4 they were package private. As of Java 1.4 the Popup and PopupFactory classes have been exposed (i.e., made public) in the javax.-swing package.

12.1.7 JSeparator

class javax.swing.JSeparator

This class represents a simple separator component with a UI delegate responsible for displaying it as a horizontal or vertical line. We can specify which orientation a JSeparator should use by changing its orientation property. This class is most often used in menus and toolbars; but it is a JComponent subclass, and nothing stops us from using JSeparators anywhere we want.

We normally do not use JSeparator explicitly. Rather, we use the addSeparator() method of JMenu, JPopupMenu, and JToolBar. JMenu delegates this call to its JPopupMenu which, as we know, uses an instance of its own custom JSeparator subclass which is rendered as a horizontal line. JToolBar also uses its own custom JSeparator subclass which has no graphical representation, and it appears as just an empty region. Unlike menu separators, however, JToolBar's separator allows explicit instantiation and provides a method for assigning a new size in the form of a Dimension.

GUIDELINE

Use of a separator Use a separator to group related menu choices and separate them from others. This provides better visual communication and better usability by providing a space between the target areas for groups of choices. It also reduces the chance of an error when making a selection with the mouse.

12.1.8 JCheckBoxMenuItem

class javax.swing.JCheckBoxMenuItem

This class extends JMenuItem and it can be selected, deselected, and rendered the same way as JCheckBox (see chapter 4). We use the isSelected()/setSelected() or getState()/setState() methods to determine/set the selection state. ActionListeners and Change-Listeners can be attached to a JCheckBoxMenuItem for notification about changes in its state (see the JMenuItem discussion for inherited functionality).

12.1.9 JRadioButtonMenuItem

class javax.swing.JRadioButtonMenuItem

This class extends JMenuItem and it can be selected, deselected, and rendered the same way as JRadioButton (see chapter 4). We use the isSelected()/setSelected() or get-State()/setState() methods to determine/set the selection state. ActionListeners and ChangeListeners can be attached to a JRadioButtonMenuItem for notification about changes in its state (see the JMenuItem discussion for inherited functionality). We often use JRadioButtonMenuItems in ButtonGroups to enforce the selection of only one item in a group at any given time.

Component overloading As a general UI design rule, it is not good to overload components by using them for two purposes. By adding check boxes or radio buttons to a menu, you are changing the purpose of a menu from one of navigation to one of selection. This is an important point to understand.

Making this change is an acceptable design technique when it will speed operation and enhance usability by removing the need for a cumbersome dialog or option pane. However, it is important to assess that it does not otherwise adversely affect usability.

Groups of radio button or check box menu items are probably best isolated using a JSeparator.

12.1.10 The MenuElement interface

abstract interface javax.swing.MenuElement

This interface must be implemented by all components that want to act as menu items. By implementing the methods of this interface, any components can act as menu items, making it quite easy to build our own custom menu items.

The getSubElements() method returns an array of MenuElements that contains the given item's sub-elements. The processKeyEvent() and processMouseEvent() methods are called to process keyboard and mouse events when the implementing component has the focus. Unlike methods with the same name in the java.awt.Component class, these two methods receive three parameters: the KeyEvent or MouseEvent, which should be processed; an array of MenuElements which forms the path to the implementing component; and the current MenuSelectionManager (see section 12.1.11). The menuSelectionChanged() method is called by the MenuSelectionManager when the implementing component is added or removed from its current selection state. The getComponent() method returns a reference to a component that is responsible for rendering the implementing component.

NOTE The getComponent() method is interesting, as it allows classes that are not Components themselves to implement the MenuElement interface and *act* as menu elements when necessary. Such a class would contain a Component used for display in a menu, and this Component would be returned by getComponent(). This design has powerful implications, as it allows us to design robust JavaBeans that encapsulate an optional GUI representation. We can imagine a complex spell-checker or dictionary class implementing the MenuElement interface and providing a custom component for display in a menu; this would be a powerful and highly object-oriented bean, indeed.

JMenuItem, JMenuBar, JPopupMenu, and JMenu all implement this interface. Note that each of their getComponent() methods simply returns a this reference. By extending any of these implementing classes, we inherit MenuElement functionality and are not required to implement it. (We won't explicitly use this interface in any examples, as the custom component we will build at the end of this chapter is an extension of JMenu.)

12.1.11 MenuSelectionManager

class javax.swing.MenuSelectionManager

MenuSelectionManager is a service class that is responsible for managing menu selection throughout a single Java session. (Unlike most other service classes in Swing, MenuSelectionManager does not register its shared instance with AppContext—see chapter 2.) When MenuElement implementations receive MouseEvents or KeyEvents, these events should not be processed directly. Rather, they should be handed off to the MenuSelectionManager so that it may forward them to subcomponents automatically. For instance, whenever a JMenuItem is activated by the keyboard or mouse, or whenever a JMenuItem selection occurs, the menu item UI delegate is responsible for forwarding the corresponding event to the MenuSelectionManager, if necessary. The following code shows how BasicMenuItemUI deals with mouse releases:

```
public void mouseReleased(MouseEvent e) {
  MenuSelectionManager manager =
    MenuSelectionManager.defaultManager();
  Point p = e.getPoint();
  if(p.x >= 0 && p.x < menuItem.getWidth() &&
   p.y >= 0 && p.y < menuItem.getHeight()) {
    manager.clearSelectedPath();
    menuItem.doClick(0);
  }
  else {
    manager.processMouseEvent(e);
  }
}
```

The static defaultManager() method returns the MenuSelectionManager shared instance, and the clearSelectedPath() method tells the currently active menu hierarchy to close and unselect all menu components. In the code shown above, clearSelectedPath() will only be called if the mouse release occurs within the corresponding JMenuItem (in which case there is no need for the event to propagate any further). If this is not the case, the event is sent to MenuSelectionManager's processMouseEvent() method, which forwards it to other subcomponents. JMenuItem doesn't have any subcomponents by default, so nothing very interesting happens in this case. However, in the case of JMenu, which considers its popup menu a subcomponent, sending a mouse-released event to the MenuSelectionManager is expected no matter what (the following code is from BasicMenuUI):

```
public void mouseReleased(MouseEvent e) {
  MenuSelectionManager manager =
    MenuSelectionManager.defaultManager();
  manager.processMouseEvent(e);
  if (!e.isConsumed())
    manager.clearSelectedPath();
}
```

`MenuSelectionManager` will fire `ChangeEvents` whenever its `setSelectedPath()` method is called (for example, each time a menu selection changes). As expected, we can attach `ChangeListeners` to listen for these events.

12.1.12 The MenuDragMouseListener interface

abstract interface javax.swing.event.MenuDragMouseListener

This listener receives notification when the mouse cursor enters, exits, is released, or is moved over a menu item.

12.1.13 MenuDragMouseEvent

class javax.swing.event.MenuDragMouseEvent

This event class is used to deliver information to `MenuDragMouseListeners`. It encapsulates the following information:

- The component source.
- The event ID.
- The time of the event.
- A bitwise OR-masked `int` specifying which mouse button and/or keys (CTRL, SHIFT, ALT, or META) were pressed at the time of the event.
- The x and y mouse coordinates.
- The number of clicks immediately preceding the event.
- Whether the event represents the platform-dependent popup trigger.
- An array of `MenuElements` leading to the source of the event.
- The current `MenuSelectionManager`.

This event inherits all `MouseEvent` functionality (see the API documentation) and it adds two methods for retrieving the array of `MenuElements` and the `MenuSelectionManager`.

12.1.14 The MenuKeyListener interface

abstract interface javax.swing.event.MenuKeyListener

This listener is notified when a menu item receives a key event corresponding to a key press, release, or type. These events don't necessarily correspond to mnemonics or accelerators; they are received whenever a menu item is simply visible on the screen.

12.1.15 MenuKeyEvent

class javax.swing.event.MenuKeyEvent

This event class is used to deliver information to `MenuKeyListeners`. It encapsulates the following information:

- The component source.
- The event ID.
- The time of the event.
- A bitwise OR-masked `int` specifying which mouse button and/or keys (CTRL, SHIFT, or ALT) were pressed at the time of the event.

- An `int` and `char` identifying the source key that caused the event.
- An array of `MenuElements` leading to the source of the event.
- The current `MenuSelectionManager`.

This event inherits all `KeyEvent` functionality (see the API documentation) and it adds two methods for retrieving the array of `MenuElements` and the `MenuSelectionManager`.

12.1.16 The MenuListener interface

abstract interface javax.swing.event.MenuListener

This listener receives notification when a menu is selected, deselected, or canceled. Three methods must be implemented by `MenuListeners`, and each takes a `MouseEvent` parameter: `menuCanceled()`, `menuDeselected()`, and `menuSelected()`.

12.1.17 MenuEvent

class javax.swing.event.MenuEvent

This event class is used to deliver information to `MenuListeners`. It simply encapsulates a reference to its source `Object`.

12.1.18 The PopupMenuListener interface

abstract interface javax.swing.event.PopupMenuListener

This listener receives notification when a `JPopupMenu` is about to become visible or hidden, or when it is canceled. Canceling a `JPopupMenu` also causes it to be hidden, so two `PopupMenu-Events` are fired in this case. (A cancel occurs when the *invoker* component is resized or when the window containing the invoker changes size or location.) Three methods must be implemented by `PopupMenuListeners`, and each takes a `PopupMenuEvent` parameter: `popupMenuCanceled()`, `popupMenuWillBecomeVisible()`, and `popupMenuWillBecomeInvisible()`.

12.1.19 PopupMenuEvent

class javax.swing.event.PopupMenuEvent

This event class is used to deliver information to `PopupMenuListeners`. It simply encapsulates a reference to its source `Object`.

12.1.20 JToolBar

class javax.swing.JToolBar

This class represents the Swing implementation of a toolbar. Toolbars are often placed directly below menu bars at the top of a frame or applet, and they act as a container for any component (buttons and combo boxes are most common). The most convenient way to add buttons to a `JToolBar` is to use `Actions`; this is discussed in section 12.1.23.

NOTE   Components often need their alignment setting tweaked to provide uniform positioning within `JToolBar`. This can be accomplished using the `setAlignmentY()` and `setAlignmentX()` methods. The need to tweak the alignment of components in `JToolBar` has been alleviated for the most part, as of JDK 1.2.2.

JToolBar also allows the convenient addition of an inner JSeparator subclass, JTool-Bar.Separator, to provide an empty space for visually grouping components. These separators can be added with either of the overloaded addSeparator() methods, one of which takes a Dimension parameter that specifies the size of the separator.

Two orientations are supported, VERTICAL and HORIZONTAL, and the current orientation is maintained by JToolBar's orientation property. It uses a BoxLayout layout manager which is dynamically changed between Y_AXIS and X_AXIS when the orientation property changes.

JToolBar can be dragged in and out of its parent container if its floatable property is set to true. When it is dragged out of its parent, a JToolBar appears as a floating window (during a mouse drag) and its border changes color depending on whether it can re-dock in its parent at a given location. If a JToolBar is dragged outside of its parent and released, it will be placed in its own JFrame which will be fully maximizable, minimizable, and closable. When this frame is closed, JToolBar will jump back into its most recent dock position in its original parent, and the floating JFrame will disappear. We recommend that you place JToolBar in one of the four sides of a container using a BorderLayout and leave the other sides unused, to allow the JToolBar to be docked in any of that container's side regions.

The protected createActionChangeListener() method is used when an Action (see section 12.1.23) is added to a JToolBar to create a PropertyChangeListener for internal use in responding to bound property changes that occur in that Action.

Uses for a toolbar   Toolbars have become ubiquitious in modern software. They are often overused or misused, and therefore, they fail to achieve their objective of increased usability. The three key uses have subtle differences and implications.

Tool selection or mode selection   Perhaps the most effective use of a toolbar is, as the name suggests, for the selection of a tool or operational mode. This is most common in drawing or image manipulation packages. The user selects the toolbar button to change the mode from "paintbrush" to "filler" to "draw box" to "cut," for example. This is a highly effective use of toolbar, as the small icons are usually sufficient to render a suitable tool image. Many images for this purpose have been adopted as a defacto standard. If you are developing a tool selection toolbar, we advise you to stick closely to icons which have been used by similar existing products.

Functional selection   The earliest use of a toolbar was to replace the selection of a specific function from the menu. This led to them being called "speedbars" or "menubars." The idea was that the small icon button was faster and easier to acquire than the menu selection and that usability was enhanced as a result. This worked well for many common functions in file-oriented applications, such as Open File, New File, Save, Cut, Copy, and Paste. In fact, most of us would recognize the small icons for all of these functions. However, with other more application-specific functions, it has become more difficult for icon designers to come up with appropriate designs. This often leads to applications which have a confusing and intimidating array of icons across the top of the screen, which therefore detracts from usability. As a general rule of thumb, stick to common cross-application functions when you're overloading menu selections with toolbar buttons. If you do need to break the rule, consider selecting annotated buttons for the toolbar.

Navigational selection   The third use for toolbars has been for navigational selection. This often means replacing or overloading menu options. These menu options are used to select a specific screen to move to the front. The toolbar buttons replace or overload the menu option and allow the navigational selection to be made by supposedly faster means. However, this usage also suffers from the problem of appropriate icon design. It is usually too difficult to devise a suitable set of icons which have clear and unambiguous meaning. Therefore, as a rule of thumb, consider the use of annotated buttons on the toolbar.

12.1.21   Custom JToolBar separators

Unfortunately, Swing does not include a toolbar-specific separator component that will display a vertical or horizontal line depending on current toolbar orientation. The following pseudocode shows how we can build such a component under the assumption that it will always have a JToolBar as a direct parent:

```
public class MyToolBarSeparator extends JComponent
{
  public void paintComponent(Graphics g) {
    super.paintComponent(g);
    if (getParent() instanceof JToolBar) {
      if (((JToolBar) getParent()).getOrientation()
      == JToolBar.HORIZONTAL) {
        // Paint a vertical line
      }
      else {
        // Paint a horizontal line
      }
    }
  }

  public Dimension getPreferredSize() {
    if (getParent() instanceof JToolBar) {
      if (((JToolBar) getParent()).getOrientation()
      == JToolBar.HORIZONTAL) {
        // Return horizontal size
      }
      else {
        // Return vertical size
      }
    }
  }
}
```

Use of a separator   The failure to include a graphical separator for toolbars really was an oversight on the part of the Swing designers. Again, the separator is used to group related functions or tools. For example, if the functions all belong on the same menu, then group them together, or if the tools (or modes) are related, such as Cut, Copy, and Paste, then group them together and separate them from others with a separator.

Grouping like this improves perceived separation by introducing a visual layer. The viewer can first acquire a group of buttons and then a specific button. He will also learn, using directional memory, the approximate position of each group. By separating the groups, you will improve the usability by helping the user to acquire the target better when using the mouse.

12.1.22   Changing JToolBar's floating frame behavior

The behavior of JToolBar's floating JFrame is certainly useful, but whether the maximization and resizability should be allowed is arguable. Though we cannot control whether a JFrame can be maximized, we can control whether it can be resized. To enforce non-resizability in JToolBar's floating JFrame (and to set its displayed title while we're at it), we need to override its UI delegate and customize the createFloatingFrame() method as follows:

```
public class MyToolBarUI
  extends javax.swing.plaf.metal.MetalToolBarUI {
  protected JFrame createFloatingFrame(JToolBar toolbar) {
    JFrame frame = new JFrame(toolbar.getName());
    frame.setTitle("My toolbar");
    frame.setResizable(false);
    WindowListener wl = createFrameListener();
    frame.addWindowListener(wl);
    return frame;
  }
}
```

To assign MyToolBarUI as a JToolBar's UI delegate, we can do the following:

```
mytoolbar.setUI(new MyToolBarUI());
```

To force the use of this delegate on a global basis, we can do the following *before* any JTool-Bars are instantiated:

```
UIManager.getDefaults().put(
  "ToolBarUI","com.mycompany.MyToolBarUI");
```

Note that we may also have to add an associated Class instance to the UIDefaults table for this to work (see chapter 21).

Use of a floating frame   It is probably best to restrict the use of a floating toolbar frame to toolbars being used for *tool or mode selection* (see the UI Guideline in section 12.1.20).

In Java 1.3 two new constructors were added to JToolBar allowing specification of a String title to use for the floating frame.

12.1.23 The Action interface

abstract interface javax.swing.Action

This interface describes a helper object which extends ActionListener and which supports a set of bound properties. We use appropriate add() methods in the JMenu, JPopupMenu, and JToolBar classes to add an Action which will use information from the given instance to create and return a component that is appropriate for that container (a JMenuItem in the case of the first two, a JButton in the case of the latter). The same Action instance can be used to create an arbitrary number of menu items or toolbar buttons.

Because Action extends ActionListener, the actionPerformed() method is inherited and it can be used to encapsulate appropriate ActionEvent handling code. When a menu item or toolbar button is created using an Action, the resulting component is registered as a PropertyChangeListener with the Action, and the Action is registered as an ActionListener with the component. Thus, whenever a change occurs to one of that Action's bound properties, all components with registered PropertyChangeListeners will receive notification. This provides a convenient means for allowing identical functionality in menus, toolbars, and popup menus with minimum code repetition and object creation.

The putValue() and getValue() methods are intended to work with a Hashtable-like structure to maintain an Action's bound properties. Whenever the value of a property changes, we are expected to fire PropertyChangeEvents to all registered listeners. As expected, methods to add and remove PropertyChangeListeners are provided.

The Action interface defines five static property keys that are intended to be used by JMenuItems and JButtons created with an Action instance:

- String DEFAULT: [Not used].
- String LONG_DESCRIPTION: Used for a lengthy description of an Action.
- String NAME: Used as the text displayed in JMenuItems and JButtons.
- String SHORT_DESCRIPTION: Used for the tooltip text of associated JMenuItems and JButtons.
- String SMALL_ICON: Used as the icon in associated JMenuItems and JButtons.

12.1.24 AbstractAction

class javax.swing.AbstractAction

This class is an abstract implementation of the Action interface. Along with the properties inherited from Action, AbstractAction defines the enabled property which provides a means of enabling/disabling all associated components registered as PropertyChangeListeners. A SwingPropertyChangeSupport instance is used to manage the firing of PropertyChangeEvents to all registered PropertyChangeListeners (see chapter 2 for more about SwingPropertyChangeSupport).

NOTE Many UI delegates define inner class subclasses of AbstractAction, and the TextAction subclass is used by DefaultEditorKit to define action-handling code corresponding to specific KeyStroke bindings (see chapter 19).

12.2 BASIC TEXT EDITOR, PART I: MENUS

In example 12.1 we begin the construction of a basic text editor application using a menu bar and several menu items. The menu bar contains two JMenus labeled "File" and "Font." The File menu contains JMenuItems for creating a new (empty) document, opening a text file, saving the current document as a text file, and exiting the application. The Font menu contains JCheckBoxMenuItems for making the document bold and/or italic, as well as JRadioButtonMenuItems organized into a ButtonGroup that allows the selection of a single font.

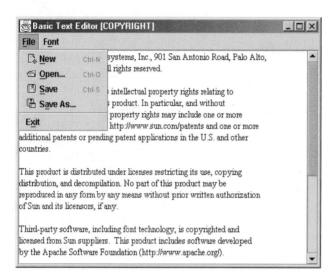

Figure 12.1
Menu containing
JMenuItems with
mnemonics and icons

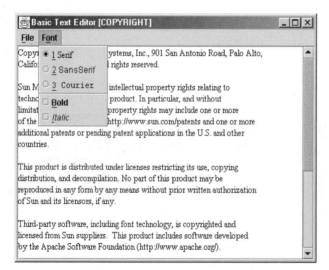

Figure 12.2
JMenu containing
JRadioButtonMenuItems
and JCheckBoxMenuItems

Example 12.1

BasicTextEditor.java

see \Chapter12\1

```java
import java.awt.*;
import java.awt.event.*;
import java.io.*;
import java.util.*;

import javax.swing.*;
import javax.swing.event.*;

public class BasicTextEditor
  extends JFrame {

  public static final String APP_NAME = "Basic Text Editor";

  public static final String FONTS[] = { "Serif", "SansSerif",
    "Courier" };
  protected Font m_fonts[];

  protected JTextArea m_editor;
  protected JMenuItem[] m_fontMenus;
  protected JCheckBoxMenuItem m_bold;
  protected JCheckBoxMenuItem m_italic;

  protected JFileChooser m_chooser;
  protected File  m_currentFile;

  protected boolean m_textChanged = false;

  public BasicTextEditor() {
    super(APP_NAME+": Part I - Menus");
    setSize(450, 350);


    m_fonts = new Font[FONTS.length];
    for (int k=0; k<FONTS.length; k++)
      m_fonts[k] = new Font(FONTS[k], Font.PLAIN, 12);

    m_editor = new JTextArea();
    JScrollPane ps = new JScrollPane(m_editor);
    getContentPane().add(ps, BorderLayout.CENTER);

    JMenuBar menuBar = createMenuBar();
    setJMenuBar(menuBar);

    m_chooser = new JFileChooser();
    try {
      File dir = (new File(".")).getCanonicalFile();
      m_chooser.setCurrentDirectory(dir);
    } catch (IOException ex) {}

    updateEditor();
    newDocument();

    WindowListener wndCloser = new WindowAdapter() {
```

❶ Creates list of fonts from font names

```
    public void windowClosing(WindowEvent e) {
      if (!promptToSave())
        return;
      System.exit(0);
    }
  };
  addWindowListener(wndCloser);
}

protected JMenuBar createMenuBar() {
  final JMenuBar menuBar = new JMenuBar();

  JMenu mFile = new JMenu("File");
  mFile.setMnemonic('f');

  JMenuItem item = new JMenuItem("New");
  item.setIcon(new ImageIcon("New16.gif"));
  item.setMnemonic('n');
  item.setAccelerator(KeyStroke.getKeyStroke(
    KeyEvent.VK_N, InputEvent.CTRL_MASK));
  ActionListener lst = new ActionListener() {
    public void actionPerformed(ActionEvent e) {
      if (!promptToSave())
        return;
      newDocument();
    }
  };
  item.addActionListener(lst);
  mFile.add(item);

  item = new JMenuItem("Open...");
  item.setIcon(new ImageIcon("Open16.gif"));
  item.setMnemonic('o');
  item.setAccelerator(KeyStroke.getKeyStroke(
    KeyEvent.VK_O, InputEvent.CTRL_MASK));
  lst = new ActionListener() {
    public void actionPerformed(ActionEvent e) {
      if (!promptToSave())
        return;
      openDocument();
    }
  };
  item.addActionListener(lst);
  mFile.add(item);

  item = new JMenuItem("Save");
  item.setIcon(new ImageIcon("Save16.gif"));
  item.setMnemonic('s');
  item.setAccelerator(KeyStroke.getKeyStroke(
    KeyEvent.VK_S, InputEvent.CTRL_MASK));
  lst = new ActionListener() {
    public void actionPerformed(ActionEvent e) {
      if (!m_textChanged)
        return;
```

2 Creates menu bar with menu items to manipulate files and fonts

3 "New" menu item clears contents of editor but prompts user to save changes before proceeding

4 "Open" menu item allows user to open an existing file; prompts user to save changes before proceeding

5 "Save" menu item saves current document; if it hasn't been saved a file chooser is used for user to select file name and destination

```
      saveFile(false);
    }
  };
  item.addActionListener(lst);
  mFile.add(item);

  item = new JMenuItem("Save As...");
  item.setIcon(new ImageIcon("SaveAs16.gif"));
  item.setMnemonic('a');
  lst = new ActionListener() {
    public void actionPerformed(ActionEvent e) {
      saveFile(true);
    }
  };
  item.addActionListener(lst);
  mFile.add(item);

  mFile.addSeparator();

  item = new JMenuItem("Exit");
  item.setMnemonic('x');
  lst = new ActionListener() {
    public void actionPerformed(ActionEvent e) {
      System.exit(0);
    }
  };
  item.addActionListener(lst);
  mFile.add(item);
  menuBar.add(mFile);

  ActionListener fontListener = new ActionListener() {
    public void actionPerformed(ActionEvent e) {
      updateEditor();
    }
  };

  JMenu mFont = new JMenu("Font");
  mFont.setMnemonic('o');

  ButtonGroup group = new ButtonGroup();
  m_fontMenus = new JMenuItem[FONTS.length];
  for (int k=0; k<FONTS.length; k++) {
    int m = k+1;
    m_fontMenus[k] = new JRadioButtonMenuItem(
      m+" "+FONTS[k]);
    m_fontMenus[k].setSelected(k == 0);
    m_fontMenus[k].setMnemonic('1'+k);
    m_fontMenus[k].setFont(m_fonts[k]);
    m_fontMenus[k].addActionListener(fontListener);
    group.add(m_fontMenus[k]);
    mFont.add(m_fontMenus[k]);
  }

  mFont.addSeparator();
```

5 "Save" menu item saves current document; if it hasn't been saved a file chooser is used for user to select file name and destination

6 "Save As" menu item uses a file changer for user to select file name and location to save the current document to

7 ActionListener invoked whenever a font menu item is selected; calls updateEditor() to change the current font in the editor

8 Create a JRadioButton corresponding to each font

```
      m_bold = new JCheckBoxMenuItem("Bold");
      m_bold.setMnemonic('b');
      Font fn = m_fonts[1].deriveFont(Font.BOLD);
      m_bold.setFont(fn);
      m_bold.setSelected(false);
      m_bold.addActionListener(fontListener);
      mFont.add(m_bold);

      m_italic = new JCheckBoxMenuItem("Italic");
      m_italic.setMnemonic('i');
      fn = m_fonts[1].deriveFont(Font.ITALIC);
      m_italic.setFont(fn);
      m_italic.setSelected(false);
      m_italic.addActionListener(fontListener);
      mFont.add(m_italic);

      menuBar.add(mFont);

      return menuBar;
  }

  protected String getDocumentName() {
      return m_currentFile==null ? "Untitled" :
        m_currentFile.getName();
  }

  protected void newDocument() {
    m_editor.setText("");
    m_currentFile = null;
    setTitle(APP_NAME+" ["+getDocumentName()+"]");
    m_textChanged = false;
    m_editor.getDocument().addDocumentListener(new UpdateListener());
  }

  protected void openDocument() {
    if (m_chooser.showOpenDialog(BasicTextEditor.this) !=
      JFileChooser.APPROVE_OPTION)
      return;
    File f = m_chooser.getSelectedFile();
    if (f == null || !f.isFile())
      return;
    m_currentFile = f;
    try {
      FileReader in = new FileReader(m_currentFile);
      m_editor.read(in, null);
      in.close();
      setTitle(APP_NAME+" ["+getDocumentName()+"]");
    }
    catch (IOException ex) {
      showError(ex, "Error reading file "+m_currentFile);
    }
    m_textChanged = false;
    m_editor.getDocument().addDocumentListener(new UpdateListener());
  }
```

9 Bold menu item changes current font in editor to its bold variant

9 Italic menu item changes current font in editor to its italic variant

```java
protected boolean saveFile(boolean saveAs) {
  if (saveAs || m_currentFile == null) {
    if (m_chooser.showSaveDialog(BasicTextEditor.this) !=
      JFileChooser.APPROVE_OPTION)
      return false;
    File f = m_chooser.getSelectedFile();
    if (f == null)
      return false;
    m_currentFile = f;
    setTitle(APP_NAME+" ["+getDocumentName()+"]");
  }

  try {
    FileWriter out = new
      FileWriter(m_currentFile);
    m_editor.write(out);
    out.close();
  }
  catch (IOException ex) {
    showError(ex, "Error saving file "+m_currentFile);
    return false;
  }
  m_textChanged = false;
  return true;
}

protected boolean promptToSave() {
  if (!m_textChanged)
    return true;
  int result = JOptionPane.showConfirmDialog(this,
    "Save changes to "+getDocumentName()+"?",
    APP_NAME, JOptionPane.YES_NO_CANCEL_OPTION,
    JOptionPane.INFORMATION_MESSAGE);
  switch (result) {
  case JOptionPane.YES_OPTION:
    if (!saveFile(false))
      return false;
    return true;
  case JOptionPane.NO_OPTION:
    return true;
  case JOptionPane.CANCEL_OPTION:
    return false;
  }
  return true;
}

protected void updateEditor() {
  int index = -1;
  for (int k=0; k<m_fontMenus.length; k++) {
    if (m_fontMenus[k].isSelected()) {
      index = k;
      break;
    }
```

⑩ Method to update the editor font based on menu item selections

```
      }
      if (index == -1)
        return;

      if (index==2) { // Courier
        m_bold.setSelected(false);
        m_bold.setEnabled(false);
        m_italic.setSelected(false);
        m_italic.setEnabled(false);
      }
      else {
        m_bold.setEnabled(true);
        m_italic.setEnabled(true);
      }

      int style = Font.PLAIN;
      if (m_bold.isSelected())
        style |= Font.BOLD;
      if (m_italic.isSelected())
        style |= Font.ITALIC;
      Font fn = m_fonts[index].deriveFont(style);
      m_editor.setFont(fn);
      m_editor.repaint();
    }

    public void showError(Exception ex, String message) {
      ex.printStackTrace();
      JOptionPane.showMessageDialog(this,
        message, APP_NAME,
        JOptionPane.WARNING_MESSAGE);
    }

    public static void main(String argv[]) {
      BasicTextEditor frame = new BasicTextEditor();
      frame.setDefaultCloseOperation(JFrame.DO_NOTHING_ON_CLOSE);
      frame.setVisible(true);
    }

    class UpdateListener implements DocumentListener {

      public void insertUpdate(DocumentEvent e) {
        m_textChanged = true;
      }

      public void removeUpdate(DocumentEvent e) {
        m_textChanged = true;
      }

      public void changedUpdate(DocumentEvent e) {
        m_textChanged = true;
      }
    }
}
```

12.2.1 Understanding the code

Class BasicTextEditor

This class extends JFrame and provides the parent frame for our example. Two class variables are declared:

- String APP_NAME: name of this example used in title bar.
- String FONTS[]: an array of font family names.

Instance variables:

- Font[] m_fonts: an array of Font instances which can be used to render our JText-Area editor.
- JTextArea m_editor: used as our text editor.
- JMenuItem[] m_fontMenus: an array of menu items representing available fonts.
- JCheckBoxMenuItem m_bold: menu item which sets/unsets the bold property of the current font.
- JCheckBoxMenuItem m_italic: menu item which sets/unsets the italic property of the current font.
- JFileChooser m_chooser: used to load and save simple text files.
- File m_currentFile: the current File instance corresponding to the current document.
- boolean m_textChanged: will be set to true if the current document has been changed; will be set to false if the document was just opened or saved. This flag is used in combination with a DocumentListener (see chapter 19) to determine whether or not to save the current document before dismissing it.

❶ The BasicTextEditor constructor populates our m_fonts array with Font instances corresponding to the names provided in FONTS[]. The m_editor JTextArea is then created and placed in a JScrollPane. This scroll pane is added to the center of our frame's content pane and we append some simple text to m_editor for display at startup. Our createMenuBar() method is called to create the menu bar to manage this application, and this menu bar is then added to our frame using the setJMenuBar() method.

❷ The createMenuBar() method creates and returns a JMenuBar. Each menu item receives an ActionListener to handle its selection. Two menus are added titled "File" and "Font". The File menu is assigned a mnemonic character, 'f', and by pressing ALT+F while the application frame is active, its popup will be displayed allowing navigation with either the mouse or keyboard. The Font menu is assigned the mnemonic character 'o'.

❸ The New menu item in the File menu is responsible for creating a new (empty) document. It doesn't really replace JTextArea's Document. Instead it simply clears the contents of our editor component. Before it does so, however, it calls our custom promptToSave() method to determine whether or not we want to continue without saving the current changes (if any). Note that an icon is used for this menu item. Also note that this menu item can be selected with the keyboard by pressing 'n' when the File menu's popup is visible, because we assigned it 'n' as a mnemonic. We also assigned it the accelerator CTRL+N. Therefore, this menu's action will be directly invoked whenever that key combination is pressed. (All other menus and menu items in this example also receive appropriate mnemonics and accelerators.)

The Open menu item brings up our m_chooser JFileChooser component (discussed in chapter 14) to allow selection of a text file to open. Once a text file is selected, we open a FileReader on it and invoke read() on our JTextArea component to read the file's content (which creates a new PlainDocument containing the selected file's content to replace the current JTextArea document, see chapter 11). The Save menu item brings up m_chooser to select a destination and file name to save the current text to (if previously not set). Once a text file is selected, we open a FileWriter on it and invoke write() on our JTextArea component to write its content to the destination file. The Save As... menu is similar to the Save menu, but prompts the user to select a new file. The Exit menu item terminates program execution. This is separated from the first three menu items with a menu separator to create a more logical display.

The Font menu consists of several menu items used to select the font and font style used in our editor. All of these items receive the same ActionListener which invokes our updateEditor() method. To give the user an idea of how each font looks, each font is used to render the corresponding menu item text. Since only one font can be selected at any given time, we use JRadioButtonMenuItems for these menu items, and add them all to a ButtonGroup instance which manages a single selection.

To create each menu item we iterate through our FONTS array and create a JRadioButtonMenuItem corresponding to each entry. Each item is set to unselected (except for the first one), assigned a numerical mnemonic corresponding to the current FONTS array index, assigned the appropriate Font instance for rendering its text, assigned our multipurpose ActionListener, and added to our ButtonGroup along with the others.

The two other menu items in the Font menu manage the bold and italic font properties. They are implemented as JCheckBoxMenuItems since these properties can be selected or unselected independently. These items also are assigned the same ActionListener as the radio button items to process changes in their selected state.

The updateEditor() method updates the current font used to render the editing component by checking the state of each check box item and determining which radio button item is currently selected. The m_bold and m_italic components are disabled and unselected if the Courier font is selected, and enabled otherwise. The appropriate m_fonts array element is selected and a Font instance is derived from it corresponding to the current state of the check box items using Font's deriveFont() method (see chapter 2).

NOTE   Surprisingly the ButtonGroup class does not provide a direct way to determine which component is currently selected. So we have to examine the m_fontMenus array elements in turn to determine the selected font index. Alternatively we could save the font index in an enhanced version of our ActionListener.

12.2.2   Running the code

Open a text file, make some changes, and save it as a new file. Change the font options and watch how the text area is updated. Select the Courier font and notice how it disables the bold and italic check box items (it also unchecks them if they were previously checked). Select another font and notice how this re-enables check box items. Figure 12.1 shows BasicText-

Editor's File menu, and figure 12.2 shows the Font menu. Notice how the mnemonics are underlined and the images appear to the left of the text by default, just like buttons.

GUIDELINE

File-oriented applications   Example 12.1 is an example of a menu being used in a file-oriented application. Menus were first developed to be used in this fashion. Including a menu in such an application is essential, as users have come to expect one. There are clearly defined platform standards for menu layout and it is best that you adhere to these. For example, the File menu almost always comes first (from the left-hand side).

Also notice the use of the elipsis "..." on the Open... and Save... options. This is a standard technique which gives a visual confirmation that a dialog will open when the menu item is selected.

Correct use of separator and component overloading   This example shows clearly how adding selection controls to a menu in a simple application can speed operation and ease usability. The separator is used to group and separate the selection of the font type from the font style.

12.3   *BASIC TEXT EDITOR, PART II: TOOLBARS AND ACTIONS*

Swing provides the Action interface to simplify the creation of menu items. As we know, implementations of this interface encapsulate both the knowledge of what to do when a menu item or toolbar button is selected (by extending the ActionListener interface) and the knowledge of how to render the component itself (by holding a collection of bound properties such as NAME and SMALL_ICON). We can create both a menu item and a toolbar button from a single Action instance, conserving code and providing a reliable means of ensuring consistency between menus and toolbars.

Example 12.2 uses the AbstractAction class to add a toolbar to our BasicTextEditor application. By converting the ActionListeners used in the example above to AbstractActions, we can use these actions to create both toolbar buttons and menu items with very little additional work.

Example 12.2

BasicTextEditor.java

see \Chapter12\2

```
import java.awt.*;
import java.awt.event.*;
import java.io.*;
import java.util.*;

import javax.swing.*;
import javax.swing.event.*;
```

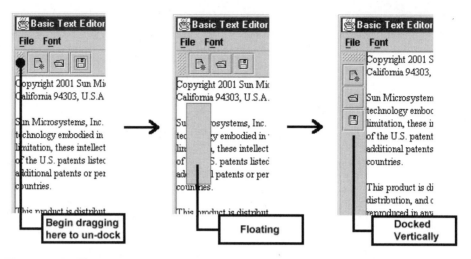

Figure 12.3 The process of undocking, dragging, and docking a `JToolBar`

Figure 12.4
A floating `JToolBar`

```
public class BasicTextEditor extends JFrame
{
  // Unchanged code from example 12.1

  protected JToolBar m_toolBar;                         ❶ Toolbar for shortcuts

  protected JMenuBar createMenuBar() {
    final JMenuBar menuBar = new JMenuBar();
    JMenu mFile = new JMenu("File");
    mFile.setMnemonic('f');

    ImageIcon iconNew = new ImageIcon("New16.gif");
    Action actionNew = new AbstractAction("New", iconNew) {
      public void actionPerformed(ActionEvent e) {     ❶ Actions are
        if (!promptToSave())                              now used
          return;                                         to create
        newDocument();                                    menu items
      }                                                   and toolbar
    };                                                    buttons
    JMenuItem item = new JMenuItem(actionNew);
    item.setMnemonic('n');
    item.setAccelerator(KeyStroke.getKeyStroke(
      KeyEvent.VK_N, InputEvent.CTRL_MASK));
    mFile.add(item);

    ImageIcon iconOpen = new ImageIcon("Open16.gif");
    Action actionOpen = new AbstractAction("Open...", iconOpen) {
```

```java
    public void actionPerformed(ActionEvent e) {
      if (!promptToSave())
        return;
      openDocument();
    }
};
item = new JMenuItem(actionOpen);
item.setMnemonic('o');
item.setAccelerator(KeyStroke.getKeyStroke(
  KeyEvent.VK_O, InputEvent.CTRL_MASK));
mFile.add(item);

ImageIcon iconSave = new ImageIcon("Save16.gif");
Action actionSave = new AbstractAction("Save", iconSave) {
    public void actionPerformed(ActionEvent e) {
      if (!m_textChanged)
        return;
      saveFile(false);
    }
};
item = new JMenuItem(actionSave);
item.setMnemonic('s');
item.setAccelerator(KeyStroke.getKeyStroke(
  KeyEvent.VK_S, InputEvent.CTRL_MASK));
mFile.add(item);

ImageIcon iconSaveAs = new ImageIcon("SaveAs16.gif");
Action actionSaveAs = new AbstractAction(
  "Save As...", iconSaveAs) {
    public void actionPerformed(ActionEvent e) {
      saveFile(true);
    }
};
item = new JMenuItem(actionSaveAs);
item.setMnemonic('a');
mFile.add(item);
mFile.addSeparator();

Action actionExit = new AbstractAction("Exit") {
    public void actionPerformed(ActionEvent e) {
      System.exit(0);
    }
};

item = mFile.add(actionExit);
item.setMnemonic('x');
menuBar.add(mFile);

m_toolBar = new JToolBar("Commands");
JButton btn1 = m_toolBar.add(actionNew);
btn1.setToolTipText("New text");
JButton btn2 = m_toolBar.add(actionOpen);
btn2.setToolTipText("Open text file");
JButton btn3 = m_toolBar.add(actionSave);
```

```
        btn3.setToolTipText("Save text file");

        // Unchanged code from example 12.1

        getContentPane().add(m_toolBar, BorderLayout.NORTH);

        return menuBar;
    }

    // Unchanged code from example 12.1
}
```

12.3.1 Understanding the code

Class BasicTextEditor

❶ This class now declares one more instance variable, JToolBar m_toolBar. The constructor remains unchanged and it is not listed here. The createMenuBar() method now creates AbstractAction instances instead of ActionListeners. These objects encapsulate the same action handling code we defined in example 12.1, as well as the text and icon to display in associated menu items and toolbar buttons. This allows us to create JMenuItems using the JMenu.add(Action a) method, and JButtons using the JToolBar.add(Action a) method. These methods return instances that we can treat like any other button component and we can do things such as set the background color or assign a different text alignment.

Our JToolBar component is placed in the NORTH region of our content pane, and we make sure to leave the EAST, WEST, and SOUTH regions empty, thereby allowing it to dock on all sides.

12.3.2 Running the code

Verify that the toolbar buttons work as expected by opening and saving a text file. Try dragging the toolbar from its handle and notice how it is represented by an empty gray window as it is dragged. The border will change to a dark color when the window is in a location where it will dock if the mouse is released. If the border does not appear dark, releasing the mouse will result in the toolbar being placed in its own JFrame. Figure 12.3 illustrates the simple process of undocking, dragging, and docking our toolbar in a new location. Figure 12.4 shows our toolbar in its own JFrame when it is undocked and released outside of a dockable region (this is also referred to as a *hotspot*).

> **NOTE**   The current JToolBar implementation does not easily allow the use of multiple floating toolbars as is common in many modern applications. We hope to see more of this functionality built into future versions of Swing.

GUIDELINE

Vertical or horizontal?   In some applications, you may prefer to leave the selection of a vertical or horizontal toolbar to the user. More often than not, you as the designer can make that choice for them. Consider whether vertical or horizontal space is more valuable for what you need to display. If, for example, you are displaying letter text then you probably need vertical space more than horizontal space. In PC applications, vertical space is usually at a premium.

When vertical space is at a premium, place the toolbar vertically to free up valuable vertical space. When horizontal space is at a premium, place the toolbar horizontally to free up valuable horizontal space.

Almost never use a floating toolbar, as it has a tendency to get lost under other windows. Floating toolbars are for advanced users who understand the full operation of the computer system, so consider the technical level of your user group before making the design choice for a floating toolbar.

12.4 BASIC TEXT EDITOR, PART III: CUSTOM TOOLBAR COMPONENTS

Using `Actions` to create toolbar buttons is easy, but it is not always desirable if we want to have complete control over our toolbar components. In this section's example 12.3, we build off of `BasicTextEditor` and place a `JComboBox` in the toolbar to allow `Font` selection. We also use instances of our own custom buttons, `SmallButton` and `SmallToggleButton`, in the toolbar. Both of these button classes use different borders to signify different states. `SmallButton` uses a raised border when the mouse passes over it, no border when the mouse is not within its bounds, and a lowered border when a mouse press occurs. `SmallToggleButton` uses a raised border when it is unselected and a lowered border when selected.

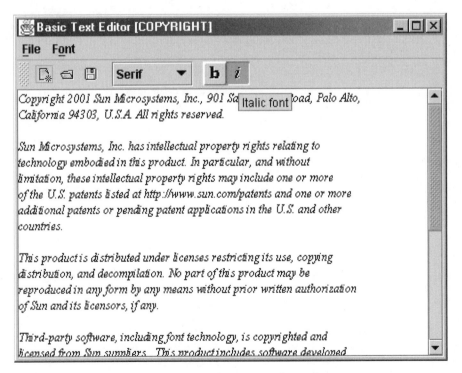

Figure 12.5 `JToolBar` with custom buttons and a `JComboBox`

Example 12.3

BasicTextEditor.java

see \Chapter12\3

```java
import java.awt.*;
import java.awt.event.*;
import java.io.*;
import java.util.*;

import javax.swing.*;
import javax.swing.event.*;

public class BasicTextEditor extends JFrame
{
  // Unchanged code from example 12.2

  protected JComboBox m_cbFonts;
  protected SmallToggleButton m_bBold;
  protected SmallToggleButton m_bItalic;

  // Unchanged code from example 12.2

  protected JMenuBar createMenuBar()
  {
    // Unchanged code from example 12.2

    m_toolBar = new JToolBar();
    JButton bNew = new SmallButton(actionNew,
      "New text");
    m_toolBar.add(bNew);

    JButton bOpen = new SmallButton(actionOpen,
      "Open text file");
    m_toolBar.add(bOpen);

    JButton bSave = new SmallButton(actionSave,
      "Save text file");
    m_toolBar.add(bSave);

    JMenu mFont = new JMenu("Font");
    mFont.setMnemonic('o');

    // Unchanged code from example 12.2

    mFont.addSeparator();

    m_toolBar.addSeparator();
    m_cbFonts = new JComboBox(FONTS);
    m_cbFonts.setMaximumSize(m_cbFonts.getPreferredSize());
    m_cbFonts.setToolTipText("Available fonts");
    ActionListener lst = new ActionListener() {
      public void actionPerformed(ActionEvent e) {
        int index = m_cbFonts.getSelectedIndex();
        if (index < 0)
```

1 Custom buttons for toolbar

2 Creates instances of custom buttons and adds them to toolbar

```
        return;
      m_fontMenus[index].setSelected(true);
      updateEditor();
  }
};
m_cbFonts.addActionListener(lst);
m_toolBar.add(m_cbFonts);

m_bold = new JCheckBoxMenuItem("Bold");
m_bold.setMnemonic('b');
Font fn = m_fonts[1].deriveFont(Font.BOLD);
m_bold.setFont(fn);
m_bold.setSelected(false);
m_bold.addActionListener(fontListener);
mFont.add(m_bold);

m_italic = new JCheckBoxMenuItem("Italic");
m_italic.setMnemonic('i');
fn = m_fonts[1].deriveFont(Font.ITALIC);
m_italic.setFont(fn);
m_italic.setSelected(false);
m_italic.addActionListener(fontListener);
mFont.add(m_italic);

menuBar.add(mFont);

m_toolBar.addSeparator();

ImageIcon img1 = new ImageIcon("Bold16.gif");
m_bBold = new SmallToggleButton(false, img1, img,
  "Bold font");
lst = new ActionListener() {
  public void actionPerformed(ActionEvent e) {
    m_bold.setSelected(m_bBold.isSelected());
    updateEditor();
  }
};
m_bBold.addActionListener(lst);
m_toolBar.add(m_bBold);

img1 = new ImageIcon("Italic16.gif");
m_bItalic = new SmallToggleButton(false, img1, img,
  "Italic font");
lst = new ActionListener() {
  public void actionPerformed(ActionEvent e) {
    m_italic.setSelected(m_bItalic.isSelected());
    updateEditor();
  }
};
m_bItalic.addActionListener(lst);
m_toolBar.add(m_bItalic);

getContentPane().add(m_toolBar, BorderLayout.NORTH);
return menuBar;
}
```

3 Custom check boxes for toolbar, to control bold and italic properties

```
//Unchanged code from example 12.2
protected void updateEditor() {
  int index = -1;
  for (int k=0; k<m_fontMenus.length; k++) {
    if (m_fontMenus[k].isSelected()) {
      index = k;
      break;
    }
  }
  if (index == -1)
    return;
  boolean isBold = m_bold.isSelected();
  boolean isItalic = m_italic.isSelected();

  m_cbFonts.setSelectedIndex(index);

  if (index==2) {   //Courier
    m_bold.setSelected(false);
    m_bold.setEnabled(false);
    m_italic.setSelected(false);
    m_italic.setEnabled(false);
    m_bBold.setSelected(false);
    m_bBold.setEnabled(false);
    m_bItalic.setSelected(false);
    m_bItalic.setEnabled(false);
  }
  else {
    m_bold.setEnabled(true);
    m_italic.setEnabled(true);
    m_bBold.setEnabled(true);
    m_bItalic.setEnabled(true);
  }

  if (m_bBold.isSelected() != isBold)
    m_bBold.setSelected(isBold);
  if (m_bItalic.isSelected() != isItalic)
    m_bItalic.setSelected(isItalic);

  int style = Font.PLAIN;
  if (isBold)
    style |= Font.BOLD;
  if (isItalic)
    style |= Font.ITALIC;
  Font fn = m_fonts[index].deriveFont(style);
  m_editor.setFont(fn);
  m_editor.repaint();
}

public static void main(String argv[]) {
  //Unchanged code from example 12.2
}
}
```

4 Keeps toolbar and menu bar settings in sync

4 Keeps toolbar and menu bar settings in sync

```
class SmallButton extends JButton implements MouseListener {
  protected Border m_raised =
    new SoftBevelBorder(BevelBorder.RAISED);
  protected Border m_lowered =
    new SoftBevelBorder(BevelBorder.LOWERED);
  protected Border m_inactive = new EmptyBorder(3, 3, 3, 3);
  protected Border m_border = m_inactive;
  protected Insets m_ins = new Insets(4,4,4,4);

  public SmallButton(Action act, String tip) {
    super((Icon)act.getValue(Action.SMALL_ICON));
    setBorder(m_inactive);
    setMargin(m_ins);
    setToolTipText(tip);
    setRequestFocusEnabled(false);
    addActionListener(act);
    addMouseListener(this);
  }

  public float getAlignmentY() {
    return 0.5f;
  }

  public Border getBorder() {
    return m_border;
  }

  public Insets getInsets() {
    return m_ins;
  }

  public void mousePressed(MouseEvent e) {
    m_border = m_lowered;
    setBorder(m_lowered);
  }

  public void mouseReleased(MouseEvent e) {
    m_border = m_inactive;
    setBorder(m_inactive);
  }

  public void mouseClicked(MouseEvent e) {}

  public void mouseEntered(MouseEvent e) {
    m_border = m_raised;
    setBorder(m_raised);
  }

  public void mouseExited(MouseEvent e) {
    m_border = m_inactive;
    setBorder(m_inactive);
  }
}
class SmallToggleButton extends JToggleButton
  implements ItemListener {
```

5 Used for small buttons in toolbar

6 Used for small toggle buttons in toolbar

```
protected Border m_raised =
  new SoftBevelBorder(BevelBorder.RAISED);
protected Border m_lowered =
  new SoftBevelBorder(BevelBorder.LOWERED);
protected Insets m_ins = new Insets(4,4,4,4);

public SmallToggleButton(boolean selected,
  ImageIcon imgUnselected, ImageIcon imgSelected, String tip) {
  super(imgUnselected, selected);
  setHorizontalAlignment(CENTER);
  setBorder(selected ? m_lowered : m_raised);
  setMargin(m_ins);
  setToolTipText(tip);
  setRequestFocusEnabled(false);
  setSelectedIcon(imgSelected);
  addItemListener(this);
}

public float getAlignmentY() {
  return 0.5f;
}

public Insets getInsets() {
  return m_ins;
}

public Border getBorder() {
  return (isSelected() ? m_lowered : m_raised);
}

public void itemStateChanged(ItemEvent e) {
  setBorder(isSelected() ? m_lowered : m_raised);
}
}
```

12.4.1   Understanding the code

Class BasicTextEditor

1 BasicTextEditor now declares three new instance variables:
- JComboBox m_cbFonts: A combo box containing available font names.
- SmallToggleButton m_bBold: A custom toggle button representing the bold font style.
- SmallToggleButton m_bItalic: A custom toggle button representing the italic font style.

2 The createMenuBar() method now creates three instances of the SmallButton class (see below) corresponding to our pre-existing New, Open, and Save toolbar buttons. These are constructed by passing the appropriate Action (which we built in part II) as well as a tooltip String to the SmallButton constructor. Then we create a combo box with all the available font names and add it to the toolbar. The setMaximumSize() method is called on the combo box to reduce its size to a necessary maximum (otherwise, it will fill all the unoccupied space in our toolbar). An ActionListener is then added to monitor combo box selection. This listener selects the corresponding font menu item (containing the same font name) because the combo box and font radio button menu items must always be in synch. It then calls our update-Editor() method.

③ Two SmallToggleButtons are created and added to our toolbar to manage the bold and italic font properties. Each button receives an ActionListener which selects/deselects the corresponding menu item (because both the menu items and toolbar buttons must be in synch) and calls our updateEditor() method.

④ Our updateEditor() method receives some additional code to provide consistency between our menu items and toolbar controls. This method relies on the state of the menu items, which is why the toolbar components first set the corresponding menu items when selected. The code added here is self-explanatory; it just involves enabling/disabling and selecting/deselecting components to preserve consistency.

Class SmallButton

⑤ SmallButton represents a small push button intended for use in a toolbar. It implements the MouseListener interface to process mouse input. Three instance variables are declared:

- Border m_raised: The border to be used when the mouse cursor is located over the button.
- Border m_lowered: The border to be used when the button is pressed.
- Border m_inactive: The border to be used when the mouse cursor is located outside the button.

The SmallButton constructor takes an Action parameter (which is added as an Action-Listener and performs an appropriate action when the button is pressed) and a String representing the tooltip text. Several familiar properties are assigned and the icon encapsulated within the Action is used for this button's icon. SmallButton also adds itself as a MouseListener and sets its tooltip text to the given String passed to the constructor. The requestFocusEnabled property is set to false so that when this button is clicked, focus will not be transferred out of our JTextArea editor component.

The getAlignmentY() method is overriden to return a constant value of 0.5f, indicating that this button should always be placed in the middle of the toolbar in the vertical direction (Note that this is only necessary in JDK 1.2.1 and earlier.). The remainder of SmallButton represents an implementation of the MouseListener interface which sets the border based on mouse events. The border is set to m_inactive when the mouse is located outside its bounds, m_active when the mouse is located inside its bounds, and m_lowered when the button is pressed.

Class SmallToggleButton

⑥ SmallToggleButton extends JToggleButton and implements the ItemListener interface to process changes in the button's selection state. Two instance variables are declared:

- Border m_raised: The border to be used when the button is unselected (unchecked).
- Border m_lowered: The border to be used when the button is selected (checked).

The SmallToggleButton constructor takes four arguments:

- boolean selected: The initial selection state.
- ImageIcon imgUnselected: The icon for use when unselected.

- `ImageIcon imgSelected:` The icon for use when selected.
- `String tip:` The tooltip message.

In the constructor, several familiar button properties are set, and a raised or lowered border is assigned depending on the initial selection state. Each instance is added to itself as an `Item-Listener` to receive notification about changes in its selection. Thus the `itemState-Changed()` method is implemented; it simply sets the button's border accordingly based on the new selected state.

12.4.2 Running the code

Verify that the toolbar components (combo box and toggle buttons) change the editor's font as expected. Notice which menu and toolbar components work in synchronization (meaning the menu item selections result in changes in the toolbar controls, and vice versa). Figure 12.5 shows our new basic text editor toolbar with a `SmallToggleButton` in the pressed state displaying its tooltip text.

GUIDELINE

Tooltip help   Tooltip Help on mouse-over is a must-have technical addition for small toolbar buttons. The relatively recent innovation of tooltips has greatly improved the usability of toolbars. Don't get caught delivering a toolbar without one—make sure that your tooltip text is meaningful to the user!

12.5 *Basic text editor, part IV: custom menu components*

In example 12.4 we will show how to build a custom menu component, `ColorMenu`, which allows the selection of a color from a grid of small colored panes (which are instances of the inner class `ColorMenu.ColorPane`). By extending `JMenu`, we inherit all `MenuElement` functionality (see section 12.1.10), making custom menu creation quite easy.

Example 12.4

BasicTextEditor.java

see \Chapter12\4

```
import java.awt.*;
import java.awt.event.*;
import java.io.*;
import java.util.*;

import javax.swing.*;
import javax.swing.event.*;
import javax.swing.border.*;

public class BasicTextEditor extends JFrame
{
```

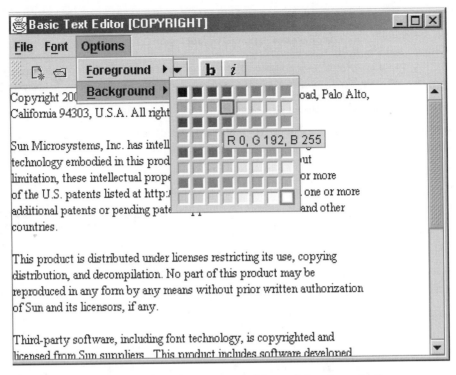

Figure 12.6 **Custom menu component used for quick color selection**

```
// Unchanged code from example 12.3

protected JMenuBar createMenuBar()
{
  // Unchanged code from example 12.3

  JMenu mOpt = new JMenu("Options");
  mOpt.setMnemonic('p');

  ColorMenu cm = new ColorMenu("Foreground");
  cm.setColor(m_monitor.getForeground());
  cm.setMnemonic('f');
  lst = new ActionListener() {
    public void actionPerformed(ActionEvent e) {
      ColorMenu m = (ColorMenu)e.getSource();
      m_editor.setForeground(m.getColor());
    }
  };
  cm.addActionListener(lst);
  mOpt.add(cm);

  cm = new ColorMenu("Background");
  cm.setColor(m_monitor.getBackground());
  cm.setMnemonic('b');
  lst = new ActionListener() {
```

1 Presents color selector for foreground color

1 Presents color selector for background color

```
    public void actionPerformed(ActionEvent e) {
      ColorMenu m = (ColorMenu)e.getSource();
      m_editor.setBackground(m.getColor());
    }
  };
  cm.addActionListener(lst);
  mOpt.add(cm);
  menuBar.add(mOpt);

  getContentPane().add(m_toolBar, BorderLayout.NORTH);
  return menuBar;
}

// Unchanged code from example 12.3
}

class ColorMenu extends JMenu
{
  protected Border m_unselectedBorder;
  protected Border m_selectedBorder;
  protected Border m_activeBorder;

  protected Hashtable m_panes;
  protected ColorPane m_selected;

  public ColorMenu(String name) {
    super(name);
    m_unselectedBorder = new CompoundBorder(
      new MatteBorder(1, 1, 1, 1, getBackground()),
      new BevelBorder(BevelBorder.LOWERED,
      Color.white, Color.gray));
    m_selectedBorder = new CompoundBorder(
      new MatteBorder(2, 2, 2, 2, Color.red),
      new MatteBorder(1, 1, 1, 1, getBackground()));
    m_activeBorder = new CompoundBorder(
      new MatteBorder(2, 2, 2, 2, Color.blue),
      new MatteBorder(1, 1, 1, 1, getBackground()));

    JPanel p = new JPanel();
    p.setBorder(new EmptyBorder(5, 5, 5, 5));
    p.setLayout(new GridLayout(8, 8));
    m_panes = new Hashtable();

    int[] values = new int[] { 0, 128, 192, 255 };
    for (int r=0; r<values.length; r++) {
      for (int g=0; g<values.length; g++) {
        for (int b=0; b<values.length; b++) {
          Color c = new Color(values[r], values[g], values[b]);
          ColorPane pn = new ColorPane(c);
          p.add(pn);
          m_panes.put(c, pn);
        }
      }
    }
    add(p);
```

1 Presents color selector for background color

2 Custom menu which presents a grid of colors to select from

3 Creates oneColorPane for each of the 64 (4*4*4) colors

```
      }
      public void setColor(Color c) {
        Object obj = m_panes.get(c);
        if (obj == null)
          return;
        if (m_selected != null)
          m_selected.setSelected(false);
        m_selected = (ColorPane)obj;
        m_selected.setSelected(true);
      }

      public Color getColor() {
        if (m_selected == null)
          return null;
        return m_selected.getColor();
      }

      public void doSelection() {
        fireActionPerformed(new ActionEvent(this,
          ActionEvent.ACTION_PERFORMED, getActionCommand()));
      }

      class ColorPane extends JPanel implements MouseListener
      {
        protected Color m_c;
        protected boolean m_selected;

        public ColorPane(Color c) {
          m_c = c;
          setBackground(c);
          setBorder(m_unselectedBorder);
          String msg = "R "+c.getRed()+", G "+c.getGreen()+
            ", B "+c.getBlue();
          setToolTipText(msg);
          addMouseListener(this);
        }

        public Color getColor() { return m_c; }

        public Dimension getPreferredSize() {
          return new Dimension(15, 15);
        }
        public Dimension getMaximumSize() { return getPreferredSize(); }
        public Dimension getMinimumSize() { return getPreferredSize(); }
        public void setSelected(boolean selected) {
          m_selected = selected;
          if (m_selected)
            setBorder(m_selectedBorder);
          else
            setBorder(m_unselectedBorder);
        }

        public boolean isSelected() { return m_selected; }
```

4 Finds a ColorPane of a given color and sets that as the selected color

5 Notifies listeners that a color selection has occurred

6 Displays a single color for selection

```
      public void mousePressed(MouseEvent e) {}

      public void mouseClicked(MouseEvent e) {}

      public void mouseReleased(MouseEvent e) {
        setColor(m_c);
        MenuSelectionManager.defaultManager().clearSelectedPath();
        doSelection();
      }

      public void mouseEntered(MouseEvent e) {
        setBorder(m_activeBorder);
      }

      public void mouseExited(MouseEvent e) {
        setBorder(m_selected ? m_selectedBorder :
          m_unselectedBorder);
      }
    }
  }
}
```

7 Sets new color, closes all menus, and notifies listeners of color change

12.5.1 Understanding the code

Class BasicTextEditor

1 The createMenuBar() method now creates a new JMenu titled "Options" and populates it with two ColorMenus. The first of these menus receives an ActionListener which requests the selected color using ColorMenu's getColor() method, and assigns it as the foreground color of our editor component. Similarly, the second ColorMenu receives an ActionListener which manages our editor's background color.

Class ColorMenu

2 This class extends JMenu and represents a custom menu component which serves as a quick color chooser. Here are the instance variables:

- Border m_unselectedBorder: The border to be used for a ColorPane (see below) when it is not selected and the mouse cursor is located outside of its bounds.
- Border m_selectedBorder: The border to be used for a ColorPane when it is selected and the mouse cursor is located outside of its bounds.
- Border m_activeBorder: The border to be used for a ColorPane when the mouse cursor is located inside its bounds.
- Hashtable m_panes: A collection of ColorPanes.
- ColorPane m_selected: A reference to the currently selected ColorPane.

3 The ColorMenu constructor takes a menu name as a parameter and creates the underlying JMenu component using that name. This creates a root menu item which can be added to another menu or to a menu bar. Selecting this menu item will display its JPopupMenu component, which normally contains several simple menu items. In our case, however, we add a JPanel to it using JMenu's add(Component c) method. This JPanel serves as a container for 64 ColorPanes (see below) which are used to display the available selectable colors, as well as the current selection. A triple for cycle is used to generate the constituent ColorPanes in 3-dimensional color space. Each ColorPane takes a Color instance as a constructor parameter, and each `ColorPane` is placed in our `Hashtable` collection, `m_panes`, using its associated `Color` as the key.

④ The `setColor()` method finds a `ColorPane` which holds a given `Color`. If such a component is found, this method clears the previously selected `ColorPane` and selects the new one by calling its `setSelected()` method. The `getColor()` method simply returns the currently selected color.

⑤ The `doSelection()` method sends an `ActionEvent` to registered listeners notifying them that an action has been performed on this `ColorMenu`, which means a new color may have been selected.

Class ColorMenu.ColorPane

⑥ This inner class is used to display a single color available for selection in a `ColorMenu`. It extends `JPanel` and implements `MouseListener` to process its own mouse events. This class uses the three `Border` variables from the parent `ColorMenu` class to represent its state, whether it is selected, unselected, or active. These are the instance variables:

- `Color m_c`: The color instance represented by this pane.
- `boolean m_selected`: A flag indicating whether this pane is currently selected.

The `ColorPane` constructor takes a `Color` instance as a parameter and stores it in our `m_c` instance variable. The only thing we need to do to display that color is to set it as the pane's background. We also add a tooltip indicating the red, green, and blue components of this color.

⑦ All `MouseListener`-related methods should be familiar by now. However, take note of the `mouseReleased()` method which plays the key role in color selection: If the mouse is released over a `ColorPane`, we first assign the associated `Color` to the parenting `ColorMenu` component using the `setColor()` method (so it can be retrieved later by any attached listeners). We then hide all opened menu components by calling the `MenuSelectionManager.clearSelected-Path()` method since menu selection is complete at this point. Finally, we invoke the `doSelection()` method on the parenting `ColorMenu` component to notify all attached listeners.

12.5.2 Running the code

Experiment with changing the editor's background and foreground colors using our custom menu component available in the Options menu. Notice that a color selection will not affect anything until the mouse is released, and a mouse release also triggers the collapse of all menu popups in the current path. Figure 12.6 shows `ColorMenu` in action.

GUIDELINE

Usability and design alternatives   A more traditional approach to this example would be to have an elipsis option in the Options menu that opens a color chooser dialog. Consider what an improvement the presented design makes to usability. Within a limited range of colors, this design allows for faster selection with the possible minor problem that there is a greater chance of a mistake being made in the selection. However, a mistake like that can be easily corrected. As you will see in the next chapter, knowing that you have a bounded range of input selections can be put to good use when you're improving a design and its usability.

Progress bars, sliders, and scroll bars

13.1 *BOUNDED-RANGE COMPONENTS OVERVIEW*

`JScrollBar`, `JSlider`, and `JProgressBar` provide visualization and selection within a bounded interval, thereby allowing the user to conveniently select a value from that interval or to simply observe its current state. In this section we'll give a brief overview of these components and the significant classes and interfaces that support them.

13.1.1 The BoundedRangeModel interface

abstract interface javax.swing.BoundedRangeModel

The `BoundedRangeModel` interface describes a data model that is used to define an integer *value* between *minimum* and *maximum* values. This value can have a subrange called an *extent*, which can be used to define the size of, for instance, a scrollbar "thumb." The extent often changes dynamically corresponding to how much of the entire range of possible values is visible. The value can never be set larger than the maximum or minimum values, and the extent always starts at the current value and never extends past the maximum. Another property called `valueIsAdjusting` is declared and is expected to be true when the value is in the state of being adjusted (for example, when a slider thumb is being dragged).

Implementations are expected to fire `ChangeEvents` when any of the `minimum`, `maximum`, `value`, `extent`, or `valueIsAdjusting` properties change state. Thus, `BoundedRangeModel` includes method declarations for adding and removing `ChangeListeners`: `addChangeListener()` and `removeChangeListener()`. This model is used by `JProgressBar`, `JSlider`, and `JScrollBar`.

GUIDELINE

Why choose a bounded range component? The bounded range components are essentially analog devices in nature. They are good at providing relative, positional, approximate, or changing (in time) data. They are also excellent at visually communicating the bounds or limits of a data selection and at communicating a percentage of the whole through approximate visual means. Where you have several values which share the same bounds (such as RGB values for a color chooser), you can easily communicate relative values of the three choices through use of a bounded range component. The position of each component shows the relative value of one against another.

Therefore, use bounded range components when there is an advantage to communicating either a range of values and/or an approximate position or changing value to the user.

13.1.2   DefaultBoundedRangeModel

class javax.swing.DefaultBoundedRangeModel

`DefaultBoundedRangeModel` is the default concrete implementation of the `BoundedRangeModel` interface. The default constructor initializes a model with 0 for `minimum`, 100 for `maximum`, and 0 for the `value` and `extent` properties. Another constructor allows the specification of each of these initial values as `int` parameters. As expected, this implementation does fire `ChangeEvents` whenever one of its properties changes.

13.1.3   JScrollBar

class javax.swing.JScrollBar

Scroll bars can be used to choose a new value from a specified interval by sliding a *knob* (often referred to as the *thumb*) between the given maximum and minimum bounds, or by using small buttons at the ends of the component. The area not occupied by the thumb and buttons is known as the *paging area*; this can also be used to change the current scroll bar value. The thumb represents the `extent` of this bounded-range component, and its `value` is stored in the `visibleAmount` property.

`JScrollBar` can be oriented horizontally or vertically, and its value increases to the right or upward, respectively. To specify orientation, which is stored in the `orientation` property, we call the `setOrientation()` method and pass it one of the `JScrollBar.HORIZONTAL` or `JScrollBar.VERTICAL` constants.

Clicking on a button moves the thumb (and thus the value—recall that a bounded-range component's value lies at the beginning of the extent) by the value of `JScrollBar`'s `unitIncrement` property. Similarly, clicking the paging area moves the thumb by the value of `JScrollBar`'s `blockIncrement` property.

NOTE   It is common to match the `visibleAmount` property with the `blockIncrement` property. This is a simple way to visually signify to the user how much of the available range of data is currently visible.

GUIDELINE

Using a scroll bar

Background   The scroll bar is really a computer-enhanced development from an original analog mechanical idea. Scroll bars are, in some respects, more advanced than sliders (see section 13.1.4). The thumb of the scroll bar can very cleverly be used to show the current data as a percentage of a whole, as described in the note above. If the scroll bar is placed onto an image and the thumb is approximately 50% of the total size, then the user is given a clear indication that the viewing area is roughly half of the total size. The ability for the thumb in a scroll bar to change size to accurately reflect this is something which could not have been achieved with a mechanical device. Scroll bars are, in this respect, a very good example of taking a metaphor based on a mechanical device and enhancing it to improve usability.

Choosing position   By far, the best use of a scroll bar is position selection. They are, by nature, analog, so the viewer only sees an approximate position. Scroll bars are used by a `JScrollPane` to select the viewing position of the component the `JScrollPane` contains. Users have become accustomed to this method of using them. For most other occasions where you want to use a sliding control for selection, a `JSlider` is probably best.

As expected, `JScrollBar` uses a `DefaultBoundedRangeModel` by default. In addition to the `ChangeEvents` fired by this model, `JScrollBar` fires `PropertyChangeEvents` when its `orientation`, `unitIncrement`, or `blockIncrement` properties change state. `JScroll-Pane` also fires `AdjustmentEvents` whenever any of its bound properties change, or when any of its model's properties change (this is done solely for backward compatibility with the AWT scroll bar class). Accordingly, `JScrollBar` provides methods to add and remove `AdjustmentListeners`; we don't need to provide methods for adding and removing `PropertyChangeListeners` because this functionality is inherited from `JComponent`.

NOTE   `AdjustmentListeners` receive `AdjustmentEvents`. Both are defined in `java.awt.event`; refer to the API documentation for more detail.

13.1.4   JSlider

class javax.swing.JSlider

Sliders can be used to choose a numerical value from a specified interval. To use a slider, slide a knob between the given borders using the mouse, arrow keys, or PageDown and PageUp. Sliders are very useful when we know in advance the range of input from which the user should be able to choose.

JSlider supports horizontal and vertical orientations, and its `orientation` property can be set to either `JSlider.HORIZONTAL` or `JSlider.VERTICAL`. The `extent` property specifies the number of values to skip forward/up or back/down when PageUp or PageDown is pressed, respectively. Tick marks can be used to denote value locations. *Minor* and *major* tick marks are supported; major ticks are usually longer and more spread apart than minor ticks. In the case where a major and minor tick fall on the same location, the major tick takes precedence and the minor tick will not be displayed. Spacing between minor tick marks is specified by the `minorTickSpacing` property, and spacing between major tick marks is specified by the `majorTickSpacing` property.

NOTE The tick spacing properties specify the number of values to be skipped between successive ticks. Their names are somewhat misleading because they actually have nothing to do with the physical space (in pixels) between ticks. They would be more appropriately named "`minorTickDisplayInterval`" and "`majorTickDisplayInterval`."

Setting either spacing property to 0 has a disabling effect, and the `paintTicks` property also provides a way of turning ticks on and off.

BUG FIX The `snapToTicks` property is intended to only allow the slider knob to lie on a tick-marked value. This feature did not work as expected in Java 1.2 FCS, but has been fixed in more recent versions of Java. Try setting this to true on a `JSlider` with the `setSnapToTicks()` method.

Major ticks can be annotated by components and, by default, each of `JSlider`'s major ticks are adorned with `JLabel`s that denote the integer tick value. We can turn this functionality on and off by changing the `paintLabels` property, and we can customize which components are used to annotate, and at what values they are placed, by passing a `Dictionary` of `Integer/Component` pairs to the `setLabelTable()` method. The `createStandardLabels()` method is used by default to set up `JSlider` with its `JLabel`s at each major tick value. This method returns a `Hashtable` (a subclass of `Dictionary`) which can then be assigned to `JSlider` using `setLabelTable()`.

By default, `JSlider`'s values increment from left to right or bottom to top depending on whether horizontal or vertical orientation is used. To reverse the incrementation direction, we can set the `inverted` property to `true`.

GUIDELINE

Using a Slider Sliders are really a close graphical and behavioral representation of a real world analog slider—a hi-fi system or an older TV volume control are good examples. As such, sliders are analog devices and they are designed to be used to determine an approximate or positional setting for something. They usually rely on direct user feedback to help select a position. With the TV volume control example, the volume would go up and down as the slider is moved and the user would stop moving it when the volume was at a comfortable level.

The Swing version of a slider is actually a digital device disguised as an analog one. Each tick of the slider is a digital increment. The slider can therefore be used to determine an accurate value, provided the user is given some additional digital feedback, such as a numeric display of the absolute value or a scale along the side of the slider. Where accurate values are important, such as with a color chooser, be sure to provide an absolute value as output alongside the slider.

Feedback   Immediate feedback is important with sliders because of their analog nature. Provide actual feedback, such as the brightness of a picture which increases or decreases as the slider is moved, or provide an absolute numeric value readout which the user can see change as the slider is moved. Judicious use of the change event with a ChangeListener is important so that the feedback mechanism can be updated—for example, to show brightness or contrast in an image.

Movement   The two default orientations of a slider are conventions which date back to the original analog electronic devices. When a slider is vertical, the down position is lower and you move it up to increase in value. When it is horizontal, the left position is lower and you move it right to increase in value. Users should be very familiar with this convention. If you wish to switch it, you should have a very very good reason for doing so. We wouldn't recommend it!

Slider vs. Scroll bar   On the whole, use a slider for choosing a value when the value needed is approximate and subjective (such as color, volume, and brightness) and when the user needs to make the subjective judgement. Conversely, use a scroll bar for positional choice, where the desired position is approximate and judged relative to the whole.

The paintTrack property specifies whether the whole slider track is filled in. The Metal look and feel UI delegate for JSlider pays attention to the client property with the key "JSlider.isFilled" and a Boolean value. Adding this property to a JSlider's client properties hashtable (using putClientProperty(); see chapter 2) with a value of Boolean.TRUE will fill in only the lower half of the slider track from the position of the knob. This client property will have no effect if the paintTrack property is set to true, and it will work only if the slider is using the Metal look and feel UI delegate.

As expected, JSlider uses a DefaultBoundedRangeModel by default. In addition to the ChangeEvents fired by this model, JSlider fires PropertyChangeEvents when any of its properties described above change state. Unlike JScrollBar, JSlider provides the ability to add and remove ChangeListeners directly.

13.1.5   JProgressBar

Class javax.swing.JProgressBar

Progress bars can be used to display how far or close a given numerical value is from the bounds of a specified interval. They are typically used to indicate progress during a certain lengthy job to show the user that the job being monitored is alive and active. As with JScrollBar and JSlider, JProgressBar can be oriented horizontally or vertically. Notice also that JProgressBar acts the same way as JSlider with respect to incrementing: left to right in horizontal orientation, bottom to top in vertical orientation.

A JProgressBar is painted and filled from the minimum value to its current value (with the exception of the Windows look and feel, which paints a series of small rectangles). A percentage representing how much of a job has been completed can optionally be displayed in the center of JProgressBar. The string property represents the String to be painted (it's usually of the form XX%, where X is a digit), stringPainted specifies whether string should be painted, and `percentComplete` is a `double` between 0 and 1 to specify how much of the job has been completed so far.

> **NOTE** We normally do not need to take control of this rendering functionality, because by setting the `string` property to `null`, and the `stringPainted` property to `true`, the `percentComplete` property is converted to the XX% form for us, and it is displayed in the progress bar.

`JProgressBar`'s foreground and background can be assigned just like any `JComponent`; however, the color used to render its status text is not directly modifiable. Instead, this is handled by the UI delegate. The easiest way to assign specific colors is to replace the appropriate UI resources in the `UIManager`'s defaults table (see chapter 21 for more about look and feel customization).

The `borderPainted` property (which defaults to `true`) specifies whether a border is rendered around `JProgressBar`. As expected, `JProgressBar` uses a `DefaultBoundedRangeModel` by default, and `ChangeListeners` can be added to receive `ChangeEvents` when any of `JProgressBar`'s properties change state.

During a monitored operation, we simply call `setValue()` on a `JProgressBar` and all updating is taken care of for us. We must be careful to make this call in the event-dispatching thread. Consider the following basic example (13.1). Figure 13.1 illustrates the output.

Figure 13.1   A basic `JProgressBar` example showing custom colors and proper updating

> **JAVA 1.4** The new `indeterminate` property has been added to `JProgressBar` in Java 1.4. Setting this to `true` with the `setIndeterminate()` method places `JProgressBar` in a new mode in which an animated rectangle moves right and left indicating an action of unknown length is taking place.

To demonstrate the new `indeterminate` property added in Java 1.4 we set it to `true` for 5 seconds then to `false` each time the start button is pressed. Also, each time the start button is pressed we toggle the `stringPainted` property. When this is set to `false`, the progress bar is changed from a solid rectangle to a sequence of small rectangles.

Example 13.1

JProgressBarDemo.java

see \Chapter13\1

```
import java.awt.*;
import java.awt.event.*;

import javax.swing.*;
import javax.swing.event.*;
```

```java
import javax.swing.border.*;

public class JProgressBarDemo extends JFrame {
    protected int m_min = 0;
    protected int m_max = 100;
    protected int m_counter = 0;
    protected JProgressBar m_progress;
    protected JButton m_start;
    protected boolean m_stringPainted = false;

    public JProgressBarDemo() {
        super("JProgressBar Demo");
        setSize(300,50);

        UIManager.put("ProgressBar.selectionBackground", Color.black);
        UIManager.put("ProgressBar.selectionForeground", Color.white);
        UIManager.put("ProgressBar.foreground", new Color(8,32,128));
        UIManager.put("ProgressBar.cellLength", new Integer(5));
        UIManager.put("ProgressBar.cellSpacing", new Integer(1));

        m_progress = new JProgressBar();
        m_progress.setMinimum(m_min);
        m_progress.setMaximum(m_max);
        m_progress.setStringPainted(m_stringPainted);

        m_start = new JButton("Start");
        ActionListener lst = new ActionListener() {
            public void actionPerformed(ActionEvent e) {
                m_stringPainted = !m_stringPainted;
                m_progress.setStringPainted(m_stringPainted);

                Thread runner = new Thread() {

                    int m_counter;
                    public void run() {
                        m_start.setEnabled(false);
                        // Pretend we're doing phase 1
                        m_progress.setIndeterminate(true);
                        try {
                            Thread.sleep(5000);
                        }
                        catch (InterruptedException ex) {}
                        m_progress.setIndeterminate(false);

                        // Pretend we're doing phase 2
                        for (m_counter=m_min; m_counter<=m_max; m_counter++) {
                            Runnable runme = new Runnable() {
                                public void run() {
                                    m_progress.setValue(m_counter);
                                }
                            };
                            SwingUtilities.invokeLater(runme);
                            try {
                                Thread.sleep(100);
                            }
```

```
                catch (InterruptedException ex) {}
            }
            m_start.setEnabled(true);
        }
    };
    runner.start();
    }
  };
  m_start.addActionListener(lst);

  getContentPane().setLayout(new BorderLayout(10,10));
  getContentPane().add(m_progress, BorderLayout.CENTER);
  getContentPane().add(m_start, BorderLayout.WEST);
}

public static void main(String[] args) {
  JProgressBarDemo frame = new JProgressBarDemo();
  frame.setDefaultCloseOperation(JFrame.EXIT_ON_CLOSE);
  frame.setVisible(true);
}
}
```

NOTE   The JProgressBar UI delegate centers the progress text horizontally and vertically. However, its centering scheme enforces a certain amount of white space around the text and has undesirable effects when using thin progress bars. In order to fix this, we can override BasicProgressBarUI's getStringPlacement() method (refer to the API documentation and the BasicProgressBarUI.java source code) to return the desired Point location where the text should be rendered.

GUIDELINE

Using progress bar long operations   Progress bars are commonly used as a filter for operations which take a long time. A long time in human interaction is often defined as one second or longer. The progress bar is usually rendered inside a JOptionPane.

You will need to pay special attention to the business logic code so that it is capable of notifying a progress bar of the progress of an operation.

Progress bars are inherently analog in nature. Analog data is particularly good for displaying change and for relative comparison. It is not good for exact measurement. In this situation, the analog nature of a progress bar means that it is good for showing that something is happening and that progress is taking place. However, it is not good for giving an exact measure of completeness. If you need to show the user exactly what percentage of the task is complete, you may need to supplement the progress bar with a digital progress reading. This is common with Internet download dialogs and option panes.

A digital readout is particularly useful when the task to be completed will take a very long time. The progress bar may give you a granularity of 3% or so for each graphic. If it takes a significantly long time to progress by such a jump, say greater than 5 seconds, the digital readout will give you a finer grained reading at 1%, and, it will change approximately three times faster than your progress bar. The combination of the two helps to pass the time for the user and it gives them the reassurance that something is happening; it also gives them a very accurate view of their progress. This is why the dual combination of digital and analog progress is popular with Internet download dialogs, as the task can be very long and its length cannot be determined by the application developer.

13.1.6 ProgressMonitor

class javax.swing.ProgressMonitor

The `ProgressMonitor` class is a convenient means of deploying a dynamic progress bar in an application that performs time-consuming operations. This class is a direct subclass of `Object`, so it does not exist in the component hierarchy.

`ProgressMonitor` displays a `JDialog` containing a `JOptionPane`-style component. The `note` property represents a `String` that can change during the course of an operation and it is displayed in a `JLabel` above the `JProgressBar` (if `null` is used, this label is not displayed).

Two buttons, OK and Cancel, are placed at the bottom of the dialog. They serve to dismiss the dialog and abort the operation, respectively. The OK button simply hides the dialog. The Cancel button hides the dialog, and it also sets the `canceled` property to `true`, providing us with a way to test whether the user has canceled the operation. Since most time-consuming operations occur in loops, we can test this property during each iteration, and abort if necessary.

The `millisToDecideToPopup` property is an `int` value that specifies the number of milliseconds to wait before `ProgressMonitor` should determine whether to pop up a dialog (it defaults to 500). This is used to allow a certain amount of time to pass before questioning whether the job is long enough to warrant a progress dialog. The `millisToPopup` property is an `int` value that specifies the minimum time a job must take in order to warrant popping up a dialog (it defaults to 2000). If `ProgressMonitor` determines that the job will take less than `millisToPopup` milliseconds, the dialog will not be shown.

The `progress` property is an `int` value that specifies the current value of the `JProgressBar`. During an operation, we are expected to update the `note` and `progress` in the event-dispatching thread.

> **WARNING**   In light of these properties, we should only use a `ProgressMonitor` for simple, predictable jobs. `ProgressMonitor` bases the estimated time to completion on the value of its `JProgressBar` from the start time to the current evaluation time, and it assumes that a constant rate of progression will exist throughout the whole job. For transferring a single file this may be a fairly valid assumption. However, the rate of progress is highly dependent on how the job is constructed.

> **NOTE**   `ProgressMonitor` does not currently give us access to its `JProgressBar` component. We hope that in future implementations it will be accounted for, as it currently makes customization more difficult.

13.1.7 ProgressMonitorInputStream

class javax.swing.ProgressMonitorInputStream

This class extends `java.io.FilterInputStream` and contains a `ProgressMonitor`. When it is used in place of an `InputStream`, this class provides a very simple means of displaying job progress. This `InputStream`'s overloaded `read()` methods read data and update the `ProgressMonitor` at the same time. We can access `ProgressMonitorInputStream`'s `ProgressMonitor` with `getProgressMonitor()`, but we cannot assign it a new one. (See the API documentation for more information about `InputStream`s.)

13.2 BASIC *JSCROLLBAR* EXAMPLE

The `JScrollBar` component is most often seen as part of a `JScrollPane`. We rarely use this component alone, unless customized scrolling is desired. In example 13.2 in this section, we'll show how to use `JScrollBar` to create a simple custom scrolling pane from scratch.

Figure 13.2
`ScrollDemo` **example showing an image in the custom scroll pane**

Example 13.2

ScrollDemo.java

see \Chapter13\2

```java
import java.awt.*;
import java.awt.event.*;

import javax.swing.*;
import javax.swing.event.*;
import javax.swing.border.*;

public class ScrollDemo
    extends JFrame {

  public ScrollDemo() {
    super("JScrollBar Demo");
    setSize(300,250);

    ImageIcon ii = new ImageIcon("earth.jpg");
    CustomScrollPane sp = new CustomScrollPane(new JLabel(ii));
```

```
            getContentPane().add(sp);
        }

        public static void main(String[] args) {
            ScrollDemo frame = new ScrollDemo();
            frame.setDefaultCloseOperation(JFrame.EXIT_ON_CLOSE);
            frame.setVisible(true);
        }
    }

    class CustomScrollPane
        extends JPanel {
```

1 Custom scroll pane class similar to JScrollPane, but with additional buttons to scroll to extremities

```
        protected JScrollBar m_vertSB;
        protected JScrollBar m_horzSB;
        protected CustomViewport m_viewport;
        protected JComponent m_comp;

        protected JButton m_btUp;
        protected JButton m_btDown;
        protected JButton m_btLeft;
        protected JButton m_btRight;

        public CustomScrollPane(JComponent comp) {
            if (comp == null)
                throw new IllegalArgumentException(
                    "Component cannot be null");

            setLayout(null);
            m_viewport = new CustomViewport();
            m_viewport.setLayout(null);
            add(m_viewport);
            m_comp = comp;
            m_viewport.add(m_comp);

            m_vertSB = new JScrollBar(JScrollBar.VERTICAL, 0, 0, 0, 0);
            m_vertSB.setUnitIncrement(5);
            add(m_vertSB);

            m_horzSB = new JScrollBar(JScrollBar.HORIZONTAL, 0, 0, 0, 0);
            m_horzSB.setUnitIncrement(5);
            add(m_horzSB);

            AdjustmentListener lst = new AdjustmentListener() {
                public void adjustmentValueChanged(AdjustmentEvent e) {
                    m_viewport.doLayout();
                }
            };
            m_vertSB.addAdjustmentListener(lst);
            m_horzSB.addAdjustmentListener(lst);

            m_btUp = new JButton(new ImageIcon("Up16.gif"));
            m_btUp.setMargin(new Insets(0,0,0,0));
            m_btUp.setBorder(new EmptyBorder(1,1,1,1));
            m_btUp.setToolTipText("Go top");
            add(m_btUp);
```

```
      ActionListener listener = new ActionListener() {
        public void actionPerformed(ActionEvent e) {
          m_vertSB.setValue(m_vertSB.getMinimum());
          validate();
        }
      };
      m_btUp.addActionListener(listener);

      m_btDown = new JButton(new ImageIcon("Down16.gif"));
      m_btDown.setMargin(new Insets(0,0,0,0));
      m_btDown.setBorder(new EmptyBorder(1,1,1,1));
      m_btDown.setToolTipText("Go bottom");
      add(m_btDown);
      l = new ActionListener() {
        public void actionPerformed(ActionEvent e) {
          m_vertSB.setValue(m_vertSB.getMaximum());
          validate();
        }
      };
      m_btDown.addActionListener(listener);

      m_btLeft = new JButton(new ImageIcon("Back16.gif"));
      m_btLeft.setMargin(new Insets(0,0,0,0));
      m_btLeft.setBorder(new EmptyBorder(1,1,1,1));
      m_btLeft.setToolTipText("Go left");
      add(m_btLeft);
      l = new ActionListener() {
        public void actionPerformed(ActionEvent e) {
          m_horzSB.setValue(m_horzSB.getMinimum());
          validate();
        }
      };
      m_btLeft.addActionListener(listener);

      m_btRight = new JButton(new ImageIcon("Forward16.gif"));
      m_btRight.setMargin(new Insets(0,0,0,0));
      m_btRight.setBorder(new EmptyBorder(1,1,1,1));
      m_btRight.setToolTipText("Go right");
      add(m_btRight);
      l = new ActionListener() {
        public void actionPerformed(ActionEvent e) {
          m_horzSB.setValue(m_horzSB.getMaximum());
          validate();
        }
      };
      m_btRight.addActionListener(l);
  }
  public void doLayout() {
    Dimension d = getSize();
    Dimension d0 = m_comp.getPreferredSize();
    Dimension d1 = m_vertSB.getPreferredSize();
    Dimension d2 = m_horzSB.getPreferredSize();
```

2 **Responsible for all layout of custom scroll pane children**

```
        int w = Math.max(d.width - d1.width-1, 0);
        int h = Math.max(d.height - d2.height-1, 0);
        m_viewport.setBounds(0, 0, w, h);

        int btW = d1.width;
        int btH = d2.height;
        m_btUp.setBounds(w+1, 0, btW, btH);
        m_vertSB.setBounds(w+1, btH+1, btW, h-2*btH);
        m_btDown.setBounds(w+1, h-btH+1, btW, btH);

        m_btLeft.setBounds(0, h+1, btW, btH);
        m_horzSB.setBounds(btW+1, h+1, w-2*btW, btH);
        m_btRight.setBounds(w-btW+1, h+1, btW, btH);

        int xs = Math.max(d0.width - w, 0);
        m_horzSB.setMaximum(xs);
        m_horzSB.setBlockIncrement(xs/5);
        m_horzSB.setEnabled(xs > 0);

        int ys = Math.max(d0.height - h, 0);
        m_vertSB.setMaximum(ys);
        m_vertSB.setBlockIncrement(ys/5);
        m_vertSB.setEnabled(ys > 0);

        m_horzSB.setVisibleAmount(m_horzSB.getBlockIncrement());
        m_vertSB.setVisibleAmount(m_vertSB.getBlockIncrement());
    }
    public Dimension getPreferredSize() {
        Dimension d0 = m_comp.getPreferredSize();
        Dimension d1 = m_vertSB.getPreferredSize();
        Dimension d2 = m_horzSB.getPreferredSize();
        Dimension d = new Dimension(d0.width+d1.width,
            d0.height+d2.height);
        return d;
    }

    class CustomViewport
        extends JPanel {

        public void doLayout() {
            Dimension d0 = m_comp.getPreferredSize();
            int x = m_horzSB.getValue();
            int y = m_vertSB.getValue();
            m_comp.setBounds(-x, -y, d0.width, d0.height);
        }
    }
}
```

3 Calculates preferred size based on preferred sizes of child components

4 Custom viewport-like panel as a container for the component to be scrolled, and is responsible for assigning the correct positioning of that component based on scroll bar values

13.2.1 Understanding the code

Class ScrollDemo

This simple frame-based class creates a CustomScrollPane instance to scroll a large image. This class is very similar to the first example in chapter 7 and does not require additional explanation.

❶ *Class CustomScrollPane*

This class extends JPanel to represent a simple custom scroll pane. Eight instance variables are declared:

- JScrollBar m_vertSB: vertical scroll bar.
- JScrollBar m_horzSB: horizontal scroll bar.
- CustomViewport m_viewport: custom viewport component.
- JComponent m_comp: component to be placed in our custom viewport.
- JButton m_btUp: vertical scroll bar up button.
- JButton m_btDown: vertical scroll bar down button.
- JButton m_btLeft: horizontal scroll bar left button.
- JButton m_btRight: horizontal scroll bar right button.

The CustomScrollPane constructor takes a component to be scrolled as a parameter. It instantiates the instance variables and adds them to itself using a null layout (because this component acts as its own layout manager). Note that the JScrollBars are created with proper orientation and zero values across the board (because these are meaningless if not based on the size of the component being scrolled). Two buttons for each scroll bar are added for setting the scroll bar value to its maximimum and minimum value.

An AdjustmentListener is created and added to both scroll bars. The adjustmentValueChanged() method calls the doLayout() method on the m_viewport component to perform the actual component scrolling according to the new scroll bars values.

❷ The doLayout() method sets the bounds for the viewport (in the center), vertical scroll bar (on the right), and horizontal scroll bar (on the bottom). New maximum values and block increment values are set for the scroll bars based on the sizes of the scrolling pane and component to be scrolled. Note that if the maximum value reaches zero, the corresponding scroll bar is disabled. The visibleAmount property of each is set to the corresponding blockIncrement value to provide proportional thumb sizes.

❹ The getPreferredSize() method simply calculates the preferred size of this component based on the preferred sizes of its children.

❹ *Class CustomViewport*

This class extends JPanel and represents a simple realization of a viewport for our custom scrolling pane. The only implemented method, doLayout(), reads the current scroll bar values and assigns bounds to the scrolling component accordingly.

13.2.2 Running the code

Figure 13.2 shows an image in the custom scroll pane. Use the horizontal and vertical scroll bars to verify that scrolling works as expected. Resize the frame component to verify that the scroll bar values and thumbs are adjusted correctly as the container's size is changed. Use the custom buttons to set the scroll bar to its maximum and minimum values.

13.3   *JSLIDER DATE CHOOSER*

In example 13.3, we'll show how three `JSliders` can be combined to allow date selection. We will also address some resizing issues and show how to dynamically change `JSlider`'s annotation components and tick spacing based on size constraints.

NOTE   While month and day are limited values, year is not. We can use a `JSlider` to select year only if we define a finite, static range of years to choose from, because `JSlider` must have a minimum and maximum value at all times. In this example we bound the year slider value between 1990 and 2010.

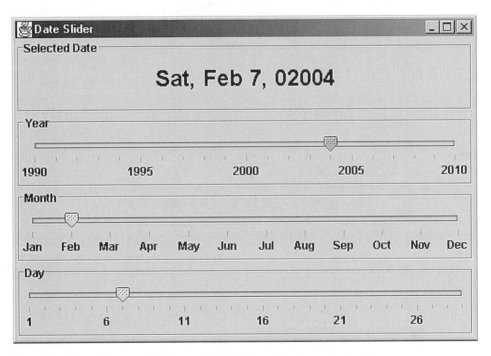

Figure 13.3 `JSliders` with dynamically changable bound values, tick spacing, and annotation components

GUIDELINE

Feedback in readable form Using sliders to pick the values for a date may be an interesting method for data input, but it does not lend itself to easy and clear output communication. It can be visually tedious to determine the actual selected date; users may need to look at each slider and put the information together themselves. This problem is fixed by the use of the clearly human readable form (the label) at the top of the dialog. This label directly follows the advice that sliders should be used to provide immediate visual feedback.

Visual noise Visual noise or clutter is avoided by spacing annotations and avoiding the temptation to annotate each day and each year. The change in rendering as the device is made smaller is also a clear example of how extra-coding and the adoption of an advanced technique can aid visual communication and usability

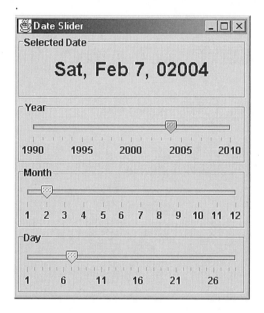

Figure 13.4
JSliders showing altered maximum bound and annotation labels

Example 13.3

DateSlider.java

see \Chapter13\3
```
import java.awt.*;
import java.awt.event.*;
import java.util.*;
import java.text.*;

import javax.swing.*;
import javax.swing.border.*;
import javax.swing.event.*;
```

```
public class DateSlider
    extends JFrame {

  public final static Dimension RIGID_DIMENSION =
      new Dimension(1,3);

  protected JLabel  m_lbDate;
  protected JSlider m_slYear;
  protected JSlider m_slMonth;
  protected JSlider m_slDay;
  protected Hashtable m_labels;
  protected GregorianCalendar m_calendar;
  protected SimpleDateFormat m_dateFormat;

  public DateSlider() {
    super("Date Slider");
    setSize(500, 340);

    m_calendar = new GregorianCalendar();
    Date currDate = new Date();
    m_calendar.setTime(currDate);
    m_dateFormat = new SimpleDateFormat("EEE, MMM d, yyyyy");

    JPanel p1 = new JPanel();
    p1.setLayout(new GridLayout(4, 1));

    JPanel p = new JPanel();
    p.setBorder(new TitledBorder(new EtchedBorder(),
        "Selected Date"));
    m_lbDate = new JLabel(
        m_dateFormat.format(currDate) + "       ");
    m_lbDate.setFont(new Font("Arial",Font.BOLD,24));
    p.add(m_lbDate);
    p1.add(p);

    m_slYear = new JSlider(JSlider.HORIZONTAL, 1990, 2010,
        m_calendar.get(Calendar.YEAR));
    m_slYear.setPaintLabels(true);
    m_slYear.setMajorTickSpacing(5);
    m_slYear.setMinorTickSpacing(1);
    m_slYear.setPaintTicks(true);
    ChangeListener lst = new ChangeListener() {
      public void stateChanged(ChangeEvent e) {
        showDate();
      }
    };
    m_slYear.addChangeListener(lst);

    p = new JPanel();
    p.setBorder(new TitledBorder(new EtchedBorder(), "Year"));
    p.setLayout(new BoxLayout(p, BoxLayout.Y_AXIS));
    p.add(Box.createRigidArea(RIGID_DIMENSION));
    p.add(m_slYear);
    p.add(Box.createRigidArea(RIGID_DIMENSION));
    p1.add(p);
```

❶ Creates calendar and date information

❷ Slider to set year

```
m_slMonth = new JSlider(JSlider.HORIZONTAL, 1, 12,
  m_calendar.get(Calendar.MONTH)+1);
String[] months = (new DateFormatSymbols()).getShortMonths();
m_labels = new Hashtable(12);
for (int k=0; k<12; k++)
  m_labels.put(new Integer(k+1), new JLabel(
    months[k], JLabel.CENTER ));
m_slMonth.setLabelTable(m_labels);
m_slMonth.setPaintLabels(true);
m_slMonth.setMajorTickSpacing(1);
m_slMonth.setPaintTicks(true);
m_slMonth.addChangeListener(lst);

p = new JPanel();
p.setBorder(new TitledBorder(new EtchedBorder(), "Month"));
p.setLayout(new BoxLayout(p, BoxLayout.Y_AXIS));
p.add(Box.createRigidArea(RIGID_DIMENSION));
p.add(m_slMonth);
p.add(Box.createRigidArea(RIGID_DIMENSION));
p1.add(p);

int maxDays = m_calendar.getActualMaximum(
  Calendar.DAY_OF_MONTH);
m_slDay = new JSlider(JSlider.HORIZONTAL, 1, maxDays,
  m_calendar.get(Calendar.DAY_OF_MONTH));
m_slDay.setPaintLabels(true);
m_slDay.setMajorTickSpacing(5);
m_slDay.setMinorTickSpacing(1);
m_slDay.setPaintTicks(true);
m_slDay.addChangeListener(lst);

p = new JPanel();
p.setBorder(new TitledBorder(new EtchedBorder(), "Day"));
p.setLayout(new BoxLayout(p, BoxLayout.Y_AXIS));
p.add(Box.createRigidArea(RIGID_DIMENSION));
p.add(m_slDay);
p.add(Box.createRigidArea(RIGID_DIMENSION));
p1.add(p);

getContentPane().add(p1, BorderLayout.CENTER);

enableEvents(ComponentEvent.COMPONENT_RESIZED);
}


protected void processComponentEvent(ComponentEvent e) {
  if (e.getID() == ComponentEvent.COMPONENT_RESIZED) {
    int w = getSize().width;

    m_slYear.setLabelTable(null);
    if (w > 200)
      m_slYear.setMajorTickSpacing(5);
    else
      m_slYear.setMajorTickSpacing(10);
```

③ Slider to set month

④ Slider to set day

⑤ Enables receipt of resize events

⑥ Reconfigures tick spacing based on width of frames

```
        m_slYear.setPaintLabels(w > 100);

        m_slMonth.setLabelTable(w > 300 ? m_labels : null);
        if (w <= 300 && w >=200)
           m_slMonth.setMajorTickSpacing(1);
        else
           m_slMonth.setMajorTickSpacing(2);
        m_slMonth.setPaintLabels(w > 100);

        m_slDay.setLabelTable(null);
        if (w > 200)
           m_slDay.setMajorTickSpacing(5);
        else
           m_slDay.setMajorTickSpacing(10);
        m_slDay.setPaintLabels(w > 100);
     }
  }
  public void showDate() {
     m_calendar.set(m_slYear.getValue(), m_slMonth.getValue()-1, 1);
     int maxDays = m_calendar.getActualMaximum(
        Calendar.DAY_OF_MONTH);

     if (m_slDay.getMaximum() != maxDays) {
        m_slDay.setValue(Math.min(m_slDay.getValue(), maxDays));
        m_slDay.setMaximum(maxDays);
        m_slDay.repaint();
     }

     m_calendar.set(m_slYear.getValue(), m_slMonth.getValue()-1,
        m_slDay.getValue());
     Date date = m_calendar.getTime();
     m_lbDate.setText(m_dateFormat.format(date));
  }
  public static void main(String argv[]) {
     DateSlider frame = new DateSlider();
     frame.setDefaultCloseOperation(JFrame.EXIT_ON_CLOSE);
     frame.setVisible(true);
  }
}
```

❼ Retrieves values from sliders to format date string in m_lbDate

13.3.1   Understanding the code

Class DateSlider

DateSlider extends JFrame and declares seven instance variables and one class constant.
This is the class constant:

- Dimension RIGID_DIMENSION: Used to create rigid areas above and below each slider.

There are seven instance variables:

- JLabel m_lbDate: The label to display the selected date.
- JSlider m_slYear: The slider to select the year.

- `JSlider m_slMonth`: The slider to select the month.
- `JSlider m_slDay`: The slider to select the day.
- `Hashtable m_labels`: A collection of labels to denote months by short names rather than numbers.
- `GregorianCalendar m_calendar`: A calendar that performs date manipulations.
- `SimpleDateFormat m_dateFormat`: The object to format the date as a string.

① The `DateSlider` constructor initializes the `m_calendar` instance defined above, and the date format `m_dateFormat`. A `JPanel` with a `GridLayout` of one column and four rows is used as a base panel, `p1`. `JLabel m_lbDate` is created and embedded in a `JPanel` with a simple `TitledBorder`, and placed in the first row.

② The `m_slYear` slider is created and placed in the second row. This slider is used to select the year from the interval 1990 to 2010. It takes its initial value from the current date. A number of settings are applied to `m_slYear`. The `paintLabels` and `paintTicks` properties are set to `true` to allow for drawing ticks and labels, `majorTickSpacing` is set to 5 to draw major ticks for every fifth value, and `minorTickSpacing` is set to 1 to draw minor ticks for every value. Finally, a `ChangeListener` is added to monitor changes to this slider's properties and update them when necessary with our custom `ShowDate()` method. Notice that `m_slYear` is placed in a `JPanel` that is surrounded by a `TitledBorder`. Two rigid areas are added to ensure vertical spacing between our slider and this parent panel (see chapter 4 for more about `Box` and its invisible `Filler` components).

③ The `m_slMonth` slider is created and placed in the third row. This slider is used to select the month from the interval 1 to 12. This component is constructed similar to `m_slYear`, but it receives a `Hashtable` of `JLabel`s to denote months by short names rather than numbers. These names are taken from an instance of the `DateFormatSymbols` class (see the API documentation) and they are used to create pairs in a local `m_labels` Hashtable in the form `Integer`/`JLabel`. The `Integer` represents slider value (from 1 to 12) as key, and the `JLabel` is used to display this value. Finally, the `setLabelTable()` method is invoked to assign these custom labels to the slider.

④ The `m_slDay` slider is created and placed in the fourth row. It is used to select the day of the month from an interval which dynamically changes depending on the current month and, for February, the year. Aside from this difference, `m_slDay` is constructed very similar to `m_slYear`.

⑤ A slider's tick annotation components may overlap each other and become unreadable if not enough space is provided, and it is up to us to account for this possibility. This becomes a more significant problem when (as in this example) slider components can be resized by simply resizing the parent frame. To work around this problem, we can simply enforce a certain size, but this may not be desirable in all situations. If we ever find ourselves in such a situation, we need to change our slider's properties dynamically depending on its size. For this reason, the `processComponentEvent()` method is overridden to process resizing events that occur on the parent frame. This event processing is enabled in the `DateSlider` constructor with the `enableEvents()` method.

⑥ The `processComponentEvent()` method only responds to `ComponentEvents` with the ID `COMPONENT_RESIZED`. For each of our three sliders, this method changes the `majorTick-`

Spacing property based on the container's width. m_slDay and m_slYear receive a spacing of 5 if the width is greater than 200; otherwise they receive a spacing of 10. m_slMonth receives a majorTickSpacing of 1 if the container's width is anywhere from 200 to 300, and it receives 2 otherwise. If this width is greater than 300, our custom set of labels is used to annotate m_slMonth's major ticks. The default numerical labels are used otherwise. For each slider, if the width is less than 100 the paintLabels property is set to false, which disables all annotations; otherwise, paintLabels is set to true.

7 Our custom showDate() method is used to retrieve values from our sliders and display them in m_lbDate as the new selected date. First, we determine the maximum number of days for the selected month by passing m_calendar a year, a month, and 1 as the day. Then, if necessary, we reset m_slDay's current and maximum values. Finally, we pass m_calendar a year, month, and the selected (possibly adjusted) day, retrieve a Date instance corresponding to these values, and invoke format() to retrieve a textual representation of the date.

> **NOTE** Java 2 does not really provide a direct way to convert a year, month, and day triplet into a Date instance (this functionality has been deprecated). We need to use Calendar. set() and Calendar.getTime() for this. Be aware that the day parameter is not checked against the maximum value for the selected month. If the day is set to 30 when the month is set to February, it will be silently treated as March 2.

13.3.2 Running the code

Notice how the date is selected and displayed, and how the range of the Day slider is adjusted when a new month is selected. Figure 13.3 shows the selection of February 7, 2004, demonstrating that this is a leap year.

> **NOTE** A leap year is a year whose last two digits are evenly divisible by 4, except for centenary years not divisible by 400.

Now try resizing the application frame to see how the slider annotations and ticks change to their more compact variants as the available space shrinks. Figure 13.4 illustrates the changes.

GUIDELINE

Exact value selection Although sliders are best used for selections where an exact value is not needed, this example gets around situations where an exact value is needed by providing an adequate gap between ticks, making an exact choice easy to achieve.

The use of a slider for the year selection is an unusual choice, as the year is not normally a bounded input. However, in certain domains it may be a more suitable choice such as this example. Once the year and the month have been displayed using sliders, it is visually attractive and consistent to use a slider for the day. There may be some debate about doing so, as the bound will change depending on the month that is selected. However, it is fair to argue that the changing bound on the day, as the month is selected, gives a clear, instant, visual feedback of how many days are in the month, which meets with the criteria of providing instant feedback when using a slider.

13.4 *JSliders in a JPEG Image Editor*

Java 2 ships with a special package, `com.sun.image.codec.jpeg`, that provides a set of classes and interfaces for working with JPEG images (this package is created at least in part by Eastman Kodak Company). Although this package is not a part of Swing, it can be very useful in Swing-based applications. By reducing image quality (which is actually a result of compression), required storage space can be decreased. Using reduced quality JPEGs in web pages increases response time by decreasing download time, and the editor application we will develop here allows us to load an existing JPEG, modify its quality, and then save the result. `JSliders` are used for the main editing components.

NOTE   JPEG stands for Joint Photographic Experts Group. It is a popular graphical format that allows images to be compressed up to 10 or 20 times.

Before we decide to use functionality in this package, you should know that, even though this package is shipped with Java 2, according to the API documentation, "... the classes in the `com.sun.image.codec.jpeg` package are not part of the core Java APIs. They are a part of Sun's JDK and JRE distributions. Although other licensees may choose to distribute these classes, developers cannot depend on their availability in non-Sun implementations. We expect that equivalent functionality will eventually be available in a core API or standard extension."

13.4.1   The JPEGDecodeParam interface

abstract interface com.sun.image.codec.jpeg.JPEGDecodeParam

This interface encapsulates the parameters used to control the decoding of a JPEG image. It provides a rich set of `getXX()` and `isXX()` accessor methods. Instances contain information about how to decode a JPEG input stream, and they are created automatically by `JPEGImage-Decoder` (see below) if none is specified when an image is decoded. A `JPEGImageDecoder`'s associated `JPEGDecoderParam` can be obtained with its `getJPEGDecodeParam()` method.

13.4.2   The JPEGEncodeParam interface

abstract interface com.sun.image.codec.jpeg.JPEGEncodeParam

This interface encapsulates parameters that are used to control the encoding of a JPEG image stream. It provides a rich set of `getXX()` and `setXX()` accessor methods. Instances contain information about how to encode a JPEG to an output stream, and a default instance will be created atomically by `JPEGImageEncoder` (see below) if none is specified when an image is encoded. A `JPEGImageEncoder`'s associated `JPEGEncodeParam` can be obtained with its `getJPEGEncodeParam()` method, or with one of its overriden `getDefaultJPEGEncode-Param()` methods.

Particularly relevant to this example are `JPEGEncodeParam`'s `xDensity`, `yDensity`, and `quality` properties, all of which can be assigned using typical `setXX()` methods. `xDensity` and `yDensity` represent horizontal and vertical pixel density, which depends on `JPEGEncoder-Param`'s current pixel density setting. The pixel density setting is controlled with `JPEGEncode-Param`'s `setDensityUnit()` method. It can be, for instance, `DENSITY_UNIT_DOTS_INCH`, which means pixel density will be interpreted as pixels per inch. The quality property is specified as a float within the range 0.0 to 1.0, where 1.0 means perfect quality. In general, 0.75 means high quality, 0.5 means medium quality, and 0.25 means low quality.

13.4.3 The JPEGImageDecoder interface

abstract interface com.sun.image.codec.jpeg.JPEGImageDecoder

This interface describes an object used to decode a JPEG data stream into an image. We invoke the decodeAsBufferedImage() method to perform the actual decoding into a Buffered-Image instance, or we invoke decodeAsRaster() to perform the decoding into a Raster instance. An instance of this interface can be obtained with one of the JPEGCodec.create-JPEGDecoder() methods, which takes the delivering data InputStream as a parameter. JPEGImageDecoder decodes according to its associated JPEGDecodeParam, and a default instance will be provided if we do not specify one.

13.4.4 The JPEGImageEncoder interface

abstract interface com.sun.image.codec.jpeg.JPEGImageEncoder

This interface describes an object used to encode an image into a JPEG data stream. We invoke the overloaded encode() method to perform the actual encoding. Instances of this interface can be obtained with one of the JPEGCodec.createJPEGEncoder() methods, which takes the destination OutputStream as a parameter. JPEGImageEncoder encodes according to its associated JPEGImageEncoder, and a default instance will be provided if we do not specify one.

13.4.5 JPEGCodec

class com.sun.image.codec.jpeg.JPEGCodec

This class contains a collection of static methods used to create JPEG encoders and decoders. Particularly useful are the overloaded createJPEGDecoder() and createJPEGEncoder() methods which take an InputStream and OutputStream, respectively, as parameters (along with an optional JPEGDecodeParam or JPEGEncodeParam instance).

Example 13.4

JPEGEditor.java

see \Chapter13\4

```
import java.awt.*;
import java.awt.event.*;
import java.awt.image.*;
import java.util.*;
import java.io.*;

import javax.swing.*;
import javax.swing.border.*;
import javax.swing.event.*;
import javax.swing.filechooser.*;

import com.sun.image.codec.jpeg.*;

public class JPEGEditor extends JFrame {

    public final static Dimension VERTICAL_RIGID_SIZE
        = new Dimension(1,3);
```

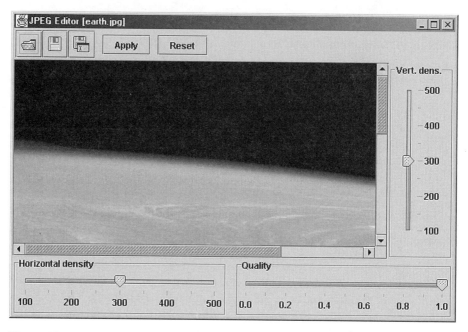

Figure 13.5 `JPEGEditor` **showing a high-quality image of Earth (using** `JSliders` **with the "isFilled" client property)**

```
public final static Dimension HORIZONTAL_RIGID_SIZE
  = new Dimension(3,1);

protected File m_currentDir;
protected File m_currentFile;

protected JFileChooser m_chooser;
  protected JPEGPanel m_panel;
  protected JSlider m_slHorzDensity;
  protected JSlider m_slVertDensity;
  protected JSlider m_slQuality;

protected BufferedImage m_bi1, m_bi2;

public JPEGEditor() {
  super("JPEG Editor");
  setSize(600, 400);

  m_chooser = new JFileChooser();
  m_chooser.setFileFilter(new SimpleFilter("jpg",
    "JPEG Image Files"));
  try {
    m_currentDir = (new File(".")).getCanonicalFile();
  }
  catch (IOException ex) {}

  m_panel = new JPEGPanel();
```

❶ Creates file chooser for selectting JPEG images

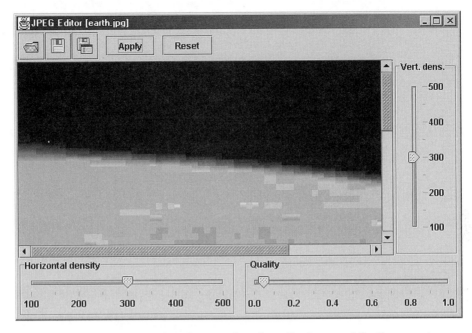

Figure 13.6 `JPEGEditor` **showing a reduced-quality image of Earth**

```
JScrollPane ps = new JScrollPane(m_panel,
   JScrollPane.VERTICAL_SCROLLBAR_ALWAYS,
   JScrollPane.HORIZONTAL_SCROLLBAR_ALWAYS);
getContentPane().add(ps, BorderLayout.CENTER);

JPanel p;
JPanel p1 = new JPanel(new GridLayout(1, 2, 10, 10));

m_slVertDensity = new JSlider(JSlider.VERTICAL,
   100, 500, 300);
m_slVertDensity.setExtent(50);
m_slVertDensity.setPaintLabels(true);
m_slVertDensity.setMajorTickSpacing(100);
m_slVertDensity.setMinorTickSpacing(50);
m_slVertDensity.setPaintTicks(true);
m_slVertDensity.putClientProperty(
   "JSlider.isFilled", Boolean.TRUE);

p = new JPanel();
p.setBorder(new TitledBorder(new EtchedBorder(),
   "Vert. dens."));
p.add(Box.createRigidArea(HORIZONTAL_RIGID_SIZE));
p.add(m_slVertDensity);
p.add(Box.createRigidArea(HORIZONTAL_RIGID_SIZE));
getContentPane().add(p, BorderLayout.EAST);

m_slHorzDensity = new JSlider(JSlider.HORIZONTAL,
   100, 500, 300);
```

❶ **Slider for JPEGEncodeParam "yDensity" property**

❶ **Slider for JPEGEncodeParam "xDensity" property**

```
    m_slHorzDensity.setExtent(50);
    m_slHorzDensity.setPaintLabels(true);
    m_slHorzDensity.setMajorTickSpacing(100);
    m_slHorzDensity.setMinorTickSpacing(50);
    m_slHorzDensity.setPaintTicks(true);
    m_slHorzDensity.putClientProperty(
      "JSlider.isFilled", Boolean.TRUE);

    p = new JPanel();
    p.setBorder(new TitledBorder(new EtchedBorder(),
      "Horizontal density"));
    p.setLayout(new BoxLayout(p, BoxLayout.Y_AXIS));
    p.add(Box.createRigidArea(VERTICAL_RIGID_SIZE));
    p.add(m_slHorzDensity);
    p.add(Box.createRigidArea(VERTICAL_RIGID_SIZE));
    p.setLayout(new BoxLayout(p, BoxLayout.X_AXIS));
    p1.add(p);

    m_slQuality = new JSlider(JSlider.HORIZONTAL,
      0, 100, 100);
    Hashtable labels = new Hashtable(6);
    for (float q = 0; q <= 1.0; q += 0.2)
      labels.put(new Integer((int)(q*100)),
      new JLabel("" + q, JLabel.CENTER ));
    m_slQuality.setLabelTable(labels);
    m_slQuality.setExtent(10);
    m_slQuality.setPaintLabels(true);
    m_slQuality.setMinorTickSpacing(10);
    m_slQuality.setPaintTicks(true);
    m_slQuality.putClientProperty(
      "JSlider.isFilled", Boolean.TRUE);

    p = new JPanel();
    p.setBorder(new TitledBorder(new EtchedBorder(),
      "Quality"));
    p.setLayout(new BoxLayout(p, BoxLayout.Y_AXIS));
    p.add(Box.createRigidArea(VERTICAL_RIGID_SIZE));
    p.add(m_slQuality);
    p.add(Box.createRigidArea(VERTICAL_RIGID_SIZE));
    p1.add(p);
    getContentPane().add(p1, BorderLayout.SOUTH);

    JToolBar tb = createToolbar();
    getContentPane().add(tb, BorderLayout.NORTH);
  }

  protected JToolBar createToolbar() {
    JToolBar tb = new JToolBar();
    tb.setFloatable(false);

    JButton bt = new JButton(new ImageIcon("Open24.gif"));
    bt.setToolTipText("Open JPEG file");
    ActionListener lst = new ActionListener() {
      public void actionPerformed(ActionEvent e) {
          m_chooser.setCurrentDirectory(m_currentDir);
```

❶ Slider for JPEGEncodeParam "xDensity" property

❶ Slider for JPEGEncodeParam "quality" property

❷ Method to create toolbar containing Open, Save, Save As, Apply and Reset buttons

```
            m_chooser.rescanCurrentDirectory();
            int result = m_chooser.showOpenDialog(JPEGEditor.this);
            repaint();
            if (result != JFileChooser.APPROVE_OPTION)
               return;
            m_currentDir = m_chooser.getCurrentDirectory();
            File fChoosen = m_chooser.getSelectedFile();
            openFile(fChoosen);
         }
   };
   bt.addActionListener(lst);
   tb.add(bt);

   bt = new JButton(new ImageIcon("Save24.gif"));
   bt.setToolTipText("Save changes to current file");
   lst = new ActionListener() {
      public void actionPerformed(ActionEvent e) {
         saveFile(m_currentFile);
      }
   };
   bt.addActionListener(lst);
   tb.add(bt);

   bt = new JButton(new ImageIcon("SaveAs24.gif"));
   bt.setToolTipText("Save changes to another file");
   lst = new ActionListener() {
      public void actionPerformed(ActionEvent e) {
         if (m_currentFile == null ||
            m_panel.getBufferedImage() == null)
         return;
         m_chooser.setCurrentDirectory(m_currentDir);
         m_chooser.rescanCurrentDirectory();
         int result = m_chooser.showSaveDialog(JPEGEditor.this);
         repaint();
         if (result != JFileChooser.APPROVE_OPTION)
            return;
         m_currentDir = m_chooser.getCurrentDirectory();
         File fChoosen = m_chooser.getSelectedFile();
         if (fChoosen!=null && fChoosen.exists()) {
            String message = "File " + fChoosen.getName()+
               " already exists. Override?";
            int result2 = JOptionPane.showConfirmDialog(
               JPEGEditor.this, message, getTitle(),
               JOptionPane.YES_NO_OPTION);
            if (result2 != JOptionPane.YES_OPTION)
               return;
         }
         setCurrentFile(fChoosen);
         saveFile(fChoosen);
      }
   };
   bt.addActionListener(lst);
   tb.add(bt);
```

4 Locates a JPEG file to open

4 Saves current JPEG using applied settings; allows selection of file name and location to save to

```
      tb.addSeparator();
      JButton btApply = new JButton("Apply");
      lst = new ActionListener() {
        public void actionPerformed(ActionEvent e) {
          apply();
        }
      };
      btApply.addActionListener(lst);

      btApply.setMinimumSize(btApply.getPreferredSize());
      btApply.setMaximumSize(btApply.getPreferredSize());
      tb.add(btApply);

      tb.addSeparator();
      JButton btReset = new JButton("Reset");
      lst = new ActionListener() {
        public void actionPerformed(ActionEvent e) {
          reset();
        }
      };
      btReset.addActionListener(lst);

      btReset.setMinimumSize(btReset.getPreferredSize());
      btReset.setMaximumSize(btReset.getPreferredSize());
      tb.add(btReset);

      return tb;
    }

    protected void setCurrentFile(File file) {
      if (file != null) {
        m_currentFile = file;
        setTitle("JPEG Editor ["+file.getName()+"]");
      }
    }

    protected void openFile(final File file) {
      if (file == null || !file.exists())
        return;
      setCurrentFile(file);

      setCursor(Cursor.getPredefinedCursor(Cursor.WAIT_CURSOR));
      Thread runner = new Thread() {
        public void run() {
          try {
            FileInputStream in = new FileInputStream(file);
            JPEGImageDecoder decoder =
              JPEGCodec.createJPEGDecoder(in);
            m_bi1 = decoder.decodeAsBufferedImage();
            m_bi2 = null;
            in.close();
            SwingUtilities.invokeLater( new Runnable() {
              public void run() { reset(); }
            });
          }
```

③ Button to apply current slider settings to JPEG image

③ Button to reset slider values to default (initial) values and reset JPEG image to original

⑤ Reads and decodes a JPEG image into a BufferedImage

⑤ Call the reset() method in the event thread because it modifies a Swing component

```
            catch (Exception ex) {
              ex.printStackTrace();
              System.err.println("openFile: "+ex.toString());
            }
            setCursor(Cursor.getPredefinedCursor(
              Cursor.DEFAULT_CURSOR));
          }
        };
        runner.start();
      }

      protected void saveFile(final File file) {
        if (file == null || m_panel.getBufferedImage() == null)
          return;

        setCursor(Cursor.getPredefinedCursor(Cursor.WAIT_CURSOR));
        Thread runner = new Thread() {
          public void run() {
            try {
              FileOutputStream out = new FileOutputStream(file);
              JPEGImageEncoder encoder = JPEGCodec.createJPEGEncoder(out);
              encoder.encode(m_panel.getBufferedImage());
              out.close();
            }
            catch (Exception ex) {
              ex.printStackTrace();
              System.err.println("apply: "+ex.toString());
            }
            setCursor(Cursor.getPredefinedCursor(Cursor.DEFAULT_CURSOR));
          }
        };
        runner.start();
      }

      protected void apply() {
        if (m_bi1 == null)
          return;

        setCursor(Cursor.getPredefinedCursor(Cursor.WAIT_CURSOR));
        Thread runner = new Thread() {
          public void run() {
            try {
              ByteArrayOutputStream out = new ByteArrayOutputStream();
              JPEGImageEncoder encoder =
                JPEGCodec.createJPEGEncoder(out);
              JPEGEncodeParam param =
                encoder.getDefaultJPEGEncodeParam(m_bi1);

              float quality = m_slQuality.getValue()/100.0f;
              param.setQuality(quality, false);

              param.setDensityUnit(
                JPEGEncodeParam.DENSITY_UNIT_DOTS_INCH);
              int xDensity = m_slHorzDensity.getValue();
              param.setXDensity(xDensity);
```

Encodes current image into a JPEG file ❻

Process image using current slider values ❼

```
            int yDensity = m_slVertDensity.getValue();
            param.setYDensity(yDensity);

            encoder.setJPEGEncodeParam(param);
            encoder.encode(m_bi1);

            ByteArrayInputStream in = new ByteArrayInputStream(
              out.toByteArray());
            JPEGImageDecoder decoder =
              JPEGCodec.createJPEGDecoder(in);
            final BufferedImage bi2 = decoder.decodeAsBufferedImage();
            SwingUtilities.invokeLater( new Runnable() {
              public void run() {
                m_panel.setBufferedImage(bi2);
              }
            });
          }
          catch (Exception ex) {
            ex.printStackTrace();
            System.err.println("apply: "+ex.toString());
          }
          setCursor(Cursor.getPredefinedCursor(Cursor.DEFAULT_CURSOR));
        }
      };
      runner.start();
  }

  protected void reset() {
    if (m_bi1 != null) {
      m_panel.setBufferedImage(m_bi1);
      m_slQuality.setValue(100);
      m_slHorzDensity.setValue(300);
      m_slVertDensity.setValue(300);
    }
  }

  public static void main(String argv[]) {
    JPEGEditor frame = new JPEGEditor();
    frame.setDefaultCloseOperation(JFrame.EXIT_ON_CLOSE);
    frame.setVisible(true);
  }
}

class JPEGPanel extends JPanel {
  protected BufferedImage m_bi = null;

  public void setBufferedImage(BufferedImage bi) {
    if (bi == null)
      return;
    m_bi = bi;
    Dimension d = new Dimension(m_bi.getWidth(this),
      m_bi.getHeight(this));
    setPreferredSize(d);
    revalidate();
    repaint();
```

7 Process image using current slider values

7 Reads input from OutputStream into BufferedImage

8 Container for a JPEG image

9 revalidate() called on this component will cause its parent JScrollPane to revalidate itself

```
      }

   public void paintComponent(Graphics g) {
      super.paintComponent(g);
      Dimension d = getSize();
      g.setColor(getBackground());
      g.fillRect(0, 0, d.width, d.height);
      if (m_bi != null)
         g.drawImage(m_bi, 0, 0, this);
   }

   public BufferedImage getBufferedImage() {
      return m_bi;
   }
}

//class SimpleFilter taken from chapter 14
```

13.4.6   Understanding the code

Class JPEGEditor

Class variables:

- Dimension VERTICAL_RIGID_SIZE: The size of the rigid area used for vertical spacing.
- Dimension HORIZONTAL_RIGID_SIZE: The size of the rigid area used for horizontal spacing.

Instance variables:

- File m_currentDir: The current directory navigated to by our JFileChooser.
- File m_currentFile: The JPEG image file currently in our editing environment.
- JFileChooser m_chooser: The file chooser used for loading and saving JPEGs.
- JPEGPanel m_panel: The custom component used to display JPEGs.
- JSlider m_slHorzDensity: The slider to choose horizontal pixel density.
- JSlider m_slVertDensity: The slider to choose vertical pixel density.
- JSlider m_slQuality: The slider to choose image quality.
- BufferedImage m_bi1: The original image.
- BufferedImage m_bi2: The modified image.

❶ JPEGEditor's constructor starts by instantiating our JFileChooser and applying a Simple-Filter (see chapter 14) file filter to it, in order to restrict file selection to JPEG images (files with a .jpg extension). The custom panel m_panel is used to display a JPEG image (see the JPEG-Panel class below) and it is added to a JScrollPane to provide scrolling capabilities. Three sliders are used to select JPEGEncodeParam properties as described above: xDensity, yDensity, and quality. Each is surrounded by a TitledBorder with an appropriate title. Similar to the previous example, RigidAreas are used to ensure proper spacing between the slider and the border. Each slider makes use of the Metal look and feel client property JSlider.isFilled with the value Boolean.TRUE to force the lower portion of each slider track to be filled.

The m_slQuality slider must represent values from 0 to 1.0. We scale this interval to [0, 100], but we display the annotation labels 0.0, 0.2, 0.4,...,1.0, which are stored in Hash-table labels. The selected image quality value is the slider's value divided by 100. Note the use of setExtent() for each slider in this example. The value of the extent property is used when the slider has focus and the user presses the PAGEUP or PAGEDN key to increment or decrement the slider's value, respectively.

2 The createToolBar() method creates and returns a JToolBar that contains five buttons: Open, Save, Save As, Apply, and Reset. Each receives its own ActionListener.

3 An Apply button is created and assigned an ActionListener to retrieve the current slider settings and apply them to the current JPEG image by calling our custom apply() method. Because of the large amount of work the apply method performs, it does not make sense to do this on-the-fly by listening for slider change events. A Reset button undoes any changes and returns the image to its original state by calling our custom reset() method. Finally, a JToolBar is created with our createToolBar() method.

4 The Open button brings up our JFileChooser for selecting a JPEG image file. After a successful selection, the current directory is stored in our m_currentDir variable for future use, and our custom openFile() method is invoked to load the image into our environment. The Save button invokes our custom saveFile() method to save the image currently in our environment. The Save As button instructs JFileChooser to prompt the user for a new name and possibly a location, to which to save the current image. This code is fairly similar to the code for the Open button, except that showSaveDialog() is used instead of show-OpenDialog(). If the selected file already exists, a request for confirmation is invoked using JOptionPane.showConfirmDialog(). (Interestingly, this is not a standard feature of JFile-Chooser—see chapter 14 for more about JFileChooser.) Finally, our saveFile() method is invoked to save the current image as the selected file.

The setCurrentFile() method stores a reference to the newly opened file in m_currentFile. This method also modifies the frame's title to display the file name. It is called whenever the Open and Save As buttons are activated.

5 The openFile() method opens a given File corresponding to a stored JPEG image. It first checks to see whether the selected file exists. If it does, a new thread is created to execute all remaining code in this method so as to avoid clogging up the event-dispatching thread. A FileInputStream is opened and a JPEGImageDecoder is created for the given file. Then a call to decodeAsBufferedImage() retrieves a BufferedImage from the JPEGImageDecoder and stores it in our m_bi1 variable. The file stream is closed and our image is passed to JPEGPanel by calling the reset() method (see below). Because our reset method directly modifies the state of Swing components, we place this call in a Runnable and send it to the event-dispatching queue with SwingUtilities.invokeLater() (see chapter 2 for more about invokeLater()).

6 The saveFile() method saves the current image in the given File. In a separate thread, a FileOutputStream is opened and a JPEGImageEncoder is created that correspond to this File. Then a call to the JPEGImageEncoder's encode() method saves the current image (retrieved by our JPEGPanel's getBufferedImage() method) to the opened stream.

7 The apply() method applies the current slider settings to the current image. In a separate thread, this method creates a ByteArrayOutputStream to stream the operations in memory. Then a JPEGImageEncoder is created for this stream, and a JPEGEncodeParam is retrieved that corresponds to the original image, m_bi1 (which is assigned in openFile()). Three property values are retrieved from our sliders and sent to a JPEGEncodeParam object via setXX() methods: quality, xDensity, and yDensity. (Note that quality is converted to a float through division by 100.0f). Then this JPEGEncodeParam object is assigned to our JPEGImageEncoder, and the encode() method is used to perform the actual encoding of the m_bi1 image. Next, a new image is retrieved from this encoder by first retrieving a Byte-ArrayInputStream from our ByteArrayOutputStream using its toByteArray() method. A JPEGImageDecoder is created for this stream, and the decodeAsBufferedImage() method retrieves a BufferedImage instance. Finally, in a Runnable sent to SwingUtilities.invokeLater(), this image is assigned to our image panel for display with JPEG-Panel's setBufferedImage() method.

The reset() method, as you might guess from its name, resets the current image to its original state (the state it was in when it was opened) and it resets the slider values.

Class JPEGPanel

8 JPEGPanel extends JPanel and provides a placeholder for JPEG images. It declares a single instance variable:

- BufferedImage m_bi: Holds the current JPEG.

The setBufferedImage() method assigns the given image to m_bi, and it changes this panel's preferred size to the size of that image. The panel is then revalidated and repainted to display the new image properly.

9 **NOTE** We learned in chapter 2 that when a revalidate() request is invoked on a component, all ancestors below the first ancestor whose validateRoot property is true get validated. JRootPane, JScrollPane, and JTextField are the only Swing components with a true validateRoot property by default. Thus, calling revalidate() on our JPEGPanel will result in validation of the JScrollPane it is contained in within our JPEGEditor application. JPEGPanel is then properly laid out and displayed; this would not occur by simply calling repaint().

The paintComponent() method clears the background and draws the current image (if there is one). The getBufferedImage() method simply returns the most recent image associated with this panel.

13.4.7   Running the code

Figure 13.6 shows JPEGEditor displaying a high-quality image of Earth. By applying our sliders to reduce the quality, and clicking the Apply button, we produce the image shown in figure 13.7. Saving this image as a new file gives us a representation that occupies much less disk space than the original. Making a decision on the balance between quality and size often needs to be done when space or latency issues are important.

GUIDELINE

Component selection   This example provides some tricky problems for the designer. The nature of the calculation means that instant feedback is not possible. However, the user needs to see what the result of a choice would mean. The Apply button solves the problem. This is justifiable in a case such as this due to the complex and time-consuming nature of the effect of the selection. Otherwise, we don't recommend it.

The shaded area on the sliders gives a clear indication that an amount or quantity rather than an exact, discrete value is being selected and that the amount is a percentage of the bounded whole. This helps the viewer understand what is happening.

13.5   *JProgressBar IN AN FTP CLIENT APPLICATION*

Example 13.5 uses a `JProgressBar` to display progress when downloading and uploading files using the File Transfer Protocol (FTP). Support for this protocol is provided in the `sun.net` and `sun.net.ftp` packages.

13.5.1   FtpClient

class sun.net.ftp.FtpClient

This class provides functionality for an FTP client. The methods particularly relevant to this example include the following:

- `FTPClient(String host)`: The constructor to create a new instance and connect to the given host address.
- `login(String user, String password)`: Login to an FTP host with the given username and password.
- `cd(String directory)`: Change the directory.
- `binary()`: Set the mode to binary for proper file transferring.
- `closeSever()`: Disconnect from the host.
- `list()`: Returns an `InputStream` that supplies the printout of the `ls -l` command (the list contents of the directories, one per line).
- `get(String filename)`: Returns an `InputStream` for retrieving the specified file from the host.
- `put(String filename)`: Returns an `OutputStream` for writing the specified file to the host.

NOTE   This application's GUI is laid out using our custom `DialogLayout2` layout manager, which we developed in chapter 4. Refer to chapter 4 for more information about how this manager works.

Figure 13.7 FTP client application with a JProgressBar to show the upload/download status

Example 13.5

FTPApp.java

see \Chapter13\5

```java
import java.awt.*;
import java.awt.event.*;
import java.util.*;
import java.io.*;
import java.net.*;
import java.lang.reflect.*;

import sun.net.ftp.*;
import sun.net.*;

import javax.swing.*;
import javax.swing.border.*;
import javax.swing.event.*;

import dl.*;

public class FTPApp extends JFrame {

    public static int BUFFER_SIZE = 2048;

    protected JTextField m_txtUser;
    protected JPasswordField m_txtPassword;
    protected JTextField m_txtURL;
    protected JTextField m_txtFile;
```

```
   protected JTextArea  m_monitor;
   protected JProgressBar m_progress;
   protected JButton m_btPut;
   protected JButton m_btGet;
   protected JButton m_btFile;
   protected JButton m_btClose;
   protected JFileChooser m_chooser;

   protected FtpClient m_client;
   protected String m_sLocalFile;
   protected String m_sHostFile;

   public FTPApp() {
      super("FTP Client");

      JPanel p = new JPanel();
      p.setLayout(new DialogLayout2(10, 5));
      p.setBorder(new EmptyBorder(10, 10, 10, 10));

      p.add(new JLabel("User name:"));
      m_txtUser = new JTextField("anonymous", 20);
      p.add(m_txtUser);

      p.add(new JLabel("Password:"));
      m_txtPassword = new JPasswordField(20);
      p.add(m_txtPassword);

      p.add(new JLabel("URL:"));
      m_txtURL = new JTextField(20);
      p.add(m_txtURL);

      p.add(new JLabel("Destination file:"));
      m_txtFile = new JTextField(20);
      p.add(m_txtFile);

      JPanel pp = new JPanel(new DialogLayout2(10, 5));
      pp.setBorder(new CompoundBorder(
         new TitledBorder(new EtchedBorder(), "Connection Monitor"),
         new EmptyBorder(3, 5, 3, 5)));

      m_monitor = new JTextArea(5, 20);
      m_monitor.setEditable(false);
      m_monitor.setLineWrap(true);
      m_monitor.setWrapStyleWord(true);
      JScrollPane ps = new JScrollPane(m_monitor);
      pp.add(ps);

      m_progress = new JProgressBar();
      m_progress.setStringPainted(true);
      m_progress.setBorder(new BevelBorder(BevelBorder.LOWERED,
         Color.white, Color.gray));
      m_progress.setMinimum(0);
      JPanel p1 = new JPanel(new BorderLayout());
      p1.add(m_progress, BorderLayout.CENTER);
      pp.add(p1);
      p.add(pp);
```

❶ Uses custom DialogLayout2 layout manager so that labels and text fields arranged opposite one another one pair per row

```java
m_btPut = new JButton("Put");
ActionListener lst = new ActionListener() {
   public void actionPerformed(ActionEvent e) {
      Thread uploader = new Thread() {
         public void run() {
            if (connect())
               putFile();
            disconnect();
         }
      };
      uploader.start();
   }
;
m_btPut.addActionListener(lst);
m_btPut.setMnemonic('p');
p.add(m_btPut);

m_btGet = new JButton("Get");
lst = new ActionListener() {
   public void actionPerformed(ActionEvent e) {
      Thread downloader = new Thread() {
         public void run() {
            if (connect())
               getFile();
            disconnect();
         }
      };
      downloader.start();
   }
};
m_btGet.addActionListener(lst);
m_btGet.setMnemonic('g');
p.add(m_btGet);

m_btFile = new JButton("File");
lst = new ActionListener() {
   public void actionPerformed(ActionEvent e) {
      if (m_chooser.showSaveDialog(FTPApp.this) !=
         JFileChooser.APPROVE_OPTION)
            return;
      File f = m_chooser.getSelectedFile();
      m_txtFile.setText(f.getPath());
   }
};
m_btFile.addActionListener(lst);
m_btFile.setMnemonic('f');
p.add(m_btFile);

m_btClose = new JButton("Close");
lst = new ActionListener() {
   public void actionPerformed(ActionEvent e) {
      if (m_client != null)
         disconnect();
```

2 ActionListener to upload a selected file

2 ActionListener to download a selected file

2 ActionListener allows user to select a local file or specify a new file name or location

2 ActionListener either disconnects from FT8 host or exits the application

```
          else
            System.exit(0);
    }
  };
  m_btClose.addActionListener(lst);
  m_btClose.setDefaultCapable(true);
  m_btClose.setMnemonic('g');
  p.add(m_btClose);

  getContentPane().add(p, BorderLayout.CENTER);
  pack();

  m_chooser = new JFileChooser();
  m_chooser.setDialogTitle(
    "Select File For Upload/Download");
  try {
    File dir = (new File(".")).getCanonicalFile();
    m_chooser.setCurrentDirectory(dir);
  } catch (IOException ex) {}
protected void setButtonStates(boolean state) {
  m_btPut.setEnabled(state);
  m_btGet.setEnabled(state);
  m_btFile.setEnabled(state);
}

protected boolean connect() {
  // Input validation
  String user = m_txtUser.getText();
  if (user.length()==0) {
    message("Please enter user name");
    return false;
  }
  String password = new String(m_txtPassword.getPassword());
  String sUrl = m_txtURL.getText();
  if (sUrl.length()==0) {
    message("Please enter URL");
    return false;
  }
  m_sLocalFile = m_txtFile.getText();
  if (m_sLocalFile.length()==0) {
    message("Please enter local file name");
    return false;
  }

  // Parse URL
  int index = sUrl.indexOf("//");
  if (index >= 0)
  sUrl = sUrl.substring(index+2);

  index = sUrl.indexOf("/");
  String host = sUrl.substring(0, index);
  sUrl = sUrl.substring(index+1);

  String sDir = "";
```

2 ActionListener
either disconnects
from FT8 host
or exits the
application

3 Connects to
specified host
with name and
password

```
index = sUrl.lastIndexOf("/");
if (index >= 0) {
   sDir = sUrl.substring(0, index);
   sUrl = sUrl.substring(index+1);
}
m_sHostFile = sUrl;

m_monitor.setText("");
setButtonStates(false);
m_btClose.setText("Cancel");
setCursor(Cursor.getPredefinedCursor(Cursor.WAIT_CURSOR));

try {
   m_progress.setIndeterminate(true);
   message("Connecting to host "+host);
   m_client = new FtpClient(host);
   m_client.login(user, password);
   message("User "+user+" login OK");
   message(m_client.welcomeMsg);
   m_client.cd(sDir);
   message("Directory: "+sDir);
   m_client.binary();
   return true;
}
catch (Exception ex) {
   message("Error: "+ex.toString());
   ex.printStackTrace();
   setButtonStates(true);
      return false;
   }
   finally {
      m_progress.setIndeterminate(false);
   }
}

protected void disconnect() {
   if (m_client != null) {
      try { m_client.closeServer(); }
      catch (IOException ex) {}
      m_client = null;
   }
   m_progress.setValue(0);
   setButtonStates(true);
   m_btClose.setText("Close");
   validate();
   setCursor(Cursor.getPredefinedCursor(
   Cursor.DEFAULT_CURSOR));
}

protected void getFile() {
   byte[] buffer = new byte[BUFFER_SIZE];
   try {
      int size = getFileSize(m_client, m_sHostFile);
      if (size > 0) {
```

③ Creates FtpClient object, logs in with user name and password, and sets "binary" mode

④ Downloads a pre-specified file

```java
      message("File " + m_sHostFile + ": " + size + " bytes");
      setProgressMaximum(size);
    }
    else
      message("File " + m_sHostFile + ": size unknown");

    File output = new File(m_sLocalFile);
    message("Output to "+output);
    FileOutputStream out = new FileOutputStream(output);

    InputStream in = m_client.get(m_sHostFile);
    int counter = 0;
    while(true) {
      int bytes = in.read(buffer);
      if (bytes < 0)
        break;

      out.write(buffer, 0, bytes);
      counter += bytes;
      if (size > 0) {
        setProgressValue(counter);
        int proc = (int) Math.round(m_progress.
          getPercentComplete() * 100);
        setProgressString(proc + " %");
      }
      else {
        int kb = counter/1024;
        setProgressString(kb + " KB");
      }
    }
    out.close();
    in.close();
  }
  catch (Exception ex) {
    message("Error: "+ex.toString());
    ex.printStackTrace();
  }
}

protected void putFile() {
  byte[] buffer = new byte[BUFFER_SIZE];
  try {
    File f = new File(m_sLocalFile);
    int size = (int)f.length();
    message("File " + m_sLocalFile + ": " + size + " bytes");
    setProgressMaximum (size);

    File input = new File(m_sLocalFile);
    FileInputStream in = new
      FileInputStream(input);
    OutputStream out = m_client.put(m_sHostFile);

    int counter = 0;
    while(true) {
      int bytes = in.read(buffer);
```

4 Reads file in 1,024 byte blocks

5 Uploads a specified file

5 Writes file in 1,024 byte blocks

```
            if (bytes < 0)
               break;
            out.write(buffer, 0, bytes);
            counter += bytes;
            setProgressValue(counter);
            int proc = (int) Math.round(m_progress.
               getPercentComplete() * 100);
            setProgressString(proc + " %");
         }

         out.close();
         in.close();
      }
      catch (Exception ex) {
         message("Error: " + ex.toString());
         ex.printStackTrace();
      }
   }

   protected void message(final String str) {
      if (str != null) {
         Runnable runner = new Runnable() {
            public void run() {
               m_monitor.append(str + '\n');
               m_monitor.repaint();
            }
         };
         SwingUtilities.invokeLater(runner);
      }
   }

   protected void setProgressValue(final int value) {
      Runnable runner = new Runnable() {
         public void run() {
            m_progress.setValue(value);
         }
      };
      SwingUtilities.invokeLater(runner);
   }

   protected void setProgressMaximum(final int value) {
      Runnable runner = new Runnable() {
         public void run() {
            m_progress.setMaximum(value);
         }
      };
      SwingUtilities.invokeLater(runner);
   }

   protected void setProgressString(final String string) {
      Runnable runner = new Runnable() {
         public void run() {
            m_progress.setString(string);
         }
```

⑤ Writes file in 1,024 byte blocks

```
        };
        SwingUtilities.invokeLater(runner);
    }

    public static void main(String argv[]) {
        FTPApp frame = new FTPApp();
        frame.setDefaultCloseOperation(JFrame.EXIT_ON_CLOSE);
        frame.setVisible(true);
    }

    public static int getFileSize(FtpClient client, String fileName)
        throws IOException {
        TelnetInputStream lst = client.list();
        String str = "";
        fileName = fileName.toLowerCase();
        while(true) {
            int c = lst.read();
            char ch = (char)c;
            if (c < 0 || ch == '\n') {
                str = str.toLowerCase();
                if (str.indexOf(fileName) >= 0) {
                    StringTokenizer tk = new StringTokenizer(str);
                    int index = 0;
                    while(tk.hasMoreTokens()) {
                        String token = tk.nextToken();
                        if (index == 4)
                            try {
                                return Integer.parseInt(token);
                            }
                            catch (NumberFormatException ex) {
                                return -1;
                            }
                        index++;
                    }
                }
                str = "";
            }
            if (c <= 0)
                break;
            str += ch;
        }
        return -1;
    }
}
```

Parses output of "ls -l" on remote host to get size of remote file **6**

13.5.2   Understanding the code

Class FTPApp

Class variable:

- int BUFFER_SIZE: The size of the buffer used for input/ouput operations.

Instance variables:

- `JTextField m_txtUser`: The login username text field.
- `JPasswordField m_txtPassword`: The login password field.
- `JTextField m_txtURL`: The field for the URL of the file to be downloaded/uploaded on the remote site.
- `JTextField m_txtFile`: The field for the file name of the file to be uploaded/downloaded on the local machine.
- `JTextArea m_monitor`: Used as a log to display various status messages.
- `JProgressBar m_progress`: Indicates the progress of an upload/download operation.
- `JButton m_btPut`: Initiates uploading.
- `JButton m_btGet`: Initiates downloading.
- `JButton m_btFile`: Brings up a file chooser dialog to choose a local file or to specify a file name and location.
- `JButton m_btClose`: Closes the application.
- `JFileChooser m_chooser`: Used to choose a local file or specify a file name and location.
- `FtpClient m_client`: The client connection to the host which manages I/O operations.
- `String m_sLocalFile`: The name of the most recent local file involved in a data transfer.
- `String m_sHostFile`: The name of the most recent host file involved in a data transfer.

1 The `FTPApp` constructor first creates a panel using a `DialogLayout2` layout manager, then it instantiates and adds our four text fields with corresponding labels (recall that our `Dialog-Layout2` manager requires that label/input field pairs are added in the specific label1, field1, label2, field2, ... order). The `m_monitor` text area is created and placed in a `JScrollPane`, and it is separated from the label/field panel. The `m_progress` `JProgressBar` is created and placed in a `JPanel` with a `BorderLayout` to ensure that `DialogLayout2` allows it to occupy the maximum width across the frame, as well as its preferred height.

2 Four buttons are created with attached `ActionListeners`. They are then added to the `DialogLayout2` panel, resulting in a horizontal row at the bottom of the frame. The button titled Put attempts to connect to a host using our `connect()` method. If it is successful, a new thread is started which calls `putFile()` to upload a selected file; it then calls `disconnect()` to terminate the connection to the host. Similarly, the button entitled Get attempts to connect to a host, and, if it is successful, it starts a thread which calls our `getFile()` method to download a file, then `disconnect()`. The button entitled File brings up our `JFileChooser` dialog to allow the user to select a local file or specify a new file name and location. The button entitled Close invokes `disconnect()` to terminate a connection to the host if an FTP transfer is in progress (if the `m_client` is not `null`). If a transfer is not in progress the application is terminated.

The `setButtonStates()` method takes a boolean parameter and enables/disables the Put, Get, and File buttons accordingly.

3 The `connect()` method establishes a connection to the remote host and returns `true` in the case of success, or `false` otherwise. This method first disables our Put, Get, and File push buttons, and it sets the text of the last button to "Cancel." This method then reads the contents of the text fields to obtain the login name, password, URL, and local file name. The URL is parsed and split into the host name, remote directory, and host file name. A new `FtpClient` instance is created to connect to the remote host, and it is stored in our m_client instance variable. Then the login() method is invoked on m_client to log in to the server using the specified username and password. If the login is successful, we change the remote directory and set the connection type to binary (which is almost always required for file transfers). If no exceptions have been thrown during this process, connect() returns true. Otherwise, it shows an exception in our m_monitor text area, re-enables our buttons, and returns false.

NOTE The connect() method code that connects to a host and changes the directory would be better off in a separate thread. We suggest this enhancement for more professional implementations. All other time-intensive code in this example is executed in separate threads.

The disconnect() method invokes closeServer() on the current m_client FTPClient instance if it is in use. It then sets the m_client reference to null, allowing garbage collection of the FTPClient object. This method also clears the progress bar component, enables all push buttons which may have been disabled by the connect() method, and restores the text of the Close button. All component updates are wrapped in a Runnable and sent to the event-dispatching queue with SwingUtilities.invokeLater().

4 The getFile() method downloads a prespecified file from the current host. While we attempt to connect to a server, the progress bar displays an animation letting the user know that something is happening. This is accomplished by setting the indeterminate property to true. If the name of the destination local file is not specified, the name of the remote file is used. This method tries to determine the size of the remote file by calling our getFile-Size() helper method (see below). If that succeeds, the file size is set as the maximum value of the progress bar (the minimum value is always 0) using our custom setProgressMaximum() method. Then a FileOutputStream is opened to write to the local file, and an InputStream is retrieved from the FTPClient to read from the remote file. A while loop is set up to perform typical read/write operations until all content of the remote file is written to the local file. During this process, the number of bytes read is accumulated in the counter local variable. If the size of the file is known, this number is assigned to the progress bar using our custom setProgressValue() method. We also calculate the percentage of download-ing that is complete with our custom getPercentComplete() method, and we display it in the progress bar using our custom setProgressString() method. If the size of the file is unknown (meaning it is less than or equal to 0), we can only display the number of kilobytes currently downloaded at any given time. To obtain this value we simply divide the current byte count, which is stored in the local counter variable, by 1024.

5 The putFile() method uploads the content of a local file to a remote pre-specified URL. If the name of the local file is not specified, a "Please enter file name" message is printed using our custom message() method, and we simply return. Otherwise, the size of the local file is determined and used as the maximum value of our progress bar using our custom setMaxi-mum() method (the minimum value is always 0). A FileInputStream is opened to read from the local file, and an OutputStream is retrieved from the FTPClient to write to the remote file. A while loop is set up to perform typical read/write operations until all the content of the local file is written to the remote host. During this process, the number of bytes written is accu-mulated in the counter local variable. This number is assigned to the progress bar using our custom setProgressValue() method. As in the getFile() method, we also calculate the percentage of downloading that is complete with our `getPercentComplete()` method, and we display it in the progress bar using our `setProgressString()` method. Since we can always determine the size of a local `File` object, there is no need to display the progress in terms of kilobytes as we did in `getFile()` above.

The `message()` method takes a `String` parameter to display in our m_monitor text area. The `setProgressValue()` and `setProgressMaximum()` methods assign selected and maximum values to our progress bar, respectively. Since each of these methods modifes the state of our progress bar component, and each is called from a custom thread, we wrap their bodies in `Runnables` and send them to the event-dispatching queue using `SwingUtilities.-invokeLater()`.

6 Unfortunately, the `FtpClient` class does not provide a direct way to determine either the size of a remote file or any other available file specifics. The only way we can get any information about files on the remote host using this class is to call its `list()` method, which returns a `TelnetInputStream` that supplies the printout of the results of an `ls -l` command. Our `getFileSize()` method uses this method in an attempt to obtain the length of a remote file specified by a given file name and `FTPClient` instance. This method captures the printout from the remote server, splits it into lines separated by "\n" characters, and uses a `StringTokenizer` to parse them into tokens. According to the syntax of the `ls -l` command output, the length of the file in bytes appears as the fifth token, and the last token contains the file name. So we go character by character through each line until a line containing a matching file name is found; the length is then returned to the caller. If this does not succeed, we return −1 to indicate that the server either does not allow its content to browsed, or that an error has occurred.

13.5.3   Running the code

Figure 13.7 shows `FTPApp` in action. Try running this application and transferring a few files. Start by entering your username and password, a URL containing the host FTP server, and (optionally) a local file name and path to act as the source or destination of a transfer. Click the Get button to download a specified remote file, or click the Put button to upload a specified local file to the host. If the required connection is established successfully, you will see the transfer progress updated incrementally in the progress bar.

In figure 13.7 we specified "anonymous" as the user name and we used an email address as the password. In our URL text field we specified the remote tutorial.zip file (the most recent Java Tutorial) on the ftp.javasoft.com FTP server in its docs directory. In our File text field, we specified tutorial.zip as the destination file in the current running directory. Clicking on Get establishes a connection, changes the remote directory to docs, determines the size of the remote tutorial.zip file, and starts retrieving and storing it as a local file in the current running directory. Try performing this transfer and watch how smoothly the progress bar updates itself (it can't hurt to keep a local copy of the Java Tutorial, but be aware that this archive is close to 10 megabytes).

> **NOTE**   In the next chapter we will customize `JFileChooser` to build a ZIP/JAR archive tool. This can be used to unpackage tutorial.zip if you do not have access to an appropriate tool.

C H A P T E R 1 4

Dialogs

14.1 DIALOGS AND CHOOSERS OVERVIEW

Swing's JDialog class allows the implementation of both modal and non-modal dialogs. In simple cases, when we need to post a short message or ask for a single value input, we can use standardized pre-built dialog boxes provided by the JOptionPane convenience class. Additionally, two special dialog classes provide powerful selection and navigation capabilities for choosing colors and files: JColorChooser and JFileChooser.

GUIDELINE

When to use a dialog Dialogs are intended for the acquisition of a set of inter-related data; for example, selecting a group of files and the type of action to perform on them. This may be the set of attributes for a particular object or group of objects. A dialog is particularly useful when validation across those attributes must be performed before the data can be accepted. The validation code can be executed when an Accept button is pressed, and the dialog will only dismiss when the data is validated as good.

Dialogs are also useful for complex manipulations or selections. For example, a dialog with two lists, "Available Players" and "Team for Saturday's Game," might allow the selection, addition, and deletion of items to and/or from each list. When the team for the Saturday game is selected, the user can accept the selection by clicking OK.

418

Data entry and complex data manipulation which requires a clear boundary or definition of acceptance are good uses for a dialog.

When to use an option pane   Option panes are best used when the system needs to hold a conversation with the user, either for simple directed data entry such as "Enter your name and password" or for navigation choices such as View, Edit, or Print.

When to use a chooser   Choosers facilitate consistency for common selections across a whole operating environment. If you need to select files or colors, you should use the appropriate chooser. The user gets the benefit of only learning one component which appears again and again across applications. Using a chooser when appropriate should improve customer acceptance of your application.

14.1.1   JDialog

class javax.swing.JDialog

This class extends `java.awt.Dialog` and is used to create a new dialog box in a separate native platform window. We typically extend this class to create our own custom dialog, as it is a container almost identical to `JFrame`.

NOTE   `JDialog` is a `JRootPane` container just like `JFrame`, and familiarity with chapter 3 is assumed here. All `WindowEvents`, default close operations, sizing and positioning, and so forth, can be controlled identically to `JFrame` and we will not repeat this material.

We can create a `JDialog` by specifying a dialog owner (`Frame` or `Dialog` instances), a dialog title, and a modal/non-modal state. We are not required to pass a valid parent, and we are free to use `null` as the parent reference. As we discussed in chapter 2, the `SwingUtilities` class maintains a non-visible `Frame` instance that is registered with the `AppContext` service mapping, which is used as the parent of all null-parent dialogs. If a valid parent is used, the dialog's icon will be that of the parent frame set with the `setIconImage()` method.

NOTE   As of Java 1.4 `JDialog` supports decorations (i.e., title bar, icons, borders, etc.) in the style of the current Look and Feel. To enable this for all `JDialogs` we use the following new static method:

```
JDialog.setDefaultLookAndFeelDecorated(true);
```

After the above method is called all newly instantiated `JDialogs` will have decorations in the style of the current look and feel. All those existing before this method was called will not be affected.

To enable this on a single `JDialog` instance we can do the following:

```
myJDialog.setUndecorated(true);
myJDialog.getRootPane().setWindowDecorationStyle(
    JRootPane.FRAME)
```

There are eight `JRootPane` constants used for the `windowDecorationStyle` property:

- `JRootPane.FRAME`
- `JRootPane.PLAIN_DIALOG`

- JRootPane.INFORMATION_DIALOG
- JRootPane.QUESTION_DIALOG
- JRootPane.ERROR_DIALOG
- JRootPane.WARNING_DIALOG
- JRootPane.COLOR_CHOOSER_DIALOG
- JRootPane.FILE_CHOOSER_DIALOG

Figure 14.1 shows eight JDialogs demonstrating each of the window decoration styles. Other than the close button and title bar icon in the FRAME style, the only differences between the other styles are color: FRAME, PLAIN_DIALOG, and INFORMATION_DIALOG are blue; QUESTION_DIALOG, COLOR_CHOOSER_DIALOG, and FILE_CHOOSER_DIALOG are green; WARNING_DIALOG is orange; ERROR_DIALOG is red.

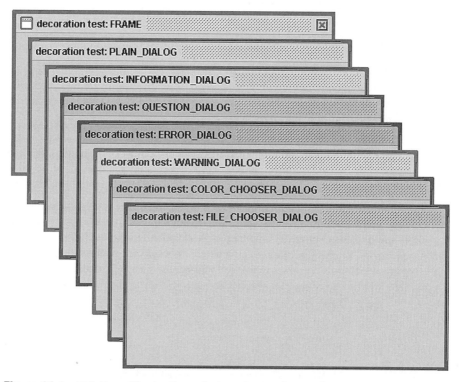

Figure 14.1 JDialogs illustrating window decoration styles

A modal dialog will not allow other windows to become active (respond to user input) at the same time that it is active. Modal dialogs also block the invoking thread of execution and do not allow it to continue until they are dismissed. Nonmodal dialogs do allow other windows to be active and do not affect the invoking thread.

To populate a dialog we use the same layout techniques discussed for JFrame, and we are prohibited from changing the layout or adding components directly. Instead we are expected to deal with the dialog's content pane.

From the design perspective, it is very common to add push buttons to a dialog. Typical buttons are OK or Save to continue with an action or save data, and Cancel or Close to close the dialog and cancel an action or avoid saving data.

As with JFrame, JDialog will appear in the upper left-hand corner of the screen unless another location is specified. It is usually more natural to use JDialog's setLocationRelativeTo- (Component c) method to center a dialog relative to a given component. If the component is not visible, the dialog will be centered relative to the screen.

> **NOTE** It is common practice to show dialogs in response to menu selections. In such cases, a menu's pop-up may remain visible and the parent frame needs to be manually repainted. Therefore, we suggest calling repaint() on the parent before displaying dialogs invoked by menus.

To display a JDialog window we can use either the show() method inherited from java.awt.Dialog or the setVisible() method inherited from java.awt.Component.

> **NOTE** When building complex dialogs, it is normally preferable that one instance of that dialog be used throughout a given Java session. We suggest instantiating such dialogs when the application/applet is started, and storing them as variables for repetitive use. This avoids the often significantly long delay time required to instantiate a dialog each time it is needed. We also suggest wrapping dialog instantiation in a separate thread to avoid clogging up the event-dispatching thread.

14.1.2   JOptionPane

class javax.swing.JOptionPane

This class provides an easy and convenient way to display the standard dialogs used for posting a message, asking a question, or prompting for simple user input. Each JOptionPane dialog is modal and will block the invoking thread of execution, as described above (this does not apply to internal dialogs; we will discuss these soon enough).

It is important to understand that JOptionPane is not itself a dialog (note that it directly extends JComponent). Rather, it acts as a container that is normally placed in a JDialog or a JInternalFrame, and it provides several convenient methods for doing so. There is nothing stopping us from creating a JOptionPane and placing it in any container we choose, but this will rarely be useful. Figure 14.2 illustrates the general JOptionPane component arrangement:

The JOptionPane class supports four pre-defined types: Message, Confirm, Input, and Option. We will discuss how to create and work with each type, but first we need to understand the constituents. To create a JOptionPane that is automatically placed in either a JDialog or JInternalFrame, we need to supply some or all of the following parameters to one if its static showXXDialog() methods (discussed below):

- A parent Component. If the parent is a Frame, the option pane will be placed in a JDialog and centered with respect to the parent. If this parameter is null, it will instead be centered with respect to the screen. If the parent is a JDesktopPane, or is contained in one, the option pane will be contained in a JInternalFrame and placed in the parent desktop's MODAL_LAYER (see chapter 15). For other types of parent components, a JDialog will be used and placed below that component on the screen.

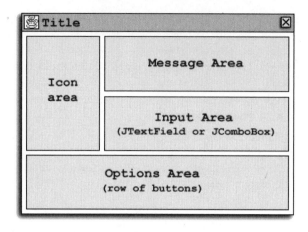

Figure 14.2
**The components
of a JOptionPane dialog**

- A message `Object` is a message to be displayed in the top right of the pane (in the Message area). Typically this is a `String` which may be broken into separate lines using "\n" characters. However this parameter has a generic `Object` type and `JOptionPane` deals with non-`String` objects in the following way:
  - `Icon`: This will be displayed in a `JLabel`.
  - `Component`: This will simply be placed in the message area.
  - `Object[]`: Dealt with as described here, these will be placed vertically in a column (this is done recursively).
  - `Object`: The `toString()` method will be called to convert this to a `String` for display in a `JLabel`.
- An `int` message type can be one of the following static constants defined in `JOptionPane`: `ERROR_MESSAGE`, `INFORMATION_MESSAGE`, `WARNING_MESSAGE`, `QUESTION_MESSAGE`, or `PLAIN_MESSAGE`. This is used by the current look and feel to customize the look of an option pane by displaying an appropriate icon (in the *Icon area*) corresponding to the message type's meaning.
- An `int` option type can be one of the following static constants defined in `JOptionPane`: `DEFAULT_OPTION`, `YES_NO_OPTION`, `YES_NO_CANCEL_OPTION`, or `OK_CANCEL_OPTION`. This parameter specifies a set of corresponding buttons to be displayed at the bottom of the pane (in the *Options area*). One of a set of similar parameters will be returned from `JOptionPane`'s `showXXDialog()` methods (see below) specifying which button was pressed: `CANCEL_OPTION`, `CLOSED_OPTION`, `NO_OPTION`, `OK_OPTION`, and `YES_OPTION`. Note that `CLOSED_OPTION` is only returned when the pane is contained in a `JDialog` or `JInternalFrame`, and that container's close button (located in the title bar) is pressed.
- An `Icon` is displayed in the left side of the pane (in the *Icon area*). If it's not explicitly specified, the icon is determined by the current look and feel based on the message type (this does not apply to panes using the `PLAIN_MESSAGE` message type).
- An array of option `Objects`. We can directly specify an array of option `Objects` to be displayed at the bottom of the pane (in the *Options area*). This array can also be specified with the `setOptions()` method. It typically contains an array of `Strings` to be displayed on a set of `JButtons`, but `JOptionPane` also honors `Icons` (which are also dis-

played in JButtons) and Components (which are placed directly in a row). Similar to message Objects, the toString() method will be called to convert all objects that are not Icons or Components to a String for display in a JButton. If null is used, the option buttons are determined by the specified option type.

- An initial value Object specifies which button or component in the *Options area* has the focus when the pane is initially displayed.

- An array of selection value Objects specifies an array of allowed choices the user can make. If this array contains more than twenty items, a JList is used to display them using the default rendering behavior (see chapter 10). If the array contains twenty or less items, a JComboBox is used to display them (also using the default JList rendering behavior). If null is used, an empty JTextField is displayed. In any case, the component used for selection is placed in the *Input area*.

- A String title is used for display as the title bar title in the parent JDialog or JInternalFrame.

The following static methods are provided for the convenient creation of JOptionPanes placed in JDialogs:

- showConfirmDialog(): This method displays a dialog with several buttons and returns an int option type corresponding to the button pressed. Four overloaded methods are provided that allow the specification of, at most, a parent component, message, title, option type, message type, and icon.

- showInputDialog(): This method displays a dialog which is intended to receive user input, and it returns a String if the input component is a text field, or an Object if the input component is a list or a combo box. Four overloaded methods are provided that allow the specification of, at most, a parent component, message, title, option type, message type, icon, array of possible selections, and an initially selected item. Two buttons are always displayed in the Options area: OK and Cancel.

JAVA 1.4 As of Java 1.4 there are two new showInputDialog() methods added to JOptionPane. One takes an Object as a parameter representing the message or question to display. The other takes two Objects, one representing the message or question and the other representing the initial input value the input field should contain. Neither of these methods takes a parent component, and by default they are centered with respect to the screen.

- showMessageDialog(): This method displays a dialog with an OK button, and it doesn't return anything. Three overloaded methods are provided that allow the specification of, at most, a parent component, message, title, message type, and icon.

- showOptionDialog(): This method displays a dialog which can be customized a bit more than the above dialogs, and it returns either the index into the array of option Objects specified, or an option type if no option Objects are specified. Only one method is provided that allows the specification of a parent component, message, title, option type, message type, icon, array of option Objects, and an option Object with the initial focus. The option Objects are laid out in a row in the Options area.

To create JOptionPanes contained in JInternalFrames rather than JDialogs, we can use the showInternalConfirmDialog(), showInternalInputDialog(), showInternal-

MessageDialog(), and showInternalOptionDialog() overloaded methods. These work the same as the methods described above, only they expect that a given parent is a JDesktop-Pane (or has a JDesktopPane ancestor).

NOTE   Internal dialogs are not modal and, as such, do not block execution of the invoking thread.

Alternatively, we can directly create a JOptionPane as illustrated by the following pseudo-code:

```
JOptionPane pane = new JOptionPane(...); // Specify parameters

pane.setXX(...); // Set additional properties

JDialog dialog = pane.createDialog(parent, title);
dialog.show();

// Process result (may be null)
Object result = pane.getValue();
```

This code creates an instance of JOptionPane and specifies several parameters (see the API documentation). Additional settings are then provided with setXX accessor methods. The createDialog() method creates a JDialog instance that contains our JOptionPane which is then displayed (we could also have used the createInternalFrame() method to wrap our pane in a JInternalFrame). Finally, the getValue() method retrieves the option selected by the user, so the program may react accordingly. This value may be null (if the user closes the dialog window). Because program execution blocks until the dialog is dismissed, getValue() will not be called until a selection is made.

NOTE   The advantage of JOptionPane is its simplicity and convenience. In general, you shouldn't need to customize it to any large extent. If you find yourself needing a different layout, we suggest writing your own container instead.

Figure 14.3 illustrates the use of JOptionPane where a custom dialog may be more suitable. Note the extremely long button, text field, and combo box. Such extreme sizes have detrimental effects on the overall usability and appearance of an application.

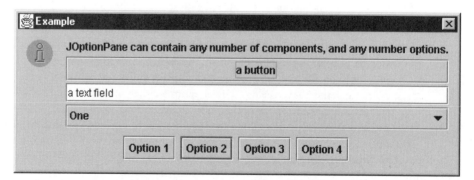

Figure 14.3   Awkward use of components in a JOptionPane (from the SwingSet demo)

CHAPTER 14   DIALOGS

GUIDELINE

JOptionPane JOptionPane is not designed as a general purpose input dialog. The primary restriction is the defined layout. JOptionPane is designed for use in conversations between the system and the user where the desired result is a navigation choice or a data selection, or where the user must be notified of an event.

Therefore, JOptionPane is best used with a single entry field or combo box selection, possibly with a set of buttons for selection or navigational choice.

For example, an Answer Phone application might require an option dialog displaying "You have 1 message," with options Play, Save, Record outgoing message, and Delete messages. Such a requirement can be met with a JOptionPane which provides a single label for the message and four buttons for each of the available choices.

14.1.3 JColorChooser

class javax.swing.JColorChooser

This class represents a powerful, pre-built component that is used for color selection. JColorChooser is normally used in a modal dialog. It consists of a tabbed pane containing three panels, each offering a different method of choosing a color: Swatches, HSB, and RGB. A color preview pane is displayed below this tabbed pane and it always displays the currently selected color. Figure 14.4 illustrates.

The static showDialog() method instantiates and displays a JColorChooser in a modal dialog, and returns the selected Color (or null if no selection is made):

```
Color color = JColorChooser.showDialog(myComponent,
  "Color Chooser", Color.red);
if (color != null)
  myComponent.setBackground(c);
```

A more complex variant is the static createDialog() method which allows two Action-Listeners to be invoked when a selection is made or canceled. We can also do the following:

- Retrieve color selection panels with the getChooserPanels() method.
- Add custom color selection panels using the addChooserPanel() method.
- Assign a new custom color preview pane using the setPreviewPanel() method.

Several classes and interfaces (discussed below) that support JColorChooser are grouped into the javax.swing.colorchooser package.

14.1.4 The ColorSelectionModel interface

abstract interface javax.swing.colorchooser.ColorSelectionModel

This is a simple interface describing the color selection model for JColorChooser. It declares methods for adding and removing ChangeListeners which are intended to be notified when the selected Color changes, and getSelectedColor()/setSelectedColor() accessors to retrieve and assign the currently selected Color, respectively.

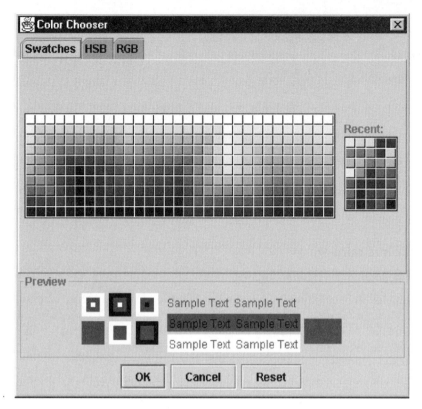

Figure 14.4 `JColorChooser` in a `JDialog`

14.1.5   DefaultColorSelectionModel

class javax.swing.colorchooser.DefaultColorSelectionModel

This is the default concrete implementation of the `ColorSelectionModel` interface. It simply implements the necessary methods as expected, stores registered `ChangeListeners` in an `EventListenerList`, and implements an additional method to perform the actual firing of `ChangeEvents` to all registered listeners.

14.1.6   AbstractColorChooserPanel

abstract class javax.swing.colorchooser.AbstractColorChooserPanel

This abstract class describes a color chooser panel which can be added to `JColorChooser` as a new tab. We can subclass `AbstractColorChooserPanel` to implement a custom color chooser panel of our own. The two most important methods that must be implemented are `buildChooser()` and `updateChooser()`. The former is normally called only once at instantiation time and is intended to perform all GUI initialization tasks. The latter is intended to update the panel to reflect a change in the associated `JColorChooser`'s `ColorSelection-Model`. Other required methods include those allowing access to a display name and icon which are used to identify the panel when it is displayed in `JColorChooser`'s tabbed pane.

14.1.7 ColorChooserComponentFactory

class javax.swing.colorchooser.ColorChooserComponentFactory

This is a very simple class that is responsible for creating and returning instances of the default color chooser panels and the preview pane used by JColorChooser. The three color chooser panels are instances of private classes: DefaultSwatchChooserPanel, DefaultRGBChooser-Panel, and DefaultHSBChooserPanel. The preview pane is an instance of Default-PreviewPane. Other private classes used in the colorchooser package include two custom layout managers, CenterLayout and SmartGridLayout; a class for convenient generation of synthetic images, SyntheticImage; and a custom text field that only allows integer input, JIntegerTextField. These undocumented classes are very interesting and we urge curious readers to spend some time with the source code. Because they are only used within the color-chooser package and are defined as a package private, we will not discuss them further here.

14.1.8 JFileChooser

class javax.swing.JFileChooser

This class represents the standard Swing directory navigation and file selection component which is normally used in a modal dialog. It consists of a JList and JTable and several button and input components all linked together to offer functionality similar to the file dialogs we are used to on our native platforms. The JList and JTable are used to display a list of files and subdirectories residing in the current directory being navigated. Figures 14.5 and 14.6 illustrate.

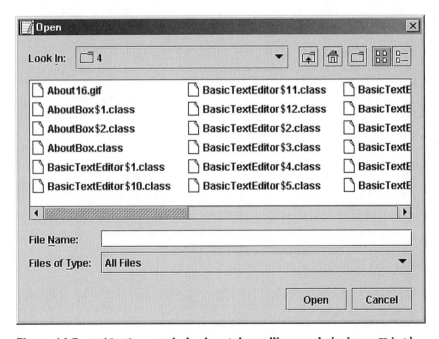

Figure 14.5 JFileChooser in horizontal scrolling mode (using a JList)

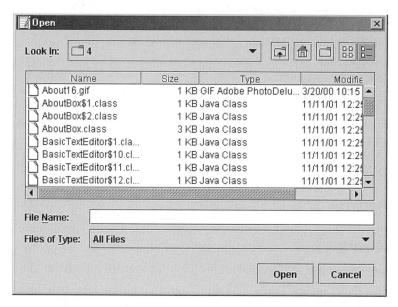

Figure 14.6 `JFileChooser` **in row mode (using a** `JTable`**)**

Cross-application consistency   The key reason for promoting the use of a standard file chooser dialog is to promote the consistency of such an operation across the whole operating system or machine environment. The user's experience is improved because file selection is always the same no matter which application he is running. This is an important goal and is worthy of recognition. Thus, if you have a requirement to manipulate files, you ought to be using the `JFileChooser` component.

The fact that such a reusable component exists and that much of the complex coding is provided as part of the implementation is merely a bonus for the developer.

We can set the current directory by passing a `String` to its `setCurrentDirectory()` method. `JFileChooser` also has the ability to use special `FileFilters` (discussed below) to allow navigation of only certain types of files. Several properties control whether directories and/ or files can be navigated and selected, and how the typical Open (*approve*) and Cancel (*cancel*) buttons are represented (see the API documentation for more on these straightforward methods.)

JAVA 1.3   As of Java 1.3 `JFileChooser` allows us to specify whether the control buttons (i.e. Cancel and Approve buttons) are shown or not with the `setControlButton-sAreShown()` method.

To use this component, we normally create an instance of it, set the desired options, and call `showDialog()` to place it in an active modal dialog. This method takes the parent component and the text to display for its Approve button as parameters. Calling `showOpenDialog()` or `showSaveDialog()` will show a modal dialog with Open or Save for the Approve button text.

NOTE   JFileChooser can take a significant amount of time to instantiate. Consider storing an instance as a variable and performing instantiation in a separate thread at startup time.

The following code instantiates a JFileChooser in an Open file dialog, verifies that a valid file is selected, and retrieves that file as a File instance:

```
JFileChooser chooser = new JFileChooser();
chooser.setCurrentDirectory(".");
if (chooser.showOpenDialog(myComponent) !=
  JFileChooser.APPROVE_OPTION)
    return;
File file = chooser.getSelectedFile();
```

JAVA 1.4   As of Java 1.4 JFileChooser allows multiple file selection (a problem we worked around in the first edition using brute force) with the new setMultiSelection-Enabled() method. The getSelectedFiles() method returns a File array representing the files selected.

JFileChooser generates PropertyChangeEvents when any of its properties change state. The Approve and Cancel buttons generate ActionEvents when they are pressed. We can register PropertyChangeListeners and ActionListeners to receive these events respectively. As any well-defined JavaBean should, JFileChooser defines several static String constants corresponding to each property name; JFileChooser.FILE_FILTER_CHANGED _PROPERTY is one example (see the API documentation for a full listing). We can use these constants in determining which property a JFileChooser-generated PropertyChangeEvent corresponds to.

JFileChooser also supports the option of inserting an *accessory* component. This component can be any component we want and it will be placed to the right of the JList. In constructing such a component, we are normally expected to implement the PropertyChangeListener interface. This way the component can be registered with the associated JFileChooser to receive notification of property state changes. The component should use these events to update its state accordingly. We use the setAccessory() method to assign an accessory component to a JFileChooser, and addPropertyChangeListener() to register it for receiving property state change notification.

REFERENCE   For a good example of an accessory component used to preview selected images, see the FileChooserDemo example that ships with Java 2. In the final example of this chapter, we will show how to customize JFileChooser in a more direct mannar.

Several classes and interfaces related to JFileChooser are grouped into the javax. swing.filechooser package.

NOTE   JFileChooser is still somewhat incomplete. For example, multi-selection mode is specified, but it has not been implemented yet. Later in this chapter we will show how to work around this, as well as how to build our own accessory-like component in a location different from that of a normal accessory.

14.1.9   FileFilter

abstract class javax.swing.filechooser.FileFilter

This abstract class is used to implement a filter for displaying only certain file types in `JFile-Chooser`. Two methods must be implemented in concrete subclasses:

- `boolean accept(File f)`: Returns `true` if the given file should be displayed, `false` otherwise.
- `String getDescription()`: Returns a description of the filter used in the `JComboBox` at the bottom of `JFileChooser`.

To manage `FileFilters`, we can use several methods in `JFileChooser`, including these:

- `addChoosableFileFilter(FileFilter f)`: Adds a new filter.
- `removeChoosableFileFilter(FileFilter f)`: Removes an existing filter.
- `setFileFilter(FileFilter f)`: Sets a filter as currently active (and adds it, if necessary).

By default in Java 1.2, `JFileChooser` uses a filter that accepts all files. Special effort must be made to remove this filter if we do not want our application to accept all files:

```
FileFilter ft = myChooser.getAcceptAllFileFilter();
myChooser.removeChoosableFileFilter(ft);
```

JAVA 1.3   As of Java 1.3 `JFileChooser` allows us to specify whether or not the accept all file filter appears with the `setAcceptAllFileFilterUsed()` method.

So how do we create a simple file filter instance to allow navigation and selection of only certain file types? The following class can be used as a template for defining most of our own filters, and we will see it used in this and future chapters:

```
class SimpleFilter extends FileFilter
{
  private String m_description = null;
  private String m_extension = null;

  public SimpleFilter(String extension, String description) {
    m_description = description;
    m_extension = "." + extension.toLowerCase();
  }

  public String getDescription() {
    return m_description;
  }

  public boolean accept(File f) {
    if (f == null)
      return false;
    if (f.isDirectory())
      return true;
    return f.getName().toLowerCase().endsWith(m_extension);
  }
}
```

This filter only shows files that match the given extension `String` that is passed into our constructor and stored as variable `m_extension`. In more robust, multipurpose filters we might store an array of legal extensions, and check for each in the `accept()` method.

NOTE   The `SimpleFilter` `accept()` method always returns `true` for directories because we normally want to be able to navigate any directory.

Notice that the description `String` passed into the constructor, and stored as the variable `m_description`, is the `String` shown in the combo box at the bottom of `JFileChooser` representing the corresponding file type. `JFileChooser` can maintain multiple filters, all added using the `addChoosableFileFilter()` method, and removable with its `removeChoosableFileFilter()` method.

14.1.10   FileSystemView

abstract class javax.swing.filechooser.FileSystemView

This class includes functionality which extracts information about files, directories, and partitions, and supplies this information to the `JFileChooser` component. This class is used to make `JFileChooser` independent from both platform-specific file system information, and the JDK/Java 2 release version (since the JDK1.1 `File` API doesn't allow access to more specific file information available in Java 2). We can provide our own `FileSystemView` subclass and assign it to a `JFileChooser` instance using the `setFileSystemView(FileSystem-View fsv)` method. Four abstract methods must be implemented:

- `createNewFolder(File containingDir)`: Creates a new folder (directory) within the given folder.
- `getRoots()`: Returns all root partitions. The notion of a root differs significantly from platform to platform.
- `isHiddenFile(File f)`: Returns whether the given `File` is hidden.
- `isRoot(File f)`: Returns whether the given `File` is a partition or drive.

These methods are called by `JFileChooser` and `FileFilter` implementations. We will, in general, have no need to extend this class unless we need to tweak the way `JFileChooser` interacts with our operating system. The static `getFileSystemView()` method currently returns a Unix- or Windows-specific instance for use by `JFileChooser` in the most likely event that one of these platform types is detected. Otherwise, a generic instance is used. Support for Macintosh, OS2, and several other operating systems is expected to be provided in future releases.

14.1.11   FileView

abstract class javax.swing.filechooser.FileView

This abstract class is used to provide customized information about files and their types (typically determined by the file extension), including icons and a string description. Each look and feel provides its own subclass of `FileView`, and we can construct our own `FileView` subclass fairly easily. Each of the five methods in this class is abstract and must be implemented by subclasses. The following generalized template can be used when creating our own `FileViews`:

```
class MyExtView extends FileView
{
  // Store icons to use for list cell renderer.
  protected static ImageIcon MY_EXT_ICON =
    new ImageIcon("myexticon.gif");
  protected static ImageIcon MY_DEFAULT_ICON =
    new ImageIcon("mydefaulticon.gif");

  // Return the name of a given file. "" corresponds to
  // a partition, so in this case we must return the path.
  public String getName(File f) {
    String name = f.getName();
    return name.equals("") ? f.getPath() : name;
  }

  // Return the description of a given file.
  public String getDescription(File f) {
    return getTypeDescription(f);
  }

  // Return the String to use for representing each specific
  // file type.  (Not used by JFileChooser in Java 2 FCS.)
  public String getTypeDescription(File f) {
    String name = f.getName().toLowerCase();
    if (name.endsWith(".ext"))
      return "My custom file type";
    else
      return "Unrecognized file type";
  }

  // Return the icon to use for representing each specific
  // file type in JFileChooser's JList cell renderer.
  public Icon getIcon(File f) {
    String name = f.getName().toLowerCase();
    if (name.endsWith(".ext"))
      return MY_EXT_ICON;
    else
      return MY_DEFAULT_ICON;
  }

  // Normally we should return true for directories only.
  public Boolean isTraversable(File f) {
    return (f.isDirectory() ? Boolean.TRUE : Boolean.FALSE);
  }
}
```

We will see how to build a custom `FileView` for JAR and ZIP archive files in the final example of this chapter.

14.2 CONSTRUCTING A LOGIN DIALOG

Numerous readers of the first edition have asked in our forum for example code of a login dialog. We've added this example as a simple beginning to those looking to build their own

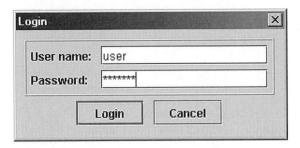

Figure 14.7
Login dialog with text
and password field

login dialog. A small module is used to verify name and password, and only a limited number of unsuccessful attempts are allowed before the application exits.

Example 14.1

LoginDialog.java

see \Chapter14\1

```java
import java.awt.*;
import java.awt.event.*;
import java.io.*;
import java.util.*;

import javax.swing.*;
import javax.swing.border.*;
import javax.swing.event.*;

import dl.*;

public class LoginDialog extends JDialog {
    private boolean m_succeeded = false;
    private JTextField m_loginNameBox;
    private JPasswordField m_passwordBox;

    private String m_loginName;
    private String m_password;

    private int m_errCounter = 0;

    public LoginDialog(Frame parent) {
        super(parent, "Login", true);

        JPanel pp = new JPanel(new DialogLayout2());
        pp.setBorder(new CompoundBorder(
            new EtchedBorder(EtchedBorder.RAISED),
            new EmptyBorder(5,5,5,5)));

        pp.add(new JLabel("User name:"));
        m_loginNameBox = new JTextField(16);
        pp.add(m_loginNameBox);

        pp.add(new JLabel("Password:"));
        m_passwordBox = new JPasswordField(16);
```

```
pp.add(m_passwordBox);

JPanel p = new JPanel(new DialogLayout2());
p.setBorder(new EmptyBorder(10, 10, 10, 10));
p.add(pp);

ActionListener lst = new ActionListener() {
  public void actionPerformed(ActionEvent evt) {
    m_loginName = m_loginNameBox.getText();
    m_password = new String(m_passwordBox.getPassword());

    if (!LoginModule.login(m_loginName, m_password)) {
      JOptionPane.showMessageDialog(LoginDialog.this,
        "System cannot login", "Login Error",
        JOptionPane.ERROR_MESSAGE);

      if (++m_errCounter >= LoginModule.MAX_LOGIN_ATTEMPTS) {
        System.out.println("All login attempts failed");
        System.exit(1);
      }
      else {
        m_passwordBox.setText("");
        return;// Try one more time
      }
    }

    // If we get here, login was successful
    m_succeeded = true;
    dispose();
  }
};

JButton saveButton = new JButton("Login");
saveButton.addActionListener(lst);
getRootPane().setDefaultButton(saveButton);
getRootPane().registerKeyboardAction(lst,
  KeyStroke.getKeyStroke(KeyEvent.VK_ENTER, 0),
  JComponent.WHEN_IN_FOCUSED_WINDOW);
p.add(saveButton);

JButton cancelButton = new JButton("Cancel");
lst = new ActionListener() {
  public void actionPerformed(ActionEvent evt) {
    dispose();
  }
};
cancelButton.addActionListener(lst);
getRootPane().registerKeyboardAction(lst,
  KeyStroke.getKeyStroke(KeyEvent.VK_ESCAPE, 0),
  JComponent.WHEN_IN_FOCUSED_WINDOW);
p.add(cancelButton);

getContentPane().add(p, BorderLayout.CENTER);
pack();
setResizable(false);
setLocationRelativeTo(parent);
```

1 Login button set as default button and **ENTER** keystroke registered to invoke login button's **ActionListener**

1 Escape keystroke registered to invoke cancel button's **ActionListener**

```
  }

  public boolean succeeded() {
    return m_succeeded;
  }

  public String getLoginName() {
    return m_loginName;
  }

  public String getPassword() {
    return m_password;
  }

  public static void main( String args[] ) {
    LoginDialog dlg = new LoginDialog(null);
    dlg.show();
    if (!dlg.succeeded()) {
      System.out.println("User cancelled login");
      System.exit(1);
    }
    System.out.println("User "+dlg.getLoginName()+" has logged in");
    System.exit(0);
  }

}

class LoginModule {
  public static final int MAX_LOGIN_ATTEMPTS = 3;

  public static boolean login(String userName, String password) {
    return userName.equalsIgnoreCase("user") &&
      password.equalsIgnoreCase("welcome");
  }
}
```

14.2.1 Understanding the code

Class LoginDialog

This dialog uses a `DialogLayout2` (described in chapter 4) to lay out its components: `JText-Field m_loginNameBox` to enter user's name, `JPasswordField m_passwordBox` to enter user's password, and two buttons used to proceed with a login or cancel. The Login button retrieves the data entered and calls the static `LoginModule.login()` in an attempt to login. If that operation is successful, the dialog will be disposed. Otherwise an error message is shown. If the number of unsuccessful attempts exceeds `LoginModule.MAX_LOGIN_ATTEMPTS` we shut down the application.

Note that the Login button is set as the *default* button. Also, a keyboard event is registered so that the login button will be effectively be pressed whenever ENTER is pressed. Similarly, the Cancel button will be effectively pressed whenever the ESCAPE key is pressed.

The `succeeded()` method returns the status of the login operation. The calling application must examine this status before continuing.

Class LoginModule

This class emulates a login layer with allowed username "user" and password "welcome". A real system would do something like connect to the database of an LDAP system to verify the user and password information.

14.2.2 Running the code

Run this example several times to observe its behavior when ESCAPE and ENTER are pressed. Try entering incorrect values for username and password and note the error message that is displayed. Keep doing this to verify that the maximum number of failed attempts feature works and the application exits. Enter username "user" and password "welcome" and the dialog is disposed indicating that the login was successful.

14.3 ADDING AN ABOUT DIALOG

Most GUI applications have at least one About dialog, usually modal, which often displays copyright, company, and other important information such as product name, version number, and authors. Example 14.2 illustrates how to add such a dialog to our text editor example we developed in chapter 12. We build a subclass of JDialog, populate it with some simple components, and store it as a variable which can be shown and hidden indefinitely without having to instantiate a new dialog each time it is requested. We also implement centering so that whenever the dialog is shown, it will appear in the center of our application's frame.

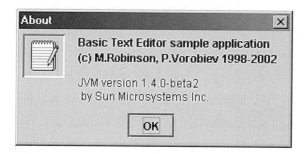

Figure 14.8
A typical About dialog

Example 14.2

BasicTextEditor.java

see \Chapter14\2

```
import java.awt.*;
import java.awt.event.*;
import java.io.*;
import java.util.*;

import javax.swing.*;
import javax.swing.event.*;
import javax.swing.border.*;
```

```java
public class BasicTextEditor extends JFrame
{
   // Unchanged code from example 12.4

   public BasicTextEditor() {
      super("\"About\" BasicTextEditor");
      setSize(450, 350);

      // Unchanged code from example 12.4
   }

   protected JMenuBar createMenuBar() {
      // Unchanged code from example 12.4

      JMenu mHelp = new JMenu("Help");
      mHelp.setMnemonic('h');

      Action actionAbout = new AbstractAction("About",
         new ImageIcon("About16.gif")) {
            public void actionPerformed(ActionEvent e) {
               AboutBox dlg = new AboutBox(BasicTextEditor.this);
               dlg.show();
            }
         };
      item =  mHelp.add(actionAbout);
      item.setMnemonic('a');
      menuBar.add(mHelp);

      getContentPane().add(m_toolBar, BorderLayout.NORTH);
      return menuBar;
   }

   // Unchanged code from example 12.4
}

class AboutBox extends JDialog {

   public AboutBox(Frame owner) {
      super(owner, "About", true);

      JLabel lbl = new JLabel(new ImageIcon("icon.gif"));
      JPanel p = new JPanel();
      Border b1 = new BevelBorder(BevelBorder.LOWERED);
      Border b2 = new EmptyBorder(5, 5, 5, 5);
      lbl.setBorder(new CompoundBorder(b1, b2));
      p.add(lbl);
      getContentPane().add(p, BorderLayout.WEST);

      String message = "Basic Text Editor sample application\n"+
         "(c) M.Robinson, P.Vorobiev 1998-2001";
      JTextArea txt = new JTextArea(message);
      txt.setBorder(new EmptyBorder(5, 10, 5, 10));
      txt.setFont(new Font("Helvetica", Font.BOLD, 12));
      txt.setEditable(false);
      txt.setBackground(getBackground());
      p = new JPanel();
      p.setLayout(new BoxLayout(p, BoxLayout.Y_AXIS));
```

New "Help" menu with "About" menu item that displays about dialog **1**

```
            p.add(txt);

            message = "JVM version " +
                System.getProperty("java.version") + "\n"+
                " by " + System.getProperty("java.vendor");
            txt = new JTextArea(message);
            txt.setBorder(new EmptyBorder(5, 10, 5, 10));
            txt.setFont(new Font("Arial", Font.PLAIN, 12));
            txt.setEditable(false);
            txt.setLineWrap(true);
            txt.setWrapStyleWord(true);
            txt.setBackground(getBackground());
            p.add(txt);

            getContentPane().add(p, BorderLayout.CENTER);

            final JButton btOK = new JButton("OK");
            ActionListener lst = new ActionListener() {
                public void actionPerformed(ActionEvent e) {
                    dispose();
                }
            };
            btOK.addActionListener(lst);
            p = new JPanel();
            p.add(btOK);
            getRootPane().setDefaultButton(btOK);
            getRootPane().registerKeyboardAction(lst,
                KeyStroke.getKeyStroke(KeyEvent.VK_ENTER, 0),
            JComponent.WHEN_IN_FOCUSED_WINDOW);
            getContentPane().add(p, BorderLayout.SOUTH);

            WindowListener wl = new WindowAdapter() {
                public void windowOpened(WindowEvent e) {
                    btOK.requestFocus();
                }
            };
            addWindowListener(wl);

            pack();
            setResizable(false);
        setLocationRelativeTo(owner);
    }
}
```

WindowListener transfers focus to "OK" button as soon as the About dialog is made visible ②

14.3.1 Understanding the code

Class BasicTextEditor

① The createMenuBar() method is modified by adding a new Help menu containing an About menu item. This menu item is created as an Action implementation, and its action-Performed() method creates our About dialog.

Class AboutBox

This class extends `JDialog` to implement our custom About dialog. The constructor creates a modal `JDialog` instance titled About Swing Menu, and populates it with some simple components. A large icon is placed in the left side and two `JTextAreas` are placed in the center to display multiline text messages with different fonts. A push button titled OK is placed at the bottom. Its `ActionListener`'s `actionPerformed()` method invokes `setVisible(false)` when pressed.

❷ A `WindowListener` is added which transfers focus to the OK button as soon as the dialog is made visible.

> **NOTE**   We could have constructed a similar About dialog using a `JOptionPane` message dialog. However, the point of this example is to demonstrate the basics of custom dialog creation, which we will be using later in chapter 20 to create several complex custom dialogs that could not be derived from `JOptionPane`.

14.3.2   Running the code

Select the About menu item which brings up the dialog shown in figure 14.8. This dialog serves only to display information, and has no functionality other than the OK button which hides it. Note that no matter where the parent frame lies on the screen, when the dialog is invoked it appears centered.

14.4   *JOPTIONPANE MESSAGE DIALOGS*

Message dialogs provided by the `JOptionPane` class can be used for many purposes in Swing applications: to post a message, ask a question, or get simple user input. Example 14.3 brings up several message boxes of different types with a common Shakespeare theme. Both internal and regular dialogs are constructed, demonstrating how to use the convenient `showXXDialog()` methods (see section 14.1.2), as well as how to manually create a `JOptionPane` component and place it in a dialog or internal frame for display. Each dialog is instantiated as needed and we perform no caching here (for purposes of demonstration). A more professional implementation might instantiate each dialog at startup and store them as variables for use throughout the application's lifetime.

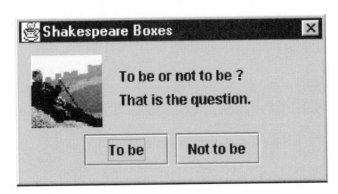

Figure 14.9
A `JOptionPane` with custom icon, message, and option button strings in a `JDialog`

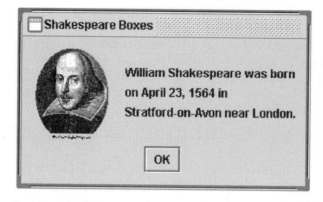

Figure 14.10
A `JOptionPane` **with custom icon and message in a** `JInternalFrame`

Example 14.3

DialogBoxes.java

see \Chapter14\3

```java
import java.awt.*;
import java.awt.event.*;

import javax.swing.*;

public class DialogBoxes extends JFrame
{
  static final String BOX_TITLE = "Shakespeare Boxes";

  public DialogBoxes() {
    super(BOX_TITLE);
    setSize(400,300);
    setLayeredPane(new JDesktopPane());

    JMenuBar menuBar = createMenuBar();
    setJMenuBar(menuBar);

}

  protected JMenuBar createMenuBar() {
    JMenuBar menuBar = new JMenuBar();

    JMenu mFile = new JMenu("File");
    mFile.setMnemonic('f');

    JMenuItem mItem = new JMenuItem("Ask Question");
    mItem.setMnemonic('q');
    ActionListener lst = new ActionListener() {
      public void actionPerformed(ActionEvent e) {
        JOptionPane pane = new JOptionPane(
          "To be or not to be ?\nThat is the question.");
        pane.setIcon(new ImageIcon("Hamlet.gif"));
        Object[] options =
          new String[] {"To be", "Not to be"};
        pane.setOptions(options);
```

1 Constructor creates empty frame with menu bar

2 Creates menus and actions which will create various dialogs

3 Question dialog with custom buttons

```
        JDialog dialog = pane.createDialog(
        DialogBoxes.this, BOX_TITLE);
        dialog.show();
        Object obj = pane.getValue();
        int result = -1;
        for (int k=0; k<options.length; k++)
          if (options[k].equals(obj))
        result = k;
        System.out.println("User's choice: "+result);
    }
};
mItem.addActionListener(lst);
mFile.add(mItem);

mItem = new JMenuItem("Info Message");
mItem.setMnemonic('i');
lst = new ActionListener() {
  public void actionPerformed(ActionEvent e) {
    String message = "William Shakespeare was born\n"+
      "on April 23, 1564 in\n"
      +"Stratford-on-Avon near London";
    JOptionPane pane = new JOptionPane(message);
    pane.setIcon(new ImageIcon("Shakespeare.gif"));
    JInternalFrame frame = pane.createInternalFrame(
      (DialogBoxes.this).getLayeredPane(), BOX_TITLE);
    getLayeredPane().add(frame);
  }
```

3 Question dialog with custom buttons

3 Creates internalframe with information dialog

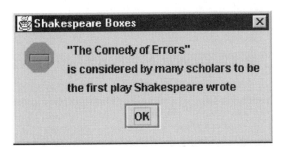

Figure 14.11
A JOptionPane Error_Message **message dialog with a multi-line message**

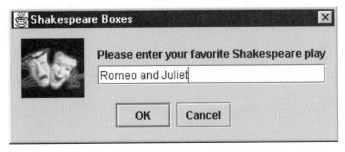

Figure 14.12 A JOptionPane INFORMATION_MESSAGE **input dialog with custom icon, message, text field**

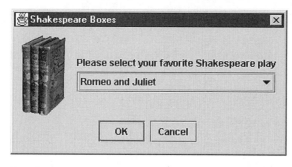

Figure 14.13 A `JOptionPane` `INFORMATION_MESSAGE` input dialog with custom icon, message, combo box input, and initial selection

Figure 14.14
A `JOptionPane` `YES_NO_OPTION` confirm dialog

```
      };
      mItem.addActionListener(lst);
      mFile.add(mItem);

      mItem = new JMenuItem("Error Message");
      mItem.setMnemonic('e');
      lst = new ActionListener() {
        public void actionPerformed(ActionEvent e) {
          String message = "\"The Comedy of Errors\"\n"+
            "is considered by many scholars to be\n"+
            "the first play Shakespeare wrote";
          JOptionPane.showMessageDialog(
            DialogBoxes.this, message,
            BOX_TITLE, JOptionPane.ERROR_MESSAGE);
        }
      };
      mItem.addActionListener(lst);
      mFile.add(mItem);

      mFile.addSeparator();

      mItem = new JMenuItem("Text Input");
      mItem.setMnemonic('t');
      lst = new ActionListener() {
        public void actionPerformed(ActionEvent e) {
          String input = (String) JOptionPane.showInputDialog(
            DialogBoxes.this,
            "Please enter your favorite Shakespeare play",
            BOX_TITLE, JOptionPane.INFORMATION_MESSAGE,
            new ImageIcon("Plays.jpg"), null,
```

Shows error dialog ❹

Shows input dialog with message, using text field ❺

```
                   "Romeo and Juliet");
             System.out.println("User's input: "+input);       Shows input dialog    ⑤
           }                                                    with message,
         };                                                     using text field
         mItem.addActionListener(lst);
         mFile.add(mItem);

         mItem = new JMenuItem("Combobox Input");
         mItem.setMnemonic('c');
         lst = new ActionListener() {
           public void actionPerformed(ActionEvent e) {
             String[] plays = new String[] {
               "Hamlet", "King Lear", "Othello", "Romeo and Juliet" };
             String input = (String) JOptionPane.showInputDialog(
               DialogBoxes.this,
               "Please select your favorite Shakespeare play",
               BOX_TITLE, JOptionPane.INFORMATION_MESSAGE,
               new ImageIcon("Books.gif"), plays,
               "Romeo and Juliet");
             System.out.println("User's input: "+input);
           }
         };
         mItem.addActionListener(lst);                      Shows input dialog    ⑤
         mFile.add(mItem);                                  with message,
                                                            using combo box
         mFile.addSeparator();

         mItem = new JMenuItem("Exit");
         mItem.setMnemonic('x');                                Shows a           ⑥
         lst = new ActionListener() {                        confirm dialog
           public void actionPerformed(ActionEvent e) {
             if (JOptionPane.showConfirmDialog(
               DialogBoxes.this,
               "Do you want to quit this application ?",
               BOX_TITLE, JOptionPane.YES_NO_OPTION)
               == JOptionPane.YES_OPTION)
                System.exit(0);
           }
         };
         mItem.addActionListener(lst);
         mFile.add(mItem);
         menuBar.add(mFile);

         return menuBar;
       }

     public static void main(String argv[]) {
       DialogBoxes frame = new DialogBoxes();
       frame.setDefaultCloseOperation(JFrame.EXIT_ON_CLOSE);
       frame.setVisible(true);
     }
   }
 }
```

14.4.1 Understanding the code

Class DialogBoxes

1 This class represents a simple frame which contains a menu bar created with our create-MenuBar() method, and a JDesktopPane (see chapter 16) which is used as the frame's layered pane. The menu bar contains a single menu, File, which holds several menu items.

2 The createMenuBar() method is responsible for populating our frame's menu bar with seven menu items, each with an ActionListener to invoke the display of a JOptionPane in either a JDialog or a JInternalFrame. The first menu item, Ask Question, creates an instance of JOptionPane, and assigns it a custom icon using its setIcon() method and custom option button Strings using setOptions(). A JDialog is created to hold this message box, and the show() method displays this dialog on the screen and waits until it is dismissed. At that point the getValue() method retrieves the user's selection as an Object, which may be null or one of the option button Strings assigned to this message box. The resulting dialog is shown in figure 14.9.

GUIDELINE

Affirmative text   The use of the affirmative and unambiguous text "To Be" and "Not to be" greatly enhances the usability of the option dialog. For example, if the text read "To be or not to be? That is the question," "Yes" or "No," would have been somewhat ambiguous and may have confused some users. The explicit text "To Be," "Not to be" is much clearer.

This is another example of how to improve usability with just a little extra coding effort.

---

3 The second menu item, Info Message, creates a JOptionPane with a multi-line message String and a custom icon. The createInternalFrame() method is used to create a JInternalFrame that holds the resulting JOptionPane message box. This internal frame is then added to the layered pane, which is now a JDesktopPane instance. The resulting internal frame is shown in figure 14.10.

4 The third menu item, Error Message, produces a standard error message box using JOption-Pane's static showMessageDialog() method and the ERROR_MESSAGE message type. The resulting dialog is shown in figure 14.11. Recall that JOptionPane dialogs appear, by default, centered with respect to the parent if the parent is a frame. This is why we don't do any manual positioning here.

5 The next two menu items, Text Input and Combobox Input, produce INFORMATION_MESSAGE JOptionPanes which take user input in a JTextField and JComboBox, respectively. The static showInputDialog() method is used to display these JOptionPanes in JDialogs. Figures 14.12 and 14.13 illustrate. The Text Input pane takes the initial text to display in its text field as a String parameter. The Combobox Input pane takes an array of Strings to display in the combo box as possible choices, as well as the initial String to be displayed by the combo box.

Added usability with constrained lists   Figures 14.12 and 14.13 clearly highlight how usability can be improved through effective component choice. The combo box with a constrained list of choices is clearly the better tool for the task at hand.

The options in this example consist of a fixed number of choices. Shakespeare is clearly dead and the plays attributed to him are widely known. Thus the combo box in figure 14.13 is a better choice. It should be populated with a list of all the known plays.

The option pane in figure 14.12 is better used for unknown data entry such as "Please enter your name."

6 The final menu item, Exit, brings up a YES_NO_OPTION confirmation JOptionPane in a JDialog (shown in figure 14.14) by calling showConfirmDialog(). The application is terminated if the user answers "Yes."

14.5   *CUSTOMIZING JCOLORCHOOSER*

In chapter 12 we developed a custom menu item that allowed quick and easy selection of a color for the background and foreground of a JTextArea. In section 14.1 we built off this example to add a simple About dialog. In this section we'll build off it further, and construct a customized JColorChooser that allows a much wider range of color selection. Our implementation in example 14.4 includes a preview component, PreviewPanel, that illustrates how text will appear with chosen background and foreground colors. We have to return both background and foreground selection values when the user dismisses the color chooser in order to update the text component properly.

Previewing improves usability   In this example, the user's goal may be to select suitable colors for a banner headline. Allowing the user to view a WYSIWYG preview improves usability. The user doesn't have to experiment with his selection, which involves opening and closing the dialog several times. Instead, he can achieve his goal on a single visit to the color chooser dialog.

Example 14.4

BasicTextEditor.java

see \Chapter14\4

```
import java.awt.*;
import java.awt.event.*;

import javax.swing.*;

public class BasicTextEditor extends JFrame
{
```

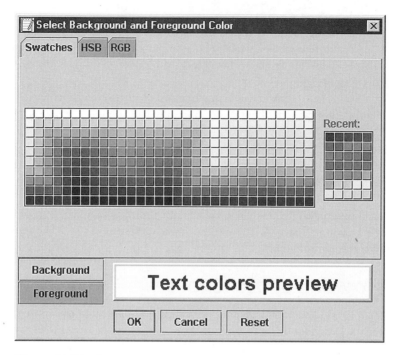

Figure 14.15 A `JColorChooser` with a custom `PreviewPanel` component capable of returning two color selections

```
// Unchanged code from example 14.2

protected JColorChooser m_colorChooser;
protected PreviewPanel m_previewPanel;
protected JDialog m_colorDialog;

public BasicTextEditor() {
  super("BasicTextEditor with JColorChooser");
  setSize(450, 350);
  ImageIcon icon = new ImageIcon("smallIcon.gif");
  setIconImage(icon.getImage());

  m_colorChooser = new JColorChooser();
  m_previewPanel = new PreviewPanel(m_colorChooser);
  m_colorChooser.setPreviewPanel(m_previewPanel);

  // Unchanged code from example 14.2
}

protected JMenuBar createMenuBar() {
  // Unchanged code from example 14.2

  Action actionChooser = new AbstractAction("Color Chooser") {
    public void actionPerformed(ActionEvent e) {
      BasicTextEditor.this.repaint();
      if (m_colorDialog == null)
        m_colorDialog = JColorChooser.createDialog(
```

❶ Constructor creates color chooser and PreviewPane and connects them

❷ Creates dialog for color chooser

```
          BasicTextEditor.this,
          "Select Background and Foreground Color",
          true, m_colorChooser, m_previewPanel, null);
        m_previewPanel.setTextForeground(
          m_monitor.getForeground());
        m_previewPanel.setTextBackground(
          m_monitor.getBackground());
        m_colorDialog.show();

        if (m_previewPanel.isSelected()) {
          m_monitor.setBackground(
            m_previewPanel.getTextBackground());
          m_monitor.setForeground(
            m_previewPanel.getTextForeground());
        }
      }
    };
    mOpt.addSeparator();
    item = mOpt.add(actionChooser);
    item.setMnemonic('c');

    menuBar.add(mOpt);

    // Unchanged code from example 14.2
  }
}

// Unchanged code from example 14.2

class PreviewPanel extends JPanel
 implements ChangeListener, ActionListener
{
  protected JColorChooser m_chooser;
  protected JLabel m_preview;
  protected JToggleButton m_btBack;
  protected JToggleButton m_btFore;
  protected boolean m_isSelected = false;

  public PreviewPanel(JColorChooser chooser) {
    this(chooser, Color.white, Color.black);
  }

  public PreviewPanel(JColorChooser chooser,
   Color background, Color foreground) {
    m_chooser = chooser;
    chooser.getSelectionModel().addChangeListener(this);

    setLayout(new BorderLayout());
    JPanel p = new JPanel(new GridLayout(2, 1, 0, 0));
    ButtonGroup group = new ButtonGroup();
    m_btBack = new JToggleButton("Background");
    m_btBack.setSelected(true);
    m_btBack.addActionListener(this);
    group.add(m_btBack);
    p.add(m_btBack);
    m_btFore = new JToggleButton("Foreground");
```

2 Creates dialog for color chooser

3 Copies colors from text area

4 After dialog is dismissed, copies out new colors

5 Panel to preview selected colors

6 First constructor creates white background and black foreground; calls second constructor

7 Background and foreground buttons in vertical grid

```
  m_btFore.addActionListener(this);
  group.add(m_btFore);
  p.add(m_btFore);
  add(p, BorderLayout.WEST);

  p = new JPanel(new BorderLayout());
  Border b1 = new EmptyBorder(5, 10, 5, 10);
  Border b2 = new BevelBorder(BevelBorder.RAISED);
  Border b3 = new EmptyBorder(2, 2, 2, 2);
  Border cb1 = new CompoundBorder(b1, b2);
  Border cb2 = new CompoundBorder(cb1, b3);
  p.setBorder(cb2);

  m_preview = new JLabel("Text colors preview",
    JLabel.CENTER);
  m_preview.setBackground(background);
  m_preview.setForeground(foreground);
  m_preview.setFont(new Font("Arial",Font.BOLD, 24));
  m_preview.setOpaque(true);
  p.add(m_preview, BorderLayout.CENTER);
  add(p, BorderLayout.CENTER);

  m_chooser.setColor(background);
}

protected boolean isSelected() {
  return m_isSelected;
}

public void setTextBackground(Color c) {
  m_preview.setBackground(c);
}

public Color getTextBackground() {
  return m_preview.getBackground();
}

public void setTextForeground(Color c) {
  m_preview.setForeground(c);
}

public Color getTextForeground() {
  return m_preview.getForeground();
}

public void stateChanged(ChangeEvent evt) {
  Color c = m_chooser.getColor();
  if (c != null) {
    if (m_btBack.isSelected())
      m_preview.setBackground(c);
    else
      m_preview.setForeground(c);
  }
}

public void actionPerformed(ActionEvent evt) {
  if (evt.getSource() == m_btBack)
```

7 Background and foreground buttons in vertical grid

7 Raised, button-like border for big label

7 Big label to show text colors

8 Called for change events on color chooser

9 Called when either the background or foreground button is pressed

```
            m_chooser.setColor(getTextBackground());
        else if (evt.getSource() == m_btFore)
            m_chooser.setColor(getTextForeground());
        else
            m_isSelected = true;
    }
}
```

14.5.1   Understanding the code

Class BasicTextEditor

This class includes three new instance variables:

- `JColorChooser m_colorChooser`: Used to store `JColorChooser` to avoid unnecessary instantiation.
- `PreviewPanel m_previewPanel`: An instance of our custom color previewing component.
- `JDialog m_colorDialog`: Used to store the `JDialog` that acts as the parent of `m_colorChooser`.

❶ The constructor instantiates `m_colorChooser` and `m_previewPanel`, assigning `m_preview-Panel` as `m_colorChooser`'s preview component using the `setPreviewPanel()` method.

❷ The menu bar receives a new menu item, Color Chooser, which is set up in the `createMenu-Bar()` method as an `Action` implementation. When selected, this item first repaints our application frame to ensure that the area covered by the pop-up menu is refreshed properly. Then it checks to see if our `m_colorDialog` has been instantiated yet. If it has not, we call `JColorChooser`'s static `createDialog()` method to wrap `m_colorChooser` in a dialog, and we use `m_previewPanel` as an `ActionListener` for the OK button (see section 14.1.3). This instantiation only occurs once.

❸ We then assign the current colors of `m_monitor` to `m_previewPanel` (recall that `m_monitor` is the `JTextArea` central to this application). We do this because the foreground and background can also be assigned by our custom menu color choosers. If this occurs, `m_previewPanel` is not notified, so we update the selected colors each time the dialog is invoked.

❹ The dialog is then shown and the main application thread waits for it to be dismissed. When the dialog is dismissed, `m_previewPanel` is checked to see whether new colors have been selected using its `isSelected()` method. If new colors have been chosen, they are assigned to `m_monitor`.

> **NOTE**   We have purposely avoided updating the selected colors in our custom color menu components. The reason we did this is that in a more professional implementation we would most likely not offer both methods for choosing text component colors. If we did want to support both methods, we would need to determine the closest color in our custom color menus that matches the corresponding color selected with `JColorChooser`, because `JColorChooser` offers a much wider range of choices.

Class PreviewPanel

⑤ This class represents our custom color preview component which is designed to be used with JColorChooser. It extends JPanel and implements two listener interfaces, Change-Listener and ActionListener. It displays selected foreground and background colors in a label, and it includes two JToggleButtons that are used to switch between background color and foreground color selection modes. There are five instance variables:

- JColorChooser m_chooser: A reference to the hosting color chooser.
- JLabel m_preview: The label to preview background and foreground colors.
- JToggleButton m_btBack: The toggle button to switch to the background color selection.
- JToggleButton m_btFore: The toggle button to switch to the foreground color selection.
- boolean m_isSelected: The flag indicating a selection has taken place.

⑥ The first PreviewPanel constructor takes a JColorChooser as a parameter and delegates its work to the second constructor, passing it the JColorChooser as well as white and black Colors for the initial background and foreground colors, respectively. As we discussed in the beginning of this chapter, JColorChooser's ColorSelectionModel fires ChangeEvents when the selected Color changes. So we start by registering this component as a Change-Listener with the given color chooser's model.

⑦ A BorderLayout is used to manage this container and two toggle buttons are placed in a 2x1 GridLayout, which is added to the WEST region. Both buttons receive a this reference as an ActionListener. A label with a large font is then placed in the CENTER region. This label is surrounded by a decorative, doubly-compounded border consisting of an EmptyBorder, a BevelBorder, and another EmptyBorder. The foreground and background colors of this label are assigned the values passed to the constructor.

⑧ Several methods are used to set and get the selected colors; they do not require any special explanation. The stateChanged() method will be called when the color chooser model fires ChangeEvents. Depending on which toggle button is selected, this method updates the background or foreground color of the preview label.

⑨ The actionPerformed() method will be called when one of the toggle buttons is pressed. It assigns the stored background or foreground, depending which button is clicked, as the color of the hosting JColorChooser. This method is also called when the OK button is clicked, in which case the m_isSelected flag is set to true.

14.5.2 Running the code

Select the Color Chooser menu item to bring up our customized JColorChooser (shown in figure 14.15). Select a background and foreground color using any of the available color panes. Verify that the preview label is updated to reflect the current color selection and the currently selected toggle button. Click the OK button to dismiss the dialog and notice that both the selected foreground and background colors are assigned to our application's text area. Also notice that clicking the Cancel button dismisses the dialog without making any color changes.

14.6 CUSTOMIZING JFILECHOOSER

Examples that use JFileChooser to load and save files are scattered throughout this book. In this section we'll take a closer look at the more advanced features of this component as we build a powerful JAR and ZIP archive creation, viewing, and extraction tool. We will see how to implement a custom FileView and FileFilter, and how to access and manipulate the internals of JFileChooser to allow multiple file selection and add our own components. Since this example deals with Java archive functionality, we will first briefly summarize the classes from the java.util.zip and java.util.jar packages we will be using.

NOTE The GUI presented in this section is extremely basic, and professional implementations would surely construct a more elaborate counterpart. We have purposely avoided this construction here due to the complex nature of the example, and to avoid straying from the JFileChooser topics central to the GUI's construction.

14.6.1 ZipInputStream

class java.util.zip.ZipInputStream

This class represents a filtered input stream which uncompresses ZIP archive data. The constructor takes an instance of InputStream as a parameter. Before we can read data from this stream, we need to find a ZIP file entry using the getNextEntry() method. Each entry corresponds to an archived file. We can read() an array of bytes from an entry, and then close it using the closeEntry() method when reading is complete.

14.6.2 ZipOutputStream

class java.util.zip.ZipOutputStream

This class represents a filtered output stream which writes binary data into an archive in the compressed (default) or uncompressed (optional) form. The constructor of this class takes an instance of OutputStream as a parameter. Before writing data to this stream, we need to create a new ZipEntry using the putNextEntry() method. Each ZipEntry corresponds to an archived file. We can write() an array of bytes to a ZipEntry, and close it using the closeEntry() method when writing is complete. We can also specify the compression method for storing ZipEntrys using ZipOutputStream's setMethod() method.

14.6.3 ZipFile

class java.util.zip.ZipFile

This class encapsulates a collection of ZipEntrys and represents a read-only ZIP archive. We can fetch an Enumeration of the contained ZipEntrys using the entries() method. The size() method tells us how many files are contained, and getName() returns the archive's full path name. We can retrieve an InputStream for reading the contents of a contained Zip-Entry using the getInputStream() method. When we are finished reading, we are expected to call the close() method to close the archive.

14.6.4 ZipEntry

class java.util.zip.ZipEntry

This class represents a single archived file or directory within a ZIP archive. It allows retrieval of its name and it can be cloned using the `clone()` method. Using typical set/get accessors, we can access a `ZipEntry`'s compression method, CRC-32 checksum, size, modification time, and a comment attachment. We can also query whether a `ZipEntry` is a directory using its `isDirectory()` method.

14.6.5 The java.util.jar package

This package contains a set of classes for managing JAR files. The relevant classes that we will be dealing with (`JarEntry`, `JarFile`, `JarInputStream`, and `JarOutputStream`) are direct subclasses of the `zip` package counterparts (`ZipEntry`, `ZipFile`, `ZipInputStream`, and `ZipOutputStream`), and thus they inherit the functionality described above.

14.6.6 Manifest

class java.util.jar.Manifest

This class represents a JAR `Manifest` file. A `Manifest` contains a collection of names and their associated attributes specific both for the archive as a whole and for a particular `JarEntry`, such as a file or directory in the archive. We are not concerned with the details of JAR manifest files in this chapter; suffice it to say that the `JarOutputStream` constructor takes a `Manifest` instance as a parameter, along with an `OutputStream`.

In example 14.5, we create a simple, two-button GUI with a status bar (a label). One button corresponds to creating a ZIP or JAR archive, and the other corresponds to decompressing an archive. In each case, two `JFileChoosers` are used to perform the operation. The first chooser allows the user to either enter an archive name to use or select an archive to decompress. The second chooser allows the user to select files to compress or decompress. (As noted above, more professional implementations would most likely include a more elaborate GUI.) A custom `FileView` class represents ZIP and JAR archives using a custom icon, and a `FileFilter` class allows ZIP (.zip) and JAR (.jar) files only to be viewed. We also work with `JFileChooser` as a container by adding our own custom component, taking advantage of the fact that it uses a y-oriented `BoxLayout` to organize its children.

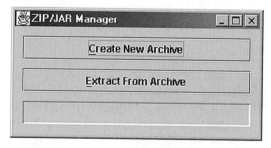

Figure 14.16   ZIP/JAR Manager
`JFileChooser` example at startup

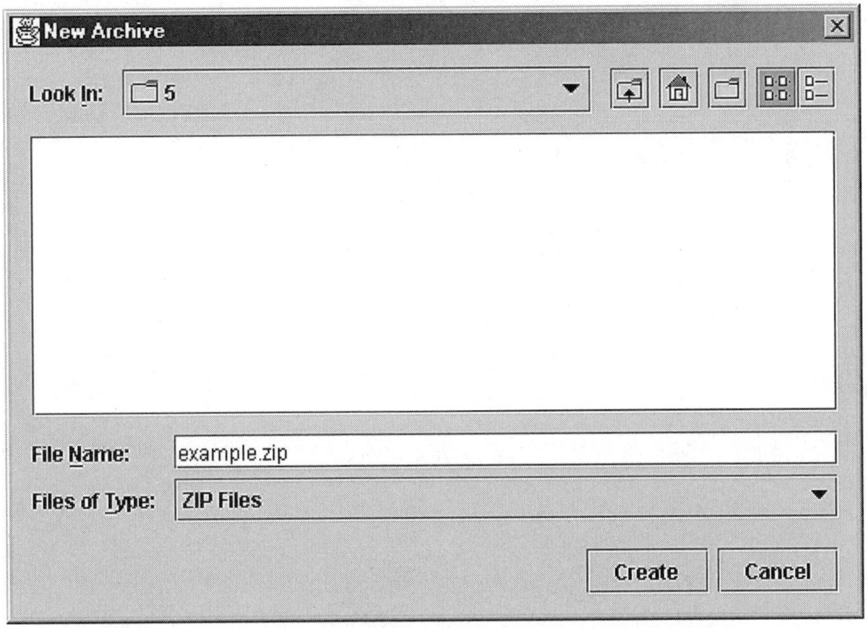

Figure 14.17 The first step in creating an archive: using JFileChooser to select an archive location and name

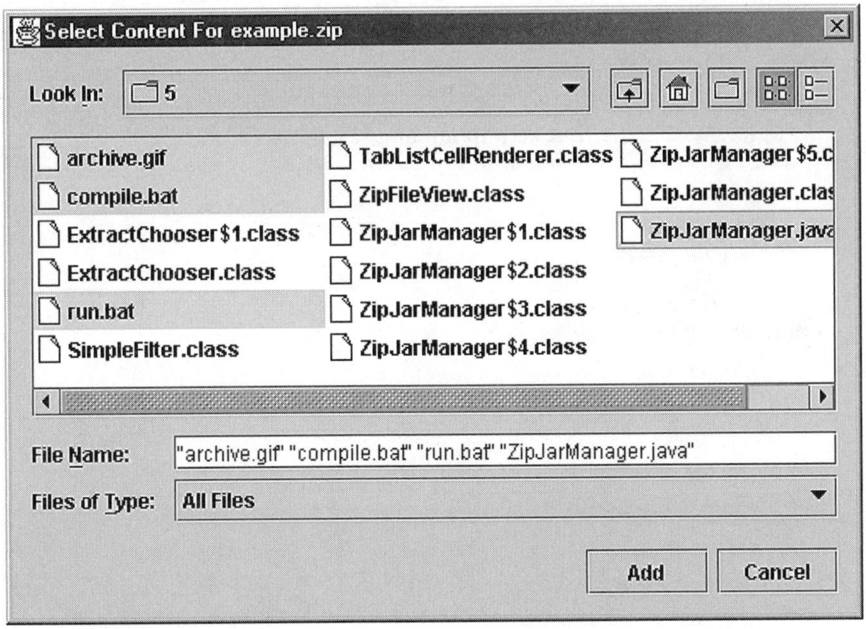

Figure 14.18 Second step in creating an archive; using JFileChooser to select archive content

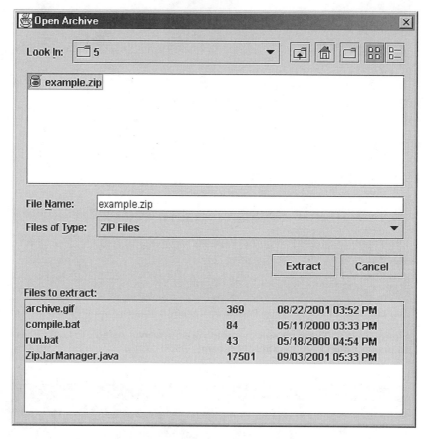

**Figure 14.19 The first step in uncompressing an archive;
using a custom component in `JFileChooser`**

Example 14.5

ZipJarManager.java

see \Chapter14\5

```
import java.awt.*;
import java.awt.event.*;
import java.io.*;
import java.util.*;
import java.util.zip.*;
import java.util.jar.*;
import java.beans.*;
import java.text.SimpleDateFormat;

import javax.swing.*;
import javax.swing.event.*;
```

```java
import javax.swing.border.*;

public class ZipJarManager
    extends JFrame {

  public static int BUFFER_SIZE = 10240;

  protected File   m_currentDir;
  protected SimpleFilter m_zipFilter;
  protected SimpleFilter m_jarFilter;
  protected ZipFileView  m_view;

  protected JButton m_btCreate;
  protected JButton m_btExtract;
  protected JLabel  m_status;

  public ZipJarManager() {
    super("ZIP/JAR Manager");
    setSize(300,150);

    JPanel p = new JPanel(new GridLayout(3, 1, 10, 10));
    p.setBorder(new EmptyBorder(10, 10, 10, 10));

    m_btCreate = new JButton("Create New Archive");
    ActionListener lst = new ActionListener() {
      public void actionPerformed(ActionEvent e) {
        m_btCreate.setEnabled(false);
        m_btExtract.setEnabled(false);
        createArchive();
        m_btCreate.setEnabled(true);
        m_btExtract.setEnabled(true);
      }
    };
    m_btCreate.addActionListener(lst);
    m_btCreate.setMnemonic('c');
    p.add(m_btCreate);

    m_btExtract = new JButton("Extract From Archive");
    lst = new ActionListener() {
      public void actionPerformed(ActionEvent e) {
        m_btCreate.setEnabled(false);
        m_btExtract.setEnabled(false);
        extractArchive();
        m_btCreate.setEnabled(true);
        m_btExtract.setEnabled(true);
      }
    };
    m_btExtract.addActionListener(lst);
    m_btExtract.setMnemonic('e');
    p.add(m_btExtract);

    m_status = new JLabel();
    m_status.setBorder(new BevelBorder(BevelBorder.LOWERED,
      Color.white, Color.gray));
    p.add(m_status);
```

```
      getContentPane().add(p, BorderLayout.CENTER);

    m_zipFilter = new SimpleFilter("zip", "ZIP Files");
    m_jarFilter = new SimpleFilter("jar", "JAR Files");
    m_view = new ZipFileView();
    try {
      m_currentDir = (new File(".")).getCanonicalFile();
    } catch (IOException ex) {}
  }

  public void setStatus(String str) {
    m_status.setText(str);
    m_status.repaint();
  }

  protected void createArchive() {
    // Show chooser to select archive
    JFileChooser archiveChooser = new JFileChooser();
    archiveChooser.addChoosableFileFilter(m_zipFilter);
    archiveChooser.addChoosableFileFilter(m_jarFilter);
    archiveChooser.setFileView(m_view);
    archiveChooser.setMultiSelectionEnabled(false);
    archiveChooser.setFileFilter(m_jarFilter);
    javax.swing.filechooser.FileFilter ft =
      archiveChooser.getAcceptAllFileFilter();
    archiveChooser.removeChoosableFileFilter(ft);

    archiveChooser.setCurrentDirectory(m_currentDir);
    archiveChooser.setDialogType(JFileChooser.SAVE_DIALOG);
    archiveChooser.setDialogTitle("New Archive");

    if (archiveChooser.showDialog(this, "Create") !=
      JFileChooser.APPROVE_OPTION)
        return;
    m_currentDir = archiveChooser.getCurrentDirectory();

    final File archiveFile = archiveChooser.getSelectedFile();
    if (!isArchiveFile(archiveFile))
      return;

    // Show chooser to select entries
    JFileChooser entriesChooser = new JFileChooser();
    entriesChooser.setCurrentDirectory(m_currentDir);
    entriesChooser.setDialogType(JFileChooser.OPEN_DIALOG);
    entriesChooser.setDialogTitle("Select Content For "
      + archiveFile.getName());
    entriesChooser.setMultiSelectionEnabled(true);
    entriesChooser.setFileSelectionMode(JFileChooser.FILES_ONLY);

    if (entriesChooser.showDialog(this, "Add") !=
      JFileChooser.APPROVE_OPTION)
        return;

    m_currentDir = entriesChooser.getCurrentDirectory();
    final File[] selected = entriesChooser.getSelectedFiles();

    String name = archiveFile.getName().toLowerCase();
```

Method to create a ZIP or JAR archive using two JFileChoosers

❶

```
      if (name.endsWith(".zip")) {
        Thread runner = new Thread() {
            public void run() {
              createZipArchive(archiveFile, selected);
            }
        };
        runner.start();
      }
      else if (name.endsWith(".jar")) {
        Thread runner = new Thread() {
            public void run() {
              createJarArchive(archiveFile, selected);
            }
        };
        runner.start();
      }
      else {
        setStatus("No JAR or ZIP file has been selected");
      }
    }

    protected void extractArchive() {
      // Show dialog to select archive and entries
      ExtractChooser extractChooser = new ExtractChooser();
      extractChooser.addChoosableFileFilter(m_zipFilter);
      extractChooser.addChoosableFileFilter(m_jarFilter);
      extractChooser.setFileView(m_view);
      extractChooser.setMultiSelectionEnabled(false);
      extractChooser.setFileFilter(m_jarFilter);
      javax.swing.filechooser.FileFilter ft =
          extractChooser.getAcceptAllFileFilter();
      extractChooser.removeChoosableFileFilter(ft);

      extractChooser.setCurrentDirectory(m_currentDir);
      extractChooser.setDialogType(JFileChooser.OPEN_DIALOG);
      extractChooser.setDialogTitle("Open Archive");
      extractChooser.setMultiSelectionEnabled(false);
      extractChooser.setPreferredSize(new Dimension(470,450));

      if (extractChooser.showDialog(this, "Extract") !=
          JFileChooser.APPROVE_OPTION)
        return;

      m_currentDir = extractChooser.getCurrentDirectory();
      final File archiveFile = extractChooser.getSelectedFile();
      if (!archiveFile.exists() || !isArchiveFile(archiveFile))
        return;

      final String[] entries = extractChooser.getSelectedEntries();
      if (entries.length == 0) {
        setStatus("No entries have been selected for extraction");
        return;
      }

      // Show dialog to select output directory
```

Extracts files from a ZIP or JAR archive using a JFileChooser and our custom ExtractChooser

❷

```java
      JFileChooser dirChooser = new JFileChooser();
      dirChooser.setCurrentDirectory(m_currentDir);
      dirChooser.setDialogType(JFileChooser.OPEN_DIALOG);
      dirChooser.setDialogTitle("Select Destination Directory For " +
        archiveFile.getName());
      dirChooser.setMultiSelectionEnabled(false);
      dirChooser.setFileSelectionMode(JFileChooser.DIRECTORIES_ONLY);

      if (dirChooser.showDialog(this, "Select") !=
          JFileChooser.APPROVE_OPTION)
        return;

      m_currentDir = dirChooser.getCurrentDirectory();
      final File outputDir = dirChooser.getSelectedFile();

      Thread runner = new Thread() {
        public void run() {
          extractFromArchive(archiveFile, entries, outputDir);
        }
      };
      runner.start();
  }

  protected void createZipArchive(File archiveFile, File[] selected) {
      try {
          byte buffer[] = new byte[BUFFER_SIZE];
          // Open archive file
          FileOutputStream stream =
            new FileOutputStream(archiveFile);
          ZipOutputStream out = new ZipOutputStream(stream);

          for (int k=0; k<selected.length; k++) {
            if (selected[k]==null || !selected[k].exists() ||
                selected[k].isDirectory())
              continue;// Just in case...
            setStatus("Adding "+selected[k].getName());

            // Add archive entry
            ZipEntry zipAdd = new ZipEntry(selected[k].getName());
            zipAdd.setTime(selected[k].lastModified());
            out.putNextEntry(zipAdd);

            // Read input & write to output
            FileInputStream in = new FileInputStream(selected[k]);
            while (true) {
              int nRead = in.read(buffer, 0, buffer.length);
              if (nRead <= 0)
                break;
              out.write(buffer, 0, nRead);
            }
            in.close();
          }

          out.close();
          stream.close();
          setStatus("ZIP archive was created successfully");
```

```
        }
        catch (Exception e) {
          e.printStackTrace();
          setStatus("Error: "+e.getMessage());
          return;
        }
}

protected void createJarArchive(File archiveFile, File[] selected) {
    try {
        byte buffer[] = new byte[BUFFER_SIZE];
        // Open archive file
        FileOutputStream stream =
          new FileOutputStream(archiveFile);
        JarOutputStream out = new JarOutputStream(stream,
          new Manifest());

        for (int k=0; k<selected.length; k++) {
            if (selected[k]==null || !selected[k].exists() ||
               selected[k].isDirectory())
               continue;// Just in case...
            setStatus("Adding "+selected[k].getName());

            // Add archive entry
            JarEntry jarAdd = new JarEntry(selected[k].getName());
            jarAdd.setTime(selected[k].lastModified());
            out.putNextEntry(jarAdd);

            // Write file to archive
            FileInputStream in = new FileInputStream(selected[k]);
            while (true) {
               int nRead = in.read(buffer, 0, buffer.length);
               if (nRead <= 0)
                 break;
               out.write(buffer, 0, nRead);
            }
            in.close();
        }

        out.close();
        stream.close();
        setStatus("JAR archive was created successfully");
    }
    catch (Exception ex) {
        ex.printStackTrace();
        setStatus("Error: "+ex.getMessage());
    }
}

protected void extractFromArchive(File archiveFile,
    String[] entries, File outputDir) {
      try {
         byte buffer[] = new byte[BUFFER_SIZE];
         // Open the archive file
         FileInputStream stream =
```

3 This method performs the actual archive extraction

```java
            new FileInputStream(archiveFile);
        ZipInputStream in = new ZipInputStream(stream);

      // Find archive entry
      while (true) {
         ZipEntry zipExtract = in.getNextEntry();
         if (zipExtract == null)
            break;
         boolean bFound = false;
         for (int k=0; k<entries.length; k++) {
            if (zipExtract.getName().equals(entries[k])) {
               bFound = true;
               break;
            }
         }
         if (!bFound) {
            in.closeEntry();
            continue;
         }
         setStatus("Extracting "+zipExtract.getName());

         // Create output file and check required directory
         File outFile = new File(outputDir,
            zipExtract.getName());
         File parent = outFile.getParentFile();
         if (parent != null && !parent.exists())
            parent.mkdirs();

         // Extract unzipped file
         FileOutputStream out =
            new FileOutputStream(outFile);
         while (true) {
            int nRead = in.read(buffer,
               0, buffer.length);
            if (nRead <= 0)
               break;
            out.write(buffer, 0, nRead);
         }
         out.close();
         in.closeEntry();
      }

      in.close();
      stream.close();
      setStatus("Files were extracted successfully");
   }
   catch (Exception ex) {
      ex.printStackTrace();
      setStatus("Error: "+ex.getMessage());
   }
}

public static boolean isArchiveFile(File f) {
   String name = f.getName().toLowerCase();
```

```
          return (name.endsWith(".zip") || name.endsWith(".jar"));
      }

      public static void main(String argv[]) {
          ZipJarManager frame = new ZipJarManager();
          frame.setDefaultCloseOperation(JFrame.EXIT_ON_CLOSE);
          frame.setVisible(true);
      }
  }

class SimpleFilter
    extends javax.swing.filechooser.FileFilter {

    private String m_description = null;
    private String m_extension = null;

    public SimpleFilter(String extension, String description) {
        m_description = description;
        m_extension = "."+extension.toLowerCase();
    }

    public String getDescription() {
        return m_description;
    }

    public boolean accept(File f) {
        if (f == null)
            return false;
        if (f.isDirectory())
            return true;
        return f.getName().toLowerCase().endsWith(m_extension);
    }
}

class ZipFileView
    extends javax.swing.filechooser.FileView {

    protected static ImageIcon ZIP_ICON = new ImageIcon("archive.gif");
    protected static ImageIcon JAR_ICON = new ImageIcon("archive.gif");

    public String getName(File f) {
        String name = f.getName();
        return name.equals("") ? f.getPath() : name;
    }

    public String getDescription(File f) {
        return getTypeDescription(f);
    }

    public String getTypeDescription(File f) {
        String name = f.getName().toLowerCase();
        if (name.endsWith(".zip"))
            return "ZIP Archive File";
        else if (name.endsWith(".jar"))
            return "Java Archive File";
        else
            return "File";
```

4 **Custom FileView to show ZIP and JAR files with appropriate icons and file type descriptions**

```
    }

    public Icon getIcon(File f) {
        String name = f.getName().toLowerCase();
        if (name.endsWith(".zip"))
            return ZIP_ICON;
        else if (name.endsWith(".jar"))
            return JAR_ICON;
        else
            return null;
    }

    public Boolean isTraversable(File f) {
        return ( f.isDirectory() ? Boolean.TRUE : Boolean.FALSE);
    }
}

class TabListCellRenderer
    extends JLabel
    implements ListCellRenderer {

    protected static Border m_noFocusBorder;
    protected FontMetrics m_fm = null;
    protected Insets m_insets = new Insets(0, 0, 0, 0);

    protected int m_defaultTab = 50;
    protected int[] m_tabs = null;

    public TabListCellRenderer() {
        super();
        m_noFocusBorder = new EmptyBorder(1, 1, 1, 1);
        setOpaque(true);
        setBorder(m_noFocusBorder);
    }

    public Component getListCellRendererComponent(JList list,
        Object value, int index, boolean isSelected,
        boolean cellHasFocus) {

        setText(value.toString());

        setBackground(isSelected ? list.getSelectionBackground()
            : list.getBackground());
        setForeground(isSelected ? list.getSelectionForeground()
            : list.getForeground());

        setFont(list.getFont());
        setBorder((cellHasFocus) ? UIManager.getBorder(
            "List.focusCellHighlightBorder") : m_noFocusBorder);

        return this;
    }

    public void setDefaultTab(int defaultTab) {
        m_defaultTab = defaultTab;
    }

    public int getDefaultTab() {
```

```
          return m_defaultTab;
   }

   public void setTabs(int[] tabs) {
      m_tabs = tabs;
   }

   public int[] getTabs() {
      return m_tabs;
   }

   public int getTab(int index) {
      if (m_tabs == null)
         return m_defaultTab*index;

      int len = m_tabs.length;
      if (index>=0 && index<len)
         return m_tabs[index];

      return m_tabs[len-1] + m_defaultTab*(index-len+1);
   }

   public void paintComponent(Graphics g) {
      super.paintComponent(g);
      m_fm = g.getFontMetrics();

      g.setColor(getBackground());
      g.fillRect(0, 0, getWidth(), getHeight());
      getBorder().paintBorder(this, g, 0, 0, getWidth(), getHeight());

      g.setColor(getForeground());
      g.setFont(getFont());
      m_insets = getInsets();
      int x = m_insets.left;
      int y = m_insets.top + m_fm.getAscent();

      StringTokenizer st = new StringTokenizer(getText(), "\t");
      while (st.hasMoreTokens()) {
         String sNext = st.nextToken();
         g.drawString(sNext, x, y);
         x += m_fm.stringWidth(sNext);

         if (!st.hasMoreTokens())
            break;
         int index = 0;
         while (x >= getTab(index))
            index++;
         x = getTab(index);
      }
   }
}

class ExtractChooser extends JFileChooser {
   protected JList m_zipEntries;

   protected JDialog createDialog(Component parent)
      throws HeadlessException {
```

⑤ Custom file chooser which displays archive contents in a JList

```
JDialog dialog = super.createDialog(parent);

m_zipEntries = new JList();
m_zipEntries.setSelectionMode(
  ListSelectionModel.MULTIPLE_INTERVAL_SELECTION);
TabListCellRenderer renderer = new TabListCellRenderer();
renderer.setTabs(new int[] {240, 300, 360});
m_zipEntries.setCellRenderer(renderer);

JPanel p = new JPanel(new BorderLayout());
p.setBorder(new EmptyBorder(0,10,10,10));
p.add(new JLabel("Files to extract:"), BorderLayout.NORTH);

JScrollPane ps = new JScrollPane(m_zipEntries);
p.add(ps, BorderLayout.CENTER);
dialog.getContentPane().add(p, BorderLayout.SOUTH);

PropertyChangeListener lst = new PropertyChangeListener() {
    SimpleDateFormat m_sdf = new SimpleDateFormat(
      "MM/dd/yyyy hh:mm a");
    DefaultListModel m_emptyModel = new DefaultListModel();

    public void propertyChange(PropertyChangeEvent e) {
      if (e.getPropertyName() ==
        JFileChooser.FILE_FILTER_CHANGED_PROPERTY) {
        m_zipEntries.setModel(m_emptyModel);
        return;
      }
      else if (e.getPropertyName() ==
        JFileChooser.SELECTED_FILE_CHANGED_PROPERTY) {
        File f = getSelectedFile();
        if (f == null) {
          m_zipEntries.setModel(m_emptyModel);
          return;
        }
        String name = f.getName().toLowerCase();
        if (!name.endsWith(".zip") && !name.endsWith(".jar")) {
          m_zipEntries.setModel(m_emptyModel);
          return;
        }
        try {
          ZipFile zipFile = new ZipFile(f.getPath());
          DefaultListModel model = new DefaultListModel();
          Enumeration en = zipFile.entries();
          while (en.hasMoreElements()) {
            ZipEntry zipEntr = (ZipEntry)en.
              nextElement();
            Date d = new Date(zipEntr.getTime());
            String str = zipEntr.getName()+'\t'+
              zipEntr.getSize()+'\t'+m_sdf.format(d);
            model.addElement(str);
          }
          zipFile.close();
          m_zipEntries.setModel(model);
```

```
                        m_zipEntries.setSelectionInterval(0,
                            model.getSize()-1);
                    }
                    catch(Exception ex) {
                        ex.printStackTrace();
                    }
                }
                else {
                    m_zipEntries.setModel(m_emptyModel);
                    return;
                }
            }
        };
        addPropertyChangeListener(lst);
        cancelSelection();

        return dialog;
    }

    public String[] getSelectedEntries() {
        Object[] selObj = m_zipEntries.getSelectedValues();
        String[] entries = new String[selObj.length];
        for (int k=0; k<selObj.length; k++) {
            String str = selObj[k].toString();
            int index = str.indexOf('\t');
            entries[k] = str.substring(0, index);
        }
        return entries;
    }
}

// Class TabListCellRenderer is taken from Chapter 10,
// section 10.3 without modification.
```

14.6.7   Understanding the code

Class ZipJarManager

This class extends JFrame to provide a very simple GUI for our ZIP/JAR archive manager application.

One class variable is defined:

- int BUFFER_SIZE: used to define the size of an array of bytes for reading and writing files.

Seven instance variables:

- File m_currentDir: the currently selected directory
- SimpleFilter m_zipFilter: filter for files with a ".zip" extension
- SimpleFilter m_jarFilter: filter for files with a ".jar" extension
- ZipFileView m_view: a custom FileView implementation for JAR and ZIP files
- JButton m_btCreate: initiates the creation of an archive
- JButton m_btExtract: initiates extraction from an archive
- JLabel m_status: label to display status messages

The `ZipJarManager` constructor first creates the buttons and labels and encapsulates them in a `JPanel` using a `GridLayout` and adds this to the content pane. The first button titled Create new Archive is assigned an `ActionListener` which invokes `createArchive()`. The second button titled Extract from Archive is assigned an `ActionListener` which invokes `extractArchive()`. Our custom `SimpleFilters` and `FileView` are then instantiated.

The `setStatus()` method simply assigns a given `String` to the `m_status` label.

❶ The `createArchive()` method is used to create a new archive file using two `JFile-Choosers`. First we add the file filters, set multiple file selection to false, and remove the "accept all" file filter. Then we set its title to New Archive and its type to `SAVE_DIALOG`. We show it in a dialog to prompt the user for a new archive name. If the dialog is dismissed by pressing Cancel or the close button we do nothing and return. Otherwise we store the current directory in our `m_currentDir` instance variable and create a `File` instance corresponding to the file specified in the chooser.

Interestingly, `JFileChooser` does not check whether the filename entered in its text field is valid with respect to its filters when the approve button pressed. So we are forced to check if our `File`'s name has a .zip or .jar extension manually using our custom `isArchiveFile()` method. If this method returns `false` we do nothing and return. Otherwise we set up a second `JFileChooser` to allow multiple selections to make up the content of the archive, and only allow file selections (by setting the `fileSelectionMode` property to `FILES_ONLY`) to avoid overcomplicating our archive processing scheme. Also note that we set the dialog title to specify the name of the archive we are creating.

We use `JFileChooser`'s `showDialog()` method to display this chooser in a `JDialog` and assign Add as its approve button text. If the approve button is not pressed we do nothing and return. Otherwise we create an array of `Files` to be placed in the specified archive using `JFileChooser`'s `getSelectedFiles()` method (which works correctly as of Java 1.4). Finally, we invoke our `createZipArchive()` method if the selected archive file has a .zip extension, or `createJarArchive()` if it has a .jar extension. These method calls are wrapped in separate threads to avoid clogging up the event–dispatching thread.

The `createZipArchive()` method takes two parameters: a ZIP archive file and an array of the files to be added to the archive. It creates a `ZipOutputStream` to write the selected archive file. Then for each file in the given array it creates a `ZipEntry` instance, places it in the `ZipOutputStream`, and performs standard read/write operations until all data has been written into the archive. The status label is updated, using our `setStatus()` method, each time a file is written and when the operation completes, to provide feedback during long operations.

The `createJarArchive()` method works almost identically to `createZipAr-chive()`, using the corresponding `java.util.jar` classes. Note that a default `Manifest` instance is supplied to the `JarOutputStream` constructor.

❷ The `extractArchive()` method extracts data from an archive file using two J-File-Choosers, one of which is an instance of our custom `ExtractChooser` class. First we create an `ExtractChooser` instance, add the file filters, set multiple file selection to `false` and remove the Accept All file filter. Then we set its title to Open Archive and its type to `OPEN_DIALOG`. We show it in a dialog to prompt the user for a new archive name. If the dialog is dismissed by pressing Cancel or the close button we do nothing and return. Otherwise we store the current directory in our `m_currentDir` instance variable and create a `File` instance corresponding to the file specified in the chooser. We then create a `String` array representing the entries selected in the `ExtractChooser` with its `getSelectedEntries()` method. If no entries were selected we display a message in the status bar and return. Otherwise a regular `JFileChooser` is used to select a directory to extract the selected archive entries in. We instantiate this and set its `fileSelectionMode` property to `DIRECTORIES_ONLY`, and enforce single selection by setting its `multiSelectionEnabled` property to `false`. We then show the chooser using Select for its approve button text. If it is dismissed we return. Otherwise we start the extraction process in a separate thread calling our custom `extractFrom-Archive()` method.

3 In the `extractFromArchive()` method we begin the extraction process by creating a `ZipInputStream` to read from the selected archive file. We then process each entry in the archive by retrieving a corresponding `ZipEntry` and verifying whether each `ZipEntry`'s name matches a `String` in the passed in array of selected files. If a match is found we create a `File` instance to write that entry to. If a `ZipEntry` includes subdirectories, we create these subdirectories using `File`'s `mkdirs()` method. Finally we perform standard read/write operations until all files have been extracted from the archive. Note that we update the status label each time a file is extracted and when the opertion completes.

Class SimpleFilter

This class represents a basic `FileFilter` that accepts files with a given `String` extension, and displays a given `String` description in `JFileChooser`'s Files of Type combo box. We have already seen and discussed this filter in section 14.1.9. It is used here to create our JAR and ZIP filters in the `ZipJarManager` constructor.

4 Class ZipFileView

This class extends `FileView` to provide a more user-friendly graphical representation of ZIP and JAR files in `JFileChooser`. Two instance variables, `ImageIcon ZIP_ICON` and `ImageIcon JAR_ICON`, represent small images corresponding to each archive type: `archive.gif`. This class is a straightforward adaptation of the sample `FileView` class presented in section 14.1.11.

5 Class ExtractChooser

Since `JFileChooser` is derived from `JComponent`, we can add our own components to it just like any other container. A quick look at the source code shows that `JFileChooser` uses a *y*-oriented `BoxLayout`. This implies that new components added to a `JFileChooser` will be placed below all other existing components (see chapter 4 for more about `BoxLayout`).

We take advantage of this knowledge in building our `ExtractChooser` class and add a `JList` component, `m_zipEntries`, to allow selection of compressed entries to be extracted from a selected archive. This `JList` component receives an instance of our custom `TabListCellRenderer` as its cell renderer to process `Strings` with tabs (see chapter 10, section 10.3). The location of `String` segments between tabs are assigned using its `setTabs()` method. Finally, this list is placed in a `JScrollPane` to provide scrolling capabilities, and added to the bottom of the component.

A `PropertyChangeListener` is added to process the user's selection. This anonymous class maintains two instance variables:

- `SimpleDateFormat m_sdf`: used to format file time stamps
- `DefaultListModel m_emptyModel`: assigned to `m_zipEntries` when non-archive files are selected, or when the file filter is changed

This listener's `propertyChange()` method will receive a `PropertyChangeEvent` when, among other things, the chooser's selection changes. The selected file can then be retrieved and if this file represents a ZIP or JAR archive, our implementation creates a `ZipFile` instance to read its content, and retrieves an `Enumeration` of `ZipEntry`s in this archive (recall that `JarFile` and `JarEntry` are subclasses of `ZipFile` and `ZipEntry`, allowing us to display the contents of a JAR or a ZIP archive identically). For each entry we form a `String` containing that entry's name, size, and time stamp. This `String` is added to a `DefaultListModel` instance. After each entry has been processed, this model is assigned to our `JList`, and all items are initially selected. The user can then modify the selection to specify entries to be extracted from the archive.

14.6.8   Running the code

Press the Create new Archive button and select a name and location for the new archive file in the first file chooser that appears. Press its OK button and then select files to be added to that archive in the second chooser. Figure 14.16 shows `ZipJarManager` in action, and figures 14.17 and 14.18 show the first and second choosers that appear during the archive creation process.

Try uncompressing an existing archive. Press the Extract from Archive button and select an existing archive file in the first chooser that appears. Note the custom list component displayed in the bottom of this chooser, figure 14.19 illustrates. Each time an archive is selected its contents are displayed in this list. Select entries to extract and press the Extract button. A second chooser will appear, shown in figure 14.20, allowing selection of a destination directory for extraction.

PART III

Advanced topics

In chapters 15 through 21 we discuss the most advanced Swing components and the classes and interfaces that support them. We start with `JLayeredPane` in chapter 15.

Chapter 16 is about `JDesktopPane` and `JInternalFrame`, the MDI components that ship with Swing.

Chapters 17 and 18 discuss the powerful and intricate tree and table components. Among other examples, we show how to build a directory browser using the tree component, and a sortable, JDBC-aware stocks application using the table component, and an expense report application.

Chapter 19 continues the text component coverage where chapter 11 left off, and it discusses them at a much lower level.

Chapter 20 presents a complete HTML editor application using `JTextPane`; several powerful custom dialogs are used to manage fonts, document properties, find and replace, hyperlink, image, and table insertion, and spell checking.

Chapter 21 discusses the pluggable look and feel architecture in detail and presents the construction of our own custom `LookAndFeel` implementation.

C H A P T E R 1 5

Layered panes

15.1   J*LAYERED*P*ANE*

class javax.swing.JLayeredPane

JLayeredPane is a container with an almost infinite number of *layers* in which components reside. Not only is there no limit to the number or type of components in each layer, but components can overlap one another.

Components within each layer of a JLayeredPane are organized by *position*. When overlapping is necessary, those components with a higher-valued position are displayed *under* those with a lower-valued position. However, components in higher layers are displayed *over* all components residing in lower layers. It is important to get this overlapping hierarchy down early, as it can often be confusing.

Component position is numbered from −1 to the number of components in the layer minus one. If we have N components in a layer, the component at position 0 will overlap the component at position 1, and the component at position 1 will overlap the component at position 2, and so on. The lowest position is N−1; it represents the same position as −1. Figure 15.1 illustrates the concept of position within a layer.

The layer at which a component resides is often referred to as its *depth*. (Heavyweight components cannot conform to this notion of depth; see chapter 1 for more information.) Each

471

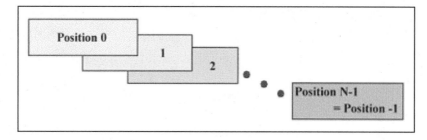

Figure 15.1   The position of components within a layer

layer is represented by an `Integer` object, and the position of a component within each layer is represented by an `int` value. The `JLayeredPane` class defines six different `Integer` object constants, representing what are intended to be commonly used layers: `FRAME_CONTENT_LAYER`, `DEFAULT_LAYER`, `PALETTE_LAYER`, `MODAL_LAYER`, `POPUP_LAYER`, and `DRAG_LAYER`.

Figure 15.2 illustrates the six standard layers and their overlap hierarchy.

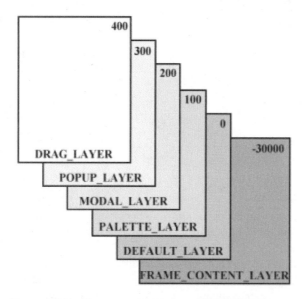

Figure 15.2   The `JLayeredPane` standard layers

We have just discussed a component's layer and position within a layer. Another value is also associated with each component within a `JLayeredPane`. This value is called the *index*. The index is the same as the position, if we were to ignore layers. That is, components are assigned indices by starting from position 0 in the highest layer and counting upward in position and downward in layer until all layers have been exhausted. The lowest component in the lowest layer will have index M–1, where M is the total number of components in the `JLayeredPane`. Similar to position, an index of –1 means the component is the bottom-most component.

(The index is really a combination of a component's layer and position. As such, there are no methods to directly change a component's index within JLayeredPane, although we can always query a component for its current index.)

There are three ways to add a component to a JLayeredPane. (Note that there is no add method defined within JLayeredPane itself.) Each method used to add a component to a JLayeredPane is defined within the Container class (see the API documentation for more information).

1 To add a component to a JLayeredPane, we use the add(Component component) method. This places the component in the layer represented by the Integer object with value 0, the DEFAULT_LAYER.

2 To add a component to a specific layer of a JLayeredPane we use the add(Component component, Object obj) method. We pass this method our component and an Integer object representing the desired layer. For layer 10, we would pass it new Integer(10). If we wanted to place it on one of the standard layers, for instance the POPUP_LAYER, we could instead pass it JLayeredPane.POPUP_LAYER.

3 To add a component to a specific position within a specific layer, we use the add(Component component, Object obj, int index) method, in which the object is specified as above, and the int is the value representing the component's position within the layer.

15.2 USING JLAYEREDPANE TO ENHANCE INTERFACES

As we mentioned earlier in chapter 4, JLayeredPane can sometimes come in handy when we want to manually position and size components. Because its layout is null, it is not prone to the effects of resizing. Thus, when its parent is resized, a layered pane's children will stay in the same position and maintain the same size. However, there are other more interesting ways to use JLayeredPane in typical interfaces. For instance, we can easily place a nice, background image behind all of our components, giving life to an otherwise dull-looking panel.

Figure 15.3
Using JLayeredPane to add a background image

Example 15.1

see \Chapter15\1

```java
import javax.swing.*;
import java.awt.*;
import java.awt.event.*;

public class TestFrame extends JFrame
{
  public TestFrame() {
    super("JLayeredPane Demo");
    setSize(256,256);

    JPanel content = new JPanel();
    content.setLayout(new BoxLayout(content, BoxLayout.Y_AXIS));
    content.setOpaque(false);

    JLabel label1 = new JLabel("Username:");
    label1.setForeground(Color.white);
    content.add(label1);

    JTextField field = new JTextField(15);
    content.add(field);

    JLabel label2 = new JLabel("Password:");
    label2.setForeground(Color.white);
    content.add(label2);

    JPasswordField fieldPass = new JPasswordField(15);
    content.add(fieldPass);

    getContentPane().setLayout(new FlowLayout());
    getContentPane().add(content);
    ((JPanel)getContentPane()).setOpaque(false);

    ImageIcon earth = new ImageIcon("earth.jpg");
    JLabel backlabel = new JLabel(earth);
    getLayeredPane().add(backlabel,
      new Integer(Integer.MIN_VALUE));
    backlabel.setBounds(0,0,earth.getIconWidth(),
      earth.getIconHeight());

    setDefaultCloseOperation(JFrame.EXIT_ON_CLOSE);
    setVisible(true);
  }

  public static void main(String[] args) {
    new TestFrame();
  }
}
```

Most of this code should look familiar. We extend JFrame and create a new JPanel with a y-oriented BoxLayout. We make this panel non-opaque so our background image will show through, then we add four simple components: two JLabels, a JTextField, and a

JPasswordField. We then set the layout of the contentPane to FlowLayout (remember that the contentPane has a BorderLayout by default), and add our panel to it. We also set the contentPane's opaque property to false, thereby ensuring that our background will show through this panel as well. Finally, we create a JLabel containing our background image, add it to our JFrame's layeredPane, and set its bounds based on the background image's size.

15.3 CREATING A CUSTOM MDI

In the first edition we stepped through the creation of a custom internal frame component and MDI container. We've removed these step-by-step examples in this edition to allow space for updated material. However, these examples have been included in the second edition .zip files, and their descriptions can still be found in the first edition text (freely available at www.manning.com/sbe). Figure 15.4 shows what our custom InnerFrame component looks like.

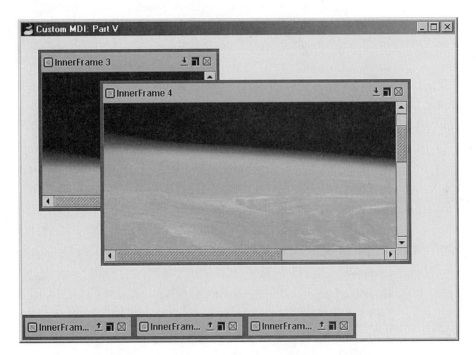

Figure 15.4   Custom InnerFrame component and MDI container

C H A P T E R   1 6

Desktops & internal frames

16.1 JDESKTOPPANE AND JINTERNALFRAME

The purpose of JDesktopPane is to provide a specialized container for JInternalFrames.

16.1.1 JDesktopPane

class javax.swing.JDesktopPane

JDesktopPane is a powerful extension of JLayeredPane that is built specifically to manage JInternalFrame children. This is Swing's version of a multiple document interface, a feature common to most modern operating system desktops. In the last chapter we created our own MDI from scratch. Both our MDI and the JDesktopPane/JInternalFrame prebuilt MDI are quite powerful. This chapter focuses on the latter.

16.1.2 JInternalFrame

class javax.swing.JInternalFrame

We can access JInternalFrame's contents in the same way we do JLayeredPane. Several additional convenience methods are defined in JDesktopPane for accessing JInternal-Frame children (see the API documentation) and attaching a DesktopManager implementation (see below).

JInternalFrames can be dragged, resized, iconified, maximized, and closed. JInternalFrame contains a JRootPane as its main container and it implements the RootPaneContainer interface. We can access a JInternalFrame's rootPane and its associated glassPane, contentPane, layeredPane, and menuBar the same way we access them in JFrame.

16.1.3 JInternalFrame.JDesktopIcon

class javax.swing.JInternalFrame.JDesktopIcon

This represents a JInternalFrame in its iconified state. In the API documentation, we are warned against using this class as it will disappear in future versions of Swing: "This API should NOT BE USED by Swing applications, as it will go away in future versions of Swing as its functionality is moved into JInternalFrame." Currently, when a JInternalFrame is iconified, it is removed from its JDesktopPane and a JDesktopIcon instance is added to represent it. In future versions of Swing, JInternalFrame will have JDesktopIcon functionality built into it. Currently, to customize the desktop icon, it is necessary to build your own DesktopIconUI subclass.

16.1.4 The DesktopManager interface

abstract interface javax.swing.DesktopManager

Each JDesktopPane has a DesktopManager object attached to it whose job it is to manage all operations performed on JInternalFrames within the desktop. DesktopManager methods are automatically called from the associated JDesktopPane when an action is invoked on a JInternalFrame within that desktop. These are usually invoked when the user performs some action on a JInternalFrame with the mouse:

- activateFrame(JInternalFrame f)
- beginDraggingFrame(JComponent f)
- beginResizingFrame(JComponent f, int direction)
- closeFrame(JInternalFrame f)
- deactivateFrame(JInternalFrame f)
- deiconifyFrame(JInternalFrame f)
- dragFrame(JComponent f, int newX, int newY)
- endDraggingFrame(JComponent f)
- endResizingFrame(JComponent f)
- iconifyFrame(JInternalFrame f)
- maximizeFrame(JInternalFrame f)
- minimizeFrame(JInternalFrame f)
- openFrame(JIntenerlFrame f)
- resizeFrame(JComponent f, int newX, int newY, int newWidth, int newHeight)
- setBoundsForFrame(JComponent f, int newX, int newY, int newWidth, int newHeight)

If we want to manually invoke iconification, for example, on a JInternalFrame, we should do the following:

```
myJInternalFrame.getDesktopPane().getDesktopManager().
    iconifyFrame(myJInternalFrame);
```

We could also directly call setIcon(true) on a JInternalFrame, but we are discouraged from doing so because it is not good practice to bypass the DesktopManager—necessary actions may be defined within the DesktopManager's iconifyFrame() method that would not be invoked. So, in general, all calls to methods of JInternalFrame that have Desktop-Manager counterparts should be delegated to the DesktopManager.

We have written an animated demo that shows when and how often each Desktop-Manager method is called. See \Chapter16\5 in the ZIP archive for this chapter and execute the DesktopManagerDemo class. Figure 16.1 illustrates.

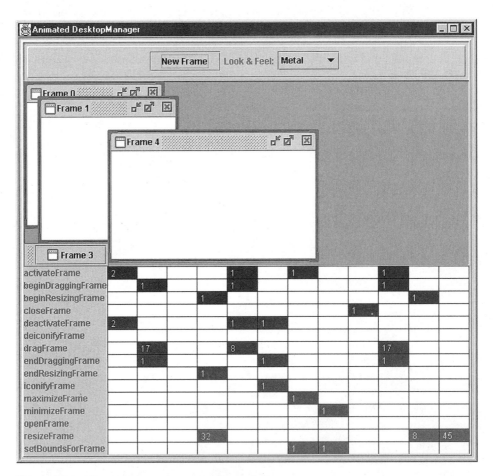

Figure 16.1 The DesktopManager animated demo

16.1.5 DefaultDesktopManager

class javax.swing.DefaultDesktopManager

This is the concrete default implementation of the `DesktopManager` interface. An instance of this class is attached to each `JDesktopPane` if a custom `DesktopManager` implementation is not specified.

16.1.6 Capturing internal frame close events

Refer to chapter 3 for a description of this interface.

To capture the closing of a `JInternalFrame` and display a confirmation dialog, we can construct the following `JInternalFrame` subclass:

```
class ConfirmJInternalFrame extends JInternalFrame
  implements VetoableChangeListener {

  public ConfirmJInternalFrame(String title, boolean resizable,
   boolean closable, boolean maximizable, boolean iconifiable) {
    super(title, resizable, closable, maximizable, iconifiable);
    addVetoableChangeListener(this);
  }

  public void vetoableChange(PropertyChangeEvent pce)
   throws PropertyVetoException {
    if (pce.getPropertyName().equals(IS_CLOSED_PROPERTY)) {
      boolean changed = ((Boolean) pce.getNewValue()).booleanValue();
      if (changed) {
        int confirm = JOptionPane.showOptionDialog(this,
          "Close " + getTitle() + "?",
          "Close Confirmation",
          JOptionPane.YES_NO_OPTION,
          JOptionPane.QUESTION_MESSAGE,
          null, null, null);
        if (confirm == 0) {
          m_desktop.remove(this);
          m_desktop.repaint();
        }
        else throw new PropertyVetoException("Cancelled",null);
      }
    }
  }
}
```

Using this class in place of `JInternalFrame` will always display a confirmation dialog when the Close button is pressed. This code checks to see if the `closed` property has changed from its previous state. This is a constrained property which we can veto if desired (see chapter 2). Luckily, this comes in quite handy for working around the `DO_NOTHING_ON_CLOSE` bug.

If the confirmation dialog is displayed and then cancelled (for example, either the NO button or the Close Dialog button is pressed), a `PropertyVetoException` is thrown which vetos the property change and the internal frame will not be closed. Figure 16.2 illustrates.

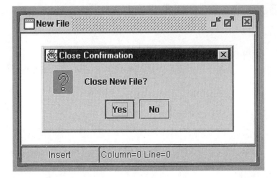

Figure 16.2
Handling internal frame closing
with a Close Confirmation dialog

16.1.7 The InternalFrameListener interface

abstract interface javax.swing.event.InternalFrameListener

Each `JInternalFrame` can have one or more `InternalFrameListeners` attached. An `InternalFrameListener` will receive `InternalFrameEvents` that allow us to capture and handle them however we like with the following methods:

- `internalFrameActivated(InternalFrameEvent e)`
- `internalFrameClosed(InternalFrameEvent e)`
- `internalFrameClosing(InternalFrameEvent e)`
- `internalFrameDeactivated(InternalFrameEvent e)`
- `internalFrameDeiconified(InternalFrameEvent e)`
- `internalFrameIconified(InternalFrameEvent e)`
- `internalFrameOpened(InternalFrameEvent e)`

`InternalFrameListener` and `DesktopManager` both exist to process changes in a `JInternalFrame`'s state. However, they can both be used to achieve different ends. `DesktopManager` allows us to define internal frame handling methods for all `JInternalFrames` within a given `JDesktopPane`, whereas `InternalFrameListener` allows us to define `InternalFrameEvent` handling unique to each *individual* `JInternalFrame`. We can attach a different `InternalFrameListener` implementation to each instance of `JInternalFrame`, whereas only one `DesktopManager` implementation can be attached to any instance of `JDesktopPane` (and thus, each of its children).

We have written an animated demo that shows when and how often each `InternalFrameListener` method is called. See \Chapter16\6 and execute the `InternalFrameListenerDemo` class. Figure 16.3 illustrates.

16.1.8 InternalFrameEvent

class javax.swing.event.InternalFrameEvent

`InternalFrameEvents` are sent to `InternalFrameListeners` whenever a `JInternalFrame` is activated, closed, about to close, deactivated, deiconified, iconified, or opened. The following static int IDs designate which type of action an `InternalFrameEvent` corresponds to:

- `INTERNAL_FRAME_ACTIVATED`
- `INTERNAL_FRAME_CLOSED`

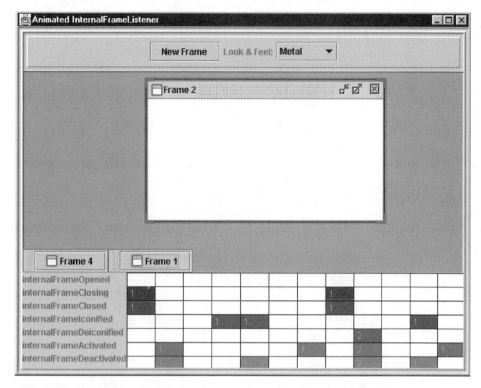

Figure 16.3 The `InternalFrameListener` animated demo

- `INTERNAL_FRAME_CLOSING`
- `INTERNAL_FRAME_DEACTIVATED`
- `INTERNAL_FRAME_DEICONIFIED`
- `INTERNAL_FRAME_ICONIFIED`
- `INTERNAL_FRAME_OPENED`

`InternalFrameEvent` extends `AWTEvent`, and thus encapsultes its source and the associated event ID (which are retrievable with `getSource()` and `getID()` respectively).

16.1.9 InternalFrameAdapter

class javax.swing.event.InternalFrameAdapter

This is a concrete implementation of the `InternalFrameListener` interface. It is intended to be extended for use by `InternalFrameListener` implementations that need to define only a subset of the `InternalFrameListener` methods. All methods defined within this adapter class have empty bodies.

16.1.10 Outline dragging mode

`JDesktopPane` supports an outline dragging mode to help with `JInternalFrame` dragging performance bottlenecks. To enable this mode on any `JDesktopPane`, we must set the `JDesktopPane.dragMode` client property:

```
myDesktopPane.putClientProperty(
  "JDesktopPane.dragMode","outline");
```

Instead of actually moving and painting the frame whenever it is dragged, an XOR'd rectangle is drawn in its place until the drag ends. Example 16.1 shows outline dragging mode in action.

16.2 CASCADING AND OUTLINE DRAGGING MODE

You are probably familiar with the cascading layout that occurs as new windows are opened in most MDI environments. In fact, if you have looked at any of the custom MDI examples of chapter 15, you will have seen that when you start each demo the InnerFrames are arranged in a cascading fashion. Example 16.1 shows how to control cascading for an arbitrary number of internal frames. Additionally, the ability to switch between any pluggable look and feel available on your system is added, and outline dragging mode is enabled in our desktop.

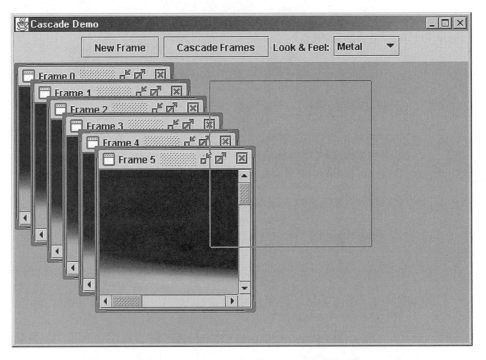

Figure 16.4 Cascading Internal Frames

Example 16.1

see \Chapter16\1

```java
import java.beans.PropertyVetoException;
import javax.swing.*;
import java.awt.event.*;
import java.awt.*;

public class CascadeDemo
    extends JFrame
    implements ActionListener {

    public static final int INI_WIDTH = 200;
    public static final int INI_HEIGHT = 200;

    private ImageIcon m_earth;
    private int m_count;
    private int m_tencount;
    private JButton m_newFrame;
    private JButton m_cascadeFrames;
    private JDesktopPane m_desktop;
    private JComboBox m_UIBox;
    private UIManager.LookAndFeelInfo[] m_infos;

    public CascadeDemo() {
        super("Cascade Demo");
        setSize(570,400);

        m_earth = new ImageIcon("earth.jpg");
        m_count = m_tencount = 0;

        m_desktop = new JDesktopPane();
        m_desktop.putClientProperty("JDesktopPane.dragMode", "outline");

        m_newFrame = new JButton("New Frame");
        m_newFrame.addActionListener(this);

        m_cascadeFrames = new JButton("Cascade Frames");
        m_cascadeFrames.addActionListener(this);

        m_infos = UIManager.getInstalledLookAndFeels();
        String[] LAFNames = new String[m_infos.length];
        for(int i=0; i<m_infos.length; i++) {
            LAFNames[i] = m_infos[i].getName();
        }

        m_UIBox = new JComboBox(LAFNames);
        m_UIBox.addActionListener(this);

        JPanel topPanel = new JPanel(true);
        topPanel.add(m_newFrame);
        topPanel.add(m_cascadeFrames);
        topPanel.add(new JLabel("Look & Feel:",SwingConstants.RIGHT));
        topPanel.add(m_UIBox);
```

1 Constructor lays out all GUI components

3 Button to create new frames

2 Provides combo box with available look and feel

```java
      getContentPane().setLayout(new BorderLayout());
      getContentPane().add(topPanel, BorderLayout.NORTH);
      getContentPane().add(m_desktop, BorderLayout.CENTER);

      Dimension dim = getToolkit().getScreenSize();
      setLocation(dim.width/2-getWidth()/2,
        dim.height/2-getHeight()/2);
   }

   public void newFrame() {                 ❸  Creates a new frame
      JInternalFrame jif = new JInternalFrame("Frame " + m_count,
        true, true, true, true);
      jif.setBounds(20*(m_count%10) + m_tencount*80,
        20*(m_count%10), INI_WIDTH, INI_HEIGHT);

      JLabel label = new JLabel(m_earth);
      jif.getContentPane().add(new JScrollPane(label));

      m_desktop.add(jif);
      jif.show();
                                          ❹   Steps to determine
      m_count++;                               the location for
      if (m_count%10 == 0)                     the next frame
{
         if (m_tencount < 3)
           m_tencount++;
         else
           m_tencount = 0;
      }
   }

   public void cascadeFrames() {            ❺   Organizes internal frames
      try {                                     in a cascading fashion
         JInternalFrame[] frames = m_desktop.getAllFrames();
         JInternalFrame selectedFrame = m_desktop.getSelectedFrame();
         int x = 0;
         int y = 0;
         for (int k=frames.length-1; k>=0; k--) {
           frames[k].setMaximum(false);
           frames[k].setIcon(false);
           frames[k].setBounds(x, y, INI_WIDTH, INI_HEIGHT);
           x += 20;
           y += 20;
         }
         if (selectedFrame != null)
           m_desktop.setSelectedFrame(selectedFrame);
      }
      catch(Exception ex) {
         ex.printStackTrace();
      }
   }

   public void actionPerformed(ActionEvent e) {    ❸  Create new frames
      if (e.getSource() == m_newFrame)
        newFrame();
```

```
        else if (e.getSource() == m_cascadeFrames)
          cascadeFrames();
        else if (e.getSource() == m_UIBox) {
        int index = m_UIBox.getSelectedIndex();       ⑤  Cascades frames
        if (index < 0)
        return;
          String lfClass = m_infos[index].getClassName();
          m_UIBox.hidePopup(); // BUG WORKAROUND
          try {
            UIManager.setLookAndFeel(lfClass);          ⑥  Changes
            SwingUtilities.updateComponentTreeUI(this);      look and feel
          }
          catch(Exception ex) {
            System.out.println("Could not load " + lfClass);
            ex.printStackTrace();
          }
          m_UIBox.setSelectedIndex(index);
        }
      }

  public static void main(String[] args) {
    CascadeDemo frame = new CascadeDemo();
    frame.setDefaultCloseOperation(JFrame.EXIT_ON_CLOSE);
    frame.setVisible(true);
  }
}
```

16.2.1   Understanding the code

Class CascadeDemo

❶ CascadeDemo extends JFrame to provide the main container for this example. The constructor is responsible for initializing and laying out all GUI components. Two class variables, INI_WIDTH and INI_HEIGHT, and several instance variables are needed:

- int INI_WIDTH: initial width of a new internal frame.
- int INI_HEIGHT: initial height of a new internal frame.
- ImageIcon m_earth: image used in each label.
- int m_count: keeps track of the number of internal frames that exist within the desktop.
- int m_tencount: incremented every time ten internal frames are added to the desktop.
- JButton m_newFrame: used to add new JInternalFrames to m_desktop.
- JButton m_cascadeFrames: used to cascade existing internal frames.
- JDesktopPane m_desktop: container for our JInternalFrames.
- JComboBox m_UIBox: used for look and feel selection.
- UIManager.LookAndFeelInfo[] m_infos: An array of LookAndFeelInfo objects used in changing look and feels.

❷ The only code that may look unfamiliar to you in the constructor is the following:

```
m_infos = UIManager.getInstalledLookAndFeels();
String[] LAFNames = new String[m_infos.length];
```

```
for(int i=0; i<m_infos.length; i++) {
  LAFNames[i] = m_infos[i].getName();
}
m_UIBox = new JComboBox(LAFNames);
```

The UIManager class is in charge of keeping track of the current look and feel as well as providing us with a way to query information about the different look and feels available on our system. Its static getInstalledLookAndFeels() method returns an array of UIManager.LookAndFeelInfo objects and we assign this array to m_infos.

Each UIManager.LookAndFeelInfo object represents a different look and feel that is currently installed on our system. Its getName() method returns a short name representing its associated look and feel (e.g., Metal, CDE/Motif, Windows, etc.). We create an array of these Strings, LAFNames, with indices corresponding to those of m_infos.

Finally we create a JComboBox, m_UIBox, using this array of Strings. In the action-Performed() method when an entry in m_UIBox is selected we match it with its corresponding UIManager.LookAndFeelInfo object in m_infos and load the associated look and feel.

③ The newFrame() method is invoked whenever the m_newButton is pressed. First this method creates a new JInternalFrame with resizable, closable, maximizable, and iconifiable properties, and a unique title based on the current frame count:

```
JInternalFrame jif = new JInternalFrame("Frame " + m_count,
  true, true, true, true);
```

The frame is then sized to 200 x 200 and its initial position within our desktop is calculated based on the value of m_count and m_tencount. The value of m_tencount is periodically reset so that each new internal frame lies within our desktop view (assuming we do not resize our desktop to have a smaller width than the maximum of 20*(m_count%10) + m_tencount*80, and a smaller height than the maximum of 20*(m_count%10). This turns out to be 420 x 180, where the maximum of m_count%10 is 9 and the maximum of m_tencount is 3).

```
jif.setBounds(20*(m_count%10) + m_tencount*80,
  20*(m_count%10), 200, 200);
```

> **NOTE**   You might imagine a more flexible cascading scheme that positions internal frames based on the current size of the desktop. In general a rigid cascading routine is sufficient, but we are certainly not limited to this.

A JLabel with an image is added to a JScrollPane, which is then added to the content-Pane of each internal frame. Each frame is added to the desktop in layer 0 (the default layer when none is specified).

④ Finally the newFrame() method increments m_count and determines whether to increment m_tencount or reset it to 0. m_tencount is only incremented after a group of 10 frames has been added (m_count%10 == 0) and is only reset after it has reached a value of 3. So 40 internal frames are created for each cycle of m_tencount (10 for m_tencount = 0, 1, 2, and 3).

```
m_count++;
if (m_count%10 == 0) {
  if (m_tencount < 3)
    m_tencount++;
```

```
        else
            m_tencount = 0;
    }
```

⑤ The `cascadeFrames()` method is invoked whenever the source of the event is the
`m_cascadeFrames` button. This method obtains an array of all existing internal frames and
iterates through it organizing them in a cascading fashion.

The `actionPerformed()` method also handles `m_newFrame` button presses and `m_UIBox`
selections. The `m_newFrame` button invokes the `newFrame()` method and selecting a look
and feel from `m_UIBox` changes the application to use that look and feel. Look and feel

⑥ switching is done by calling the `UIManager setLookAndFeel()` method and passing it the
classname of the look and feel to use (which we stored in the `m_infos` array in the constructor). Calling `SwingUtilities.updateComponentTreeUI(this)` changes the look and
feel of everything contained within the `CascadeDemo` frame (refer to chapter 2).

16.2.2   Running the code

Figure 16.4 shows `CascadeDemo` in action. This figure shows a `JInternalFrame` in the
process of being dragged in outline dragging mode. Try creating plenty of frames to make sure
that cascading is working properly. Experiment with different look and feels.

16.3   *ADDING MDI TO A TEXT EDITOR APPLICATION*

In this example we add an MDI to our basic text editor application developed in chapter 12.
We also add a commonly included function in MDI applications: a "Window" menu which
allows you to switch focus among open documents.

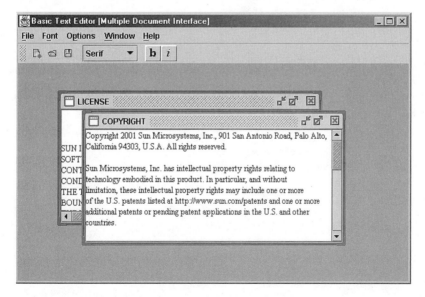

Figure 16.5   Basic text editor application with MDI

Example 16.2

see \Chapter16\2

```java
import java.awt.*;
import java.awt.event.*;
import java.io.*;
import java.util.*;

import javax.swing.*;
import javax.swing.border.*;
import javax.swing.event.*;

public class BasicTextEditor extends JFrame {

// Unchanged code from example 12.4

    protected JDesktopPane m_desktop;
    protected EditorFrame m_activeFrame;
    protected JMenu m_windowMenu;
    protected ButtonGroup  m_windowButtonGroup;

    public static final int INI_WIDTH = 400;
    public static final int INI_HEIGHT = 200;
    protected int m_frameCounter = 0;

    public BasicTextEditor() {
        super(APP_NAME+" [Multiple Document Interface]"
        setSize(600, 400);

        // Unchanged code from example 12.4

        m_desktop = new JDesktopPane();
        getContentPane().add(m_desktop, BorderLayout.CENTER);

        newDocument();

        JMenuBar menuBar = createMenuBar();
        setJMenuBar(menuBar);

        // Unchanged code from exmample 12.4

        WindowListener wndCloser = new WindowAdapter() {
            public void windowClosing(WindowEvent e) {
                if (!promptAllToSave())
                    return;
                System.exit(0);
            }
        };
        addWindowListener(wndCloser);
    }

    public JTextArea getEditor() {
        if (m_activeFrame == null)
            return null;
        return m_activeFrame.m_editor;
```

Desktop for internal frames ❶

Gives user chance to save any changes before exiting application ❶

```
    }

    public void addEditorFrame(File f) {
        EditorFrame frame = new EditorFrame(f);

        frame.setBounds(m_frameCounter*30, m_frameCounter*20,
            INI_WIDTH, INI_HEIGHT);
        m_frameCounter = (m_frameCounter+1) % 10;

        JRadioButtonMenuItem item = frame.m_frameMenuItem;
        m_windowMenu.add(item);
        m_windowButtonGroup.add(item);
        item.setSelected(true);

        frame.addInternalFrameListener(frame.new FrameListener());
        m_desktop.add(frame);
        frame.show();
        activateInternalFrame(frame);
    }

    public void activateInternalFrame(EditorFrame frame) {
        m_activeFrame = frame;
        JRadioButtonMenuItem item = frame.m_frameMenuItem;
        item.setSelected(true);

        JTextArea editor = frame.m_editor;
        Font font = editor.getFont();
        int index = 0;
        for (int k=0; k<FONTS.length; k++) {
            if (font.getName().equals(FONTS[k])) {
                index = k;
                break;
            }
        }
        m_fontMenus[index].setSelected(true);
        m_bold.setSelected(font.isBold());
        m_italic.setSelected(font.isItalic());
        updateEditor();
        m_cmFrg.setColor(editor.getForeground());
        m_cmBkg.setColor(editor.getBackground());
    }

    protected JMenuBar createMenuBar() {
        final JMenuBar menuBar = new JMenuBar();

// Unchanged code from example 12.4

        ImageIcon iconNew = new ImageIcon("New16.gif");
        Action actionNew = new AbstractAction("New", iconNew) {
            public void actionPerformed(ActionEvent e) {
                newDocument();
            }
        };
        JMenuItem item = new JMenuItem(actionNew);
        item.setMnemonic('n');
        item.setAccelerator(KeyStroke.getKeyStroke(
```

❷ Creates a new internal frame containing a given file in a text component

❸ Sets menu items corresponding to newly active internal frame

```java
      KeyEvent.VK_N, InputEvent.CTRL_MASK));
mFile.add(item);

ImageIcon iconOpen = new ImageIcon("Open16.gif");
Action actionOpen = new AbstractAction("Open...", iconOpen) {
   public void actionPerformed(ActionEvent e) {
      openDocument();
   }
};
item = new JMenuItem(actionOpen);
item.setMnemonic('o');
item.setAccelerator(KeyStroke.getKeyStroke(
   KeyEvent.VK_O, InputEvent.CTRL_MASK));
mFile.add(item);

ImageIcon iconSave = new ImageIcon("Save16.gif");
Action actionSave = new AbstractAction("Save", iconSave) {
   public void actionPerformed(ActionEvent e) {
      if (m_activeFrame != null)
         m_activeFrame.saveFile(false);
   }
};
item = new JMenuItem(actionSave);
item.setMnemonic('s');
item.setAccelerator(KeyStroke.getKeyStroke(
   KeyEvent.VK_S, InputEvent.CTRL_MASK));
mFile.add(item);

ImageIcon iconSaveAs = new ImageIcon("SaveAs16.gif");
Action actionSaveAs = new AbstractAction(
"Save As...", iconSaveAs) {
   public void actionPerformed(ActionEvent e) {
      if (m_activeFrame != null)
         m_activeFrame.saveFile(true);
   }
};
item = new JMenuItem(actionSaveAs);
item.setMnemonic('a');
mFile.add(item);

// Unchanged code from example 12.4

Action actionChooser = new AbstractAction("Color Chooser") {
   public void actionPerformed(ActionEvent e) {
      BasicTextEditor.this.repaint();
      JTextArea editor = getEditor();
      if (editor == null)
         return;

      // Unchanged code from example 12.4

   }
};

m_windowMenu = new JMenu("Window");
m_windowMenu.setMnemonic('w');
```

④ **Window menu to control a menu item corresponding to each internal frame**

```
      menuBar.add(m_windowMenu);
   m_windowButtonGroup = new ButtonGroup();

   Action actionCascade = new AbstractAction("Cascade") {
      public void actionPerformed(ActionEvent e) {
         cascadeFrames();
      }
   };
   item = new JMenuItem(actionCascade);
   item.setMnemonic('c');
   m_windowMenu.add(item);
   m_windowMenu.addSeparator();

   // Unchanged code from example 12.4

   return menuBar;
}

protected boolean promptAllToSave() {
   JInternalFrame[] frames = m_desktop.getAllFrames();
   for (int k=0; k<frames.length; k++) {
      EditorFrame frame = (EditorFrame)frames[k];
      if (!frame.promptToSave())
         return false;
   }
   return true;
}

public void cascadeFrames() {

   // Identical to cascadeFrames() method in example 16.1

}

protected void updateEditor() {
   JTextArea editor = getEditor();
   if (editor == null)
      return;

   // Unchanged code from example 12.4

}

class EditorFrame extends JInternalFrame {

   protected JTextArea m_editor;
   protected File m_currentFile;
   protected JRadioButtonMenuItem m_frameMenuItem;

   protected boolean m_textChanged = false;

   public EditorFrame(File f) {
      super("", true, true, true, true);
      m_currentFile = f;
      setTitle(getDocumentName());
      setDefaultCloseOperation(DO_NOTHING_ON_CLOSE);

      m_editor = new JTextArea();
      JScrollPane ps = new JScrollPane(m_editor);
```

5 Gives user chance to save all files

6 Internal frame class containing a text editor

```
      getContentPane().add(ps, BorderLayout.CENTER);

   m_frameMenuItem = new JRadioButtonMenuItem(getTitle());
   m_frameMenuItem.addActionListener(new ActionListener() {
      public void actionPerformed(ActionEvent evt) {
         if(isSelected())
            return;
         try {
            if (isIcon())
               setIcon(false);
            setSelected(true);
         } catch (java.beans.PropertyVetoException e) { }
   }});

   if (m_currentFile != null) {
      try {
         FileReader in = new FileReader(m_currentFile);
         m_editor.read(in, null);
         in.close();
      }
      catch (IOException ex) {
         showError(ex, "Error reading file "+m_currentFile);
      }
   }
   m_editor.getDocument().addDocumentListener(new UpdateListener());
}

public String getDocumentName() {
   return m_currentFile==null ? "Untitled "+(m_frameCounter+1) :
      m_currentFile.getName();
}

public boolean saveFile(boolean saveAs) {      ❼ Saves current
   if (!saveAs && !m_textChanged)                  document to file
      return true;
   if (saveAs || m_currentFile == null) {
      if (m_chooser.showSaveDialog(BasicTextEditor.this) !=
         JFileChooser.APPROVE_OPTION)
         return false;
      File f = m_chooser.getSelectedFile();
      if (f == null)
         return false;
      m_currentFile = f;
      setTitle(getDocumentName());
      m_frameMenuItem.setText(getDocumentName());
   }

   try {
      FileWriter out = new FileWriter(m_currentFile);
      m_editor.write(out);
      out.close();
   }
   catch (IOException ex) {
      showError(ex, "Error saving file "+m_currentFile);
```

```
        return false;
      }
      m_textChanged = false;
      return true;
    }

    public boolean promptToSave() {
      if (!m_textChanged)
        return true;
      int result = JOptionPane.showConfirmDialog(
        BasicTextEditor.this,
        "Save changes to "+getDocumentName()+"?",
        APP_NAME, JOptionPane.YES_NO_CANCEL_OPTION,
        JOptionPane.INFORMATION_MESSAGE);
      switch (result) {
        case JOptionPane.YES_OPTION:
          if (!saveFile(false))
            return false;
          return true;
        case JOptionPane.NO_OPTION:
          return true;
        case JOptionPane.CANCEL_OPTION:
          return false;
      }
      return true;
    }

    class UpdateListener implements DocumentListener {

      public void insertUpdate(DocumentEvent e) {
        m_textChanged = true;
      }

      public void removeUpdate(DocumentEvent e) {
        m_textChanged = true;
      }

      public void changedUpdate(DocumentEvent e) {
        m_textChanged = true;
      }
    }

    class FrameListener extends InternalFrameAdapter {

      public void internalFrameClosing(InternalFrameEvent e) {
        if (!promptToSave())
          return;
        m_windowMenu.remove(m_frameMenuItem);
        dispose();
      }

      public void internalFrameActivated(InternalFrameEvent e) {
        m_frameMenuItem.setSelected(true);
        activateInternalFrame(EditorFrame.this);
      }
    }
  }
```

❽ Prompts user to save current document if any changes have been made

Deletes when user attempts to close an internal frame and when a new internal frame is selected ❾

```
        }
    }

    // Unchanged code from example 12.4
```

16.3.1   Understanding the code

Class BasicTextEditor

This class has four additional instance variables:

- JDesktopPane m_desktop: desktop pane containing the internal frames.
- EditorFrame m_activeFrame: represents the currently selected internal frame.
- JMenu m_windowMenu: menu used to switch windows or cascade current windows.
- ButtonGroup m_windowButtonGroup: button group for m_windowMenu's items.

Three new class constants are also added:

- int INI_WIDTH: initial width of internal frames.
- int INI_HEIGHT: initial height of internal frames.
- int m_frameCounter: counter used to track number of internal frames created.

1 The desktop pane is added to the content pane and the WindowListener is modified to call the custom promptAllToSave() method before exiting the application.

The getEditor() method returns a reference to the active EditorFrame's JTextArea, or null if there isn't one.

2 The addEditorFrame() method takes a File as a parameter and creates a new Editor-Frame to add to the desktop pane. The File is passed to the EditorFrame constructor and displayed in the contained JTextArea for editing. The EditorFrame's bounds are set based on the state of m_frameCounter and a new JRadioButtonMenuItem is added to m_windowMenu to represent this new EditorFrame. Whenever an EditorFrame is added to the desktop an instance of the EditorFrame.FrameListener inner class is attached to it to control what happens when the user attempts to close the editor frame. Finally our custom activateInternalFrame() method is called.

3 The activateInternalFrame() method takes an EditorFrame as parameter and sets the menu bar and toolbar state according to the properties of the current editor frame and its JTextArea.

4 The createMenuBar() method includes several revisions to support the new MDI. The new m_windowMenu is added to contain items corresponding to all existing internal frames. A new action is also added to allow cascading of existing frames. The custom cascadeFrames() method is identical to that introduced in example 16.1.

5 The promptAllToSave() method iterates through all existing EditorFrames and calls the promptToSave() method on each. If the user cancels out of any dialogs that appear this method will return false. Otherwise it will return true.

6 *BasicTextEditor.EditorFrame*

This class represents an internal frame with a contained text editor. The m_currentFile variable is used to hold a reference to the File instance being edited in this frame's text area.

The constructor sets the title of the frame to the document's name using the custom `getDoc-`
`umentName()` method. It also creates a new `JRadioButtonMenuItem` to represent this
frame in the parent MDI. To this menu item is added an `ActionListener` which, when
activated, will deiconify an existing frame (if needed) and set its state to `selected`. The constructor also opens the `File` passed into the constructor and reads its contents into the editor's text area using a `FileReader`.

❼ The `saveFile()` method is responsible for saving the current document to the `File`. If the
`saveAs` parameter is `true` a `JFileChooser` is shown allowing the user to choose a new
name and/or destination for the file. This method will immediately return if no changes have
been made to the document (i.e., `m_textChanged` is `false`), unless `saveAs` is `true`.

❽ The `promptToSave()` method checks the `m_textChanged` variable to see if any document
changes have been made. If so an option pane is shown asking whether or not the user wants
to save these changes. If this process is canceled the method will return `false`; otherwise it
will return `true`.

❾ The inner `FrameListener` class is used to intercept whenever the frame is requested to close
and ask the user whether or not they want to save changes through use of the `prompt-`
`ToSave()` method. It is also used to properly synchronize state of the GUI whenever a frame
is activated.

16.3.2 Running the code

Figure 16.5 shows our basic text editor MDI in action. Try opening several documents and
switch between them using the Window menu. Try modifying a document and attempt to
close an internal frame before making changes. Note the dialogs that prompt you to save
changes. Try modifying several documents in various frames and close the application. Note
the series of dialogs that are displayed prompting you to save changes before closing.

16.4 EXAMPLES FROM THE FIRST EDITION

In chapter 16 of the first edition we covered the creation of an X-windows-like resizable pager
component to show the position of internal frames within a desktop pane. We also stepped
through the creation of a multiuser (collaborative) desktop environment using sockets. Both
examples are included in the second edition ZIP files, and the full explanation of the code
remains freely available in the online first edition manuscript. Figures 16.6–16.9 illustrate
these examples (see \Chapter16\3 and \Chapter16\4).

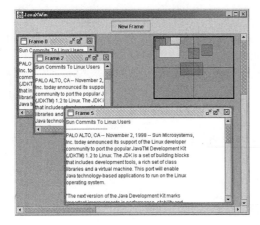

Figure 16.6
MDI with an X-windows like pager component

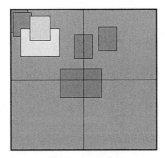

Figure 16.7
X-windows like pager component

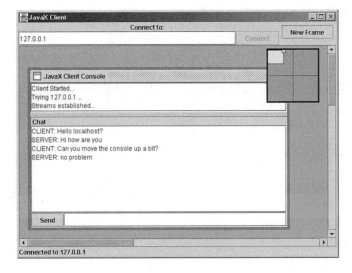

Figure 16.8
Collaborative MDI client

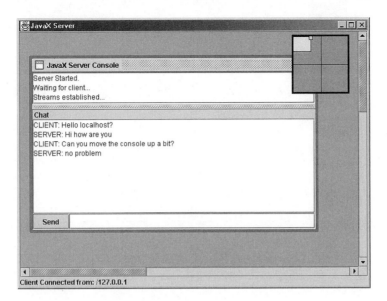

Figure 16.9   Collaborative MDI server

C H A P T E R   1 7

Trees

17.1   *JTREE*

JTree is a perfect tool for the display, navigation, and editing of hierarchical data. Because of its complex nature, JTree has a whole package devoted to it: javax.swing.tree. This package consists of a set of classes and interfaces which we will briefly review before moving on to several examples. But first, what is a tree?

17.1.1   Tree concepts and terminology

The tree is a very important and heavily used data structure throughout computer science—for example, it's used in compiler design, graphics, and artificial intelligence. This data structure consists of a logically arranged set of *node*s, which are containers for data. Each tree contains one *root* node, which serves as that tree's top-most node. Any node can have an arbitrary number of child (*descendant*) nodes. In this way, each descendant node is the root of a *subtree*.

Each node is connected by an *edge*. An edge signifies the relationship between two nodes. A node's direct predecessor is called its *parent* node, and all predecesors (above and including the parent) are called its *ancestor* nodes. A node that has no descendants is called a *leaf* node. All direct child nodes of a given node are *sibling* nodes.

A *path* from one node to another is a sequence of nodes with edges from one node to the next. The *level* of a node is the number of nodes visited in the path between the root and that node. The *height* of a tree is its largest level—the length of its longest path.

17.1.2   Tree traversal

It is essential that we be able to systematically visit each and every node of a tree. (The term "visit" here refers to performing some task before moving on.) There are three common traversal orders used for performing such an operation: *preorder, inorder,* and *postorder*. Each is recursive and can be summarized as follows:

- *Preorder*
  Recursively do the following: If the tree is not empty, visit the root and then traverse all subtrees in ascending order.
- *Inorder* (often referred to as *breadth first*):
  Start the traversal by visiting the main tree root. Then, in ascending order, visit the root of each subtree. Continue visiting the roots of all subtrees in this manner, in effect visiting the nodes at each *level* of the tree in ascending order.
- *Postorder* (often referred to as *depth first*):
  Recursively do the following: If the tree is not empty, traverse all subtrees in ascending order, and then visit the root.

17.1.3   JTree

class javax.swing.JTree

So how does Swing's `JTree` component deal with all this structure? Implementations of the `TreeModel` interface encapsulate all tree nodes, which are implementations of the `TreeNode` interface. The `DefaultMutableTreeNode` class (which is an implementation of `TreeNode`) provides us with the ability to perform preorder, inorder, and postorder tree traversals.

> **NOTE** Nothing stops us from using `TreeModel` as a data structure class without actually displaying it in a GUI. However, since this book and the Swing library are devoted to GUI, we will not discuss these possibilities further.

`JTree` graphically displays each node similarly to the way in which `JList` displays its elements: in a vertical column of cells. Also, each cell can be rendered with a custom renderer (an implementation of `TreeCellRenderer`) and can be edited with a custom `TreeCellEditor`. Each tree cell shows a non-leaf node as being *expanded* or *collapsed*, and each can represent node relationships (meaning edges) in various ways. Expanded nodes show their subtree nodes, and collapsed nodes hide this information.

The selection of tree cells is similar to `JList`'s selection mechanism, and it is controlled by a `TreeSelectionModel`. Selection also involves keeping track of paths between nodes as instances of `TreePath`. Two kinds of events are used specifically with trees and tree selections: `TreeModelEvent` and `TreeExpansionEvent`. Other AWT and Swing events also apply to `JTree`. For instance, we can use `MouseListeners` to intercept mouse presses and clicks. Keep in mind that `JTree` implements the `Scrollable` interface (see chapter 7), and it is intended to be placed in a `JScrollPane`.

A `JTree` can be constructed using either the default constructor, by providing a `Tree-Node` to use for the root node, by providing a `TreeModel` that contains all constituent nodes, or by providing a one-dimensional array, `Vector`, or `Hashtable` of objects. In the latter case, if any element in the given structure is a multi-element structure itself, it is recursively used to build a subtree (this functionality is handled by an inner class called `DynamicUtilTree-Node`).

We will see how to construct and work with all aspects of a `JTree` soon enough. But first we need to develop a more solid understanding of its underlying constituents and how they interact.

GUIDELINE

When to use a tree:

As a selection device   The tree component allows users to select items from large hierarchical data sets without having to use a Search mechanism. As such, `JTree` falls between listing and search data as a component which can improve usability by easing the process of finding something, providing that the item to be found (or selected) is hidden within a hierarchical data set.

Let's use finding an employee by name as an example. For a small data set, a simple list may be sufficient. As the data set grows, it may be easier for the user if you sort the names alphabetically or by department in which they work. By doing so, you have introduced a hierarchy and you may now use a tree component. Use of the tree component may help and speed random selection from the data set, providing that the hierarchical structure used exists in reality—don't introduce artificial hierarchies and expect users to understand them.

As a data set rises to become very large, the tree component may again be of little value and you will need to introduce a full search facility.

As a general rule, when using a tree as a selection device, start with the tree collapsed and allow the user to expand it as they search for the item they are looking for. If there is a default selection or a current selection, then we advize expanding that part of the tree to show that selection.

As a visual layering device   Even with a small data set, you may find it advantageous to display a hierarchical structure to aid visual comprehension and visual searching. With the employee example you may prefer to layer by department or by alphabetical order. When a tree is selected for display only (meaning no selection is taking place), then you are definitely using the tree as a visual layering device.

As a general rule, when you use a tree as a visual layering device, you will, by default, expand the tree in full, revealing the full hierarchy.

How you use a tree and which options to select from the many selection and display variants can be affected by how they are used, as we will demonstrate later.

17.1.4   The TreeModel interface

abstract interface javax.swing.tree.TreeModel

This model handles the data to be used in a `JTree`, assuming that each node maintains an array of child nodes. Nodes are represented as `Objects`, and a separate root node accessor is defined. A set of methods is intended to: retrieve a node based on a given parent node and index, return the number of children of a given node, return the index of a given node based on a given parent, check if a given node is a leaf node (has no children), and notify `JTree` that a node which is the destination of a given `TreePath` has been modified. It also provides method declarations for adding and removing `TreeModelListeners` which should be notified when any nodes are added, removed, or changed. A `JTree`'s `TreeModel` can be retrieved and assigned with its `getModel()` and `setModel()` methods, respectively.

17.1.5   DefaultTreeModel

class javax.swing.tree.DefaultTreeModel

`DefaultTreeModel` is the default concrete implementation of the `TreeModel` interface. It defines the root and each node of the tree as `TreeNode` instances. It maintains an `EventListenerList` of `TreeModelListeners` and provides several methods for firing `TreeModelEvents` when anything in the tree changes. It defines the `asksAllowedChildren` flag, which is used to confirm whether a node allows children to be added *before* actually attempting to add them. `DefaultTreeModel` also defines methods for: returning an array of nodes from a given node to the root node, inserting and removing nodes, and reloading/refreshing a tree from a specified node. We normally build off this class when implementing a tree model.

> **JAVA 1.4**   As of Java 1.4 `DefaultTreeModel` allows a `null` root node.

17.1.6   The TreeNode interface

abstract interface javax.swing.tree.TreeNode

`TreeNode` describes the base interface which all tree nodes must conform to in a `DefaultTreeModel`. So, implementations of this interface represent the basic building block of `JTree`'s default model. This interface declares methods for specifying whether a node: is a leaf or a parent, allows the addition of child nodes, determines the number of children, obtains a `TreeNode` child at a given index or the parent node, and obtains an `Enumeration` of all child nodes.

17.1.7   The MutableTreeNode interface

abstract interface javax.swing.tree.MutableTreeNode

This interface extends `TreeNode` to describe a more sophisticated tree node which can carry a user object. This is the object that represents the data of a given tree node. The `setUserObject()` method declares how the user object should be assigned (it is assumed that implementations of this interface will provide the equivalent of a `getUserObject()` method, even though none is included here). This interface also provides method declarations for inserting and removing child nodes from a given node, and changing its parent node.

17.1.8   DefaultMutableTreeNode

class javax.swing.tree.DefaultMutableTreeNode

`DefaultMutableTreeNode` is a concrete implementation of the `MutableTreeNode` interface. The `getUserObject()` method returns the data object encapsulated by this node. It stores all child nodes in a `Vector` called `children`, which is accessible with the `children()` method, which returns an `Enumeration` of all child nodes. We can also use the `getChildAt()` method to retreive the node corresponding to a given index. There are many methods for, among other things, retrieving and assigning tree nodes, and they are all self-explanatory (or they can be understood through simple reference of the API documentation). The only methods that deserve special mention here are the overridden `toString()` method, which returns the `String` given by the user object's `toString()` method, and the tree traversal methods which return an `Enumeration` of nodes in the order in which they can be visited. As discussed above, three types of traversal are supported: preorder, inorder, and postorder. The corresponding methods are `preorderEnumeration()`, `breadthFirstEnumeration()`, `depthFirstEnumeration()`, and `postorderEnumeration()` (the last two methods do the same thing).

17.1.9 TreePath

class javax.swing.tree.TreePath

A `TreePath` represents the path to a node as a set of nodes starting from the root. (Recall that nodes are `Objects`, not necessarily `TreeNodes`.) `TreePaths` are read-only objects and they provide functionality for comparison between other `TreePaths`. The `getLastPath-Component()` gives us the final node in the path, `equals()` compares two paths, `getPathCount()` gives the number of nodes in a path, `isDescendant()` checks whether a given path is a descendant of (is completely contained in) a given path, and `pathByAddingChild()` returns a new `TreePath` instance resulting from adding the given node to the path.

> **JAVA 1.4** New to JTree in Java 1.4 is the `getNextMatch()` method which returns a `TreePath` to the next tree element (by searching up or down) that starts with a given prefix.

17.1.10 The TreeCellRenderer interface

abstract interface javax.swing.tree.TreeCellRenderer

This interface describes the component used to render a cell of the tree. The `getTreeCell-RendererComponent()` method is called to return the component to use for rendering a given cell and that cell's selection, focus, and tree state (i.e. whether it is a leaf or a parent, and whether it is expanded or collapsed). This works similarly to custom cell rendering in `JList` and `JComboBox` (see chapters 9 and 10). To assign a renderer to `JTree`, we use its `setCellRenderer()` method. Recall that renderer components are not at all interactive and simply act as "rubber stamps" for display purposes only.

17.1.11 DefaultTreeCellRenderer

class javax.swing.tree.DefaultTreeCellRenderer

`DefaultTreeCellRenderer` is the default concrete implementation of the `TreeCell-Renderer` interface. It extends `JLabel` and maintains several properties used to render a tree cell based on its current state, as described above. These properties include `Icons` used to represent the node in any of its possible states (leaf, parent collapsed, or parent expanded) and background and foreground colors to use based on whether the node is selected or unselected. Each of these properties is self-explanatory and typical get/set accessors are provided.

17.1.12 CellRendererPane

class javax.swing.CellRendererPane

In chapter 2 we discussed the painting and validation process in detail, but we purposely avoided the discussion of how renderers actually work behind the scenes because they are only used by a few specific components. The component returned by a renderer's getXX-RendererComponent() method is placed in an instance of CellRendererPane. The Cell-RendererPane is used to act as the component's parent so that any validation and repaint requests that occur do not propogate up the ancestry tree of the container it resides in. It does this by overriding the paint() and invalidate() methods with empty implementations.

Several paintComponent() methods are provided to render a given component onto a given graphical context. These are used by the JList, JTree, and JTable UI delegates to actually paint each cell, which results in the "rubber stamp" behavior we have referred to.

17.1.13 The CellEditor interface

abstract javax.swing.CellEditor

Unlike renderers, cell editors for JTree and JTable are defined from a generic interface. This interface is CellEditor and it declares the following methods for controlling: when editing will start and stop, retrieving a new value resulting from an edit, and whether an edit request changes the component's current selection.

- Object getCellEditorValue(): Used by JTree and JTable after an accepted edit to retrieve the new value.
- boolean isCellEditable(EventObject anEvent): Used to test whether the given event should trigger a cell edit. For instance, to accept a single mouse click as an edit invocation, we would override this method to test for an instance of MouseEvent and check its click count. If the click count is 1, return true; otherwise, return false.
- boolean shouldSelectCell(EventObject anEvent): Used to specify whether the given event causes a cell that is about to be edited to also be selected. This will cancel all previous selection and for components that want to allow editing during an ongoing selection, we would return false here. It is most common to return true, as we normally think of the cell being edited as the currently selected cell.
- boolean stopCellEditing(): Used to stop a current cell edit. This method can be overriden to perform input validation. If a value is found to be unacceptable we can return false, indicating to the component that editing should not be stopped.
- void cancelCellEditing(): Used to stop a current cell edit and ignore any new input.

This interface also declares methods for adding and removing CellEditorListeners which should receive ChangeEvents whenever an edit is stopped or canceled. So stopCell-Editing() and cancelCellEditing() are responsible for firing ChangeEvents to any registered listeners.

Normally, cell editing starts with the user clicking on a cell a specified number of times which can be defined in the isCellEditable() method. The component containing the cell then replaces the current renderer pane with its editor component (JTree's editor component is returned by TreeCellEditor's getTreeCellEditorComponent() method). If should-SelectCell() returns true then the component's selection state changes to only contain the cell being edited. A new value is entered using the editor and an appropriate action takes place which invokes either stopCellEditing() or cancelCellEditing(). Finally, if the edit was stopped and not canceled, the component retrieves the new value from the editor, using getCellEditorValue(), and overwrites the old value. The editor is then replaced by the renderer pane which is updated to reflect the new data value.

17.1.14   The TreeCellEditor interface

abstract interface javax.swing.tree.TreeCellEditor

This interface extends CellEditor and describes the behavior of a component to be used in editing the cells of a tree. The getTreeCellEditorComponent() method is called prior to the editing of a new cell to set the initial data for the component it returns as the editor, based on a given cell and that cell's selection, focus, and its expanded/collapsed states. We can use any interactive component we want as an editor. To assign a TreeCellEditor to JTree, we use its setCellEditor() method.

17.1.15   DefaultCellEditor

class javax.swing.DefaultCellEditor

This is a concrete implementation of the TreeCellEditor interface as well as the TableCell-Editor interface (see section 18.1.11). This editor allows the use of JTextField, JComboBox, or JCheckBox components to edit data. It defines a protected inner class called Editor-Delegate, which is responsible for returning the current value of the editor component in use when the getCellEditorValue() method is invoked. DefaultCellEditor is limited to three constructors for creating a JTextField, JComboBox, or a JCheckBox editor.

> **NOTE**   The fact that the only constructors provided are component-specific makes Default-CellEditor a bad candidate for extensibility.

DefaultCellEditor maintains an int property called clickCountToStart which specifies how many mouse click events should trigger an edit. By default this is 2 for JTextFields and 1 for JComboBox and JCheckBox editors. As expected, ChangeEvents are fired when stopCellEditing() and cancelCellEditing() are invoked.

> **JAVA 1.3**   As of Java 1.3 this class extends the new javax.Swing.AbstractCellEditor interface.

17.1.16   DefaultTreeCellEditor

class javax.swing.tree.DefaultTreeCellEditor

DefaultTreeCellEditor extends DefaultCellEditor, and it is the default concrete implementation of the TreeCellEditor interface. It uses a JTextField for editing a node's data (an instance of DefaultTreeCellEditor.DefaultTextField). stopCellEditing() is called when ENTER is pressed in this text field.

An instance of DefaultTreeCellRenderer is needed to construct this editor, allowing renderer icons to remain visible while editing (this is accomplished by embedding the editor in an instance of `DefaultTreeCellEditor.EditorContainer`). It fires `ChangeEvents` when editing begins and ends. As expected, we can add `CellEditorListeners` to intercept and process these events.

By default, editing starts (if it is enabled) when a cell is triple-clicked or when a pause of 1200ms occurs between two single mouse clicks (the latter is accomplished using an internal `Timer`). We can set the click count requirement using the `setClickCountToStart()` method, or check for it directly by overriding `isCellEditable()`.

17.1.17 The RowMapper interface

abstract interface javax.swing.text.RowMapper

`RowMapper` declares a single method, `getRowsForPaths()`, which is intended to map an array of tree paths to an array of tree rows. A tree row corresponds to a tree cell, and as we discussed, these are organized similar to `JList` cells. `JTree` selections are based on rows and tree paths, and we can choose which to deal with depending on the needs of our application. (We aren't expected to have the need to implement this interface unless we decide to build our own `JTree` UI delegate.)

17.1.18 The TreeSelectionModel interface

abstract interface javax.swing.tree.TreeSelectionModel

The `TreeSelectionModel` interface describes a base interface for a tree's selection model. Three modes of selection are supported, similar to `JList` (see chapter 10), and implementations allow for setting this mode through the `setSelectionMode()` method: `SINGLE_TREE_SELECTION`, `DISCONTIGUOUS_TREE_SELECTION`, and `CONTIGUOUS_TREE_SELECTION`. Implementations are expected to maintain a `RowMapper` instance. The `getSelectionPath()` and `getSelectionPaths()` methods are intended to return a `TreePath` and an array of `TreePaths` respectively, allowing access to the currently selected paths. The `getSelectionRows()` method should return an `int` array that represents the indices of all rows currently selected. The *lead* selection refers to the most recently added path to the current selection. Whenever the selection changes, implementations of this interface should fire `TreeSelectionEvents`. Appropriately, add/remove `TreeSelectionListener` methods are also declared. All other methods are, for the most part, self explanatory (see the API documentation). The tree selection model can be retrieved using `JTree`'s `getSelectionModel()` method.

NOTE `JTree` defines the inner class `EmptySelectionModel`, which does not allow any selection at all.

There is also a new `removeDescendantSelectedPaths()` method which removes all `TreePaths` from the current selection that are descendants of the given path passed in a parameter.

17.1.19 DefaultTreeSelectionModel

class javax.swing.tree.DefaultTreeSelectionModel

`DefaultTreeSelectionModel` is the default concrete implementation of the `TreeSelectionModel` interface. This model supports `TreeSelectionListener` notification when changes are made to a tree's path selection. Several methods are defined for, among other things, modifying and retrieving a selection, and firing `TreeSelectionEvents` when a modification occurs.

17.1.20 The TreeModelListener interface

abstract interface javax.swing.event.TreeModelListener

The `TreeModelListener` interface describes a listener which receives notifications about changes in a tree's model. `TreeModelEvents` are normally fired from a `TreeModel` when nodes are modified, added, or removed. We can register/unregister a `TreeModelListener` with a `JTree`'s model using `TreeModel`'s `addTreeModelListener()` and `removeTreeModelListener()` methods respectively.

17.1.21 The TreeSelectionListener interface

abstract interface javax.swing.event.TreeSelectionListener

The `TreeSelectionListener` interface describes a listener which receives notifications about changes in a tree's selection. It declares only one method, `valueChanged()`, accepting a `TreeSelectionEvent`. These events are normally fired whenever a tree's selection changes. We can register/unregister a `TreeSelectionListener` with a tree's selection model using `JTree`'s `addTreeSelectionListener()` and `removeTreeSelectionListener()` methods.

17.1.22 The TreeExpansionListener interface

abstract interface javax.swing.event.TreeExpansionListener

The `TreeExpansionListener` interface describes a listener which receives notifications about tree expansions and collapses. Implementations must define `treeExpanded()` and `tree-Collapsed()` methods, which take a `TreeExpansionEvent` as a parameter. We can register/unregister a `TreeExpansionListener` with a tree using `JTree`'s `addTreeExpansion-Listener()` and `removeTreeExpansionListener()` methods respectively.

17.1.23 The TreeWillExpandListener interface

abstract interface javax.swing.event.TreeWillExpandListener

The `TreeWillExpandListener` interface describes a listener which receives notifications when a tree is *about* to expand or collapse. Unlike `TreeExpansionListener`, this listener will be notified before the actual change occurs. Implementations are expected to throw an `ExpandVetoException` if it is determined that a pending expansion or collapse should not be carried out. Its two methods, treeWillExpand() and treeWillCollapse(), take a Tree-ExpansionEvent as a parameter. We can register/unregister a TreeWillExpandListener with a tree using JTree's addTreeWillExpandListener() and removeTreeWillExpand-Listener() methods.

17.1.24 TreeModelEvent

class javax.swing.event.TreeModelEvent

TreeModelEvent is used to notify TreeModelListeners that all or part of a JTree's data has changed. This event encapsulates a reference to the source component, and a single Tree-Path or an array of path Objects leading to the topmost affected node. We can extract the source as usual, using getSource(), and we can extract the path(s) using either of the get-Path() or getTreePath() methods (the former returns an array of Objects, the latter returns a TreePath). Optionally, this event can also carry an int array of node indices and an array of child nodes. These can be extracted using the getChildIndices() and getChildren() methods respectively.

17.1.25 TreeSelectionEvent

class javax.swing.event.TreeSelectionEvent

TreeSelectionEvent is used to notify TreeSelectionListeners that the selection of a JTree has changed. One variant of this event encapsulates: a reference to the source component, the selected TreePath, a flag specifying whether the tree path is a new addition to the selection (true if so), and the new and old lead selection paths (remember that the lead selection path is the newest path added to a selection). The second variant of this event encapsulates: a reference to the source component, an array of selected TreePaths, an array of flags specifying whether each path is a new addition, and the new and old lead selection paths. Typical getXX() accessor methods allow extraction of this data.

> **NOTE** An interesting and unusual method defined in this class is cloneWithSource(). When passed a component, this method returns a clone of the event, but with a reference to the given component parameter as the event source.

> **JAVA 1.3** New to TreeSelectionEvent in Java 1.3 is the isAddedPath() method which takes an int index as parameter. If the TreePath at the given index was added, this method returns true; if not it returns false.

17.1.26 TreeExpansionEvent

class javax.swing.event.TreeExpansionEvent

TreeExpansionEvent is used to encapsulate a TreePath corresponding to a recently, or possibly pending, expanded or collapsed tree path. This path can be extracted with the get-Path() method.

17.1.27 ExpandVetoException

class javax.swing.tree.ExpandVetoException

ExpandVetoException may be thrown by TreeWillExpandListener methods to indicate that a tree path expansion or collapse is prohibited, and should be vetoed.

17.1.28 JTree client properties and UI defaults

When using the Metal look and feel, JTree uses a specific line style to represent the edges between nodes. The default is no edges, but we can set JTree's lineStyle client property so that each parent node appears connected to each of its child nodes by an angled line:

```
myJTree.putClientProperty("JTree.lineStyle", "Angled");
```

We can also set this property so that each tree cell is separated by a horizontal line:

```
myJTree.putClientProperty("JTree.lineStyle", "Horizontal");
```

To disable the line style, do this:

```
myJTree.putClientProperty("JTree.lineStyle", "None");
```

As with any Swing component, we can also change the UI resource defaults used for all instances of the JTree class. For instance, to change the color of the lines used for rendering the edges between nodes as described above, we can modify the entry in the UI defaults table for this resource as follows:

```
UIManager.put("Tree.hash",
    new ColorUIResource(Color.lightGray));
```

To modify the open node icons used by all trees when a node's children are shown:

```
UIManager.put("Tree.openIcon", new IconUIResource(
    new ImageIcon("myOpenIcon.gif")));
```

We can do a similar thing for the closed, leaf, expanded, and collapsed icons using Tree. closedIcon, Tree.leafIcon, Tree.expandedIcon, and Tree.collapsedIcon respectively. (See the BasicLookAndFeel source code for a complete list of UI resource defaults.)

> **NOTE** We used the ColorUIResource and IconUIResource wrapper classes found in the javax.swing.plaf package to wrap our resources before placing them in the UI defaults table. If we do not wrap our resources in UIResource objects, they will persist through look and feel changes (which may or may not be desirable). See chapter 21 for more about look and feel and resource wrappers.

17.1.29 Controlling JTree appearance

Though we haven't concentrated heavily on UI delegate customization for each component throughout this book, Swing certainly provides us with a high degree of flexibility in this area. It is particularly useful with JTree because no methods are provided in the component itself to control the indentation spacing of tree cells (note that the row height can be specified with JTree's setRowHeight() method). The JTree UI delegate also provides methods for setting expanded and collapsed icons, allowing us to assign these on a per-component basis rather than a global basis (which is done using `UIManager`; see section 17.1.28). The following `BasicTreeUI` methods provide this control, and figure 17.1 illustrates:

- `void setCollapsedIcon(Icon newG)`: The icon used to specify that a node is in the collapsed state.
- `void setExpandedIcon(Icon newG)`: The icon used to specify that a node is in the expanded state.
- `void setLeftChildIndent(int newAmount)`: Used to assign a distance between the left side of a parent node and the center of an expand/collapse box of a child node.
- `void setRightChildIndent(int newAmount)`: Used to assign a distance between the center of the expand/collapse box of a child node to the left side of that child node's cell renderer.

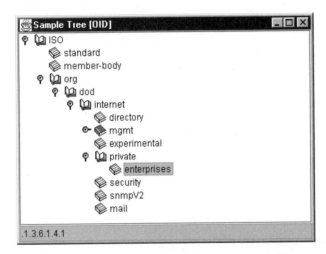

Figure 17.1
The `JTree` UI delegate icon and indentation properties

To actually use these methods, we first have to obtain the target tree's UI delegate. For example, to assign a left indent of 8 and a right indent of 10:

```
BasicTreeUI basicTreeUI = (BasicTreeUI) myJTree.getUI();
basicTreeUI.setRightChildIndent(10);
basicTreeUI.setLeftChildIndent(8);
```

17.2 BASIC JTREE EXAMPLE

As we know very well by now, `JTree` is suitable for the display and editing of a hierarchical set of objects. To demonstrate this in an introductory-level example, we will consider a set of Object Identifiers (OIDs) used in the Simple Network Management Protocol (SNMP). In example 17.1 we will show how to build a simple `JTree` that displays the initial portion of the OID tree.

SNMP is used extensively to manage network components, and it is particularly important in managing Internet routers and hosts. Every object managed by SNMP must have a unique OID. An OID is built from a sequence of numbers separated by periods. Objects are organized hierarchically and have an OID with a sequence of numbers equal in length to their *level* (see section 17.1.1) in the OID tree. The International Organization of Standards (ISO) establishes rules for building OIDs.

Understanding SNMP is certainly not necessary to understand this example. The purpose of this example is to show how to construct a tree using the following items:

- A `DefaultTreeModel` with `DefaultMutableTreeNodes` containing custom user objects.
- A customized `DefaultTreeCellRenderer`.
- A `TreeSelectionListener` which displays information in a status bar based on the `TreePath` encapsulated in the `TreeSelectionEvents` it receives.

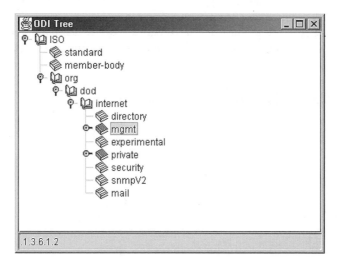

Figure 17.2
JTree with custom cell renderer icons, selection listener, and visible root

Example 17.1

Tree1.java

see \Chapter17\1

```
import java.awt.*;
import java.awt.event.*;
import java.util.*;

import javax.swing.*;
import javax.swing.tree.*;
import javax.swing.event.*;

public class Tree1 extends JFrame
{
  protected JTree  m_tree = null;
  protected DefaultTreeModel m_model = null;
  protected JTextField m_display;

  public Tree1() {
    super("Sample Tree [OID]");
    setSize(400, 300);

    Object[] nodes = new Object[5];
    DefaultMutableTreeNode top = new DefaultMutableTreeNode(
```

❶ **Constructor creates several DefaultMutableTreeNodes, each containing an OidNode**

```
    new OidNode(1, "ISO"));
DefaultMutableTreeNode parent = top;
  nodes[0] = top;

DefaultMutableTreeNode node = new DefaultMutableTreeNode(
  new OidNode(0, "standard"));
parent.add(node);
node = new DefaultMutableTreeNode(new OidNode(2,
  "member-body"));
parent.add(node);
node = new DefaultMutableTreeNode(new OidNode(3, "org"));
parent.add(node);
parent = node;
nodes[1] = parent;

node = new DefaultMutableTreeNode(new OidNode(6, "dod"));
parent.add(node);
parent = node;
nodes[2] = parent;

node = new DefaultMutableTreeNode(new OidNode(1, "internet"));
parent.add(node);
parent = node;
nodes[3] = parent;

node = new DefaultMutableTreeNode(new OidNode(1, "directory"));
parent.add(node);
node = new DefaultMutableTreeNode(new OidNode(2, "mgmt"));
parent.add(node);
nodes[4] = node;
node.add(new DefaultMutableTreeNode(new OidNode(1, "mib-2")));
node = new DefaultMutableTreeNode(new OidNode(3,
  "experimental"));
parent.add(node);
node = new DefaultMutableTreeNode(new OidNode(4, "private"));
node.add(new DefaultMutableTreeNode(new OidNode(1,
  "enterprises")));
parent.add(node);
node = new DefaultMutableTreeNode(new OidNode(5, "security"));
parent.add(node);
node = new DefaultMutableTreeNode(new OidNode(6, "snmpV2"));
parent.add(node);
node = new DefaultMutableTreeNode(new OidNode(7,
  "mail"));
parent.add(node);

m_model = new DefaultTreeModel(top);
m_tree = new JTree(m_model);

DefaultTreeCellRenderer renderer = new
  DefaultTreeCellRenderer();
renderer.setOpenIcon(new ImageIcon("opened.gif"));
renderer.setClosedIcon(new ImageIcon("closed.gif"));
renderer.setLeafIcon(new ImageIcon("leaf.gif"));
m_tree.setCellRenderer(renderer);
```

2 Creates a JTree pointing to the top node

```
      m_tree.setShowsRootHandles(true);
      m_tree.setEditable(false);
      TreePath path = new TreePath(nodes);
      m_tree.setSelectionPath(path);

      m_tree.addTreeSelectionListener(new
        OidSelectionListener());

      JScrollPane s = new JScrollPane(m_tree);
      getContentPane().add(s, BorderLayout.CENTER);

      m_display = new JTextField();
      m_display.setEditable(false);
      getContentPane().add(m_display, BorderLayout.SOUTH);

      setDefaultcloseOperation(JFrame.EXIT_ON_CLOSE);
      setVisible(true);
    }
    public static void main(String argv[]) {
      new Tree1();
    }

    class OidSelectionListener implements TreeSelectionListener
    {
      public void valueChanged(TreeSelectionEvent e) {
        TreePath path = e.getPath();
        Object[] nodes = path.getPath();
        String oid = "";
        for (int k=0; k<nodes.length; k++) {
          DefaultMutableTreeNode node =
            (DefaultMutableTreeNode)nodes[k];
          OidNode nd = (OidNode)node.getUserObject();
          oid += "."+nd.getId();
        }
        m_display.setText(oid);
      }
    }
  }

class OidNode
{
  protected int    m_id;
  protected String m_name;

  public OidNode(int id, String name) {
    m_id = id;
    m_name = name;
  }

  public int getId() { return m_id; }

  public String getName() { return m_name; }

  public String toString() { return m_name; }
}
```

③ Adds a JScrollPane, with the tree in the viewport

④ Listens for node selections, then follows the path from the root to the node to build the ID string

⑤ Simple object identifier encapsulated at each node

17.2.1 Understanding the code

Class Tree1

This class extends `JFrame` to implement the frame container for our `JTree`. Three instance variables are declared:

- `JTree m_tree`: Our OID tree.
- `DefaultTreeModel m_model`: The tree model to manage data.
- `JTextField m_display`: Used as a status bar to display the selected object's OID.

1 The constructor first initializes the parent frame object. Then a number of `DefaultMutable-TreeNodes` encapsulating `OidNodes` (see below) are created. These objects form a hierarchical structure with `DefaultMutableTreeNode top` at the root. During the construction of these nodes, the `Object[]` nodes array is populated with a path of nodes leading to the `mgmt` node.

2 `DefaultTreeModel m_model` is created with the `top` node as the root, and `JTree m_tree` is created to manage this model. Then specific options are set for this tree component. First, we replace the default icons for opened, closed, and leaf icons with our custom icons, using a `DefaultTreeCellRenderer` as our tree's cell renderer:

```
DefaultTreeCellRenderer renderer = new
    DefaultTreeCellRenderer();
renderer.setOpenIcon(new ImageIcon("opened.gif"));
renderer.setClosedIcon(new ImageIcon("closed.gif"));
renderer.setLeafIcon(new ImageIcon("leaf.gif"));
m_tree.setCellRenderer(renderer);
```

Then we set the `showsRootHandles` property to `true` and the `editable` property to `false`, and we select the path determined by the `nodes` array formed above:

```
m_tree.setShowsRootHandles(true);
m_tree.setEditable(false);
TreePath path = new TreePath(nodes);
m_tree.setSelectionPath(path);
```

Our custom `OidSelectionListener` (see below) `TreeSelectionListener` is added to the tree to receive notification when our tree's selection changes.

3 A `JScrollPane` is created to provide scrolling capabilities, and our tree is added to its `JViewport`. This `JScrollPane` is then added to the center of our frame. A non-editable `JTextField m_display` is created and added to the south region of our frame's content pane to display the currently selected OID.

Class Tree1.OidSelectionListener

4 This inner class implements the `TreeSelectionListener` interface to receive notifications about when our tree's selection changes. Our `valueChanged()` implementation extracts the `TreePath` corresponding to the current selection and visits each node, starting from the root, accumulating the OID in .N.N.N form as it goes (where N is a digit). This method ends by displaying the resulting OID in our text field status bar.

Class OidNode

⑤ This class encapsulates a single object identifier as a number and a `String` name describing the associated object. Both values are passed to the `OidNode` constructor. Instances of this class are passed directly to the `DefaultMutableTreeNode` constructor to act as a node's user object. The overridden `toString()` method is used to return the name `String` so that our tree's cell renderer will display each node correctly. Recall that, by default, `DefaultTree-CellRenderer` will call a node's user object `toString()` method for rendering.

17.2.2   Running the code

Figure 17.2 shows our OID tree in action. Try selecting various tree nodes and notice how the selected OID is displayed at the bottom of the frame.

GUIDELINE

Icons and root handles   In this example, we are visually reinforcing the data hierarchy with icons. The icons communicate whether an element is a document or a container and whether that container is open or closed. The book icon has two variants to communicate "open book" and "closed book." The icons are communicating the same information as the root handles. Therefore, it is technically possible to remove the root handles. In some problem domains, hidden root handles may be more appropriate, providing that the users are comfortable with interpreting the book icons and realize that a "closed book" icon means that the node can be expanded.

17.3   *DIRECTORY TREE, PART I: DYNAMIC NODE RETRIEVAL*

Example 17.2 in this section uses the `JTree` component to display and navigate through a tree of directories located on drives accessible from the user's machine. We will show how to build a custom tree cell renderer as well as how to create and insert tree nodes dynamically.

The main problem encountered in building this application is the fact that it is not practical to read all directories for all accessible drives before displaying our tree component. This would take an extremely long time. To deal with this issue, we initially display only the roots (such as disk partitions or network drives), and then we dynamically expand the tree as the user navigates through it. This requires the use of threads and `SwingUtilities.invokeLater()` for thread-safe updating of our tree.

Example 17.2

DirTree.java

see \Chapter17\2

```
import java.awt.*;
import java.awt.event.*;
import java.io.*;
import java.util.*;

import javax.swing.*;
```

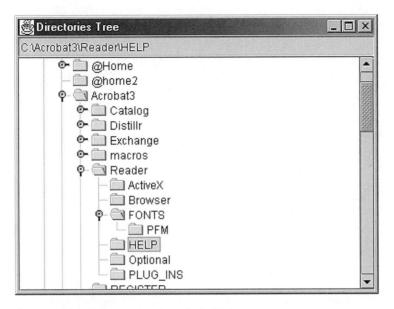

Figure 17.3 A dynamic, threaded directory tree with a custom cell renderer and angled line style

```
import javax.swing.tree.*;
import javax.swing.event.*;

public class DirTree extends JFrame
{
  public static final String APP_NAME = "DIRECTORIES TREE";
  public static final ImageIcon ICON_FOLDER =
    new ImageIcon("computer.gif");
  public static final ImageIcon ICON_DISK =
    new ImageIcon("disk.gif");
  public static final ImageIcon ICON_FOLDER =
    new ImageIcon("folder.gif");
  public static final ImageIcon ICON_EXPANDEDFOLDER =
    new ImageIcon("expandedfolder.gif");

  protected JTree  m_tree;
  protected DefaultTreeModel m_model;
  protected JTextField m_display;

  public DirTree() {
    super(APP_NAME);
    setSize(400, 300);

    DefaultMutableTreeNode top = new DefaultMutableTreeNode(
      new IconData(ICON_COMPUTER, null, "Computer"));

    DefaultMutableTreeNode node;
      File[] roots = File.listRoots();
    for (int k=0; k<roots.length; k++) {
```

① Constructor creates tree with nodes representing all disk partitions and network nodes

```
        node = new DefaultMutableTreeNode(
          new IconData(ICON_DISK,
          null, new FileNode(roots[k])));
        top.add(node);
        node.add(new DefaultMutableTreeNode(
        new Boolean(true)));
      }

      m_model = new DefaultTreeModel(top);
      m_tree = new JTree(m_model);

      m_tree.getSelectionModel().setSelectionMode(
        TreeSelectionModel.SINGLE_TREE_SELECTION);
      m_tree.putClientProperty("JTree.lineStyle", "Angled");
      TreeCellRenderer renderer = new IconCellRenderer();
      m_tree.setCellRenderer(renderer);
      m_tree.addTreeExpansionListener(new DirExpansionListener());
      m_tree.addTreeSelectionListener(new DirSelectionListener());
      m_tree.setShowsRootHandles(true);
      m_tree.setEditable(false);

      JScrollPane s = new JScrollPane();
      s.getViewport().add(m_tree);
      getContentPane().add(s, BorderLayout.CENTER);

      m_display = new JTextField();
      m_display.setEditable(false);
      getContentPane().add(m_display, BorderLayout.NORTH);

      setDefaultCloseOperation(JFrame.EXIT_ON_CLOSE);
      setVisible(true);
    }

    DefaultMutableTreeNode getTreeNode(TreePath path) {
      return (DefaultMutableTreeNode) (path.getLastPathComponent());
    }

    FileNode getFileNode(DefaultMutableTreeNode node) {
      if (node == null)
        return null;
      Object obj = node.getUserObject();
      if (obj instanceof IconData)
        obj = ((IconData)obj).getObject();
      if (obj instanceof FileNode)
        return (FileNode)obj;
      else
        return null;
    }

    // Make sure expansion is threaded and updating the tree model
    // only occurs within the event dispatching thread.
    class DirExpansionListener implements TreeExpansionListener
    {
      public void treeExpanded(TreeExpansionEvent event) {
        final DefaultMutableTreeNode node = getTreeNode(
          event.getPath());
```

① Creates one TreeNode holding icon and file info

② Creates tree with top node as root

③ Gets the TreeNode at the end of the path

③ Gets the FileNode from a TreeNode

④ Listens for tree expansion events

```
          final FileNode fnode = getFileNode(node);

      Thread runner = new Thread() {
        public void run() {
          if (fnode != null && fnode.expand(node)) {
            Runnable runnable = new Runnable() {
              public void run() {
                m_model.reload(node);
              }
            };
            SwingUtilities.invokeLater(runnable);
          }
        }
      };
      runner.start();
    }

    public void treeCollapsed(TreeExpansionEvent event) {}
  }

  class DirSelectionListener implements TreeSelectionListener
  {
    public void valueChanged(TreeSelectionEvent event) {
      DefaultMutableTreeNode node = getTreeNode(event.getPath());
        FileNode fnode = getFileNode(node);
        if (fnode != null)
          m_display.setText(fnode.getFile().getAbsolutePath());
        else
          m_display.setText("");
    }
  }

  public static void main(String argv[]) { new FileTree1(); }
}

class IconCellRenderer extends JLabel implements TreeCellRenderer
{
  protected Color m_textSelectionColor;
  protected Color m_textNonSelectionColor;
  protected Color m_bkSelectionColor;
  protected Color m_bkNonSelectionColor;
  protected Color m_borderSelectionColor;

  protected boolean m_selected;

  public IconCellRenderer() {
    super();
    m_textSelectionColor = UIManager.getColor(
      "Tree.selectionForeground");
    m_textNonSelectionColor = UIManager.getColor(
      "Tree.textForeground");
    m_bkSelectionColor = UIManager.getColor(
      "Tree.selectionBackground");
    m_bkNonSelectionColor = UIManager.getColor(
      "Tree.textBackground");
```

4 Does expansion work in the background?

5 Resets the tree on the event-dispatch thread

6 Listens for tree selection events; updates m_display with selected path

7 Renders TreeNodes with icons and text

```
      m_borderSelectionColor = UIManager.getColor(
        "Tree.selectionBorderColor");
      setOpaque(false);
    }

    public Component getTreeCellRendererComponent(JTree tree,
     Object value, boolean sel, boolean expanded, boolean leaf,
     int row, boolean hasFocus)
    {
      DefaultMutableTreeNode node = (DefaultMutableTreeNode)value;
      Object obj = node.getUserObject();
      setText(obj.toString());
```

8 Indicates node
in midst of being
expanded

```
      if (obj instanceof Boolean)
        setText("Retrieving data...");

      if (obj instanceof IconData) {
        IconData idata = (IconData)obj;
        if (expanded)
          setIcon(idata.getExpandedIcon());
        else
          setIcon(idata.getIcon());
      }
      else
        setIcon(null);

      setFont(tree.getFont());
      setForeground(sel ? m_textSelectionColor :
        m_textNonSelectionColor);
      setBackground(sel ? m_bkSelectionColor :
        m_bkNonSelectionColor);
      m_selected = sel;
      return this;
    }

    public void paintComponent(Graphics g) {
      Color bColor = getBackground();
      Icon icon = getIcon();
```

9 Just paints text
background color;
text is drawn in
base class method

```
      g.setColor(bColor);
      int offset = 0;
      if(icon != null && getText() != null)
        offset = (icon.getIconWidth() + getIconTextGap());
      g.fillRect(offset, 0, getWidth() - 1 - offset,
        getHeight() - 1);

      if (m_selected) {
        g.setColor(m_borderSelectionColor);
        g.drawRect(offset, 0, getWidth()-1-offset, getHeight()-1);
      }
      super.paintComponent(g);
    }
  }
```

```java
class IconData
{
  protected Icon    m_icon;
  protected Icon    m_expandedIcon;
  protected Object m_data;

  public IconData(Icon icon, Object data) {
    m_icon = icon;
    m_expandedIcon = null;
    m_data = data;
  }

  public IconData(Icon icon, Icon expandedIcon, Object data) {
    m_icon = icon;
    m_expandedIcon = expandedIcon;
    m_data = data;
  }

  public Icon getIcon() { return m_icon; }

  public Icon getExpandedIcon() {
    return m_expandedIcon!=null ? m_expandedIcon : m_icon;
  }

  public Object getObject() { return m_data; }

  public String toString() { return m_data.toString(); }
}

class FileNode
{
  protected File m_file;

  public FileNode(File file) { m_file = file; }

  public File getFile() { return m_file; }

  public String toString() {
    return m_file.getName().length() > 0 ? m_file.getName() :
      m_file.getPath();
  }

  public boolean expand(DefaultMutableTreeNode parent) {
    DefaultMutableTreeNode flag =
      (DefaultMutableTreeNode)parent.getFirstChild();
    if (flag==null)        // No flag
      return false;
    Object obj = flag.getUserObject();
    if (!(obj instanceof Boolean))
      return false;        // Already expanded

    parent.removeAllChildren();  // Remove flag

    File[] files = listFiles();
    if (files == null)
      return true;

    Vector v = new Vector();
```

⑩ Encapsulates "closed" and "open" icons, and a data object that is either a FileNode or a Boolean

⑪ Stores file information, and can be expanded to contain child FileNodes

⑫ Expands a node by adding new nodes corresponding to the subdirectory of the starting node

⑬ Determines whether node has no children, is already expanded, or needs to do more work to expand it

⑭ Gets list of files in directory

```
      for (int k=0; k<files.length; k++) {
        File f = files[k];
        if (!(f.isDirectory()))
          continue;

        FileNode newNode = new FileNode(f);

        boolean isAdded = false;
        for (int i=0; i<v.size(); i++) {
          FileNode nd = (FileNode)v.elementAt(i);
          if (newNode.compareTo(nd) < 0) {
            v.insertElementAt(newNode, i);
            isAdded = true;
            break;
          }
        }
        if (!isAdded)
        v.addElement(newNode);
      }

      for (int i=0; i<v.size(); i++) {
        FileNode nd = (FileNode)v.elementAt(i);
        IconData idata = new IconData(FileTree1.ICON_FOLDER,
          FileTree1.ICON_EXPANDEDFOLDER, nd);
        DefaultMutableTreeNode node =
          new DefaultMutableTreeNode(idata);
        parent.add(node);

        if (nd.hasSubDirs())
          node.add(new DefaultMutableTreeNode(
            new Boolean(true)));
      }
      return true;
    }

  public boolean hasSubDirs() {
    File[] files = listFiles();
    if (files == null)
      return false;
    for (int k=0; k<files.length; k++) {
      if (files[k].isDirectory())
        return true;
    }
    return false;
  }

  public int compareTo(FileNode toCompare) {
    return  m_file.getName().compareToIgnoreCase(
      toCompare.m_file.getName());
  }

  protected File[] listFiles() {
    if (!m_file.isDirectory())
      return null;
```

15 Creates a new FileNode for each file in directory

16 Performs insertion sort

17 Creates IconDatas for each FileNode

17 If new node has children, creates the Boolean child to mark it for further expansion

```
      try {
        return m_file.listFiles();
      }
      catch (Exception ex) {
        JOptionPane.showMessageDialog(null,
          "Error reading directory "+m_file.getAbsolutePath(),
          "Warning", JOptionPane.WARNING_MESSAGE);
            return null;
      }
    }
}
```

17.3.1   Understanding the code

Class DirTree

Four custom icons are loaded as static ImageIcon variables: ICON_COMPUTER, ICON_DISK, ICON_FOLDER, and ICON_EXPANDEDFOLDER, and three instance variables are declared:

- JTree m_tree: The tree component to display the directory nodes.
- DefaultTreeModel m_model: The tree model to manage the nodes.
- JTextField m_display: The component to display the selected directory (acts as a status bar).

❶ The DirTree constructor creates and initializes all GUI components. A root node Computer hosts child nodes for all disk partitions and network drives in the system. These nodes encapsulate Files retrieved with the static File.listRoots() method (which is a valuable addition to the File class in Java 2). Note that IconData objects (see below) encapsulate Files in the tree. Also note that each newly created child node immediately receives a child node containing a Boolean user object. This Boolean object allows us to display an expanding message for nodes when they are in the process of being expanded. Exactly how we expand them will be explained soon enough.

❷ We then create a DefaultTreeModel and pass our Computer node as the root. This model is used to instantiate our JTree object:

```
m_model = new DefaultTreeModel(top);
m_tree = new JTree(m_model);
```

We then set the lineStyle client property so that angled lines will represent the edges between parent and child nodes:

```
m_tree.putClientProperty("JTree.lineStyle", "Angled");
```

We also use a custom tree cell renderer, as well as a tree expansion listener and a tree selection listener: these are instances of IconCellRenderer, DirExpansionListener, and DirSelectionListener, respectively.

The actual contents of our tree nodes represent directories. Each node is a DefaultMutableTreeNode with an IconData user object. Each user object is an instance of IconData, and each IconData contains an instance of FileNode. Each FileNode contains a java.io.File object. Thus we have a four-layer nested structure:

- `DefaultMutableTreeNode` is used for each node to represent a directory or disk (as well as the Computer root node). When we retrieve a node at the end of a given `Tree-Path`, using the `getLastPathComponent()` method, we are provided with an instance of this class.
- `IconData` (see below) sits inside `DefaultMutableTreeNode` and provides custom icons for our tree cell renderer, and encapsulation of a `FileNode` object. `IconData` can be retrieved using `DefaultMutableTreeNode`'s `getUserObject()` method. We need to cast the returned `Object` to an `IconData` instance.
- `FileNode` (see below) sits inside `IconData` and encapsulates a `File` object. A `File-Node` can be retrieved using `IconData`'s `getObject()` method, which also requires a subsequent cast.
- A `File` object sits inside a `FileNode` and can be retrieved using `FileNode`'s `get-File()` method.

Figure 17.4 illustrates this structure.

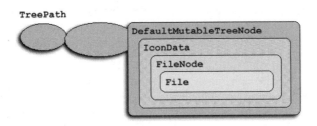

**Figure 17.4
The nested structure
of our tree nodes**

❸ To keep things simple, two helper methods are provided to work with these encapsulated nodes: `getTreeNode()` retrieves a `DefaultMutableTreeNode` from a given `TreePath`, and `getFileNode()` retrieves the `FileNode` (or `null`) from a `DefaultMutableTreeNode`. We will see where these methods are needed shortly.

Class DirTree.DirExpansionListener

❹ This inner class implements `TreeExpansionListener` to listen for tree expansion events. When a node is expanded, the `treeExpanded()` method retrieves the `FileNode` instance for that node and if the instance is not `null`, it calls the `expand()` method on it (see below). This call is wrapped in a separate thread because it can often be a very time-consuming process and we do not want the application to freeze. Inside this thread, once `expand()` has completed,
❺ we need to update the tree model with any new nodes that are retrieved. As we learned in chapter 2, updating the state of a component should only occur within the event-dispatching thread. For this reason we wrap the call to `reload()` in a `Runnable` and send it the event-dispatching queue using `SwingUtilities.invokeLater()`:

```
Runnable runnable = new Runnable() {
  public void run() {
    m_model.reload(node);
  }
};
SwingUtilities.invokeLater(runnable);
```

As we will see below in our discussion of `IconCellRenderer`, placing a `Boolean` user object in a dummy child node of each non-expanded node, allows a certain `String` to be displayed while a node is in the process of being expanded. In our case, "Retrieving data..." is shown below a node until it is finished expanding.

Class DirTree.DirSelectionListener

6 This inner class implements `TreeSelectionListener` to listen for tree selection events. When a node is selected, the `valueChanged()` method extracts the `FileNode` instance contained in that node, and if the instance is not `null`, it displays the absolute path to that directory in the `m_display` text field.

Class IconCellRenderer

7 This class implements the `TreeCellRenderer` interface and extends `JLabel`. The purpose of this renderer is to display custom icons and access `FileNodes` contained in `IconData` instances.

First, we declare five `Colors` and retrieve them from the current look and feel in use through `UIManager`'s `getColor()` method. The `getTreeCellRendererComponent()` method is then implemented to set the proper text and icon (which are retrieved from the underlying

8 `IconData` object). If the user object happens to be a `Boolean`, this signifies that a node is in the process of being expanded:

```
if (obj instanceof Boolean)
    setText("Retrieving data...");
```

The reason we do this is slightly confusing. In the `FileNode` `expand()` method (see below), when each new node is added to our tree, it receives a node containing a `Boolean` user object only if the corresponding directory has subdirectories. When we click on this node, the `Boolean` child will be immediately shown, and we also generate an expansion event that is received by our `DirExpansionListener`. As we discussed above, this listener extracts the encapsulated `FileNode` and calls the `FileNode` `expand()` method on it. The child node containing the `Boolean` object is removed before all new nodes are added. Until this update occurs, the `JTree` will display the `Boolean` child node, in effect telling us that the expansion is not yet complete. So if our cell renderer detects a `Boolean` user object, we simply display Receiving data... for its text.

9 The `paintComponent()` method is overridden to fill the text background with the appropriate color set in the `getTreeCellRendererComponent()` method. Fortunately we don't need to explicitly draw the text and icon because we have extended `JLabel`, which can do this for us.

Class IconData

10 Instances of this class are used as our `DefaultMutableTreeNode` user data objects, and they encapsulate a generic `Object` `m_data` and two `Icons` for use by `IconCellRenderer`. These icons can be retrieved with our `getIcon()` and `getExpandedIcon()` methods. The icon retrieved with `getExpandedIcon()` represents an expanded folder, and the icon retrieved with `getIcon()` represents a collapsed/non-expanded folder. Notice that the `toString()` method invokes toString() on the m_data object. In our example this object is either a FileNode, in the case of an expanded folder, or a Boolean, in the case of a non-expanded folder.

Class FileNode

⑪ This class encapsulates a File object, which is in turn encapsulated in an IconData object in a DefaultMutableTreeNode.

As we discussed above, the toString() method determines the text to be displayed in each tree cell containing a FileNode. It returns File.getName() for regular directories and File.getPath() for partitions.

⑫ The most interesting and complex method of this class is expand(), which attempts to expand a node by dynamically inserting new DefaultMutableTreeNodes corresponding to each subdirectory. This method returns true if nodes are added, and false otherwise. We first need to discuss the mechanism of dynamically reading information (of any kind) into a tree:

- Before we add any new node to the tree, we must somehow determine whether it has children (we don't need a list of children yet, just a yes or no answer).
- If a newly created node has children, a fake child to be used as a flag will be added to it. This will signify that the parent node has not been expanded.
- When a node is expanded, its list of children is examined. Three situations are possible:
- No children. This node is a leaf and cannot be expanded (remember, we've previously checked whether any newly created node has children).
- One flag child is present. That node has children which have not been added yet, so we create these children and add new nodes to the parent node.
- One or more non-flag children are present. This node has already been processed, so expand it as usual.

⑬ The FileNode.expand() method implements this dynamic tree expansion strategy, and it takes a parent node as a parameter. In the process of expansion it also alphabetically sorts each node for a more organized display structure. Initially this method checks the first child of the given parent node:

```
DefaultMutableTreeNode flag =
  (DefaultMutableTreeNode)parent.getFirstChild();
if (flag==null)        // No flag
  return false;
Object obj = flag.getUserObject();
if (!(obj instanceof Boolean))
  return false;      // Already expanded

parent.removeAllChildren();  // Remove Flag
```

If no child is found, it can only mean that this node was already checked and was found to be a true leaf (a directory with no subdirectories). If this isn't the case, then we extract the associated data object and check whether it is an instance of Boolean. If it is, the flag child is removed and our method proceeds to add nodes corresponding to each subdirectory. Otherwise, we conclude that this node has already been processed and return, allowing it to be expanded as usual.

⑭ We process a newly expanded node by retrieving an array of File objects representing files contained in the corresponding directory.

```
File[] files = listFiles();
if (files == null)
  return true;
```

15 If the contents have been successfully read, we check for subdirectories and create new File-Nodes for each.

```
Vector v = new Vector();

for (int k=0; k<files.length; k++) {
  File f = files[k];
  if (!(f.isDirectory()))
    continue;

  FileNode newNode = new FileNode(f);
```

16 To perform an alphabetical sorting of child nodes, we store them in a temporary collection Vector v, and iterate through our array of Files, inserting them accordingly.

```
boolean isAdded = false;
for (int i=0; i<v.size(); i++) {
  FileNode nd = (FileNode)v.elementAt(i);
  if (newNode.compareTo(nd) < 0) {
    v.insertElementAt(newNode, i);
    isAdded = true;
    break;
  }
}
if (!isAdded)
  v.addElement(newNode);
}
```

17 We then wrap each newly created FileNode object in an IconData to encapsulate them with folder icons, and we add the sorted nodes to the given parent node. At the same time, flags are added to new nodes if they contain any subdirectories themselves (this is checked by the has-SubDirs() method):

```
for (int i=0; i<v.size(); i++) {
  FileNode nd = (FileNode)v.elementAt(i);
  IconData idata = new IconData(FileTree1.ICON_FOLDER,
  FileTree1.ICON_EXPANDEDFOLDER, nd);
  DefaultMutableTreeNode node = new
    DefaultMutableTreeNode(idata);
  parent.add(node);
  if (nd.hasSubDirs())
    node.add(new DefaultMutableTreeNode(
      new Boolean(true)));
}
return true;
```

The rest of FileNode class implements three methods which do not require much explanation at this point:

- boolean hasSubDirs(): Returns true if this directory has subdirectories; returns false otherwise.

- `int compareTo(FileNode toCompare)`: returns the result of the alphabetical comparison of this directory with another given as parameter.
- `File[] listFiles()`: Reads a list of contained files in this directory. If an exception occurs (this is possible when reading from a floppy disk or network drive), this method displays a warning message and returns `null`.

17.3.2 Running the code

Figure 17.3 shows our directory tree at work. Notice the use of custom icons for partition roots. Try selecting various directories and notice how the selected path is reflected at the top of the frame in our status bar. Also notice that when large directories are expanded, "Retrieving data" will be displayed underneath the corresponding node. Because we have properly implemented multithreading, we can go off and expand other directories while this one is being processed. The tree is always updated correctly when the expanding procedure completes because we have made sure to only change its state in the event-dispatching thread using `invokeLater()`.

GUIDELINE

When to use connecting lines   Angled connecting lines (or edges) add visual noise and clutter to a tree display. Reduced visual clutter leads to recognition and comprehension; this is a clear advantage to leaving them out of the design. So when is it appropriate to include them?

Include the line edges when one or more of these scenarios is likely:

(a) Several nodes may be expanded at one time, and/or

(b) The data set is very large and a node may expand off the bottom of the screen and possibly go several screens deep. In this case, introducing lines helps to give the user a clear picture of how many layers deep in the hierarchy he is. It also makes it easier for him to trace back to the original root node.

17.4 DIRECTORY TREE, PART II: POPUP MENUS AND TreeNode MANAGEMENT

Example 17.2 in the previous section can be extended in numerous ways to serve as a framework for a much more flexible application. In example 17.3 in this section, we'll add a toolbar to the frame and a popup menu to our tree, both containing the same actions. The popup menu will be displayed in response to a right-click, with the content dependent on the clicked node. (We discussed popup menus in chapter 12.)

Our popup menu contains either an Expand or Collapse item, depending on the status of the corresponding node nearest to the mouse click. These items will programmatically invoke an expand or collapse of the given node. Both our toolbar and popup menu also contain Create, Delete, and Rename actions.

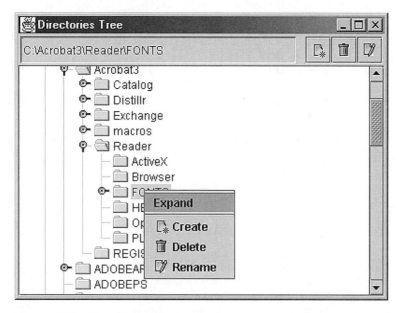

Figure 17.5 Node-dependent popup menus that allow programmatic expansion, collapse, creation of a child node, deletion, and renaming.

Example 17.3

see \Chapter17\3

```java
import java.awt.*;
import java.awt.event.*;
import java.io.*;
import java.util.*;

import javax.swing.*;
import javax.swing.tree.*;
import javax.swing.event.*;
import javax.swing.border.*;

public class DirTree extends JFrame {

  // Unchanged code from Example 17.2

  protected DefaultTreeCellEditor m_editor;
  protected FileNode m_editingNode;
  protected JPopupMenu m_popup;
  protected Action m_expandAction;
  protected TreePath m_clickedPath;

  public DirTree() {

    // Unchanged code from example 17.2
```

```
m_model = new DefaultTreeModel(top);
m_tree = new JTree(m_model) {
    public boolean isPathEditable(TreePath path) {
        if (path == null || path.getPathCount() < 3)
            return false;
        FileNode node = getFileNode(getTreeNode(path));
        if (node == null)
            return false;
        File dir = node.getFile();
        if (dir != null && dir.isDirectory()) {
            m_editingNode = node;
            return true;
        }
        return false;
    }
};

// Unchanged code from example 17.2

CellEditorListener cel = new CellEditorListener() {
    public void editingStopped(ChangeEvent e) {
        if (m_editingNode != null) {
            String newName = m_editor.getCellEditorValue().toString();
            File dir = m_editingNode.getFile();
            File newDir = new File(dir.getParentFile(), newName);
            dir.renameTo(newDir);
            // Update tree
            TreePath path = m_tree.getSelectionPath();
            DefaultMutableTreeNode node = getTreeNode(path);
            IconData idata = new IconData(DirTree.ICON_FOLDER,
                DirTree.ICON_EXPANDEDFOLDER, new FileNode(newDir));
            node.setUserObject(idata);
            m_model.nodeStructureChanged(node);
            m_display.setText(newDir.getAbsolutePath());
        }
        m_editingNode = null;
    }

    public void editingCanceled(ChangeEvent e) {
        m_editingNode = null;
    }
};
m_editor = new DefaultTreeCellEditor(m_tree, renderer);
m_editor.addCellEditorListener(cel);
m_tree.setCellEditor(m_editor);
m_tree.setEditable(true);

JToolBar tb = new JToolBar();
tb.setFloatable(false);
m_display = new JTextField();
m_display.setEditable(false);
m_display.setBorder(new SoftBevelBorder(BevelBorder.LOWERED));
tb.add(m_display);
tb.addSeparator();
```

1 Overridden to stop user from editing root node and its directory children which represent disk/ hard drives

2 Listener responsible for renaming a directory once it is renamed in the tree

```
m_popup = new JPopupMenu();
m_expandAction = new AbstractAction() {
   public void actionPerformed(ActionEvent e) {
      if (m_clickedPath==null)
         return;
      if (m_tree.isExpanded(m_clickedPath))
         m_tree.collapsePath(m_clickedPath);
      else
         m_tree.expandPath(m_clickedPath);
   }
};
m_popup.add(m_expandAction);
m_popup.addSeparator();

Action a1 = new AbstractAction("Create",
   new ImageIcon("New16.gif")) {
      public void actionPerformed(ActionEvent e) {
         m_tree.repaint();
         TreePath path = m_tree.getSelectionPath();
         if (path == null || path.getPathCount() < 2)
            return;
         DefaultMutableTreeNode treeNode = getTreeNode(path);
         FileNode node = getFileNode(treeNode);
         if (node == null)
            return;

         File dir = node.getFile();
         int index = 0;
         File newDir = new File(dir, "New Directory");
         while (newDir.exists()) {
            index++;
            newDir = new File(dir, "New Directory"+index);
         }
         newDir.mkdirs();

         IconData idata = new IconData(DirTree.ICON_FOLDER,
            DirTree.ICON_EXPANDEDFOLDER, new FileNode(newDir));
         DefaultMutableTreeNode newNode = new
            DefaultMutableTreeNode(idata);
         treeNode.add(newNode);
         m_model.nodeStructureChanged(treeNode);

         path = path.pathByAddingChild(newNode);
         m_tree.scrollPathToVisible(path);
         m_tree.startEditingAtPath(path);
      }
};
m_popup.add(a1);
JButton bt = tb.add(a1);
bt.setToolTipText("Create new directory");

Action a2 = new AbstractAction("Delete",
   new ImageIcon("Delete16.gif")) {
   public void actionPerformed(ActionEvent e) {
```

3 Action to control expand/collapse from popup menu

4 Action to create a new directory

4 Action to delete a directory

```
        m_tree.repaint();
        TreePath path = m_tree.getSelectionPath();
        if (path == null || path.getPathCount() < 3)
           return;
        DefaultMutableTreeNode treeNode = getTreeNode(path);
        FileNode node = getFileNode(treeNode);
        if (node == null)
           return;
        File dir = node.getFile();
        if (dir != null && dir.isDirectory()) {
           if (JOptionPane.showConfirmDialog(DirTree.this,
             "Do you want to delete \ndirectory \""
               + dir.getName() + "\" ?",
             DirTree.APP_NAME, JOptionPane.YES_NO_OPTION)
               != JOptionPane.YES_OPTION)
             return;

           setCursor(Cursor.getPredefinedCursor(Cursor.WAIT_CURSOR));
           deleteDirectory(dir);
           setCursor(Cursor.getPredefinedCursor(Cursor.DEFAULT_CURSOR));

           TreeNode parent = treeNode.getParent();
           treeNode.removeFromParent();
           m_model.nodeStructureChanged(parent);
           m_display.setText("");
        }
     }
  };
  m_popup.add(a2);
  bt = tb.add(a2);
  bt.setToolTipText("Delete directory");
  m_tree.registerKeyboardAction(a2,
     KeyStroke.getKeyStroke(KeyEvent.VK_DELETE, 0),
     JComponent.WHEN_FOCUSED);

  Action a3 = new AbstractAction("Rename",
     new ImageIcon("Edit16.gif")) {
        public void actionPerformed(ActionEvent e) {
           m_tree.repaint();
           TreePath path = m_tree.getSelectionPath();
           if (path == null)
              return;
           m_tree.scrollPathToVisible(path);
           m_tree.startEditingAtPath(path);
        }
  };
  m_popup.add(a3);
  bt = tb.add(a3);
  bt.setToolTipText("Rename directory");

  getContentPane().add(tb, BorderLayout.NORTH);
  m_tree.add(m_popup);
  m_tree.addMouseListener(new PopupTrigger());
```

❹ Action to rename a directory

```
}

DefaultMutableTreeNode getTreeNode(TreePath path) {
   return (DefaultMutableTreeNode)(path.getLastPathComponent());
}

FileNode getFileNode(DefaultMutableTreeNode node) {

   // Unchanged code from example 17.2

}

class PopupTrigger extends MouseAdapter {
   public void mouseReleased(MouseEvent e) {
      if (e.isPopupTrigger() || e.getButton() == MouseEvent.BUTTON3) {
         int x = e.getX();
         int y = e.getY();
         TreePath path = m_tree.getPathForLocation(x, y);
         if (path == null)
            return;

         if (m_tree.isExpanded(path))
            m_expandAction.putValue(Action.NAME, "Collapse");
         else
            m_expandAction.putValue(Action.NAME, "Expand");

         m_tree.setSelectionPath(path);
         m_tree.scrollPathToVisible(path);
         m_popup.show(m_tree, x, y);
         m_clickedPath = path;
      }
   }
}

class DirExpansionListener implements TreeExpansionListener {
   // Unchanged code from example 17.2
}

class DirSelectionListener implements TreeSelectionListener {
   // Unchanged code from example 17.2
}

public static void deleteDirectory(File dir) {
   if (dir == null || !dir.isDirectory() || dir.isHidden())
      return;
   File[] files = dir.listFiles();
   if (files != null)
      for (int k=0; k<files.length; k++) {
         File f = files[k];
         if (f.isDirectory())
            deleteDirectory(f);
         else
            f.delete();
      }
   dir.delete();
}
```

⑤ Controls display of popup menu

```
      public static void main(String argv[]) {
         DirTree frame = new DirTree();
         frame.setDefaultCloseOperation(JFrame.EXIT_ON_CLOSE);
         frame.setVisible(true);
      }
   }

   // Unchanged code from example 17.2
```

17.4.1   Understanding the code

Class DirTree

This example adds five new instance variables:

- `DefaultTreeCellEditor m_editor`: A custom cell editor to allow renaming of folders.
- `FileNode m_editingNode`: Used to keep a reference to the node currently being edited.
- `JPopupMenu m_popup`: The popup menu component.
- `Action m_expandAction`: The expand/collapse action.
- `TreePath m_clickedPath`: The currently selected tree path.

① The new code in the constructor first overrides `JTree`'s `isPathEditable()` method to stop the user from editing the root node and directory children which represent disk/hard drives.

② Then a custom `CellEditorListener` implementation is created which is responsible for renaming a directory once editing is completed on a tree cell. This listener is then added to a new `DefaultTreeCellEditor` instance which we use for our `JTree`'s editor. Then we make sure to make the `JTree` editable.

   A nonfloatable toolbar is created and the status text field is added to it first.

③ The popup menu is then created and the expand/collapse action is created and added to it. This action expands the selected node if it is currently collapsed and collapses it if it is currently expanded. Because this operation depends on the state of a given node, it is not added to the toolbar.

④ The Create, Delete, and Rename actions are then created and added to both the popup menu and the toolbar. Note that whenever a node is added or deleted we call the tree model's `nodeStructureChanged()` method to allow `JTree` to handle these changes properly. Also note that we've registered a keyboard action with our `JTree` to detect when the DELETE key is pressed and invoke the Delete action accordingly, which relies on our custom `deleteDirectory()` method.

⑤ *Class DirTree.PopupTrigger*

This class extends `MouseAdapter` to trigger the display of our popup menu. This menu should be displayed when the right mouse button is released. So we override the `mouseReleased()` method and check whether `isPopupTrigger()` is true (unfortunately in Windows this can correspond to the mouse scroll button) or whether BUTTON3 was pressed (in Windows this can correspond to the right mouse button which should be the popup trigger). In this case we determine the coordinates of the click and retrieve the `TreePath` corresponding to that coordinate with the `getPathForLocation()` method. If a path is not found (i.e., the click does not occur on a tree node or leaf) we do nothing. Otherwise we adjust the title of the first menu item accordingly, display our popup menu with the `show()` method, and store our recently clicked path in the `m_clickedPath` instance variable (for use by the expand/collapse action.

17.4.2 Running the code

Figure 17.5 shows our directory tree application as it displays a context-sensitive popup menu. Notice how the first menu item is changed depending on whether the selected tree node is collapsed or expanded. The tree can be manipulated (expanded or collapsed) programmatically by choosing the Collapse or Expand popup menu item. Try creating, deleting, and renaming directories to verify the functionality.

GUIDELINE

Visually reinforcing variations in behavior   If you intend to introduce context-dependent popup menus on tree cells, then this is an ideal time to consider using a tree cell renderer which incorporates an icon. The differing icons help to reinforce the idea that the data in the cells are different types; consequently, when the behavior is slightly different across nodes, it is less surprising. The icon visually reinforces the difference in behavior.

17.5 DIRECTORY TREE, PART III: TOOLTIPS

As we discussed in chapter 5, tooltips are commonly used to display helpful information. In example 17.4, we will show how to use tooltips specific to each tree cell. The key point (which is mentioned in the `JTree` documentation, but can be easily overlooked) is to register the tree component with the `ToolTipManager` shared instance:

```
ToolTipManager.sharedInstance().registerComponent(myTree);
```

Without doing this, no tooltips will appear over our tree (refer back to chapter 2, section 2.5, for more about shared instances and service classes).

The `JTree` component overrides the `getToolTipText(MouseEvent ev)` method that is inherited from `JComponent`, and it delegates this call to the tree's cell renderer component. By implementing the `getToolTipText(MouseEvent ev)` method in our renderer, we can allow cell-specific tooltips. Specifically, we can can return the tooltip text as a `String` depending on the last node passed to the `getTreeCellRendererComponent()` method. Alternatively, we can subclass our `JTree` component and provide our own `getToolTipText()` implementation. We use the latter method here.

Example 17.4

DirTree.java

see \Chapter17\4

```
import java.awt.*;
import java.awt.event.*;
import java.io.*;
import java.util.*;
```

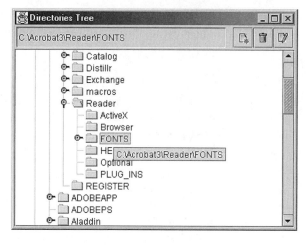

Figure 17.6
JTree with node-specific tooltips

```java
import javax.swing.*;
import javax.swing.tree.*;
import javax.swing.event.*;
import javax.swing.border.*;

public class DirTree extends JFrame {

    // Unchanged code from example 17.3

    public DirTree() {

        // Unchanged code from example 17.3

        m_model = new DefaultTreeModel(top);
        m_tree = new JTree(m_model) {
            public boolean isPathEditable(TreePath path) {
                if (path == null || path.getPathCount() < 3)
                    return false;
                FileNode node = getFileNode(getTreeNode(path));
                if (node == null)
                    return false;
                File dir = node.getFile();
                if (dir != null && dir.isDirectory()) {
                    m_editingNode = node;
                    return true;
                }
                return false;
            }

            public String getToolTipText(MouseEvent ev) {
                if(ev == null)
                    return null;
                TreePath path = m_tree.getPathForLocation(ev.getX(),
                    ev.getY());
                if (path != null) {
                    FileNode fnode = getFileNode(getTreeNode(path));
                    if (fnode==null)
                        return null;
```

```
        File f = fnode.getFile();
        return (f==null ? null : f.getPath());
    }
    return null;
  }
};
ToolTipManager.sharedInstance().registerComponent(m_tree);

// The rest of the code is unchanged from example 17.3
```

17.5.1 Understanding the code

Class DirTree

This example anonymously subclasses the JTree component to override getToolTip-Text(MouseEvent ev), which finds the path closest to the current mouse location, determines the FileNode at the end of that path, and returns the full file path to that node as a String for use as tooltip text. Our JTree component is manually registered with the shared instance of ToolTipManager, as discussed above.

17.5.2 Running the code

Figure 17.6 shows our directory tree application displaying a tooltip with text specifying the full path of the directory corresponding to the node nearest to the current mouse location.

GUIDELINE

Tooltips as an aid to selection   Tooltips have two really useful advantages for tree cells. Trees have a habit of wandering off to the right-hand side of a display, particularly when you're in deep hierarchies. This may result in cell labels being clipped. Using the tooltip to display the full-length cell label will speed selection and prevent the need for scrolling.

The second use is shown clearly in this example. The tooltip is used to unravel the hierarchy. This would be particularly useful when the original root node is off screen. The user can quickly see the full hierarchical path to the selected cell. This is a very powerful aid in correctly selecting items, and it's another example of additional coding effort providing improved usability.

CHAPTER 18

Tables

18.1 JTABLE

JTable is extremely useful for displaying, navigating, and editing tabular data. Because of its complex nature, JTable has a whole package devoted just to it: javax.swing.table. This package consists of a set of classes and interfaces which we will review briefly in this chapter. In the examples that follow, we construct—in a step-wise fashion—a table-based application that displays stock market data. (In chapter 22, we enhance this application further to allow printing and print preview.) This chapter concludes with an expense report application that demonstrates the use of different components as table cell editors and renderers, and the completion of the JavaBeans property editor we started to build in chapter 4.

18.1.1 JTable

class javax.swing.JTable

This class represents Swing's table component and provides a rich API for managing its behavior and appearance. JTable directly extends JComponent, and it implements the TableModel-

Listener, TableColumnModelListener, ListSelectionListener, CellEditor-Listener, and Scrollable interfaces (it is meant to be placed in a JScrollPane). Each JTable has three models: TableModel, TableColumnModel, and ListSelectionModel. All table data is stored in a TableModel, normally in a two-dimensional structure such as a 2-D array or a Vector of Vectors. TableModel implementations specify how this data is stored, as well as how to manage the addition, manipulation, and retrieval of this data. Table-Model also plays a role in dictating whether specific cells can be edited, as well as the data type of each column of data. The location of data in a JTable's TableModel does not directly correspond to the location of that data as it is displayed by JTable itself. This part is controlled at the lowest level by TableColumnModel.

A TableColumnModel is designed to maintain instances of TableColumn, each of which represents a single column of TableModel data. The TableColumn class is responsible for managing column display in the actual JTable GUI. Each TableColumn has an associated cell renderer, cell editor, table header, and cell renderer for the table header. When a JTable is placed in a JScrollPane, these headers are placed in the scroll pane's COLUMN_HEADER viewport, and they can be dragged and resized to reorder and change the size of columns. A TableColumn's header renderer is responsible for returning a component that renders the column header, and the cell renderer is responsible for returning a component that renders each cell. As with JList and JTree renderers, these renderers also act as rubber stamps and they are not at all interactive. The component returned by the cell editor, however, is completely interactive. Cell renderers are instances of TableCellRenderer and cell editors are instances of TableCellEditor. If none are explicitly assigned, default versions will be used based on the Class type of the corresponding TableModel column data.

TableColumnModel's job is to manage all TableColumns, providing control over order, column selections, and margin size. To support several different modes of selection, Table-ColumnModel maintains a ListSelectionModel which, as we learned in chapter 10, allows single, single-interval, and multiple-interval selections. JTable takes this flexibility even further by providing functionality to customize any row, column, and/or cell-specific selection schemes we can come up with.

We can specify one of several resizing policies which dictate how columns react when another column is resized, as well as whether grid lines between rows and/or columns should appear. We can also specify: margin sizes between rows and columns, the selected and unselected cell foreground and background colors, the height of rows, and the width of each column on a column-by-column basis.

With tables come two new kinds of events in Swing: TableModelEvent and Table-ColumnModelEvent. Regular Java events apply to JTable as well. For instance, we can use MouseListeners to process double mouse clicks. ChangeEvents and ListSelection-Events are also used for communication in TableColumnModel.

NOTE Although JTable implements several listener interfaces, it does not provide any methods to register listeners other than those inherited from JComponent. To attach listeners for detecting any of the above events, we must first retrieve the appropriate model.

A number of constructors are provided for building a JTable component. We can use the default constructor or pass each of the table's data and column names as a separate Vector.

We can build an empty `JTable` with a specified number of rows and columns. We can also pass table data to the constructor as a two-dimensional array of data `Objects` along with an `Object` array of column names. Other constructors allow for the creation of a `JTable` with specific models. In all cases, if a specific model is not assigned in the constructor, `JTable` will create default implementations with its protected `createDefaultColumnModel()`, `cre-ate-DefaultDataModel()`, and `createDefaultSelectionModel()` methods. It will do the same for each `TableColumn` renderer and editor, as well as for its `JTableHeader`, using `create-DefaultEditors()`, `createDefaultRenderers()`, and `createDefaultTable-Headers()`.

`JTable` is one of the most complex Swing components; keeping track of its constituents and how they interact is intially a challenge. Before we begin the step-wise construction of our stocks table application, we must make our way through all of these details. The remainder of this section is devoted to a discussion of the classes and interfaces that define the underlying mechanics of `JTable`.

18.1.2 The TableModel interface

abstract interface javax.swing.table.TableModel

Instances of `TableModel` are responsible for storing a table's data in a two-dimensional structure such as a two-dimensional array or a `Vector` of `Vectors`. A set of methods is declared to retrieve data from a table's cells. The `getValueAt()` method should retrieve data from a given row and column index as an `Object`, and `setValueAt()` should assign the provided data object to the specified location (if valid). `getColumnClass()` should return the `Class` that describes the data objects stored in the specified column (used to assign a default renderer and editor for that column), and `getColumnName()` should return the `String` name associated with the specified column (often used for that column's header). The `getColumn-Count()` and `getRowCount()` methods should return the number of contained columns and rows, respectively.

> **NOTE** `getRowCount()` is called frequently by `JTable` for display purposes; therefore, it should be designed with efficiency in mind.

The `isCellEditable()` method should return `true` if the cell at the given row and column index can be edited. The `setValueAt()` method should be designed so that if `isCellEdit-able()` returns `false`, the object at the given location will not be updated.

This model supports the attachment of `TableModelListeners` which should be notified about changes to this model's data. As expected, methods for adding and removing these listeners are provided (`addTableModelListener()` and `removeTableModelListener()`) and implementations are responsible for dispatching `TableModelEvents` to those registered.

Each `JTable` uses one `TableModel` instance which can be assigned/retrieved using `JTable`'s `setModel()` and `getModel()` methods respectively.

> **NOTE** The position of a row or column in the model does not correspond to `JTable`'s GUI representation of that row or column. Rather, each column is represented by an instance of `TableColumn` which maps to a unique model column. When a `TableColumn` is moved in the GUI, the associated data in the `TableModel` model stays put, and vice versa.

18.1.3 AbstractTableModel

abstract class javax.swing.table.AbstractTableModel

AbstractTableModel is an abstract class that implements the TableModel interface. It provides default code for firing TableModelEvents with the fireTableRowsDeleted(), fireTableCellUpdated(), and fireTableChanged() methods. It also manages all registered TableModelListeners in an EventListenerList (see chapter 2).

The findColumn() method searches for the index of a column with the given String name. This search is performed in a linear fashion (this is referred to as "naive" in the documentation) and it should be overridden for large table models for more efficient searching.

Three methods need to be implemented in concrete subclasses: getRowCount(), get-ColumnCount(), and getValueAt(int row, int column), and we are expected to use this class as a base for building our own TableModel implementations, rather than Default-TableModel, see below.

18.1.4 DefaultTableModel

class javax.swing.tableDefaultTableModel

DefaultTableModel is the default concrete TableModel implementation used by JTable when no model is specified in the constructor. It uses a Vector of Vectors to manage its data, which is one major reason why extending AbstractTableModel is often more desirable—AbstractTableModel gives you complete control over how data storage and manipulation is implemented. This Vector can be assigned with the overloaded setDataVector() method and retrieved with the getDataVector() method. Internally, two overloaded, protected convertToVector() methods are used for converting Object arrays to Vectors when inserting rows, columns, or assigning a new data Vector. Methods for adding, inserting, removing, and moving columns and rows of data are also provided.

Along with the TableModelEvent functionality inherited from AbstractTableModel, this class implements three new event-dispatching methods, each taking a TableModelEvent as parameter: newDataAvailable(), newRowsAdded(), and rowsRemoved(). The newRows-Added() method ensures that new rows (see the discussion of TableModelEvent below) have the correct number of columns by either removing excess elements or using null for each missing cell. If null is passed to any of these methods, they will construct and fire a default TableModelEvent which assumes that all table model data has changed.

18.1.5 TableColumn

class javax.swing.table.TableColumn

TableColumn is the basic building block of JTable's visual representation, and it provides the main link between the JTable GUI and its model. TableColumn does not extend java.awt.Component, and thus it is not a component. Rather, it acts more like a model that maintains all the properties of a column displayed in a JTable. An instance of TableColumn represents a specific column of data stored in a TableModel. TableColumn maintains the index of the TableModel column it represents as property modelIndex. We can get/set this index with the getModelIndex() and setModelIndex() methods. It is important to remember that the position of a `TableColumn` in `JTable` does not at all correspond to its corresponding `TableModel` column index.

A `TableColumn` is represented graphically by a column header renderer, cell renderer, and, optionally, a cell editor. The renderers must be instances of `TableCellRenderer`, and the editor must be an instance of `TableCellEditor`. A column's header is rendered by a renderer stored as the `headerRenderer` property. By default, this is an instance of `DefaultTable-CellRenderer` (which supplies a `JLabel` with a beveled border; see below) and it is created with `TableColumn`'s protected `createDefaultHeaderRenderer()` method. This renderer simply renders the `String` returned by the `toString()` method of the `Object` referred to by the `headerValue` property. The header renderer and value can be assigned/retrieved with the `setHeaderRenderer()`/`getHeaderRenderer()` and `setHeaderValue()`/`getHeader-Value()` methods, respectively. `headerValue` often directly corresponds to the column name retrieved using `TableModel`'s `getColumnName()` method. If `headerValue` is not explicitly set, it defaults to `null`.

The column cell renderer and editor also default to `null`, and unless they are explicitly specified using `setCellRenderer()` or `setCellEditor()`, they are automatically assigned based on the `Class` type of the data stored in the associated column in the `TableModel` (this is retrieved using `TableModel`'s `getColumnClass()` method). Explicity specified renderers and editors are referred to as *column-based*, whereas those determined by data type are referred to as *class-based* (we will discuss renderers and editors in more detail later in this section).

Each `TableColumn` has an `identifier` property which also defaults to `null`. This property can be assigned and retrieved using typical set/get accessors, and the `getIdenti-fier()` method will return the `headerValue` property if `identifier` is `null`. When search-ing for a `TableColumn` by name (using `TableColumnModel`'s `getColumnIndex()` method or `JTable`'s `getColumn()` method), the given `Object` will be compared, using `Object`'s `equals()` method, to each `TableColumn` `identifier`. Since it is possible that more than one `TableColumn` will use the same `identifier`, the first match is returned as the answer.

`TableColumn` maintains three properties: `minWidth`, `maxWidth`, and `width`. The first two specify the minimum and maximum allowable widths for column rendering, and the `width` property stores the current width. Each property can be retrieved and assigned with typ-ical get/set methods: `getMinWidth()`/`setMinWidth()`, `getMaxWith()`/`setMaxWidth()`, and `getWidth()`/`setWidth()`. `minWidth` defaults to 15, `maxWidth` defaults to `Integer.-MAX_VALUE`, and `width` defaults to 75. When a `JTable` is resized, it will try to maintain its width, and it will never exceeed its maximum or shrink smaller than its minimum.

NOTE   All other visual aspects of each column are controlled by either `JTable` or `Table-ColumnModel` (see below).

`TableColumn` also maintains an `isResizable` property, which specifies whether its width can be changed by the user (this does not apply to programmatic calls to `setWidth()`). We will discuss resizing in more detail below.

An interesting and rarely used property maintained by `TableColumn` is called `resized-PostingDisabledCount`. It is used to enable and disable the posting of `PropertyChange-Events` when a `TableColumn`'s width changes. This property is an `int` value that is incremented on each call to `disableResizedPosting()`, and it is decremented on each call to `enableResizedPosting()`. Events will only be fired if this value is less than or equal to 0.

The logic behind this is that if two separate sources both call the `disableResizedPost()` method, then two calls should be required to re-enable it.

JAVA 1.3   The `resizedPostingDisabledCount` property is not actually used anywhere and it does not play a role in `PropertyChangeEvent` firing. This property and the associated methods have been deprecated in Java 1.3.

`TableColumn` fires `PropertyChangeEvents` when any of the `width`, `cellRenderer`, `headerRenderer`, or `headerValue` bound properties change. Thus we can add and remove `PropertyChangeListeners` to be notified of these changes. The corresponding property names are COLUMN_WIDTH_PROPERTY, COLUMN_RENDERER_PROPERTY, HEADER_RENDERER_PROPERTY, and HEADER_VALUE_PROPERTY.

BUG ALERT!   In some situations, such as when the first column of your table consists of small icons, you may want the header value of your first table column to be empty "". You'll be in for a bit of a surprise, as this choice will lead to dramatic consequences: the whole header of your table will disappear (if you haven't seen this before, try it now for your viewing pleasure).

The reason for this lies in an optimization made in javax.swing.plaf.basic.Basic-TableHeaderUI, and is explained in an associated comment:

```
// If the header value is empty (== "") in the
// first column (and this column is set up
// to use the default renderer) we will
// return zero from this routine and the header
// will disappear altogether. Avoiding the calculation
// of the preferred size is such a performance win for
// most applications that we will continue to
// use this cheaper calculation, handling these
// issues as 'edge cases'.
```

So if you're on the edge case, just use one space (" ") instead of an empty string.

18.1.6   The TableColumnModel interface

abstract interface javax.swing.table.TableColumnModel

This model is designed to maintain a `JTable`'s `TableColumns`, and it provides control over column selections and margin size. `TableColumnModel` controls how `JTable` displays its `TableModel` data. The `addColumn()` method should append a given `TableColumn` to the end of the structure that is used to maintain them (this is usually a `Vector`), `removeColumn()` should remove a given `TableColumn`, and `moveColumn()` should change the location of a given `TableColumn` within that structure.

The index of a `TableColumn` in a `TableColumnModel`'s storage structure directly corresponds to its position in the `JTable` GUI. The `moveColumn()` method is called whenever the user drags a column to a new position.

NOTE When creating a JTable, if no TableColumnModel is specified, one will automatically be constructed for us. It will contain TableColumns that display TableModel data in the same order it appears in the model. This will only occur if JTable's auto-CreateColumnsFromModel property is set to true, which it is by default. Though this is very helpful, it often has the undesirable side effect of completely rebuilding the TableColumnModel whenever TableModel changes. Thus, it is common to set this property to false once a JTable has been created or after a new TableModel is assigned.

The getColumnCount() method returns the number of TableColumns currently being maintained, getColumns() returns an Enumeration of all contained TableColumns, and getColumn() returns the TableColumn at the given index. The getColumnIndex() method returns the index of the TableColumn whose identifier property is equal to the given Object (the equality is determined by using Object's equals() method). getColumnIndexAtX() returns the index of the TableColumn at the given x-coordinate in the table's coordinate system (if getColumnIndexAtX() is passed either a coordinate that maps to the margin space between adjacent columns or any x-coordinate that does not correspond to a table column, it will return –1). setColumnMargin() and getColumnMargin() allow the assignment and retrieval of an int value to be used as the margin space on each side of each table column. The getTotalColumnWidth() method returns the sum of the current width of all TableColumns, including all margin space.

NOTE The margin size does not correspond to the width of the separating grid lines between columns in JTable. In fact, the width of these lines is always 1, and it cannot be changed without customizing JTable's UI delegate.

TableColumnModel declares methods for controlling the selection of its TableColumns, and it allows the assignment and retrieval of a ListSelectionModel implementation to store information about the current column selection with the methods setSelectionModel() and getSelectionModel(). The setColumnSelectionAllowed() method turns on/off column selection capabilities, and getColumnSelectionAllowed() returns a boolean that specifies whether selection is currently allowed. For convenience, JTable's setColumn-SelectionAllowed() method delegates its traffic to the method of the same signature in this interface.

TableColumnModel also declares support for TableColumnModelListeners (see below). TableColumnModel implementations are expected to fire a TableColumnModelEvent whenever a TableColumn is added, removed, or moved; a ChangeEvent whenever margin size is changed; and a ListSelectionEvent whenever a change in column selection occurs.

18.1.7 DefaultTableColumnModel

class javax.swing.table.DefaultTableColumnModel

This class is the concrete default implementation of the TableColumnModel interface used by JTable when none is specifically assigned or provided at construction time. All Table-ColumnModel methods are implemented as expected, and the following protected methods are provided to fire events: fireColumnAdded(), fireColumnRemoved(), fireColumn-Moved(), fireColumnSelectionChanged(), and fireColumnMarginChanged(). A value-

Changed() method is provided to listen for column selection changes and fire a List-SelectionEvent when necessary, and a propertyChanged() method is used to update the totalColumnWidth property when the width of a contained TableColumn changes.

18.1.8 The TableCellRenderer interface

abstract interface javax.swing.table.TableCellRenderer

This interface describes the renderer used to display cell data in a TableColumn. Each TableColumn has an associated TableCellRender which can be assigned and retrieved with the setCellRenderer() and getCellRenderer() methods. The getTableCellRenderer-Component() method is the only method declared by this interface, and it is expected to return a Component that will be used to actually render a cell. It takes the following parameters:

- JTable table: The table instance that contains the cell to be rendered.
- Object value: The value used to represent the data in the given cell.
- boolean isSelected: Specifies whether the given cell is selected.
- boolean hasFocus: Specifies whether the given cell has the focus (true if it was clicked last).
- int row: Used to a renderer component specific to a row or cell.
- int column: Specify a renderer component specific to a column or cell.

We are expected to customize or vary the returned component based on the given parameters. For instance, given a value that is an instance of Color, we might return a special JLabel subclass that paints a rectangle in the given color. This method can be used to return different renderer components on a column, row, or cell-specific basis, and it is similar to JTree's TreeCell-Renderer getTreeCellRendererComponent() method. As with JTree and JList, the renderer component returned acts as a "rubber stamp" that is used strictly for display purposes.

NOTE   The row and column parameters refer to the location of data in the TableModel, not a cell location in the TableColumnModel.

When JTable's UI delegate repaints a certain region of a table, it must query that table to determine the renderer to use for each cell that it needs to repaint. This is accomplished through JTable's getCellRenderer() method, which takes row and column parameters and returns the component returned by the getTableCellRendererComponent() method of the TableCellRenderer assigned to the appropriate TableColumn. If no specific renderer is assigned to that TableColumn (recall that this is the case by default), the TableModel's getColumnClass() method is used to recursively determine an appropriate renderer for the given data type. If no specific class-based renderer is available for a given class, getColumnClass() searches for one that corresponds to the superclass. This process will, in the most generic case, stop at Object, for which a DefaultTableCellRenderer is used (see below).

A DefaultTreeCellRenderer is also used if the class is of type Icon or Number (its subclasses are BigDecimal, BigInteger, Byte, Double, Float, Integer, Long, and Short). If the type happens to be a Boolean, a JCheckBox is used. We can specify additional class-based renderers with JTable's setDefaultRenderer() method. Remember that class-based renderers will only be used if no column-based renderer has been explicitly assigned to the `TableColumn` containing the given cell.

18.1.9 DefaultTableCellRenderer

class javax.swing.table.DefaultTableCellRenderer

This is the concrete default implementation of the `TableCellRenderer` interface. `Default-TableCellRenderer` extends `JLabel` and is used as the default class-based renderer for `Number`, `Icon`, and `Object` data types. Two private `Color` variables are used to hold selected foreground and background colors which render the cell if it is editable and if it has the current focus. These colors can be assigned with `DefaultTableCellRenderer`'s overridden `setBackground()` and `setForeground()` methods.

A protected `Border` property is used to store the border that is used when the cell does not have the current focus. By default, this is an `EmptyBorder` with a top and bottom space of 1 and a left and right space of 2. Unfortunately, `DefaultTableCellRenderer` does not provide a method to change this border.

`DefaultTableCellRenderer` renders the value object passed as parameter to its `get-TableCellRenderer()` method by setting its label text to the `String` returned by that object's `toString()` method. All default `JLabel` attributes are used in rendering. We can do anything to this renderer component that we can do to a `JLabel`, such as assign a tooltip or a disabled/enabled state.

NOTE   `JTable` can have a tooltip assigned to it just as any other Swing component. However, tooltips assigned to renderers take precedence over those assigned to `JTable`, and in the case that both are used, the renderer's tooltip text will be displayed when the mouse lies over a cell using it.

18.1.10 The TableCellEditor interface

abstract interface javax.swing.table.TableCellEditor

This interface extends `CellEditor` and describes the editor used to edit cell data in a `Table-Column`. Each `TableColumn` has an associated `TableCellEditor` which can be assigned and retrieved with the `setCellEditor()` and `getCellEditor()` methods. The `getTable-CellEditorComponent()` method is the only method declared by this interface, and it is expected to return a `Component` that will be used to allow editing of a cell's data value. It takes the following parameters:

- `JTable table`: The table instance containing the cell to be rendered.
- `Object value`: The value used to represent the data in the given cell.
- `boolean isSelected`: Specifies whether the given cell is selected.
- `int row`: Used to a renderer component specific to a row or cell.
- `int column`: Specify a renderer component specific to a column or cell.

We are expected to customize or vary the returned component based on the given parameters. For instance, given a `value` that is an instance of `Color`, we might return a special `JComboBox` which lists several color choices. This method can be used to return different editor components on a column, row, or cell-specific basis, and it is similar to `JTree`'s `Tree-CellEditor getTreeCellEditorComponent()` method.

NOTE The row and column parameters refer to the location of data in the TableModel, not a cell location in the TableColumnModel.

Just like table cell renderers, each TableColumn has a column-based editor associated with it. By default, this editor is null and it can be assigned and retrieved with TableColumn's setCellEditor() and getCellEditor() methods. Unlike renderers, table cell editors are completely interactive and do not simply act as rubber stamps.

TableCellEditor implementations must also implement methods defined in the CellEditor interface: addCellEditorListener(), removeCellEditorListener(), cancelCellEditing(), stopCellEditing(), isCellEditable(), shouldSelectCell(), and getCellEditorValue(). The isCellEditable() method is expected to be used in combination with TableModel's isCellEditable() method to determine whether a given cell can be edited. Only in the case that both return true is editing allowed. (See the discussion of the CellEditor interface in section 17.1.13 for more about each of these methods.)

To initiate cell editing on a given cell, JTable listens for mouse presses and invokes its editCellAt() method in response. This method queries both the TableModel and the appropriate cell editor to determine if the given cell can be edited. If it can, the editor component is retrieved with getTableCellEditorComponent() and placed in the given cell (its bounds are adjusted so that it will fit within the current cell bounds). Then JTable adds itself as a listener to the editor component (recall that JTable implements the CellEditorListener interface) and the same mouse event that sparked the edit gets sent to the editor component. Finally, the cell editor's shouldSelectCell() method is invoked to determine whether the row containing that cell should become selected.

The default implementation of TableCellEditor is provided as DefaultCellEditor. Unfortunately, DefaultCellEditor is not easily extensible and we are often forced to implement all TableCellEditor and CellEditor functionality ourselves.

18.1.11 DefaultCellEditor

class javax.swing.DefaultCellEditor

DefaultCellEditor is a concrete implementation of both the TableCellEditor interface and the TreeCellEditor interface. This editor is designed to return either a JTextField, JComboBox, or JCheckBox for cell editing. It is used by both JTable and JTree components and is discussed in section 17.1.15.

18.1.12 The TableModelListener interface

abstract interface javax.swing.event.TableModelListener

This interface describes an object that listens to changes in a TableModel. The tableChanged() method will be invoked to notify us of these changes. TableModel's addTableModelListener() and removeTableModelListener() methods are used to add and remove TableModelListeners respectively (they are not added directly to JTable).

18.1.13 TableModelEvent

class javax.swing. TableModelEvent

This event extends `EventObject` and is used to notify `TableModelListeners` registered with a `TableModel` about changes in that model. This class consists of four properties, which are each accessible with typical `get` methods:

- `int column`: Specifies the column affected by the change. `TableModelEvent.ALL_COLUMNS` is used to indicate that more than one column is affected.
- `int firstRow`: Specifies the first row affected. `TableModelEvent.HEADER_ROW` can be used here to indicate that the name, type, or order of one or more columns has changed.
- `int lastRow`: Specifies the last row affected. This value should always be greater than or equal to `firstRow`.
- `int type`: Specifies the type of change that occurred. It can be `TableModelEvent.INSERT`, `TableModelEvent.DELETE`, or `TableModelEvent.UPDATE`. `INSERT` and `DELETE` indicate the insertion and deletion of rows. `UPDATE` indicates that values have changed but the number of rows and columns has not changed.

As with any `EventObject`, we can retrieve the source of a `TableModelEvent` with `getSource()`.

18.1.14 The TableColumnModelListener interface

abstract interface javax.swing.event. TableColumnModelListener

This interface describes an object that listens to changes in a `TableColumnModel`: the adding, removing, and movement of columns, as well as changes in margin size and the current selection. `TableColumnModel` provides two methods for adding and removing these listeners: `addTableColumnModelListener()` and `removeTableColumnModelListener()`. (As is the case with `TableModelListeners`, `TableColumnModelListeners` are not directly added to `JTable`.)

Five methods are declared in this interface and they must be defined by all implementations: `columnAdded(TableColumnModelEvent)`, `columnRemoved(TableColumnModelEvent)`, `columnMoved(TableColumnModelEvent)`, `columnMarginChanged(TableColumnModel-Event)`, and `columnSelectionChanged(ListSelectionEvent)`. `ListSelectionEvents` are forwarded to `TableColumnModel`'s `ListSelectionModel`.

18.1.15 TableColumnModelEvent

class javax.swing.event. TableColumnModelEvent

This event extends `EventObject` and is used to notify a `TableColumnModel` about changes to a range of columns. These events are passed to `TableColumnModelListeners`. The `fromIndex` property specifies the lowest index of the column in the `TableColumnModel` affected by the change. The `toIndex` specifies the highest index. Both can be retrieved with typical `get` accessors. A `TableColumnModel` fires a `TableColumnModelEvent` whenever a column move, removal, or addition occurs. The event source can be retrieved with `getSource()`.

18.1.16 JTableHeader

class javax.swing.table.JTableHeader

This GUI component (which looks like a set of buttons for each column) is used to display a table's column headers. By dragging these headers, the user can rearrange a table's columns dynamically. This component is used internally by JTable. It can be retrieved with JTable's getTableHeader() method and assigned with setTableHeader(). When a JTable is placed in a JScrollPane, a default JTableHeader corresponding to each column is added to that scroll pane's COLUMN_HEADER viewport (see section 7.1.3). Each JTable uses one JTableHeader instance.

JTableHeader extends JComponent and implements TableColumnModelListener. Though JTableHeader is a Swing component, it is not used for display purposes. Instead, each TableColumn maintains a specific TableCellRenderer implementation used to represent its header. By default this is an instance of DefaultTableCellRenderer (see section 18.1.8).

NOTE   It is more common to customize the header renderer of a TableColumn than it is to customize a table's JTableHeader. In most cases, the default headers provided by JTable are satisfactory.

The resizingAllowed property specifies whether columns can be resized (if this property is false, it overpowers the isResizable property of each TableColumn). The reorderingAllowed property specifies whether columns can be reordered, and the updateTableInRealTime property specifies whether the whole column is displayed along with the header as it is dragged (this is only applicable if reorderingAllowed is true). All three of these properties are true by default.

JAVA 1.3   As of Java 1.3 the updateTableInRealTime property is obsolete. Regardless of this setting, columns will always be repainted in response to column dragging and resizing.

UI GUIDELINE

Column resizing   It is best to isolate columns which need to be a fixed width— for example, say you have a table in which monetary amounts might be ten significant figures with two decimal places. Such a column requires a fixed width. It doesn't need to be bigger and it doesn't want to be smaller. Allow the other columns to vary in size around the fixed columns.

For example, in a two-column table displaying Product Description and Price, fix the size of the Price column and allow Product Description to resize.

Draggable columns, added flexibility, and added complexity   If you don't need the flexibility of draggable table columns, it is best to switch them off. If a user accidentally picks up a JHeader component and rearranges a table, the table could quickly become confusing. The user may not realise what he has done or how to restore the table to its original form.

At any given time during a column drag we can retrieve the distance, in table coordinates, that the column has been dragged with respect to its original position from the draggedDistance property. JTableHeader also maintains a reference to the TableColumn it represents as well as the JTable it is part of, using the tableColumn and table properties, respectively.

18.1.17 JTable selection

JTable supports two selection models: one for row selections and one for column selections. JTable also supports the selection of individual table cells. Column selections are managed by a ListSelectionModel which is maintained by a TableColumnModel implementation, and row selections are managed by a ListSelectionModel which is maintained by JTable itself (both are DefaultListSelectionModels by default). As we learned in chapter 10, List-SelectionModels support three selection modes: SINGLE_SELECTION, SINGLE_INTERVAL_SELECTION, and MULTIPLE_INTERVAL_SELECTION. JTable provides the setSelectionMode() methods which will set both selection models to the given mode. Note, however, that getSelectionMode() only returns the current row selection mode.

To assign a specific selection mode to JTable's row ListSelectionModel:

```
myJTable.getSelectionModel().setSelectedMode(
    ListSelectionModel.XX_SELECTION);
```

To assign a specific selection mode to JTable's column ListSelectionModel:

```
myJTable.getColumnModel().getSelectionModel().setSelectionMode(
    ListSelectionModel.XX_SELECTION);
```

Row selection mode defaults to MULTIPLE_INTERVAL_SELECTION, and column selection mode defaults to SINGLE_SELECTION_MODE.

JTable provides control over whether rows and columns can be selected. We can query these modes and turn them on and off, with getRowSelectionAllowed() / getColumnSelectionAllowed(), and setRowSelectionAllowed() / setColumnSelectionAllowed(), respectively. When row selection is enabled (true by default), and cell selection is disabled (see below), clicking on a cell will select the entire row that cell belongs to. Similarly, when column selection is enabled (false by default), the whole column that cell belongs to will be selected. Nothing is stopping us from having both row and column selection active simultaneously.

JTable also provides control over whether individual cells can be selected with its cellSelectionEnabled property. We can turn this on or off with setCellSelectionEnabled() and query its state using getCellSelectionEnabled(). If cell selection is enabled (false by default), a cell can only be selected if both row selection and column selection are also enabled. If cell selection is not enabled, whenever a row or column containing that cell is selected (assuming that either row and/or column selection is enabled), that cell is also considered selected.

JTable provides several additional methods for querying the state of a selection. If at least one cell is selected, the following methods apply:

- getSelectedColumn() Returns the index (in the TreeModel) of the most recently selected column (-1 if no selection exists).
- getSelectedRow() Returns the index (in the TreeModel) of the most recently selected row (-1 if no selection exists).
- getSelectedColumns() and getSelectedRows(): Return the TreeModel indices of all currently selected columns and rows respectively (int[0] if no selection exists).

- getSelectedColumnCount() and getSelectedRowCount(): Return the current number of selected columns and rows respectively (0 if no selection exists).
- isColumnSelected() and isRowSelected(): Return a boolean specifying whether the given column or row is currently selected.
- isCellSelected(): Returns a boolean specifying whether the cell at the given TreeModel row and column index is selected.

The following methods can be used to programatically change JTable's selection, assuming the corresponding selection properties are enabled:

- clearSelection(): Unselects all rows, columns, and cells.
- selectAll(): Selects all rows, columns, and cells.
- addColumnSelectionInterval() and addRowSelectionInterval(): Allow programmatic selection of a contiguous group of columns and rows respectively. These methods can be called repeatedly to build a multiple-interval selection if the MULTIPLE_INTERVAL_SELECTION mode is active in the corresponding selection models.
- removeColumnSelectionInterval() and removeRowSelectionInterval(): Allow programmatic deselection of a contiguous interval of columns and rows respectively. These methods can also be used repeatedly to affect multiple-interval selections.
- setColumnSelectionInterval() and setRowSelectionInterval(): Clear the current column and row selection, and select the specified contiguous interval.

Interestingly, when cell selection is enabled, JTable considers the columns and rows that contain selected cells as selected themselves (even though they aren't highlighted). For example, if cells (1,5) and (3,6) are selected with row and column selection enabled and cell selection enabled, getSelectedColumns() will return {5,6} and getSelectedRows() will return {1,3}. Oddly enough, those two cells will be highlighted and considered selected by JTable, along with cells (1,6) and (3,5)! This is due to the fact that JTable bases cell selection solely on whether or not both the row and column containing a cell are selected. *When selected rows and columns intersect, the cells at the intersection points are considered selected.*

If these same cells are selected when cell selection is disabled and row and column selection are enabled, all cells in rows 1 and 3, and all cells in columns 5 and 6 will be considered selected. If they are selected with cell selection and only row selection is enabled, all cells in rows 1 and 3 will be considered selected. Similarly, if these two cells are selected with cell selection and only column selection is enabled, all cells in columns 5 and 6 will be considered selected. If cell selection is *not* enabled, and row and/or column selection is enabled, a cell will be considered selected if either a column or row containing it is selected.

NOTE   Multiple single-cell selections can be made by holding down the CTRL key and using the mouse for selection. A contiguous selection can be made by holding down the SHIFT key and using the mouse to select a range of cells.

We are typically interested in determining cell, row, and/or column selection based on a mouse click. JTable supports MouseListeners just as any other JComponent does, and we can use the getSelectedColumn() and getSelectedRow() methods to determine which cell was clicked in MouseListener's mouseClicked() method:

```
myJTable.addMouseListener(new MouseAdapter() {
    public void mouseClicked(MouseEvent e) {
```

```
      // Get the most recently selected row index
      int row = myJTable.getSelectedRow();
      // Get the most recently selected column index
      int column = myJTable.getSelectedColumn();
      if (row == -1 || column == -1)
        return; // Can't determine the selected cell
      else
        // Do something cell-specific
  }
});
```

This listener is not very robust because it will only give us a cell if both a row and a column have recently been selected, which in turn can only occur if both row selection and column selection is enabled. Thankfully, JTable provides methods for retrieving a row and column index corresponding to a given Point: rowAtPoint() and columnAtPoint() will return –1 if no row or column is found, respectively. Since MouseEvent carries a Point specifying the location where the event occurred, we can use these methods in place of the getSelectedRow() and getSelectedColumn() methods. This is particularly useful when row, column, and/or cell selection is not enabled.

As with JList, JTable does not directly support double mouse-click selections. However, as we learned in chapter 10, we can capture a double click and determine which cell was clicked by adding a listener to JTable similar to the following:

```
myJTable.addMouseListener(new MouseAdapter() {
  public void mouseClicked(MouseEvent e) {
    if (e.getClickCount() == 2) {
      Point origin = e.getPoint();
      int row = myJTable.rowAtPoint(origin);
      int column = myJTable.columnAtPoint(origin);
      if (row == -1 || column == -1)
        return; // no cell found
      else
        // Do something cell-specific
    }
  }
});
```

18.1.18 Column width and resizing

When a column's width increases, JTable must decide how other columns will react. One or more columns must shrink. Similarly, when a column's width decreases, JTable must decide how other columns will react to the newly available amount of space. JTable's autoResize-Mode property can take on any of five different values; each handles these cases differently.

- JTable.AUTO_RESIZE_ALL_COLUMNS: All columns gain or lose an equal amount of space corresponding to the width lost or gained by the resizing column.
- JTable.AUTO_RESIZE_LAST_COLUMN: The rightmost column shrinks or grows in direct correspondence with the amount of width lost or gained from the column being resized. All other columns are not affected.

- JTable.AUTO_RESIZE_NEXT_COLUMN: The column to the immediate right of the column being resized shrinks or grows in direct correspondence with the amount of width lost or gained from the resizing column. All other columns are not affected.
- JTable.AUTO_RESIZE_OFF: Resizing only affects the column being sized. All columns to the right of the column being resized are shifted right or left accordingly while maintaining their current sizes. Columns to the left are not affected.
- JTable.AUTO_RESIZE_SUBSEQUENT_COLUMNS: All columns to the right of the column being resized gain or lose an equal amount of space corresponding to the width lost or gained by the resizing column. Columns to the left are not affected.

TableColumn's width defaults to 75. Its minimum width defaults to 15 and its maximum width defaults to Integer.MAX_VALUE. When a JTable is first displayed, it attempts to size each TableColumn according to its width property. If that table's autoResizeMode property is set to AUTO_RESIZE_OFF, this will occur successfully. Otherwise, TableColumns are adjusted according to the current autoResizeMode property.

A TableColumn will never be sized larger than its maximum width or smaller than its minimum. For this reason it is possible that a JTable will occupy a larger or smaller area than that available (usually in a parent JScrollPane's main viewport), which may result in part of the table being clipped from view. If a table is contained in a JScrollPane and it occupies more than the available visible width, a horizontal scroll bar will be presented by default.

TableColumnModel's getTotalColumnWidth() method returns the sum of the current width of all TableColumns, including all margin space.

We can specify the amount of empty space between rows with JTable's setRowMargin() method, and we can assign all rows a specific height with setRowHeight(). JTable's setIntercellSpacing() method takes a Dimension instance and uses it to assign a new width and height to be used as margin space between cells (this method will repaint the table it is invoked on after all sizes have been changed).

18.1.19 JTable appearance

We can change the background and foreground colors used to highlight selected cells by setting the selectedBackground and SelectedForeground properties.

The default colors used for each TableColumn's table header renderer are determined from the current JTableHeader's background and foreground colors (recall that JTable-Header extends JComponent).

We can turn on and off horizontal and vertical grid lines (which always have a thickness of 1 pixel) by changing the showHorizontalLines and showVerticalLines properties. The showGrid property will overpower these properties when it is set with setShowGrid() because this method reassigns them to the specified value. So setShowGrid() turns on and off both vertical and horizontal lines as specified. The gridColor property specifies the Color to use for both vertical and horizontal grid lines. setGridColor() will assign the specified value to this property and then repaint the whole table.

GUIDELINE

Visual noise   Grid lines add visual noise to the display of a table. Removing some of them can aid the user in reading the table data. If you intend for the user to read rows across, then switch off the vertical grid lines. If you have columns of figures, for example, then you might prefer to switch off the horizontal grid lines, thereby making the columns easier to read.

When switching off the horizontal grid lines on the table, you may want to use the column cell renderer to change the background color of alternate table rows to make it easier to read rows. This combination of visual techniques, grid lines to distinguish columns and color to distinguish rows, helps guide the reader to better interpret data.

JAVA 1.3   As of Java 1.3 `JTable` allows the specification of row height for each individual row. This is supported by the new `setRowHeight()` and `getRowHeight()` methods. Example 18.6 in section 18.7 demonstrates this new functionality.

18.1.20   JTable scrolling

`JTable` implements the `Scrollable` interface (see section 7.1.4) and it is intended to be placed in a `JScrollPane`. `JTableHeaders` will not be displayed if `JTable` isn't placed in a `JScrollPane`, and the ability to resize columns would be lost because the table headers give us that capability. Among the required `Scrollable` methods, `JTable` implements `getScrollableTracksViewportWidth()` to return `true`, which forces `JTable` to attempt to size itself horizontally to fit within the current scroll pane viewport width. `getScrollableTracksViewportHeight()`, however, returns `false` as it is most common for tables to be vertically scrolled but not horizontally scrolled. Horizontal scrolling is often awkward and we suggest you avoid it whenever possible.

`JTable`'s vertical block increment is the number of visible rows less one, and its vertical unit increment is the row height of the next cell. The horizontal block increment is the width of the viewport, and the horizontal unit increment defaults to 100.

GUIDELINE

Small grids, no column headers   If you need to show two or three pieces of data grouped and aligned together, consider using a `JTable` without a `JScrollPane`. This gives you a small grid which is already aligned, neat, and tidy for display without column headers.

18.2   STOCKS TABLE, PART I: BASIC JTABLE EXAMPLE

This basic example shows how to construct a `JTable` to display information about stock market data for a given day. Despite its simplicity, the example demonstrates some of the most fundamental features of `JTable` and serves as a good basis for the more advanced examples that follow.

Stocks and stock trading is characterized by many attributes. The following are selected for display in our example:

Name	Type	Description
Symbol	String	Stock's symbol (NYSE or NASDAQ)
Name	String	Company name
Last	double	Price at the beginning of the trade day
Open	double	Price at the end of the trade day
Change	double	Absolute change in price with respect to previous closing
Change %	double	Percent change in price with respect to previous closing
Volume	long	Day's volume of trade (in $) for this stock

Each stock attribute represents a column in our table, and each row represents a specific company's stock information.

Example 18.1

StocksTable.java

see \Chapter18\1

```java
import java.awt.*;
import java.awt.event.*;
import java.util.*;
import java.io.*;
import java.text.*;

import javax.swing.*;
import javax.swing.border.*;
import javax.swing.event.*;
import javax.swing.table.*;

public class StocksTable extends JFrame {
    protected JTable m_table;
```

Stock Quotes at 12/18/2004

Symbol	Name	Last	Open	Change	Change %	Volume
ORCL	Oracle Corp.	23.6875	25.375	-1.6875	-6.42	24976600
EGGS	Egghead.com	17.25	17.4375	-0.1875	-1.43	2146400
T	AT&T	65.1875	66.0	-0.8125	-0.1	554000
LU	Lucent Technology	64.625	59.9375	4.6875	9.65	29856300
FON	Sprint	104.5625	106.375	-1.8125	-1.82	1135100
ENML	Enamelon Inc.	4.875	5.0	-0.125	0.0	35900
CPQ	Compaq Computers	30.875	31.25	-0.375	-2.18	11853900
MSFT	Microsoft Corp.	94.0625	95.1875	-1.125	-0.92	19836900
DELL	Dell Computers	46.1875	44.5	1.6875	6.24	47310000
SUNW	Sun Microsystems	140.625	130.9375	10.0	10.625	17734600
IBM	Intl. Bus. Machines	183.0	183.125	-0.125	-0.51	4371400
HWP	Hewlett-Packard	70.0	71.0625	-1.4375	-2.01	2410700
UIS	Unisys Corp.	28.25	29.0	-0.75	-2.59	2576200
SNE	Sony Corp.	96.1875	95.625	1.125	1.18	330600

Figure 18.1   Table in a `JScrollPane` with 7 TableColumns and 16 rows of data

```java
   protected StockTableData m_data;
   protected JLabel m_title;

   public StocksTable() {
      super("Stocks Table");
      setSize(600, 300);

      UIManager.put("Table.focusCellHighlightBorder",
         new LineBorder(Color.black, 0));

      m_data = new StockTableData();

      m_title = new JLabel(m_data.getTitle(),
         new ImageIcon("money.gif"), SwingConstants.CENTER);
      m_title.setFont(new Font("Helvetica",Font.PLAIN,24));
      getContentPane().add(m_title, BorderLayout.NORTH);

      m_table = new JTable();
      m_table.setAutoCreateColumnsFromModel(false);
      m_table.setModel(m_data);

      for (int k = 0; k < m_data.getColumnCount(); k++) {
         DefaultTableCellRenderer renderer = new
            DefaultTableCellRenderer();
         renderer.setHorizontalAlignment(
         StockTableData.m_columns[k].m_alignment);
         TableColumn column = new TableColumn(k,
         StockTableData.m_columns[k].m_width, renderer, null);
         m_table.addColumn(column);
      }

      JTableHeader header = m_table.getTableHeader();
      header.setUpdateTableInRealTime(false);

      JScrollPane ps = new JScrollPane();
      ps.getViewport().setBackground(m_table.getBackground());
      ps.getViewport().add(m_table);
      getContentPane().add(ps, BorderLayout.CENTER);
   }

   public static void main(String argv[]) {
      StocksTable frame = new StocksTable();
      frame.setDefaultCloseOperation(JFrame.EXIT_ON_CLOSE);
      frame.setVisible(true);
   }
}

class StockData {
   public String m_symbol;
   public String m_name;
   public Double m_last;
   public Double m_open;
   public Double m_change;
   public Double m_changePr;
   public Long m_volume;

   public StockData(String symbol, String name, double last,
```

❶ Creates StockTableData and passes it to JTable

❶ We're creating our own columns

❷ Creates each TableColumn with the specified alignment and width

❸ Only shows column header when dragging

❹ Puts primitive in Object-derived classes for easier data interchange

```
                double open, double change, double changePr, long volume) {
                m_symbol = symbol;
                m_name = name;
                m_last = new Double(last);
                m_open = new Double(open);
                m_change = new Double(change);
                m_changePr = new Double(changePr);
                m_volume = new Long(volume);
            }
        }

        class ColumnData {
            public String m_title;
            public int m_width;
            public int m_alignment;

            public ColumnData(String title, int width, int alignment) {
                m_title = title;
                m_width = width;
                m_alignment = alignment;
            }
        }

        class StockTableData extends AbstractTableModel {
            static final public ColumnData m_columns[] = {
                new ColumnData( "Symbol", 100, JLabel.LEFT ),
                new ColumnData( "Name", 160, JLabel.LEFT ),
                new ColumnData( "Last", 100, JLabel.RIGHT ),
                new ColumnData( "Open", 100, JLabel.RIGHT ),
                new ColumnData( "Change", 100, JLabel.RIGHT ),
                new ColumnData( "Change %", 100, JLabel.RIGHT ),
                new ColumnData( "Volume", 100, JLabel.RIGHT )
            };

            protected SimpleDateFormat m_frm;
            protected Vector m_vector;
            protected Date m_date;

            public StockTableData() {
                m_frm = new SimpleDateFormat("MM/dd/yyyy");
                m_vector = new Vector();
                setDefaultData();
            }

            public void setDefaultData() {
                try {
                    m_date = m_frm.parse("12/18/2004");
                }
                catch (java.text.ParseException ex) {
                    m_date = null;
                }

                m_vector.removeAllElements();
                m_vector.addElement(new StockData("ORCL", "Oracle Corp.",
                    23.6875, 25.375, -1.6875, -6.42, 24976600));
```

5 **Encapsulates information about each TableColumn**

6 **Data model for JTable**

7 **Static list of column names, widths, and alignments**

```
m_vector.addElement(new StockData("EGGS", "Egghead.com",
    17.25, 17.4375, -0.1875, -1.43, 2146400));
m_vector.addElement(new StockData("T", "AT&T",
    65.1875, 66, -0.8125, -0.10, 554000));
m_vector.addElement(new StockData("LU", "Lucent Technology",
    64.625, 59.9375, 4.6875, 9.65, 29856300));
m_vector.addElement(new StockData("FON", "Sprint",
    104.5625, 106.375, -1.8125, -1.82, 1135100));
m_vector.addElement(new StockData("ENML", "Enamelon Inc.",
    4.875, 5, -0.125, 0, 35900));
m_vector.addElement(new StockData("CPQ", "Compaq Computers",
    30.875, 31.25, -0.375, -2.18, 11853900));
m_vector.addElement(new StockData("MSFT", "Microsoft Corp.",
    94.0625, 95.1875, -1.125, -0.92, 19836900));
m_vector.addElement(new StockData("DELL", "Dell Computers",
    46.1875, 44.5, 1.6875, 6.24, 47310000));
m_vector.addElement(new StockData("SUNW", "Sun Microsystems",
    140.625, 130.9375, 10, 10.625, 17734600));
m_vector.addElement(new StockData("IBM", "Intl. Bus. Machines",
    183, 183.125, -0.125, -0.51, 4371400));
m_vector.addElement(new StockData("HWP", "Hewlett-Packard",
    70, 71.0625, -1.4375, -2.01, 2410700));
m_vector.addElement(new StockData("UIS", "Unisys Corp.",
    28.25, 29, -0.75, -2.59, 2576200));
m_vector.addElement(new StockData("SNE", "Sony Corp.",
    96.1875, 95.625, 1.125, 1.18, 330600));
m_vector.addElement(new StockData("NOVL", "Novell Inc.",
    24.0625, 24.375, -0.3125, -3.02, 6047900));
m_vector.addElement(new StockData("HIT", "Hitachi, Ltd.",
    78.5, 77.625, 0.875, 1.12, 49400));
}

public int getRowCount() {
    return m_vector==null ? 0 : m_vector.size();
}

public int getColumnCount() {
    return m_columns.length;
}

public String getColumnName(int column) {
    return m_columns[column].m_title;
}

public boolean isCellEditable(int nRow, int nCol) {
    return false;
}

public Object getValueAt(int nRow, int nCol) {
    if (nRow < 0 || nRow>=getRowCount())
        return "";
    StockData row = (StockData)m_vector.elementAt(nRow);
    switch (nCol) {
        case 0: return row.m_symbol;
```

8 Can be called before constructor, so needs to check for initialization

```
          case 1: return row.m_name;
          case 2: return row.m_last;
          case 3: return row.m_open;
          case 4: return row.m_change;
          case 5: return row.m_changePr;
          case 6: return row.m_volume;
      }
      return "";
  }

  public String getTitle() {
      if (m_date==null)
          return "Stock Quotes";
      return "Stock Quotes at "+m_frm.format(m_date);
  }
}
```

18.2.1 Understanding the code

Class StocksTable

This class extends JFrame to implement the frame container for our table. Three instance variables are declared (to be used extensively in more complex examples that follow):

- JTable m_table: table component to display stock data.
- StockTableData m_data: TableModel implementation to manage stock data.
- JLabel m_title: used to display stocks table title (date which stock prices are referenced).

1 The StocksTable constructor first initializes the parent frame object and builds an instance of StockTableData. StockTableData's getTitle() method is invoked to set the text for the title label which is added to the northern region of the content pane. Then a JTable is created by passing the StockTableData instance to the constructor. Note that the auto-CreateColumnsFromModel method is set to false because we plan on creating our own TableColumns.

As we will see, the static array m_columns of the StockTableData class describes all columns of our table. It is used here to create each TableColumn instance and set their text alignment and width.

2 The setHorizontalAlignment() method (inherited by DefaultTableCellRenderer from JLabel) is used to set the proper alignment for each TableColumn's cell renderer. The TableColumn constructor takes a column index, width, and renderer as parameters. Note that TableCellEditor is set to null since we don't want to allow editing of stock data. Finally, columns are added to the table's TableColumnModel (which JTable created by default because we didn't specify one) with the addColumn() method.

3 In the next step, an instance of JTableHeader is created for this table, and the update-TableInRealTime property is set to false (this is done to demonstrate the effect this has on column dragging—only a column's table header is displayed during a drag).

Lastly a JScrollPane instance is used to provide scrolling capabilities, and our table is added to its JViewport. This JScrollPane is then added to the center of our frame's content pane.

Class StockData

This class encapsulates a unit of stock data as described in the previous table. The instance variables defined in this class have the following meaning:

- `String m_symbol`: stock's symbol (NYSE or NASDAQ)
- `String m_name`: company name
- `Double m_last`: the price of the last trade
- `Double m_open`: price at the beginning of the trade day
- `Double m_change`: absolute change in price with respect to previous closing
- `Double m_changePr`: percent change in price with respect to previous closing
- `Long m_volume`: day's volume of trade (in $) for this stock

4 Note that all numerical data are encapsulated in `Object`-derived classes. This design decision simplifies data exchange with the table (as we will see). The only constructor provided assigns each of these variables from the data passed as parameters.

> **NOTE** We use `public` instance variables in this and several other classes in this chapter to avoid overcomplication. In most professional apps these would either be protected or private properties with associated accessor methods.

5 Class ColumnData

This class encapsulates data describing the visual characteristics of a single `TableColumn` of our table. The instance variables defined in this class have the following meaning:

- `String m_title`: column title
- `int m_width`: column width in pixels
- `int m_alignment`: text alignment as defined in `JLabel`

The only constructor provided assigns each of these variables the data passed as parameters.

6 Class StockTableData

This class extends `AbstractTableModel` to serve as the data model for our table. Recall that `AbstractTableModel` is an abstract class, and three methods must be implemented to instantiate it:

- `public int getRowCount()`: returns the number of rows in the table.
- `public int getColumnCount()`: returns the number of columns in the table.
- `public Object getValueAt(int row, int column)`: returns data in the specified cell as an `Object` instance.

> **NOTE** An alternative approach is to extend the `DefaultTableModel` class which is a concrete implementation of `AbstractTableModel`. However, this is not recommended, as the few abstract methods in `AbstractTableModel` can be easily implemented. Usage of `DefaultTableModel` often creates unnecessary overhead.

7 By design, this class manages all information about our table, including the title and column data. A static array of `ColumnData`, `m_columns`, is provided to hold information about our table's columns (it is used in the `StocksTable` constructor). Three instance variables have the following meaning:

- `SimpleDateFormat m_frm`: used to format dates

- `Date m_date`: date of currently stored market data
- `Vector m_vector`: collection of `StockData` instances for each row in the table

The only constructor of the `StockTableData` class initializes two of these variables and calls the `setDefaultData()` method to assign the predefined default data to `m_date` and `m_vector`. (In a later example we'll see how to use JDBC to retrieve data from a database rather than using hard-coded data as we do here.)

As we discussed, the `getRowCount()` and `getColumnCount()` methods should return the number of rows and columns, respectively. So their implementation is fairly obvious. The only catch is that they may be called by the `AbstractTableModel` constructor before any member variable is initialized. So we have to check for a null instance of `m_vector`. Note that `m_columns`, as a static variable, will be initialized before any nonstatic code is executed (so we don't have to check `m_columns` against `null`).

The remainder of the `StockTableData` class implements the following methods:

- `getColumnName()`: returns the column title.
- `isCellEditable()`: always returns `false`, because we want to disable all editing.
- `getValueAt()`: retrieves data for a given cell as an `Object`. Depending on the column index, one of the `StockData` fields is returned.
- `getTitle()`: returns our table's title as a `String` to be used in a `JLabel` in the northern region of our frame's content pane.

18.2.2 Running the code

Figure 18.1 shows `StocksTable` in action displaying our hard-coded stock data. Note that the `TableColumns` resize properly in response to the parent frame size. Also note that the selected row in our table can be changed with the mouse or arrow keys, but no editing is allowed.

18.3 STOCKS TABLE, PART II: CUSTOM RENDERERS

Now we'll extend `StocksTable` to use color and small icons in rendering our table cells. To enhance data visibility, we'll make the following two enhancements:

- Render absolute and percent changes in green for positive values and red for negative values.
- Add an icon next to each stock symbol: arrow up for positive changes and arrow down for negative.

To do this we need to build our own custom `TreeCellRenderer`.

Example 18.2

StocksTable.java

see \Chapter18\2

```
import java.awt.*;
import java.awt.event.*;
```

	Symbol	Name	Last	Open	Change	Change %	Volume
↓	ORCL	Oracle Corp.	23.6875	25.375	-1.6875	-6.42	24,976,600
↓	EGGS	Egghead.com	17.25	17.4375	-0.1875	-1.43	2,146,400
↓	T	AT&T	65.1875	66.0	-0.8125	-0.1	554,000
↑	LU	Lucent Technology	64.625	59.9375	4.6875	9.65	29,856,300
↓	FON	Sprint	104.5625	106.375	-1.8125	-1.82	1,135,100
↓	ENML	Enamelon Inc.	4.875	5.0	-0.125	0.0	35,900
↓	CPQ	Compaq Computers	30.875	31.25	-0.375	-2.18	11,853,900
↓	MSFT	Microsoft Corp.	94.0625	95.1875	-1.125	-0.92	19,836,900
↑	DELL	Dell Computers	46.1875	44.5	1.6875	6.24	47,310,000
↑	SUNW	Sun Microsystems	140.625	130.9375	10.0	10.625	17,734,600
↓	IBM	Intl. Bus. Machines	183.0	183.125	-0.125	-0.51	4,371,400
↓	HWP	Hewlett-Packard	70.0	71.0625	-1.4375	-2.01	2,410,700
↓	UIS	Unisys Corp.	28.25	29.0	-0.75	-2.59	2,576,200
↑	SNE	Sony Corp.	96.1875	95.625	1.125	1.18	330,600

Figure 18.2   Table using a custom cell renderer

```
import java.util.*;
import java.io.*;
import java.text.*;

import javax.swing.*;
import javax.swing.border.*;
import javax.swing.event.*;
import javax.swing.table.*;

public class StocksTable extends JFrame {
    protected JTable m_table;
    protected StockTableData m_data;
    protected JLabel m_title;

    public StocksTable() {
        // Unchanged code from example 18.1

        for (int k = 0; k < m_data.getColumnCount(); k++) {
            DefaultTableCellRenderer renderer = new
                ColoredTableCellRenderer();
            renderer.setHorizontalAlignment(
            StockTableData.m_columns[k].m_alignment);
            TableColumn column = new TableColumn(k,
            StockTableData.m_columns[k].m_width, renderer, null);
            m_table.addColumn(column);
        }
        // Unchanged code from example 18.1
    }

    public static void main(String argv[]) {
        StocksTable frame = new StocksTable();
        frame.setDefaultCloseOperation(JFrame.EXIT_ON_CLOSE);
        frame.setVisible(true);
```

❶ Use custom cell renderer

```
      }
    }

    class ColoredTableCellRenderer extends DefaultTableCellRenderer {
      public void setValue(Object value) {
        if (value instanceof ColorData) {
          ColorData cvalue = (ColorData)value;
          setForeground(cvalue.m_color);
          setText(cvalue.m_data.toString());
        }
        else if (value instanceof IconData) {
          IconData ivalue = (IconData)value;
          setIcon(ivalue.m_icon);
          setText(ivalue.m_data.toString());
        }
        else
          super.setValue(value);
      }
    }

    class ColorData {
      public Color m_color;
      public Object m_data;
      public static Color GREEN = new Color(0, 128, 0);
      public static Color RED = Color.red;

      public ColorData(Color color, Object data) {
        m_color = color;
        m_data = data;
      }

      public ColorData(Double data) {
        m_color = data.doubleValue() >= 0 ? GREEN : RED;
        m_data = data;
      }

      public String toString() {
        return m_data.toString();
      }
    }

    class IconData {
      public ImageIcon m_icon;
      public Object m_data;

      public IconData(ImageIcon icon, Object data) {
        m_icon = icon;
        m_data = data;
      }

      public String toString() {
        return m_data.toString();
      }
    }

    class StockData {
```

2 Custom cell renderer to render colored text and icons

3 Binds a color value to data

4 Binds an icon image to data

5 Similar to previous version, but encodes icon and color information with some of the existing fields

```java
// Unchanged code from example 18.1

public StockData(String symbol, String name, double last,
    double open, double change, double changePr, long volume) {
    m_symbol = new IconData(getIcon(change), symbol);
    m_name = name;
    m_last = new Double(last);
    m_open = new Double(open);
    m_change = new ColorData(new Double(change));
    m_changePr = new ColorData(new Double(changePr));
    m_volume = new Long(volume);
}

public static ImageIcon getIcon(double change) {
    return (change>0 ? ICON_UP : (change<0 ? ICON_DOWN :
        ICON_BLANK));
}
}

// Unchanged code from example 18.1

class StockTableData extends AbstractTableModel {
    // Unchanged code from example 18.1

    protected SimpleDateFormat m_frm;
    protected NumberFormat m_volumeFormat;
    protected Vector m_vector;
    protected Date m_date;

    public StockTableData() {
        m_frm = new SimpleDateFormat("MM/dd/yyyy");
        m_volumeFormat = NumberFormat.getInstance();
        m_volumeFormat.setGroupingUsed(true);
        m_volumeFormat.setMaximumFractionDigits(0);

        m_vector = new Vector();
        setDefaultData();
    }

    public void setDefaultData() {
        // Unchanged code from example 18.1
    }

    // Unchanged code from example 18.1

    public Object getValueAt(int nRow, int nCol) {
        if (nRow < 0 || nRow>=getRowCount())
            return "";
        StockData row = (StockData)m_vector.elementAt(nRow);
        switch (nCol) {
            case 0: return row.m_symbol;
            case 1: return row.m_name;
            case 2: return row.m_last;
            case 3: return row.m_open;
            case 4: return row.m_change;
            case 5: return row.m_changePr;
```

6 New NumberFormat used to format Volume data

```
      case 6: return m_volumeFormat.format(row.m_volume);
   }
   return "";
}

// Unchanged code from example 18.1
}
```

18.3.1 Understanding the code

Class StocksTable

1 The only change we need to make in the base frame class is to change the column renderer to an instance of our custom `ColoredTableCellRenderer` class.

2 *Class ColoredTableCellRenderer*

This class extends `DefaultTableCellRenderer` and overrides only one method: `set-Value()`. This method will be called prior to the rendering of a cell to retrieve its corresponding data (of any nature) as an `Object`. Our overridden `setValue()` method is able to recognize two specific kinds of cell data: `ColorData`, which adds color to a data object, and `IconData`, which adds an icon. If a `ColorData` instance is detected, its encapsulated color is set as the foreground for the renderer. If an `IconData` instance is detected, its encapsulated icon is assigned to the renderer with the `setIcon()` method (which is inherited from `JLabel`). If the value is neither a `ColorData` or an `IconData` instance we call the super-class `setValue()` method.

3 *Class ColorData*

This class is used to bind a specific color, `m_color`, to a data object of any nature, `m_data`. Two constructors are provided for this class. The first constructor takes `Color` and `Object` parameters and assigns them to instance variables `m_color` and `m_data` respectively. The second constructor takes a `Double` parameter which gets assigned to `m_data`, and `m_color` is assigned the color green if the parameter is positive, and red if negative. The `toString()` method simply calls the `toString()` method of the data object.

4 *Class IconData*

This class is used to bind `ImageIcon m_icon` to a data object of any nature, `m_data`. Its only constructor takes `ImageIcon` and `Object` parameters. The `toString()` method simply calls the `toString()` method of the data object.

5 *Class StockData*

This class has been enhanced from its previous version to provide images and new variable data types. We've prepared three static `ImageIcon` instances holding images: arrow up, arrow down, and a blank (completely transparent) image. The static `getIcon()` method returns one of these images depending on the sign of the given double parameter. We've also changed three instance variables to bind data with the color and image attributes according to the following table:

Field	New type	Data object	Description
m_symbol	IconData	String	Stock's symbol (NYSE or NASDAQ)
m_change	ColorData	Double	Absolute change in price
m_changePr	ColorData	Double	Percent change in price

The corresponding changes are also required in the `StockData` constructor.

Class StockTableData

6 This class has an additional instance variable `m_volumeFormat` of type `NumberFormat`. This is used to format the volume data in a locale dependent fashion. The `setGroupingUsed()` method is used to turn on grouping separators (in English these are ","s), and the `setMaximumFractionDigits()` method is used to specify that no fractional decimal places should be shown.

The switch statement in the `getValueAt()` method is modified to format the volume data on the fly in the current locale.

18.3.2 Running the code

Figure 18.2 shows `StocksTable` with custom rendering in action. Note the correct usage of color and icons, which considerably enhances the visualization of our data.

GUIDELINE

Improving visual communication   Tables can be data intensive and consequently it can be very difficult for the viewer to quickly pick out the important information. The table in figure 18.1 highlighted this. In figure 18.2, we are improving the visual communication with the introduction of visual layers. The icons in the first column quickly tell the viewer whether a price is rising or falling. This is visually reinforced with the red and green introduced on the change columns.

Red particularly is a very strong color. By introducing red and green only on the change columns and not across the entire row, we avoid the danger of the red becoming overpowering. If we had introduced red and green across the full width of the table, the colors may have become intrusive and impaired the visual communication.

18.4   *STOCKS TABLE, PART III: SORTING COLUMNS*

In this section we add the ability to sort any column in ascending or descending order. The most suitable graphical element for selection of sort order are the column headers. We adopt the following model for our sorting functionality:

- A single click on the header of a certain column causes the table to resort based on this column.
- A repeated click on the same column changes the sort direction from ascending to descending and vice versa.
- The header of the column which provides the current sorting should be marked to indicate which direction the column is sorted in.

To do this we add a mouse listener to the table header to capture mouse clicks and trigger a table sort. Sorting can be accomplished fairly easily using the `Collections` API.

NOTE   Class `java.util.Collections` contains a set of static methods used to manipulate Java collections, including `java.util.Vector` which is used in this example.

We use the `java.util.Collections.sort(List lst, Comparator c)` method to sort any collection implementing the `java.util.List` interface based on a given `Comparator`. A `Comparator` implementation requires two methods:

- `int compare(Object o1, Object o2)`: Compares two objects and returns the result as an `int` (zero if equal, negative value if the first is less than the second, positive value if the first is more than the second).
- `boolean equals(Object obj)`: Returns `true` if the given object is equal to this `Comparator`.

Example 18.3

StocksTable.java

see \Chapter18\3

```java
import java.awt.*;
import java.awt.event.*;
import java.util.*;
import java.io.*;
import java.text.*;

import javax.swing.*;
import javax.swing.border.*;
import javax.swing.event.*;
import javax.swing.table.*;

public class StocksTable extends JFrame {
    protected JTable m_table;
    protected StockTableData m_data;
    protected JLabel m_title;
```

	Symbol	Name	Last	Open	▽ Change	Change %	Volume
♊	SUNW	Sun Microsystems	140.625	130.9375	10.0	10.625	17,734,600
♊	LU	Lucent Technology	64.625	59.9375	4.6875	9.65	29,856,300
♊	DELL	Dell Computers	46.1875	44.5	1.6875	6.24	47,310,000
♊	SNE	Sony Corp.	96.1875	95.625	1.125	1.18	330,600
♊	HIT	Hitachi, Ltd.	78.5	77.625	0.875	1.12	49,400
♊	ENML	Enamelon Inc.	4.875	5.0	-0.125	0.0	35,900
♊	IBM	Intl. Bus. Machines	183.0	183.125	-0.125	-0.51	4,371,400
♊	EGGS	Egghead.com	17.25	17.4375	-0.1875	-1.43	2,146,400
♊	NOVL	Novell Inc.	24.0625	24.375	-0.3125	-3.02	6,047,900
♊	CPQ	Compaq Computers	30.875	31.25	-0.375	-2.18	11,853,900
♊	UIS	Unisys Corp.	28.25	29.0	-0.75	-2.59	2,576,200
♊	T	AT&T	65.1875	66.0	-0.8125	-0.1	554,000
♊	MSFT	Microsoft Corp.	94.0625	95.1875	-1.125	-0.92	19,836,900
♊	HWP	Hewlett-Packard	70.0	71.0625	-1.4375	-2.01	2,410,700

Figure 18.3   Table with ascending and descending sorting of all columns.

```
public StocksTable() {
   super("Stocks Table");
   setSize(600, 300);

   // Unchanged code from example 18.2

   for (int k = 0; k < m_data.getColumnCount(); k++) {
     DefaultTableCellRenderer renderer = new
        ColoredTableCellRenderer();
     renderer.setHorizontalAlignment(
        StockTableData.m_columns[k].m_alignment);
     TableColumn column = new TableColumn(k,
        StockTableData.m_columns[k].m_width, renderer, null);
     column.setHeaderRenderer(createDefaultRenderer());
     m_table.addColumn(column);
   }

   JTableHeader header = m_table.getTableHeader();
   header.setUpdateTableInRealTime(true);
   header.addMouseListener(new ColumnListener());
   header.setReorderingAllowed(true);

   // Unchanged code from example 18.2
}

protected TableCellRenderer createDefaultRenderer() {
   DefaultTableCellRenderer label =
     new DefaultTableCellRenderer() {
       public Component getTableCellRendererComponent(
       JTable table, Object value, boolean isSelected,
       boolean hasFocus, int row, int column) {
         if (table != null) {
           JTableHeader header = table.getTableHeader();
           if (header != null) {
             setForeground(header.getForeground());
             setBackground(header.getBackground());
             setFont(header.getFont());
           }
         }
         setText((value == null) ? "" : value.toString());
         setBorder(UIManager.getBorder("TableHeader.cellBorder"));
         return this;
       }
     };
   label.setHorizontalAlignment(JLabel.CENTER);
   return label;
}

public static void main(String argv[]) {
   StocksTable frame = new StocksTable();
   frame.setDefaultCloseOperation(JFrame.EXIT_ON_CLOSE);
   frame.setVisible(true);
}
```

1 Moves listener added to table header to allow sorting; allow reordering of columns

2 Returns a custom renderer for use in table headers

```
class ColumnListener extends MouseAdapter {
   public void mouseClicked(MouseEvent e) {
      TableColumnModel colModel = m_table.getColumnModel();
      int columnModelIndex = colModel.getColumnIndexAtX(e.getX());
      int modelIndex =
         colModel.getColumn(columnModelIndex).getModelIndex();

      if (modelIndex < 0)
         return;
      if (m_data.m_sortCol == modelIndex)
         m_data.m_sortAsc = !m_data.m_sortAsc;
      else
         m_data.m_sortCol = modelIndex;

      for (int i=0; i < m_data.getColumnCount(); i++) {
         TableColumn column = colModel.getColumn(i);
         int index = column.getModelIndex();
         JLabel renderer = (JLabel)column.getHeaderRenderer();
         renderer.setIcon(m_data.getColumnIcon(index));
      }
      m_table.getTableHeader().repaint();

      m_data.sortData();
      m_table.tableChanged(new TableModelEvent(m_data));
      m_table.repaint();
   }
}
}
```

③ Used to intercept mouse events on table header and assign appropriate sorting direction icon

④ Enhanced to support sorting of data and to track currently sorted column as well as direction of sort

```
// Unchanged code from example 18.2

class StockTableData extends AbstractTableModel {

   // Unchanged code from example 18.2

   public static ImageIcon COLUMN_UP = new ImageIcon("SortUp.gif");
   public static ImageIcon COLUMN_DOWN = new ImageIcon("SortDown.gif");


   protected SimpleDateFormat m_frm;
   protected NumberFormat m_volumeFormat;
   protected Vector m_vector;
   protected Date m_date;

   public int m_sortCol = 0;
   public boolean m_sortAsc = true;

   public void setDefaultData() {
      // Unchanged code from example 18.2
      sortData();
   }

   // Unchanged code from example 18.2

   public Icon getColumnIcon(int column)
      if (column==m_sortCol)
         return m_sortAsc ? COLUMN_UP : COLUMN_DOWN;
```

```
        return null;
    }

    public void sortData() {
        Collections.sort(m_vector, new
            StockComparator(m_sortCol, m_sortAsc));
    }
}

class StockComparator implements Comparator {
    protected intm_sortCol;
    protected boolean m_sortAsc;

    public StockComparator(int sortCol, boolean sortAsc) {
        m_sortCol = sortCol;
        m_sortAsc = sortAsc;
    }

    public int compare(Object o1, Object o2) {
        if(!(o1 instanceof StockData) || !(o2 instanceof StockData))
            return 0;
        StockData s1 = (StockData)o1;
        StockData s2 = (StockData)o2;
        int result = 0;
        double d1, d2;
        switch (m_sortCol) {
            case 0:// symbol
                String str1 = (String)s1.m_symbol.m_data;
                String str2 = (String)s2.m_symbol.m_data;
                result = str1.compareTo(str2);
                break;
            case 1:// name
                result = s1.m_name.compareTo(s2.m_name);
                break;
            case 2:// last
                d1 = s1.m_last.doubleValue();
                d2 = s2.m_last.doubleValue();
                result = d1<d2 ? -1 : (d1>d2 ? 1 : 0);
                break;
            case 3:// open
                d1 = s1.m_open.doubleValue();
                d2 = s2.m_open.doubleValue();
                result = d1<d2 ? -1 : (d1>d2 ? 1 : 0);
                break;
            case 4:// change
                d1 = ((Double)s1.m_change.m_data).doubleValue();
                d2 = ((Double)s2.m_change.m_data).doubleValue();
                result = d1<d2 ? -1 : (d1>d2 ? 1 : 0);
                break;
            case 5:// change %
                d1 = ((Double)s1.m_changePr.m_data).doubleValue();
                d2 = ((Double)s2.m_changePr.m_data).doubleValue();
                result = d1<d2 ? -1 : (d1>d2 ? 1 : 0);
                break;
```

⑤ Implements the rules of comparison between StockData objects

```
        case 6:// volume
            long l1 = s1.m_volume.longValue();
            long l2 = s2.m_volume.longValue();
            result = l1<l2 ? -1 : (l1>l2 ? 1 : 0);
            break;
    }

    if (!m_sortAsc)
        result = -result;
    return result;
}

public boolean equals(Object obj) {
    if (obj instanceof StockComparator) {
        StockComparator compObj = (StockComparator)obj;
        return (compObj.m_sortCol==m_sortCol) &&
            (compObj.m_sortAsc==m_sortAsc);
    }
    return false;
}
```

18.4.1 Understanding the code

Class StocksTable

1 In the `StocksTable` constructor we add an instance of the `ColumnListener` class as a mouse listener to the table's header and allow reordering of columns. We also use our custom **2** `createDefaultRenderer()` to provide the header renderer for our table columns. This renderer is used by `ColumnListener` to show the direction of a column sort.

3 *Class StockTable.ColumnListener*

This class extends `MouseAdapter` and is used to intercept mouse events on our table column headers to perform a column sort.

The `mouseClicked()` method is invoked when the user clicks on a header. First it determines the index of the `TableColumn` clicked based on the coordinate of the click. If for any reason the returned index is negative (i.e., the column cannot be determined) the method cannot continue and we return. Otherwise, we check whether this index corresponds to the column which already has been selected for sorting. If so, we invert the `m_sortCol` flag to reverse the sorting order. If the index corresponds to the newly selected column we store the new sorting index in the `m_sortCol` variable.

Then we refresh the headers by iterating through the `TableColumn`s and assigning the appropriate renderer an icon (or `null`) using `StockTableData`'s `getColumnIcon()` method. Finally our table data is resorted by calling `StockTableData`'s `sortData()` method. We then refresh the table by calling `tableChanged()` and `repaint()`.

4 *Class StockTableData*

Here we declare two new instance variables: `int m_sortCol` to hold the index of the current column chosen for sorting, and `boolean m_sortAsc`, which is `true` when sorting in ascending order, and `false` when sorting in descending order. These variables determine the initial sorting order. To be consistent we sort our table initially by calling the new sortData() method in our setDefaultData() method (which is called from the Stock-TableData constructor).

We've also added two new ImageIcon class variables, COLUMN_UP and COLUMN_DOWN, representing images used in the header renderer to indicate a column's sorting direction. The getColumnIcon() method returns the appropriate icon based on the state of m_sortAsc and the given column index (this method will return null if the given index does not match m_sortCol–the currently sorted column index).

The sortData() method invokes the static Collections.sort() method to sort our table data using an instance of our custom StockComparator class.

❺ *Class StockComparator*

This class implements the rule of comparison for two objects, which in our case are Stock-Datas. Instances of the StockComparator class are passed to the Collections.sort() method to perform data sorting.

Two instance variables are defined:

- int m_sortCol represents the index of the column which performs the comparison
- boolean m_sortAsc is true for ascending sorting and false for descending

The StockComparator constructor takes two parameters and stores them in these instance variables.

The compare() method takes two objects to be compared and returns an integer value according to the rules determined in the Comparator interface:

- 0 if object 1 equals 2
- A positive number if object 1 is greater than object 2
- A negative number if object 1 is less than object 2

Since we are dealing only with StockData objects, first we cast both objects and return 0 if this cast isn't possible. The next issue is to define what it means when one StockData objects is greater, equal, or less than another. This is done in a switch-case structure, which, depending on the index of the comparison column, extracts two fields and forms an integer result of the comparison. When the switch-case structure finishes, we know the result of an ascending comparison. For descending comparison we simply need to invert the sign of the result.

The equals() method takes another Comparator instance as parameter and returns true if that parameter represents the same Comparator. We determine this by comparing Comparator instance variables: m_sortCol and m_sortAsc.

18.4.2 Running the code

Figure 18.3 shows StocksTable sorted by decreasing Change %. Click different column headers and note that resorting occurs as expected. Click the same column header twice and note that sorting order flips from ascending to descending and vice versa. Also note that the currently selected sorting column header is marked with an informative icon. This sorting functionality is very useful. Particularly, for stock market data we can instantly determine which stocks have the highest price fluctuations or the most heavy trading.

GUIDELINE

Sort by header selection idiom   Introducing table sorting using the column headers is introducing another design idiom to the User Interface. This design idiom is becoming widely accepted and widely used in many applications. It is a useful and powerful technique which you can introduce when sorting table data is a requirement. The technique is not intuitive and there is little visual affordance to suggest that clicking a column header will have any effect. So consider that the introduction of this technique may require additional UI training.

18.5   STOCKS TABLE, PART IV: JDBC

Despite all of our sorting functionality and enhanced data display, our application is relatively useless because it displays only data for a predefined day. In the real world we would need to connect such an application to the source of fresh information such as a database. Very often tables are used to display data retrieved from databases, or to edit data to be stored in databases. In this section we show how to feed our `StocksTable` data extracted from a database using the Java Database Connectivity (JDBC) API.

First, we need to create the database. We chose to use two SQL tables (do not confuse SQL table with `JTable`) whose structure precisely corresponds to the market data structure described in section 18.2.

Table 18.1 Symbols

Field name	Type
symbol	Text
name	Text

Table 18.2 Data

Field name	Type
symbol	Text
date 1	Date/Time
last	Number
change	Number
changeproc	Number
open	Number
volume	Number

For this example we use the JDBC-ODBC bridge which has been a standard part of Java since the 1.1 release. This bridge links Java programs to Microsoft Access databases. If you are using another database engine, you can work with this example as well, but you must make sure that the structure of your tables is the same. Before running the example in a Windows environment you need to register a database in an ODBC Data Source Administrator which is accessible through the Control Panel (this is not a JDBC tutorial, so we'll skip the details).

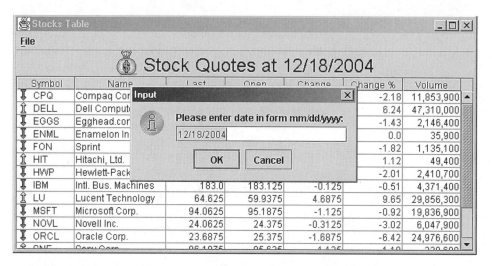

Figure 18.4 Retrieving stock data from a database for display in JTable

Example 18.4

see \Chapter18\4

StocksTable.java

```java
import java.awt.*;
import java.awt.event.*;
import java.util.*;
import java.io.*;
import java.text.*;
import java.util.Date;
import java.sql.*;

import javax.swing.*;
import javax.swing.border.*;
import javax.swing.event.*;
import javax.swing.table.*;

public class StocksTable extends JFrame {
   protected JTable m_table;
   protected StockTableData m_data;
   protected JLabel m_title;

   public StocksTable() {
      // Unchanged code from example 18.3

      setJMenuBar(createMenuBar());

      JScrollPane ps = new JScrollPane();
      ps.getViewport().setBackground(m_table.getBackground());
      ps.getViewport().add(m_table);
      getContentPane().add(ps, BorderLayout.CENTER);
```

```
    }

    // Unchanged code from example 18.3
    protected JMenuBar createMenuBar() {
      JMenuBar menuBar = new JMenuBar();

      JMenu mFile = new JMenu("File");
      mFile.setMnemonic('f');

      JMenuItem mData = new JMenuItem("Retrieve Data...");
      mData.setMnemonic('r');
      ActionListener lstData = new ActionListener() {
        public void actionPerformed(ActionEvent e) {
          retrieveData();
        }
      };
      mData.addActionListener(lstData);
      mFile.add(mData);
      mFile.addSeparator();

      JMenuItem mExit = new JMenuItem("Exit");
      mExit.setMnemonic('x');
      ActionListener lstExit = new ActionListener() {
        public void actionPerformed(ActionEvent e) {
          System.exit(0);
        }
      };
      mExit.addActionListener(lstExit);
      mFile.add(mExit);
      menuBar.add(mFile);

      return menuBar;
    }

    public void retrieveData() {
      Runnable updater = new Runnable() {
        public void run() {
          SimpleDateFormat frm = new SimpleDateFormat("MM/dd/yyyy");
          String currentDate = frm.format(m_data.m_date);
          String result =
          (String)JOptionPane.showInputDialog(StocksTable.this,
            "Please enter date in form mm/dd/yyyy:", "Input",
            JOptionPane.INFORMATION_MESSAGE, null, null,
            currentDate);
          if (result==null)
            return;

          java.util.Date date = null;
          try {
            date = frm.parse(result);
          }
          catch (java.text.ParseException ex) {
            date = null;
          }
```

1 New "Retrieve Data" menu item

2 Retrieves data from database, updates table model, and repaints JTable

```
          if (date == null) {
            JOptionPane.showMessageDialog(StocksTable.this,
              result+" is not a valid date",
              "Warning", JOptionPane.WARNING_MESSAGE);
            return;
          }

          setCursor(Cursor.getPredefinedCursor(Cursor.WAIT_CURSOR));
          try {
            m_data.retrieveData(date);
          }
          catch (Exception ex) {
            JOptionPane.showMessageDialog(StocksTable.this,
              "Error retrieving data:\n"+ex.getMessage(),
              "Error", JOptionPane.ERROR_MESSAGE);
          }
          setCursor(Cursor.getPredefinedCursor(Cursor.DEFAULT_CURSOR));
          m_title.setText(m_data.getTitle());
          m_table.tableChanged(new TableModelEvent(m_data));
        }
      };
    SwingUtilities.invokeLater(updater);
  }

  // Unchanged code from example 18.3
}

// Unchanged code from example 18.3
```

Updated to allow retrieval of data from a database using JDBC and SQL ❸

```
class StockTableData extends AbstractTableModel {
  // Unchanged code from example 18.3

  static final String QUERY = "SELECT data.symbol, symbols.name, "+
    "data.last, data.open, data.change, data.changeproc, "+
    "data.volume FROM DATA INNER JOIN SYMBOLS "+
    "ON DATA.symbol = SYMBOLS.symbol WHERE "+
    "month(data.date1)=? AND day(data.date1)=?"+
    " AND year(data.date1)=?";

  public void retrieveData(Date date)
    throws SQLException, ClassNotFoundException {

    GregorianCalendar calendar = new GregorianCalendar();
    calendar.setTime(date);
    int month = calendar.get(Calendar.MONTH)+1;
    int day = calendar.get(Calendar.DAY_OF_MONTH);
    int year = calendar.get(Calendar.YEAR);

    m_date = date;
    m_vector = new Vector();
    Connection conn = null;
    PreparedStatement pst = null;
    try {
      // Load the JDBC-ODBC bridge driver
      Class.forName("sun.jdbc.odbc.JdbcOdbcDriver");
```

```
        conn = DriverManager.getConnection(
            "jdbc:odbc:Market", "admin", "");

        pst = conn.prepareStatement(QUERY);
        pst.setInt(1, month);
        pst.setInt(2, day);
        pst.setInt(3, year);
        ResultSet results = pst.executeQuery();

        while (results.next()) {
            Stringsymbol = results.getString(1);
            Stringname = results.getString(2);
            doublelast = results.getDouble(3);
            doubleopen = results.getDouble(4);
            doublechange = results.getDouble(5);
            doublechangePr = results.getDouble(6);
            long volume = results.getLong(7);
            m_vector.addElement(new StockData(symbol, name, last,
                open, change, changePr, volume));
        }
        sortData();
    }
    finally {
        if (pst != null)
            pst.close();
        if (conn != null)
            conn.close();
    }
  }
}

// Unchanged code from example 18.3
```

18.5.1   Understanding the code

Class StocksTable

A JMenuBar instance is created with our custom createMenuBar() method and added to our frame.

1 The createMenuBar() method creates a menu bar containing a single menu titled File. Two menu items are added: Retrieve Data... and Exit with a separator in between. Anonymous ActionListeners are added to each. The first calls our custom retrieveData() method, and the second simply kills the application using System.exit(0).

2 The retrieveData() method is called in response to a Retrieve Data... menu item activation. First it prompts the user to enter the date by displaying a JOptionPane dialog. Once the date has been entered, this method parses it using a SimpleDateFormat object. If the entered string cannot be parsed into a valid date, the method shows a warning message and returns. Otherwise, we connect to JDBC and retrieve new data. To indicate that the program will be busy for some time the wait mouse cursor is displayed. The main job is performed by our new StockTableData retrieveData() method, which is invoked on the m_data object. If an exception occurs an error message is displayed, and no changes in the table model are made. Otherwise table model is updated and repainted.

③ *Class StockTableData*

First note that a minor change was required in the import statements. In addition to importing the entire `java.util` package and `java.sql` package we've also explicitly imported `java.util.Date`. Since both packages include a `Date` class, this extra import tells Java that whenever we refer to a `Date` instance we are referring to an instance of `java.util.Date` unless otherwise specified with a fully qualified class name (i.e., `java.sql.Date`).

A new instance variable is added to store the result of a data retrieval request in the `retrieveData()` method. As mentioned, `retrieveData()` retrieves a table's data for a given date of trade. Our implementation uses the JDBC bridge driver and should be familiar to JDBC-aware readers. The first thing we do is construct an SQL statement. Since we cannot compare a `java.util.Date` object and an SQL date stored in the database, we have to extract the date's components (year, month, and day) and compare them separately. An instance of `GregorianCalendar` is used to manipulate the date object.

We load the JDBC-ODBC bridge driver to Microsoft Access by using the `Class.forName` method, and then connect to a database with the `DriverManager.getConnection()` method. If no exception is thrown, we can create a `Statement` instance for the newly created `Connection` object and retrieve a `ResultSet` by executing the previously constructed query. While new data is available we retrieve this data using basic `getXX()` methods. We create a new `StockData` instance to encapsulate this new data and add it to `m_vector`. Once we've retrieved all the data we sort it with the `sortData()` method. Finally, we close our `PreparedStatement` and `Connection` instances.

18.5.2 Running the code

Figure 18.4 shows `StocksTable` in action. Try loading data for different dates in your database. A sample Microsoft Access database, market.mdb, containing some real market data, can be found in the \swing\2nd-edition\Chapter18 directory.

18.6 STOCKS TABLE, PART V: COLUMN ADDITION AND REMOVAL

`JTable` allows us to dynamically add and remove `TableColumns` on the fly. Recall that the `TableColumnModel` interface provides the methods `addColumn()` and `removeColumn()` to programmatically add or remove a `TableColumn` respectively. In this section we add dynamic column addition and removal to our `StocksTable` application.

Example 18.5

`StocksTable.java`

see \Chapter18\5

```
// Unchanged code from example 18.4
public class StocksTable extends JFrame {
```

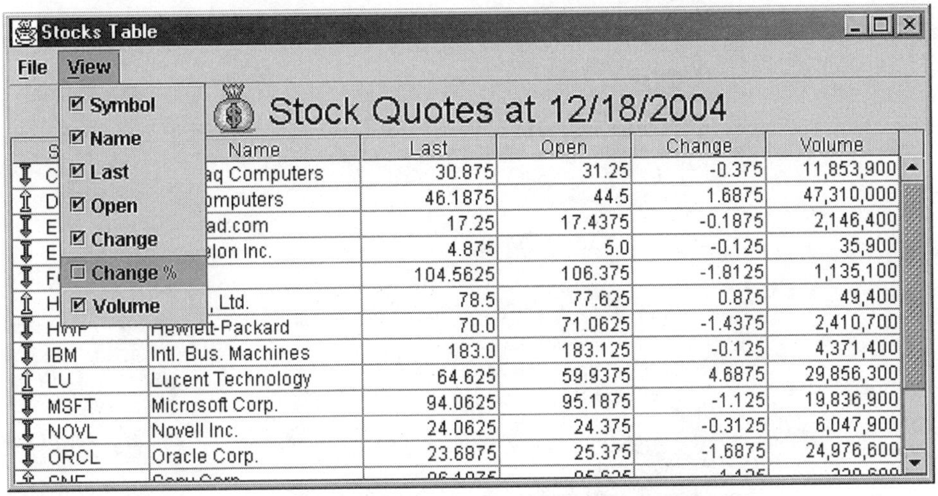

Figure 18.5 `JTable` with dynamic column addition and removal

```java
protected JTable m_table;
protected StockTableData m_data;
protected JLabel m_title;

public StocksTable() {
   super("Stocks Table");
   setSize(600, 300);

   // Unchanged code from example 18.4

   m_table.getColumnModel().addColumnModelListener(m_data);

   setJMenuBar(createMenuBar());

   JScrollPane ps = new JScrollPane();
   ps.getViewport().setBackground(m_table.getBackground());
   ps.getViewport().add(m_table);
   getContentPane().add(ps, BorderLayout.CENTER);
}

// Unchanged code from example 18.4

protected JMenuBar createMenuBar() {
   JMenuBar menuBar = new JMenuBar();

   // Unchanged code from example 18.4

   JMenu mView = new JMenu("View");
   mView.setMnemonic('v');
   TableColumnModel model = m_table.getColumnModel();
   for (int k = 0; k < m_data.getColumnCount(); k++) {
      JCheckBoxMenuItem item = new JCheckBoxMenuItem(
         StockTableData.m_columns[k].m_title);
      item.setSelected(true);
      TableColumn column = model.getColumn(k);
```

1 StockTableData now implements
TableColumnModelListener

2 New "View"
menu with
a check box
menu item
corresponding
to each table
column

```
        item.addActionListener(new ColumnKeeper(column,
            StockTableData.m_columns[k]));
        mView.add(item);
    }
    menuBar.add(mView);

    return menuBar;
}
```

② New "View" menu with a check box menu item corresponding to each table column

```
// Unchanged code from example 18.4

public static void main(String argv[]) {
    StocksTable frame = new StocksTable();
    frame.setDefaultCloseOperation(JFrame.EXIT_ON_CLOSE);
    frame.setVisible(true);
}

class ColumnKeeper implements ActionListener {
    protected TableColumn m_column;
    protected ColumnData m_colData;

    public ColumnKeeper(TableColumn column, ColumnData colData) {
        m_column = column;
        m_colData = colData;
    }

    public void actionPerformed(ActionEvent e) {
        JLabel renderer = (JLabel)m_column.getHeaderRenderer();
        renderer.setIcon(null);
        JCheckBoxMenuItem item = (JCheckBoxMenuItem)e.getSource();
        TableColumnModel model = m_table.getColumnModel();
        if (item.isSelected()) {
            model.addColumn(m_column);
        }
        else {
            model.removeColumn(m_column);
        }
        m_table.tableChanged(new TableModelEvent(m_data));
        m_table.repaint();
    }
}
}
```

③ Keeps track of which columns are added and removed

```
// Unchanged code from example 18.4

class StockTableData extends AbstractTableModel
    implements TableColumnModelListener{

    // Unchanged code from example 18.4

    protected SimpleDateFormat m_frm;
    protected NumberFormat m_volumeFormat;
    protected Vector m_vector;
    protected Date m_date;
    protected int m_columnsCount = m_columns.length;

    public int m_sortCol = 0;
```

④ Now implements TableColumnModelListener to keep track of how many columns are visible

```
public boolean m_sortAsc = true;

// Unchanged code from example 18.4

public int getColumnCount() {
  return m_columnsCount;
}

// Unchanged code from example 18.4

public void columnAdded(TableColumnModelEvent e) {
  m_columnsCount++;
}

public void columnRemoved(TableColumnModelEvent e) {
  m_columnsCount--;
  if (m_sortCol >= m_columnsCount)
    m_sortCol = -1;
}

public void columnMarginChanged(ChangeEvent e) {}
public void columnMoved(TableColumnModelEvent e) {}
public void columnSelectionChanged(ListSelectionEvent e) {}
}
```

// Unchanged code from example 18.4

18.6.1   Understanding the code

Class StocksTable

1 The StocksTable constructor now adds m_data, our instance of StockTableData which now implements TableColumnModelListener, to our table's TableColumnModel to listen for column additions and removals.

2 Our createMenuBar() method now adds several check box menu items to a new View menu—one for each column. Each of these check box menu items receives a ColumnKeeper instance as ActionListener.

3 ### Class StocksTable.ColumnKeeper

This inner class implements the ActionListener interface and serves to keep track of when the user removes and adds columns to the table. The constructor receives a TableColumn instance and a ColumnData object. The actionPerformed() method adds this column to the model with the addColumn() method if the corresponding menu item is checked, and removes this column from the model with removeColumn() if it is unchecked. To update the table to properly reflect these changes, we call its tableChanged() method followed by a repaint() request.

4 ### Class StockTableData

StockTableData now implements TableColumnModelListener and contains instance variable m_columnsCount to keep track of the current column count. This variable is decremented and incremented in the columnRemoved() and columnAdded(). It is also used in StockTable's createMenuBar() method for creating the appropriate number of check box menu items (one corresponding to each column).

18.6.2 Running the code

Figure 18.5 shows the new View menu with an unchecked Change % menu item, and the corresponding column hidden. Reselecting this menu item will place the column back in the table at the end position. Verify that each menu item functions similarly.

18.7 EXPENSE REPORT APPLICATION

In constructing our `StocksTable` application we talked mostly about displaying and retrieving data in `JTable`. In this section we will construct a basic expense report application, and in doing so we will concentrate on table cell editing. We will also see how to implement dynamic addition and removal of table rows.

The editing of data generally follows this scheme:

- Create an instance of the `TableCellEditor` interface. We can use the `Default-CellEditor` class or implement our own. The `DefaultCellEditor` class takes a GUI component as a parameter to its constructor: `JTextField`, `JCheckBox`, or `JComboBox`. This component will be used for editing.
- If we are developing a custom editor, we need to implement the `getTableCellEditorComponent()` method which will be called each time a cell is about to be edited.
- In our table model we need to implement the `setValueAt(Object value, int nRow, int nCol)` method which will be called to change a value in the table when an edit ends. This is where we can perform any necessary data processing and validation.

The data model for this example is designed as follows (where each row represents a column in our `JTable`):

Name	Type	Description
Date	String	Date of expense
Amount	Double	Amount of expense
Category	Integer	Category from pre-defined list
Approved	Boolean	Sign of approval for this expense
Description	String	Brief description

Example 18.6

ExpenseReport.java

see \Chapter18\6

```
import java.awt.*;
import java.awt.event.*;
import java.util.*;
import java.io.*;
import java.text.*;

import javax.swing.*;
import javax.swing.border.*;
import javax.swing.event.*;
```

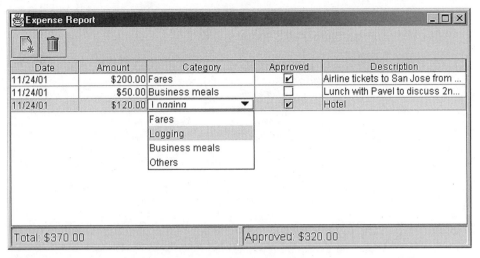

Figure 18.6 An expense report application illustrating custom cell editing, rendering, and row addition/removal

```java
import javax.swing.table.*;

public class ExpenseReport extends JFrame{

  protected JTable m_table;
  protected ExpenseReportData m_data;
  protected JLabel m_tolatLbl;
  protected JLabel m_approvedLbl;
  protected NumberFormat m_moneyFormat =
        NumberFormat.getCurrencyInstance(Locale.US);

  static {
    UIManager.put("ComboBox.foreground",
      UIManager.getColor("Table.foreground"));
    UIManager.put("ComboBox.background",
      UIManager.getColor("Table.background"));
    UIManager.put("ComboBox.selectionForeground",
      UIManager.getColor("Table.selectionForeground"));
    UIManager.put("ComboBox.selectionBackground",
      UIManager.getColor("Table.selectionBackground"));
    UIManager.put("ComboBox.font",
      UIManager.getFont("Table.font"));
  }

  public ExpenseReport() {
    super("Expense Report");
    setSize(600, 300);

    m_data = new ExpenseReportData(this);

    m_table = new JTable();
    m_table.setAutoCreateColumnsFromModel(false);
    m_table.setModel(m_data);
    m_table.setSelectionMode(ListSelectionModel.SINGLE_SELECTION);
```

Creates table model and JTable ❶

```
for (int k = 0; k < m_data.getColumnCount(); k++) {
  TableCellRenderer renderer = null;
  TableCellEditor editor = null;
  switch (k) {
  case ExpenseReportData.COL_DATE:
    SimpleDateFormat dateFormat =
      new SimpleDateFormat("MM/dd/yy");
    renderer = new FormattedCellRenderer(dateFormat);
    editor = new FormattedCellEditor(
      new JFormattedTextField(dateFormat));
    break;

  case ExpenseReportData.COL_AMOUNT:
    renderer = new FormattedCellRenderer(m_moneyFormat);
    editor = new FormattedCellEditor(
      new JFormattedTextField(m_moneyFormat));
    break;

  case ExpenseReportData.COL_CATEGORY:
    renderer = new DefaultTableCellRenderer();
    JComboBox combo = new JComboBox(
      ExpenseReportData.CATEGORIES);
    combo.setRequestFocusEnabled(false);
    editor = new DefaultCellEditor(combo);
    break;

  case ExpenseReportData.COL_APPROVED:
    renderer = new CheckCellRenderer();
    JCheckBox chBox = new JCheckBox();
    chBox.setHorizontalAlignment(JCheckBox.CENTER);
    chBox.setBackground(m_table.getBackground());
    editor = new DefaultCellEditor(chBox);
    break;

  case ExpenseReportData.COL_DESCRIPTION:
    renderer = new DefaultTableCellRenderer();
    JTextField txt = new JTextField();
    txt.setBorder(null);
    editor = new DefaultCellEditor(txt);
    break;
  }
  if (renderer instanceof JLabel)
    ((JLabel)renderer).setHorizontalAlignment(
      ExpenseReportData.m_columns[k].m_alignment);
  if (editor instanceof DefaultCellEditor)
    ((DefaultCellEditor)editor).setClickCountToStart(2);

  TableColumn column = new TableColumn(k,
    ExpenseReportData.m_columns[k].m_width,
    renderer, editor);
  m_table.addColumn(column);
}

JTableHeader header = m_table.getTableHeader();
header.setUpdateTableInRealTime(false);
```

2 Create cell renderers and editors for each column based on date type

```
      JScrollPane ps = new JScrollPane();
      ps.getViewport().setBackground(m_table.getBackground());
      ps.setSize(550, 150);
      ps.getViewport().add(m_table);
      getContentPane().add(ps, BorderLayout.CENTER);

      JToolBar tb = createToolbar();                         ❸  Toolbar with buttons
      getContentPane().add(tb, BorderLayout.NORTH);              to add and delete rows

      JPanel p = new JPanel(new GridLayout(1, 2, 5, 5));

      m_tolatLbl = new JLabel("Total: ");
      m_tolatLbl.setFont(new Font("Helvetica", Font.PLAIN, 14));
      m_tolatLbl.setBorder(new SoftBevelBorder(BevelBorder.LOWERED));
      p.add(m_tolatLbl);

      m_approvedLbl = new JLabel("Approved: ");
      m_approvedLbl.setFont(new Font("Helvetica", Font.PLAIN, 14));
      m_approvedLbl.setBorder(new SoftBevelBorder(BevelBorder.LOWERED));
      p.add(m_approvedLbl);

      getContentPane().add(p, BorderLayout.SOUTH);

      calcTotal();
   }

public void calcTotal() {                              ❹  Calculates total amount
   double total = 0;                                       of expenses and updates labels
   double approved = 0;
   for (int k=0; k<m_data.getRowCount(); k++) {
      Double amount = (Double)m_data.getValueAt(k,
         ExpenseReportData.COL_AMOUNT);
      total += amount.doubleValue();

      Boolean flag = (Boolean)m_data.getValueAt(k,
         ExpenseReportData.COL_APPROVED);
      if (flag.booleanValue())
         approved += amount.doubleValue();
   }
   m_tolatLbl.setText("Total: "+m_moneyFormat.format(total));
   m_approvedLbl.setText("Approved: "+m_moneyFormat.format(approved));
}

protected JToolBar createToolbar() {                   ❸  Toolbar with buttons
   JToolBar tb = new JToolBar();                           to insert and delete rows
   tb.setFloatable(false);

   JButton bt = new JButton(new ImageIcon("Insert24.gif"));
   bt.setToolTipText("Insert Row");
   bt.setRequestFocusEnabled(false);
   ActionListener lst = new ActionListener() {
      public void actionPerformed(ActionEvent e) {
         int nRow = m_table.getSelectedRow()+1;
         m_data.insert(nRow);

         m_table.tableChanged(new TableModelEvent(
            m_data, nRow, nRow, TableModelEvent.ALL_COLUMNS,
```

```
            TableModelEvent.INSERT));
          m_table.setRowSelectionInterval(nRow, nRow);
        }
      };
      bt.addActionListener(lst);
      tb.add(bt);

      bt = new JButton(new ImageIcon("Delete24.gif"));
      bt.setToolTipText("Delete Row");
      bt.setRequestFocusEnabled(false);
      lst = new ActionListener() {
        public void actionPerformed(ActionEvent e) {
          int nRow = m_table.getSelectedRow();
          if (m_data.delete(nRow)) {
            m_table.tableChanged(new TableModelEvent(
              m_data, nRow, nRow, TableModelEvent.ALL_COLUMNS,
              TableModelEvent.DELETE));
            m_table.clearSelection();
            calcTotal();
          }
        }
      };
      bt.addActionListener(lst);
      tb.add(bt);

      return tb;
    }

    public static void main(String argv[]) {
      ExpenseReport frame = new ExpenseReport();
      frame.setDefaultCloseOperation(JFrame.EXIT_ON_CLOSE);
      frame.setVisible(true);
    }
  }

  class CheckCellRenderer extends JCheckBox
    implements TableCellRenderer {
    protected static Border m_noFocusBorder =
      new EmptyBorder(1, 1, 1, 1);
    protected static Border m_focusBorder = UIManager.getBorder(
      "Table.focusCellHighlightBorder");

    public CheckCellRenderer() {
      super();
      setOpaque(true);
      setBorderPainted(true);
      setBorder(m_noFocusBorder);
      setHorizontalAlignment(JCheckBox.CENTER);
    }

    public Component getTableCellRendererComponent(JTable table,
      Object value, boolean isSelected, boolean hasFocus,
      int nRow, int nCol)
    {
      if (value instanceof Boolean) {
```

5 **Cell renderer which uses check boxes to be consistent with corresponding editor**

```
      Boolean b = (Boolean)value;
      setSelected(b.booleanValue());
    }

    setBackground(isSelected && !hasFocus ?
      table.getSelectionBackground() : table.getBackground());
    setForeground(isSelected && !hasFocus ?
      table.getSelectionForeground() : table.getForeground());
    setFont(table.getFont());
    setBorder(hasFocus ? m_focusBorder : m_noFocusBorder);

    return this;
  }
}

class FormattedCellRenderer extends DefaultTableCellRenderer {
  protected Format m_format;

  public FormattedCellRenderer(Format format) {
    m_format = format;
  }

  public Component getTableCellRendererComponent(JTable table,
   Object value, boolean isSelected, boolean hasFocus,
   int nRow, int nCol)
  {
    return super.getTableCellRendererComponent(table,
      value==null ? null : m_format.format(value),
      isSelected, hasFocus, nRow, nCol);
  }
}

class FormattedCellEditor extends DefaultCellEditor {
  public FormattedCellEditor(
   final JFormattedTextField formattedTextField)
  {
    super(formattedTextField);
    formattedTextField.removeActionListener(delegate);
    delegate = new EditorDelegate() {
      public void setValue(Object value) {
        formattedTextField.setValue(value);
      }
      public Object getCellEditorValue() {
        return formattedTextField.getValue();
      }
    };
    formattedTextField.addActionListener(delegate);
    formattedTextField.setBorder(null);
  }
}

class ExpenseData {
  public Datem_date;
  public Doublem_amount;
  public Integer m_category;
```

6 Cell renderer used to format data using a given Format object

7 Cell editor to provide custom editing capability using a JFormattedTextField

8 Represents a row of table data

```
      public Boolean m_approved;
      public Stringm_description;

      public ExpenseData() {
         m_date = new Date();
         m_amount = new Double(0);
         m_category = new Integer(1);
         m_approved = new Boolean(false);
         m_description = "";
      }

      public ExpenseData(Date date, double amount, int category,
       boolean approved, String description)
      {
         m_date = date;
         m_amount = new Double(amount);
         m_category = new Integer(category);
         m_approved = new Boolean(approved);
         m_description = description;
      }
   }

class ColumnData {                          ⑨  Holds column metadata
   public Stringm_tolatLbl;
   int m_width;
   int m_alignment;

   public ColumnData(String title, int width, int alignment) {
      m_tolatLbl = title;
      m_width = width;
      m_alignment = alignment;
   }
}

class ExpenseReportData extends AbstractTableModel {    ⑩  Custom table model
   public static final ColumnData m_columns[] = {               with overwritten
      new ColumnData( "Date", 80, JLabel.LEFT ),                setValueAt() method
      new ColumnData( "Amount", 80, JLabel.RIGHT ),
      new ColumnData( "Category", 130, JLabel.LEFT ),
      new ColumnData( "Approved", 80, JLabel.CENTER ),
      new ColumnData( "Description", 180, JLabel.LEFT )
   };

   public static final int COL_DATE = 0;
   public static final int COL_AMOUNT = 1;
   public static final int COL_CATEGORY = 2;
   public static final int COL_APPROVED = 3;
   public static final int COL_DESCRIPTION = 4;

   public static final String[] CATEGORIES = {
      "Fares", "Logging", "Business meals", "Others"
   };

   protected ExpenseReport m_parent;
   protected Vector m_vector;
```

```java
public ExpenseReportData(ExpenseReport parent) {
  m_parent = parent;
  m_vector = new Vector();
  setDefaultData();
}

public void setDefaultData() {
  m_vector = new Vector();
  try {
    SimpleDateFormat f = new SimpleDateFormat("MM/dd/yy");
    m_vector.addElement(new ExpenseData(
      f.parse("12/06/04"), 200, 0, true,
      "Airline tickets"));
    m_vector.addElement(new ExpenseData(
      f.parse("12/05/04"), 50, 2, false,
      "Lunch with client"));
    m_vector.addElement(new ExpenseData(
      f.parse("12/05/04"), 120, 1, true,
      "Hotel"));
  }
  catch (java.text.ParseException ex) {}
}

public int getRowCount() {
  return m_vector==null ? 0 : m_vector.size();
}

public int getColumnCount() {
  return m_columns.length;
}

public String getColumnName(int nCol) {
  return m_columns[nCol].m_tolatLbl;
}

public boolean isCellEditable(int nRow, int nCol) {
  return true;
}

public Object getValueAt(int nRow, int nCol) {
  if (nRow < 0 || nRow>=getRowCount())
    return "";
  ExpenseData row = (ExpenseData)m_vector.elementAt(nRow);
  switch (nCol) {
    case COL_DATE:
      return row.m_date;
    case COL_AMOUNT:
      return row.m_amount;
    case COL_CATEGORY:
      return CATEGORIES[row.m_category.intValue()];
    case COL_APPROVED:
      return row.m_approved;
    case COL_DESCRIPTION:
      return row.m_description;
  }
```

```
          return "";
    }

    public void setValueAt(Object value, int nRow, int nCol) {
        if (nRow < 0 || nRow>=getRowCount() || value == null)
            return;
        ExpenseData row = (ExpenseData)m_vector.elementAt(nRow);
        String svalue = value.toString();

        switch (nCol) {
            case COL_DATE:
                row.m_date = (Date)value;
                break;
            case COL_AMOUNT:
                if (value instanceof Double)
                    row.m_amount = (Double)value;
                else
                    row.m_amount = new Double(((Number)value).doubleValue());
                m_parent.calcTotal();
                break;
            case COL_CATEGORY:
                for (int k=0; k<CATEGORIES.length; k++)
                    if (svalue.equals(CATEGORIES[k])) {
                        row.m_category = new Integer(k);
                        break;
                    }
                break;
            case COL_APPROVED:
                row.m_approved = (Boolean)value;
                m_parent.calcTotal();
                break;
            case COL_DESCRIPTION:
                row.m_description = svalue;
                break;
        }
    }

    public void insert(int nRow) {
        if (nRow < 0)
            nRow = 0;
        if (nRow > m_vector.size())
            nRow = m_vector.size();
        m_vector.insertElementAt(new ExpenseData(), nRow);
    }

    public boolean delete(int nRow) {
        if (nRow < 0 || nRow >= m_vector.size())
            return false;
        m_vector.remove(nRow);
        return true;
    }
}
```

18.7.1 Understanding the code

Class ExpenseReport

Class ExpenseReport extends JFrame and defines three instance variables:

- JTable m_table: table to edit data
- ExpenseReportData m_data: data model for this table
- JLabel m_total: label to dynamically display total amount of expenses
- JLabel m_approvedLbl: label to dynamically display total amount of approved expenses only
- NumberFormat m_moneyFormat: used to format data in the Amount column and the m_total and m_approvedLbl labels

1 The ExpenseReport constructor first instantiates our table model, m_data, and then instantiates our table, m_table. The selection mode is set to single selection and we iterate through the number of columns creating cell renderers and editors based on each specific column.

2 These renderers and editors are instances of our custom FormattedCellEditor and FormattedCellRenderer classes or DefaultTableCellEditor and DefaultTableCellRenderer. The only exception is the Approved column which uses an instance of our custom CheckCellRenderer class as renderer.

The component used for editing varies: the Category column uses a JComboBox, the Approved column uses a JCheckBox, the Amount and Date columns use a JFormattedTextField and the Description column uses a JTextField.

3 A JToolBar is created with our custom createToolBar() method and added to the top of the frame. This toolbar contains two buttons that are responsible for inserting and deleting rows. The delete button (shown with a trash can icon) deletes the currently selected row. The insert button inserts a new row below the selected row. Note that when inserting a new row we are careful to make the new row the selected row once it is added. Both buttons invoke respective insert() and delete() methods on the ExpenseReportData instance to perform the actual deletion of the data from the model. The table is updated and repainted after this is complete.

The m_total and m_approvedLbl labels are added to the bottom of the frame.

4 The calcTotal() method calculates the total amount of expenses in column COL_AMOUNT using our table's data model, m_data.

5 ### Class CheckCellRenderer

Since we use check boxes to edit our table's Approved column, to be consistent we also need to use check boxes for that column's cell renderer (recall that cell renderers just act as rubber stamps and are not at all interactive). The only GUI component which can be used in the existing DefaultTableCellRenderer is JLabel, so we have to provide our own implementation of the TableCellRenderer interface. This class, CheckCellRenderer, uses JCheckBox as a superclass. Its constructor sets the border to indicate whether the component has the focus and sets its opaque property to true to indicate that the component's background will be filled with the background color.

The only method which must be implemented in the `TableCellRenderer` interface is `getTableCellRendererComponent()`. This method will be called each time the cell is about to be rendered to deliver new data to the renderer. It takes six parameters:

- `JTable table`: reference to table instance
- `Object value`: data object to be sent to the renderer
- `boolean isSelected`: true if the cell is currently selected
- `boolean hasFocus`: true if the cell currently has the focus
- `int row`: cell's row
- `int column`: cell's column

Our implementation sets whether the `JCheckBox` is checked depending on the `value` passed as `Boolean`. Then it sets the background, foreground, font, and border to ensure that each cell in the table has a similar appearance.

6 *Class FormattedCellRenderer*

This class extends `DefaultTableCellRenderer` to format table data using a given Format object. The `getTableCellRendererComponent()` method is implemented to simply format the data for a given cell with the `Format` instance.

7 *Class FormattedCellEditor*

This class extends `DefaultCellEditor` to provide custom editing capability using a `JFormattedTextField`. The `EditorDelegate` is replaced by one that behaves appropriately in setting and retrieving the value from `JFormattedTextField`.

> **NOTE**   `DefaultCellEditor` contains an internal class called `EditorDelegate`. By replacing the `EditorDelegate` of a `DefaultCellEditor` we can customize editor behavior without changing the editor itself.

8 *Class ExpenseData*

Class `ExpenseData` represents a single row in the table. It holds five variables corresponding to our data structure described in the beginning of this section.

9 *Class ColumnData*

Class `ColumnData` holds each column's title, width, and header alignment.

10 *Class ExpenseReportData*

`ExpenseReportData` extends `AbstractTableModel` and should look somewhat familiar from previous examples in this chapter (e.g., `StockTableData`), so we will not discuss this class in complete detail. However, we should take a closer look at the `setValueAt()` method, which is new for this example (all previous examples did not accept new data). This method is called each time an edit is made to a table cell. First we determine which `ExpenseData` instance (table's row) is affected, and if it is invalid we simply return. Otherwise, depending on the column of the changed cell, we define several cases in a switch structure to accept and store a new value, or to reject it:

- For the Date column the input string is parsed using our `SimpleDateFormat` instance. If parsing is successful, a new date is saved as a `Date` object, otherwise an error message is displayed.

- For the Amount column the input string is parsed as a `Double` and stored in the table if parsing is successful. Also new total and approved amounts are recalculated and displayed in the corresponding labels.
- For the Category column the input string is placed in the `CATEGORIES` array at the corresponding index and is stored in the table model.
- For the Approved column the input object is cast to a `Boolean` and stored in the table model. Also new total and approved amounts are recalculated and displayed in the corresponding labels.
- For the Description column the input string is directly saved in our table model.

18.7.2   Running the code

Try editing different columns and note how the corresponding cell editors work. Experiment with adding and removing table rows and note how the total amount is updated each time the Amount column is updated. Also note how the approved amount is updated each time the Approved column is updated. Figure 18.7 shows `ExpenseReport` with a combo box opened to change a cell's value.

18.8   EXPENSE REPORT APPLICATION WITH VARIABLE HEIGHT ROWS

As of Java 1.3 `JTable` allows variable height rows through use of the new `setRowHeight()` method which takes two `int` parameters specifying target row index and height for that row. Internally `JTable` makes use of the new `javax.swing.SizeSequence` class to track and update each row's height. This example builds off of the expense report application in section 18.7 to allow variable height rows with wrapping cell text.

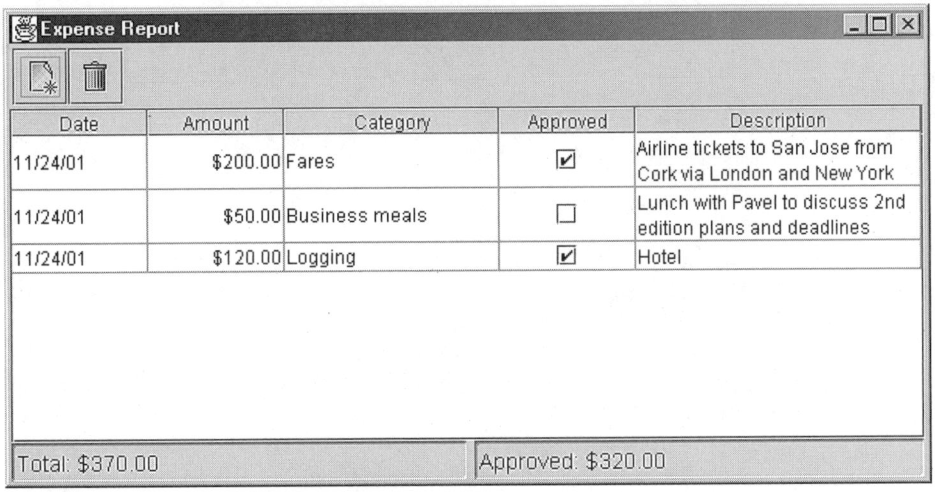

Figure 18.7   Expense report application with variable height rows

Example 18.7

ExpenseReport.java

see \Chapter18\7

```java
import java.awt.*;
import java.awt.event.*;
import java.util.*;
import java.io.*;
import java.text.*;

import javax.swing.*;
import javax.swing.border.*;
import javax.swing.event.*;
import javax.swing.table.*;

public class ExpenseReport extends JFrame {

  // Unchanged code from example 18.6

  public ExpenseReport() {
    // Unchanged code from example 18.6

    for (int k = 0; k < m_data.getColumnCount(); k++) {
      TableCellRenderer renderer = null;
      TableCellEditor editor = null;
      switch (k) {

        // Unchanged code from example 18.6

        case ExpenseReportData.COL_DESCRIPTION:
          renderer = new TextAreaCellRenderer();
          editor = new TextAreaCellEditor();
          break;
      }
      // Unchanged code from example 18.6
    }

    // Unchanged code from example 18.6
  }

  // Unchanged code from example 18.6
}

// Unchanged code from example 18.6

class TextAreaCellRenderer extends JTextArea
 implements TableCellRenderer
{
  protected static Border m_noFocusBorder =
    new EmptyBorder(1, 1, 1, 1);
  protected static Border m_focusBorder = UIManager.getBorder(
      "Table.focusCellHighlightBorder");

  public TextAreaCellRenderer() {
    setEditable(false);
    setLineWrap(true);
```

❶ Description column now uses a custom text area renderer

❷ Custom JTextArea-based cell renderer which allows variable height JTable rows based on amount of text

```
    setWrapStyleWord(true);
    setBorder(m_noFocusBorder);
  }

  public Component getTableCellRendererComponent(JTable table,
    Object value, boolean isSelected, boolean hasFocus,
    int nRow, int nCol)
  {
    if (value instanceof String)
      setText((String)value);

    setBackground(isSelected && !hasFocus ?
      table.getSelectionBackground() : table.getBackground());
    setForeground(isSelected && !hasFocus ?
      table.getSelectionForeground() : table.getForeground());
    setFont(table.getFont());
    setBorder(hasFocus ? m_focusBorder : m_noFocusBorder);

    // Adjust row's height
    int width = table.getColumnModel().getColumn(nCol).getWidth();
    setSize(width, 1000);
    int rowHeight = getPreferredSize().height;
    if (table.getRowHeight(nRow) != rowHeight)
      table.setRowHeight(nRow, rowHeight);

    return this;
  }

  public String getToolTipText(MouseEvent event) {
    return null;
  }
}

// Unchanged code from example 18.6

class TextAreaCellEditor extends AbstractCellEditor
  implements TableCellEditor
{
  public static int CLICK_COUNT_TO_EDIT = 2;
  protected JTextArea m_textArea;
  protected JScrollPane m_scroll;

  public TextAreaCellEditor() {
    m_textArea = new JTextArea();
    m_textArea.setLineWrap(true);
    m_textArea.setWrapStyleWord(true);

    m_scroll = new JScrollPane(m_textArea,
      JScrollPane.VERTICAL_SCROLLBAR_AS_NEEDED,
      JScrollPane.HORIZONTAL_SCROLLBAR_NEVER);
  }

  public Component getTableCellEditorComponent(JTable table,
    Object value, boolean isSelected,
    int nRow, int nCol)
  {
    m_textArea.setBackground(table.getBackground());
```

❶ JTextArea-based cell editor allowing mutiple line input in a single cell

```
        m_textArea.setForeground(table.getForeground());
        m_textArea.setFont(table.getFont());
        m_textArea.setText(value==null ? "" : value.toString());

        return m_scroll;
    }

    public Object getCellEditorValue() {
        return m_textArea.getText();
    }

    public boolean isCellEditable(EventObject anEvent) {
        if (anEvent instanceof MouseEvent) {
            int click = ((MouseEvent)anEvent).getClickCount();
            return click >= CLICK_COUNT_TO_EDIT;
        }
        return true;
    }
}

// Unchanged code from example 18.6
```

18.8.1   Understanding the code

Class ExpenseReport

1 The Description column now uses instances of our custom `TextAreaCellRenderer` and `TextAreaCellEditor` as its renderer and editor respectively.

2 *Class TextAreaCellRenderer*

This class extends `JTextArea` and implements `TableCellRenderer`. Because this renderer inherits base functionality from `JTextArea` it is fully capably of allowing word and line wrapping. This is enabled in the constructor.

The `getTableCellRendererComponent()` method is implemented to adjust the corresponding row's height according to the preferred height of the renderer. This is accomplished through use of `JTable`'s `setRowHeight()` method.

3 *Class TextAreaCellEditor*

This class extends `AbstractCellEditor` and implements `TableCellEditor`. It consists of a line and word-wrapping enabled `JTextArea` within a `JScrollPane`. The `getTableCellEditorComponent()` method is implemented to return a reference to the `JScrollPane`. In this way any amount of text can be entered into a cell in the "Description" column in a WYSIWYG (what you see is what you get) fashion.

18.8.2   Running the code

Try entering large amounts of text in the Description column. Note that a row's height will not change until editing is completed and the cell editor is replaced with the renderer.

18.9 A JavaBeans Property Editor

Now that we're familiar with the table API we can complete the JavaBeans container introduced in chapter 4 and give it the capability to edit the properties of JavaBeans. This dramatically increases the possible uses of our simple container and makes it quite a powerful tool for studying JavaBeans.

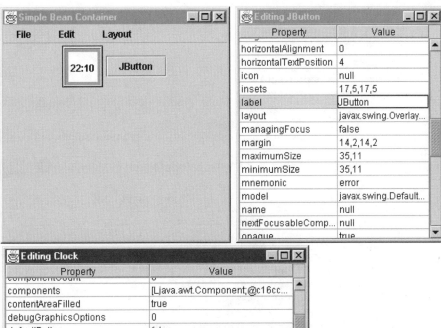

Figure 18.8 The `BeanContainer` JavaBeans property editor using `JTables` as editing forms

Example 18.8

BeanContainer.java

see \Chapter18\8

```java
import java.awt.*;
import java.awt.event.*;
import java.io.*;
import java.beans.*;
import java.lang.reflect.*;
import java.util.*;

import javax.swing.*;
import javax.swing.table.*;
import javax.swing.event.*;

import dl.*;

public class BeanContainer extends JFrame implements FocusListener
{
  protected Hashtable m_editors = new Hashtable();

  // Unchanged code from example 4.8

  protected JMenuBar createMenuBar() {
    // Unchanged code from example 4.8

    JMenu mEdit = new JMenu("Edit");
    mItem = new JMenuItem("Delete");
    lst = new ActionListener() {
      public void actionPerformed(ActionEvent e) {
        if (m_activeBean == null)
          return;
        Object obj = m_editors.get(m_activeBean);
        if (obj != null) {
          BeanEditor editor = (BeanEditor)obj;
          editor.dispose();
          m_editors.remove(m_activeBean);
        }
        getContentPane().remove(m_activeBean);
        m_activeBean = null;
        validate();
        repaint();
      }
    };
    mItem.addActionListener(lst);
    mEdit.add(mItem);

    mItem = new JMenuItem("Properties...");
    lst = new ActionListener() {
      public void actionPerformed(ActionEvent e) {
        if (m_activeBean == null)
          return;
        Object obj = m_editors.get(m_activeBean);
```

1 Hashtable storing editors for Beans

3 Deleting active bean also removes an existing BeanEditor

2 Menu item to create or reactivate a BeanEditor

```
        if (obj != null) {
          BeanEditor editor = (BeanEditor)obj;
          editor.setVisible(true);
          editor.toFront();
        }
        else {
          BeanEditor editor = new BeanEditor(m_activeBean);
          m_editors.put(m_activeBean, editor);
        }
      }
    };
    mItem.addActionListener(lst);
    mEdit.add(mItem);
    menuBar.add(mEdit);

    // Unchanged code from example 4.8

    return menuBar;
  }

  // Unchanged code from example 4.8
}

class BeanEditor extends JFrame implements PropertyChangeListener
{
  protected Component m_bean;
  protected JTable m_table;
  protected PropertyTableData m_data;

  public BeanEditor(Component bean) {
    m_bean = bean;
    m_bean.addPropertyChangeListener(this);

    Point pt = m_bean.getLocationOnScreen();
    setBounds(pt.x+50, pt.y+10, 400, 300);
    getContentPane().setLayout(new BorderLayout());

    m_data = new PropertyTableData(m_bean);
    m_table = new JTable(m_data);

    JScrollPane ps = new JScrollPane();
    ps.getViewport().add(m_table);
    getContentPane().add(ps, BorderLayout.CENTER);

    setDefaultCloseOperation(HIDE_ON_CLOSE);
    setVisible(true);
  }

  public void propertyChange(PropertyChangeEvent evt) {
    m_data.setProperty(evt.getPropertyName(), evt.getNewValue());
  }

  class PropertyTableData extends AbstractTableModel
  {
    protected String[][] m_properties;
    protected int m_numProps = 0;
    protected Vector m_v;
```

2 Menu item to create or reactivate a BeanEditor

5 Listens for property change events on the Bean

4 Positions frame slightly offset from Bean

6 Table model with one row for each property/value pair from the Bean

```java
public PropertyTableData(Component bean) {
  try {
    BeanInfo info = Introspector.getBeanInfo(
      m_bean.getClass());
    BeanDescriptor descr = info.getBeanDescriptor();
    setTitle("Editing "+descr.getName());
    PropertyDescriptor[] props = info.getPropertyDescriptors();
    m_numProps = props.length;

    m_v = new Vector(m_numProps);
    for (int k=0; k<m_numProps; k++) {
      String name = props[k].getDisplayName();
      boolean added = false;
      for (int i=0; i<m_v.size(); i++) {
        String str = ((PropertyDescriptor)m_v.elementAt(i)).
          getDisplayName();
        if (name.compareToIgnoreCase(str) < 0) {
          m_v.insertElementAt(props[k], i);
          added = true;
          break;
        }
      }
      if (!added)
        m_v.addElement(props[k]);
    }

    m_properties = new String[m_numProps][2];
    for (int k=0; k<m_numProps; k++) {
      PropertyDescriptor prop =
        (PropertyDescriptor)m_v.elementAt(k);
      m_properties[k][0] = prop.getDisplayName();
      Method mRead = prop.getReadMethod();
      if (mRead != null &&
       mRead.getParameterTypes().length == 0) {
        Object value = mRead.invoke(m_bean, null);
        m_properties[k][1] = objToString(value);
      }
      else
        m_properties[k][1] = "error";
    }
  }
  catch (Exception ex) {
    ex.printStackTrace();
    JOptionPane.showMessageDialog(
      BeanEditor.this, "Error: "+ex.toString(),
      "Warning", JOptionPane.WARNING_MESSAGE);
  }
}

public void setProperty(String name, Object value) {
  for (int k=0; k<m_numProps; k++)
    if (name.equals(m_properties[k][0])) {
      m_properties[k][1] = objToString(value);
```

7 Gets property descriptors from Bean, using Introspection

8 Sorts by property name

9 Reads property values by indirectly executing the "read" method, using Reflection to get the actual method

10 Called from fired events to set a new property value

```
        m_table.tableChanged(new TableModelEvent(this, k));
        m_table.repaint();
        break;
      }
  }

  public int getRowCount() { return m_numProps; }

  public int getColumnCount() { return 2; }

  public String getColumnName(int nCol) {
    return nCol==0 ? "Property" : "Value";
  }

  public boolean isCellEditable(int nRow, int nCol) {
      return (nCol==1);
  }

  public Object getValueAt(int nRow, int nCol) {
    if (nRow < 0 || nRow>=getRowCount())
      return "";
    switch (nCol) {
      case 0: return m_properties[nRow][0];
      case 1: return m_properties[nRow][1];
    }
    return "";
  }

  public void setValueAt(Object value, int nRow, int nCol) {
    if (nRow < 0 || nRow>=getRowCount())
      return;
    String str = value.toString();
    PropertyDescriptor prop = (PropertyDescriptor)m_v.
      elementAt(nRow);
    Class cls = prop.getPropertyType();
    Object obj = stringToObj(str, cls);
    if (obj==null)
      return;          // Can't process

    Method mWrite = prop.getWriteMethod();
    if (mWrite == null || mWrite.getParameterTypes().length != 1)
      return;
    try {
      mWrite.invoke(m_bean, new Object[]{ obj });
      m_bean.getParent().doLayout();
      m_bean.getParent().repaint();
      m_bean.repaint();
    }
    catch (Exception ex) {
      ex.printStackTrace();
      JOptionPane.showMessageDialog(
        BeanEditor.this, "Error: "+ex.toString(),
        "Warning", JOptionPane.WARNING_MESSAGE);
    }
    m_properties[nRow][1] = str;
  }
```

11 Can only edit values in the second column

12 Writes new property value to Bean, using Reflection to get method to call

```
public String objToString(Object value) {
  if (value==null)
    return "null";
  if (value instanceof Dimension) {
    Dimension dim = (Dimension)value;
    return ""+dim.width+","+dim.height;
  }
  else if (value instanceof Insets) {
    Insets ins = (Insets)value;
    return ""+ins.left+","+ins.top+","+ins.right+","+ins.bottom;
  }
  else if (value instanceof Rectangle) {
    Rectangle rc = (Rectangle)value;
    return ""+rc.x+","+rc.y+","+rc.width+","+rc.height;
  }
  else if (value instanceof Color) {
    Color col = (Color)value;
    return ""+col.getRed()+","+col.getGreen()+","+col.getBlue();
  }
  return value.toString();
}

public Object stringToObj(String str, Class cls) {
  try {
    if (str==null)
      return null;
    String name = cls.getName();
    if (name.equals("java.lang.String"))
      return str;
    else if (name.equals("int"))
      return new Integer(str);
    else if (name.equals("long"))
      return new Long(str);
    else if (name.equals("float"))
      return new Float(str);
    else if (name.equals("double"))
      return new Double(str);
    else if (name.equals("boolean"))
      return new Boolean(str);
    else if (name.equals("java.awt.Dimension")) {
      int[] i = strToInts(str);
      return new Dimension(i[0], i[1]);
    }
    else if (name.equals("java.awt.Insets")) {
      int[] i = strToInts(str);
      return new Insets(i[0], i[1], i[2], i[3]);
    }
    else if (name.equals("java.awt.Rectangle")) {
      int[] i = strToInts(str);
      return new Rectangle(i[0], i[1], i[2], i[3]);
    }
    else if (name.equals("java.awt.Color")) {
```

13 Provides specialized "toString" behavior

14 Builds conversion of object to given class

14 These cases expect string in format produced by objToString() method

```
        int[] i = strToInts(str);
        return new Color(i[0], i[1], i[2]);
      }
      return null;      // Not supported
    }
    catch(Exception ex) { return null; }
  }
  public int[] strToInts(String str) throws Exception {
    int[] i = new int[4];
    StringTokenizer tokenizer = new StringTokenizer(str, ",");
    for (int k=0; k<i.length &&
      tokenizer.hasMoreTokens(); k++)
        i[k] = Integer.parseInt(tokenizer.nextToken());
    return i;
  }
}
}
```

14 These cases expect string in format produced by objToString() method

18.9.1   Understanding the code

Class BeanContainer

1 This class (formerly BeanContainer from section 4.7) has received a new collection, Hashtable m_editors, which has been added as an instance variable. This Hashtable holds references to BeanEditor frames (used to edit beans, see below) as values, and the corresponding Components being edited as keys.

2 A new menu item titled Properties... is added to the Edit menu. This item is used to either create a new editor for the selected bean or activate an existing one (if any). The attached ActionListener looks for an existing BeanEditor that corresponds to the currently selected m_activeBean component in the m_editors collection. If such an editor is found, it is made visible and brought to the front. Otherwise, a new instance of BeanEditor is created to edit the currently active m_activeBean component, and it is added to the m_editors collection.

3 The ActionListener attached to the Delete menu item, which removes the currently active component, receives additional functionality. The added code looks for an existing BeanEditor that corresponds to the currently selected m_activeBean component in the m_editors collection. If such an editor is found, it is disposed of and its reference is removed from the hashtable.

Class BeanEditor

This class extends JFrame and implements the PropertyChangeListener interface. BeanEditor is used to display and edit the properties exposed by a given JavaBean. Three instance variables are declared:

- Component m_bean: The JavaBean component to be edited.
- JTable m_table: The table component to display a bean's properties.
- PropertyTableData m_data: The table model for m_table.

The BeanEditor constructor takes a reference to the JavaBean component to be edited and **4** stores it in instance variable m_bean. The initial location of the editor frame is selected depending on the location of the component being edited.

The table component, m_table, is created and added to a JScrollPane to provide scrolling capabilities. We do not add a WindowListener to this frame. Instead we use the HIDE_ON_CLOSE default close operation (see chapter 3):

```
setDefaultCloseOperation(HIDE_ON_CLOSE);
setVisible(true);
```

Upon closing, this frame will be hidden but not disposed of. Its reference will still be present in the m_editors collection, and this frame will be reactivated if the user chooses to see the properties of the associated bean again.

5 Note that an instance of the BeanEditor class is added as a PropertyChangeListener to the corresponding bean being edited. The propertyChange() method is invoked if the bean has changed its state during editing and a PropertyChangeEvent has been fired. This method simply triggers a call to the setProperty() method of the table model.

Class BeanEditor.PropertyTableData

6 PropertyTableData extends AbstractTableModel and provides the table model for each bean editor. Three instance variables are declared:

- String[][] m_properties: An array of data displayed in the table.
- int m_numProps: The number of bean properties (this corresponds to the number of rows in the table).
- Vector m_v: A collection of PropertyDescriptor objects sorted in alphabetical order.

7 The constructor of the PropertyTableData class takes a given bean instance and retrieves its properties. It first uses the Introspector.getBeanInfo() method to get a BeanInfo instance:

```
BeanInfo info = Introspector.getBeanInfo(
  m_bean.getClass());
BeanDescriptor descr = info.getBeanDescriptor();
setTitle("Editing "+descr.getName());
PropertyDescriptor[] props = info.getPropertyDescriptors();
m_numProps = props.length;
```

8 This provides us with all the available information about a bean (see chapter 2). We determine the bean's name and use it as the editor frame's title (note that this is an inner class, so set-Title() refers to the parent BeanEditor instance). We then extract an array of Property-Descriptors which will provide us with the actual information about a bean's properties.

Bean properties are sorted by name in alphabetical order. The name of each property is determined by the getDisplayName() method. The sorted PropertyDescriptors are stored in our m_v Vector collection. Then we can create the two-dimensional array, m_properties, **9** which holds data to be displayed in the table. This array has m_numProps rows and two columns (for property name and value). To determine a property's value, we need to obtain a reference to its getXX() method with getReadMethod() and make a call using the reflection API. We can call only getXX() methods without parameters (since we don't know anything about these parameters). Note that our `objToString()` helper method is invoked to translate a property's value into a display string (see below).

10 The `setProperty()` method searches for the given name in the 0th column of the `m_proper-ties` array. If such a property is found, this method sets its new value and updates the table component.

11 Several other simple methods included in this class have already been presented in previous examples and need not be explained again here. However, note that the `isCellEditable()` method returns `true` only for cells in the second column (property names, obviously, cannot be changed).

12 The `setValueAt()` method deserves additional explanation because it not only saves the modified data in the table model, but it also sends these modifications to the bean component itself. To do this we obtain a `PropertyDescriptor` instance that is stored in the `m_v` Vec-tor collection. The modified property value is always a `String`, so we first need to convert it into its proper object type using our `stringToObj()` helper method (if we can do this; see below). If the conversion succeeds (if the result is not `null`), we can continue.

To modify a bean value we determine the reference to its `setXX()` method (which corresponds to a certain property) and invoke it. An anonymous array containing one element is used as a parameter; these constructions are typical when dealing with the reflection API. Then the bean component and its container (which can also be affected by changes in such properties as size and color) are refreshed to reflect the bean's new property value. Finally, if the above procedures were successful, we store the new value in the `m_properties` data array.

13 The `objToString()` helper method converts a given `Object` into a `String` that is suitable for editing. In many cases the `toString()` method returns a long string starting with the class name. This is not very appropriate for editable data values, so for several classes we provide our own conversion into a string of comma-delimited numbers. For instance, a `Dimension` object is converted into a "width, height" form, `Color` is converted into a "red, green, blue" form, and so on. If no special implementation is provided, an object's `toString()` string is returned.

14 The `stringToObj()` helper method converts a given `String` into an `Object` of the given `Class`. The class's name is analyzed and a conversion method is chosen to build the correct type of object based on this name. The simplest case is the `String` class: we don't need to do any conversion at all in this case. For the primitive data types such as `int` or `boolean`, we return the corresponding encapsulating (wrapper class) objects. For the several classes which receive special treatment in the `objToString()` method (such as a `Dimension` or `Color` object), we parse the comma-delimited string of numbers and construct the proper object. For all other classes (or if a parsing exception occurs) we return `null` to indicate that we cannot perform the required conversion.

18.9.2   Running the code

Figure 18.8 shows the `BeanContainer` container and two editing frames displaying the properties of `Clock` and `JButton` components. This application provides a simple but powerful tool for investigating Swing and AWT components as well as custom JavaBeans. We can see all the exposed properties and modify many of them. If a component's properties change as a result of user interaction, our component properly notifies its listeners and we see an automatic editor table update. Try serializing a modified component and restoring it from its file. Notice how the previously modified properties are saved as expected.

It is natural to imagine using this example as a base for constructing a custom Swing IDE (Integrated Development Environment). `BeanContainer`, combined with the custom resize edge components developed in chapters 15 and 16, provides a fairly powerful base to work from.

C H A P T E R   1 9

Inside text components

19.1 TEXT PACKAGE OVERVIEW

A truly exhaustive discussion of the text package is beyond the scope of this book. However, in this chapter we hope to provide enough information about text components and their underlying constituents to leave you with a solid understanding of their inner workings. Picking up where chapter 11 left off, we continue our discussion of the most significant aspects of the text package classes and interfaces. In the next chapter, we'll continue our study of text components with the development of a full-featured HTML editor application. The examples in chapter 20 demonstrate practical applications of many of the complex topics covered in this chapter.

> **NOTE**   If, after reading this chapter, you want a more detailed treatment of the text package, we recommend *Java Swing*, by Robert Eckstein, Marc Loy, and Dave Wood, O'Reilly & Associates, 1998. This book includes roughly 300 pages of detailed text-related class and interface descriptions. In particular, the discussion of Views and EditorKits provides indispensable knowledge for any developer working on support for a custom content type.

19.1.1 More about JTextComponent

abstract class javax.swing.text.JTextComponent

Associated with each JTextComponent is a set of Actions which are normally bound to specific KeyStrokes (see section 2.13) and are managed in a hierarchically resolving set of Keymaps

605

(see section 19.1.23). We can retrieve a text component's `Actions` as an array with the `get-Actions()` method and we can retrieve and assign a new `Keymap` with `getKeymap()` and `setKeymap()`, respectively.

All text components share a set of default `Actions`. Each of these `Actions` are instances of `TextAction` by default (see section 19.1.24). `JTextComponent` provides a private static `EditorKit` (see section 19.1.25) which consists of a set of four pre-built `TextActions` shared by all text components through the use of a default `Keymap` instance (see section 19.1.26).

`JTextComponent` maintains a private reference to the text component that most recently had the keyboard focus. `TextActions` are designed to take advantage of this, and each `Text-Action` will operate on this component when it's invoked in the event that the source of the invoking event is not a text component.

`Document` content is structured hierarchically by `Element` implementations (see section 19.1.9). Each `Element` maintains a set of attributes encapsulated in implementations of the `AttributeSet` interface (see section 19.1.12). Many `Elements` also contain one or more child `Elements`. Attributes that apply to one element also apply to all child `Elements`, but not vice versa. Each `Element` has an associated start and end `Position` (see section 19.1.6).

`AttributeSets` can be applied manually to a region of text. However, it is often more convenient to use `Styles` (see section 19.1.14). `Styles` are `AttributeSet` implementations that we do not instantiate directly. Rather, `Styles` are created and maintained by instances of `StyleContext` (see section 19.1.16), and each `Style` has an associated name that allows easy reference. `StyleContext` also provides a means for sharing `AttributeSets` across a document or possibly multiple documents, and it is particularly useful in large documents.

The cursor of a text component is defined by implementations of the `Caret` interface (see section 19.1.19). We can retrieve the current `Caret` with `getCaret()`, and assign a new one with `setCaret()`. A text component's `Caret` is instantiated (but not maintained) by its UI delegate. So when the look and feel of a particular text component changes, the `Caret` in use will also change. `JTextComponent` supports the addition of `CaretListeners` that will receive `CaretEvents` whenever the position of the `Caret` changes.

Text components also support an arbitrary number of highlights through implementations of the `Highlighter` interface (see section 19.1.17). `Highlighters` are most often used to indicate a specific selection. They can also be used for many other things, such as marking new text additions. `Highlighter` maintains each highlighted region as an implementation of `High-lighter.Highlight`, and each `Highlight` can be rendered using a `Highlighter.High-lightPainter` implementation. As with `Carets`, a text area's `Highlighter` is instantiated by its UI delegate. We can assign and retrieve a text component's `Highlighter` with `setHigh-lighter()` and `getHighlighter()`, respectively.

`JTextComponent` also maintains a bound `focusAccelerator` property, as we discussed in chapter 11. This property is a `char` that is used to transfer focus to a text component when the corresponding key is pressed simultaneously with the ALT key. `JTextComponent` defines a private `Action` called `focusAction` whose `actionPerformed()` method calls `requestFocus()`. Initially, `focusAction` is not attached to the text component (that is, it is turned off). To activate it we use the `setFocusAccelerator()` method. Sending '\0' to the `setFocusAccelerator()` method turns it off. Internally, this method searches through all registered `KeyStrokes` and checks whether any are associated with `focusAction`, using the `getActionForKeyStroke()` method. If any are found, they are unregistered using the `unregisterKeyboardAction()` method of `JComponent`. Finally, the character passed in is used to construct a `KeyStroke` to register and associate with `focusAction`. This action is registered such that it will be invoked whenever the top-level window containing the given text component has the focus:

```
// From JTextComponent.java
registerKeyboardAction(
    focusAction,KeyStroke.getKeyStroke(aKey,ActionEvent.ALT_MASK),
    JComponent.WHEN_IN_FOCUSED_WINDOW);
```

Each text component uses a subclass of `BasicTextUI` as its UI delegate. As we mentioned earlier, each text component also has an `EditorKit` for storing `Actions`. This `EditorKit` is referenced by the UI delegate. `JTextField` and `JTextArea` have default editor kits assigned by the UI delegate, whereas `JEditorPane` and `JTextPane` maintain their own editor kits independent of their UI delegate.

Unlike most Swing components, a text component's UI delegate does not directly define how that text component is rendered and laid out. Rather, it implements the `View-Factory` interface (see section 19.1.29) which requires the implementation of one method: `create(Element e)`. This method returns a `View` instance (see section 19.1.28) which is responsible for rendering the given `Element`. Each `Element` has an associated `View` that is used to render it. Many different views are provided in the text package, and we will rarely need to implement our own (although this is certainly possible). `JTextArea`, `JTextField`, and `JPasswordField` have specific `Views` returned by their UI delegate's `create()` method. `JEditorPane` and `JTextPane` `Views` are created by the current `EditorKit`.

We can retrieve a `Point` location in the coordinate system of a text component corresponding to a character offset with `JTextComponent`'s `viewToModel()` method. Similarly, we can retrieve a `Rectangle` instance that describes the size and location of the `View` which is responsible for rendering an `Element` occupying a given character offset with `modelToView()`.

`JTextComponent`'s `margin` property specifies the space to use between its border and its document content. Standard clipboard operations can be programmatically performed with the `cut()`, `copy()`, and `paste()` methods.

JAVA 1.4   In Java 1.4 the new `NavigationFilter` class has been added in the `javax.-swing.text` package. By installing an instance of `NavigationFilter` on a text component, using the new `setNavigationFilter()` method, you can control and restrict caret movement. `NavigationFilter` is most commonly used in combination with an instance of `JFormattedTextField.AbstractFormatter` (see section 11.3).

Java 1.4 also includes a new `DocumentFilter` class in the `javax.swing.text` package. When an instance of `DocumentFilter` is installed on a `Document`, all invocations of `insertString()`, `remove()`, and `replace()` get forwarded on to the `DocumentFilter`. This allows clean encapsulation of all custom document mutation code. In this way different filters can be applied to various documents without the need to change a given `Document` instance. To support `Document-Filters`, `AbstractDocument` includes the new `setDocumentFilter()` and `getDocumentFilter()` methods. `DocumentFilter` is most commonly used in combination with an instance of `JFormattedTextField.AbstractFormatter` (see section 11.3).

19.1.2 The Document interface

abstract interface javax.swing.text.Document

In MVC terms, the model of a text component contains the text itself, and the `Document` interface describes this model. A hierarchical set of `Elements` (see section 19.1.9) define the structure of a `Document`. Each `Document` contains one or more root `Elements`, potentially allowing more than one way of structuring the same content. Most documents only have one structure, and hence one root element. This element can be accessed with `getDefault-RootElement()`. All root elements, including the default root element, are accessible with `getRoot-Elements()`, which returns an `Element` array.

NOTE   We will not discuss the details of maintaining multiple structures, as this is very rarely desired. See the API documentation for examples of situations in which multiple structures might be useful.

`Documents` maintain two `Positions` which keep track of the beginning and end positions of the content. These can be accessed with `getStartPosition()` and `getEndPosition()`, respectively. `Documents` also maintain a `length` property, which is accessible with `get-Length()`, that maintains the number of contained characters.

The `Document` interface declares methods for adding and removing `Document-Listeners` (see section 19.1.8), for notification of any content changes, and for `Undoable-EditListeners` (allowing easy access to built-in undo/redo support; refer to chapter 11 for an example of adding undo/redo support to a text area).

Methods for retrieving, inserting, and removing content are also declared: `getText()`, `insertString()`, and `remove()`. Each of these throws a `BadLocationException` if an illegal (nonexistent) location in the document is specified. The `insertString()` method requires an `AttributeSet` instance that describes the attributes to apply to the given text (`null` can be used for this parameter). Plain text components will not pay any attention to this attribute set. Text components using a `StyledDocument` instance most likely will pay attention to these attributes.

The `createPosition()` method inserts a `Position` instance at a given index, and the `putProperty()` and `getProperty()` methods insert and retrieve various properties that are stored in an internal collection.

The `render()` method is unique. It takes a `Runnable` as a parameter, and it ensures thread safety by not allowing document content to change while that `Runnable` is running. This method is used by each text component's UI delegate during painting.

19.1.3 The StyledDocument interface

abstract interface javax.swing.StyledDocument

This interface extends the `Document` interface to add functionality for working with `Styles` and other `AttributeSets`. Implementations are expected to maintain a collection of `Style` implementations. This interface also declares the notion of character and paragraph attributes, and logical styles. What these mean is specific to each `StyledDocument` implementation (we will discuss these more when we talk about `DefaultStyledDocument` in section 19.1.11).

The `setCharacterAttributes()` method assigns a given set of attributes to a given range of document content. A `boolean` parameter is also required; it specifies whether preexisting attributes of the affected content should be overwritten (`true`) or merged (`false`—only new attributes are assigned). The `setParagraphAttributes()` method works the same way as `setCharacterAttributes()`, but it applies to the number of paragraphs spanned by a given range of content. The `getFont()`, `getBackground()`, and `getForeground()` methods take an `AttributeSet` parameter, and they are used for convenient access to the corresponding attribute in the given set (if it exists).

`StyledDocuments` are meant to allow `Styles` to be added, removed, and retrieved from an internal collection of `Styles`. The `addStyle()` method takes a `String` and a parent `Style` as parameters and returns a new `Style` with the given name and given `Style` as its resolving parent. The `getLogicalStyle()` method returns a `Style` that corresponds to the paragraph containing the given character offset. The `setLogicalStyle()` method assigns a `Style` to the paragraph that contains the given character offset. The `getStyle()` and `removeStyle()` methods retrieve and remove a `Style` with the given name, respectively, in the internal collection.

The `getCharacterElement()` and `getParagraphElement()` methods allow the retrieval of `Elements` that correspond to a given character offset. The definition of these methods will vary based on the definition of paragraph and character `Elements` in a `StyledDocument` implementation. Typically, a character `Element` represents a range of text containing a given offset, and a paragraph `Element` represents a paragraph containing the given offset.

19.1.4 AbstractDocument

abstract class javax.swing.text.AbstractDocument

`AbstractDocument` implements the `Document` interface and provides a base implementation for text component models. Two provided classes that extend `AbstractDocument` are used by the Swing text components as their default model: `PlainDocument` and `DefaultStyledDocument`. `PlainDocument` is used by all the plain text components, such as `JTextArea`, `JTextField`, and its subclass, `JPasswordField`. It provides support for character data content only and does not support markup (such as multiple fonts and colors) of this content. `DefaultStyledDocument` is used by more sophisticated text components such as `JEditorPane` and its subclass, `JTextPane`. It provides support for text markup by implementing the `StyledDocument` interface.

`AbstractDocument` specifies a mechanism that separates character data storage from the structuring of that data. Thus, we have the capability to store our text however we like without concern for how the document is structured and marked up. Similarly, we can structure a document with little concern for how its data is stored. The significance of this structure-storage separation will make more sense after we have discussed `Elements` and attributes below. Character data is stored in an instance of the inner `Content` interface which we will also discuss below.

This class defines the functionality for a basic read/write locking scheme. This scheme enforces the rule that no write can occur while a read is occurring. However, multiple reads can occur simultaneously. To obtain a read lock, we use the `render()` method, which releases the read lock when it finishes executing the `Runnable` passed to it. No other access methods acquire such a lock (making them not thread-safe). The `getText()` method, for example, does not acquire a read lock. In a multithreaded environment, any text retrieved with this method may be corrupted if a write occurred at the time the text was retrieved.

The read lock is basically just an increment in an internal variable that keeps track of the number of readers. The readLock() method does this for us, and it will force the current thread to wait until no write locks exist. When the Runnable finishes executing, the internal reader-count variable is decremented—this is done by the readUnlock() method. Both of these methods will simply do nothing and return if the current thread is the writer thread. A StateInvariantError exception will be thrown if a read unlock is requested when there are no readers.

The write lock is a reference to the writing thread. The writeLock() and write-Unlock() methods take care of this for us. Whenever a modification is requested, the write lock must first be obtained. If the writer thread is not null, and it is not the same as the invoking thread, writeLock() blocks the current thread until the current writer releases the lock by calling writeUnlock().

If we intend to use the protected reader- and writer-locking methods ourselves in a subclass, we should make sure that a readUnlock() call will be made no matter what happens in the try block, using the following semantics:

```
// From AbstractDocument.java
try {
  readLock();
// Do something
} finally {
  readUnlock();
}
```

All methods that modify document content must obtain a write lock before any modification can take place. These methods include insertString() and remove().

AbstractDocument's dump() method prints the document's Element hierarchy to the given PrintStream for debugging purposes. For example, the following class will dump a JTextArea's Element hierarchy to standard output.

```
import java.awt.*;
import java.awt.event.*;
import javax.swing.*;
import javax.swing.text.*;

public class DumpDemo extends JFrame
{
  JTextArea m_editor;

  public DumpDemo() {
    m_editor = new JTextArea();

    JScrollPane js1 = new JScrollPane(m_editor);
    getContentPane().add(js1, BorderLayout.CENTER);

    JButton dumpButton = new JButton("Dump");
    dumpButton.addActionListener(new ActionListener() {
      public void actionPerformed(ActionEvent e) {
        ((PlainDocument) m_editor.getDocument()).dump(System.out);
      }
```

```
    });

    JPanel buttonPanel = new JPanel();
    buttonPanel.add(dumpButton);

    getContentPane().add(buttonPanel, BorderLayout.SOUTH);

    setSize(300,300);
    setVisible(true);
  }

  public static void main(String[] args) {
    new DumpDemo();
  }
}
```

Typing this text in the JTextArea:

```
Swing is
powerful!!
```

produces the following output when the dump() method is invoked (this will make more sense after we discuss Elements in section 19.1.9).

```
<paragraph>
  <content>
    [0,9][Swing is
]
  <content>
    [9,20][powerful!!
]
  <content>
    [20,21][
]
<bidi root>
  <bidi level
    bidiLevel=0
  >
    [0,21][Swing is
powerful!!
]
```

AbstractDocument also includes several significant inner classes and interfaces. We will discuss most of them in this chapter. A brief overview is appropriate here:

- abstract class AbstractDocument.AbstractElement: Implements the Element and MutableAttributeSet interfaces, allowing instances to act both as Elements and the mutable AttributeSets that describe them. This class also implements the TreeNode interface, providing an easy means of displaying document structure with a JTree.
- class AbstractDocument.BranchElement: A concrete subclass of AbstractDocument.AbstractElement that represents an Element which can contain multiple child Elements (see section 19.1.9).
- class AbstractDocument.LeafElement: A concrete subclass of AbstractDocument. AbstractElement that represents an Element which cannot contain child Elements (see section 19.1.9).

- static abstract interface AbstractDocument.Content: Defines the data storage mechanism used by AbstractDocument subclasses (see section 19.1.9).
- static abstract interface AbstractDocument.AttributeContext: Used for efficient AttributeSet management (see section 19.1.16).
- static class AbstractDocument.ElementEdit: Extends AbstractUndoableEdit, implements DocumentEvent.ElementChange (see section 19.1.7), and allows document changes to be undone and redone.
- class AbstractDocument.DefaultDocumentEvent: Extends CompoundEdit and implements DocumentEvent (see section 19.1.7). Instances of this class are used by documents to create UndoableEdits, which can be used to create UndoableEditEvents for dispatching to UndoableEditListeners. Instances of this class are also fired to any registered DocumentListeners (see section 19.1.8) for change notification.

19.1.5 The Content interface

abstract static interface javax.swing.text.AbstractDocument.Content

In order to implement a data storage mechanism for text, AbstractDocument provides the static Content interface. Every Document character storage mechanism must implement this interface. (Images and other embedded objects are not considered to be part of a document's content.) Each Content instance represents a sequence of character data, and each provides the ability to insert, remove, and retrieve character data with the insertString(), remove(), getString(), and getChars() methods.

> **NOTE** A special convenience class called Segment allows users to access fragments of actual document text without having to copy characters into a new array for processing. This class is used internally by text components to speed up searching and rendering large documents.

Implementations of Content must also provide the ability to create position markers that keep track of a certain location between characters in storage with the createPosition() method. These markers are implementations of the Position interface.

Content implementations provide UndoableEdit objects that represent the state of storage before and after any change is made. The insertString() and remove() methods are meant to return such an object each time they are invoked, allowing insertions and removals to be undone and redone.

Two Content implementations are included in the javax.swing.text package: StringContent and GapContent. StringContent stores character data in a normal char array. GapContent also stores data in a char array but it purposefully leaves an empty space, a gap, in this array. According to the API documentation, "The gap is moved to the location of changes to take advantage of common behavior where most changes are in the same location. Changes that occur at a gap boundary are generally cheap and moving the gap is generally cheaper than moving the array contents directly to accommodate the change." This gap is strictly used for internal efficiency purposes and is not accessible outside of this class.

NOTE   `StringContent` was used in earlier implementations of `PlainDocument` and `DefaultStyledDocument`, but it has been replaced by `GapContent`, which extends a package private class called `GapVector`. The gap buffer algorithm used in `GapContent` is very efficient for keeping track of large numbers of `Position`s and, interestingly, it is used in the popular emacs editor.

19.1.6   The Position interface

abstract interface javax.swing.text.Position

This interface consists of one method, `getOffset()`, which returns an `int` value representing the location, or *offset*, from the beginning of the document's content. Figure 19.1 illustrates what happens to a `Position` marker when text is inserted and removed from storage. This figure starts by showing a document containing "Swing text" as its content. There are initially `Position` markers at offsets 0, 4, and 7. When we remove the characters from offset 4 through 9, the `Position` at offset 7 is moved to offset 4. At this point there are two `Position`s at offset 4 and the document content is "Swin." When we insert "g is" at offset 4, both `Position`s at offset 4 are moved to offset 8 and the document content becomes "Swing is."

NOTE   The term *range* refers to a sequence of characters between two `Position` markers as shown in figure 19.1.

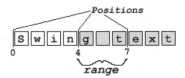

After deleting

After inserting

Figure 19.1
Position movement

19.1.7   The DocumentEvent interface

abstract interface javax.swing.event.DocumentEvent

Changes to a `Document`'s content are encapsulated in implementations of the `DocumentEvent` interface, the default implementation of which is `AbstractDocument.DefaultDocumentEvent`. Three types of changes can be made to document content: CHANGE, INSERT, and REMOVE (these fields are defined within the `DocumentEvent.EventType` inner class). `DocumentEvent` also defines an interface within it called `ElementChange`. Implementations of this interface, the default of which is `AbstractDocument.ElementEdit`, are responsible for storing information about changes to the structure of a document for use in

TEXT PACKAGE OVERVIEW   *613*

undo and redo operations, among other things. `AbstractDocument` handles the firing of `Default-DocumentEvents` appropriately with its `fireXXUpdate()` methods.

The `getChange()` method takes an `Element` instance as a parameter and returns an instance of `DocumentEvent.ElementChange` describing the elements that were added and/or removed, as well as the location of a change. The `getDocument()` method returns a reference to the `Document` instance that generated this event. The `getLength()` method returns the length of a change, and the `getOffset()` method returns the offset at which a change began. The `getType()` method returns an instance of `Document.EventType` specifying the type of change that occurred to the document.

19.1.8   The DocumentListener interface

abstract interface javax.swing.event.DocumentListener

Instances of this interface can be attached to `Documents` and each `Document` will notify its attached `DocumentListeners` whenever a change occurs to its content. It is important to note that this notification will always occur *after* any content has been updated. Knowing this, it is even more important to realize that we should not perform any changes to the content of a document from within a `DocumentListener`. This can potentially result in an infinite loop in situations where a document event causes another to be fired.

> **NOTE**   Never modify the contents of a document from within a `DocumentListener`.

The `insertUpdate()` and `removeUpdate()` methods give notification of content insertions and removals. The `changedUpdate()` method provides notification of attribute changes.

19.1.9   The Element interface

abstract interface javax.swing.text.Element

`Elements` provide a hierarchical means of structuring a `Document`'s content. Associated with each `Element` is a set of attributes encapsulated in an `AttributeSet` implementation. These attributes provide a way to specify the markup of content associated with each `Element`. `AttributeSets` most often take the form of `Style` implementations and they are grouped together inside a `StyleContext` object. `StyleContext` objects are used by `Styled-Document` implementations such as `DefaultStyledDocument`. The objects that are responsible for actually rendering text components are implementations of the abstract `View` class. Each `Element` has a separate `View` object associated with it, and each `View` recognizes a predefined set of attributes used in the actual rendering and layout of that `Element`.

> **NOTE**   `Elements` are objects that impose structure on a text component's content. They are actually part of the document model, but they are also used by views for text component rendering.

The `getAttributes()` method retrieves an `AttributeSet` collection of attributes describing an `Element`. The `getElement()` method fetches a child `Element` at the given index, where the index is given in terms of the number of child `Elements`. The `getElement-Count()` method returns the index of the `Element` closest to the provided document content offset. The `getElementCount()` method returns the number of child `Elements` an Element contains (it returns 0 if the parent `Element` is itself a leaf). The `isLeaf()` method tells us whether an `Element` is a leaf element, and `getParentElement()` returns an `Element`'s parent `Element`.

The `getDocument()` method retrieves the `Document` instance an `Element` belongs to. The `getStartOffset()` and `getEndOffset()` methods return the offset of the beginning and end of an `Element`, respectively, from the beginning of the document. The `getName()` method returns a short `String` description of an `Element`.

`AbstractDocument` defines the inner class `AbstractElement`, which implements the `Element` interface. As we mentioned earlier, two subclasses of `AbstractElement` are defined within `AbstractDocument`: `LeafElement` and `BranchElement`. Each `LeafElement` has a specific *range* of content text associated with it (this range can change when content is inserted, removed, or replaced—figures 19.2 and 19.3 illustrate). `LeafElements` cannot have any child `Elements`. `BranchElements` can have any number of child `Elements`. The range of content text associated with `BranchElements` is the union of all content text associated with their child `LeafElements`. (Thus the start offset of a `BranchElement` is the lowest start offset of all its child `LeafElements`, and its end offset is the highest end offset of all its child `LeafElements`.) `DefaultStyledDocument` provides a third type of element called `Section-Element` which extends `BranchElement`.

The text package also includes an `ElementIterator` class, which traverses an `Element` hierarchy in a depth-first fashion (meaning postorder; see section 17.1.2). The `first()`, `current()`, `depth()`, `next()`, and `previous()` methods can be used to obtain information about, and programmatically traverse, an `Element` hierarchy. We can construct an `Element-Iterator` object by providing either a `Document` or an `Element` to the `ElementIterator` constructor. If a `Document` is provided, the default root `Element` of that document is used as the root of the `Element` hierarchy traversed by `ElementIterator`.

NOTE   `ElementIterator` does not provide any thread safety by default, so it is our responsibility to make sure that no `Element` changes occur during traversal.

19.1.10   PlainDocument

class javax.swing.text.PlainDocument

This class extends `AbstractDocument` and it is used by the basic text components `JText-Field`, `JPasswordField`, and `JTextArea`. When we are enforcing certain input, usually in a `JTextField`, we normally override `AbstractDocument`'s `insertString()` method in a `PlainDocument` subclass (see the discussion of `JTextField` in chapter 11 for an example).

`PlainDocument` uses a `BranchElement` as its root and has only `LeafElements` as children. In this case, each `LeafElement` represents a line of text and the root `BranchElement` represents the whole document text. `PlainDocument` identifies a `BranchElement` as "paragraph" and a `LeafElement` as "content." The notion of a paragraph in `PlainDocument` is much different than our normal notion of a paragraph. We usually think of paragraphs as sections of text separated by line breaks. However, `PlainDocument` considers each section of text ending with a line break as a line of "content" in its never-ending "paragraph." Figures 19.2 and 19.3 show the structure of a sample `PlainDocument`, and they illustrate how `Elements` and their associated `Positions` can change when document content changes.

Figure 19.2 shows a `PlainDocument` that contains three elements. Two `LeafElements` represent two lines of text and are children of the root `BranchElement`. The root element begins at offset 0, the start offset of the first `LeafElement`, and it ends at 19, the end offset of the last `LeafElement`. This document would be displayed in a `JTextArea` as:

```
Swing is
powerful!!
```

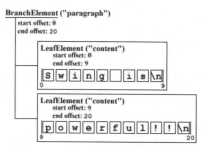

Figure 19.2
A sample `PlainDocument` structure

NOTE   The line break at the end of the second `LeafElement` is always present at the end of the last `Element` in any `PlainDocument`. It does not represent a line break that was actually inserted into the document and it is not counted when the document length is queried using the `getLength()` method. Thus the length of the document shown in figure 19.2 would be returned as 19.

Now suppose we insert two line breaks at offset 5. Figure 19.3 shows the structure that would result from this addition.

This document would now be displayed in a `JTextArea` as:

```
Swing

 is
powerful!!
```

`JTextArea`, `JTextField`, and `JPasswordField` use `PlainDocument` as their model. Only `JTextArea` allows its document to contain multiple `LeafElements`. `JTextField` and its `JPasswordField` subclass allow only one `LeafElement`.

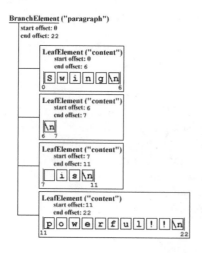

Figure 19.3
A sample `PlainDocument` structure
after inserting two line breaks at offset

19.1.11 DefaultStyledDocument

class javax.swing.text.DefaultStyledDocument

DefaultStyledDocument provides significantly more power than the PlainDocument structure described above. This StyledDocument implementation (see section 19.1.3) is used for marked-up (styled) text. JTextPane uses an instance of DefaultStyledDocument by default, although this instance may change based on JTextPane's content type.

DefaultStyledDocument uses an instance of its inner SectionElement class as its root Element; the root has only instances of AbstractDocument.BranchElement as children. These BranchElements represent paragraphs, which are referred to as *paragraph* Elements, and they contain instances of AbstractDocument.LeafElement as children. These LeafElements represent what are referred to as *character* Elements. Character Elements represent regions of text (possibly multiple lines within a paragraph) that share the same attributes.

We can retrieve the character Element that occupies a given offset with the get-CharacterElement() method, and we can retrieve the paragraph Element that occupies a given offset with the getParagraphElement() method.

We will discuss attributes, AttributeSets, and their usage details soon enough. However, it is important to understand here that AttributeSets assigned to DefaultStyled-Document Elements resolve hierarchically. For instance, a character Element will inherit all attributes assigned to itself, as well as those assigned to the parent paragraph Element. Character Element attributes override those of the same type that are defined in the parent paragraph Element's AttributeSet.

> **NOTE** The Elements used by DefaultStyledDocument are derived from Abstract-Document.AbstractElement, which implements both the Element and MutableAttributeSet interfaces. This allows these Elements to act as their own AttributeSets and use each other as resolving parents.

Figure 19.4 shows a simple DefaultStyledDocument in a JTextPane with two paragraphs.

Figure 19.4
A two-paragraph DefaultStyledDocument,
with several different attributes, in a JTextPane

Using AbstractDocument's dump() method to display this document's Element structure to standard output (see section 19.1.4), we get the following:

```
<section>
  <paragraph
    RightIndent=0.0
    LeftIndent=0.0
    resolver=NamedStyle:default {name=default,nrefs=2}
    FirstLineIndent=0.0
  >
```

```
        <content
          underline=false
          bold=true
          foreground=java.awt.Color[r=0,g=128,b=0]
          size=22
          italic=false
          family=SansSerif
        >
          [0,6][Swing
    ]
      <paragraph
        RightIndent=0.0
        LeftIndent=0.0
        resolver=NamedStyle:default {name=default,nrefs=2}
        FirstLineIndent=0.0
      >
        <content
          underline=false
          bold=false
          foreground=java.awt.Color[r=0,g=0,b=0]
          size=12
          italic=false
          family=SansSerif
        >
          [6,9][is ]
        <content
          underline=false
          bold=false
          foreground=java.awt.Color[r=0,g=0,b=0]
          size=12
          italic=false
          family=SansSerif
        >
          [9,19][extremely ]
        <content
          underline=false
          bold=false
          foreground=java.awt.Color[r=0,g=0,b=192]
          size=18
          italic=true
          family=SansSerif
        >
          [19,27][powerful]
        <content
          underline=false
          bold=true
          foreground=java.awt.Color[r=255,g=0,b=0]
          size=20
          italic=false
          family=SansSerif
        >
          [27,28][!]
```

```
    <content>
      [28,29][
]
<bidi root>
  <bidi level
    bidiLevel=0
  >
    [0,29][Swing
is extremely powerful!
]
```

Note the use of <section>, <paragraph>, and <content> to denote SectionElement, BranchElement, and LeafElement, respectively. Also note that the <paragraph> and <content> tags each contain several attributes. The <paragraph> attributes represent paragraph Element attributes and the <content> attributes represent character Element attributes. We will discuss specific attributes in more detail later. The <bidi root> tag specifies a second root Element that allows bidirectional text (this functionality is incomplete as of Java 2 FCS).

We can assign paragraph and character attributes to a region of text with the setParagraphAttributes() and setCharacterAttributes() methods. These methods require a start and end offset that specifies the region to apply the attributes to, as well as an AttributeSet that contains the attributes, and a boolean flag that specifies whether to replace pre-existing attributes with the new attributes.

Regarding the range of text, paragraph attributes will be applied to paragraph Elements that contain at least some portion of the specified range. Character attributes will be applied to all character Elements that intersect that range. If the specified range only partially extends into a paragraph Element, that Element will be split into two, so that only the specified range of text will receive the new attributes (this splitting is handled by an instance of the ElementBuffer inner class).

If the boolean flag is true, all pre-existing paragraph Element attributes are removed before the new set is applied. Otherwise, the new set is merged with the old set, and any new attributes overwrite pre-existing attributes. Character attributes work in a similar way, but they do not change paragraph attributes at all—they simply override them.

DefaultStyledDocument also defines the notion of *logical* paragraph Styles. A logical paragraph Style acts as the resolving parent of a paragraph Element's AttributeSet. So attributes defined in a paragraph Element's AttributeSet override those defined in that paragraph's logical Style. We can change a specific paragraph Element's logical style with the setLogicalStyle() method. The logical style of each paragraph defaults to StyleContext.DEFAULT_STYLE (which is empty by default).

JTextPane implements the getParagraphAttributes(), setParagraphAttributes(), getLogicalStyle(), and setLogicalStyle() methods which communicate directly with its StyledDocument. JTextPane's paragraph attributes and logical style setXX() methods apply to the paragraph the caret currently resides in if there is no selection. If there is a selection, these methods apply to all paragraphs included in the selected region. JTextPane's paragraph attributes and logical style getXX() methods apply to the paragraph currently containing the caret.

JTextPane also implements the getCharacterAttributes() and setCharacter-Attributes() methods. If there is a selection, the setCharacterAttributes() method will act as described above, splitting Elements as needed. If there is no selection, this method will modify JTextPane's *input* attributes.

NOTE JTextPane's input attributes are an AttributeSet which changes with the location of the caret. This reference always points to the attributes of the character Element at the current caret location. We can retrieve it at any time with JText-Pane's getInputAttributes() method. Whenever text is inserted in a JText-Pane, the current input attributes will be applied to that text by default. However, any attributes explicitly assigned to newly inserted text will override those defined by the current input attributes.

A StyleContext instance (see section 19.1.16) is associated with each DefaultStyled-Document. As we mentioned in the beginning of this chapter, the Style interface describes a named mutable AttributeSet, and the StyledDocument interface describes a Document which manages a set of Styles. A DefaultStyledDocument's StyleContext instance is what performs the actual management, creation, and assignment of that document's Styles. If a StyleContext is not provided to the DefaultStyledDocument constructor, a default version is created.

JTextPane defines several methods for adding, removing, and retrieving Styles, as well as specific attributes within a given AttributeSet (such as the getFont() and getFore-ground() methods). Calls to these methods are forwarded to methods of the same signature in JTextPane's StyledDocument, and, in the case of DefaultStyledDocument, these calls are forwarded to the StyleContext in charge of all the Styles.

DefaultStyledDocument also includes several significant inner classes:

- static class DefaultStyledDocument.AttributeUndoableEdit: This class extends AbstractUndoableEdit to allow AttributeSet undo/redo functionality with Elements.
- class DefaultStyledDocument.ElementBuffer: Instances of this class are used to manage structural changes in a DefaultStyledDocument, such as the splitting of Elements, or the insertion and removal of text that results in the modification of, and the insertion and/or removal of, various Elements. This class also plays a critical role in constructing AbstractDocument.DefaultDocumentEvents (see section 19.1.4).
- static class DefaultStyledDocument.ElementSpec: This class describes an Element that can be created and inserted into a document in the future with an ElementBuffer.
- protected class DefaultStyledDocument.SectionElement: This class extends AbstractDocument.BranchElement and acts as a DefaultStyledDocument's default root Element. It contains only BranchElement children (which represent paragraphs).

19.1.12   The AttributeSet interface

abstract interface javax.swing.text.AttributeSet

An attribute is simply a *key/value* pair (as in a Hashtable) that should be recognized by some View implementation available to the text component being used. As we know from our discussion above, each `Element` in a `DefaultStyledDocument` has an associated set of attributes which resolves hierarchically. The attributes play a critical role in how that piece of the document will be rendered by a `View`. For example, one commonly used attribute is `FontFamily`. The `FontFamily` attribute key is an `Object` consisting of the `String` "family." The `FontFamily` attribute *value* is a `String` representing the name of a font (such as "monospaced"). Other examples of attribute keys include "Icon" and "Component," whose values are instances of `Icon` and `Component`.

If an attribute is not recognized by a `View`, the `Element` associated with that view will not be rendered correctly. Thus, a predefined set of attributes is recognized by the Swing `View` classes, and these attribute keys should be considered reserved—in other words, all new attributes should use new keys. These predefined attribute keys are all accessible as static `Object`s in the `StyleConstants` class (see section 19.1.15).

Sets of attributes are encapsulated in implementations of either the `AttributeSet` interface, the `MutableAttributeSet` interface (see section 19.1.13), or the `Style` interface (see section 19.1.14). `Style` extends `MutableAttributeSet`, which, in turn, extends `AttributeSet`. The `AttributeSet` interface describes a read-only set of attributes because it does not provide methods for changing, adding, or removing attributes from that set.

The `containsAttribute()` and `containsAttributes()` methods are used to check whether an `AttributeSet` contains a given attribute key/value pair or any number of such pairs. The `copyAttributes()` method returns a fresh, immutable copy of the `AttributeSet` it is invoked on. The `getAttributeCount()` method returns the number of attributes contained in a set, and `getAttributeNames()` retrieves an `Enumeration` of the keys that describe each attribute. The `isDefined()` method checks whether a given attribute key corresponds to an attribute directly stored in the `AttributeSet` the method is invoked on (the resolving parents are not searched). The `isEqual()` method compares two `AttributeSet`s and returns whether they contain identical attribute key/value pairs. The `getResolveParent()` method returns a reference to an `AttributeSet`'s resolving parent, if any, and the `getAttribute()` method returns the value of an attribute corresponding to a given key.

The `AttributeSet` interface also provides four empty static interfaces: `CharacterAttribute`, `ColorAttribute`, `FontAttribute`, and `ParagraphAttribute`. The only reason these interfaces exist is to provide a signature (for example, information about the class in which it is defined), which is expected of each attribute key. This signature can be used to verify whether an attribute belongs to a certain category (see section 19.1.15).

Only one direct implementation of the `AttributeSet` interface exists within the text package: `StyleContext.SmallAttributeSet`. A `SmallAttributeSet` is an array of attribute *key*/*value* pairs stored in the alternating pattern: key1, value1, key2, value2, and so on (thus the number of attributes contained in a `SmallAttributeSet` is actually half the size of its array). An array is used for storage because `AttributeSet` describes a read-only set of attributes, and using an array is more memory-efficient than dynamically resizable storage such as that provided by a `Hashtable`. However, it is less time-efficient to search through an array than a `Hashtable`. For this reason, `SmallAttributeSet` is used only for small sets of attributes. These sets are usually shared between several `Element`s. Because of the way sharing works (see section 19.1.16), the smaller the set of attributes is, the better candidate that set is for being shared.

19.1.13 The MutableAttributeSet interface

abstract interface javax.swing.text.MutableAttributeSet

The `MutableAttributeSet` interface extends the `AttributeSet` interface and declares additional methods that allow attribute addition and removal, and resolving parent assignment: `addAttribute()`, `addAttributes()`, `setResolveParent()`, `removeAttribute()`, and two variations of `removeAttributes()`.

`MutableAttributeSet` also has two direct implementations within the text package: `AbstractDocument.AbstractElement` and `SimpleAttributeSet`. The fact that `AbstractElement` implements `MutableAttributeSet` allows such `Element`s to act as resolving parents to one another. It also reduces object overhead by combining structural information about a region of text with that region's stylistic attributes.

`SimpleAttributeSet` uses a `Hashtable` to store attribute key/value pairs because it must be dynamically resizable. By nature, a `Hashtable` is less efficient than an array in memory usage, but it is more efficient in look-up speed. For this reason, `SimpleAttributeSets` are used for large sets of attributes that are not shared.

NOTE   In the past few sections we have alluded to the importance of efficiency in attribute storage. Efficiency here refers to both memory usage and the speed of attribute location. Here's a quick summary of the issues: A `View` uses attributes to determine how to render its associated `Element`. These attribute *value*s must be located, by *key*, within that `Element`'s attribute set hierarchy. The faster this location occurs, the more quickly the view is rendered and the more responsive the user interface becomes. So look-up speed is a large factor in deciding how to store attribute *key/ value* pairs.

Memory usage is also a large issue. Obtaining efficient look-up speed involves sacrificing efficient memory usage, and vice versa. This necessary trade-off is taken into account through the implementation of the different attribute storage mechanisms described above, and the intelligent management of when each mechanism is used. We will soon see that the `StyleContext` class acts as, this intelligent manager, among other things.

19.1.14 The Style interface

abstract interface javax.swing.text.Style

The `Style` interface extends `MutableAttributeSet` and it provides the ability to attach listeners for notification of changes to its set of attributes. `Style` also adds a `String` that is used for name identification. The only direct implementation of the `Style` interface is provided by `StyleContext.NamedStyle`. Internally, `NamedStyle` maintains its own private `AttributeSet` implementation that contains all its attributes. This `AttributeSet` can be an instance of `StyleContext.SmallAttributeSet` or `SimpleAttributeSet`, and it may switch back and forth between these types over the course of its lifetime (this will become clear after our discussion of `StyleContext`).

19.1.15 StyleConstants

class javax.swing.text.StyleConstants

The StyleConstants class categorizes predefined attribute keys into members of four static inner classes: CharacterConstants, ColorConstants, FontConstants, and Paragraph-Constants. These Objects are all aliased from their outer class, StyleConstants, so they are more easily accessible (*aliasing* here means providing a reference to an object of an inner class). Also, both ColorConstants and FontConstants keys are aliased by Character-Constants to provide a sensible hierarchy of attribute key organization.

> **NOTE** Not all aliased keys use the same name in each class. For instance, FontFamily in StyledConstants is an alias of Family in StyledConstants.Character-Constants. However, Family in StyledConstants.CharacterConstants is an alias of Family (the actual key) in StyledConstants.FontConstants. Each is a reference to the same key object and it makes no difference which one we use.

The meanings of most keys are self-explanatory. The StyleConstants API documentation page contains a helpful diagram that illustrates the meaning of some of the less self-explanatory attribute keys that apply to paragraphs of styled text. (Each of the keys illustrated in this diagram is an alias of the actual key defined in StyleConstants.ParagraphConstants.)

StyleConstants also defines static methods for assigning and retrieving many predefined attributes in an AttributeSet. For example, to assign a specific font family attribute to an AttributeSet (assuming it is mutable), we can use StyleConstants' setFontFamily() method.

19.1.16 StyleContext

class javax.swing.text.StyleContext

StyleContext implements the AbstractDocument.AttributeContext interface, and it declares a set of methods that are used to modify or fetch new instances of AttributeSet implementations. AbstractContext was designed with the understanding that the implementor may use more than one type of AttributeSet implementation to store sets of attributes. The decision to use one type over another may be based on any number of factors, and StyleContext takes full advantage of this design.

StyleContext's main role is to act as a container for Styles that may be used by one or more DefaultStyledDocuments. It maintains a private NamedStyle instance that is used to store its Styles and allow access by name. Each of these contained Styles is also an instance of NamedStyle. So, to clarify, StyleContext maintains a NamedStyle instance whose key/value pairs are of the form String/NamedStyle.

StyleContext also maintains a subset of these NamedStyle values in a Hashtable. Only those NamedStyle's whose AttributeSet contains nine or fewer attributes are stored in this Hashtable and their AttributeSets are maintained as instances of SmallAttribute-Set. Those NamedStyles with an AttributeSet containing ten or more attributes are not stored in the Hashtable, and their AttributeSets are maintained as instances of Simple-AttributeSet.

This partitioning is managed dynamically by StyleContext, and it is the result of combining the AbstractContext design with the use of a *compression threshold* (a hard-coded `int` value of 9). Whenever an attribute is added or removed, `StyleContext` checks the number of attributes in the target `AttributeSet`. If the resulting set will contain nine or fewer attributes, it remains or is converted to a `SmallAttributeSet`, and it is added to the `Hashtable` if it wasn't already there. If the resulting set will contain ten or more attributes, it remains or is converted to a `SimpleAttributeSet`, and it is removed from the `Hashtable` if it was already there.

The reason for this partitioning is to support efficient `AttributeSet` sharing. Most styled documents contain many distinct regions of identically styled text. These regions normally have a small number of attributes associated with them. It is clear that the best thing to do in this situation is to assign the same `AttributeSet` to each of these regions, and the best `AttributeSet` implementation to use for this is `SmallAttributeSet` because of its superior memory efficiency, since look-up speed is a minor issue with a very small number of attributes. Larger sets of attributes are, in general, rare. The best `AttributeSet` implementation to use for this is `SimpleAttributeSet` because of its superior look-up capabilities, since memory usage will most likely be a minor issue with a relatively small number of `SimpleAttributeSet`s.

19.1.17   The Highlighter interface

abstract interface javax.swing.text.Highlighter

This interface describes how specific regions of text can be marked up with instances of the inner `Highlighter.Highlight` interface. A `Highlight` maintains a beginning and end offset, and a reference to an instance of the inner `Highlighter.HighlightPainter` interface. A `HighlightPainter`'s only responsibility is to render the background of a specific region of text.

A text component's UI delegate is responsible for maintaining its `Highlighter`. For this reason, the `Highlighter` can change when a text component's look and feel changes. `JTextComponent` provides methods for working with a text component's `Highlighter` so we generally ignore the fact that such methods really get forwarded to the UI delegate.

A `Highlighter` maintains an array of `Highlighter.Highlight` instances, and we are able to add to this array using the `addHighlight()` method. This method takes two `int`s that define the range of text to highlight, as well as a `Highlighter.HighlightPainter` instance that specifies how that `Highlight` should be rendered. Thus, by defining various `HighlightPainter`s, we can add an arbitrary number of highlighted regions with distinct visual effects.

The range a `Highlight` encompasses is modified with the `changeHighlight()` method, and `Highlight`s can be removed from a `Highlighter`'s array with the `removeAllHighlights()` or `removeHighlight()` methods. The `paint()` method manages the rendering of all of a `Highlighter`'s `Highlight`s.

We can assign a new `Highlighter` with `JTextComponent`'s `setHighlighter()` method. Similarly, we can retrieve a reference to the existing one with `JTextComponent`'s `getHighlighter()` method. Each `JTextComponent` also maintains a `selectionColor` property which specifies the color to use in rendering default highlights.

19.1.18 DefaultHighlighter

class javax.swing.text.DefaultHighlighter

`DefaultHighlighter` extends the abstract `LayeredHighlighter` class. `LayeredHighlighter` implements the `Highlighter` interface and defines a `paintLayeredHighlights()` method, which is responsible for managing potentially multiple overlapping `Highlights`. `LayeredHighlighter` also declares an inner abstract static class called `LayerPainter` from which the static `DefaultHighlighter.DefaultHighlightPainter` extends. This implementation paints a solid background behind the specified region of text, in the current text component selection color.

19.1.19 The Caret interface

abstract interface javax.swing.text.Caret

This interface describes a text component's cursor. The `paint()` method is responsible for rendering the caret, and the `setBlinkRate()` and `getBlinkRate()` methods assign and retrieve a specific caret blink interval (normally in milliseconds). The `setVisible()` and `isVisible()` methods hide/show the caret and check for caret visibility, respectively.

The `setDot()` and `getDot()` methods assign and retrieve the offset of the caret within the current document. The `getMark()` method returns a location in the document where the caret's *mark* has been assigned. The `moveDot()` method assigns a mark position, and moves the caret to a new location while highlighting the text between the dot and the mark. The `setSelectionVisible()` and `isSelectionVisible()` methods assign and query the visible state of the highlight that specifies the currently selected text.

The `setMagicCaretPosition()` and `getMagicCaretPosition()` methods manage a dynamic caret position that is used when moving the caret up and down between lines with the arrow keys. When moving up and down between lines with an unequal number of characters, the magic position places the caret as close to the same location within each line as possible. If the magic position is greater than the length of the current line, the caret is placed at the end of the line. This feature is common in almost all modern text applications, and it is implemented for us in the `DefaultCaret` class.

The `Caret` interface also declares methods for the registration of `ChangeListeners` for notification of changes in the caret's position: `addChangeListener()` and `removeChangeListener()`.

19.1.20 DefaultCaret

class javax.swing.text.DefaultCaret

This class extends `java.awt.Rectangle`, and it represents a concrete implementation of the `Caret` interface that is used by all text components by default. It is rendered as a blinking vertical line in the color specified by its associated text component's `caretColor` property. `DefaultCaret` also implements the `FocusListener`, `MouseListener`, and `MouseMotionListener` interfaces.

The only `MouseListener` methods without empty implementations are `mouseClicked()` and `mousePressed()`. If a mouse click occurs with the left mouse button, and the click count is two (it's a double-click), `mouseClicked()` will invoke the `Action` returned by DefaultEditorKit.selectWordAction() to select the word containing the caret. If the click count is three, mouseClicked() will invoke the Action returned by Default-EditorKit.selectLineAction() to select the line of text containing the caret. The mousePressed() method sends its MouseEvent parameter to DefaultCaret's position-Caret() method, which sets the dot property to the document offset corresponding to the mouse press and clears the magicCaretPosition property. The mousePressed() method also checks to see if the text component is enabled and, if it is, its requestFocus() method is invoked.

The only MouseMotionListener method without an empty implementation is mouse-Dragged(). This method simply passes its MouseEvent parameter to DefaultCaret's moveCaret() method. The moveCaret() method determines the offset of the caret destination by passing the MouseEvent's coordinates to the text component's viewToModel() method. The moveDot() method is then invoked to actually move the caret to the determined position (recall that the moveDot() method sets the mark property and selects the text between the mark position and the new dot position).

Both FocusListener methods are non-empty. The focusGained() method checks whether the text component is editable and, if it is, the caret is made visible. The focusLost() method simply hides the caret. These methods are invoked when the text component gains or loses the focus.

We can customize the way a selection's highlight appears by overriding DefaultCaret's getSelectionPainter() method to return our own Highlighter.HighlightPainter implementation. We can also customize the appearance of a caret by overriding the paint() method. If we do reimplement the paint() method, however, we must also override the damage() method. The damage() method is passed a Rectangle that represents the region of the text component to repaint when the caret is moved.

For instance, the following is a simple DefaultCaret subclass that renders a wide black caret.

```
class WideCaret extends DefaultCaret
{
  protected int caretWidth = 6;

  protected void setWidth(int w) {
    caretWidth = w;
  }

  // Since DefaultCaret extends Rectangle, it inherits
  // the x, y, width, and height variables which are
  // used here to allow proper repainting.
  protected synchronized void damage(Rectangle r) {
    if (r != null) {
      x = r.x - width;
      y = r.y;
      width = width;
      height = r.height;
      repaint();
    }
  }

  public void paint(Graphics g) {
```

```
    if(isVisible()) {
      try {
        TextUI mapper = getComponent().getUI();
        Rectangle r = mapper.modelToView(
          getComponent(), getComponent().getCaretPosition());
        g.setColor(getComponent().getCaretColor());
        g.fillRect(r.x, r.y, caretWidth, r.height - 1);
      }
      catch (Exception e) {
        System.err.println("Problem painting cursor");
      }
    }
  }
}
```

NOTE   We have implemented a short example in a Swing Connection "Tips and Tricks" article that shows you how to use a similar custom caret for designating an overwrite mode. In the same article, we also show you how to customize a `Plain-Document` model to allow insert and overwrite modes, and how to track caret position with a `CaretListener`. See http://java.sun.com/products/jfc/tsc/

19.1.21   The CaretListener interface

abstract interface javax.swing.event.CaretListener

This interface describes a listener that is notified whenever a change occurs in a text component's caret position. It declares one method, `caretUpdate()`, which takes a `CaretEvent` as a parameter. We can attach and remove `CaretListeners` to any `JTextComponent` with the `addCaretListener()` and `removeCaretListener()` methods.

19.1.22   CaretEvent

class javax.swing.event.CaretEvent

This event simply encapsulates a reference to its source object (which is normally a text component). `CaretEvents` are passed to all attached `CaretListeners` whenever the associated text component's caret position changes.

19.1.23   The Keymap interface

abstract interface javax.swing.text.Keymap

This interface describes a collection of bindings between `KeyStrokes` (see section 2.13.2) and `Actions` (see section 12.1.23). We add new `KeyStroke`/`Action` bindings to a `Keymap` with the `addActionForKeyStroke()` method. Like `AttributeSets`, `Keymaps` resolve hierarchically. Like `Styles`, `Keymaps` have a name they are referenced by.

We query the `Action` that corresponds to a specific `KeyStroke` with the `getAction()` method. If no corresponding `Action` is located in the `Keymap`, its resolving parents should be searched until either no more resolving parents exist, or a match is found. Similarly, we retrieve an array of `KeyStrokes` that are mapped to a given `Action` with the `getKeyStrokesFor-Action()` method. The `isLocallyDefined()` method checks whether a given `KeyStroke` is bound to an `Action` in the `Keymap` that is under investigation. The `removeBindings()` method removes all bindings in a `Keymap`, and the `removeKeyStrokeBinding()` method removes only those bindings corresponding to a given `KeyStroke`.

By default, all `JTextComponents` share the same `Keymap` instance. This is what enables the default functionality of the Backspace, Delete, and left and right arrow keys on any text component. For this reason, it is not a good idea to retrieve a text component's `Keymap` and modify it directly. Rather, we are encouraged to create our own `Keymap` instance and assign the default `Keymap` as its resolving parent. By assigning a resolving parent of `null`, we can effectively disable all bindings on a text component, other than those in the given component's `Keymap` itself (the underlying role `Keymaps` play in text components will become clear after we discuss `DefaultEditorKit`, below).

We can obtain a text component's `Keymap` with either of `JTextComponent`'s `getKeymap()` methods. We can assign a text component a new `Keymap` with the `setKeymap()` method, and we can add a new `Keymap` anywhere within the `Keymap` hierarchy with the `addKeymap()` method. We can also remove a `Keymap` from the hierarchy with the `removeKeymap()` method.

For example, to create and add a new `Keymap` to a `JTextField` and use the default text component `Keymap` as a resolving parent, we might do something like the following:

```
Keymap keymap = myJTextField.getKeymap();
Keymap myKeymap = myJTextField.addKeymap("MyKeymap", keymap);
```

We can then add `KeyStroke`/`Action` pairs to `myKeymap` with the `addActionForKeyStroke()` method (we will see an example of this in the next section).

NOTE Recall from section 2.13.4 that `KeyListeners` will receive key events before a text component's `Keymap`. Although using `Keymaps` is encouraged, handling keyboard events with `KeyListeners` is still allowed.

19.1.24 TextAction

abstract class javax.swing.text.TextAction

`EditorKits` are, among other things, responsible for making a set of `Actions` available for performing common text editor functions based on a given content type. `EditorKits` normally use inner subclasses of `TextAction` for this, as it extends `AbstractAction` (see section 12.1.24), and provides a relatively powerful means of determining the target component to invoke the action on (by taking advantage of the fact that `JTextComponent` keeps track of the most recent text component with the focus, retrievable with its static `getFocusedComponent()` method). The `TextAction` constructor takes the `String` to be used as that action's name, and passes it to its super-class constructor. When subclassing `TextAction`, we normally define an `actionPerformed()` method, which performs the desired action when it is passed an `ActionEvent`. Within this method, we can use `TextAction`'s `getText-Component()` method to determine which text component the action should be invoked on.

19.1.25 EditorKit

abstract class javax.swing.text.EditorKit

EditorKits are responsible for the following functionality:

- Support for an appropriate Document model. An EditorKit specifically supports one type of content, a String description of which is retrievable with the getContent-Type() method. A corresponding Document instance is returned by the create-DefaultDocument() method, and the EditorKit is able to read() and write() that Document to InputStreams/OutputStreams and Readers/Writers, respectively.

- Support for View production through a ViewFactory implementation. This behavior is actually optional, as View production will default to a text component's UI delegate if its EditorKit's getViewFactory() method returns null (see sections 19.1.28 and 19.1.29 for more about Views and the ViewFactory interface).

- Support for a set of Actions that can be invoked on a text component using the appropriate Document. Normally these Actions are instances of TextAction and are defined as inner classes. An EditorKit's Actions can be retrieved in an array with its getActions() method.

19.1.26 DefaultEditorKit

class javax.swing.text.DefaultEditorKit

DefaultEditorKit extends EditorKit, and it defines a series of TextAction subclasses and corresponding name Strings (see the API documentation). Eight of these forty-six inner action classes are public, and they can be instantiated with a default constructor: BeepAction, Copy-Action, CutAction, DefaultKeyTypedAction, InsertBreakAction, InsertContent-Action, InsertTabAction, and PasteAction. DefaultEditorKit maintains instances of all its inner Action classes in an array that can be retrieved with its getActions() method. We can access any of these Actions easily by defining a Hashtable with Action.NAME keys and Action values. See *Java Swing* by Robert Eckstein, Marc Loy, and Dave Wood, O'Reilly & Associates, 1998, p. 918.

```
Hashtable actionTable = new Hashtable
Action[] actions = myEditorKit.getActions();
for (int i=0; i < actions.length; i++) {
  String actionName = (String) actions[i].getValue(Action.NAME);
  actionTable.put(actionName, actions[i]);
}
```

We can then retrieve any of these Actions with DefaultEditorKit's static String fields. For example, the following code retrieves the action that is responsible for selecting all text in a document:

```
Action selectAll = (Action) actionTable.get(
  DefaultEditorKit.selectAllAction);
```

These Actions can be used in menus and toolbars, or with other controls, for convenient control of plain text components.

DefaultEditorKit's getViewFactory() method returns null, which means the UI delegate is responsible for creating the hierarchy of Views necessary for rendering a text component correctly. As we mentioned in the beginning of this chapter, JTextField, JPasswordField, and JTextArea all use a DefaultEditorKit.

Although EditorKits are responsible for managing a set of Actions and their corresponding names, they are not actually directly responsible for making these Actions accessible to specific text components. This is where Keymaps fit in. For instance, take a look at the following code that shows how the default JTextComponent Keymap is created (this is from JTextComponent.java):

```
/**
 * This is the name of the default keymap that will be shared by all
 * JTextComponent instances unless they have had a different
 * keymap set.
 */
public static final String DEFAULT_KEYMAP = "default";

/**
 * Default bindings for the default keymap if no other bindings
 * are given.
 */
static final KeyBinding[] defaultBindings = {
  new KeyBinding(KeyStroke.getKeyStroke(KeyEvent.VK_BACK_SPACE, 0),
    DefaultEditorKit.deletePrevCharAction),
  new KeyBinding(KeyStroke.getKeyStroke(KeyEvent.VK_DELETE, 0),
    DefaultEditorKit.deleteNextCharAction),
  new KeyBinding(KeyStroke.getKeyStroke(KeyEvent.VK_RIGHT, 0),
    DefaultEditorKit.forwardAction),
  new KeyBinding(KeyStroke.getKeyStroke(KeyEvent.VK_LEFT, 0),
    DefaultEditorKit.backwardAction)
};

static {
  try {
    keymapTable = new Hashtable(17);
    Keymap binding = addKeymap(DEFAULT_KEYMAP, null);
    binding.setDefaultAction(new
      DefaultEditorKit.DefaultKeyTypedAction());
    EditorKit kit = new DefaultEditorKit();
    loadKeymap(binding, defaultBindings, kit.getActions());
  } catch (Throwable e) {
    e.printStackTrace();
    keymapTable = new Hashtable(17);
  }
}
```

19.1.27 StyledEditorKit

class javax.swing.text.StyledEditorKit

This class extends DefaultEditorKit and defines seven additional inner Action classes, each of which is publicly accessible: AlignmentAction, BoldAction, FontFamilyAction,

FontSizeAction, ForegroundAction, ItalicAction, and UnderlineAction. All seven Actions are subclasses of the inner StyledTextAction convenience class which extends TextAction.

Each of StyledEditorKit's Actions applies to styled text documents, and they are used by JEditorPane and JTextPane. StyledEditorKit does not define its own capabilities for reading and writing styled text. Instead, this functionality is inherited from Default-EditorKit, which only provides support for saving and loading plain text. The two StyledEditorKit subclasses included with Swing, javax.swing.text.html.HTML-EditorKit and javax.swing.text.rtf.RTFEditorKit, do support styled text saving and loading for HTML and RTF content types respectively.

StyledEditorKit's getViewFactory() method returns an instance of a private static inner class called StyledViewFactory which implements the ViewFactory interface as follows (this is from StyledEditorKit.java):

```
static class StyledViewFactory implements ViewFactory {
  public View create(Element elem) {
    String kind = elem.getName();
  if (kind != null) {
    if (kind.equals(AbstractDocument.ContentElementName)) {
        return new LabelView(elem);
    } else if (kind.equals(AbstractDocument.ParagraphElementName)) {
      return new ParagraphView(elem);
    } else if (kind.equals(AbstractDocument.SectionElementName)) {
      return new BoxView(elem, View.Y_AXIS);
    } else if (kind.equals(StyleConstants.ComponentElementName)) {
      return new ComponentView(elem);
    } else if (kind.equals(StyleConstants.IconElementName)) {
      return new IconView(elem);
    }
  }
  // Default to text display
  return new LabelView(elem);
 }
}
```

The Views returned by this factory's create() method are based on the name property of the Element that is passed as a parameter. If an Element is not recognized, a LabelView is returned. In summary, because StyledEditorKit's getViewFactory() method doesn't return null, styled text components depend on their EditorKits rather than their UI delegatesfor providing Views. The opposite is true with plain text components, which rely on their UI delegates for View creation.

19.1.28 View

abstract class javax.swing.text.View

This class describes an object that is responsible for graphically representing a portion of a text component's document model. The text package includes several extensions of this class that are meant to be used by various types of Elements. We will not discuss these classes in detail, but a brief overview will be enough to provide a high-level understanding of how text components are actually rendered.

We have only included the most commonly used set of text component Views in this list. Several others are responsible for significant text-rendering functionality. See the O'Reilly book listed in the bibliography, and the API documentation for details.

- abstract interface TabableView: Used by Views whose size depends on the size of the tabs.
- abstract interface TabExpander: Extends TabableView and is used by Views that support TabStops and TabSets (a set of TabStops). A TabStop describes the positioning of a tab character and the text appearing immediately after it.
- class ComponentView: Used as a gateway View to a fully interactive embedded Component.
- class IconView: Used as a gateway View to an embedded Icon.
- class PlainView: Used for rendering one line of non-wrapped text with one font and one color.
- class FieldView: Extends PlainView and adds specialized functionality for representing a single-line editor view (such as the ability to center text in a JTextField).
- class PasswordView: Extends FieldView and adds the ability to render its content using the echo character of the associated component if it is a JPasswordField.
- class LabelView: Used to render a range of styled text.
- abstract class CompositeView: A View containing multiple child Views. All Views can contain child Views, but only instances of CompositeView and BasicTextUI's RootView (discussed below) actually contain child Views by default.
- class BoxView: Extends CompositeView and arranges a group of child Views in a rectangular box.
- class ParagraphView: Extends BoxView and is responsible for rendering a paragraph of styled text. ParagraphView is made up of a number of child Elements organized as, or within, Views representing single rows of styled text. This View supports line wrapping, and if an Element within the content paragraph spans multiple lines, more than one View will be used to represent it.
- class WrappedPlainView: Extends BoxView and is responsible for rendering multi-line, plain text with line wrapping.

JAVA 1.3 In Java 1.3 the new AsynchBoxView has been added which performs view layout asynchronously so that layout occurs without blocking the event dispatching thread. This is particularly useful when loading large documents and/or documents being loaded through a slow connection (such as an HTML document).

Also new to Java 1.3 is a ZoneView class which acts as a placeholder for actual View objects until they are needed. With large documents there are potentially a large number of Views that can demand an equally large amount of memory. To address this the Swing team has created the low-footprint ZoneView class to represent actual Views until they are needed (i.e., until that portion of the document is made visible).

All text components in Swing use UI delegates derived from BasicTextUI by default. This class defines an inner class called RootView which acts as a gateway between a text component and the actual View hierarchy used to render it.

19.1.29 The ViewFactory interface

abstract interface javax.swing.text.ViewFactory

This interface declares one method: `create(Element elem)`. This method returns a `Tom View` (which possibly contains a hierarchy of `View`s) that is used to render a given `Element`. `BasicTextUI` implements this interface, and unless a text component's `Editor-Kit` provides its own `ViewFactory`, `BasicTextUI`'s `create()` method will provide all `View`s. This is the case with the plain text components: `JTextField`, `JPasswordField`, and `JTextArea`. However, the styled text components, `JEditorPane` and `JTextPane`, vary greatly depending on their current content type. For this reason their `View`s are provided by the currently installed `EditorKit`. In this way, custom `View`s can render different types of styled content.

C H A P T E R   2 0

Constructing an HTML Editor Application

This chapter is devoted to the construction of a fully functional HTML editor application. The examples in this chapter demonstrate practical applications of many of the topics covered in chapter 19. The main focus throughout is working with styled text documents, and the techniques discussed here can be applied to almost any styled text editor.

NOTE   Chapter 20 in the first edition of this book was titled "Constructing a word processor" and was devoted to the construction of a fully functional RTF word processor application. This chapter and examples from the first edition remain freely available at www.manning.com/sbe.

20.1 HTML EDITOR, PART I: INTRODUCING HTML

In this section we introduce an example demonstrating the use of JTextPane and HTML-EditorKit to display and edit HTML documents. The following features are included:

- Creating a new HTML document
- Opening an existing HTML document
- Saving changes
- Saving the document under a new name/location
- Prompting the user to save changes before loading a new document or exiting the application

This example serves as the foundation for our HTML editor application that will be expanded upon throughout this chapter.

NOTE   The Swing HTML package supports HTML 3.2 but not 4.0. Support for 4.0 has been deferred to a future release of J2SE.

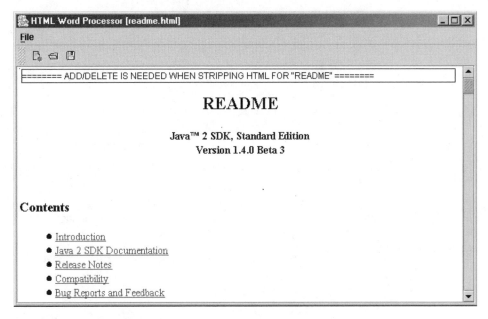

Figure 20.1   JTextPane displaying an HTML document

Example 20.1

HtmlProcessor.java

see \Chapter20\1

```
import java.awt.*;
import java.awt.event.*;
import java.io.*;
import java.util.*;
```

```java
import javax.swing.*;
import javax.swing.text.*;
import javax.swing.event.*;
import javax.swing.border.*;
import javax.swing.text.html.*;

public class HtmlProcessor extends JFrame {

    public static final String APP_NAME = "HTML Word Processor";

    protected JTextPane m_editor;
    protected StyleSheet m_context;
    protected HTMLDocument m_doc;
    protected HTMLEditorKit m_kit;
    protected SimpleFilter m_htmlFilter;
    protected JToolBar m_toolBar;

    protected JFileChooser m_chooser;
    protected File m_currentFile;

    protected boolean m_textChanged = false;

    public HtmlProcessor() {
        super(APP_NAME);
        setSize(650, 400);

        m_editor = new JTextPane();
        m_kit = new HTMLEditorKit();
        m_editor.setEditorKit(m_kit);

        JScrollPane ps = new JScrollPane(m_editor);
        getContentPane().add(ps, BorderLayout.CENTER);

        JMenuBar menuBar = createMenuBar();
        setJMenuBar(menuBar);

        m_chooser = new JFileChooser();
        m_htmlFilter = new SimpleFilter("html", "HTML Documents");
        m_chooser.setFileFilter(m_htmlFilter);
        try {
            File dir = (new File(".")).getCanonicalFile();
            m_chooser.setCurrentDirectory(dir);
        } catch (IOException ex) {}

        newDocument();

        WindowListener wndCloser = new WindowAdapter() {
            public void windowClosing(WindowEvent e) {
                if (!promptToSave())
                    return;
                System.exit(0);
            }
            public void windowActivated(WindowEvent e) {
                m_editor.requestFocus();
            }
        };
        addWindowListener(wndCloser);
    }
```

❶ Ensure user has opportunity to save changes before closing

```java
protected JMenuBar createMenuBar() {
  JMenuBar menuBar = new JMenuBar();

  JMenu mFile = new JMenu("File");
  mFile.setMnemonic('f');

  ImageIcon iconNew = new ImageIcon("New16.gif");
  Action actionNew = new AbstractAction("New", iconNew) {
    public void actionPerformed(ActionEvent e) {
      if (!promptToSave())
        return;
      newDocument();
    }
  };
  JMenuItem item = new JMenuItem(actionNew);
  item.setMnemonic('n');
  item.setAccelerator(KeyStroke.getKeyStroke(
    KeyEvent.VK_N, InputEvent.Ctrl_MASK));
  mFile.add(item);

  ImageIcon iconOpen = new ImageIcon("Open16.gif");
  Action actionOpen = new AbstractAction("Open...", iconOpen) {
    public void actionPerformed(ActionEvent e) {
      if (!promptToSave())
        return;
      openDocument();
    }
  };
  item = new JMenuItem(actionOpen);
  item.setMnemonic('o');
  item.setAccelerator(KeyStroke.getKeyStroke(
    KeyEvent.VK_O, InputEvent.Ctrl_MASK));
  mFile.add(item);

  ImageIcon iconSave = new ImageIcon("Save16.gif");
  Action actionSave = new AbstractAction("Save", iconSave) {
    public void actionPerformed(ActionEvent e) {
      saveFile(false);
    }
  };
  item = new JMenuItem(actionSave);
  item.setMnemonic('s');
  item.setAccelerator(KeyStroke.getKeyStroke(
    KeyEvent.VK_S, InputEvent.Ctrl_MASK));
  mFile.add(item);

  ImageIcon iconSaveAs = new ImageIcon("SaveAs16.gif");
  Action actionSaveAs =
  new AbstractAction("Save As...", iconSaveAs) {
    public void actionPerformed(ActionEvent e) {
      saveFile(true);
    }
  };
  item = new JMenuItem(actionSaveAs);
```

❷ Creates a menu bar with New, Open, Save, Save As, and Exit menu items

```
    item.setMnemonic('a');
    mFile.add(item);

    mFile.addSeparator();

    Action actionExit = new AbstractAction("Exit") {
      public void actionPerformed(ActionEvent e) {
        System.exit(0);
      }
    };

    item =mFile.add(actionExit);
    item.setMnemonic('x');
    menuBar.add(mFile);

    m_toolBar = new JToolBar();
    JButton bNew = new SmallButton(actionNew,
      "New document");
    m_toolBar.add(bNew);

    JButton bOpen = new SmallButton(actionOpen,
      "Open HTML document");
    m_toolBar.add(bOpen);

    JButton bSave = new SmallButton(actionSave,
      "Save HTML document");
    m_toolBar.add(bSave);

    getContentPane().add(m_toolBar, BorderLayout.NORTH);

    return menuBar;
  }

  protected String getDocumentName() {
    return m_currentFile==null ? "Untitled" :
      m_currentFile.getName();
  }

  protected void newDocument() {
    m_doc = (HTMLDocument)m_kit.createDefaultDocument();
    m_context = m_doc.getStyleSheet();

    m_editor.setDocument(m_doc);
    m_currentFile = null;
    setTitle(APP_NAME+" ["+getDocumentName()+"]");

    SwingUtilities.invokeLater(new Runnable() {
      public void run() {
        m_editor.scrollRectToVisible(new Rectangle(0,0,1,1));
        m_doc.addDocumentListener(new UpdateListener());
        m_textChanged = false;
      }
    });
  }

  protected void openDocument() {
    if (m_chooser.showOpenDialog(HtmlProcessor.this) !=
      JFileChooser.APPROVE_OPTION)
```

❸ Returns name of current file

❹ Creates new HTML document

❺ Uses JFileChooser and FileInputStream to read in an HTML file

```
      return;
   File f = m_chooser.getSelectedFile();
   if (f == null || !f.isFile())
      return;
   m_currentFile = f;
   setTitle(APP_NAME+" ["+getDocumentName()+"]");

   HtmlProcessor.this.setCursor(
      Cursor.getPredefinedCursor(Cursor.WAIT_CURSOR));

   try {
      InputStream in = new FileInputStream(m_currentFile);
      m_doc = (HTMLDocument)m_kit.createDefaultDocument();
      m_kit.read(in, m_doc, 0);
      m_context = m_doc.getStyleSheet();
      m_editor.setDocument(m_doc);
      in.close();
   }
   catch (Exception ex) {
      showError(ex, "Error reading file "+m_currentFile);
   }
   HtmlProcessor.this.setCursor(Cursor.getPredefinedCursor(
      Cursor.DEFAULT_CURSOR));

   SwingUtilities.invokeLater(new Runnable() {
      public void run() {
         m_editor.setCaretPosition(1);
         m_editor.scrollRectToVisible(new Rectangle(0,0,1,1));
         m_doc.addDocumentListener(new UpdateListener());
         m_textChanged = false;
      }
   });
}

protected boolean saveFile(boolean saveAs) {
   if (!saveAs && !m_textChanged)
      return true;
   if (saveAs || m_currentFile == null) {
      if (m_chooser.showSaveDialog(HtmlProcessor.this) !=
         JFileChooser.APPROVE_OPTION)
         return false;
      File f = m_chooser.getSelectedFile();
      if (f == null)
         return false;
      m_currentFile = f;
      setTitle(APP_NAME+" ["+getDocumentName()+"]");
   }

   HtmlProcessor.this.setCursor(
      Cursor.getPredefinedCursor(Cursor.WAIT_CURSOR));
   try {
      OutputStream out = new FileOutputStream(m_currentFile);
      m_kit.write(out, m_doc, 0, m_doc.getLength());
      out.close();
```

⑥ Uses JFileChooser and FileOutputStream to save current document to file

```
      m_textChanged = false;
    }
    catch (Exception ex) {
      showError(ex, "Error saving file "+m_currentFile);
    }
    HtmlProcessor.this.setCursor(Cursor.getPredefinedCursor(
      Cursor.DEFAULT_CURSOR));
    return true;
  }

  protected boolean promptToSave() {
    if (!m_textChanged)
      return true;
    int result = JOptionPane.showConfirmDialog(this,
      "Save changes to "+getDocumentName()+"?",
      APP_NAME, JOptionPane.YES_NO_CANCEL_OPTION,
      JOptionPane.INFORMATION_MESSAGE);
    switch (result) {
    case JOptionPane.YES_OPTION:
      if (!saveFile(false))
        return false;
      return true;
    case JOptionPane.NO_OPTION:
      return true;
    case JOptionPane.CANCEL_OPTION:
      return false;
    }
    return true;
  }

  public void showError(Exception ex, String message) {
    ex.printStackTrace();
    JOptionPane.showMessageDialog(this,
      message, APP_NAME,
      JOptionPane.WARNING_MESSAGE);
  }

  public static void main(String argv[]) {
    JFrame.setDefaultLookAndFeelDecorated(true);
    JDialog.setDefaultLookAndFeelDecorated(true);

    HtmlProcessor frame = new HtmlProcessor();
    frame.setDefaultCloseOperation(JFrame.DO_NOTHING_ON_CLOSE);
    frame.setVisible(true);
  }

  class UpdateListener implements DocumentListener {

    public void insertUpdate(DocumentEvent e) {
      m_textChanged = true;
    }

    public void removeUpdate(DocumentEvent e) {
      m_textChanged = true;
    }
```

7 Prompts user to save

8 Displays error messages in dialogs

9 Used to change the flag which indicates whether a document has been modified

```
        public void changedUpdate(DocumentEvent e) {
            m_textChanged = true;
        }
    }
}

// Class SmallButton unchanged from section 12.4

// Class SimpleFilter unchanged from section 14.1.9
```

20.1.1   Understanding the code

Class HtmlProcessor

This class extends `JFrame` to provide the supporting frame for this example. Several instance variables are declared:

- `JTextPane m_editor`: main text component.
- `StyleContext m_context`: a group of styles and their associated resources for the documents in this example.
- `HTMLDocument m_doc`: current document model.
- `HTMLEditorKit m_kit`: editor kit that knows how to read/write HTML documents.
- `SimpleFilter m_HTMLFilter`: file filter for ".HTML" files.
- `JToolBar m_toolBar`: toolbar containing New, Open, Save buttons.
- `JFileChooser m_chooser`: file chooser used to load and save HTML files.
- `File m_currentFile`: currently opened HTML file (if any).
- `boolean m_textChanged`: keeps track of whether any changes have been made since the document was last saved.

The `HtmlProcessor` constructor first instantiates our `JTextPane` and `HTMLEditorKit`, and assigns the editor kit to the text pane (it is important that this is done before any documents are created). The editor component is then placed in a `JScrollPane` which is placed in the center of the frame. The `JFileChooser` component is created and an instance of our `Simple-Filter` class (developed in chapter 14) is used as a filter to only allow the choice of HTML documents. A `WindowListener` is added to call our custom `promptToSave()` method to ensure that the user has the opportunity to save any changes before closing the application. This `WindowListener` also ensures that our editor component automatically receives the focus when this application regains the focus.

The `createMenuBar()` method creates a menu bar with a single menu titled "File" and a toolbar with three buttons. Actions for New, Open, Save, Save As, and Exit are created and added to the File menu. The New, Open, and Save actions are also added to the toolbar. This code is very similar to the code used in the examples of chapter 12. The important difference is that we use `InputStreams` and `OutputStreams` rather than `Readers` and `Writers`. The reason for this is that HTML uses 1-byte encoding which is incompatible with the 2-byte encoding used by readers and writers.

The `getDocumentName()` method simply returns the name of the file corresponding to the current document, or untitled if it hasn't been saved to disk.

The `newDocument()` method is responsible for creating a new `HTMLDocument` instance using `HTMLEditorKit`'s `createDefaultDocument()` method. Once created our `StyleContext` variable, m_context, is assiged to this new document's stylesheet with HTMLDocument's get-StyleSheet() method. The title of the frame is then updated and a Runnable instance is created and sent to the SwingUtilities.invokeLater() method to scroll the document to the beginning when it is finished loading. Finally, an instance of our custom UpdateListener class is added as a DocumentListener, and the m_textChanged variable is set to false to indicate that no changes to the document have been made yet.

5 The openDocument() is similar to the newDocument() method but uses the JFileChooser to allow selection of an existing HTML file to load, and uses an InputStream object to read the contents of that file.

6 The saveFile() method takes a boolean parameter specifying whether the method should act as a Save As process or just a regular Save. If true, indicating a Save As process, the JFileChooser is displayed to allow the user to specify the file and location to save the document to. An OutputStream is used to write the contents of the document to the destination File.

7 The promptToSave() method checks the m_textChanged flag and, if true, displays a JOptionPaneasking whether or not the current document should be saved. This method is called before a new document is created, a document is opened, or the application is closed to ensure that the user has a chance to save any changes to the current document before losing them.

8 The showError() method is used to display error messages in a JOptionPane. It is often useful to display exceptions to users so that they know an error happened and so that they may eventually report errors back to you if they are in fact bugs.

Class UpdateListener

9 This DocumentListener subclass is used to modify the state of our m_textChanged variable. Whenever an insertion, removal, or document change is made this variable is set to true. This allows HtmlProcessor's promptToSave() method to ensure the user has the option of saving any changes before loading a new document or exiting the application.

20.1.2 Running the code

Figure 20.1 shows our HTML editor in action. Use menu or toolbar buttons to open an HTML file. Save the HTML file and open it in another HTML-aware application (such as Netscape) to verify compatibility. Try modifying a document and exiting the application before saving it. Note the dialog that is displayed asking whether or not you'd like to save the changes you've made before exiting.

20.2 *HTML EDITOR, PART II: MANAGING FONTS*

The following example adds the ability to:
- Select any font available on the system
- Change font size
- Select bold and italic characteristics

This functionality is similar to the font functionality used in the examples of chapter 12. The important difference here is that the selected font applies not to the whole text component (the only possible thing with plain text documents), but to the selected region of our HTML–styled document text.

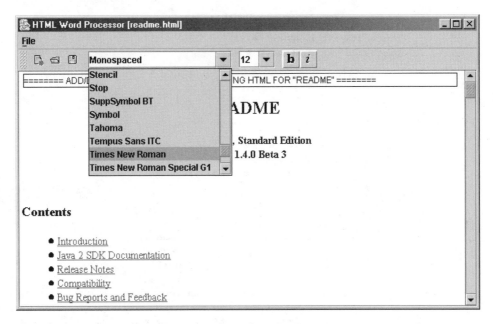

Figure 20.2   JTextPane word processor allowing font attribute assignments to selected text

Example 20.2

HtmlProcessor.java

see \Chapter20\2

```java
import java.awt.*;
import java.awt.event.*;
import java.io.*;
import java.util.*;

import javax.swing.*;
import javax.swing.text.*;
import javax.swing.event.*;
import javax.swing.border.*;
import javax.swing.text.html.*;

public class HtmlProcessor extends JFrame {

// Unchanged code from example 20.1

  protected JComboBox m_cbFonts;
  protected JComboBox m_cbSizes;
  protected SmallToggleButton m_bBold;
  protected SmallToggleButton m_bItalic;

  protected String m_fontName = "";
  protected int m_fontSize = 0;
```

```
    protected boolean m_skipUpdate;

    protected int m_xStart = -1;
    protected int m_xFinish = -1;

    public HtmlProcessor() {
       super(APP_NAME);
       setSize(650, 400);

// Unchanged code from example 20.1

       CaretListener lst = new CaretListener() {
          public void caretUpdate(CaretEvent e) {
             showAttributes(e.getDot());
          }
       };
       m_editor.addCaretListener(lst);

       FocusListener flst = new FocusListener() {
          public void focusGained(FocusEvent e) {
             int len = m_editor.getDocument().getLength();
             if (m_xStart>=0 && m_xFinish>=0 &&
               m_xStart<len && m_xFinish<len)
               if (m_editor.getCaretPosition()==m_xStart) {
                  m_editor.setCaretPosition(m_xFinish);
                  m_editor.moveCaretPosition(m_xStart);
               }
               else
                  m_editor.select(m_xStart, m_xFinish);
          }

          public void focusLost(FocusEvent e) {
             m_xStart = m_editor.getSelectionStart();
             m_xFinish = m_editor.getSelectionEnd();
          }
       };
       m_editor.addFocusListener(flst);

       newDocument();

       // Unchanged code from example 20.1
    }

    protected JMenuBar createMenuBar() {
       JMenuBar menuBar = new JMenuBar();

       // Unchanged code from example 20.1

       GraphicsEnvironment ge = GraphicsEnvironment.
         getLocalGraphicsEnvironment();
       String[] fontNames = ge.getAvailableFontFamilyNames();

       m_toolBar.addSeparator();
       m_cbFonts = new JComboBox(fontNames);
       m_cbFonts.setMaximumSize(new Dimension(200, 23));
       m_cbFonts.setEditable(true);
```

❶ Caret listener used to update toolbar state when caret moves

❷ Focus listener to save and restore the caret position when selection occurs in another text component

❸ Get complete list of available font names

❹ New font choice combo box

```
ActionListener lst = new ActionListener() {
   public void actionPerformed(ActionEvent e) {
      m_fontName = m_cbFonts.getSelectedItem().toString();
      MutableAttributeSet attr = new SimpleAttributeSet();
      StyleConstants.setFontFamily(attr, m_fontName);
      setAttributeSet(attr);
      m_editor.grabFocus();
   }
};
m_cbFonts.addActionListener(lst);
m_toolBar.add(m_cbFonts);

m_toolBar.addSeparator();
m_cbSizes = new JComboBox(new String[] {"8", "9", "10",
   "11", "12", "14", "16", "18", "20", "22", "24", "26",
   "28", "36", "48", "72"});
m_cbSizes.setMaximumSize(new Dimension(50, 23));
m_cbSizes.setEditable(true);

lst = new ActionListener() {
   public void actionPerformed(ActionEvent e) {
      int fontSize = 0;
      try {
         fontSize = Integer.parseInt(m_cbSizes.
            getSelectedItem().toString());
      }
      catch (NumberFormatException ex) { return; }

      m_fontSize = fontSize;
      MutableAttributeSet attr = new SimpleAttributeSet();
      StyleConstants.setFontSize(attr, fontSize);
      setAttributeSet(attr);
      m_editor.grabFocus();
   }
};
m_cbSizes.addActionListener(lst);
m_toolBar.add(m_cbSizes);

m_toolBar.addSeparator();
ImageIcon img1 = new ImageIcon("Bold16.gif");
m_bBold = new SmallToggleButton(false, img1, img1,
   "Bold font");
lst = new ActionListener() {
   public void actionPerformed(ActionEvent e) {
      MutableAttributeSet attr = new SimpleAttributeSet();
      StyleConstants.setBold(attr, m_bBold.isSelected());
      setAttributeSet(attr);
      m_editor.grabFocus();
   }
};
m_bBold.addActionListener(lst);
m_toolBar.add(m_bBold);
```

Applies new font to selected text ❺

New font sizes combo box ❻

Applies new font size to selected text ❻

Toggle button to manage bold property ❼

```
      img1 = new ImageIcon("Italic16.gif");
      m_bItalic = new SmallToggleButton(false, img1, img1,
        "Italic font");
      lst = new ActionListener() {
        public void actionPerformed(ActionEvent e) {
          MutableAttributeSet attr = new SimpleAttributeSet();
          StyleConstants.setItalic(attr, m_bItalic.isSelected());
          setAttributeSet(attr);
          m_editor.grabFocus();
        }
      };
      m_bItalic.addActionListener(lst);
      m_toolBar.add(m_bItalic);

      getContentPane().add(m_toolBar, BorderLayout.NORTH);

      return menuBar;
}
```

Toggle button to manage italic property ❺

```
// Unchanged code from example 20.1

protected void newDocument() {
  // Unchanged code from example 20.1

    SwingUtilities.invokeLater(new Runnable() {
      public void run() {
        showAttributes(0);
        m_editor.scrollRectToVisible(new Rectangle(0,0,1,1));
        m_doc.addDocumentListener(new UpdateListener());
        m_textChanged = false;
      }
    });
}

protected void openDocument() {
  // Unchanged code from example 20.1

    SwingUtilities.invokeLater(new Runnable() {
      public void run() {
        m_editor.setCaretPosition(1);
        showAttributes(1);
        m_editor.scrollRectToVisible(new Rectangle(0,0,1,1));
        m_doc.addDocumentListener(new UpdateListener());
        m_textChanged = false;
      }
    });
}

// Unchanged code from example 20.1

protected void showAttributes(int p) {
  m_skipUpdate = true;
  AttributeSet attr = m_doc.getCharacterElement(p).
    getAttributes();
  String name = StyleConstants.getFontFamily(attr);
  if (!m_fontName.equals(name)) {
```

❽ Sets state of toolbar buttons based on position of caret

```
        m_fontName = name;
        m_cbFonts.setSelectedItem(name);
      }
      int size = StyleConstants.getFontSize(attr);
      if (m_fontSize != size) {
        m_fontSize = size;
        m_cbSizes.setSelectedItem(Integer.toString(m_fontSize));
      }
      boolean bold = StyleConstants.isBold(attr);
      if (bold != m_bBold.isSelected())
        m_bBold.setSelected(bold);
      boolean italic = StyleConstants.isItalic(attr);
      if (italic != m_bItalic.isSelected())
        m_bItalic.setSelected(italic);
      m_skipUpdate = false;
    }

    protected void setAttributeSet(AttributeSet attr) {
      if (m_skipUpdate)
        return;
      int xStart = m_editor.getSelectionStart();
      int xFinish = m_editor.getSelectionEnd();
      if (!m_editor.hasFocus()) {
        xStart = m_xStart;
        xFinish = m_xFinish;
      }
      if (xStart != xFinish) {
        m_doc.setCharacterAttributes(xStart, xFinish - xStart,
          attr, false);
      }
      else {
        MutableAttributeSet inputAttributes =
          m_kit.getInputAttributes();
        inputAttributes.addAttributes(attr);
      }
    }

  public static void main(String argv[]) {
    HtmlProcessor frame = new HtmlProcessor();
    frame.setDefaultCloseOperation(JFrame.DO_NOTHING_ON_CLOSE);
    frame.setVisible(true);
  }

  // Unchanged code from example 20.1
}

// Unchanged code from example 20.1

// Class SmallToggleButton unchanged from section 12.4
```

❾ Used to assign a given set of attributes to currently selected text

20.2.1 Understanding the code

Class HtmlProcessor

Several new instance variables have been added:

- JComboBox m_cbFonts: toolbar component to select the font name.
- JComboBox m_cbSizes: toolbar component to select the font size.
- SmallToggleButton m_bBold: toolbar component to select the bold font style.
- SmallToggleButton m_bItalic: toolbar component to select the italic font style.
- String m_fontName: current font name.
- int m_fontSize: current font size.
- boolean m_skipUpdate: flag used to skip word processor update (see below).
- int m_xStart: used to store the selection start position.
- int m_xFinish: used to store the selection end position.

1 The HtmlProcessor constructor adds a CaretListener to our m_editor text pane. The caretUpdate() method of this listener is invoked whenever the caret position is changed. caretUpdate() calls our showAttributes() method to update the toolbar component's states to display the currently selected font attributes.

2 A FocusListener is also added to our m_editor component. The two methods of this listener, focusGained() and focusLost(), will be invoked when the editor gains and loses the focus respectively. The purpose of this implementation is to save and restore the starting and end positions of the text selection. The reason we do this is because Swing supports only one text selection at any given time. This means that if the user selects some text in the editor component to modify its attributes, and then goes off and makes a text selection in some other component, the original text selection will disappear. This can potentially be very annoying to the user. To fix this problem we save the selection before the editor component loses the focus. When the focus is gained we restore the previously saved selection. We distinguish between two possible situations: when the caret is located at the beginning of the selection and when it is located at the end of the selection. In the first case we position the caret at the end of the stored interval with the setCaretPosition() method, and then move the caret backward to the beginning of the stored interval with the moveCaretPosition() method. The second situation is easily handled using the select() method.

4 The createMenuBar() method creates new components to manage font properties for the selected text interval. First, the m_cbFonts combo box is used to select the font family name. Unlike the example in chapter 12, which used several predefined font names, this example uses all fonts available to the user's system. A complete list of the available font names can be

3 obtained through the getAvailableFontFamilyNames() method of GraphicsEnvironment (see section 2.8). Also note that the editable property of this combo box component is set to true, so the font name can be both selected from the drop-down list and entered in by hand.

5 Once a new font name is selected, it is applied to the selected text through the use of an attached ActionListener. The selected font family name is assigned to a SimpleAttributeSet instance with the StyleConstants.setFontFamily() method. Then our custom setAttributeSet() method is called to modify the attributes of the selected text according to this SimpleAttributeSet.

6 The `m_cbSizes` combo box is used to select the font size. It is initiated with a set of pre-defined sizes. The `editable` property is set to `true` so the font size can be both selected from the drop-down list and entered by hand. Once a new font size is selected, it is applied to the selected text through the use of an attached `ActionListener`. The setup is similar to that used for the `m_cbFonts` component. The `StyleConstants.setFontSize()` method is used to set the font size. Our custom `setAttributeSet()` method is then used to apply this attribute set to the selected text.

7 The bold and italic properties are managed by two `SmallToggleButtons` (a custom button class we developed in chapter 12): `m_bBold` and `m_bItalic` respectively. These buttons receive `ActionListeners` which create a `SimpleAttributeSet` instance with the bold or italic property with `StyleConstants.setBold()` or `StyleConstants.setItalic()`. Then our custom `setAttributeSet()` method is called to apply this attribute set.

8 The `showAttributes()` method is called to set the state of the toolbar components described earlier according to the font properties of the text at the given caret position. This method sets the `m_skipUpdate` flag to `true` at the beginning and `false` at the end of its execution (the purpose of this will be explained soon). Then an `AttributeSet` instance corresponding to the character element at the current caret position in the editor's document is retrieved with the `getAttributes()` method. The `StyleConstants.getFontFamily()` method is used to retrieve the current font name from this attribute set. If it is not equal to the previously selected font name (stored in the `m_fontName` instance variable) it is selected in the `m_cbFonts` combo box. The other toolbar controls are handled in a similar way.

9 The `setAttributeSet()` method is used to assign a given set of attributes to the currently selected text. Note that this method does nothing (simply returns) if the `m_skipUpdate` flag is set to `true`. This is done to prevent the backward link with the `showAttributes()` method. As soon as we assign some value to a combo box in the `showAttributes()` method (e.g., font size) this internally triggers a call to the `setAttributeSet()` method (because `Action-Listeners` attached to combo boxes are invoked even when selection changes occur programmatically). The purpose of `showAttributes()` is to simply make sure that the attributes corresponding to the character element at the current text position are accurately reflected in the toolbar components. To prevent the combo box `ActionListeners` from invoking unnecessary operations we prohibit any text property updates from occuring in `setAttributeSet()` while the `showAttributes()` method is being executed (this is the whole purpose of the `m_skipUpdate` flag).

`setAttributeSet()` first determines the start and end positions of the selected text. If `m_editor` currently does not have the focus, the stored bounds, `m_xStart` and `m_xFinish`, are used instead. If the selection is not empty (`xStart != xFinish`), the `setCharacter-Attributes()` method is called to assign the given set of attributes to the selection. Note that this new attribute set does not have to contain a complete set of attributes. It simply replaces only the existing attributes for which it has new values, leaving the remainder unchanged. If the selection is empty, the new attributes are added to the input attributes of the editor kit (recall that `StyledEditorKit`'s input attributes are those attributes that will be applied to newly inserted text–`HTMLEditorKit` extends `StyledEditorKit`).

20.2.2   Running the code

Figure 20.2 shows our editor with a font combo box selection in process. Open an existing HTML file and move the cursor to various positions in the text. Note that the text attributes displayed in the toolbar components are updated correctly. Select a portion of text and use the toolbar components to modify the selection's font attributes. Type a new font name and font size in the editable combo box and press Enter. This has the same effect as selecting a choice from the drop-down list. Save the HTML file and open it in another HTML-aware application to verify that your changes were saved correctly.

20.3   *HTML EDITOR, PART III: DOCUMENT PROPERTIES*

In this example we add the following features to our HTML editor application:

- Image insertion
- Hyperlink insertion
- Foreground color selection
- An HTML page properties dialog to assign text color, link colors, background color and title
- An HTML source dialog that allows editing

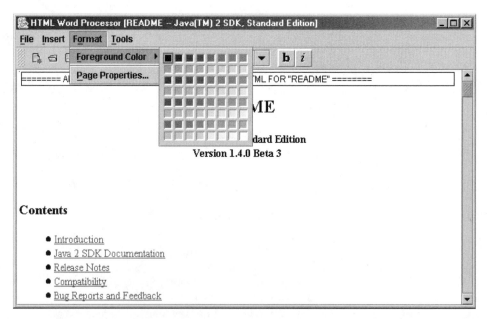

Figure 20.3   `HtmlProcessor` **showing foreground color selection component**

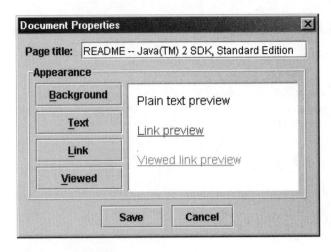

Figure 20.4
**HtmlProcessor's docu-
ment properties dialog**

Example 20.3

see \Chapter20\3

```java
import java.awt.*;
import java.awt.event.*;
import java.io.*;
import java.net.*;
import java.util.*;

import javax.swing.*;
import javax.swing.text.*;
import javax.swing.event.*;
import javax.swing.border.*;
import javax.swing.text.html.*;

import dl.*;

public class HtmlProcessor extends JFrame {

    public static final String APP_NAME = "HTML HTML Editor";

    protected JTextPane m_editor;
    protected StyleSheet m_context;
    protected MutableHTMLDocument m_doc;
    protected CustomHTMLEditorKit m_kit;
    protected SimpleFilter m_htmlFilter;
    protected JToolBar m_toolBar;

// Unchanged code from example 20.2

    protected int m_xStart = -1;
    protected int m_xFinish = -1;

    protected ColorMenu m_foreground;

// Unchanged code from example 20.2
```

❶ Custom document and editor
kit classes are now used

❷ Menu component used
to select foreground color

Figure 20.5
HtmlProcessor's
HTML source dialog

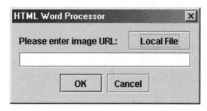

Figure 20.6
HtmlProcessor's
insert image dialog

```java
protected JMenuBar createMenuBar() {
   JMenuBar menuBar = new JMenuBar();

   JMenu mFile = new JMenu("File");
   mFile.setMnemonic('f');
  // Unchanged code from example 20.2

   JMenu mInsert = new JMenu("Insert");
   mInsert.setMnemonic('i');

   item = new JMenuItem("Image...");
   item.setMnemonic('i');
   lst = new ActionListener() {
      public void actionPerformed(ActionEvent e) {
         String url = inputURL("Please enter image URL:", null);}
         if (url == null)
            return;
         try {
            ImageIcon icon = new ImageIcon(new URL(url));
```

3 New menu item allowing
insertion of an image

Figure 20.7
HtmlProcessor's insert link dialog

```java
        int w = icon.getIconWidth();
        int h = icon.getIconHeight();
        if (w<=0 || h<=0) {
           JOptionPane.showMessageDialog(HtmlProcessor.this,
              "Error reading image URL\n"+
              url, APP_NAME,
              JOptionPane.WARNING_MESSAGE);
              return;
        }

        MutableAttributeSet attr = new SimpleAttributeSet();
        attr.addAttribute(StyleConstants.NameAttribute,
        HTML.Tag.IMG);
        attr.addAttribute(HTML.Attribute.SRC, url);
        attr.addAttribute(HTML.Attribute.HEIGHT,
        Integer.toString(h));
        attr.addAttribute(HTML.Attribute.WIDTH,
        Integer.toString(w));
        int p = m_editor.getCaretPosition();
        m_doc.insertString(p, " ", attr);
      }
      catch (Exception ex) {
         showError(ex, "Error: "+ex);
      }
   }
};
item.addActionListener(lst);
mInsert.add(item);

item = new JMenuItem("Hyperlink...");
item.setMnemonic('h');
lst = new ActionListener(){
   public void actionPerformed(ActionEvent e) {
      String oldHref = null;

      int p = m_editor.getCaretPosition();
      AttributeSet attr = m_doc.getCharacterElement(p).
         getAttributes();
      AttributeSet anchor =
         (AttributeSet)attr.getAttribute(HTML.Tag.A);
      if (anchor != null)
         oldHref = (String)anchor.getAttribute(HTML.Attribute.HREF);

      String newHref = inputURL("Please enter link URL:", oldHref);
      if (newHref == null)
```

3 New menu item allowing
insertion of a hyperlink

```
              return;

          SimpleAttributeSet attr2 = new SimpleAttributeSet();
          attr2.addAttribute(StyleConstants.NameAttribute, HTML.Tag.A);
          attr2.addAttribute(HTML.Attribute.HREF, newHref);
          setAttributeSet(attr2, true);
          m_editor.grabFocus();
        }
    };
    item.addActionListener(lst);
    mInsert.add(item);

    menuBar.add(mInsert);

    JMenu mFormat = new JMenu("Format");
    mFormat.setMnemonic('o');

    m_foreground = new ColorMenu("Foreground Color");
    m_foreground.setColor(m_editor.getForeground());
    m_foreground.setMnemonic('f');
    lst = new ActionListener() {
      public void actionPerformed(ActionEvent e) {
        MutableAttributeSet attr = new SimpleAttributeSet();
        StyleConstants.setForeground(attr,
        m_foreground.getColor());
        setAttributeSet(attr);
      }
    };
    m_foreground.addActionListener(lst);
    mFormat.add(m_foreground);

    MenuListener ml = new MenuListener() {
      public void menuSelected(MenuEvent e) {
        int p = m_editor.getCaretPosition();
        AttributeSet attr = m_doc.getCharacterElement(p).
          getAttributes();
        Color c = StyleConstants.getForeground(attr);
        m_foreground.setColor(c);
      }
      public void menuDeselected(MenuEvent e) {}
      public void menuCanceled(MenuEvent e) {}
    };
    m_foreground.addMenuListener(ml);
    mFormat.addSeparator();

    item = new JMenuItem("Page Properties...");
    item.setMnemonic('p');
    lst = new ActionListener(){
      public void actionPerformed(ActionEvent e) {
        DocumentPropsDlg dlg = new
        DocumentPropsDlg(HtmlProcessor.this, m_doc);
        dlg.show();
        if (dlg.succeeded())
          documentChanged();
```

4 Menu item allowing selection of foreground color

4 Menu item to display page properties dialog

```
        }
      };
      item.addActionListener(lst);
      mFormat.add(item);

      menuBar.add(mFormat);

      JMenu mTools = new JMenu("Tools");
      mTools.setMnemonic('t');

      item = new JMenuItem("HTML Source...");
      item.setMnemonic('s');
      lst = new ActionListener(){
        public void actionPerformed(ActionEvent e) {
          try {
            StringWriter sw = new StringWriter();
            m_kit.write(sw, m_doc, 0, m_doc.getLength());
            sw.close();

            HtmlSourceDlg dlg = new HtmlSourceDlg(
              HtmlProcessor.this, sw.toString());
            dlg.show();
            if (!dlg.succeeded())
              return;

            StringReader sr = new StringReader(dlg.getSource());
            m_doc = (MutableHTMLDocument)m_kit.createDocument();
            m_context = m_doc.getStyleSheet();
            m_kit.read(sr, m_doc, 0);
            sr.close();
            m_editor.setDocument(m_doc);
            documentChanged();
          }
          catch (Exception ex) {
            showError(ex, "Error: "+ex);
          }
        }
      };
      item.addActionListener(lst);
      mTools.add(item);

      menuBar.add(mTools);

      getContentPane().add(m_toolBar, BorderLayout.NORTH);

      return menuBar;
  }
  protected String getDocumentName() {
    String title = m_doc.getTitle();
    if (title != null && title.length() > 0)
      return title;
    return m_currentFile==null ? "Untitled" :
      m_currentFile.getName();
  }
```

5 Menu item to display HTML source dialog

```
protected void newDocument() {
    m_doc = (MutableHTMLDocument)m_kit.createDocument();
    m_context = m_doc.getStyleSheet();

    m_editor.setDocument(m_doc);
    m_currentFile = null;
    setTitle(APP_NAME+" ["+getDocumentName()+"]");

    SwingUtilities.invokeLater(new Runnable() {
        public void run() {
            showAttributes(0);
            m_editor.scrollRectToVisible(new Rectangle(0,0,1,1));
            m_doc.addDocumentListener(new UpdateListener());
            m_textChanged = false;
        }
    });
}

protected void openDocument() {
    // Unchanged code from example 20.2

    HtmlProcessor.this.setCursor(
        Cursor.getPredefinedCursor(Cursor.WAIT_CURSOR));
    try {
        InputStream in = new FileInputStream(m_currentFile);
        m_doc = (MutableHTMLDocument)m_kit.createDocument();
        m_kit.read(in, m_doc, 0);
        m_context = m_doc.getStyleSheet();
        m_editor.setDocument(m_doc);
        in.close();
    }
    catch (Exception ex) {
        showError(ex, "Error reading file "+m_currentFile);
    }
    HtmlProcessor.this.setCursor(Cursor.getPredefinedCursor(
        Cursor.DEFAULT_CURSOR));

    // Unchanged code from example 20.2
}

// Unchanged code from example 20.2
protected void setAttributeSet(AttributeSet attr) {
    setAttributeSet(attr, false);
}

protected void setAttributeSet(AttributeSet attr,
    boolean setParagraphAttributes) {
    if (m_skipUpdate)
        return;
    int xStart = m_editor.getSelectionStart();
    int xFinish = m_editor.getSelectionEnd();
    if (!m_editor.hasFocus()) {
        xStart = m_xStart;
        xFinish = m_xFinish;
    }
```

❻ Updated to allow specification paragraph or character attributes

```
      if (setParagraphAttributes)
        m_doc.setParagraphAttributes(xStart,
          xFinish - xStart, attr, false);
      else if (xStart != xFinish)
        m_doc.setCharacterAttributes(xStart,
          xFinish - xStart, attr, false);
      else {
        MutableAttributeSet inputAttributes =
          m_kit.getInputAttributes();
        inputAttributes.addAttributes(attr);
      }
  }

  protected String inputURL(String prompt, String initialValue) {
    JPanel p = new JPanel();
    p.setLayout(new BoxLayout(p, BoxLayout.X_AXIS));
    p.add(new JLabel(prompt));
    p.add(Box.createHorizontalGlue());
    JButton bt = new JButton("Local File");
    bt.setRequestFocusEnabled(false);
    p.add(bt);

    final JOptionPane op = new JOptionPane(p,
      JOptionPane.PLAIN_MESSAGE, JOptionPane.OK_CANCEL_OPTION);
    op.setWantsInput(true);
    if (initialValue != null)
      op.setInitialSelectionValue(initialValue);

    ActionListener lst = new ActionListener() {
      public void actionPerformed(ActionEvent e) {
        JFileChooser chooser = new JFileChooser();
        if (chooser.showOpenDialog(HtmlProcessor.this) !=
          JFileChooser.APPROVE_OPTION)
          return;
        File f = chooser.getSelectedFile();
        try {
          String str = f.toURL().toString();
          op.setInitialSelectionValue(str);
        }
        catch (Exception ex) {
          ex.printStackTrace();
        }
      }
    };
    bt.addActionListener(lst);

    JDialog dlg = op.createDialog(this, APP_NAME);
    dlg.show();
    dlg.dispose();

Object value = op.getInputValue();
    if (value == JOptionPane.UNINITIALIZED_VALUE)
      return null;
    String str = (String)value;
```

Method to insert a URL (either an image or hyperlink in this example) ❼

```
      if (str != null && str.length() == 0)
        str = null;
      return str;
    }

    public void documentChanged() {
      m_editor.setDocument(new HTMLDocument());
      m_editor.setDocument(m_doc);
      m_editor.revalidate();
      m_editor.repaint();
      setTitle(APP_NAME+" ["+getDocumentName()+"]");
      m_textChanged = true;
    }
```

8 **Brute force method at updating document display**

```
  // Unchanged code from example 20.2
}

// Unchanged code from example 20.2

// Class ColorMenu unchanged from chapter 12

class Utils
{
  // Copied from javax.swing.text.html.CSS class
  // because it is not publicly accessible there.
  public static String colorToHex(Color color) {
    String colorstr = new String("#");
```

9 **Returns the hot value for a given color**

```
    // Red
    String str = Integer.toHexString(color.getRed());
    if (str.length() > 2)
      str = str.substring(0, 2);
    else if (str.length() < 2)
      colorstr += "0" + str;
    else
      colorstr += str;

    // Green
    str = Integer.toHexString(color.getGreen());
    if (str.length() > 2)
      str = str.substring(0, 2);
    else if (str.length() < 2)
      colorstr += "0" + str;
    else
      colorstr += str;

    // Blue
    str = Integer.toHexString(color.getBlue());
    if (str.length() > 2)
      str = str.substring(0, 2);
    else if (str.length() < 2)
      colorstr += "0" + str;
    else
      colorstr += str;
    return colorstr;
  }
```

```
   }

class CustomHTMLEditorKit extends HTMLEditorKit {
   public Document createDocument() {
      StyleSheet styles = getStyleSheet();
      StyleSheet ss = new StyleSheet();

      ss.addStyleSheet(styles);

      MutableHTMLDocument doc = new MutableHTMLDocument(ss);
      doc.setParser(getParser());
      doc.setAsynchronousLoadPriority(4);
      doc.setTokenThreshold(100);
      return doc;
   }
}

class MutableHTMLDocument extends HTMLDocument {
   public MutableHTMLDocument(StyleSheet styles) {
      super(styles);
   }

   public Element getElementByTag(HTML.Tag tag) {
      Element root = getDefaultRootElement();
      return getElementByTag(root, tag);
   }

   public Element getElementByTag(Element parent, HTML.Tag tag) {
      if (parent == null || tag == null)
         return null;
      for (int k=0; k<parent.getElementCount(); k++) {
         Element child = parent.getElement(k);
         if (child.getAttributes().getAttribute(
               StyleConstants.NameAttribute).equals(tag))
            return child;
         Element e = getElementByTag(child, tag);
         if (e != null)
            return e;
      }
      return null;
   }

   public String getTitle() {
      return (String)getProperty(Document.TitleProperty);
   }

   // This will work only if the <title> element was
   // previously created. Looks like a bug in the HTML package.
   public void setTitle(String title) {
      Dictionary di = getDocumentProperties();
      di.put(Document.TitleProperty, title);
      setDocumentProperties(di);
   }

   public void addAttributes(Element e, AttributeSet attributes) {
      if (e == null || attributes == null)
```

10 Custom editor kit to return **MutableHTMLDocuments**

11 Custom **HTMLDocument** with enhancement to locate text elements corresponding to a given HTML tag

```
        return;
      try {
        writeLock();
        MutableAttributeSet mattr =
          (MutableAttributeSet)e.getAttributes();
        mattr.addAttributes(attributes);
        fireChangedUpdate(new DefaultDocumentEvent(0, getLength(),
          DocumentEvent.EventType.CHANGE));
      }
      finally {
        writeUnlock();
      }
    }
  }
}

class DocumentPropsDlg extends JDialog {
  protected boolean m_succeeded = false;
  protected MutableHTMLDocument m_doc;

  protected Color m_backgroundColor;
  protected Color m_textColor;
  protected Color m_linkColor;
  protected Color m_viewedColor;

  protected JTextField m_titleTxt;
  protected JTextPane m_previewPane;

  public DocumentPropsDlg(JFrame parent, MutableHTMLDocument doc) {
    super(parent, "Page Properties", true);
    m_doc = doc;

    Element body = m_doc.getElementByTag(HTML.Tag.BODY);
    if (body != null) {
      AttributeSet attr = body.getAttributes();
      StyleSheet syleSheet = m_doc.getStyleSheet();
      Object obj = attr.getAttribute(HTML.Attribute.BGCOLOR);
      if (obj != null)
        m_backgroundColor = syleSheet.stringToColor((String)obj);
      obj = attr.getAttribute(HTML.Attribute.TEXT);
      if (obj != null)
        m_textColor = syleSheet.stringToColor((String)obj);
      obj = attr.getAttribute(HTML.Attribute.LINK);
      if (obj != null)
        m_linkColor = syleSheet.stringToColor((String)obj);
      obj = attr.getAttribute(HTML.Attribute.VLINK);
      if (obj != null)
        m_viewedColor = syleSheet.stringToColor((String)obj);
    }

    ActionListener lst;
    JButton bt;

    JPanel pp = new JPanel(new DialogLayout2());
    pp.setBorder(new EmptyBorder(10, 10, 5, 10));

    pp.add(new JLabel("Page title:"));
```

(12) Custom dialog class to modify HTML document properties such as title, background color, text color, hyperlink color, and viewed hyperlink color

```java
m_titleTxt = new JTextField(m_doc.getTitle(), 24);
pp.add(m_titleTxt);

JPanel pa = new JPanel(new BorderLayout(5, 5));
Border ba = new TitledBorder(new EtchedBorder(
    EtchedBorder.RAISED), "Appearance");
pa.setBorder(new CompoundBorder(ba, new EmptyBorder(0, 5, 5, 5)));

JPanel pb = new JPanel(new GridLayout(4, 1, 5, 5));
bt = new JButton("Background");
bt.setMnemonic('b');
lst = new ActionListener() {
    public void actionPerformed(ActionEvent e) {
        m_backgroundColor =
        JColorChooser.showDialog(DocumentPropsDlg.this,
            "Document Background", m_backgroundColor);
        showColors();
    }
};
bt.addActionListener(lst);
pb.add(bt);

bt = new JButton("Text");
bt.setMnemonic('t');
lst = new ActionListener() {
    public void actionPerformed(ActionEvent e) {
        m_textColor = JColorChooser.showDialog(DocumentPropsDlg.this,
            "Text Color", m_textColor);
        showColors();
    }
};
bt.addActionListener(lst);
pb.add(bt);

bt = new JButton("Link");
bt.setMnemonic('l');
lst = new ActionListener() {
    public void actionPerformed(ActionEvent e) {
        m_linkColor = JColorChooser.showDialog(DocumentPropsDlg.this,
            "Links Color", m_linkColor);
        showColors();
    }
};
bt.addActionListener(lst);
pb.add(bt);

bt = new JButton("Viewed");
bt.setMnemonic('v');
lst = new ActionListener() {
    public void actionPerformed(ActionEvent e) {
        m_viewedColor = JColorChooser.showDialog(DocumentPropsDlg.this,
            "Viewed Links Color", m_viewedColor);
        showColors();
    }
```

```
      };
      bt.addActionListener(lst);
      pb.add(bt);
      pa.add(pb, BorderLayout.WEST);

      m_previewPane = new JTextPane();
      m_previewPane.setBackground(Color.white);
      m_previewPane.setEditable(false);
      m_previewPane.setBorder(new CompoundBorder(
        new BevelBorder(BevelBorder.LOWERED),
        new EmptyBorder(10, 10, 10, 10)));
      showColors();
      pa.add(m_previewPane, BorderLayout.CENTER);

      pp.add(pa);

      bt = new JButton("Save");
      lst = new ActionListener() {
        public void actionPerformed(ActionEvent e) {
          saveData();
          dispose();
        }
      };
      bt.addActionListener(lst);
      pp.add(bt);

      bt = new JButton("Cancel");
      lst = new ActionListener() {
        public void actionPerformed(ActionEvent e) {
          dispose();
        }
      };
      bt.addActionListener(lst);
      pp.add(bt);

      getContentPane().add(pp, BorderLayout.CENTER);
      pack();
      setResizable(false);
      setLocationRelativeTo(parent);
    }

    public boolean succeeded() {
      return m_succeeded;
    }

    protected void saveData() {
      m_doc.setTitle(m_titleTxt.getText());

      Element body = m_doc.getElementByTag(HTML.Tag.BODY);
      MutableAttributeSet attr = new SimpleAttributeSet();
      if (m_backgroundColor != null)
        attr.addAttribute(HTML.Attribute.BGCOLOR,
          Utils.colorToHex(m_backgroundColor));
      if (m_textColor != null)
        attr.addAttribute(HTML.Attribute.TEXT,
          Utils.colorToHex(m_textColor));
```

```
         if (m_linkColor != null)
            attr.addAttribute(HTML.Attribute.LINK,
               Utils.colorToHex(m_linkColor));
         if (m_viewedColor != null)
            attr.addAttribute(HTML.Attribute.VLINK,
               Utils.colorToHex(m_viewedColor));
         m_doc.addAttributes(body, attr);

         m_succeeded = true;
      }

      protected void showColors() {
         DefaultStyledDocument doc = new DefaultStyledDocument();

         SimpleAttributeSet attr = new SimpleAttributeSet();
         StyleConstants.setFontFamily(attr, "Arial");
         StyleConstants.setFontSize(attr, 14);
         if (m_backgroundColor != null) {
            StyleConstants.setBackground(attr, m_backgroundColor);
            m_previewPane.setBackground(m_backgroundColor);
         }

         try {
            StyleConstants.setForeground(attr, m_textColor!=null ?
               m_textColor : Color.black);
            doc.insertString(doc.getLength(),
             "Plain text preview\n\n", attr);

            StyleConstants.setForeground(attr, m_linkColor!=null ?
               m_linkColor : Color.blue);
            StyleConstants.setUnderline(attr, true);
            doc.insertString(doc.getLength(), "Link preview\n\n", attr);

            StyleConstants.setForeground(attr, m_viewedColor!=null ?
               m_viewedColor : Color.magenta);
            StyleConstants.setUnderline(attr, true);
            doc.insertString(doc.getLength(), "Viewed link preview\n", attr);
         }
         catch (BadLocationException be) {
            be.printStackTrace();
         }
         m_previewPane.setDocument(doc);
      }
   }

   class HtmlSourceDlg extends JDialog {
      protected boolean m_succeeded = false;

      protected JTextArea m_sourceTxt;

      public HtmlSourceDlg(JFrame parent, String source) {
         super(parent, "HTML Source", true);

         JPanel pp = new JPanel(new BorderLayout());
         pp.setBorder(new EmptyBorder(10, 10, 5, 10));

         m_sourceTxt = new JTextArea(source, 20, 60);
```

13 Custom dialog to allow viewing and editing of HTML source

```
m_sourceTxt.setFont(new Font("Courier", Font.PLAIN, 12));
JScrollPane sp = new JScrollPane(m_sourceTxt);
pp.add(sp, BorderLayout.CENTER);

JPanel p = new JPanel(new FlowLayout());
JPanel p1 = new JPanel(new GridLayout(1, 2, 10, 0));
JButton bt = new JButton("Save");
ActionListener lst = new ActionListener() {
  public void actionPerformed(ActionEvent e) {
    m_succeeded = true;
    dispose();
  }
};
bt.addActionListener(lst);
p1.add(bt);

bt = new JButton("Cancel");
lst = new ActionListener() {
  public void actionPerformed(ActionEvent e) {
    dispose();
  }
};
bt.addActionListener(lst);
p1.add(bt);
p.add(p1);
pp.add(p, BorderLayout.SOUTH);

getContentPane().add(pp, BorderLayout.CENTER);
pack();
setResizable(true);
setLocationRelativeTo(parent);
}

public boolean succeeded() {
  return m_succeeded;
}

public String getSource() {
  return m_sourceTxt.getText();
}
}
```

20.3.1 Understanding the code

Class HtmlProcessor

1 Two instance variables have changed class type:

- MutableHTMLDocument m_doc: the main text component's Document is now an instance of our custom HTMLDocument subclass.
- CustomHTMLEditorKit m_kit: the editor kit is now an instance of our custom HTML-EditorKit subclass.

2 One new instance variable has been added to this example:

- ColorMenu m_foreground: used to choose the selected text foreground color.

3 The `createMenuBar()` method adds three new menus. An Insert menu is added with menu items Image and Hyperlink. These menu items are responsible for inserting images and hyperlinks respectively. Their `ActionListeners` both use our custom `inputURL()` method to display a dialog that allows specification of the path to the image or hyperlink. Given a URL to an image or hyperlink, note how we use the `HTML.Attribute` and `HTML.Tag` classes to insert tags and attributes respectively.

Also note that before displaying the input dialog for inserting a hyperlink, our code checks whether there is already a hyperlink at the current caret position. If there is, this hyperlink is displayed in the insert hyperlink dialog so that it may be modified (a more professional implementation might allow us to right-click on the hyperlink to display a popup menu in which one of the options would be to edit it).

4 A Format menu is added with menu items Foreground Color and Page Properties. The Foreground Color item is an instance of our custom `ColorMenu` class developed in chapter 12 as a simple color selection menu item (see section 12.5). This item sets the foreground color attribute of the selected text to the color chosen in the `ColorMenu` component. A `MenuListener` is added to the `ColorMenu` component to set its selected color to the foreground color of the text at the current carret location when this menu is displayed. The Page Properties menu item creates an instance of our custom `DocumentPropsDlg` dialog which is used to change the text and background color page properties, as well as the document title. If changes are made with the `DocumentPropsDlg` we call our `documentChanged()` method to update our editor properly with the modified document.

5 A Tools menu is added with item HTML Source. The HTML Source item displays the HTML source code behind the current document in an instance of our custom `HtmlSourceDlg` dialog. A `StringWriter` is used to convert the current document to a `String` which is passed to the `HtmlSourceDlg` constructor. If changes have been made to the HTML by `HtmlSourceDlg` we use a `StringReader` to bundle the new source from `HtmlSourceDlg`'s `getSource()` method, create a new document using our custom editor kit, read the contents of the `StringReader` into the document, and set this new document as our editor's current `Document` instance. Then we call our `documentChanged()` method to update our editor properly with the new document.

The `getDocumentName()` method is modified to return the contents of the title tag, or if undefined, the current file name.

The `newDocument()` method is modified to create a new instance of our custom `Mutable-HTMLDocument` class using our custom editor kit implementation. The `openDocument()` method is modified similarly.

6 There are now two `setAttributeSet()` methods. The main `setAttributeSet()` method takes an `AttributeSet` parameter and a `boolean` parameter. The `boolean` parameter specifies whether or not the given `AttributeSet` should be applied as paragraph or character attributes. If `true` the attributes will be applied to the currently selected paragraph(s).

7 The `inputURL()` method takes two `String` parameters representing a message to display and an initial value. This method creates a `JOptionPane` with a custom panel and given initial value. The panel consists of a label containing the given message string and a button called Local File. This button is used to navigate the local computer for a file and, if selected, the path to the file will appear in the JOptionPane's input field. Once the JOptionPane is dismissed the inputURL() method returns the chosen string URL.

8 The documentChanged() method updates the text pane with the current Document instance after it has been changed by an outside source.

> **BUG ALERT!** Unfortunately we were forced to resort to rather barbaric techniques in order to properly handle Document updates that occur outside of the editor. Because simply calling JTextPane's setDocument() method does not properly update the editor, we assign it a completely new Document, then reassign it our modified document and then revalidate and repaint the editor. We encourage you to search for a better solution to this problem if one exists, and we hope that this problem is addressed in a future version of JTextPane.

Class Utils

9 This class consists of the static colorToHex() method which was copied from the javax.swing.text.html.CSS class. This method takes a Color parameter and returns a String representing a hex value used in HTML documents to specify a color.

> **NOTE** We copied this method directly from Swing source code and placed it in this separate class because, unfortunately, the method is private in the CSS class. We are unsure why it is private and hope to see this changed in a future release.

10 Class CustomHTMLEditorKit

This class extends HTMLEditorKit and overrides its createDocument() method to return an instance of our custom MutableHTMLDocument class.

11 Class MutableHTMLDocument

This class extends HTMLDocument to add functionality for locating Elements corresponding to a specific HTML tag, retrieving and setting the document <title> tag value, and adding attributes to an Element corresponding to a specific HTML tag.

12 Class DocumentPropsDlg

This class extends JDialog and has eight instance variables:

- boolean m_succeeded: flag set to true if new attributes are successfully added.
- MutableHTMLDocument m_doc: reference to the HTML document passed into the constructor.
- Color m_backgroundColor: used to store the HTML document's background color.
- Color m_textColor: used to store the HTML document's text foreground color.
- Color m_linkColor: used to store the HTML document's hyperlink color.
- Color m_viewedColor: used to store the HTML document's visited hyperlink color.
- JTextField m_titleTxt: input field used to change the HTML document's title value.
- JTextPane m_previewPane: text pane to preview HTML document color settings.

The DocumentPropsDlg constructor takes JFrame and MutableHTMLDocument parameters. The document passed in represents the HTML document whose properties are to be modified by this dialog. The <body> element is located and the color variables are initialized based on this element's attributes. A panel is created to contain the input field, preview pane, and a series of buttons used for displaying a `JColorChooser` to change each color variable and update the preview panel. Whenever a color change is made the `showColors()` method is called to update the preview panel. A Save button and a Cancel button are also added to this panel to save changes or abort them respectively. This panel is added to the content pane and the dialog is centered with respect to the `JFrame` parent.

The `succeeded()` method simply returns `m_succeeded` which indicates whether or not attempts to change the document's attributes were successful.

The `saveData()` method is called when the Save button is pressed. This method updates the `<body>` element's attributes in the HTML document and sets the `m_succeeded` variable to `true` if it succeeds.

The `showColors()` method updates the preview text pane with a new `Default-Styled-Document`. Text is added to this document with attributes corresponding to the text and hyperlink colors to demonstrate the current selections. The text pane's background is also set to the currently selected background color.

⑬ Class HtmlSourceDlg

This class extends `JDialog` and has two instance variables:

- `boolean m_succeeded`: flag set to `true` if the Save button is pressed.
- `JTextArea m_sourceTxt`: text area used for displaying and editing HTML source code.

The `HtmlSourceDlg` constructor takes `JFrame` and `String` parameters. The `String` represents the HTML source code and is placed in the text area. The text area is placed in a `JScrollPane` and added to a panel. A Save button and a Cancel button are also added to this panel to save changes or abort them respectively. This panel is added to the content pane and the dialog is centered with respect to the `JFrame` parent.

The `succeeded()` method simply returns `m_succeeded` which indicates whether or not attempts to change the document's attributes were successful.

The `getSource()` method returns the current contents of the `JTextArea` representing the HTML source code.

20.3.2 Running the code

Figure 20.3 shows our editor with the color menu open. Figures 20.4 through 20.7 show our page properties, HTML source, image, and URL insertion dialogs. Open an existing HTML file, select a portion of text, and use the custom color menu component to modify its foreground. From the Document menu select the page properties dialog and the HTML source dialog to modify internal aspects of the document. Verify that these dialogs work as expected. Try inserting hyperlinks and images. Save the HTML file and open it in another HTML-aware application to verify that your changes have been saved correctly.

20.4 HTML EDITOR, PART IV: WORKING WITH HTML STYLES AND TABLES

Using Styles to manage a set of attributes as a single named entity can greatly simplify editing. The user only has to apply a known style to a paragraph of text rather than selecting all appropriate text attributes from the provided toolbar components. By adding a combo box allowing the choice of styles, we can not only save the user time and effort, but we can also

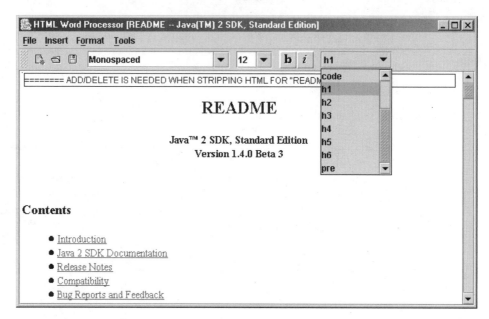

Figure 20.8   HtmlProcessor with style management

provide more uniform text formatting throughout the resulting document. In this section we'll add the following features:

- Ability to apply HTML styles to paragraphs of text.
- A dialog to create HTML tables.

Example 20.4

HtmlProcessor.java

see \Chapter20\4

```
import java.awt.*;
import java.awt.event.*;
import java.io.*;
import java.net.*;
import java.util.*;
import javax.swing.*;

import javax.swing.text.*;
import javax.swing.event.*;
import javax.swing.border.*;
import javax.swing.text.html.*;
```

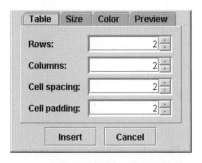

Figure 20.9
HtmlProcessor's table creation
dialog–Table pane

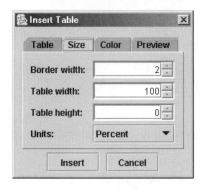

Figure 20.10
HtmlProcessor's table
creation dialog–Size pane

```
import dl.*;

public class HtmlProcessor extends JFrame {

    public static final String APP_NAME = "HTML HTML Editor";

    // Unchanged code from example 20.3

    protected JComboBox m_cbStyles;
    public static HTML.Tag[] STYLES = {
       HTML.Tag.P, HTML.Tag.BLOCKQUOTE, HTML.Tag.CENTER,
       HTML.Tag.CITE, HTML.Tag.CODE, HTML.Tag.H1, HTML.Tag.H2,
       HTML.Tag.H3, HTML.Tag.H4, HTML.Tag.H5, HTML.Tag.H6,
       HTML.Tag.PRE };

    public HtmlProcessor() {
      // Unchanged code from example 20.3
    }

    protected JMenuBar createMenuBar() {

// Unchanged code from example 20.3

        item = new JMenuItem("Table...");
        item.setMnemonic('t');
        lst = new ActionListener(){
```

① New combo box
containing HTML styles

② Menu item to invoke table dialog
for creating an HTML table

Figure 20.11
HtmlProcessor's table creation dialog–Color pane

Figure 20.12
HtmlProcessor's table creation dialog–Preview pane

```java
public void actionPerformed(ActionEvent e) {
    TableDlg dlg = new TableDlg(HtmlProcessor.this, m_doc);
    dlg.show();
    if (dlg.succeeded()) {
        String tableHtml = dlg.generateHTML();
        Element ep = m_doc.getParagraphElement(
          m_editor.getSelectionStart());
        try {
            m_doc.insertAfterEnd(ep, tableHtml);
        }
        catch (Exception ex) {
            ex.printStackTrace();
        }
        documentChanged();
    }
  }
};
item.addActionListener(lst);
mInsert.add(item);

menuBar.add(mInsert);

JMenu mFormat = new JMenu("Format");
mFormat.setMnemonic('o');

// Unchanged code from example 20.3
```

```java
      m_toolBar.addSeparator();
      m_cbStyles = new JComboBox(STYLES);
      m_cbStyles.setMaximumSize(new Dimension(100, 23));
      m_cbStyles.setRequestFocusEnabled(false);
      m_toolBar.add(m_cbStyles);

      lst = new ActionListener() {
        public void actionPerformed(ActionEvent e) {
          HTML.Tag style = (HTML.Tag)m_cbStyles.getSelectedItem();
          if (style == null)
            return;
          MutableAttributeSet attr = new SimpleAttributeSet();
          attr.addAttribute(StyleConstants.NameAttribute, style);
          setAttributeSet(attr, true);
          m_editor.grabFocus();
        }
      };
      m_cbStyles.addActionListener(lst);

      getContentPane().add(m_toolBar, BorderLayout.NORTH);

      return menuBar;
    }

// Unchanged code from example 20.3

  protected void showAttributes(int p) {

// Unchanged code from example 20.3

    Element ep = m_doc.getParagraphElement(p);
    HTML.Tag attrName = (HTML.Tag)ep.getAttributes().
      getAttribute(StyleConstants.NameAttribute);

    int index = -1;
    if (attrName != null) {
      for (int k=0; k<STYLES.length; k++) {
        if (STYLES[k].equals(attrName)) {
          index = k;
          break;
        }
      }
    }
    m_cbStyles.setSelectedIndex(index);

    m_skipUpdate = false;
  }

// Unchanged code from example 20.3

}

// Unchanged code from example 20.3

class TableDlg extends JDialog {
  protected boolean m_succeeded = false;
  protected MutableHTMLDocument m_doc;
```

3 Styles combo box applies selected HTML.Tag to current paragraph

4 Custom dialog to create an HTML table allowing specification of # of rows, # of columns, cell spacing, cell padding, border width, table width, table height, table units, border color, and background color; also includes a preview of proposed table

```
protected JSpinner m_rowsSpn;
protected JSpinner m_colsSpn;
protected JSpinner m_spacingSpn;
protected JSpinner m_paddingSpn;

protected JSpinner m_borderWidthSpn;
protected JSpinner m_tableWidthSpn;
protected JSpinner m_tableHeightSpn;
protected JComboBox m_tableUnitsCb;

protected JTextPane m_previewPane;

protected Color m_borderColor;
protected Color m_backgroundColor;

protected HTMLEditorKit m_kit = new HTMLEditorKit();

public TableDlg(JFrame parent, MutableHTMLDocument doc) {
    super(parent, "Insert Table", true);
    m_doc = doc;

    ActionListener lst;
    JButton bt;

    JPanel pp = new JPanel(new DialogLayout2());
    pp.setBorder(new EmptyBorder(10, 10, 5, 10));

    JPanel p1 = new JPanel(new DialogLayout2());
    p1.setBorder(new EmptyBorder(10, 10, 5, 10));

    p1.add(new JLabel("Rows:"));
    m_rowsSpn = new JSpinner(new SpinnerNumberModel(
        new Integer(2), new Integer(0), null, new Integer(1)));
    p1.add(m_rowsSpn);

    p1.add(new JLabel("Columns:"));
    m_colsSpn = new JSpinner(new SpinnerNumberModel(
        new Integer(2), new Integer(0), null, new Integer(1)));
    p1.add(m_colsSpn);

    p1.add(new JLabel("Cell spacing:"));
    m_spacingSpn = new JSpinner(new SpinnerNumberModel(
        new Integer(2), new Integer(0), null, new Integer(1)));
    p1.add(m_spacingSpn);

    p1.add(new JLabel("Cell padding:"));
    m_paddingSpn = new JSpinner(new SpinnerNumberModel(
        new Integer(2), new Integer(0), null, new Integer(1)));
    p1.add(m_paddingSpn);

    JPanel p2 = new JPanel(new DialogLayout2());
    p2.setBorder(new EmptyBorder(10, 10, 5, 10));

    p2.add(new JLabel("Border width:"));
    m_borderWidthSpn = new JSpinner(new SpinnerNumberModel(
        new Integer(2), new Integer(0), null, new Integer(1)));
    p2.add(m_borderWidthSpn);

    p2.add(new JLabel("Table width:"));
```

```
m_tableWidthSpn = new JSpinner(new SpinnerNumberModel(
   new Integer(100), new Integer(0), null, new Integer(1)));
p2.add(m_tableWidthSpn);

p2.add(new JLabel("Table height:"));
m_tableHeightSpn = new JSpinner(new SpinnerNumberModel(
   new Integer(0), new Integer(0), null, new Integer(1)));
p2.add(m_tableHeightSpn);

p2.add(new JLabel("Units:"));
m_tableUnitsCb = new JComboBox(new String[]
 {"Percent", "Pixels" });
p2.add(m_tableUnitsCb);

JPanel p3 = new JPanel(new FlowLayout());
p3.setBorder(new EmptyBorder(10, 10, 5, 10));
JPanel pb = new JPanel(new GridLayout(2, 1, 5, 5));
p3.add(pb);

bt = new JButton("Border");
bt.setMnemonic('b');
lst = new ActionListener() {
   public void actionPerformed(ActionEvent e) {
      m_borderColor = JColorChooser.showDialog(
      TableDlg.this, "Border Color", m_borderColor);
   }
};
bt.addActionListener(lst);
pb.add(bt);

bt = new JButton("Background");
bt.setMnemonic('c');
lst = new ActionListener() {
   public void actionPerformed(ActionEvent e) {
      m_backgroundColor = JColorChooser.showDialog(
      TableDlg.this, "Background Color", m_backgroundColor);
   }
};
bt.addActionListener(lst);
pb.add(bt);

JPanel p4 = new JPanel(new BorderLayout());
p4.setBorder(new EmptyBorder(10, 10, 5, 10));

m_previewPane = new JTextPane();
m_previewPane.setEditorKit(m_kit);
m_previewPane.setBackground(Color.white);
m_previewPane.setEditable(false);
JScrollPane sp = new JScrollPane(m_previewPane);
sp.setPreferredSize(new Dimension(200, 100));
p4.add(sp, BorderLayout.CENTER);

final JTabbedPane tb = new JTabbedPane();
tb.addTab("Table", p1);
tb.addTab("Size", p2);
tb.addTab("Color", p3);
```

```java
        tb.addTab("Preview", p4);
        pp.add(tb);

        ChangeListener chl = new ChangeListener() {
           public void stateChanged(ChangeEvent e) {
              if (tb.getSelectedIndex() != 3)
                 return;
              setCursor(Cursor.getPredefinedCursor(
                 Cursor.WAIT_CURSOR));
              try {
                 HTMLDocument doc =
                 (HTMLDocument)m_kit.createDefaultDocument();
                 doc.setAsynchronousLoadPriority(0);
                 StringReader sr = new StringReader(generateHTML());
                 m_kit.read(sr, doc, 0);
                 sr.close();

                 m_previewPane.setDocument(doc);
                 validate();
                 repaint();
              }
              catch (Exception ex) {
                 ex.printStackTrace();
              }
              finally {
                 setCursor(Cursor.getPredefinedCursor(
                    Cursor.DEFAULT_CURSOR));
              }
           }
        };
        tb.addChangeListener(chl);

        bt = new JButton("Insert");
        lst = new ActionListener() {
           public void actionPerformed(ActionEvent e) {
              m_succeeded = true;
              dispose();
           }
        };
        bt.addActionListener(lst);
        pp.add(bt);

        bt = new JButton("Cancel");
        lst = new ActionListener() {
           public void actionPerformed(ActionEvent e) {
              dispose();
           }
        };
        bt.addActionListener(lst);
        pp.add(bt);

        getContentPane().add(pp, BorderLayout.CENTER);
        pack();
        setResizable(true);
```

```java
        setLocationRelativeTo(parent);
    }

    public boolean succeeded() {
        return m_succeeded;
    }

    protected String generateHTML() {
        StringBuffer buff = new StringBuffer();
        buff.append("<table");

        int tableWidth =
          ((Integer) m_tableWidthSpn.getValue()).intValue();
        int tableHeight =
          ((Integer)m_tableHeightSpn.getValue()).intValue();
        String unit = "";
        if (m_tableUnitsCb.getSelectedIndex()==0)
            unit = "%";
        if (tableWidth > 0)
            buff.append(" width=\"").append(
            tableWidth).append(unit).append("\"");
        if (tableHeight > 0)
            buff.append(" height=\"").append(
            tableHeight).append(unit).append("\"");

        buff.append(" cellspacing=\"").append(
        m_spacingSpn.getValue()).append("\"");
        buff.append(" cellpadding=\"").append(
        m_paddingSpn.getValue()).append("\"");
        buff.append(" border=\"").append(
        m_borderWidthSpn.getValue()).append("\"");
        if (m_borderColor != null)
            buff.append(" bordercolor=\"").append(
            Utils.colorToHex(m_borderColor)).append("\"");
        if (m_backgroundColor != null)
            buff.append(" bgcolor=\"").append(
            Utils.colorToHex(m_backgroundColor)).append("\"");
        buff.append(">\n");

        int nRows = ((Integer)m_rowsSpn.getValue()).intValue();
        int nCols = ((Integer)m_colsSpn.getValue()).intValue();
        for (int k=0; k<nRows; k++) {
            buff.append("<tr>\n");
            for (int s=0; s<nCols; s++)
                buff.append("<td> </td>\n");
            buff.append("</tr>\n");
        }

        buff.append("</table>\n");
        return buff.toString();
    }
}
```

20.4.1   Understanding the code

Class HtmlProcessor

❶ One new instance variable has been added:

- JComboBox m_cbStyles: toolbar component to apply HTML styles.

A new static array of HTML.Tags is also added:

- HTML.Tag[] STYLES: used to hold tags for all HTML styles.

❷ The createMenuBar() method creates a new Table menu item added to the Insert menu, and a new combo box for HTML style selection is added to the toolbar. The Table menu item displays an instance of our custom TableDlg class for inserting a new HTML table. This item's ActionListener is responsible for creating the TableDlg instance and inserting the resulting HTML code, retrieved using TableDlg's generateHTML() method, after the paragraph the cursor is currently in.

❸ The editable styles combo box, m_cbStyles, holds the STYLES list of HTML styles. It receives an ActionListener which applies the selected HTML.Tag to the paragraph the cursor currently resides in.

The showAttributes() method receives additional code to manage the new style's combo box when the caret moves through the document. It retrieves the style corresponding to the paragraph based on caret position and selects the appropriate entry in the combo box.

❹ *Class TableDlg*

This class extends JDialog and has several instance variables:

- boolean m_succeeded: flag set to true if the Save button is pressed.
- MutableHTMLDocument m_doc: reference to the HTML document passed into the constructor.
- JSpinner m_rowsSpn: used to select number of table rows.
- JSpinner m_colsSpn: used to select number of table columns.
- JSpinner m_spacingSpn: used to select table cell spacing size.
- JSpinner m_paddingSpn: used to select table cell padding size.
- JSpinner m_borderWidthSpn: used to select table border width.
- JSpinner m_tableWidthSpn: used to select table width.
- JSpinner m_tableHeightSpn: used to select table height.
- JComboBox m_tableUnitsCb: used to choose units with which to measure HTML table dimensions (either percentage of available space or pixels).
- JTextPane m_previewPane: text component to display a preview of the HTML table.
- Color m_borderColor: used to maintain the HTML table's border color.
- Color m_backgroundColor: used to maintain the HTML table's background color.
- HTMLEditorKit m_kit: editor kit used to create new preview pane document.

The TableDlg constructor takes JFrame and MutableHTMLDocument as parameters. The document represents the HTML document to which a table will be added. A JTabbedPane is created with four tabs: Table, Size, Color, and Preview. Each of these tabs receives its own panel of components.

The Table tab consists of four JSpinners used to select number of table rows and columns, and values for table cell spacing and padding.

The Size tab consists of three JSpinners used to select table border width, table width, and table height. It also contains a JComboBox used to select whether the spinner values for table width and height in this tab are using Percent or Pixels as units. Percent refers to percentage of available space the table should occupy, whereas Pixels refers to actual pixel values.

The Color tab contains buttons called Border, and Background which are responsible for setting the table border color and table background colors respectively through use of a JColorChooser.

The Preview tab consists of a text pane to show a preview of the proposed HTML table. A ChangeListener is added to the tabbed pane to detect when the Preview tab is selected and update the text pane in response using our custom generateHTML() method.

An Insert button and a Cancel button are also added to this dialog. The Insert button sets the m_succeeded flag to true before the dialog is disposed; the Cancel button simply diposes of the dialog.

The getSucceeded() method returns the m_succeeded flag.

The generateHTML() method returns a String representing the HTML code for a table based on the current values of the input components in the Table, Size, and Color tabs.

20.4.2 Running the code

Figure 20.8 shows our editor with the styles combo box open. Figures 20.9 through 20.12 show each tab of our HTML table dialog. Open an existing HTML file and verify that the selected style is automatically updated while the caret moves through the document. Place the caret in a different paragraph and select a different style from the styles combo box. Note how all text properties are updated according to the new style. Use the Insert menu and select Table to insert an HTML table.

20.5 *HTML* EDITOR, PART *V:* CLIPBOARD AND UNDO/REDO

Clipboard and undo/redo operations have become common and necessary components of all modern text editing environments. We have discussed these features in chapters 11 and 19, and in this section we show how to integrate them into our HTML editor application.

Example 20.5

HtmlProcessor.java

see \Chapter20\5

```
import java.awt.*;
import java.awt.event.*;
import java.io.*;
import java.net.*;
import java.util.*;

import javax.swing.*;
import javax.swing.text.*;
import javax.swing.event.*;
import javax.swing.border.*;
import javax.swing.text.html.*;
```

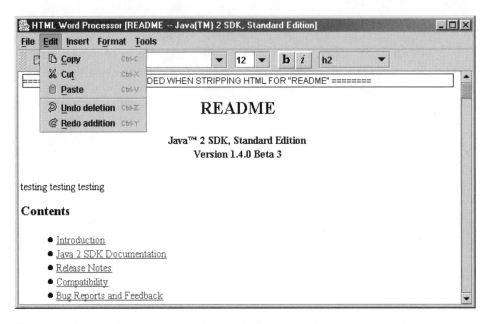

Figure 20.13 `HtmlProcessor` **with undo/redo and clipboard functionality**

```
import javax.swing.undo.*;

import dl.*;

public class HtmlProcessor extends JFrame {

    // Unchanged code from example 20.4

    protected UndoManager m_undo = new UndoManager();
    protected Action m_undoAction;
    protected Action m_redoAction;

    // Unchanged code from example 20.4

    protected JMenuBar createMenuBar() {
        JMenuBar menuBar = new JMenuBar();

        // Unchanged code from example 20.4

        JMenu mEdit = new JMenu("Edit");
        mEdit.setMnemonic('e');

            Action action = new AbstractAction("Copy",
        new ImageIcon("Copy16.gif"))
        {
            public void actionPerformed(ActionEvent e) {
                m_editor.copy();
            }
        };
        item = mEdit.add(action);
```

Action to invoke a copy of currently selected text ❶

```
item.setMnemonic('c');
item.setAccelerator(KeyStroke.getKeyStroke(KeyEvent.VK_C,
  KeyEvent.Ctrl_MASK));

  action = new AbstractAction("Cut",
new ImageIcon("Cut16.gif"))
{
  public void actionPerformed(ActionEvent e) {
    m_editor.cut();
  }
};
item = mEdit.add(action);
item.setMnemonic('t');
item.setAccelerator(KeyStroke.getKeyStroke(KeyEvent.VK_X,
  KeyEvent.Ctrl_MASK));

  action = new AbstractAction("Paste",
new ImageIcon("Paste16.gif"))
{
  public void actionPerformed(ActionEvent e) {
    m_editor.paste();}
};
item = mEdit.add(action);
item.setMnemonic('p');
item.setAccelerator(KeyStroke.getKeyStroke(KeyEvent.VK_V,
  KeyEvent.Ctrl_MASK));

  mEdit.addSeparator();

  m_undoAction = new AbstractAction("Undo",
new ImageIcon("Undo16.gif"))
{
  public void actionPerformed(ActionEvent e) {
    try {
      m_undo.undo();
    }
    catch (CannotUndoException ex) {
      System.err.println("Unable to undo: " + ex);
    }
    updateUndo();
  }
};
item = mEdit.add(m_undoAction);
item.setMnemonic('u');
item.setAccelerator(KeyStroke.getKeyStroke(KeyEvent.VK_Z,
  KeyEvent.Ctrl_MASK));

  m_redoAction = new AbstractAction("Redo",
new ImageIcon("Redo16.gif"))
{
  public void actionPerformed(ActionEvent e) {
    try {
      m_undo.redo();
    }
```

Action to invoke a copy of currently selected text ❶

Action to invoke a cut of currently selected text ❶

Action to invoke a paste of current clipboard text ❶

Action to invoke an Undo ❷

Action to invoke a Redo ❷

```
            catch (CannotRedoException ex) {
               System.err.println("Unable to redo: " + ex);
            }
            updateUndo();
         }
      };
      item =mEdit.add(m_redoAction);
      item.setMnemonic('r');
      item.setAccelerator(KeyStroke.getKeyStroke(KeyEvent.VK_Y,
         KeyEvent.Ctrl_MASK));

         menuBar.add(mEdit);

      // Unchanged code from example 20.4

      return menuBar;
   }
   // Unchanged code from example 20.4

   protected void newDocument() {
      // Unchanged code from example 20.4

      SwingUtilities.invokeLater(new Runnable() {
         public void run() {
            showAttributes(0);
            m_editor.scrollRectToVisible(new Rectangle(0,0,1,1));
            m_doc.addDocumentListener(new UpdateListener());
            m_doc.addUndoableEditListener(new Undoer());
            m_textChanged = false;
         }
      });
   }

   protected void openDocument() {
     // Unchanged code from example 20.4

      SwingUtilities.invokeLater(new Runnable() {
         public void run() {
            m_editor.setCaretPosition(1);
            showAttributes(1);
            m_editor.scrollRectToVisible(new Rectangle(0,0,1,1));
            m_doc.addDocumentListener(new UpdateListener());
            m_doc.addUndoableEditListener(new Undoer());
            m_textChanged = false;
         }
      });
   }

// Unchanged code from example 20.4

   protected void updateUndo() {
      if(m_undo.canUndo()) {
         m_undoAction.setEnabled(true);
         m_undoAction.putValue(Action.NAME,
         m_undo.getUndoPresentationName());
      }
```

2 Action to invoke a Redo

3 Updates undo and redo Actions based on undo stack

```
      else {
        m_undoAction.setEnabled(false);
        m_undoAction.putValue(Action.NAME, "Undo");
      }
      if(m_undo.canRedo()) {
        m_redoAction.setEnabled(true);
        m_redoAction.putValue(Action.NAME,
          m_undo.getRedoPresentationName());
      }
      else {
        m_redoAction.setEnabled(false);
        m_redoAction.putValue(Action.NAME, "Redo");
      }
    }

  public static void main(String argv[]) {
    HtmlProcessor frame = new HtmlProcessor();
    frame.setDefaultCloseOperation(JFrame.DO_NOTHING_ON_CLOSE);
    frame.setVisible(true);
  }

// Unchanged code from example 20.4

  class Undoer implements UndoableEditListener {
    public Undoer() {
      m_undo.die();
      updateUndo();
    }

    public void undoableEditHappened(UndoableEditEvent e) {
      UndoableEdit edit = e.getEdit();
      m_undo.addEdit(e.getEdit());
      updateUndo();
    }
  }
}
```

Adds undoable edit events to UndoManager and updates state of undo/redo components ❹

`// Unchanged code from example 20.4`

20.5.1   Understanding the code

Class HtmlProcessor

We now import the `javax.swing.undo` package and add three new instance variables:

- `UndoManager m_undo`: used to manage undo/redo operations.
- `Action m_undoAction`: used for a menu item/action to perform undo operations.
- `Action m_redoAction`: used for a menu item/action to perform redo operations.

❶ The `createMenuBar()` method now creates a menu titled Edit (which traditionally follows the File menu) containing menu items titled Copy, Cut, Paste, Undo, and Redo. The first three items merely trigger calls to the `copy()`, `cut()`, and `paste()` methods of our `m_editor` text pane. These methods perform basic clipboard operations. They are available when the editor has the current focus and the appropriate keyboard accelerator is pressed.

The Undo menu item is created from an `AbstractAction` whose `actionPerformed()` method first invokes `undo()` on the `UndoManager`, and then invokes our custom `update-Undo()` method to update our Undo/Redo menu items appropriately. Similarly, the Redo menu item is created from an `AbstractAction` which invokes `redo()` on the `UndoManager`, and then calls our `updateUndo()` method.

The `newDocument()` and `openDocument()` methods now add an instance of our custom `Undoer` class as an `UndoableEditListener` to all newly created or loaded documents.

❸ The `updateUndo()` method enables or disables the Undo and Redo menu items, and updates their names according to the operation which can be undone/redone (if any). If the `Undo-Manager`'s `canUndo()` method returns `true`, the `m_undoAction` is enabled and its name is set to the string returned by `getUndoPresentationName()`. Otherwise it is disabled and its name is set to Undo. The Redo menu item is handled similarly.

Class HtmlProcessor.Undoer

❹ This inner class implements the `UndoableEditListener` interface to receive notifications about undoable operations. The `undoableEditHappened()` method receives `Undoable-EditEvents`, retrieves their encapsulated `UndoableEdit` instances, and passes them to the `UndoManager`. The `updateUndo()` method is also invoked to update the undo/redo menu items appropriately.

20.5.2 Running the code

Figure 20.13 shows our editor with the Edit menu open. Open an existing HTML file and verify that copy, cut, and paste clipboard operations transfer text successfully. Make some changes to the textual content or styles and note that the title of the Undo menu item is updated. Select this menu item, or press its keyboard accelerator (Ctrl-Z) to undo a series of changes. This will enable the Redo menu item. Use this menu item or press its keyboard accelerator (Ctrl-Y) to redo a series of changes.

20.6 *HTML EDITOR, PART VI: ADVANCED FONT MANAGEMENT*

In section 20.2 we used toolbar components to change font properties. This is useful for making a quick modification without leaving the main application frame, and is typical for word processor applications. However, all serious editor applications also provide a dialog for the editing of all available font properties from one location. In this section's example we'll show how to create such a dialog, which includes components to select various font properties and preview the result.

Example 20.6

HtmlProcessor.java

see \Chapter20\6

```
import java.awt.*;
import java.awt.event.*;
import java.io.*;
import java.net.*;
```

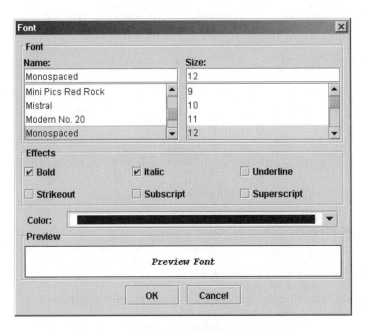

Figure 20.14   Font properties and preview dialog

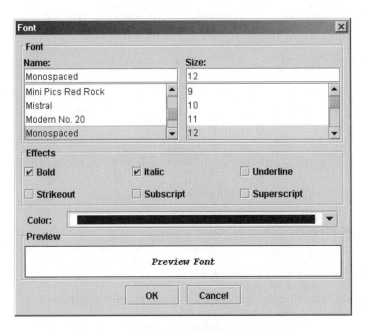

**Figure 20.15   Font dialog displaying custom list and
list cell renderer for foreground color selection**

```
import java.util.*;

import javax.swing.*;
import javax.swing.text.*;
import javax.swing.event.*;
import javax.swing.border.*;
import javax.swing.text.html.*;
import javax.swing.undo.*;

import dl.*;

public class HtmlProcessor extends JFrame {

   public static final String APP_NAME = "HTML HTML Editor";

// Unchanged code from example 20.5

   protected String[] m_fontNames;
   protected String[] m_fontSizes;

   // Unchanged code from example 20.5

   protected JMenuBar createMenuBar() {
      JMenuBar menuBar = new JMenuBar();

// Unchanged code from example 20.5

      GraphicsEnvironment ge = GraphicsEnvironment.
         getLocalGraphicsEnvironment();
      m_fontNames = ge.getAvailableFontFamilyNames();

      m_toolBar.addSeparator();
      m_cbFonts = new JComboBox(m_fontNames);
      m_cbFonts.setMaximumSize(new Dimension(200, 23));
      m_cbFonts.setEditable(true);

      ActionListener lst = new ActionListener() {
         public void actionPerformed(ActionEvent e) {
            m_fontName = m_cbFonts.getSelectedItem().toString();
            MutableAttributeSet attr = new SimpleAttributeSet();
            StyleConstants.setFontFamily(attr, m_fontName);
            setAttributeSet(attr);
            m_editor.grabFocus();
         }
      };
      m_cbFonts.addActionListener(lst);

      m_toolBar.add(m_cbFonts);

      m_toolBar.addSeparator();
      m_fontSizes = new String[] {"8", "9", "10",
         "11", "12", "14", "16", "18", "20", "22", "24", "26",
         "28", "36", "48", "72"};
      m_cbSizes = new JComboBox(m_fontSizes);
      m_cbSizes.setMaximumSize(new Dimension(50, 23));
      m_cbSizes.setEditable(true);
```

```
        // Unchanged code from example 20.5

        item = new JMenuItem("Font...");
        item.setMnemonic('o');
        lst = new ActionListener() {
            public void actionPerformed(ActionEvent e) {
                FontDialog dlg = new FontDialog(HtmlProcessor.this,
                    m_fontNames, m_fontSizes);
                AttributeSet a = m_doc.getCharacterElement(
                    m_editor.getCaretPosition()).getAttributes();
                dlg.setAttributes(a);
                dlg.show();
                if (dlg.succeeded()) {
                    setAttributeSet(dlg.getAttributes());
                    showAttributes(m_editor.getCaretPosition());
                }
            }
        };
        item.addActionListener(lst);
        mFormat.add(item);
        mFormat.addSeparator();

        return menuBar;
    }

// Unchanged code from example 20.5

}

// Unchanged code from example 20.5

class FontDialog extends JDialog {
    protected boolean m_succeeded = false;
    protected OpenList m_lstFontName;
    protected OpenList m_lstFontSize;
    protected MutableAttributeSet m_attributes;
    protected JCheckBox m_chkBold;
    protected JCheckBox m_chkItalic;
    protected JCheckBox m_chkUnderline;

    protected JCheckBox m_chkStrikethrough;
    protected JCheckBox m_chkSubscript;
    protected JCheckBox m_chkSuperscript;

    protected JComboBox m_cbColor;
    protected JLabel m_preview;

    public FontDialog(JFrame parent,
        String[] names, String[] sizes)
    {
        super(parent, "Font", true);
        JPanel pp = new JPanel();
        pp.setBorder(new EmptyBorder(5,5,5,5));
        pp.setLayout(new BoxLayout(pp, BoxLayout.Y_AXIS));

        JPanel p = new JPanel(new GridLayout(1, 2, 10, 2));
        p.setBorder(new TitledBorder(new EtchedBorder(), "Font"));
```

❶ New menu item to invoke custom FontDialog for font management

❷ Custom font dialog allows specification of font properties such as size, name, bold, italic, underline, strikethrough, subscript, superscript, color and also includes a preview illustrating selections

```
m_lstFontName = new OpenList(names, "Name:");
p.add(m_lstFontName);

m_lstFontSize = new OpenList(sizes, "Size:");
p.add(m_lstFontSize);
pp.add(p);
```

❸ Custom OpenList components used to select font name and size

```
p = new JPanel(new GridLayout(2, 3, 10, 5));
p.setBorder(new TitledBorder(new EtchedBorder(), "Effects"));
m_chkBold = new JCheckBox("Bold");
p.add(m_chkBold);
m_chkItalic = new JCheckBox("Italic");
p.add(m_chkItalic);
m_chkUnderline = new JCheckBox("Underline");
p.add(m_chkUnderline);
m_chkStrikethrough = new JCheckBox("Strikeout");
p.add(m_chkStrikethrough);
m_chkSubscript = new JCheckBox("Subscript");
p.add(m_chkSubscript);
m_chkSuperscript = new JCheckBox("Superscript");
p.add(m_chkSuperscript);
pp.add(p);
pp.add(Box.createVerticalStrut(5));
```

Check boxes for various font properties ❸

```
p = new JPanel();
p.setLayout(new BoxLayout(p, BoxLayout.X_AXIS));
p.add(Box.createHorizontalStrut(10));
p.add(new JLabel("Color:"));
p.add(Box.createHorizontalStrut(20));
m_cbColor = new JComboBox();

int[] values = new int[] { 0, 128, 192, 255 };
for (int r=0; r<values.length; r++) {
  for (int g=0; g<values.length; g++) {
    for (int b=0; b<values.length; b++) {
      Color c = new Color(values[r], values[g], values[b]);

m_cbColor.addItem(c);
      }
    }
  }
```

Create combo box used to select font color using custom ColorComboRenderer ❸

```
m_cbColor.setRenderer(new ColorComboRenderer());
p.add(m_cbColor);
p.add(Box.createHorizontalStrut(10));
pp.add(p);

ListSelectionListener lsel = new ListSelectionListener() {
  public void valueChanged(ListSelectionEvent e) {
    updatePreview();
  }
};
m_lstFontName.addListSelectionListener(lsel);
m_lstFontSize.addListSelectionListener(lsel);
```

Updates preview component wherever font name or size changes ❺

```
        ActionListener lst = new ActionListener() {
          public void actionPerformed(ActionEvent e) {
            updatePreview();
          }
        };
        m_chkBold.addActionListener(lst);
        m_chkItalic.addActionListener(lst);
        m_cbColor.addActionListener(lst);

        p = new JPanel(new BorderLayout());
        p.setBorder(new TitledBorder(new EtchedBorder(), "Preview"));
        m_preview = new JLabel("Preview Font", JLabel.CENTER);
        m_preview.setBackground(Color.white);
        m_preview.setForeground(Color.black);
        m_preview.setOpaque(true);
        m_preview.setBorder(new LineBorder(Color.black));
        m_preview.setPreferredSize(new Dimension(120, 40));
        p.add(m_preview, BorderLayout.CENTER);
        pp.add(p);

        p = new JPanel(new FlowLayout());
        JPanel p1 = new JPanel(new GridLayout(1, 2, 10, 0));
        JButton btOK = new JButton("OK");
        lst = new ActionListener() {
          public void actionPerformed(ActionEvent e) {
            m_succeeded = true;
            dispose();
          }
        };
        btOK.addActionListener(lst);
        p1.add(btOK);

        JButton btCancel = new JButton("Cancel");
        lst = new ActionListener() {
          public void actionPerformed(ActionEvent e) {
            dispose();
          }
        };
        btCancel.addActionListener(lst);
        p1.add(btCancel);
        p.add(p1);
        pp.add(p);

        getContentPane().add(pp, BorderLayout.CENTER);
        pack();
        setResizable(false);
        setLocationRelativeTo(parent);
      }

      public void setAttributes(AttributeSet a) {
        m_attributes = new SimpleAttributeSet(a);
        String name = StyleConstants.getFontFamily(a);
        m_lstFontName.setSelected(name);
        int size = StyleConstants.getFontSize(a);
```

Preview panel showing sample of selected font attributes changes ④

Placing buttons inside GridLayout inside FlowLayout ensures the buttons are equally sized and centered ⑥

Used to assign initial attribute to selection components when font dialog is invoked ⑦

```
      m_lstFontSize.setSelectedInt(size);
      m_chkBold.setSelected(StyleConstants.isBold(a));
      m_chkItalic.setSelected(StyleConstants.isItalic(a));
      m_chkUnderline.setSelected(StyleConstants.isUnderline(a));
      m_chkStrikethrough.setSelected(
        StyleConstants.isStrikeThrough(a));
      m_chkSubscript.setSelected(StyleConstants.isSubscript(a));
      m_chkSuperscript.setSelected(StyleConstants.isSuperscript(a));
      m_cbColor.setSelectedItem(StyleConstants.getForeground(a));
      updatePreview();
   }

   public AttributeSet getAttributes() {
      if (m_attributes == null)
         return null;
      StyleConstants.setFontFamily(m_attributes,
         m_lstFontName.getSelected());
      StyleConstants.setFontSize(m_attributes,
         m_lstFontSize.getSelectedInt());
      StyleConstants.setBold(m_attributes,
         m_chkBold.isSelected());
      StyleConstants.setItalic(m_attributes,
         m_chkItalic.isSelected());
      StyleConstants.setUnderline(m_attributes,
         m_chkUnderline.isSelected());
      StyleConstants.setStrikeThrough(m_attributes,
         m_chkStrikethrough.isSelected());
      StyleConstants.setSubscript(m_attributes,
         m_chkSubscript.isSelected());
      StyleConstants.setSuperscript(m_attributes,
         m_chkSuperscript.isSelected());
      StyleConstants.setForeground(m_attributes,
         (Color)m_cbColor.getSelectedItem());
      return m_attributes;
   }

   public boolean succeeded() {
      return m_succeeded;
   }

   protected void updatePreview() {
      String name = m_lstFontName.getSelected();
      int size = m_lstFontSize.getSelectedInt();
      if (size <= 0)
         return;
      int style = Font.PLAIN;
      if (m_chkBold.isSelected())
         style |= Font.BOLD;
      if (m_chkItalic.isSelected())
         style |= Font.ITALIC;

      // Bug Alert! This doesn't work if only style is changed.
      Font fn = new Font(name, style, size);
      m_preview.setFont(fn);
```

8 Used to retrieve current attributes selected in the font dialog

9 Updates preview panel with current font dialog selections

```
      Color c = (Color)m_cbColor.getSelectedItem();
      m_preview.setForeground(c);
      m_preview.repaint();
   }
}

class OpenList extends JPanel                                    ⑩ Custom component
   implements ListSelectionListener, ActionListener               resembling a
{                                                                  permanently open
   protected JLabel m_title;                                       combo box
   protected JTextField m_text;
   protected JList m_list;
   protected JScrollPane m_scroll;

   public OpenList(String[] data, String title) {
      setLayout(null);
      m_title = new JLabel(title, JLabel.LEFT);
      add(m_title);
      m_text = new JTextField();
      m_text.addActionListener(this);
      add(m_text);
      m_list = new JList(data);
      m_list.setVisibleRowCount(4);
      m_list.addListSelectionListener(this);
      m_list.setFont(m_text.getFont());
      m_scroll = new JScrollPane(m_list);
      add(m_scroll);
   }

   public void setSelected(String sel) {
      m_list.setSelectedValue(sel, true);
      m_text.setText(sel);
   }

   public String getSelected() { return m_text.getText(); }

   public void setSelectedInt(int value) {
      setSelected(Integer.toString(value));
   }

   public int getSelectedInt() {
      try {
         return Integer.parseInt(getSelected());
      }
      catch (NumberFormatException ex) { return -1; }
   }

   public void valueChanged(ListSelectionEvent e) {
      Object obj = m_list.getSelectedValue();
      if (obj != null)
         m_text.setText(obj.toString());
   }

   public void actionPerformed(ActionEvent e) {
      ListModel model = m_list.getModel();
      String key = m_text.getText().toLowerCase();
```

```
      for (int k=0; k<model.getSize(); k++) {
        String data = (String)model.getElementAt(k);
        if (data.toLowerCase().startsWith(key)) {
          m_list.setSelectedValue(data, true);
          break;
        }
      }
    }

    public void addListSelectionListener(ListSelectionListener lst) {
      m_list.addListSelectionListener(lst);
    }

    public Dimension getPreferredSize() {
      Insets ins = getInsets();
      Dimension d1 = m_title.getPreferredSize();
      Dimension d2 = m_text.getPreferredSize();
      Dimension d3 = m_scroll.getPreferredSize();
      int w = Math.max(Math.max(d1.width, d2.width), d3.width);
      int h = d1.height + d2.height + d3.height;
      return new Dimension(w+ins.left+ins.right,
        h+ins.top+ins.bottom);
    }

    public Dimension getMaximumSize() {
      Insets ins = getInsets();
      Dimension d1 = m_title.getMaximumSize();
      Dimension d2 = m_text.getMaximumSize();
      Dimension d3 = m_scroll.getMaximumSize();
      int w = Math.max(Math.max(d1.width, d2.width), d3.width);
      int h = d1.height + d2.height + d3.height;
      return new Dimension(w+ins.left+ins.right,
        h+ins.top+ins.bottom);
    }

    public Dimension getMinimumSize() {
      Insets ins = getInsets();
      Dimension d1 = m_title.getMinimumSize();
      Dimension d2 = m_text.getMinimumSize();
      Dimension d3 = m_scroll.getMinimumSize();
      int w = Math.max(Math.max(d1.width, d2.width), d3.width);
      int h = d1.height + d2.height + d3.height;
      return new Dimension(w+ins.left+ins.right,
        h+ins.top+ins.bottom);
    }

    public void doLayout() {
      Insets ins = getInsets();
      Dimension d = getSize();
      int x = ins.left;
      int y = ins.top;
      int w = d.width-ins.left-ins.right;
      int h = d.height-ins.top-ins.bottom;

      Dimension d1 = m_title.getPreferredSize();
```

⓫ All layout at this component is handled here

```
        m_title.setBounds(x, y, w, d1.height);
        y += d1.height;
        Dimension d2 = m_text.getPreferredSize();
        m_text.setBounds(x, y, w, d2.height);
        y += d2.height;
        m_scroll.setBounds(x, y, w, h-y);
    }
}

class ColorComboRenderer extends JPanel implements ListCellRenderer
{
    protected Color m_color = Color.black;
    protected Color m_focusColor =
        (Color) UIManager.get("List.selectionBackground");
    protected Color m_nonFocusColor = Color.white;

    public Component getListCellRendererComponent(JList list,
     Object obj, int row, boolean sel, boolean hasFocus)
    {
        if (hasFocus || sel)
            setBorder(new CompoundBorder(
                new MatteBorder(2, 10, 2, 10, m_focusColor),
                new LineBorder(Color.black)));
        else
            setBorder(new CompoundBorder(
                new MatteBorder(2, 10, 2, 10, m_nonFocusColor),
                new LineBorder(Color.black)));

        if (obj instanceof Color)
            m_color = (Color) obj;
        return this;
    }

    public void paintComponent(Graphics g) {
        setBackground(m_color);
        super.paintComponent(g);
    }
}
```

Custom list cell renderer used to display Colors in a presentable fashion ⑫

20.6.1   Understanding the code

Class HtmlProcessor

Two new instance variables are added:

- String[] m_fontNames: array of available font family names.
- String[] m_fontSizes: array of font sizes.

These arrays were used earlier as local variables to create the toolbar combo box components. Since we need to use them in our font dialog as well, we decided to make them instance variables (this requires minimal changes to the createMenuBar() method).

NOTE   Reading the list of available fonts takes a significant amount of time. For performance reasons it is best to do this only once in an application's lifetime.

❶ A new menu item titled Font... is now added to the Format menu. When the corresponding `ActionListener` is invoked an instance of our custom `FontDialog` is created and the attributes of the character element corresponding to the current caret position are retrieved as an `AttributeSet` instance and passed to the dialog for selection (using its `setAttributes()` method), and the dialog is centered relative to the parent frame and displayed. If the dialog is closed with the OK button (determined by checking whether its `succeeded()` method returns `true`), we retrieve the new font attributes with `FontDialog`'s `getAttributes()` method, and assign these attributes to the selected text with our `setAttributeSet()` method. Finally, our toolbar components are updated with our `showAttributes()` method.

❷ *Class FontDialog*

This class extends `JDialog` and acts as a font properties editor and previewer for our HTML editor application. Several instance variables are declared:

- `boolean m_succeeded`: a flag that will be set to `true` if font changes are accepted.
- `OpenList m_lstFontName`: custom `JList` subclass for selecting the font family name.
- `OpenList m_lstFontSize`: custom `JList` subclass for selecting the font size.
- `MutableAttributeSet m_attributes`: a collection of font attributes used to preserve the user's selection.
- `JCheckBox m_chkBold`: check box to select the bold attribute.
- `JCheckBox m_chkItalic`: check box to select the italic attribute.
- `JCheckBox m_chkUnderline`: check box to select the font underline attribute.
- `JCheckBox m_chkStrikethrough`: check box to select the font strikethrough attribute.
- `JCheckBox m_chkSubscript`: check box to select the font subscript attribute.
- `JCheckBox m_chkSuperscript`: check box to select the font superscript attribute.
- `JComboBox m_cbColor`: combo box to select the font foreground color.
- `JLabel m_preview`: label to preview the selections.

The `FontDialog` constructor first creates a superclass modal dialog titled Font. The constructor creates and initializes all GUI components used in this dialog. A *y*-oriented `BoxLayout` is used to place component groups from top to bottom.

❸ Two `OpenList` components are placed at the top to select an available font family name and font size. These components encapsulate a label, text box, and list components which work together. They are similar to editable combo boxes that always keep their drop-down list open. Below the `OpenLists`, a group of six check boxes are placed for selecting bold, italic, underline, strikethrough, subscript, and superscript font attributes. `JComboBox m_cbColor` is placed below this group, and is used to select the font foreground color. Sixty-four `Colors` are added, and an instance of our custom `ColorComboRenderer` class is used as its list cell renderer. **❹** `JLabel m_preview` is used to preview the selected font before applying it to the editing text, and is placed below the foreground color combo box.

❺ The `m_lstFontName` and `m_lstFontSize` `OpenList` components each receive the same `ListSelectionListener` instance which calls our custom `updatePreview()` method whenever the list selection is changed. Similarly, the check boxes and the foreground color combo box receive an `ActionListener` which does the same thing. This provides dynamic preview of the selected font attributes as soon as any is changed.

BUG ALERT! Underline, strikethrough, subscript, and superscript font properties are not supported by the AWT Font class, so they cannot be shown in the JLabel component. This is why the corresponding check box components do not receive an ActionListener. As we will see, the strikethrough, subscript, and superscript properties also do not work properly in HTML documents. They are included in this dialog for completeness, in the hopes that they will work properly in a future Swing release.

❶ Two buttons labeled OK and Cancel are placed at the bottom of the dialog. They are placed in a panel managed by a 1x2 GridLayout, which is in turn placed in a panel managed by a FlowLayout. This is to ensure the equal sizing and central placement of the buttons. Both receive ActionListeners which dispose of the dialog. The OK button also sets the m_succeeded flag to true to indicate that the changes made in the font dialog should be applied.

The dialog window is packed to give it a natural size, and is then centered with respect to the parent frame.

❼ The setAttributes() method takes an AttributeSet instance as a parameter. It copies this attribute set into a SimpleAttributeSet stored as our m_attributes instance variable. Appropriate font attributes are extracted using StyleConstants methods, and used to assign values to the dialog's controls. Finally the preview label is updated according to these new settings by calling our updatePreview() method. Note that the setAttributes() method is public and is used for data exchange between this dialog and its owner (in our case HtmlProcessor).

❽ The getAttributes() method plays an opposite role with respect to setAttributes(). It retrieves data from the dialog's controls, packs them into an AttributeSet instance using StyleConstants methods, and returns this set to the caller.

The succeeded() method simply returns the m_succeeded flag.

❾ The updatePreview() method is called to update the font preview label when a font attribute is changed. It retrieves the selected font attributes (family name, size, bold, and italic properties) and creates a new Font instance to render the label. The selected color is retrieved from the m_cbColor combo box and set as the label's foreground.

❿ *Class OpenList*

This component consists of a title label, a text field, and a list in a scroll pane. The user can either select a value from the list, or enter it in the text box manually. OpenList extends JPanel and maintains the following four instance variables:

- JLabel m_title: title label used to identify the purpose of this component.
- JTextField m_text: editable text field.
- JList m_list: list component.
- JScrollPane m_scroll: scroll pane containing the list component.

The OpenList constructor assigns a null layout manager because this container manages its child components on its own. The four components are instantiated and simply added to this container.

The setSelected() method sets the text field text to that of the given String, and selects the corresponding item in the list (which is scrolled to display the newly selected value). The getSelected() method retrieves and returns the selected item as a String.

Methods setSelectedInt()/getSelectedInt() do the same but with int values. These methods are implemented to simplify working with a list of ints.

The valueChanged() and actionPerformed() methods provide coordination between the list component and the text field. The valueChanged() method is called whenever the list selection changes, and will assign the result of a toString() call on the selected item as the text field's text. The actionPerformed() method will be called when the user presses Enter while the text field has the current focus. This implementation performs a case-insensitive search through the list items in an effort to find an item which begins with the entered text. If such an item is found, it is selected.

The public addListSelectionListener() method adds a ListSelectionListener to our list component (which is protected). In this way, external objects can dynamically receive notifications about changes in that list's selection.

The getPreferredSize(), getMaximumSize(), and getMinimumSize() methods calculate and return a preferred, maximum, and minimum dimension of this container respectively. They assume that the three child components (label, text field, and scroll pane containing the list) will be laid out one under another from top to bottom, receiving an equal width and their preferable heights. The doLayout() method actually lays out the components according to this scheme. Note that the insets (resulting from an assigned border, for instance) must always be taken into account (see chapter 4 for more about custom layout management).

⑫ *Class ColorComboRenderer*

This class implements the ListCellRenderer interface (discussed in chapters 9 and 10) and is used to represent various Colors. Three instance variables are defined:

- Color m_color: used for the main background color to represent a Color.
- Color m_focusColor: used for the thick border color of a selected item.
- Color m_nonFocusColor: used for the thick border color of an unselected item.

The getListCellRendererComponent() method is called prior to the rendering of each list item (in our HtmlProcessor example this list is contained within our foreground colors combo box). The Color instance is retrieved and stored in the m_color instance variable. This color is used as the renderer's background, while a white matte border is used to surround unselected cells, and a light blue matte border is used to surround a selected cell. The paintComponent() method simply sets the background to m_color and calls the superclass paintComponent() method.

20.6.2 Running the code

Figure 20.14 shows our custom FontDialog in action and figure 20.15 shows the foreground color combo box open, displaying our custom list cell renderer. Open an existing HTML file, select a portion of text, and bring up the font dialog. Verify that the initial values correspond to the font attributes of the paragraph of text at the current caret position. Try selecting different font attributes and note that the preview component is updated dynamically. Press the OK button to apply the selected attributes to the current paragraph. Also verify that clicking Cancel does not apply any changes.

20.7 HTML EDITOR, PART VII: FIND AND REPLACE

Along with font and paragraph dialogs, find and replace functionality has also become a fairly common tool in GUI-based text editing environments. It is safe to assume that most users would be sadly disappointed if this functionality was not included in a new word processor application. In this section we will show how to add this functionality. Traditionally such tools are represented in an Edit menu and can be activated by keyboard accelerators. We will use a dialog containing a single tabbed pane with tabs for finding and replacing a specific region of text. We will also provide several options for searching: match case, search whole words only, and search up or down.

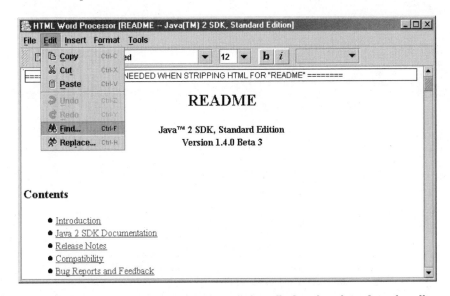

Figure 20.16 HtmlProcessor **with complete find and replace functionality; Find... and Replace... menu items shown here**

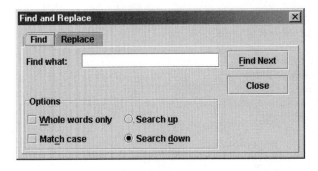

Figure 20.17 Find tab of our custom find and replace dialog

Example 20.7

see \Chapter20\7

```java
import java.awt.*;
import java.awt.event.*;
import java.io.*;
import java.net.*;
import java.util.*;

import javax.swing.*;
import javax.swing.text.*;
import javax.swing.event.*;
import javax.swing.border.*;
import javax.swing.text.html.*;
import javax.swing.undo.*;

import dl.*;

public class HtmlProcessor extends JFrame {

   public static final String APP_NAME = "HTML HTML Editor";

// Unchanged code from example 20.6

   protected FindDialog m_findDialog;

// Unchanged code from example 20.6

   protected JMenuBar createMenuBar() {

      JMenuBar menuBar = new JMenuBar();

      // Unchanged code from example 20.6

      Action findAction = new AbstractAction("Find...",
       new ImageIcon("Find16.gif"))
      {
        public void actionPerformed(ActionEvent e) {
          if (m_findDialog==null)
            m_findDialog = new FindDialog(HtmlProcessor.this, 0);
          else
            m_findDialog.setSelectedIndex(0);
          m_findDialog.show();
        }
      };
      item = mEdit.add(findAction);
      item.setMnemonic('f');
      item.setAccelerator(KeyStroke.getKeyStroke(KeyEvent.VK_F,
        KeyEvent.Ctrl_MASK));
```

Action to invoke find dialog ❶

```
    Action replaceAction = new AbstractAction("Replace...",
     new ImageIcon("Replace16.gif")) {
       public void actionPerformed(ActionEvent e) {
          if (m_findDialog==null)
             m_findDialog = new FindDialog(HtmlProcessor.this, 1);
          else
             m_findDialog.setSelectedIndex(1);
          m_findDialog.show();
       }
    };
    item = mEdit.add(replaceAction);
    item.setMnemonic('l');
    item.setAccelerator(KeyStroke.getKeyStroke(KeyEvent.VK_H,
       KeyEvent.Ctrl_MASK));

    menuBar.add(mEdit);

// Unchanged code from example 20.6

    return menuBar;
  }

  public Document getDocument() {
    return m_doc;
  }

  public JTextPane getTextPane() {
    return m_editor;
  }

  public void setSelection(int xStart, int xFinish, boolean moveUp) {
    if (moveUp) {
      m_editor.setCaretPosition(xFinish);
      m_editor.moveCaretPosition(xStart);
    }
    else
      m_editor.select(xStart, xFinish);
    m_xStart = m_editor.getSelectionStart();
    m_xFinish = m_editor.getSelectionEnd();
  }

  // Unchanged code from example 20.6
}

// Unchanged code from example 20.6

class Utils
{
  // Unchanged code from example 20.6

  public static final char[] WORD_SEPARATORS = {' ', '\t', '\n',
    '\r', '\f', '.', ',', ':', '-', '(', ')', '[', ']', '{',
    '}', '<', '>', '/', '|', '\\', '\'', '\"'};
```

Action to invoke find dialog with Replace tab selected ❶

Methods to allow easier access by external services ❷

Word separator characters ❸

```java
   public static boolean isSeparator(char ch) {
     for (int k=0; k<WORD_SEPARATORS.length; k++)
       if (ch == WORD_SEPARATORS[k])
         return true;
     return false;
   }
}
```

❸ **Method returns true if a given character is a separator character**

```java
// Unchanged code from example 20.6

class FindDialog extends JDialog {
   protected HtmlProcessor m_owner;
   protected JTabbedPane m_tb;
   protected JTextField m_txtFind1;
   protected JTextField m_txtFind2;
   protected Document m_docFind;
   protected Document m_docReplace;
   protected ButtonModel m_modelWord;
   protected ButtonModel m_modelCase;
   protected ButtonModel m_modelUp;
   protected ButtonModel m_modelDown;

   protected int m_searchIndex = -1;
   protected boolean m_searchUp = false;
   protected Stringm_searchData;

   public FindDialog(HtmlProcessor owner, int index) {
     super(owner, "Find and Replace", false);
     m_owner = owner;

     m_tb = new JTabbedPane();

     // "Find" panel
     JPanel p1 = new JPanel(new BorderLayout());

     JPanel pc1 = new JPanel(new BorderLayout());

     JPanel pf = new JPanel();
     pf.setLayout(new DialogLayout2(20, 5));
     pf.setBorder(new EmptyBorder(8, 5, 8, 0));
     pf.add(new JLabel("Find what:"));

     m_txtFind1 = new JTextField();
     m_docFind = m_txtFind1.getDocument();
     pf.add(m_txtFind1);
     pc1.add(pf, BorderLayout.CENTER);

     JPanel po = new JPanel(new GridLayout(2, 2, 8, 2));
     po.setBorder(new TitledBorder(new EtchedBorder(),
       "Options"));

     JCheckBox chkWord = new JCheckBox("Whole words only");
     chkWord.setMnemonic('w');
     m_modelWord = chkWord.getModel();
     po.add(chkWord);

     ButtonGroup bg = new ButtonGroup();
```

❹ **Dialog with tabbed pane for performing "Find" and "Replace" functionality**

❺ **Dialog is not modal**

```java
JRadioButton rdUp = new JRadioButton("Search up");
rdUp.setMnemonic('u');
m_modelUp = rdUp.getModel();
bg.add(rdUp);
po.add(rdUp);

JCheckBox chkCase = new JCheckBox("Match case");
chkCase.setMnemonic('c');
m_modelCase = chkCase.getModel();
po.add(chkCase);

JRadioButton rdDown = new JRadioButton("Search down", true);
rdDown.setMnemonic('d');
m_modelDown = rdDown.getModel();
bg.add(rdDown);
po.add(rdDown);
pc1.add(po, BorderLayout.SOUTH);

p1.add(pc1, BorderLayout.CENTER);

JPanel p01 = new JPanel(new FlowLayout());
JPanel p = new JPanel(new GridLayout(2, 1, 2, 8));

ActionListener findAction = new ActionListener() {
  public void actionPerformed(ActionEvent e) {
    findNext(false, true);
  }
};
JButton btFind = new JButton("Find Next");
btFind.addActionListener(findAction);
btFind.setMnemonic('f');
p.add(btFind);

ActionListener closeAction = new ActionListener() {
  public void actionPerformed(ActionEvent e) {
    setVisible(false);
  }
};
JButton btClose = new JButton("Close");
btClose.addActionListener(closeAction);
btClose.setDefaultCapable(true);
p.add(btClose);
p01.add(p);
p1.add(p01, BorderLayout.EAST);

m_tb.addTab("Find", p1);

// "Replace" panel
JPanel p2 = new JPanel(new BorderLayout());

JPanel pc2 = new JPanel(new BorderLayout());

JPanel pc = new JPanel();
pc.setLayout(new DialogLayout2(20, 5));
pc.setBorder(new EmptyBorder(8, 5, 8, 0));

pc.add(new JLabel("Find what:"));
```

```
m_txtFind2 = new JTextField();
m_txtFind2.setDocument(m_docFind);
pc.add(m_txtFind2);

pc.add(new JLabel("Replace:"));
JTextField txtReplace = new JTextField();
m_docReplace = txtReplace.getDocument();
pc.add(txtReplace);
pc2.add(pc, BorderLayout.CENTER);

po = new JPanel(new GridLayout(2, 2, 8, 2));
po.setBorder(new TitledBorder(new EtchedBorder(),
    "Options"));

chkWord = new JCheckBox("Whole words only");
chkWord.setMnemonic('w');
chkWord.setModel(m_modelWord);
po.add(chkWord);

bg = new ButtonGroup();
rdUp = new JRadioButton("Search up");
rdUp.setMnemonic('u');
rdUp.setModel(m_modelUp);
bg.add(rdUp);
po.add(rdUp);

chkCase = new JCheckBox("Match case");
chkCase.setMnemonic('c');
chkCase.setModel(m_modelCase);
po.add(chkCase);

rdDown = new JRadioButton("Search down", true);
rdDown.setMnemonic('d');
rdDown.setModel(m_modelDown);
bg.add(rdDown);
po.add(rdDown);
pc2.add(po, BorderLayout.SOUTH);

p2.add(pc2, BorderLayout.CENTER);

JPanel p02 = new JPanel(new FlowLayout());
p = new JPanel(new GridLayout(3, 1, 2, 8));

ActionListener replaceAction = new ActionListener() {
  public void actionPerformed(ActionEvent e) {
    findNext(true, true);
  }
};
JButton btReplace = new JButton("Replace");
btReplace.addActionListener(replaceAction);
btReplace.setMnemonic('r');
p.add(btReplace);

ActionListener replaceAllAction = new ActionListener() {
  public void actionPerformed(ActionEvent e) {
    int counter = 0;
    while (true) {
```

```
            int result = findNext(true, false);
            if (result < 0)
                return;
            else if (result == 0)
            break;
            counter++;
        }
        JOptionPane.showMessageDialog(m_owner,
            counter+" replacement(s) have been done",
            HtmlProcessor.APP_NAME,
            JOptionPane.INFORMATION_MESSAGE);
    }
};
JButton btReplaceAll = new JButton("Replace All");
btReplaceAll.addActionListener(replaceAllAction);
btReplaceAll.setMnemonic('a');
p.add(btReplaceAll);

btClose = new JButton("Close");
btClose.addActionListener(closeAction);
btClose.setDefaultCapable(true);
p.add(btClose);
p02.add(p);
p2.add(p02, BorderLayout.EAST);

// Make button columns the same size
p01.setPreferredSize(p02.getPreferredSize());

m_tb.addTab("Replace", p2);

m_tb.setSelectedIndex(index);

JPanel pp = new JPanel(new BorderLayout());
pp.setBorder(new EmptyBorder(5,5,5,5));
pp.add(m_tb, BorderLayout.CENTER);
getContentPane().add(pp, BorderLayout.CENTER);

pack();
setResizable(false);
setLocationRelativeTo(owner);

WindowListener flst = new WindowAdapter() {
    public void windowActivated(WindowEvent e) {
        m_searchIndex = -1;
    }

    public void windowDeactivated(WindowEvent e) {
        m_searchData = null;
    }
};
addWindowListener(flst);
}

public void setSelectedIndex(int index) {
    m_tb.setSelectedIndex(index);
    setVisible(true);
```

6 Make tab panels same size so that shared components stay in same position

```
      m_searchIndex = -1;
   }

   public int findNext(boolean doReplace, boolean showWarnings) {
      JTextPane monitor = m_owner.getTextPane();
      int pos = monitor.getCaretPosition();
      if (m_modelUp.isSelected() != m_searchUp) {
         m_searchUp = m_modelUp.isSelected();
         m_searchIndex = -1;
      }

      if (m_searchIndex == -1) {
         try {
            Document doc = m_owner.getDocument();
            if (m_searchUp)
               m_searchData = doc.getText(0, pos);
            else
               m_searchData = doc.getText(pos, doc.getLength()-pos);
            m_searchIndex = pos;
         }
         catch (BadLocationException ex) {
            warning(ex.toString());
            return -1;
         }
      }

      String key = "";
      try {
         key = m_docFind.getText(0, m_docFind.getLength());
      }
      catch (BadLocationException ex) {}
      if (key.length()==0) {
         warning("Please enter the target to search");
         return -1;
      }
      if (!m_modelCase.isSelected()) {
         m_searchData = m_searchData.toLowerCase();
         key = key.toLowerCase();
      }
      if (m_modelWord.isSelected()) {
         for (int k=0; k<Utils.WORD_SEPARATORS.length; k++) {
            if (key.indexOf(Utils.WORD_SEPARATORS[k]) >= 0) {
               warning("The text target contains an illegal "+
                  "character \'"+Utils.WORD_SEPARATORS[k]+"\'");
               return -1;
            }
         }
      }

      String replacement = "";
      if (doReplace) {
         try {
            replacement = m_docReplace.getText(0,
               m_docReplace.getLength());
```

Performs actual find/replace operation ⑦

Get string to search for and optionally convert both search text and target to lowercase ⑧

⑨ **Retrieves replacement text**

```
      } catch (BadLocationException ex) {}
  }

  int xStart = -1;
  int xFinish = -1;
  while (true)
  {
    if (m_searchUp)
      xStart = m_searchData.lastIndexOf(key, pos-1);
    else
      xStart = m_searchData.indexOf(key, pos-m_searchIndex);
    if (xStart < 0) {
      if (showWarnings)
        warning("Text not found");
      return 0;
    }

    xFinish = xStart+key.length();

    if (m_modelWord.isSelected()) {
      boolean s1 = xStart>0;
      boolean b1 = s1 && !Utils.isSeparator(m_searchData.charAt(
        xStart-1));
      boolean s2 = xFinish<m_searchData.length();
      boolean b2 = s2 && !Utils.isSeparator(m_searchData.charAt(
        xFinish));

      if (b1 || b2)// Not a whole word
      {
        if (m_searchUp && s1)// Can continue up
        {
          pos = xStart;
          continue;
        }
        if (!m_searchUp && s2)// Can continue down
        {
          pos = xFinish+1;
          continue;
        }
        // Found, but not a whole word, and we cannot continue
        if (showWarnings)
          warning("Text not found");
        return 0;
      }
    }
    break;
  }

  if (!m_searchUp) {
    xStart += m_searchIndex;
    xFinish += m_searchIndex;
  }
  if (doReplace) {
    m_owner.setSelection(xStart, xFinish, m_searchUp);
```

9 Retrieves replacement text

Searches backward or forward (up or down) for search string **10**

Bl and b2 determine whether the found string is in a word boundary **12**

Does actual replacement **12**

```
        monitor.replaceSelection(replacement);
        m_owner.setSelection(xStart, xStart+replacement.length(),
          m_searchUp);
        m_searchIndex = -1;
      }
      else
        m_owner.setSelection(xStart, xFinish, m_searchUp);
      return 1;
    }

  protected void warning(String message) {
    JOptionPane.showMessageDialog(m_owner,
      message, HtmlProcessor.APP_NAME,
      JOptionPane.INFORMATION_MESSAGE);
  }
}
```

Does actual replacement **12**

20.7.1   Understanding the code

Class HtmlProcessor

HtmlProcessor declares one new instance variable:

- FindDialog m_findDialog: custom dialog for finding and replacing a section of text.

1 Two new menu items titled Find... and Replace..., are added to the Edit menu. These items are activated with keyboard accelerators Ctrl-F and Ctrl-H respectively. When pressed, both items create an instance of FindDialog (if m_findDialog is null) or activate the existing instance, and the dialog is then displayed. The only difference between the two is that the Find... menu item activates the 0-indexed tabbed pane tab, and the Replace... menu item activates the tab at index 1.

2 Three new public methods have been added to this class to make access to our text pane component, and related objects, easier from external sources. The getDocument() method retrieves the text pane's current Document instance, and the getTextPane() method retrieves the text pane itself. The setSelection() method selects a portion of text between given start and end positions, and positions the caret at the beginning or end of the selection, depending on the value of the moveUp boolean parameter. The coordinates of such a selection are then stored in the m_xStart and m_xFinish instance variables (recall that these variables always hold the coordinates of the current text selection and are used to restore this selection when our text pane regains the focus).

Class Utils

3 A simple static utility method and an array of chars representing word separator characters is added to this class. The isSeparator() method simply checks whether a given character belongs to the static WORD_SEPARATORS char array.

4 ### Class FindDialog

This class is a modal JDialog subclass encapsulating our find and replace functionality. It contains a tabbed pane with two tabs, Find and Replace. Both tabs contain several common controls that should always be in synch: a check box for whole words only, a check box for match case, a radio button for search up, a radio button for search down, and a text field for the text we are searching for.

Since the components can exist in only one container, we need to place identical components in each tab. To simplify the task of maintaining consistency in component states, each pair of common components is assigned the same model.

FindDialog maintains the following instance variables:

- HtmlProcessor m_owner: an explicit reference to our HtmlProcessor parent application frame.
- JTabbedPane m_tb: the tabbed pane containing the find and replace pages.
- JTextField m_txtFind1: used to enter the string to find.
- JTextField m_txtFind2: used to enter the string to replace.
- Document m_docFind: a shared data model for the Find text fields.
- Document m_docReplace: a data model for the Replace text field.
- ButtonModel m_modelWord: a shared data model for the Whole words only check boxes.
- ButtonModel m_modelCase: a shared data model for the Match case check boxes.
- ButtonModel m_modelUp: a shared data model for the Search up radio buttons.
- ButtonModel m_modelDown: a shared data model for the Search down radio buttons.
- int m_searchIndex: position in the document to start searching from.
- boolean m_searchUp: a search direction flag.
- String m_searchData: string to search for.

5 The FindDialog constructor creates a superclass nonmodal dialog instance titled Find and Replace. The main tabbed pane, m_tb, is created, and JPanel p1 (the main container of the Find tab) receives the m_txtFind1 text field along with a Find what: label. This text field is used to enter the target string to be searched for. Note that the Document instance associated with this textbox is stored in the m_docFind instance variable (which will be used to facilitate sharing between another text field).

> **NOTE** In a more sophisticated implementation you might use editable combo boxes with memory in place of text fields, similar to those discussed in the final examples of chapter 9.

Two check boxes titled Whole words only and Match case, and two radio buttons, Search up and Search down, (initially selected) are placed at the bottom of the p1 panel. These components are surrounded by a titled Options border. Two JButtons titled Find Next and Close are placed at the right side of the panel. The first button calls our findNext() method when pressed. The second button hides the dialog. Finally the p1 panel is added to m_tb with a tab title of Find.

6 JPanel p2 (the main container of the Replace tab) receives the m_txtFind2 text field along with a "Find what:" label. It also receives another pair labeled Replace. An instance of our custom layout manager, DialogLayout (discussed in chapter 4), is used to lay out these text fields and corresponding labels without involving any intermediate containers. The same layout is used in the Find panel. We also synchronize the preferred size of the two panels to avoid movement of the synchronized components when a new page is activated.

Note that the `m_docFind` data object is set as the document for the `m_txtFind2` text field. This ensures consistency between the two different Find text fields in the two tabbed panels.

Two check boxes and two radio buttons are placed at the bottom of the panel to control the replacement options. They have identical meaning and representation as the corresponding four controls in the Find panel, and to ensure consistency between them, the data models are shared between each identical component.

Three `JButtons` titled Replace, Replace All, and Close are placed at the right side of the panel. The Replace button makes a single call to our `findNext()` method when pressed. The Replace All button is associated with an `actionPerformed()` method which repeatedly invokes `findNext()` to perform replacement until it returns `-1` to signal an error, or `0` to signal that no more replacements can be made. If an error occurs this method returns, the `action-Performed()` method simple returns (since an error will be properly reported to the user by the `findNext()` method). Otherwise the number of replacements made is reported to the user in a `JOptionPane` message dialog. The Close button hides the dialog. Finally the p2 panel is added to the `m_tb` tabbed pane with a tab title of Replace.

Since this is a nonmodal dialog, the user can freely switch to the main application frame and return back to the dialog while each remains visible (a typical find-and-replace feature). Once the user leaves the dialog he/she can modify the document's content, or move the caret position. To account for this, we add a `WindowListener` to the dialog whose `windowActi-vated()` method sets `m_searchIndex` to `-1`. This way, the next time `findNext()` is called the search data will be reinitialized, allowing the search to continue as expected, corresponding to the new caret position and document content.

The `setSelectedIndex()` method activates a page with the given index and makes this dialog visible. This method is intended mostly for use externally by our app when it wants to display this dialog with a specific tab selected.

7 The `findNext()` method is responsible for performing the actual find and replace operations. It takes two arguments:

- `boolean doReplace`: if `true`, find and replace, otherwise just find.
- `boolean showWarnings`: if `true`, display a message dialog if target text cannot be found, otherwise do not display a message.

`findNext()` returns an `int` result with the following meaning:

- `-1`: an error has occurred.
- `0`: the target text cannot be found.
- `1`: a find or find and replace was completed successfully.

The `m_searchIndex == -1` condition specifies that the portion of text to be searched through must be refreshed. In this case we store the portion of text from the beginning of the document to the current caret position if we are searching up, or between the current caret position and the end of the document if we are searching down. This text is stored in the `m_searchData` instance variable. The current caret position is stored in the `m_search-Index` variable.

NOTE   This solution may not be adequate for large documents. However, a more sophisticated solution would take us too far from the primary goal of this example.

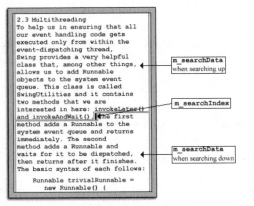

```
2.3 Multithreading
To help us in ensuring that all
our event handling code gets
executed only from within the
event-dispatching thread,
Swing provides a very helpful          m_searchData
class that, among other things,        when searching up
allows us to add Runnable
objects to the system event
queue. This class is called
SwingUtilities and it contains         m_searchIndex
two methods that we are
interested in here: invokeLater()
and invokeAndWait(). The first
method adds a Runnable to the
system event queue and returns
immediately. The second                m_searchData
method adds a Runnable and             when searching down
waits for it to be dispatched,
then returns after it finishes.
The basic syntax of each follows:

    Runnable trivialRunnable =
      new Runnable() {
```

Figure 20.18
Usage of instance variables for searching up and down through document text

8 The text to search for is retrieved from the m_docFind shared Document. If the case-insensitive option is selected, both the m_searchData text and the text to search for are converted into lower case. If the Whole words only option is selected, we check whether the text to search for contains any separator characters defined in our Util utilities class.

> **NOTE** If a given String is already in all lower or upper case, the toLowerCase() (or toUpperCase()) method returns the original String without creating a new object.

9 After this, if the doReplace parameter is true, we retrieve the replacement text from our m_docReplace Document. At this point we're ready to actually perform a search. We take advantage of existing String functionality to accomplish this:

```
if (m_searchUp)
  xStart = m_searchData.lastIndexOf(key, pos-1);
else
  xStart = m_searchData.indexOf(key, pos-m_searchIndex);
```

10 If we are seaching up, we search for the last occurrence of the target string from the current caret position. Otherwise we search for the first occurrence of the target string from the current caret position. If the target string is not found, we cannot continue the search, and a warning is displayed if the showWarnings parameter is true.

11 This simple scheme is complicated considerably if the Whole words only option is selected. In this case we need to verify whether symbols on the left and on the right of a matching region of text are either word separators defined in our Utils class, or the string lies at the end of the data being searched. If these conditions are not satisfied, we attempt to continue searching, unless the end of the search data is reached.

12 In any case, if we locate an acceptable match, we select the located text. If the replace option is selected, we replace this selected region with the specified replacement text and then select the new replacement text. In this latter case we also set m_searchIndex to -1 to force the m_searchData variable to be updated. This is necessary for continued searching because the data being searched most likely changes after each replace. The location of the caret also usually changes.

Figure 20.16 shows our editor's Find and Replace menu items. Figures 20.17 and 20.18 show our custom `FindDialog`'s Find and Replace tabs respectively. Open an existing HTML file and use the Edit menu, or the appropriate keyboard accelerator, to bring up the Find and Replace dialog with the Find tab selected. Enter some text to search for, select some search options, and press the Find Next button. If your target text is found, the matching region will be highlighted in the base document. Click this button again to find subsequent entries (if any). Verify that the Whole words only and Match case options function as discussed earlier. Change focus to the main application window and modify the document and/or change the caret position. Return to the Find and Replace dialog and note that the search continues as expected.

Select the Replace tab and verify that the state of all search options, including the search target string, are preserved from the Find tab (and vice versa when switching between tabs). Enter a replacement string and verify that the Replace and Replace All buttons work as expected.

20.8 *HTML EDITOR, PART IX: SPELL CHECKER (USING JDBC AND SQL)*

Most modern word processor applications offer tools and utilities which help the user in finding grammatical and spelling mistakes in a document. In this section we will add spell-checking to our HTML editor application. To do this we will need to perform some of our own multithreading, and use JDBC to connnect to a database containing a dictionary of words. We will use a simple database with one table, Data, which has the following structure:

Name	Type	Description
word	String	A single English word
sound	String	A 4-letter SOUNDEX code

An example of this database, populated with words from several Shakespeare comedies and tragedies, is provided in this example's directory: Shakespeare.mdb. (This database must be a registered database in your database manager prior to using it. This is not a JDBC tutorial, so we'll skip the details.)

NOTE The custom SOUNDEX algorithm used in this example hashes words for efficiency by using a simple model which approximates the sound of the word when spoken. Each word is reduced to a four character string, the first character being an upper case letter and the remaining three being digits. (This algorithm was created and patented by Robert C. Russell in 1918.)

Example 20.8

HtmlProcessor.java

see \Chapter20\8

```java
import java.awt.*;
import java.awt.event.*;
import java.io.*;
import java.net.*;
import java.util.*;
import java.sql.*;

import javax.swing.*;
import javax.swing.text.*;
import javax.swing.event.*;
import javax.swing.border.*;
import javax.swing.text.html.*;
import javax.swing.undo.*;

import dl.*;

public class HtmlProcessor extends JFrame {

  public static final String APP_NAME = "HTML HTML Editor";

  // Unchanged code from example 20.7

  protected JMenuBar createMenuBar() {
    JMenuBar menuBar = new JMenuBar();
```

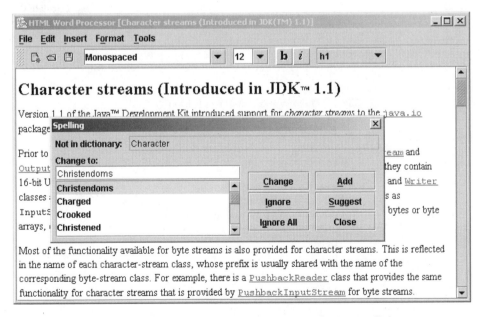

Figure 20.19   **HtmlProcessor's** `SpellChecker.SpellingDialog` **dialog**

```
      // Unchanged code from example 20.7

      Action spellAction = new AbstractAction("Spelling...",
       new ImageIcon("SpellCheck16.gif"))
      {
         public void actionPerformed(ActionEvent e) {
            SpellChecker checker = new SpellChecker(HtmlProcessor.this);
            HtmlProcessor.this.setCursor(Cursor.getPredefinedCursor(
               Cursor.WAIT_CURSOR));
            checker.start();
         }
      };
      item =mTools.add(spellAction);
      item.setMnemonic('s');
      item.setAccelerator(KeyStroke.getKeyStroke(
         KeyEvent.VK_F7, 0));

      menuBar.add(mTools);

      // Unchanged code from example 20.7

      return menuBar;
   }

   // Unchanged code from example 20.7
}

// Unchanged code from example 20.7
class Utils
{
   // Unchanged code from example 20.7

   public static String soundex(String word) {
      char[] result = new char[4];
      result[0] = word.charAt(0);
      result[1] = result[2] = result[3] = '0';
      int index = 1;

      char codeLast = '*';
      for (int k=1; k<word.length(); k++) {
         char ch = word.charAt(k);
         char code = ' ';
         switch (ch) {
            case 'b': case 'f': case 'p': case 'v':
               code = '1';
               break;
            case 'c': case 'g': case 'j': case 'k':
            case 'q': case 's': case 'x': case 'z':
               code = '2';
               break;
            case 'd': case 't':
               code = '3';
               break;
            case 'l':
               code = '4';
               break;
```

**New menu item
initiates spell checking** ❶

❷ **Calculate the SOUNDEX
code of a given word**

```
                    case 'm': case 'n':
                       code = '5';
                       break;
                    case 'r':
                       code = '6';
                       break;
                    default:
                       code = '*';
                       break;
                 }
                 if (code == codeLast)
                    code = '*';
                 codeLast = code;
                 if (code != '*') {
                    result[index] = code;
                    index++;
                    if (index > 3)
                       break;
                 }
              }
           }
           return new String(result);
        }

        public static boolean hasDigits(String word) {
           for (int k=1; k<word.length(); k++) {
              char ch = word.charAt(k);
              if (Character.isDigit(ch))
                 return true;
           }
           return false;
        }

        public static String titleCase(String source) {
           return Character.toUpperCase(source.charAt(0)) +
              source.substring(1);
        }
     }

     // Unchanged code from example 20.7

     class OpenList extends JPanel
        implements ListSelectionListener, ActionListener
     {
        protected JLabel m_title;
        protected JTextField m_text;
        protected JList m_list;
        protected JScrollPane m_scroll;

        public OpenList(String[] data, String title) {
           setLayout(null);
           m_title = new JLabel(title, JLabel.LEFT);
           add(m_title);
           m_text = new JTextField();
           m_text.addActionListener(this);
```

3 Returns true if given word contains digits

3 Converts first character of given String to upper case

4 OpenList component modified to populate list with ResultSet data

```
            add(m_text);
            m_list = new JList(data);
            m_list.setVisibleRowCount(4);
            m_list.addListSelectionListener(this);
            m_list.setFont(m_text.getFont());
            m_scroll = new JScrollPane(m_list);
            add(m_scroll);
        }

        public OpenList(String title, int numCols) {
            setLayout(null);
            m_title = new JLabel(title, JLabel.LEFT);
            add(m_title);
            m_text = new JTextField(numCols);
            m_text.addActionListener(this);
            add(m_text);
            m_list = new JList();
            m_list.setVisibleRowCount(4);
            m_list.addListSelectionListener(this);
            m_scroll = new JScrollPane(m_list);
            add(m_scroll);
        }

        public void appendResultSet(ResultSet results, int index,
          boolean toTitleCase)
        {
            m_text.setText("");
            DefaultListModel model = new DefaultListModel();
            try {
                while (results.next()) {
                    String str = results.getString(index);
                    if (toTitleCase)
                        str = Utils.titleCase(str);
                    model.addElement(str);
                }
            }
            catch (SQLException ex) {
                System.err.println("appendResultSet: "+ex.toString());
            }
            m_list.setModel(model);
            if (model.getSize() > 0)
                m_list.setSelectedIndex(0);
        }
        // Unchanged code from example 20.7
    }

// Unchanged code from example 20.7

class SpellChecker extends Thread {
    protected static String SELECT_QUERY =
        "SELECT Data.word FROM Data WHERE Data.word = ";
    protected static String SOUNDEX_QUERY =
        "SELECT Data.word FROM Data WHERE Data.soundex = ";
```

5 Custom thread that performs actual spell checking from current caret position down

```java
protected HtmlProcessor m_owner;
protected Connection m_conn;
protected DocumentTokenizer m_tokenizer;
protected Hashtablem_ignoreAll;
protected SpellingDialog m_dlg;

public SpellChecker(HtmlProcessor owner) {
  m_owner = owner;
}

public void run() {
  JTextPane monitor = m_owner.getTextPane();
  m_owner.setEnabled(false);
  monitor.setEnabled(false);

  m_dlg = new SpellingDialog(m_owner);
  m_ignoreAll = new Hashtable();

  try {
    // Load the JDBC-ODBC bridge driver
    Class.forName("sun.jdbc.odbc.JdbcOdbcDriver");
    m_conn = DriverManager.getConnection(
      "jdbc:odbc:Shakespeare", "admin", "");
    Statement selStmt = m_conn.createStatement();

    Document doc = m_owner.getDocument();
    int pos = monitor.getCaretPosition();
    m_tokenizer = new DocumentTokenizer(doc, pos);
      String word, wordLowCase;

    while (m_tokenizer.hasMoreTokens()) {
      word = m_tokenizer.nextToken();
      if (word.equals(word.toUpperCase()))
        continue;
      if (word.length()<=1)
        continue;
      if (Utils.hasDigits(word))
        continue;
      wordLowCase = word.toLowerCase();
      if (m_ignoreAll.get(wordLowCase) != null)
        continue;

      ResultSet results = selStmt.executeQuery(
        SELECT_QUERY+"'"+wordLowCase+"'");
      if (results.next())
        continue;

      results = selStmt.executeQuery(SOUNDEX_QUERY+
        "'"+Utils.soundex(wordLowCase)+"'");
      m_owner.setSelection(m_tokenizer.getStartPos(),
        m_tokenizer.getEndPos(), false);
      if (!m_dlg.suggest(word, results))
        break;
    }
    m_conn.close();
```

6 Before doing work, disables components

7 Looks at each word in the document

7 If word is found in the database then it is spelled correctly

If it is an unknown word **8** try to find words that sound like it to suggest as replacements

```
        System.gc();
        monitor.setCaretPosition(pos);
    }
    catch (Exception ex) {
      ex.printStackTrace();
      System.err.println("SpellChecker error: "+ex.toString());
    }

    monitor.setEnabled(true);
    m_owner.setEnabled(true);
    m_owner.setCursor(Cursor.getPredefinedCursor(
      Cursor.DEFAULT_CURSOR));
}

protected void replaceSelection(String replacement) {
    int xStart = m_tokenizer.getStartPos();
    int xFinish = m_tokenizer.getEndPos();
    m_owner.setSelection(xStart, xFinish, false);
    m_owner.getTextPane().replaceSelection(replacement);
    xFinish = xStart+replacement.length();
    m_owner.setSelection(xStart, xFinish, false);
    m_tokenizer.setPosition(xFinish);
}

protected void addToDB(String word) {
    String sdx = Utils.soundex(word);
    try {
      Statement stmt = m_conn.createStatement();
      stmt.executeUpdate(
        "INSERT INTO DATA (Word, Soundex) VALUES ('"+
        word+"', '"+sdx+"')");
    }
    catch (Exception ex) {
      ex.printStackTrace();
      System.err.println("SpellChecker error: "+ex.toString());
    }
}

class SpellingDialog extends JDialog {
    protected JTextField m_txtNotFound;
    protected OpenList m_suggestions;

    protected String m_word;
    protected booleanm_continue;

    public SpellingDialog(HtmlProcessor owner) {
      super(owner, "Spelling", true);

      JPanel p = new JPanel();
      p.setBorder(new EmptyBorder(5, 5, 5, 5));
      p.setLayout(new BoxLayout(p, BoxLayout.X_AXIS));
      p.add(new JLabel("Not in dictionary:"));
      p.add(Box.createHorizontalStrut(10));
      m_txtNotFound = new JTextField();
      m_txtNotFound.setEditable(false);
```

(9) If the word was misspelled and the user accepted a replacement, this does the replacement

(9) Adds a word to the "known" database

(10) Dialog that prompts the user for an action on a misspelled word

(11) Text field containing misspelled word

```
            p.add(m_txtNotFound);
            getContentPane().add(p, BorderLayout.NORTH);

            m_suggestions = new OpenList("Change to:", 12);
            m_suggestions.setBorder(new EmptyBorder(0, 5, 5, 5));
            getContentPane().add(m_suggestions, BorderLayout.CENTER);

            JPanel p1 = new JPanel();
            p1.setBorder(new EmptyBorder(20, 0, 5, 5));
            p1.setLayout(new FlowLayout());
            p = new JPanel(new GridLayout(3, 2, 8, 2));

            JButton bt = new JButton("Change");
            ActionListener lst = new ActionListener() {
              public void actionPerformed(ActionEvent e) {
                replaceSelection(m_suggestions.getSelected());
                m_continue = true;
                setVisible(false);
              }
            };
            bt.addActionListener(lst);
            bt.setMnemonic('c');
            p.add(bt);

            bt = new JButton("Add");
            lst = new ActionListener() {
              public void actionPerformed(ActionEvent e) {
                addToDB(m_word.toLowerCase());
                m_continue = true;
                setVisible(false);
              }
            };
            bt.addActionListener(lst);
            bt.setMnemonic('a');
            p.add(bt);

            bt = new JButton("Ignore");
            lst = new ActionListener() {
              public void actionPerformed(ActionEvent e) {
                m_continue = true;
                setVisible(false);
              }
            };
            bt.addActionListener(lst);
            bt.setMnemonic('i');
            p.add(bt);

            bt = new JButton("Suggest");
            lst = new ActionListener() {
              public void actionPerformed(ActionEvent e) {
                try {
                  m_word = m_suggestions.getSelected();
                  Statement selStmt = m_conn.createStatement();
                  ResultSet results = selStmt.executeQuery(
                    SELECT_QUERY+"'"+m_word.toLowerCase()+"'");
```

11 List containing replacement suggestions

12 Replaces misspelled word with selected suggestion

13 Adds misspelled word to database

14 Adds words to suggestions list that "sound like" selected suggestion

```
                boolean toTitleCase = Character.isUpperCase(
                    m_word.charAt(0));
                m_suggestions.appendResultSet(results, 1,
                    toTitleCase);
            }
            catch (Exception ex) {
                ex.printStackTrace();
                System.err.println("SpellChecker error: "+
                    ex.toString());
            }
        }
    };
    bt.addActionListener(lst);
    bt.setMnemonic('s');
    p.add(bt);

    bt = new JButton("Ignore All");
    lst = new ActionListener() {
        public void actionPerformed(ActionEvent e) {
            m_ignoreAll.put(m_word.toLowerCase(), m_word);
            m_continue = true;
            setVisible(false);
        }
    };
    bt.addActionListener(lst);
    bt.setMnemonic('g');
    p.add(bt);

    bt = new JButton("Close");
    lst = new ActionListener() {
        public void actionPerformed(ActionEvent e) {
            m_continue = false;
            setVisible(false);
        }
    };
    bt.addActionListener(lst);
    bt.setDefaultCapable(true);
    p.add(bt);
    p1.add(p);
    getContentPane().add(p1, BorderLayout.EAST);

    pack();
    setResizable(false);
    setLocationRelativeTo(owner);
}
public boolean suggest(String word, ResultSet results) {
    m_continue = false;
    m_word = word;
    m_txtNotFound.setText(word);
    boolean toTitleCase = Character.isUpperCase(
        word.charAt(0));
    m_suggestions.appendResultSet(results, 1, toTitleCase);
    show();
```

14 Adds words to suggestions list that "sound like" selected suggestion

15 Skips word, and will skip all ocurrences of word in this document

16 Called during spell checking to populate the dialog with a misspelled word and its replacement suggestion

```
            return m_continue;
        }
    }
}

class DocumentTokenizer {
    protected Document m_doc;
    protected Segmentm_seg;
    protected int m_startPos;
    protected int m_endPos;
    protected int m_currentPos;

    public DocumentTokenizer(Document doc, int offset) {
        m_doc = doc;
        m_seg = new Segment();
        setPosition(offset);
    }

    public boolean hasMoreTokens() {
        return (m_currentPos < m_doc.getLength());
    }

    public String nextToken() {
        StringBuffer s = new StringBuffer();
        try {
            // Trim leading separators
            while (hasMoreTokens()) {
                m_doc.getText(m_currentPos, 1, m_seg);
                char ch = m_seg.array[m_seg.offset];
                if (!Utils.isSeparator(ch)) {
                    m_startPos = m_currentPos;
                    break;
                }
                m_currentPos++;
            }

            // Append characters
            while (hasMoreTokens()) {
                m_doc.getText(m_currentPos, 1, m_seg);
                char ch = m_seg.array[m_seg.offset];
                if (Utils.isSeparator(ch)) {
                    m_endPos = m_currentPos;
                    break;
                }
                s.append(ch);
                m_currentPos++;
            }
        }
        catch (BadLocationException ex) {
            System.err.println("nextToken: "+ex.toString());
            m_currentPos = m_doc.getLength();
        }
        return s.toString();
    }
```

7 Used like StreamTokenizer, but keeps track of the character position from each token

18 Returns the next token, starting at the position in the document

```
public int getStartPos() { return m_startPos; }

public int getEndPos() { return m_endPos; }

public void setPosition(int pos) {
    m_startPos = pos;
    m_endPos = pos;
    m_currentPos = pos;
}
}
```

20.8.1   Understanding the code

Class HtmlProcessor

1 This class now imports the `java.sql` package to make use of JDBC functionality. The `createMenuBar()` method now creates a new menu item in the Tools menu titled Spelling... . This menu item can also be invoked with keyboard accelerator F7. When selected it creates and starts a `SpellChecker` thread, passing a reference to the main application frame as a parameter.

Class Utils

2 Three new static methods are added to this class. The `soundex()` method calculates and returns the SOUNDEX code of the given word. To calculate that code we use the first character of the given word and add a three-digit code that represents the first three remaining consonants. The conversion is made according to the following table:

Code	Letters
1	B,P,F,V
2	C,S,G,J,K,Q,X,Z
3	D,T
4	L
5	M,N
6	R
*	(all others)

3 The `hasDigits()` method returns `true` if a given string contains digits, and the `titleCase()` method converts the first character of a given string to upper case.

4 ### Class OpenList

This custom component receives new functionality for use in our new spell checker dialog. First, we add a new constructor which assigns a given number of columns to the text field, and does not initialize the list component.

Second, we add the `appendResultSet()` method which populates the list component with the data supplied in the given `ResultSet` instance at the given position. If the third parameter is set to `true`, this tells the method to convert all string data to the 'title case' (which means that the first letter is in upper case, and the rest of the string is unchanged). This is accomplished through use of the `Utils.titleCase()` method.

⑤ *Class SpellChecker*

This class extends `Thread` to perform spell checking of the current document from the current caret position moving downward. Two class variables are declared:

- `String SELECT_QUERY`: SQL query text used to select a word equal to a given string.
- `String SOUNDEX_QUERY`: SQL query text used to select a word matching a given SOUNDEX value.

Five instance variables are declared:

- `HtmlProcessor m_owner`: a reference to the main application frame.
- `Connection m_conn`: JDBC connection to a database.
- `DocumentTokenizer m_tokenizer`: a custom object used to retrieve each word in a document.
- `Hashtable m_ignoreAll`: a collection of words to ignore in a search, added to with the Ignore All button.
- `SpellingDialog m_dlg`: our custom dialog used for processing spelling mistakes.

The `SpellChecker` constructor takes a reference to the application's frame as a parameter and stores it in the `m_owner` instance variable.

⑥ The `run()` method is responsible for the most significant activity of this thread. To prevent the user from modifying the document during spell checking we first disable the main application frame and our text pane contained within it.

> **NOTE** Unlike AWT, Swing containers do not disable their child components when they themselves are disabled. It is not clear whether this is a bug, an intended feature, or an oversight.

Then we create a new `SpellingDialog` instance to provide the user interface, and instantiate the `m_ignoreAll` collection. In a try/catch block we process all JDBC interactions to allow proper handling of any potential errors. This code creates a JDBC connection to our Shakespeare database, retrieves the current caret position, and creates an instance of `Docu-` **⑦** `mentTokenizer` to parse the document from the current caret position. In a while loop we perform spell checking on each word fetched until there are no more tokens. Words in all upper case, containing only one letter, or containing digits, are skipped (this behavior can easily be customized). Then we convert the word under examination to lower case and search for it in the `m_ignoreAll` collection. If it is not found, we try to find it in the database. If the **⑧** SQL query does not return any results, we try to locate a similar word in the database with the same SOUNDEX value to suggest to the user in the dialog. The word in question is then selected in our text pane to show the user which word is currently under examination. Finally we call our `SpellingDialog`'s `suggest()` method to request that the user make a decision about what to do with this word. If the `suggest()` method returns `false`, the user has chosen to terminate the spell checking process, so we exit the loop. Once outside the loop we close the JDBC connection, restore the original caret position, explicitly call the garbage collector, and reenable the main application frame and our text pane editor contained within it.

⑨ The following two methods are invoked by the `SpellingDialog` instance associated with this `SpellChecker`:

- `replaceSelection()` is used to replace the most recently parsed word with the given replacement string.
- `addToDB()` adds a given word and it's SOUNDEX value to the database by executing an insert query.

⑩ *Class SpellChecker.SpellingDialog*

This inner class represents a dialog which prompts the user to verify or correct a certain word if it is not found in the database. The user can select one of several actions in response: ignore the given word, ignore all occurrences of that word in the document, replace that word with another word, add this word to the database and consider it correct in any future matches, or cancel the spell check. Four instance variables are declared:

- `JTextField m_txtNotFound`: used to display the word under investigation.
- `OpenList m_suggestions`: editable list component to select or enter a replacement word.
- `String m_word`: the word under investigation.
- `boolean m_continue`: a flag indicating that spell checking should continue.

⑪ The `SpellingDialog` constructor places the `m_txtNotFound` component and corresponding label at the top of the dialog window. The `m_suggestions` `OpenList` is placed in the center, and six buttons are grouped to the right.

⑫ The Change button replaces the word under investigation with the word currently selected in the list or entered by the user. Then it stores `true` in the `m_continue` flag and hides the dialog window. This terminates the modal state of the dialog and makes the `show()` method return, which in turn allows the program's execution to continue (recall that modal dialogs block the calling thread until they are dismissed).

⑬ The Add button adds the word in question to the spelling database. This word will then be considered correct in future queries. In this way we allow the spell checker to "learn" new words (i.e., add them to the dictionary).

⑭ The Suggest button populates the `m_suggestions` list with all SOUNDEX matches to the word under investigation. This button is intended for use in situations where the user is not satisfied with the initial suggestions.

The Ignore button simply skips the current word and continues spell checking the remaining text.

⑮ The Ignore All button does the same as the Ignore, but also stores the word in question in the collection of words to ignore, so the next time the spell checker finds this word it will be deemed correct. The difference between Ignore All and Add is that ignored words will only be ignored during a single spell check, whereas words added to the database will persist as long as the database data does.

The Close button stores `false` in the `m_continue` flag and hides the dialog window. This results in the termination of the spell checking process (see the `suggest()` method).

⑯ The `suggest()` method is used to display this `SpellingDialog` each time a questionable word is located during the spell check. It takes a `String` and a `ResultSet` containing suggested substitutions as parameters. It sets the text of the `m_txtNotFound` component to the

String passed in, and calls `appendResultSet()` on the `OpenList` to display an array of suggested corrections. Note that the first character of these suggestions will be converted to upper case if the word in question starts with a capital letter. Finally, the `show()` method displays this dialog in the modal state. As soon as this state is terminated by one of the push buttons, or by directly closing the dialog, the `suggest()` method returns the `m_continue` flag. If this flag is set to `false`, this indicates that the calling program should terminate the spell checking cycle.

⑰ *Class DocumentTokenizer*

This helper class was built to parse the current text pane document. Unfortunately we cannot use the standard `StreamTokenizer` class for this purpose, because it provides no way of querying the position of a token within the document (we need this information to allow word replacement). Several instance variables are declared:

- `Document m_doc`: a reference to the document to be parsed.
- `Segment m_seg`: used for quick delivery of characters from the document being parsed.
- `int m_startPos`: the start position of the current word from the beginning of the document.
- `int m_endPos`: the end position of the current word from the beginning of the document.
- `int m_currentPos`: the current position of the parser from the beginning of the document.

The `DocumentTokenizer` constructor takes a reference to the document to be parsed and the offset to start at as parameters. It initializes the instance variables described previously.

The `hasMoreTokens()` method returns `true` if the current parsing position lies within the document.

⑱ The `nextToken()` method extracts the next token (a group of characters separated by one or more characters defined in the `WORD_SEPARATORS` array from our `Utils` class) and returns it as a `String`. The positions of the beginning and the end of the token are stored in the `m_startPos` and `m_endPos` instance variables respectively. To access a portion of document text with the least possible overhead we use the `Document.getText()` method which takes three parameters: offset from the beginning of the document, length of the text fragment, and a reference to an instance of the `Segment` class. (Recall from chapter 19 that the `Segment` class provides an efficient means of directly accessing an array of document characters.)

We look at each character in turn, passing over separator characters until the first non-separator character is reached. This position is marked as the beginning of a new word. Then a `StringBuffer` is used to accumulate characters until a separator character, or the end of document, is reached. The resulting characters are returned as a `String`.

NOTE This variant of the `getText()` method gives us direct access to the characters contained in the document through a `Segment` instance. These characters should not be modified.

20.8.2   Running the code

Figure 20.19 shows our editor application with the spell checker dialog open. Open an existing HTML file and try running a complete spell check. Try adding some words to the dictionary and use the Ignore All button to avoid questioning a word again during that spell check.

Try using the Suggest button to query the database for more suggestions based on our SOUN-DEX algorithm. Click Change to accept a suggestion or a change typed into the text field. Click Ignore to ignore the current word being questioned.

NOTE　　The Shakespeare vocabulary database supplied for this example is neither complete nor contemporary. It does not include such words as "software" or "Internet." However, you can easily add them, when encountered during a spell check, by clicking the Add button.

CHAPTER 21

Pluggable look and feel

21.1   *PLUGGABLE LOOK AND FEEL OVERVIEW*

The pluggable look and feel architecture is one of Swing's greatest achievements. It allows seamless changes in the appearance of an application and the way an application interacts with the user. This can occur without modifying or recompiling the application, and it can be invoked programmatically *during* any single JVM session. In this chapter we'll discuss how look and feel works and how custom look and feel can be implemented for standard Swing components.

NOTE   In chapter 1, we introduced the basic concepts behind look and feel and UI delegates. You might find it helpful to review this material before moving on.

In examining Swing component source code, you will quickly notice that these classes do not contain any code for sophisticated rendering. All this drawing code is stored somewhere else. As we learned in chapter 1, this code is defined within various UI delegates, which act as both a component's view and controller. Before we jump into the examples, we need to discuss how the most significant look and feel-related classes and interfaces function and interact in more detail.

21.1.1 LookAndFeel

abstract class javax.swing.LookAndFeel

This abstract class serves as the superclass of the central class of any pluggable look and feel implementation. The `getDefaults()` method returns an instance of `UIDefaults` (see section 21.1.2). The `getDescription()` method returns a one-to-two sentence description of the look and feel. The `getID()` method returns a simple, unique string that identifies a look and feel. The `getName()` method returns a short string that represents the name of that look and feel, such as "Malachite," or "Windows."

> **NOTE** The `getID()` method is actually not used by Swing, but as a rule it is a good idea to provide `LookAndFeel` implementations with a unique identifier.

The `isNativeLookAndFeel()` method queries the `System` class to determine whether the given `LookAndFeel` corresponds to that which emulates the operating system platform the running VM is designed for. The `isSupportedLookAndFeel()` method determines whether the given `LookAndFeel` is supported by the operating system the running VM is designed for. Due to legal issues, some `LookAndFeels` will not be supported by certain operating systems, even though they have the ability to function perfectly well.

> **NOTE** We will not go into the details of how to work around this limitation Sun has imposed (although it is relatively easy), specifically because of the legal issues involved.

The `initialize()` and `uninitialize()` methods are called when a `LookAndFeel` is installed and uninstalled, respectively. The `toString()` method returns the description returned by `getDescription()`, as well as the fully qualified class name.

Several convenient static methods are also provided for assigning and unassigning borders, colors, and fonts to components: `installBorder()`, `installColors()`, `installColorsAndFont()`, and `uninstallBorder()`. `LookAndFeel` implements these so that the specified properties only change if the current property value of the given component is a `UIResource` (see section 21.1.4) or `null`. The static methods `makeKeyBindings()` and `makeIcon()` are convenience methods for building a list of text component key bindings and creating a `UIDefaults.LazyValue` (see section 21.1.2) which can create an `ImageIcon UIResource`.

21.1.2 UIDefaults

class javax.swing.UIDefaults

This class extends `Hashtable` and manages a collection of custom resources (such as objects and primitives) used in this look and feel. The `put(Object key, Object value)` and `putDefaults(Object[] keyValueList)` methods store data (in the latter case they must be placed in a one-dimensional array in this order: key1, value1, key2, value2, etc.). The `get(Object key)` method retrieves a stored resource.

`UIDefaults` also defines two inner classes: `LazyValue` and `ActiveValue`. A `LazyValue` is an entry in the `UIDefaults` hashtable that is not instantiated until it is looked up with its associated key name. Large objects that take a long time to instantiate and which are rarely used can benefit from being implemented as `LazyValues`. An `ActiveValue` is instantiated each time it is looked up with its associated key name. Those resources that must be unique in each place they are used are often implemented as `ActiveValues`.

Both interfaces require the definition of the `createValue()` method. The following code shows a simple `LazyValue` that constructs a new border.

```
Object myBorderLazyValue = new UIDefaults.LazyValue() {
  public Object createValue(UIDefaults table) {
    return new BorderFactory.createLoweredBevelBorder();
  }
};
myUIDefaults.put("MyBorder", borderLazyValue);
```

Note that the `createValue()` method will only be called once for `LazyValues`, whereas with `ActiveValues` it will be called each time that resource is requested.

JAVA 1.3   Performance analysis during the development of Java 1.3 indicated that one of the main reasons for the slow startup of Swing applications is due to class loading, not instance creation (which was previously thought to be the problem). Since `Lazy-Value` implementations in Swing were in the form of anonymous inner classes, each time a look and feel was loaded there would be a class load for each `Lazy-Value` implementation. In Java 1.3 there is a new concrete implementation of `LazyValue` in `UIDefaults` (`UIDefaults.UIDefaultProxy`) which uses reflection to load the appropriate class when requested. In this way there is only one `LazyValue` class load versus the many that occurred in previous versions.

21.1.3   UIManager

public class javax.swing.UIManager

This class provides a set of static methods that are used to manage the current look and feel. The current look and feel is actually made up of a three-level `UIDefaults` hierarchy: user defaults, current look and feel defaults, and system defaults. Particularly important methods are `getUI(JComponent target)`, which retrieves an instance of `ComponentUI` for the specified component, and `getDefaults()`, which retrieves a shared instance of the `UIDefaults` class.

21.1.4   The UIResource interface

abstract interface javax.swing.plaf.UIResource

This interface declares no methods and is used solely to mark resource objects created for a component's UI delegate. Several classes used to wrap component UI resources implement this interface—for example: `InsetsUIResource`, `FontUIResource`, `IconUIResource`, `BorderUIResource`, and `ColorUIResource`. These wrapper classes are used for assigning resources that will be relinquished when a component's UI delegate is changed. In other words, if we were to assign an instance of `JLabel` a background of `Color.Yellow`, this background setting would persist even through a UI delegate change. However, if we were to assign that `JLabel` a background of `new ColorUIResource(Color.Yellow)`, the background would only persist until another UI delegate is installed. When the next UI delegate is installed, the label will receive a new label background based on the look and feel the new UI delegate belongs to.

21.1.5   ComponentUI

abstract class javax.swing.plaf.ComponentUI

This abstract class represents a common superclass of all component UI delegate classes each implemented by different look and feel packages. The `createUI(JComponent c)` static method creates an instance of `ComponentUI` for a given component. See section 1.4.1, for a description of each `ComponentUI` method.

Abstract classes in the `javax.swing.plaf` package extend `ComponentUI` to represent the base class from which each Swing component's UI should extend: `ButtonUI`, `TreeUI`, and so on. Each of these classes has a concrete default implementation in the `javax.swing.-plaf.basic` package: `BasicButtonUI`, `BasicTreeUI`, and so on. In turn, these basic UI classes can be, and are intended to be, extended by other look and feel implementations. For example, the classes mentioned above are extended by `MetalButtonUI` and `MetalTreeUI`, which are defined in the `javax.swing.plaf.metal` package.

21.1.6   BasicLookAndFeel

class javax.swing.plaf.basic.BasicLookAndFeel

This class provides the basic implementation of `javax.swing.LookAndFeel`. It creates all resources used by UI classes defined in the `basic` package. Custom look and feel classes are expected to extend this class, rather than `LookAndFeel` directly, to replace only those resources that need to be customized.

> **NOTE** Though we will not go into the details of each basic UI delegate implementation in this book (indeed this is a large topic and deserves a whole volume unto itself), note that the basic package contains a class called `BasicGraphicsUtils`, which consists of several static methods used for drawing various types of rectangles most commonly used for borders. The basic package also contains several other quite useful utility-like classes, and a quick browse through the basic package API documentation will reveal some of these interesting members.

21.1.7   How look and feel works

Now we'll discuss how the pluggable look and feel mechanism works and what actually happens when a Swing component is created and painted and when the user changes the application's look and feel during a Java session.

All Swing component constructors call the `updateUI()` method which is inherited from `JComponent`. This method may also be called with the `SwingUtilities.updateCompo-nentTreeUI()` helper method. The latter method recursively updates the UI delegate of each child of the specified component (we've already seen how this is used in chapters 1 and 16).

The `updateUI()` method overridden by most Swing components typically has an implementation similar to the following:

```
setUI((MenuUI)UIManager.getUI(this));
```

This invokes the static `UIManager.getUI()` method and passes a `this` component reference as a parameter. This method, in turn, triggers a call to `getUI()` on the shared `UIDe-faults` instance retrieved with the `getDefaults()` method.

The `UIDefaults.getUI()` method actually creates the `ComponentUI` object for a given `JComponent`. It first calls `getUIClassID()` on that component to discover the unique string ID associated with that class. For example, the `JTree.getUIClassID()` call returns the string "TreeUI."

Prior to the process described above, the `UIDefaults` instance (which extends `Hashtable`) is initialized by the subclass of `LookAndFeel` which is currently in charge. For instance, the Java look and feel (also referred to as Metal) is defined by `javax.swing.plaf.metal.MetalLookAndFeel`. This class fills that look and feel's shared `UIDefaults` instance with key-value pairs. For each component which has a corresponding UI delegate implementation in the current look and feel, a component ID `String` and a fully qualified UI delegate class name is added as a key/value pair to `UIDefaults`. For instance, the `TreeUI` ID key corresponds to the value in `MetalLookAndFeel`'s look and feel `UIDefaults`. If a particular `LookAndFeel` implementation does not specify a UI delegate for some component, a value from the parent `javax.swing.plaf.BasicLookAndFeel` class is used.

Using these key/value pairs, the `UIDefaults.getUI()` method determines the fully qualified class name and calls the `createUI()` method on that class using the Java reflection API. This static method returns an instance of the proper UI delegate, such as `MetalTreeUI`.

Now let's go back to the `updateUI()` method. The retrieved `ComponentUI` object is passed to the `setUI()` method and stored into `protected` variable, `ComponentUI ui`, which is inherited from the `JComponent` base class. This completes the creation of a UI delegate.

Recall that UI delegates are normally in charge of performing the associated component's rendering, as well as processing user input directed to that component. The `update()` method of a UI delegate is normally responsible for painting a component's background, if it is opaque, and then calling `paint()`. A UI delegate's `paint()` method is what actually paints a component's content, and it is the method we most often override when building our own delegates.

Now let's review this process from a higher-level perspective:

1   The currently installed look and feel provides an application with information about UI delegates to be used for all Swing components instantiated in that application.

2   Using this information, an instance of a UI delegate class can be instantiated on demand for a given component.

3   This UI delegate is passed to the component and it generally takes responsibility for providing the complete user interface (view and controller).

4   The UI delegate can be easily replaced with another one at run-time without affecting the underlying component or its data (such as its model).

21.1.8   Selecting a look and feel

The Swing API shipped with Java 2 includes three standard look and feels: Metal, Motif, and Windows (the latter is available only for Microsoft Windows users). The first one is not associated with any existing platform and is also known as the "Java look and feel." Metal is the default, and it will be used automatically unless we explicitly change look and feels in our application.

REFERENCE   Apple provides the MacOS look and feel which is available for download at http://www.apple.com/macos/java/text/download.html.

Swing also provides a Multiplexing look and feel which allows more than one UI delegate to be associated with a component at the same time. This look and feel is intended for, but not limited to, use with accessible technologies.

To select a particular look and feel, we call the `UIManager.setLookAndFeel()` method and specify the fully qualified class name of a subclass of `javax.swing.LookAndFeel` which defines the desired look and feel. The following code shows how to force an application to use the Motif look and feel:

```
try {
  UIManager.setLookAndFeel(
    "com.sun.java.swing.plaf.motif.MotifLookAndFeel");
}
catch (Exception e) {
  System.out.println ("Couldn't load Motif look and feel " + e);
}
```

Note that this should be called *before* we instantiate any components. Alternatively we can call this method and then use the `SwingUtilities updateComponentTreeUI()` method to change the current look and feel of a container and all its children, as discussed previously.

GUIDELINE

Design balance is affected by look and feel selection   Beware! Although it is technically possible to update look and feel on-the-fly, this may often be visually undesirable. Different look and feels use different graphical weights for each component, such as bezel thickness on buttons. Therefore, a display which is designed to look good in a particular look and feel may be visually unbalanced and inelegant when switched to another look and feel. This could be due to the change in white space which balances against the graphical weight of elements such as bezels, or it may be a change in alignment. For example, the Malachite look and feel is visually heavy; as a rough guide, more white space will be required for a well-balanced effect when it's compared to the Metal look and feel.

21.1.9   Creating a custom LookAndFeel implementation

Swing provides the complete flexibility of implementing our own custom look and feel, and distributing it with our application. This task usually involves overriding the rendering functionality of all Swing components supported by our look and feel (default implementations are then used for each remaining component we are not interested in customizing). In general, this is not a simple project, and it will almost always require referencing Swing `plaf` source code.

The first step is to establish a basic idea of how we will provide consistent UI delegate appearances. This includes some thought as to what colors and icons will be used for each component, and whether these choices fit well together.

Then we move on to the most significant step in creating a custom look and feel, which is the implementation of a `javax.swing.LookAndFeel` subclass. The following six abstract methods are the minimum that should be overridden:

- `String getID()`: Returns the string ID of this look and feel (such as "Motif").

- `String getName()`: Returns a short string describing this look and feel (such as "CDE/Motif").
- `String getDescription()`: Returns a one-line string description of this look and feel.
- `boolean isNativeLookAndFeel()`: Returns `true` if the look and feel corresponds to the current underlying native platform.
- `boolean isSupportedLookAndFeel()`: Returns `true` if the the current underlying native platform supports and/or permits this look and feel.
- `UIDefaults getDefaults()`: Returns the look and feel-specific `Hashtable` of resources (discussed above). This is the most important method of any `LookAndFeel` implementation.

However, to make implementation simpler, it is normally expected that we extend `javax.swing.plaf.basic.BasicLookAndFeel` instead of `javax.swing.LookAndFeel` directly. In this case, we override some of the following `BasicLookAndFeel` methods (along with a few `LookAndFeel` methods in the list above):

- `void initClassDefaults(UIDefaults table)`: Fills a given `UIDefaults` instance with key/value pairs that specify IDs and fully qualified class names of UI delegates for each component supported by this look and feel.
- `void initComponentDefaults(UIDefaults table)`: Fills a given `UIDefaults` instance with key/value pairs using information (typically drawing resources such as colors, images, and borders) that is specific to this look and feel.
- `void initSystemColorDefaults(UIDefaults table)`: Fills a given `UIDefaults` instance with color information specific to this look and feel.
- `void loadSystemColors(UIDefaults table, String[] systemColors, boolean useNative)`: Fills a given `UIDefaults` instance with color information specific to the underlying platform.

The first two methods are the most significant, and we will discuss them in a bit more detail here.

21.1.10   Defining default component resources

The following code shows how to override the `initComponentDefaults()` method to store custom resources in a given `UIDefaults` instance. These resources will be used to construct a `JButton` UI delegate that corresponds to this look and feel (this is an imaginary implementation for now):

```
protected void initComponentDefaults(UIDefaults table) {
  super.initComponentDefaults(table);
  Object[] defaults = {
    "Button.font", new FontUIResource("Arial", Font.BOLD, 12 ),
    "Button.background", new ColorUIResource(4, 108, 2),
    "Button.foreground", new ColorUIResource(236, 236, 0),
    "Button.margin", new InsetsUIResource(8, 8, 8, 8)
  };
  table.putDefaults( defaults );
}
```

Note that the super class `initComponentDefaults()` method is called *before* putting our custom information in the table, since we only want to override button UI resources. Also note that the resource objects are encapsulated in special wrapper classes which are defined in the `javax.swing.plaf` package (Font instances are placed in `FontUIResources`, `Colors` in `ColorUIResources`, and so on.). This is necessary to correctly load and unload resources when the current look and feel is changed.

NOTE Resource keys start with the component name, minus the "J" prefix. So "Button.font" defines the font resource for `JButtons`, while "RadioButton.font" defines the font resource for `JRadioButtons`. Unfortunately these standard resource keys are not documented, but they can all be found directly in the Swing look and feel source code. For example, see MetalLookAndFeel.java in package `javax.swing.plaf.metal`.

21.1.11 Defining class defaults

Providing custom resources, such as colors and fonts, is the simplest way to create a custom look and feel. However, to provide more powerful customizations, we need to develop custom extensions of `ComponentUI` classes for specific components: custom UI delegates. We also need to provide a means of locating our custom UI delegate classes so that `UIManager` can successfully switch a component's look and feel on demand.

The following code overrides the `initClassDefaults()` method to store information about our imaginary `myLF.MyLFButtonUI` class (a member of the imaginary `myLF` look and feel package), which extends `javax.swing.plaf.ButtonUI`. It will be used to provide a custom look and feel for `JButton`:

```
protected void initClassDefaults(UIDefaults table) {
    super.initClassDefaults(table);
    try {
        String className = "myLF.MyLFButtonUI";
        Class buttonClass = Class.forName(className);
        table.put("ButtonUI", className);
        table.put(className, buttonClass);
    }
    catch (Exception ex) {
        ex.printStackTrace();
    }
}
```

The `initClassDefaults()` implementation of the super class is called *before* (not after) we populate the table with our custom information, since we don't intend to override all UI class mappings for all components. Instead, we use the default settings for all but "ButtonUI." (We did a similar thing above in `initComponentDefaults()`.) Also note that we place *both* the fully qualified class name of the delegate, as well as the `Class` instance itself, in the table.

NOTE Placing only the class name in the defaults table does not provide correct functionality. As of Java 2 FCS, without a corresponding `Class` instance in the table as well, `getUI()` will not be able to retrieve instances of custom look and feel delegates. We will see that this is the case in the examples below.

21.1.12 Creating custom UI delegates

Now it's time to show a simple pseudocode implementation of the imaginary `myLF.MyLF-ButtonUI` class to which we've been relating our discussion:

```
package myLF;

public class MyLFButtonUI extends  BasicButtonUI {
  private final static MyLFButtonUI m_buttonUI =
    new MyLFButtonUI();

  protected Color  m_backgroundNormal = null;
  // Declare variables for other resources.

  public static ComponentUI createUI( JComponent c ) {
    return m_buttonUI;

  }
  public void installUI(JComponent c) {

    super.installUI(c);
    m_backgroundNormal = UIManager.getColor(
      "Button.background");
    // Retrieve other resources and store them
    // as instance variables.
    // Add listeners. These might be registered to receive
    // events from a component's model or the component itself.
  }

  public void uninstallUI(JComponent c) {
    super.uninstallUI(c);
    // Provide cleanup.
    // Remove listeners.
  }

  public void update(Graphics g, JComponent c) {
    // Provide custom background painting if the component is
    // opaque, then call paint().
  }

  public void paint(Graphics g, JComponent c) {
    // Provide custom rendering for the given component.
  }

  // Provide implementation for listeners.
}
```

This class extends `javax.swing.plaf.basic.BasicButtonUI` to override some of its functionality and it relies on `basic` look and feel defaults for the rest. The shared instance, `MyLFButtonUI m_buttonUI`, is created once and retrieved using the `createUI()` method. Thus, only one instance of this delegate will exist, and it will act as the view and controller for all `JButton` instances with the `myLF` look and feel.

The `installUI()` method retrieves `myLF`-specific resources that correspond to `JButton` (refer to our discussion of `initComponentDefaults()` above). We might also use this method to add mouse and key listeners to provide look and feel-specific functionality. For instance, we might design our button UI so that an associated `JButton`'s text changes color each time the mouse cursor rolls over it. An advantage of this approach is that we don't need to modify our application—we can still use normal `JButtons`. Once `myLF` is installed, this functionality will automatically appear.

The `uninstallUI()` method performs all the necessary cleanup, including removing any listeners that this delegate might have attached to the component or its model.

The `update()` method will paint the given component's background if it is opaque, and then immediately call `paint()` (do not confuse this method with `JComponent`'s `paint()` method).

> **NOTE** We recommend that you always implement painting functionality in this way, but in reality the background of Swing components are more often painted directly within the `paint()` method (a quick skim through Swing UI delegate source code illustrates this; for an example, see BasicRadioButtonUI.java). If this is not the case, the resulting background will be painted by `JComponent`'s painting routine. For this reason we often find no background rendering code at all in UI delegates.
>
> This is a relatively minor issue. Just make sure that if you do want to take control of a component's background rendering, it is best to do so in UI delegate `update()` methods. This rendering should occur only if the associated component's opaque property is set to `true`, and it should be called *before* the main detail of its view is painted (`update()` should end with a call to `paint()`).

The `paint()` method renders a given component using a given graphical context. To use a look and feel successfully, the component class should not implement any rendering functionality for itself. Instead, it should allow its painting to be controlled by UI delegate classes so that all rendering is look and feel-specific (refer to chapter 2 for further discussion of painting issues).

> **NOTE** Implementing a custom look and feel will make much more sense once we step through the first two examples. We suggest that you reference the above discussion often as you make your way through this chapter. Reviewing the discussion of MVC in chapter 1 may also be helpful at this point.

21.1.13 Metal themes

class javax.swing.plaf.metal.MetalTheme

Themes are sets of color and font definitions that can be dynamically plugged into `Metal-LookAndFeel`, and immediately used by a Swing application on-the-fly if Metal is the current look and feel. To create a theme, we simply subclass `MetalTheme` (or `DefaultMetalTheme`) and override a selection of its numerous `getXX()` methods to return a specific font or color. A quick browse through these methods shows implementations for all the colors and fonts used throughout the Metal look and feel, allowing us to customize the Metal appearance however we like. `MetalLookAndFeel` contains `createDefaultTheme()`, a protected method used to create the default metal theme, and it provides us with the `setCurrentTheme()` method which allows us to plug in a new theme. The effects of plugging in a new theme are seen immediately. Themes offer a simple alternative to building a custom `LookAndFeel` when all that is desired are some simple appearance changes.

21.2 CUSTOM LOOK AND FEEL, PART I: USING CUSTOM RESOURCES

GUIDELINE

When to consider a custom look and feel Developing a custom look and feel is not a trivial undertaking. Almost certainly, more effort is needed for the design rather than the coding. Consider a custom look and feel in these situations:

- You are designing a single-use system, such as a self-service kiosk.
- You are intending to roll out a suite of enterprise applications which will work together and you want the look and feel to reflect the corporate image or identity.
- You are developing a family of software products and want to develop a unique environment or corporate identity. This was exactly Sun's intention with the Metal look and feel which closely reflects the colors and styles used in the Sun corporate identity. Other examples of custom designed environments are Lotus Notes, Lotus eSuite, and Sun HotJava Views.

The easiest way to create a custom look and feel is simply to customize default component resources (colors, borders, fonts, etc.) without actually implementing any custom UI delegates. In this case, the only thing we need to do is extend BasicLookAndFeel (see the above discussion), or another existing LookAndFeel implementation, and provide a set of resources. Example 21.1 demonstrates how this can be done by beginning the implementation of our custom Malachite look and feel.

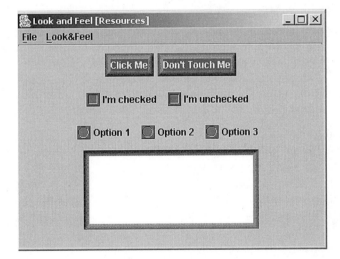

**Figure 21.1
The Malachite look
and feel in action**

Example 21.1

Button1.java

see \Chapter21\1

```java
import java.awt.*;
import java.awt.event.*;
import java.util.*;

import javax.swing.*;
import javax.swing.event.*;

import Malachite.*;

public class Button1 extends JFrame
{
  protected Hashtable  m_lfs;

  public Button1() {
    super("Look and Feel [Resources]");
    setSize(400, 300);
    getContentPane().setLayout(new FlowLayout());

    JMenuBar menuBar = createMenuBar();
    setJMenuBar(menuBar);

    JPanel p = new JPanel();
    JButton bt1 = new JButton("Click Me");
    p.add(bt1);

    JButton bt2 = new JButton("Don't Touch Me");
    p.add(bt2);
    getContentPane().add(p);

    p = new JPanel();
    JCheckBox chk1 = new JCheckBox("I'm checked");
    chk1.setSelected(true);
    p.add(chk1);

    JCheckBox chk2 = new JCheckBox("I'm unchecked");
    chk2.setSelected(false);
    p.add(chk2);
    getContentPane().add(p);

    p = new JPanel();
    ButtonGroup grp = new ButtonGroup();
    JRadioButton rd1 = new JRadioButton("Option 1");
    rd1.setSelected(true);
    p.add(rd1);
    grp.add(rd1);

    JRadioButton rd2 = new JRadioButton("Option 2");
    p.add(rd2);
    grp.add(rd2);

    JRadioButton rd3 = new JRadioButton("Option 3");
    p.add(rd3);
```

1 Creates an ordinary frame with several ordinary components

```
        grp.add(rd3);
        getContentPane().add(sp);

        JTextArea txt = new JTextArea(5, 30);
        JScrollPane sp =  new JScrollPane (text);
        getContentPane().add(text);

        SetDefaultCloseOperation(JFrame.EXIT_ON_CLOSE);
        setVisible(true);
    }

    protected JMenuBar createMenuBar() {
        JMenuBar menuBar = new JMenuBar();
        JMenu mFile = new JMenu("File");
        mFile.setMnemonic('f');

        JMenuItem mItem = new JMenuItem("Exit");
        mItem.setMnemonic('x');
        ActionListener lstExit = new ActionListener() {
            public void actionPerformed(ActionEvent e) {
                System.exit(0);
            }
        };
        mItem.addActionListener(lstExit);
        mFile.add(mItem);
        menuBar.add(mFile);

        ActionListener lst = new ActionListener() {
            public void actionPerformed(ActionEvent e) {
                String str = e.getActionCommand();
                Object obj = m_lfs.get(str);
                if (obj != null)
                try {
                  String className = (String)obj;
                  Class lnfClass = Class.forName(className);
                  UIManager.setLookAndFeel(
                     (LookAndFeel)(lnfClass.newInstance()));
                  SwingUtilities.updateComponentTreeUI(
                     Button1.this);
                }
                catch (Exception ex) {
                  ex.printStackTrace();
                  System.err.println(ex.toString());
                }
            }
        };

        m_lfs = new Hashtable();
        UIManager.LookAndFeelInfo lfs[] =
           UIManager.getInstalledLookAndFeels();
        JMenu mLF = new JMenu("Look&Feel");
        mLF.setMnemonic('l');
        for (int k = 0; k < lfs.length; k++ ) {
           String name = lfs[k].getName();
           JMenuItem lf = new JMenuItem(name);
```

2 Selects and updates new LookAndFeel from menu selection

2 Creates array of LookAndFeel objects obtained from UIManager

```
        m_lfs.put(name, lfs[k].getClassName());
        lf.addActionListener(lst);
        mLF.add(lf);
      }
    menuBar.add(mLF);

    return menuBar;
  }

  public static void main(String argv[]) {
    try {
      LookAndFeel malachite = new Malachite.MalachiteLF();
      UIManager.LookAndFeelInfo info =
        new UIManager.LookAndFeelInfo(malachite.getName(),
      malachite.getClass().getName());
      UIManager.installLookAndFeel(info);
      UIManager.setLookAndFeel(malachite);
    }
    catch (Exception ex) {
      ex.printStackTrace();
      System.err.println(ex.toString());
    }
    new Button1();
  }
}
```

② Creates array of LookAndFeel objects obtained from UIManager

③ Creates Malachite LookAndFeel and sets it as the current LookAndFeel

MalachiteLF.java

see \Chapter21\1\Malachite

```
package Malachite;

import java.awt.*;

import javax.swing.*;
import javax.swing.plaf.*;
import javax.swing.plaf.basic.*;

public class MalachiteLF extends BasicLookAndFeel
 implements java.io.Serializable
{
  public String getID() { return "Malachite"; }
  public String getName() { return "Malachite Look and Feel"; }
  public String getDescription() { return "Sample look and feel from Swing";
}
  public boolean isNativeLookAndFeel() { return false; }
  public boolean isSupportedLookAndFeel() { return true; }

  protected void initComponentDefaults(UIDefaults table) {
    super.initComponentDefaults(table);

    ColorUIResource commonBackground =
      new ColorUIResource(152, 208, 128);
    ColorUIResource commonForeground =
      new ColorUIResource(0, 0, 0);
    ColorUIResource buttonBackground =
```

④ Initializes default resource settings for this LookAndFeel

```
  new ColorUIResource(4, 108, 2);
ColorUIResource buttonForeground =
  new ColorUIResource(236, 236, 0);
ColorUIResource menuBackground =
  new ColorUIResource(128, 192, 128);

BorderUIResource borderRaised = new
  BorderUIResource(new MalachiteBorder(
MalachiteBorder.RAISED));
BorderUIResource borderLowered = new
  BorderUIResource(new MalachiteBorder(
   MalachiteBorder.LOWERED));

FontUIResource commonFont = new
  FontUIResource("Arial", Font.BOLD, 12 );

Icon ubox = new ImageIcon("Malachite/ubox.gif");
Icon ubull = new ImageIcon("Malachite/ubull.gif");

Object[] defaults = {
  "Button.font", commonFont,
  "Button.background", buttonBackground,
  "Button.foreground", buttonForeground,
  "Button.border", borderRaised,
  "Button.margin", new InsetsUIResource(8, 8, 8, 8),
  "Button.textIconGap", new Integer(4),
  "Button.textShiftOffset", new Integer(2),

  "CheckBox.font", commonFont,
  "CheckBox.background", commonBackground,
  "CheckBox.foreground", commonForeground,
  "CheckBox.icon", new IconUIResource(ubox),

  "MenuBar.font", commonFont,
  "MenuBar.background", menuBackground,
  "MenuBar.foreground", commonForeground,

  "Menu.font", commonFont,
  "Menu.background", menuBackground,
  "Menu.foreground", commonForeground,
  "Menu.selectionBackground", buttonBackground,
  "Menu.selectionForeground", buttonForeground,

  "MenuItem.font", commonFont,
  "MenuItem.background", menuBackground,
  "MenuItem.foreground", commonForeground,
  "MenuItem.selectionBackground", buttonBackground,
  "MenuItem.selectionForeground", buttonForeground,
  "MenuItem.margin", new InsetsUIResource(2, 2, 2, 2),

  "Panel.background", commonBackground,
  "Panel.foreground", commonForeground,

  "RadioButton.font", commonFont,
  "RadioButton.background", commonBackground,
  "RadioButton.foreground", commonForeground,
  "RadioButton.icon", new IconUIResource(ubull),
```

```
        "ScrollPane.margin", new InsetsUIResource(8, 8, 8, 8),
        "ScrollPane.border", borderLowered
        "ScrollPane.background", commonBackground,

        "ScrollPane.track", menuBackground,
        "ScrollBar.thumb", buttonBackground,
    };

    table.putDefaults( defaults );
  }
}
```

MalachiteBorder.java

see \Chapter21\1\Malachite

```
package Malachite;

import java.awt.*;

import javax.swing.*;
import javax.swing.border.*;
import javax.swing.event.*;

public class MalachiteBorder implements Border
{
  public static final int RAISED = 0;
  public static final int LOWERED = 1;

  static final String IMAGE_DIR = "Malachite/";
  static final ImageIcon IMAGE_NW = new ImageIcon(
    IMAGE_DIR+"nw.gif");
  static final ImageIcon IMAGE_N  = new ImageIcon(
    IMAGE_DIR+"n.gif");
  static final ImageIcon IMAGE_NE = new ImageIcon(
    IMAGE_DIR+"ne.gif");
  static final ImageIcon IMAGE_E  = new ImageIcon(
    IMAGE_DIR+"e.gif");
  static final ImageIcon IMAGE_SE = new ImageIcon(
    IMAGE_DIR+"se.gif");
  static final ImageIcon IMAGE_S  = new ImageIcon(
    IMAGE_DIR+"s.gif");
  static final ImageIcon IMAGE_SW = new ImageIcon(
    IMAGE_DIR+"sw.gif");
  static final ImageIcon IMAGE_W  = new ImageIcon(
    IMAGE_DIR+"w.gif");

  static final ImageIcon IMAGE_L_NW = new ImageIcon(
    IMAGE_DIR+"l_nw.gif");
  static final ImageIcon IMAGE_L_N  = new ImageIcon(
    IMAGE_DIR+"l_n.gif");
  static final ImageIcon IMAGE_L_NE = new ImageIcon(
    IMAGE_DIR+"l_ne.gif");
  static final ImageIcon IMAGE_L_E  = new ImageIcon(
    IMAGE_DIR+"l_e.gif");
  static final ImageIcon IMAGE_L_SE = new ImageIcon(
```

```
  IMAGE_DIR+"l_se.gif");
static final ImageIcon IMAGE_L_S  = new ImageIcon(
  IMAGE_DIR+"l_s.gif");
static final ImageIcon IMAGE_L_SW = new ImageIcon(
  IMAGE_DIR+"l_sw.gif");
static final ImageIcon IMAGE_L_W  = new ImageIcon(
  IMAGE_DIR+"l_w.gif");

protected int m_w = 7;
protected int m_h = 7;

protected boolean m_isRaised = true;

public MalachiteBorder() {}

public MalachiteBorder(int type) {
  if (type != RAISED && type != LOWERED)
    throw new IllegalArgumentException(
      "Type must be RAISED or LOWERED");
  m_isRaised = (type == RAISED);
}

public Insets getBorderInsets(Component c) {
  return new Insets(m_h, m_w, m_h, m_w);
}

public  boolean isBorderOpaque() { return true; }

public void paintBorder(Component c, Graphics g,
 int x, int y, int w, int h)
{
  int x1 = x+m_w;
  int x2 = x+w-m_w;
  int y1 = y+m_h;
  int y2 = y+h-m_h;
  int xx, yy;

  if (m_isRaised) {
    for (xx=x1; xx<=x2; xx += IMAGE_N.getIconWidth())
      g.drawImage(IMAGE_N.getImage(), xx, y, c);
    for (yy=y1; yy<=y2; yy += IMAGE_E.getIconHeight())
      g.drawImage(IMAGE_E.getImage(), x2, yy, c);
    for (xx=x1; xx<=x2; xx += IMAGE_S.getIconWidth())
      g.drawImage(IMAGE_S.getImage(), xx, y2, c);
    for (yy=y1; yy<=y2; yy += IMAGE_W.getIconHeight())
      g.drawImage(IMAGE_W.getImage(), x, yy, c);
    g.drawImage(IMAGE_NW.getImage(), x, y, c);
    g.drawImage(IMAGE_NE.getImage(), x2, y, c);
    g.drawImage(IMAGE_SE.getImage(), x2, y2, c);
    g.drawImage(IMAGE_SW.getImage(), x, y2, c);
  }
  else {
    for (xx=x1; xx<=x2; xx += IMAGE_L_N.getIconWidth())
      g.drawImage(IMAGE_L_N.getImage(), xx, y, c);
    for (yy=y1; yy<=y2; yy += IMAGE_L_E.getIconHeight())
      g.drawImage(IMAGE_L_E.getImage(), x2, yy, c);
```

❺ Paints prepared images to present Malachite border

```
                 for (xx=x1; xx<=x2; xx += IMAGE_L_S.getIconWidth())
                   g.drawImage(IMAGE_L_S.getImage(), xx, y2, c);
                 for (yy=y1; yy<=y2; yy += IMAGE_L_W.getIconHeight())
                   g.drawImage(IMAGE_L_W.getImage(), x, yy, c);
                 g.drawImage(IMAGE_L_NW.getImage(), x, y, c);
                 g.drawImage(IMAGE_L_NE.getImage(), x2, y, c);
                 g.drawImage(IMAGE_L_SE.getImage(), x2, y2, c);
                 g.drawImage(IMAGE_L_SW.getImage(), x, y2, c);
               }
           }
       }
```

21.2.1 Understanding the code

Class Button1

1 This class represents a simple frame container that is populated by several components: JButtons, JCheckBoxes, JRadioButtons, and JTextArea. Code in the constructor should be familiar, so it requires no special explanation here.

2 The createMenuBar() method is responsible for creating this frame's menu bar. A menu entitled look and feel is populated with menu items corresponding to LookAndFeel implementations available on the current JVM. An array of UIManager.LookAndFeelInfo instances is retrieved using the UIManager.getInstalledLookAndFeels() method. Look and feel class names stored in each info object are placed into the m_lfs Hashtable for future use. A brief text description of a particular look and feel retrieved using the getName() method is used to create each corresponding menu item.

When a menu item is selected, the corresponding ActionListener updates the look and feel for our application. This listener locates the class name corresponding to the selected menu item, and a new instance of that class is created, through reflection, and it is set as the current look and feel using the UIManager.setLookAndFeel() method.

3 The main() method creates an instance of our custom look and feel, MalachiteLF (defined in the Malachite package) makes it available to Java session using UIManager.install-LookAndFeel(), and sets it as the current look and feel using UIManager.setLookAnd-Feel(). Our example frame is then created; it initially uses Malachite resources.

Class Malachite.MalachiteLF

This class defines our Malachite look and feel. It extends BasicLookAndFeel to override its functionality and resources only where necessary. This look and feel is centered around a green malachite palette.

> **NOTE**   Malachite is a green mineral containing copper. This mineral can be found in the Ural Mountains of Russia, in Australia, and in Arizona in the United States of America. Since ancient times it has been used as a gemstone.

4 The getID(), getName(), and getDescription() methods return a short ID, the name, and a text description of this look and feel, respectively. As we've discussed earlier, the init-ComponentDefaults() method fills a given UIDefaults instance with key/value pairs representing information specific to this look and feel. In our implementation, we customize resources for the following components (recall that the "J" prefix is not used): Button, Check-Box, RadioButton, ScrollPane, ScrollBar, MenuBar, Menu, MenuItem, and Panel.

We did not define the `initClassDefaults()` method because we have not implemented any custom UI delegates (we will do this in the next section).

Class Malachite.MalachiteBorder

5 This class defines our custom Malachite implementation of the `Border` interface. This border is intended to provide the illusion of a 3-D frame cut out of a green gemstone. It can be drawn in two forms: lowered or raised. A 3-D effect is produced through the proper combination of previously prepared images. The actual rendering is done in the `paintBorder()` method, which simply draws a set of these images to render the border.

21.2.2 Running the code

Figure 21.1 shows our `Button1` example frame populated with controls using the Malachite look and feel. Note that these controls are lifeless. We cannot click buttons, check or uncheck boxes, or select radio buttons. Try using the menu to select another look and feel available on your system and note the differences.

The components are actually fully functional when using the Malachite look and feel, but they do not have the ability to change their appearance in response to user interaction. More functionality needs to be added to provide mouse and key listener capabilities, as well as additional resources for use in representing the selected state of the button components. We will do this in the next section.

NOTE The UI delegate used for each of these components is the corresponding `basic` look and feel version, because we did not override any class defaults in `MalachiteLF`. A quick look in the source code for these delegates shows that the rendering functionality for selected and focused states is not implemented. All subclasses corresponding to specific look and feels are responsible for implementing this functionality themselves.

21.3 CUSTOM LOOK AND FEEL, PART II: CREATING CUSTOM UI DELEGATES

The next step in the creation of a custom look and feel is to implement custom UI delegates that correspond to each supported component. In example 21.2, we'll show how to implement custom Malachite UI delegates for three relatively simple Swing components: `JButton`, `JCheckBox`, and `JRadioButton`.

Example 21.2

MalachiteLF.java

see \Chapter21\2\Malachite

```
package Malachite;

import java.awt.*;
```

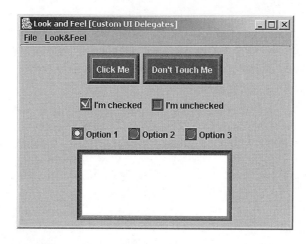

Figure 21.2
Malachite look and feel with custom Malachite UI delegates

```java
import javax.swing.*;
import javax.swing.plaf.*;
import javax.swing.plaf.basic.*;

public class MalachiteLF extends BasicLookAndFeel
 implements java.io.Serializable
{
  // Unchanged code from example 21.1

  protected void initClassDefaults(UIDefaults table) {
    super.initClassDefaults(table);
    putDefault(table, "ButtonUI");
    putDefault(table, "CheckBoxUI");
    putDefault(table, "RadioButtonUI");
  }

  protected void putDefault(UIDefaults table, String uiKey) {
    try   {
      String className = "Malachite.Malachite"+uiKey;
      Class buttonClass = Class.forName(className);
      table.put(uiKey, className);
      table.put(className, buttonClass);
    }
    catch (Exception ex) {
      ex.printStackTrace();
    }
  }

  protected void initComponentDefaults(UIDefaults table) {
    super.initComponentDefaults(table);

    // Unchanged code from example 21.1

    Icon ubox = new ImageIcon("Malachite/ubox.gif");
    Icon ubull = new ImageIcon("Malachite/ubull.gif");

    Icon cbox = new ImageIcon("Malachite/cbox.gif");
    Icon pcbox = new ImageIcon("Malachite/p_cbox.gif");
    Icon pubox = new ImageIcon("Malachite/p_ubox.gif");
```

1 Initializes component type classes from base class method, but replaces component type classes for button, check box, and radio button

1 Stores a UIDefaults entry to look up the component class name from the short component type name, and one entry to look up the class object from the class name

2 This version of this method places more defaults into the UIDefaults table

```java
    Icon cbull = new ImageIcon("Malachite/cbull.gif");
    Icon pcbull = new ImageIcon("Malachite/p_cbull.gif");
    Icon pubull = new ImageIcon("Malachite/p_ubull.gif");

  Object[] defaults = {
    "Button.font", commonFont,
    "Button.background", buttonBackground,
    "Button.foreground", buttonForeground,
    "Button.border", borderRaised,
    "Button.margin", new InsetsUIResource(8, 8, 8, 8),
    "Button.textIconGap", new Integer(4),
    "Button.textShiftOffset", new Integer(2),

    "Button.focusBorder", focusBorder,
    "Button.borderPressed", borderLowered,
    "Button.activeForeground", new
      ColorUIResource(255, 255, 255),
    "Button.pressedBackground", new
      ColorUIResource(0, 96, 0),

    "CheckBox.font", commonFont,
    "CheckBox.background", commonBackground,
    "CheckBox.foreground", commonForeground,
    "CheckBox.icon", new IconUIResource(ubox),

    "CheckBox.focusBorder", focusBorder,
    "CheckBox.activeForeground", activeForeground,
    "CheckBox.iconPressed", new IconUIResource(pubox),
    "CheckBox.iconChecked", new IconUIResource(cbox),
    "CheckBox.iconPressedChecked", new IconUIResource(pcbox),
    "CheckBox.textIconGap", new Integer(4),

    // Unchanged code from example 21.1

    "RadioButton.font", commonFont,
    "RadioButton.background", commonBackground,
    "RadioButton.foreground", commonForeground,
    "RadioButton.icon", new IconUIResource(ubull),

    "RadioButton.focusBorder", focusBorder,
    "RadioButton.activeForeground", activeForeground,
    "RadioButton.iconPressed", new IconUIResource(pubull),
    "RadioButton.iconChecked", new IconUIResource(cbull),
    "RadioButton.iconPressedChecked", new IconUIResource(pcbull),
    "RadioButton.textIconGap", new Integer(4),

    "ScrollPane.margin", new InsetsUIResource(8, 8, 8, 8),
    "ScrollPane.border", borderLowered,
    "ScrollPane.background", commonBackground,

    "ScrollPane.track", menuBackground,
    "ScrollPane.thumb", buttonBackground,
  };

  table.putDefaults( defaults );
  }
}
```

see \Chapter21\2\Malachite

```java
package Malachite;

import java.awt.*;
import java.awt.event.*;

import javax.swing.*;
import javax.swing.border.*;
import javax.swing.plaf.*;
import javax.swing.plaf.basic.*;

public class MalachiteButtonUI extends BasicButtonUI
 implements java.io.Serializable, MouseListener, KeyListener
{
  private final static MalachiteButtonUI m_buttonUI =
    new MalachiteButtonUI();

  protected Border m_borderRaised = null;
  protected Border m_borderLowered = null;
  protected Color  m_backgroundNormal = null;
  protected Color  m_backgroundPressed = null;
  protected Color  m_foregroundNormal = null;
  protected Color  m_foregroundActive = null;
  protected Color  m_focusBorder = null;

  public MalachiteButtonUI() {}

  public static ComponentUI createUI( JComponent c ) {
    return m_buttonUI;
  }

  public void installUI(JComponent c) {
    super.installUI(c);

    m_borderRaised = UIManager.getBorder(
      "Button.border");
    m_borderLowered = UIManager.getBorder(
      "Button.borderPressed");
    m_backgroundNormal = UIManager.getColor(
      "Button.background");
    m_backgroundPressed = UIManager.getColor(
      "Button.pressedBackground");
    m_foregroundNormal = UIManager.getColor(
      "Button.foreground");
    m_foregroundActive = UIManager.getColor(
      "Button.activeForeground");
    m_focusBorder = UIManager.getColor(
      "Button.focusBorder");

    c.addMouseListener(this);
    c.addKeyListener(this);
  }

  public void uninstallUI(JComponent c) {
```

❸ Malachite UI delegate for JButton

❹ Retrieves rendering resources from defaults table

```
    super.uninstallUI(c);
    c.removeMouseListener(this);
    c.removeKeyListener(this);
  }

  public void paint(Graphics g, JComponent c) {
    AbstractButton b = (AbstractButton) c;
    Dimension d = b.getSize();

    g.setFont(c.getFont());
    FontMetrics fm = g.getFontMetrics();

    g.setColor(b.getForeground());
    String caption = b.getText();
    int x = (d.width - fm.stringWidth(caption))/2;
    int y = (d.height + fm.getAscent())/2;
    g.drawString(caption, x, y);

    if (b.isFocusPainted() && b.hasFocus()) {
      g.setColor(m_focusBorder);
      Insets bi = b.getBorder().getBorderInsets(b);
      g.drawRect(bi.left, bi.top, d.width-bi.left-bi.right-1,
        d.height-bi.top-bi.bottom-1);
    }
  }

  public Dimension getPreferredSize(JComponent c) {
    Dimension d = super.getPreferredSize(c);
    if (m_borderRaised != null) {
      Insets ins = m_borderRaised.getBorderInsets(c);
      d.setSize(d.width+ins.left+ins.right,
        d.height+ins.top+ins.bottom);
    }
    return d;
  }

  public void mouseClicked(MouseEvent e) {}

  public void mousePressed(MouseEvent e) {
    JComponent c = (JComponent)e.getComponent();
    c.setBorder(m_borderLowered);
    c.setBackground(m_backgroundPressed);
  }

  public void mouseReleased(MouseEvent e) {
    JComponent c = (JComponent)e.getComponent();
    c.setBorder(m_borderRaised);
    c.setBackground(m_backgroundNormal);
  }

  public void mouseEntered(MouseEvent e) {
    JComponent c = (JComponent)e.getComponent();
    c.setForeground(m_foregroundActive);
    c.repaint();
  }

  public void mouseExited(MouseEvent e) {
    JComponent c = (JComponent)e.getComponent();
```

5 Renders button text and focus rectangle with given graphics context

6 Overridden to add in border size

7 Changes button background and border when pressed or released

7 Changes foreground color when mouse enters or exits bounds of component

```
      c.setForeground(m_foregroundNormal);
      c.repaint();
    }

  public void keyTyped(KeyEvent e) {}

  public void keyPressed(KeyEvent e) {
    int code = e.getKeyCode();
    if (code == KeyEvent.VK_ENTER || code == KeyEvent.VK_SPACE) {
      JComponent c = (JComponent)e.getComponent();
      c.setBorder(m_borderLowered);
      c.setBackground(m_backgroundPressed);
    }
  }

  public void keyReleased(KeyEvent e) {
    int code = e.getKeyCode();
    if (code == KeyEvent.VK_ENTER || code == KeyEvent.VK_SPACE) {
      JComponent c = (JComponent)e.getComponent();
      c.setBor-
der(m_borderRaised);
      c.setBackground(m_backgroundNormal);
    }
  }
}
```

⑦ Changes foreground color when mouse enters or exits bounds of component

⑧ Pressing the Spacebar or Enter while mouse cursor is within component is the same as a button click

MalachiteCheckBoxUI.java

see \Chapter21\2\Malachite

```
package Malachite;

import java.awt.*;
import java.awt.event.*;

import javax.swing.*;
import javax.swing.border.*;
import javax.swing.plaf.*;
import javax.swing.plaf.basic.*;

public class MalachiteCheckBoxUI extends BasicCheckBoxUI
  implements java.io.Serializable, MouseListener
{
  private final static MalachiteCheckBoxUI m_buttonUI =
    new MalachiteCheckBoxUI();

  protected Color  m_backgroundNormal = null;
  protected Color  m_foregroundNormal = null;
  protected Color  m_foregroundActive = null;
  protected Icon   m_checkedIcon = null;
  protected Icon   m_uncheckedIcon = null;
  protected Icon   m_pressedCheckedIcon = null;
  protected Icon   m_pressedUncheckedIcon = null;
  protected Color  m_focusBorder = null;
  protected int    m_textIconGap = -1;
```

⑨ UI delegate for JCheckBox to provide Malachite look and feel

```
public MalachiteCheckBoxUI() {}

public static ComponentUI createUI( JComponent c ) {
  return m_buttonUI;
}

public void installUI(JComponent c) {
  super.installUI(c);
  m_backgroundNormal = UIManager.getColor(
    "CheckBox.background");
  m_foregroundNormal = UIManager.getColor(
    "CheckBox.foreground");
  m_foregroundActive = UIManager.getColor(
    "CheckBox.activeForeground");
  m_checkedIcon = UIManager.getIcon(
    "CheckBox.iconChecked");
  m_uncheckedIcon = UIManager.getIcon(
    "CheckBox.icon");
  m_pressedCheckedIcon = UIManager.getIcon(
    "CheckBox.iconPressedChecked");
  m_pressedUncheckedIcon = UIManager.getIcon(
    "CheckBox.iconPressed");
  m_focusBorder = UIManager.getColor(
    "CheckBox.focusBorder");
  m_textIconGap = UIManager.getInt(
    "CheckBox.textIconGap");

  c.setBackground(m_backgroundNormal);
  c.addMouseListener(this);
}

public void uninstallUI(JComponent c) {
  super.uninstallUI(c);
  c.removeMouseListener(this);
}

public void paint(Graphics g, JComponent c) {
  AbstractButton b = (AbstractButton)c;
  ButtonModel model = b.getModel();
  Dimension d = b.getSize();

  g.setFont(c.getFont());
  FontMetrics fm = g.getFontMetrics();

  Icon icon = m_uncheckedIcon;
  if (model.isPressed() && model.isSelected())
    icon = m_pressedCheckedIcon;
  else if (model.isPressed() && !model.isSelected())
    icon = m_pressedUncheckedIcon;
  else if (!model.isPressed() && model.isSelected())
    icon = m_checkedIcon;

  g.setColor(b.getForeground());
  int x = 0;
  int y = (d.height - icon.getIconHeight())/2;
  icon.paintIcon(c, g, x, y);
```

⑩ Like MalachiteButtonUI, retrieves rendering resources from defaults table

```
      String caption = b.getText();
      x = icon.getIconWidth() + m_textIconGap;
      y = (d.height + fm.getAscent())/2;
      g.drawString(caption, x, y);

      if (b.isFocusPainted() && b.hasFocus()) {
        g.setColor(m_focusBorder);
        Insets bi = b.getBorder().getBorderInsets(b);
        g.drawRect(x-2, y-fm.getAscent()-2, d.width-x,
        fm.getAscent()+fm.getDescent()+4);
      }
    }

  public void mouseClicked(MouseEvent e) {}
  public void mousePressed(MouseEvent e) {}
  public void mouseReleased(MouseEvent e) {}

  public void mouseEntered(MouseEvent e) {
    JComponent c = (JComponent)e.getComponent();
    c.setForeground(m_foregroundActive);
    c.repaint();
  }

  public void mouseExited(MouseEvent e) {
    JComponent c = (JComponent)e.getComponent();
    c.setForeground(m_foregroundNormal);
    c.repaint();
  }
}
```

(11) Provides rollover effect

MalachiteRadioButtonUI.java

see \Chapter21\2\Malachite

```
package Malachite;

import java.awt.*;
import java.awt.event.*;

import javax.swing.*;
import javax.swing.border.*;
import javax.swing.plaf.*;
import javax.swing.plaf.basic.*;
```

(12) Very similar to MalachiteCheckBoxUI

```
public class MalachiteRadioButtonUI extends MalachiteCheckBoxUI
  implements java.io.Serializable, MouseListener
{
  private final static MalachiteRadioButtonUI m_buttonUI =
    new MalachiteRadioButtonUI();

  public MalachiteRadioButtonUI() {}

  public static ComponentUI createUI( JComponent c ) {
    return m_buttonUI;
  }

  public void installUI(JComponent c) {
    super.installUI(c);
```

```
    m_backgroundNormal = UIManager.getColor(
      "RadioButton.background");
    m_foregroundNormal = UIManager.getColor(
      "RadioButton.foreground");
    m_foregroundActive = UIManager.getColor(
      "RadioButton.activeForeground");
    m_checkedIcon = UIManager.getIcon(
      "RadioButton.iconChecked");
    m_uncheckedIcon = UIManager.getIcon(
      "RadioButon.icon");
    m_pressedCheckedIcon = UIManager.getIcon(
      "RadioButton.iconPressedChecked");
    m_pressedUncheckedIcon = UIManager.getIcon(
      "RadioButton.iconPressed");
    m_focusBorder = UIManager.getColor(
      "RadioButton.focusBorder");
    m_textIconGap = UIManager.getInt(
      "RadioButton.textIconGap");

    c.setBackground(m_backgroundNormal);
    c.addMouseListener(this);
  }
}
```

12 **Different icons used to paint UI**

21.3.1 Understanding the code

Class Malachite.MalachiteLF

1 The initClassDefaults() method inherited from BasicLookAndFeel is now overridden. As we've discussed earlier, this method will be called to fill a given UIDefaults instance with information about the specific classes responsible for providing a component's UI delegate for this look and feel. Our implementation calls the super class's initClassDefaults() method to provide all default options. It then replaces the delegate classes for our three supported button components by calling our putDefault() custom method. This helper method puts two entries into the given UIDefaults instance: the UI delegate fully qualified class name, and a corresponding instance of java.lang.Class (see selection 21.1.11).

2 The initComponentDefaults() method now places more custom resources into the given UIDefaults instance, including six custom icons. These resources are needed by our custom Malachite UI delegates, as we will see below.

Class Malachite.MalachiteButtonUI

3 This class provides a custom UI delegate for JButton. It extends BasicButtonUI to reuse much of its functionality, and it implements MouseListener and KeyListener to capture and process user input.

There is one class variable:

- MalachiteButtonUI m_buttonUI: A shared instance of this class which is returned by the createUI() method.

There are seven instance variables:

- `Border m_borderRaised`: The border when the button is not pressed.
- `Border m_borderLowered`: The border when the button is pressed.
- `Color m_backgroundNormal`: The background color when the button is not pressed.
- `Color m_backgroundPressed`: The background color when the button is pressed.
- `Color m_foregroundNormal`: The foreground color.
- `Color m_foregroundActive`: The foreground color when the mouse cursor rolls over.
- `Color m_focusBorder`: The focus rectangle color.

4 The `installUI()` method retrieves rendering resources from the defaults table by calling static methods which are defined in the `UIManager` class (these resources were stored by `MalachiteLF` as described above). It also attaches `this` as a `MouseListener` and `KeyListener` to the specified component. The `uninstallUI()` method simply removes these listeners.

5 The `paint()` method renders a given component using the given graphical context. Rendering of the background and border is done automatically by `JComponent` (see section 21.1.12), so the responsibility of this method is to simply render a button's text and focus rectangle.

6 The `getPreferredSize()` method is overridden since the default implementation in the `BasicButtonUI` class does not take into account the button's border (interestingly enough). Since we use a relatively thick border in Malachite, we need to override this method and add the border's insets to the width and height returned by the superclass implementation.

7 The next five methods represent an implementation of the `MouseListener` interface. To indicate that a button component is currently pressed, the `mousePressed()` method changes a button's background and border, which in turn causes that component to be repainted. The `mouseReleased()` method restores these attributes. To provide an additional rollover effect, the `mouseEntered()` method changes the associated button's foreground color, which is then restored in the `mouseExited()` method.

8 The remaining three methods represent an implementation of the `KeyListener` interface. Pressing the Space bar or Enter key while the button is in focus produces the same effect as performing a button click.

Class Malachite.MalachiteCheckBoxUI

9 This class extends `BasicCheckBoxUI` to provide a custom UI delegate for our `JCheckBox` component.

There is one class variable:

- `MalachiteCheckBoxUI m_buttonUI`: A shared instance of this class which is returned by the `createUI()` method.

There are the instance variables:

- `Color m_backgroundNormal`: The component's background.
- `Color m_foregroundNormal`: The foreground color.
- `Color m_foregroundActive`: The rollover foreground color.
- `Icon m_checkedIcon`: The icon displayed when the check box is checked and not pressed.
- `Icon m_uncheckedIcon`: The icon displayed when the check box is not checked and not pressed.

- Icon m_pressedCheckedIcon: The icon displayed when the check box is checked and pressed.
- Icon m_pressedUncheckedIcon: The icon displayed when the check box is not checked and pressed.
- Color m_focusBorder: The focus rectangle color.
- int m_textIconGap: The gap between the icon and the text.

⑩ Similar to MalachiteButtonUI, the installUI() method retrieves rendering resources from the defaults table and stores them in instance variables. It also attaches this as a Mouse-Listener to the given component.

The paint() method renders the given component using a given graphical context. It draws an icon, text, and focus rectangle when appropriate (this code is fairly straightforward and does not require detailed explanation here).

⑪ The next five methods represent an implementation of the MouseListener interface which provides a similar rollover effect to that of MalachiteButtonUI.

Class Malachite.MalachiteRadioButtonUI

⑫ This class extends MalachiteCheckBoxUI. The only major difference between this class and its parent is that this class uses a different set of icons to render the radio button. The paint() method is not overridden. The installUI() method is modified to retrieve the necessary resources.

21.3.2 Running the code

Figure 21.2 shows our example frame from the previous section with our new Malachite UI delegates in action. You can see that the push buttons here are bigger because their size now properly includes the border thickness. The most significant difference appears when the buttons are clicked, and when boxes are checked/unchecked using using the mouse and keyboard.

At this point we leave the implementation of Malachite UI delegates for other existing Swing components up to you. You should now have a good idea of how to approach the task for any component.

21.4 EXAMPLES FROM THE FIRST EDITION

In chapter 15 of the first edition we developed a custom MDI internal frame component called InnerFrame. Chapter 21 then went on to show how to build UI delegates for this custom component for both our custom Malachite look and feel as well as the existing look and feels. We've removed these examples in the 2nd edition to allow space for updated material. However, they remain in the first edition .zip files and manuscript (freely available at www.manning.com/sbe). Figures 21.3 through 21.6 illustrate the custom InnerFrame UI delegates in action.

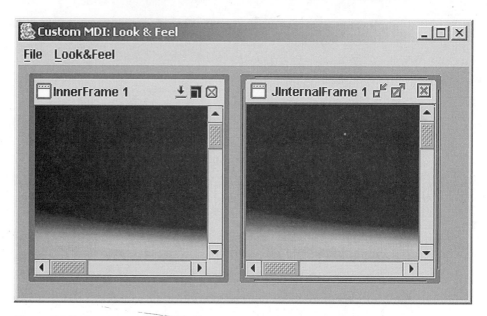

Figure 21.3   `InnerFrame` and `JInternalFrame` in the Metal look and feel

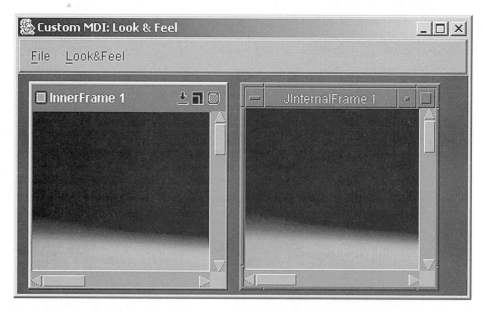

Figure 21.4   `InnerFrame` and `JInternalFrame` in the Motif look and feel

LOOK AND FEEL FOR CUSTOM COMPONENTS, PART I

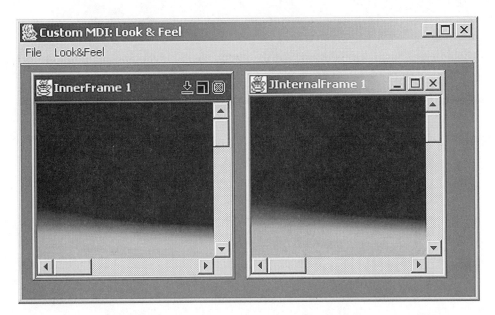

Figure 21.5 `InnerFrame` and `JInternalFrame` in the Windows look and feel

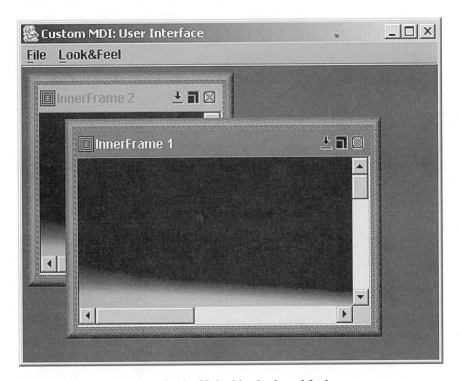

Figure 21.6 `InnerFrame` in the Malachite look and feel

PART IV

Special topics

In the following three chapters we cover several topics which relate directly to the use of Swing. Chapter 22 discusses the powerful Java printing API. We construct examples showing how to: print an image on multiple pages, construct a print preview component, print text, and print `JTable` data (in both portrait and landscape modes).

Chapter 23 focuses on using Swing to work with XML, the lingua franca of the Internet. Examples cover the step-wise implementation of a Swing-based XML editor tool.

Chapter 24 covers Drag and Drop in Swing. As of Java 1.4 Drag and Drop support is built into most Swing components.

C H A P T E R   2 2

Printing

22.1   JAVA PRINTING OVERVIEW

Java includes a considerably advanced printing API. Java veterans may recall that JDK 1.0 didn't provide printing capabilities at all. JDK 1.1 provided access to native print jobs, but multi-page printing was a real problem for that API.

Now Java developers are able to perform multi-page printing using page count selection and other typical specifications in the native Print dialog, as well as page format selection in the native platform-specific Page Setup dialog. The printing-related API is concentrated in the `java.awt.print` package, and we'll start this chapter with an overview of these classes and interfaces.

JAVA 1.4   As of Java 1.4 there is a new `javax.print` package allowing more detailed control of print jobs and communication with printers. Coverage of this new package is beyond the scope of this book, as it is deserving of a much more extensive treatment than we can provide here. This chapter should be considered a primer on printing with Swing, and for those issues that cannot be solved using the material here we would suggest digging into the new `javax.print` package and it is not part of the Swing library.

757

22.1.1 PrinterJob

class java.awt.print.PrinterJob

This is the main class which controls printing in Java. It is used to store print job properties, to initiate printing when necessary, and to control the display of Print dialogs. A typical printing process is shown in the following code:

```
PrinterJob prnJob = PrinterJob.getPrinterJob();
prnJob.setPrintable(myPrintable);
if (!prnJob.printDialog())
    return;
prnJob.print();
```

This code retrieves an instance of `PrinterJob` with the static `getPrinterJob()` method, passes a `Printable` instance to it (which is used to render a specific page on demand—see below), invokes a platform-dependent Print dialog by calling `PrinterJob`'s `printDialog()` method, and, if this method returns `true` (indicating the "OK" to print), starts the actual printing process by calling the `print()` method on that `PrinterJob`.

The Print dialog will look familiar, as it is the typical dialog used by most other applications on the user's system. For example, figure 22.1 shows a Windows 2000 Print dialog:

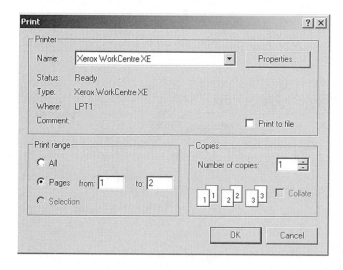

**Figure 22.1
A Windows 2000 Print
dialog, about to print
a pageable job**

Though the `PrinterJob` is the most important constituent of the printing process, it can do nothing without a `Printable` instance that specifies how to actually perform the necessary rendering for each page.

22.1.2 The Printable interface

abstract interface java.awt.print.Printable

This interface defines only one method: `print()`, which takes three parameters:

* `Graphics graphics`: The graphical context into which the page will be drawn.

- `PageFormat pageFormat`: An object containing information about the size and orientation of the page being drawn (see below).
- `int pageIndex`: The zero-based index of the page to be drawn.

The `print()` method will be called to print a portion of the `PrinterJob` corresponding to a given `pageIndex`. An implementation of this method should perform rendering of a specified page, using a given graphical context and a given `PageFormat`. The return value from this method should be `PAGE_EXISTS` if the page is rendered successfully, or `NO_SUCH_ PAGE` if the given page index is too large and does not exist. (These are static ints defined in `Printable`.)

NOTE We never call a `Printable`'s `print()` method ourselves. This is handled deep inside the actual platform-specific `PrinterJob` implementation which we aren't concerned with here.

A class that implements `Printable` is said to be a *page painter*. When a `PrinterJob` uses only one page painter to print each page, it is referred to as a *printable job*. The notion of a document being separated into a certain number of pages is not predefined in a printable job. In order to print a specific page, a printable job will actually render all pages leading up to that page first, and then it will print the specified page. This happens because it does not maintain information about how much space each page will occupy when rendered with the given page painter. For example, if we specify in our Print dialog that we want to print pages 3 and 5 only, then pages 0 through 4 (because pages are 0-indexed) will be rendered with the `print()` method, but only 2 and 4 will actually be printed.

WARNING Since the system only knows how many pages a printable job will span *after* the rendering of the complete document takes place (meaning after `paint()` has been called), Print dialogs will not display the correct number of pages to be printed. This is because there is no pre-print communication between a `PrinterJob` and the system that determines how much space the printable job requires. For this reason you will often see a range such as 1 to 9999 in Print dialogs when printing printable jobs. (This is not the case for pageable jobs.)

In reality, it is often the case that `print()` will be called for each page more than once.

NOTE In the first edition we emphasized several major performance and memory problems associated with printing images. Most of these have been addressed in Java 1.3 and 1.4, and we are happy to report that we no longer have any trouble printing from the examples in this chapter.

22.1.3   The Pageable interface

abstract interface java.awt.print.Pageable

It is possible to support multiple page painters in a single `PrinterJob`. As we know, each page printer can correspond to a different scheme of printing because each `Printable` implements its own `print()` method. Implemenatations of the `Pageable` interface are designed to manage groups of page painters, and a print job that uses multiple page painters is referred to as a *pageable job*. Each page in a pageable job can use a different page printer and `PageFormat` to perform its rendering.

Unlike printable jobs, pageable jobs *do* maintain the predefined notion of a document as a set of separate pages. For this reason, pages of a pageable job can be printed in any order without having to render all pages leading up to a specific page (as is the case with printable jobs). Also, a `Pageable` instance carries with it an explicit page count which can be communicated to the native printing system when a `PrinterJob` is established. So when it's printing a pageable job, the native Print dialog will know the correct range of pages to display, unlike a printable job. (Note that this does not mean pageable jobs are not subject to the inherent limitations described above; we will see the same repetitive calling of `print()` that we do in printable jobs.)

When we are constructing a pageable `PrinterJob`, instead of calling `PrinterJob`'s `setPrintable()` method (see section 22.1.1), we call its `setPageable()` method. Figure 22.1 shows a Windows 2000 Print dialog about to print a pageable job. Notice that the range of pages is not 1 to 9999.

We won't be working with pageable jobs in this chapter because all the documents we will be printing require only one `Printable` implementation, even if documents can span multiple pages. In most real-world applications, each page of a document is printed with identical orientation, margins, and other sizing characteristics. However, if greater flexibility is desired, `Pageable` implementations such as `Book` (see below) can be useful.

22.1.4   The PrinterGraphics interface

abstract interface java.awt.print.PrinterGraphics

This interface defines only one method: `getPrinterJob()`, which retrieves the `PrinterJob` instance controlling the current printing process. It is implemented by `Graphics` objects that are passed to `Printable` objects to render a page. (We will not need to use this interface at all, as it is used deep inside `PrinterJob` instances to define the `Graphics` objects that are passed to each `Printable`'s `paint()` method during printing.)

22.1.5   PageFormat

class java.awt.print.PageFormat

This class encapsulates a `Paper` object and adds to it an orientation property (landscape or portrait). We can force a `Printable` to use a specific `PageFormat` by passing one to `PrinterJob`'s overloaded `setPrintable()` method. For instance, the following would force a printable job to use a specific `PageFormat` with a landscape orientation:

```
PrinterJob prnJob = PrinterJob.getPrinterJob();
PageFormat pf = job.defaultPage();
pf.setOrientation(PageFormat.LANDSCAPE);
prnJob.setPrintable(myPrintable, pf);
if (!prnJob.printDialog())
  return;
prnJob.print();
```

`PageFormat` defines three orientations:

- LANDSCAPE: The origin is at the bottom left-hand corner of the paper with the x-axis pointing up and the y-axis pointing to the right.

- PORTRAIT (most common): The origin is at the top left-hand corner of the paper with the x-axis pointing to the right and the y-axis pointing down.
- REVERSE_LANDSCAPE: The origin is at the top right-hand corner of the paper with the x-axis pointing down and the y-axis pointing to the left.

We can optionally display a Page Setup dialog in which the user can specify page characteristics such as orientation, paper size, and margin size. This dialog will return a new PageFormat to use in printing. The Page Setup dialog is meant to be presented before the Print dialog and it can be displayed using PrinterJob's pageDialog() method. The following code brings up a Page Setup dialog, and it uses the resulting PageFormat for printing a printable job:

```
PrinterJob prnJob = PrinterJob.getPrinterJob();
PageFormat pf = job.pageDialog(job.defaultPage());
prnJob.setPrintable(myPrintable, pf);
if (!prnJob.printDialog())
  return;
prnJob.print();
```

We need to pass the pageDialog() method a PageFormat instance, as it uses it to clone and modify as the user specifies. If the changes are accepted, the cloned and modified version is returned. If they are not, the original version passed in is returned. Figure 22.2 shows a Windows 2000 Page Setup dialog.

22.1.6   Paper

class java.awt.print.Paper

This class holds the size and margins of the paper used for printing. The getImageableX() and getImageableY() methods retrieve the coordinates of the top-left corner of the printable area in 1/72nds of an inch (which is approximately equal to one screen pixel—referred to as a "point" in typography). The getImageableWidth() and getImageableHeight() methods retrieve the width and height of the printable area (also in 1/72nds of an inch). We can also change the size of the useable region of the paper using its setImageableArea() method.

We can access the Paper object associated with a PageFormat using PageFormat's getPaper() and setPaper() methods.

22.1.7   Book

class java.awt.print.Book

This class represents a collection of Printable instances with corresponding PageFormats to represent a complex document whose pages may have different formats. The Book class implements the Pageable interface, and Printables are added to a Book using one of its append() methods. This class also defines several methods that allow specific pages to be manipulated and replaced. (A page in terms of a Book is a Printable/PageFormat pair. Each page does correspond to an actual printed page.) See the API documentation and the Java tutorial for more information about this class.

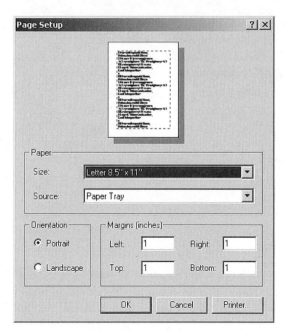

Figure 22.2
A Windows 2000
Page Setup dialog

22.1.8 PrinterException

class java.awt.print.PrinterException

This exception may be thrown to indicate an error during a printing procedure. It has two concrete subclasses: `PrinterAbortException` and `PrinterIOException`. The former indicates that a print job was terminated by the application or the user while printing, and the latter indicates that there was a problem outputting to the printer.

22.2 PRINTING IMAGES

In this section, we add printing capabilities to the `JPEGEditor` application introduced in chapter 13. The material presented in example 22.1 will form a solid basis for the subsequent printing examples. Here we show how to implement the `Printable` interface to construct a custom panel with a `print()` method that can manage the printing of large images by splitting them up into a matrix of pages.

Example 22.1

JPEGEditor.java

see \Chapter22\1

```
import java.awt.*;
import java.awt.event.*;
import java.awt.image.*;
import java.util.*;
import java.io.*;
```

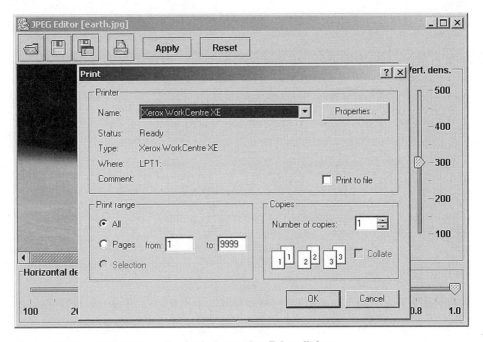

Figure 22.3 JPEGEditor **displaying a native Print dialog**

```
import javax.swing.*;
import javax.swing.border.*;
import javax.swing.event.*;
import javax.swing.filechooser.*;

import com.sun.image.codec.jpeg.*;

import java.awt.print.*;

// Unchanged code from example 13.4

public class JPEGEditor extends JFrame
{
    // Unchanged code from example 13.4

protected JToolBar createToolBar {
    // Unchanged code from example 13.4

    tb.addSeparator();
    bt = new JButton(new ImageIcon("Print24.gif"));
    bt.setToolTipText("Print image");
    lst = new ActionListener() {
      public void actionPerformed(ActionEvent e) {
        Thread runner = new Thread() {
          public void run() {
            if (m_panel.getBufferedImage() != null)
              printData();
          }
        };
    };
```

❶ If image is loaded, this button will process the image for printing

```
        runner.start();
    }
};
bt.addActionListener(lst);
tb.add(bt);

// Unchanged code from example 13.4

}

// Unchanged code from example 13.4

  public void printData() {
    try {
      PrinterJob prnJob = PrinterJob.getPrinterJob();
      prnJob.setPrintable(m_panel);
      if (!prnJob.printDialog())
        return;
      setCursor( Cursor.getPredefinedCursor(
        Cursor.WAIT_CURSOR));
      prnJob.print();
      setCursor( Cursor.getPredefinedCursor(
        Cursor.DEFAULT_CURSOR));
      JOptionPane.showMessageDialog(this,
        "Printing completed successfully", "JPEGEditor2",
        JOptionPane.INFORMATION_MESSAGE);
    }
    catch (PrinterException e) {
      e.printStackTrace();
      System.err.println("Printing error: "+e.toString());
    }
  }

  public static void main(String argv[])
  {
    JPEGEditor frame = new JPEGEditor();
    frame.setDefaultCloseOperation(JFrame.EXIT_ON_CLOSE);
    frame.setVisible(true);
  }
}

class JPEGPanel extends JPanel implements Printable
{
  protected BufferedImage m_bi = null;

  public int m_maxNumPage = 1;

  // Unchanged code from example 13.4

  public int print(Graphics pg, PageFormat pageFormat,
    int pageIndex) throws PrinterException {
    if (pageIndex >= m_maxNumPage || m_bi == null)
      return NO_SUCH_PAGE;

    pg.translate((int)pageFormat.getImageableX(),
      (int)pageFormat.getImageableY());
```

1 If image is loaded, this button will process the image for printing

2 Sets Printable object into PrinterJob and attempts to print it

3 Printable panel which contains a JPEG image

4 Shifts graphics context origin and calculates width and height of drawing area

```
        int wPage = (int)pageFormat.getImageableWidth();
        int hPage = (int)pageFormat.getImageableHeight();

        int w = m_bi.getWidth(this);
        int h = m_bi.getHeight(this);
        if (w == 0 || h == 0)
          return NO_SUCH_PAGE;
        int nCol = Math.max((int)Math.ceil((double)w/wPage), 1);
          int nRow = Math.max((int)Math.ceil((double)h/hPage), 1);
        m_maxNumPage = nCol*nRow;

        int iCol = pageIndex % nCol;
        int iRow = pageIndex / nCol;
        int x = iCol*wPage;
        int y = iRow*hPage;
        int wImage = Math.min(wPage, w-x);
        int hImage = Math.min(hPage, h-y);

        pg.drawImage(m_bi, 0, 0, wImage, hImage,
          x, y, x+wImage, y+hImage, this);
        System.gc();

        return PAGE_EXISTS;
    }
  }
```

4 Shifts graphics context origin and calculates width and height of drawing area

5 Calculates number of pages needed to print image

6 From desired page number, calculates column, row, and dimensions of image portion

7 Draws the image portion to the graphics context, and tries to release memory immediately after

22.2.1   Understanding the code

Class JPEGEditor

1 The `java.awt.print` package is imported to provide printing capabilities. A new toolbar button entitled Print... has been added to this application. If this item is selected and an image has been loaded, our new custom `printData()` method is called.

2 The `printData()` method retrieves a `PrinterJob` instance and passes it our `m_panel` component (this is an instance of `JPEGPanel`, which now implements the `Printable` interface as shown below). It then invokes a native Print dialog and initializes printing by calling `print()`. If no exception was thrown, a "Printing completed successfully" message is displayed when printing completes. Otherwise, the exception trace is printed.

Class JPEGPanel

3 This class, which was originally designed to just display an image, now implements the `Printable` interface and is able to print a portion of its displayed image upon request. A new instance variable, `m_maxNumPage`, holds a maximum page number available for this printing. This number is set initially to one and its actual value is calculated in the `print()` method (see below).

The `print()` method prints a portion of the current image corresponding to the given page index. If the current image is larger than a single page, it will be split into several pages which are arranged as several rows and columns (a matrix). When printed, they can be placed in this arrangement to form one big printout.

④ This method first shifts the origin of the graphics context to take into account the page's margins, and it calculates the width and height of the area available for drawing: the results are wPage and hPage.

```
pg.translate((int)pageFormat.getImageableX(),
    (int)pageFormat.getImageableY());
int wPage = (int)pageFormat.getImageableWidth();
int hPage = (int)pageFormat.getImageableHeight();
```

⑤ The local variables w and h represent the width and height of the whole BufferedImage to be printed. (If any of these happens to be 0, we return NO_SUCH_PAGE.) Comparing these dimensions with the width and height of a single page, we can calculate the number of columns (not fewer than 1) and rows (not fewer than 1) in which the original image should be split to fit to the page's size:

```
int nCol = Math.max((int)Math.ceil((double)w/wPage), 1);
int nRow = Math.max((int)Math.ceil((double)h/hPage), 1);
m_maxNumPage = nCol*nRow;
```

The product of rows and columns gives us the number of pages in the print job, m_maxNumPage.

⑥ Now, because we know the index of the current page to be printed (it was passed as the parameter pageIndex) we can determine the current column and row indices (note that enumeration is made from left to right and then from top to bottom); these indices are iCol and iRow.

```
int iCol = pageIndex % nCol;
int iRow = pageIndex / nCol;
int x = iCol*wPage;
int y = iRow*hPage;
int wImage = Math.min(wPage, w-x);
int hImage = Math.min(hPage, h-y);
```

We also can calculate the coordinates of the top-left corner of the portion of the image to be printed on this page (x and y), and the width and height of this region (wImage and hImage). Note that in the last column or row of our image matrix, the width and/or height of a portion can be less than the maximum values (which we calculated above: wPage and hPage).

⑦ Now we have everything ready to actually print a region of the image to the specified graphics context. We now need to extract this region and draw it at (0, 0), as this will be the origin (upper-left hand corner) of our printed page. The Graphics drawImage() method does the job. It takes ten parameters: an Image instance, four coordinates of the destination area (top-left and bottom-right—*not* width and height), four coordinates of the source area, and an ImageObserver instance.

```
pg.drawImage(m_bi, 0, 0, wImage, hImage,
    x, y, x+wImage, y+hImage, this);
System.gc();
```

NOTE Because the print() method may be called many times for the same page (see below), it makes good sense to explicitly invoke the garbage collector in this method. Otherwise, we may run out of memory.

22.2.2   Running the code

Figure 22.3 shows a Print dialog brought up by our program when it was run on a Windows 2000 platform. Try loading and printing images of various sizes.

22.3   PRINT PREVIEW

Print preview functionality has became a standard feature provided by most modern print-enabled applications. It only makes sense to include this service in Java applications. Example 22.2 in this section shows how to construct a print preview component.

NOTE   An additional reason for Java developers to add print preview to their applications is that this feature can be very useful for debugging print code.

The print preview component displays small images of the printed pages as they would appear after printing. A GUI attached to the preview component typically allows you to change the scale of the preview images and to invoke a print. Example 22.2 demonstrates such a component which can be easily added to any print-aware Swing application. Figure 22.4 shows how the image will appear.

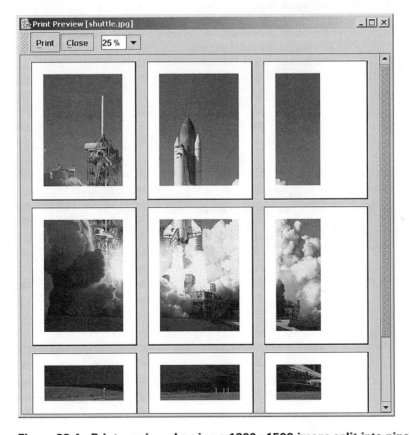

Figure 22.4   Print preview showing a 1200 x1500 image split into nine parts

Example 22.2

JPEGEditor.java

see \Chapter22\2

```java
public class JPEGEditor extends JFrame
{
  // Unchanged code from example 22.1

  protected JMenuBar createMenuBar() {
    // Unchanged code from example 22.1

    bt = new JButton(new ImageIcon("PrintPreview24.gif"));
    bt.setToolTipText("Print preview");
    lst = new ActionListener() {
      public void actionPerformed(ActionEvent e) {
        if (m_panel.getBufferedImage() != null) {
          Thread runner = new Thread() {
            public void run() {
              setCursor( Cursor.getPredefinedCursor(
                Cursor.WAIT_CURSOR));
              PrintPreview preview = new PrintPreview(m_panel,
                "Print Preview ["+m_currentFile.getName()+"]");
              preview.setVisible(true);
              setCursor(Cursor.getPredefinedCursor(
                Cursor.DEFAULT_CURSOR));
            }
          };
          runner.start();
        }
      }
    };
    bt.addActionListener(lst);
    tb.add(bt);
```

① Toolbar button to create print preview display

```java
// The rest of the code is unchanged from example 22.1
```

PrintPreview.java

see \Chapter22\2

```java
import java.awt.*;
import java.awt.event.*;
import java.awt.image.*;
import java.util.*;
import java.awt.print.*;

import javax.swing.*;
import javax.swing.border.*;
import javax.swing.event.*;

public class PrintPreview extends JFrame
{
```

② Frame to display preview of print job before printing

```
protected int m_wPage;
protected int m_hPage;
protected Printable m_target;
protected JComboBox m_cbScale;
protected PreviewContainer m_preview;

public PrintPreview(Printable target) {
  this(target, "Print Preview");
}

public PrintPreview(Printable target, String title) {
  super(title);
  setSize(600, 400);
  m_target = target;

  JToolBar tb = new JToolBar();
  JButton bt = new JButton("Print", new ImageIcon("print.gif"));
  ActionListener lst = new ActionListener() {
    public void actionPerformed(ActionEvent e) {
      try {
        // Use default printer, no dialog
        PrinterJob prnJob = PrinterJob.getPrinterJob();
        prnJob.setPrintable(m_target);
        setCursor( Cursor.getPredefinedCursor(
          Cursor.WAIT_CURSOR));
        prnJob.print();
        setCursor( Cursor.getPredefinedCursor(
          Cursor.DEFAULT_CURSOR));
        dispose();
      }
      catch (PrinterException ex) {
        ex.printStackTrace();
        System.err.println("Printing error: "+ex.toString());
      }
    }
  };
  bt.addActionListener(lst);
  bt.setAlignmentY(0.5f);
  bt.setMargin(new Insets(4,6,4,6));
  tb.add(bt);

  bt = new JButton("Close");
  lst = new ActionListener() {
    public void actionPerformed(ActionEvent e) {
      dispose();
    }
  };
  bt.addActionListener(lst);
  bt.setAlignmentY(0.5f);
  bt.setMargin(new Insets(2,6,2,6));
  tb.add(bt);

  String[] scales = { "10 %", "25 %", "50 %", "100 %" };
  m_cbScale = new JComboBox(scales);
```

**Toolbar button
to directly print
preview image** ③

```
lst = new ActionListener() {
  public void actionPerformed(ActionEvent e) {
    Thread runner = new Thread() {
      public void run() {
        String str = m_cbScale.getSelectedItem().
          toString();
        if (str.endsWith("%"))
          str = str.substring(0, str.length()-1);
        str = str.trim();
          int scale = 0;
        try { scale = Integer.parseInt(str); }
        catch (NumberFormatException ex) { return; }
        int w = (int)(m_wPage*scale/100);
        int h = (int)(m_hPage*scale/100);

        Component[] comps = m_preview.getComponents();
        for (int k=0; k<comps.length; k++) {
          if (!(comps[k] instanceof PagePreview))
            continue;
          PagePreview pp = (PagePreview)comps[k];
            pp.setScaledSize(w, h);
        }
        m_preview.doLayout();
        m_preview.getParent().getParent().validate();
      }
    };
    runner.start();
  }
};
m_cbScale.addActionListener(lst);
m_cbScale.setMaximumSize(m_cbScale.getPreferredSize());
m_cbScale.setEditable(true);
tb.addSeparator();
tb.add(m_cbScale);
getContentPane().add(tb, BorderLayout.NORTH);

m_preview = new PreviewContainer();

PrinterJob prnJob = PrinterJob.getPrinterJob();
PageFormat pageFormat = prnJob.defaultPage();
if (pageFormat.getHeight()==0 || pageFormat.getWidth()==0) {
  System.err.println("Unable to determine default page size");
    return;
}
m_wPage = (int)(pageFormat.getWidth());
m_hPage = (int)(pageFormat.getHeight());
int scale = 10;
int w = (int)(m_wPage*scale/100);
int h = (int)(m_hPage*scale/100);

int pageIndex = 0;
try {
  while (true) {
    BufferedImage img = new BufferedImage(m_wPage,
```

4 Action on Scale combo box to scale the previewed image size up or down

5 Scales each PagePreview object individually

6 Renders each portion of the original image into individual PagePreview objects

```
                  m_hPage, BufferedImage.TYPE_INT_RGB);
              Graphics g = img.getGraphics();
              g.setColor(Color.white);
              g.fillRect(0, 0, m_wPage, m_hPage);
              if (target.print(g, pageFormat, pageIndex) !=
               Printable.PAGE_EXISTS)
                break;
              PagePreview pp = new PagePreview(w, h, img);
              m_preview.add(pp);
              pageIndex++;
          }
      }
    catch (PrinterException e) {
      e.printStackTrace();
        System.err.println("Printing error: "+e.toString());
    }

    JScrollPane ps = new JScrollPane(m_preview);
    getContentPane().add(ps, BorderLayout.CENTER);

    setDefaultCloseOperation(DISPOSE_ON_CLOSE);
    setVisible(true);
  }

  class PreviewContainer extends JPanel
  {
    protected int H_GAP = 16;
    protected int V_GAP = 10;

    public Dimension getPreferredSize() {
      int n = getComponentCount();
      if (n == 0)
        return new Dimension(H_GAP, V_GAP);
      Component comp = getComponent(0);
      Dimension dc = comp.getPreferredSize();
      int w = dc.width;
      int h = dc.height;

      Dimension dp = getParent().getSize();
      int nCol = Math.max((dp.width-H_GAP)/(w+H_GAP), 1);
      int nRow = n/nCol;
      if (nRow*nCol < n)
        nRow++;

      int ww = nCol*(w+H_GAP) + H_GAP;
      int hh = nRow*(h+V_GAP) + V_GAP;
      Insets ins = getInsets();
      return new Dimension(ww+ins.left+ins.right,
        hh+ins.top+ins.bottom);
    }

    public Dimension getMaximumSize() {
      return getPreferredSize();
    }

    public Dimension getMinimumSize() {
```

6 Renders each portion of the original image into individual **PagePreview** objects

7 Panel to layout **PagePreview** objects, with special layout requirements

```
      return getPreferredSize();
  }

  public void doLayout() {
    Insets ins = getInsets();
    int x = ins.left + H_GAP;
    int y = ins.top + V_GAP;

    int n = getComponentCount();
    if (n == 0)
      return;
    Component comp = getComponent(0);
    Dimension dc = comp.getPreferredSize();
    int w = dc.width;
    int h = dc.height;

    Dimension dp = getParent().getSize();
    int nCol = Math.max((dp.width-H_GAP)/(w+H_GAP), 1);
    int nRow = n/nCol;
    if (nRow*nCol < n)
      nRow++;

    int index = 0;
    for (int k = 0; k<nRow; k++) {
      for (int m = 0; m<nCol; m++) {
        if (index >= n)
          return;
        comp = getComponent(index++);
        comp.setBounds(x, y, w, h);
        x += w+H_GAP;
      }
      y += h+V_GAP;
      x = ins.left + H_GAP;
    }
  }
}

class PagePreview extends JPanel
{
  protected int m_w;
  protected int m_h;
  protected Image m_source;
  protected Image m_img;

  public PagePreview(int w, int h, Image source) {
    m_w = w;
    m_h = h;
    m_source= source;
    m_img = m_source.getScaledInstance(m_w, m_h,
      Image.SCALE_SMOOTH);
    m_img.flush();
    setBackground(Color.white);
    setBorder(new MatteBorder(1, 1, 2, 2, Color.black));
  }
```

8 **Panel to contain a single PagePreview object**

```
        public void setScaledSize(int w, int h) {
          m_w = w;
          m_h = h;
          m_img = m_source.getScaledInstance(m_w, m_h,
            Image.SCALE_SMOOTH);
          repaint();
        }

        public Dimension getPreferredSize() {
          Insets ins = getInsets();
          return new Dimension(m_w+ins.left+ins.right,
            m_h+ins.top+ins.bottom);
        }

        public Dimension getMaximumSize() {
          return getPreferredSize();
        }

        public Dimension getMinimumSize() {
          return getPreferredSize();
        }

        public void paint(Graphics g) {
          g.setColor(getBackground());
          g.fillRect(0, 0, getWidth(), getHeight());
          g.drawImage(m_img, 0, 0, this);
          paintBorder(g);
        }
      }
    }
  }
```

22.3.1 Understanding the code

Class JPEGEditor

1 Compared with its counterpart in the previous example, this class has only one difference: it creates a Print Preview toolbar button. When it's selected, this item creates an instance of the PrintPreview class (see below). This class's constructor takes two parameters: a reference to a Printable instance and a text string for the frame's title. As we saw in example 22.1, our m_panel component implements the Printable interface and provides the actual printing functionality, so we use it to create the PrintPreview instance. This call is wrapped in a thread because when it's used with large images, creating a PrintPreview instance can take a significant amount of time.

> **NOTE** As you can see, we only need to have a reference to an instance of the Printable interface to create a PrintPreview component. Thus, this component can be added to any print-aware application with only a couple of lines of code. We will use it in the remaining examples as well, because it is such a simple feature to add.

Class PrintPreview

2 This class represents a JFrame-based component which is capable of displaying the results of printing before actual printing occurs. Several instance variables are used:

- Printable m_target: An object whose printout will be previewed.

- `int m_wPage`: The width of the default printing page.
- `int m_hPage`: The height of the default printing page.
- `JComboBox m_cbScale`: A combo box which selects a scale for preview.
- `PreviewContainer m_preview`: The container which holds the previewing pages.

Two `public` constructors are provided. The first one takes an instance of the `Printable` interface and passes control to the second constructor, using the `Printable` along with the "Print Preview" `String` as parameters. The second constructor takes two parameters: an instance of the `Printable` interface and the title string for the frame. This second constructor is the one that actually sets up the `PrintPreview` component.

❸ First, a toolbar is created and a button entitled Print is added to perform the printing of the `m_target` instance as described in the previous example. The only difference is that no Print dialog is invoked, and the default system printer is used (this approach is typical for print preview components). When the printing is complete, this print preview component is disposed of. The second button added to the toolbar is labeled Close, and it merely disposes of this frame component.

❹ The third (and last) component added to the toolbar is the editable combo box `m_cbScale`, which selects a percent scale to zoom the previewed pages. Along with several pre-defined choices (10 %, 25 %, 50 %, and 100 %), any percent value can be entered. As soon as that value is selected and the corresponding `ActionListener` is involved, the zoom scale value is extracted and stored in the local variable `scale`. This determines the width and height of each `PreviewPage` component we will be creating:

```
int w = (int)(m_wPage*scale/100);
int h = (int)(m_hPage*scale/100);
```

❺ Then all child components of the `m_preview` container in turn are cast to `PagePreview` components (each child is expected to be a `PagePreview` instance, but `instanceof` is used for precaution), and the `setScaledSize()` method is invoked to assign a new size to the preview pages. Finally, `doLayout()` is invoked on `m_preview` to lay out the resized child components, and `validate()` is invoked on the scroll pane. This scroll pane is the parent of the `m_preview` component in the second generation (the first parent is a `JViewport` component, see chapter 7). This last call is necessary to display/hide scroll bars as needed for the new size of the `m_preview` container. This whole process is wrapped in a thread to avoid clogging up the event-dispatching thread.

❻ When the toolbar construction is complete, the `m_preview` component is created and filled with the previewed pages. To do this, we first retrieve a `PrinterJob` instance for a default system printer without displaying a Page Setup dialog, and we retrieve a default `PageFormat` instance. We use this to determine the initial size of the previewed pages by multiplying its dimensions by the computed scaling percentile (which is 10% at initialization time, because `scale` is set to 10).

To create these scalable preview pages we set up a `while` loop to continuously call the `print()` method of the given `Printable` instance, using a page index that gets incremented with each iteration, until it returns something other than `Printable.PAGE_EXISTS`.

Each page is rendered into a separate image in memory. To do this, an instance of Buffered-Image is created with width m_wPage and height m_hPage. A Graphics instance is retrieved from that image using getGraphics():

```
BufferedImage img = new BufferedImage(m_wPage,
    m_hPage, BufferedImage.TYPE_INT_RGB);
Graphics g = img.getGraphics();
g.setColor(Color.white);
g.fillRect(0, 0, m_wPage, m_hPage);
if (target.print(g, pageFormat, pageIndex) !=
    Printable.PAGE_EXISTS)
    break;
```

After filling the image's area with a white background (most paper is white), this Graphics instance, along with the PageFormat and current page index, pageIndex, are passed to the print() method of the Printable object.

NOTE The BufferedImage class in the java.awt.image package allows direct image manipulation in memory.

If the call to the print() method returns PAGE_EXISTS, indicating success in rendering the new page, a new PagePreview component is created:

```
PagePreview pp = new PagePreview(w, h, img);
m_preview.add(pp);
pageIndex++;
```

Our newly created BufferedImage is passed to the PagePreview constructor as one of the parameters. This is done so that we can use it now and in the future for scaling each Page-Preview component separately. The other parameters are the width and height to use, which, at creation time, are 10% of the page size (as discussed above).

Each new component is added to our m_preview container. Finally, when the Printable's print() method finishes, our m_preview container is placed in a JScrollPane to provide scrolling capabilities. This scroll pane is then added to the center of the PrintPreview frame, and our frame is then made visible.

Class PrintPreview.PreviewContainer

7 This inner class extends JPanel to serve as a container for PagePreview components. The only reason this custom container is developed is because we have specific layout requirements. What we want here is a layout which places its child components from left to right, without any resizing (using their preferred size), leaving equal gaps between them. When the available container's width is filled, a new row should be started from the left edge, without regard to the available height (we assume scrolling functionality will be made available).

You may want to refer back to our discussion of layouts in chapter 4. The code constituting this class does not require much explanation and it provides a good exercise for custom layout development (even though this class is not explicitly a layout manager).

Class PrintPreview.PagePreview

8 This inner class extends JPanel to serve as a placeholder for the image of each printed page preview. Four instance variables are used:

- `int m_w`: The current component's width (without insets).
- `int m_h`: The current component's height (without insets).
- `Image m_source`: The source image depicting the previewed page in full scale.
- `Image m_img`: The scaled image currently used for rendering.

The constructor of the `PagePreview` class takes its initial width and height and the source image. It creates a scaled image by calling the `getScaledInstance()` method and sets its border to `MatteBorder(1, 1, 2, 2, Color.black)` to imitate a page lying on a flat surface.

The `setScaledSize()` method may be called to resize this component. It takes a new width and height as parameters and creates a new scaled image that corresponds to the new size. Using the `SCALE_SMOOTH` option for scaling is essential to get a preview image which looks like a zoomed printed page (although it is not the fastest option).

The `paint()` method draws a scaled image and draws a border around the component.

22.3.2 Running the code

Figure 22.4 shows a preview of the large image which will be printed on the nine pages. Select various zoom factors in the combo box and see how the size of the previewed pages is changed. Then click the Print button to print to the default printer directly from the preview frame.

22.4 PRINTING TEXT

In this section we'll add print and print preview functionality to our MDI basic text editor application developed in chapter 12 and extended in chapters 14 and 16. Printing text would be easy if `JTextArea` implemented the `Printable` interface and provided capability to print its contents. Unfortunately this is not the case, so we need to get fairly creative and implement our own solution.

NOTE In the first edition we implemented a solution to allow printing styled text in an RTF Word Processor application. This was accomplished by implementing a custom `BoxView` subclass (see chapter 19) to specifically handle printing. This example and its explanation remain freely available in chapter 22 of the first edition at www.manning.com/sbe.

Example 22.3

BasicTextEditor.java

see \Chapter22\3

```
import java.awt.*;
import java.awt.event.*;
import java.io.*;
import java.util.*;
import java.awt.print.*;

import javax.swing.*;
import javax.swing.border.*;
import javax.swing.event.*;
```

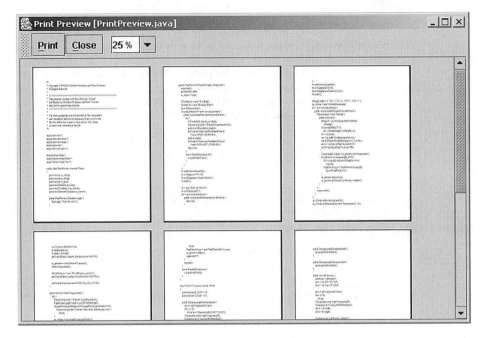

Figure 22.5   Print Preview showing six pages of a text document

```java
public class BasicTextEditor extends JFrame {
  // Unchanged code from example 16.2

  protected JMenuBar createMenuBar() {
    // Unchanged code from example 16.2

    Action actionPrint = new AbstractAction("Print...",
      new ImageIcon("Print16.gif")) {
      public void actionPerformed(ActionEvent e) {
        Thread runner = new Thread() {
          public void run() {
            printData();
          }
        };
        runner.start();
      }
    };
    item =  mFile.add(actionPrint);
    item.setMnemonic('p');

    Action actionPrintPreview = new AbstractAction("Print Preview",
      new ImageIcon("PrintPreview16.gif")) {
      public void actionPerformed(ActionEvent e) {
        Thread runner = new Thread() {
          public void run() {
            if (m_activeFrame == null)
              return;
```

1 Action to invoke a print

1 Action to invoke a print preview

```
              setCursor(Cursor.getPredefinedCursor(
                Cursor.WAIT_CURSOR));
              PrintPreview preview = new PrintPreview(
                m_activeFrame,
                "Print Preview ["+m_activeFrame.getDocumentName()+"]");
              preview.setVisible(true);
              setCursor(Cursor.getPredefinedCursor(
                Cursor.DEFAULT_CURSOR));
            }
          };
          runner.start();
        }
      };
      item =  mFile.add(actionPrintPreview);
      item.setMnemonic('v');
      mFile.addSeparator();

      // Unchanged code from example 16.2

      JButton bPrint = new SmallButton(actionPrint,
        "Print text file");
      m_toolBar.add(bPrint);

      getContentPane().add(m_toolBar, BorderLayout.NORTH);

      // Unchanged code from example 16.2
    }

    // Unchanged code from example 16.2

    public void printData() {
      if (m_activeFrame == null)
        return;
      try {
        PrinterJob prnJob = PrinterJob.getPrinterJob();
        prnJob.setPrintable(m_activeFrame);
        if (!prnJob.printDialog())
          return;
        setCursor( Cursor.getPredefinedCursor(
          Cursor.WAIT_CURSOR));
        prnJob.print();
        setCursor( Cursor.getPredefinedCursor(
          Cursor.DEFAULT_CURSOR));
        JOptionPane.showMessageDialog(this,
          "Printing completed successfully", APP_NAME,
          JOptionPane.INFORMATION_MESSAGE);
      }
      catch (PrinterException ex) {
        showError(ex, "Printing error: "+ex.toString());
      }
    }

    // Unchanged code from example 16.2

    class EditorFrame extends JInternalFrame
```

2 Creates a printer job, invokes print, and shows any exceptions in a JOptionPane dialog

3 EditorFrame now implements the Printable interface

```
    implements Printable
{
  // Unchanged code from example 16.2

  private Vector m_lines;

  public int print(Graphics pg, PageFormat pageFormat,
    int pageIndex) throws PrinterException {
    pg.translate((int)pageFormat.getImageableX(),
      (int)pageFormat.getImageableY());
    int wPage = (int)pageFormat.getImageableWidth();
    int hPage = (int)pageFormat.getImageableHeight();
    pg.setClip(0, 0, wPage, hPage);

    pg.setColor(m_editor.getBackground());
    pg.fillRect(0, 0, wPage, hPage);
    pg.setColor(m_editor.getForeground());

    Font font = m_editor.getFont();
    pg.setFont(font);
    FontMetrics fm = pg.getFontMetrics();
    int hLine = fm.getHeight();

    if (m_lines == null)
      m_lines = getLines(fm, wPage);

    int numLines = m_lines.size();
    int linesPerPage = Math.max(hPage/hLine, 1);
    int numPages =
      (int)Math.ceil((double)numLines/(double)linesPerPage);
    if (pageIndex >= numPages) {
      m_lines = null;
      return NO_SUCH_PAGE;
    }

    int x = 0;
    int y = fm.getAscent();
    int lineIndex = linesPerPage*pageIndex;
    while (lineIndex < m_lines.size() && y < hPage) {
      String str = (String)m_lines.get(lineIndex);
      pg.drawString(str, x, y);
      y += hLine;
      lineIndex++;
    }

    return PAGE_EXISTS;
  }

    public static final int TAB_SIZE = 4;

  protected Vector getLines(FontMetrics fm, int wPage) {
    Vector v = new Vector();

    String text = m_editor.getText();
    String prevToken = "";
    StringTokenizer st = new StringTokenizer(text, "\n\r", true);
```

4 Prints a given page of text to the given Graphics Object

5 Specifies number of spaces a tab character is equal to

6 Returns a Vector of lines representing the current plain text document

```
      while (st.hasMoreTokens()) {
        String line = st.nextToken();
        if (line.equals("\r"))
          continue;

        // StringTokenizer will ignore empty lines,
        // so it's a bit tricky to get them...
        if (line.equals("\n") && prevToken.equals("\n"))
          v.add("");
        prevToken = line;
        if (line.equals("\n"))
          continue;

        StringTokenizer st2 = new StringTokenizer(line, " \t", true);
        String line2 = "";
        while (st2.hasMoreTokens()) {
          String token = st2.nextToken();

          if (token.equals("\t")) {
            int numSpaces = TAB_SIZE - line2.length()%TAB_SIZE;
            token = "";
            for (int k=0; k<numSpaces; k++)
              token += " ";
          }

          int lineLength = fm.stringWidth(line2 + token);
          if (lineLength > wPage && line2.length() > 0) {
            v.add(line2);
            line2 = token.trim();
            continue;
          }
          line2 += token;
        }
        v.add(line2);
      }

      return v;
    }

// Unchanged code from example 16.2
  }
}

// Unchanged code from example 16.2
```

22.4.1   Understanding the code

Class BasicTextEditor

1 The `createMenuBar()` method includes the creation of two new `Actions`, one for invoking a print by calling our custom `printData()` method in a separate thread; the other for invoking a print preview. Both are used to create menu items in the File menu, and the Print action is also used to create a toolbar button.

② The `printData()` method creates a printer job with the current `EditorFrame` as the `Printable` instance and invokes `print()` on it, showing any errors in a `JOptionPane` if exceptions occur.

Class BasicTextEditor.EditorFrame

③ This class now implements the `Printable` interface to provide printing functionality.

An `m_lines` `Vector` is used to hold all lines of text during the printing process.

④ The `print()` method is called to print a given page of text. First this method determines the size and origin of the printable area using a `PageFormat` instance as we've seen before. We then set a clip area of the graphics context to the size of this printable area. Then we fill the background with the background color of the text area and set the current color to its foreground color. The height of each line of text is determined by retrieving the height of the current font.

If `m_lines` is `null` we reinitialize it with our `getLines()` method. Then, based on the number of lines of text in `m_lines` and the line height and page height, we determine the number of lines that should appear on each printed page, and from that we determine how many pages the print job consists of. If the page index passed into the `print()` method is greater than the estimated number of pages, the method returns. Similarly, if `m_lines` is null at this point, meaning there is no text to print, the method returns.

Then the `print()` method determines the line index at which to start rendering the current page by multiplying the lines per page by the page index. It then draws each line of the page using the calculated lines per page and line height, and returns `PAGE_EXISTS` to indicate a successful render.

> **NOTE** You might imagine a more complicated version of this process for printing styled text documents. However, this would not be practical. We would recommend taking advantage of the text component `View` architecture to render styled document contents for printing. Chapter 22 in the first edition covers this and remains freely available at www.manning.com/sbe.

⑤ The `TAB_SIZE` variable is used to specify the number of spaces a tab character (`"\t"`) should be replaced with by the `getLines()` method.

⑥ The `getLines()` method is responsible for returning a `Vector` of lines representing the current plain text document in `EditorFrame`'s `JTextArea`. Several `StringTokenizers` are used to accomplish this by replacing tab characters with spaces and detecting empty lines.

22.4.2 Running the code

Figure 22.5 shows a preview of a plain text document which will occupy eight pages when printed. Try previewing and printing `PrintPreview.java` as a test.

22.5 *PRINTING TABLES*

In this section we'll add printing capabilities to the `JTable` application we developed earlier in chapter 18. Unlike other examples in this chapter, a printed table should not resemble the `JTable` component as it is displayed on the screen. This requires us to add detailed code for

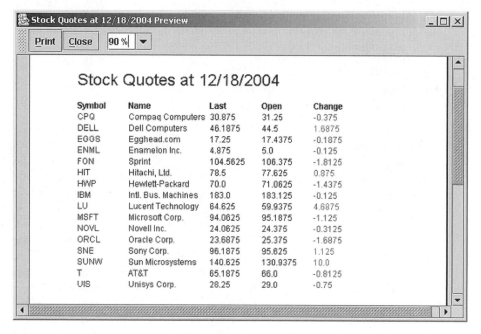

Figure 22.6 The print preview of `JTable` data

the rendering of the table's contents as they should be displayed in a printout. The resulting code, however, does not depend on the table's structure and it can be easily used for printing any table component. Thus, the code presented here in example 22.4 can be plugged into any `JTable` application that needs printing functionality. Combined with our print preview component (see the previous examples), the amount of work we need to do to support table printing in professional applications is minimal.

Example 22.4

StocksTable.java

see \Chapter22\4

```
import java.awt.*;
import java.awt.event.*;
import java.util.*;
import java.io.*;
import java.text.*;
import java.util.Date;
import java.sql.*;
import java.awt.print.*;

import javax.swing.*;
import javax.swing.border.*;
import javax.swing.event.*;
import javax.swing.table.*;
```

```
public class StocksTable extends JFrame implements Printable
{
  protected JTable m_table;
  protected StockTableData m_data;
  protected JLabel m_title;

  protected int m_maxNumPage = 1;

  // Unchanged code from example 18.5

  protected JMenuBar createMenuBar() {
    // Unchanged code from example 18.5

    JMenuItem mPrint = new JMenuItem("Print...");
    mPrint.setMnemonic('p');
    ActionListener lstPrint = new ActionListener() {
      public void actionPerformed(ActionEvent e) {
        Thread runner = new Thread() {
          public void run() {
            printData();
          }
        };
        runner.start();
      }
    };
    mPrint.addActionListener(lstPrint);
    mFile.add(mPrint);

    JMenuItem mPreview = new JMenuItem("Print Preview");
    mPreview.setMnemonic('v');
    ActionListener lstPreview = new ActionListener() {
      public void actionPerformed(ActionEvent e) {
        Thread runner = new Thread() {
          public void run() {
            setCursor(Cursor.getPredefinedCursor(
              Cursor.WAIT_CURSOR));
            new PrintPreview(StocksTable.this,
            m_title.getText()+" preview");
            setCursor(Cursor.getPredefinedCursor(
              Cursor.DEFAULT_CURSOR));
          }
        };
        runner.start();
      }
    };
    mPreview.addActionListener(lstPreview);
    mFile.add(mPreview);
    mFile.addSeparator();

    // Unchanged code from example 18.5
  }

  public void printData() {
    try {
      PrinterJob prnJob = PrinterJob.getPrinterJob();
      prnJob.setPrintable(this);
```

① **Print menu item to call printData() method**

```
      if (!prnJob.printDialog())
        return;
      m_maxNumPage = 1;
      prnJob.print();
    }
    catch (PrinterException e) {
      e.printStackTrace();
      System.err.println("Printing error: "+e.toString());
    }
  }

  public int print(Graphics pg, PageFormat pageFormat,
   int pageIndex) throws PrinterException {
    if (pageIndex >= m_maxNumPage)
      return NO_SUCH_PAGE;

    pg.translate((int)pageFormat.getImageableX(),
      (int)pageFormat.getImageableY());
    int wPage = 0;
    int hPage = 0;
    if (pageFormat.getOrientation() == pageFormat.PORTRAIT) {
      wPage = (int)pageFormat.getImageableWidth();
      hPage = (int)pageFormat.getImageableHeight();
    }
    else {
      wPage = (int)pageFormat.getImageableWidth();
      wPage += wPage/2;
      hPage = (int)pageFormat.getImageableHeight();
      pg.setClip(0,0,wPage,hPage);
    }

    int y = 0;
    pg.setFont(m_title.getFont());
    pg.setColor(Color.black);
    Font fn = pg.getFont();
    FontMetrics fm = pg.getFontMetrics();
    y += fm.getAscent();
    pg.drawString(m_title.getText(), 0, y);
    y += 20; // Space between title and table headers

    Font headerFont = m_table.getFont().deriveFont(Font.BOLD);
    pg.setFont(headerFont);
    fm = pg.getFontMetrics();

    TableColumnModel colModel = m_table.getColumnModel();
    int nColumns = colModel.getColumnCount();
    int x[] = new int[nColumns];
    x[0] = 0;

    int h = fm.getAscent();
    y += h; // Add ascent of header font because of baseline
            // positioning (see figure 2.10)

    int nRow, nCol;
    for (nCol=0; nCol<nColumns; nCol++) {
```

2 Checks for valid page index

3 Shifts graphics context and calculates size of drawing area

4 Increases width by half for landscape

5 Keeps track of current vertical position and starts rendering

6 X-coordinates of each column's upper-left corner

```
      TableColumn tk = colModel.getColumn(nCol);
      int width = tk.getWidth();
      if (x[nCol] + width > wPage) {
        nColumns = nCol;
        break;
      }
      if (nCol+1<nColumns)
        x[nCol+1] = x[nCol] + width;
      String title = (String)tk.getIdentifier();
      pg.drawString(title, x[nCol], y);
    }

    pg.setFont(m_table.getFont());
    fm = pg.getFontMetrics();

    int header = y;
    h = fm.getHeight();
    int rowH = Math.max((int)(h*1.5), 10);
    int rowPerPage = (hPage-header)/rowH;
    m_maxNumPage = Math.max((int)Math.ceil(m_table.getRowCount()/
      (double)rowPerPage), 1);

    TableModel tblModel = m_table.getModel();
    int iniRow = pageIndex*rowPerPage;
    int endRow = Math.min(m_table.getRowCount(),
      iniRow+rowPerPage);

    for (nRow=iniRow; nRow<endRow; nRow++) {
      y += h;
      for (nCol=0; nCol<nColumns; nCol++) {
        int col = m_table.getColumnModel().getColumn(nCol).getModelIndex();
        Object obj = m_data.getValueAt(nRow, col);
        String str = obj.toString();
        if (obj instanceof ColorData)
          pg.setColor(((ColorData)obj).m_color);
        else
          pg.setColor(Color.black);
          pg.drawString(str, x[nCol], y);
      }
    }

    System.gc();
    return PAGE_EXISTS;
  }
```

7 Draws all the column headers that will fit in the page width

8 After headers, figures out how many body rows will fit on page

9 Prints the rows allotted to this page

```
// Remaining code unchanged from example 18.5
```

22.5.1   Understanding the code

Class StocksTable

1 In comparison with the table examples of chapter 18, we now implement the Printable interface. In our createMenuBar() method, we add a Print... menu item which calls our new `printData()` method, which acts just like the `printData()` methods we implemented in the earlier examples.

② In our implementation of the `print()` method, we first determine whether a valid page index has been specified by comparing it to the maximum number of pages, `m_maxNumPage`:

```
if (pageIndex > m_maxNumPage)
    return NO_SUCH_PAGE;
```

The catch is that we don't know this maximum number in advance. So we assign an initial value of 1 to `m_maxNumPage` (the code above works for the 0-th page), and we adjust `m_max-NumPage` to the real value later in the code, just as we've done in earlier examples in this chapter.

③ We then translate the origin of the graphics context to the origin of the given `PageFormat` instance and determine the width and height of the area available for printing. These dimensions are used to determine how much data can fit on the given page. This same technique was

④ also used in the previous examples. However, in this example we've added the ability to print with a landscape orientation because tables can be quite wide, and we normally don't want table data to span multiple pages (at least horizontally). In order to do this, we have to first check the orientation of the given `PageFormat` instance. If it is `PORTRAIT`, we determine its width and height as we have always done. If it is not `PORTRAIT`, then it must be either `LANDSCAPE` or `REVERSE_LANDSCAPE` (see section 22.1.5). In this case we need to increase the width of the page because the default is not adequate. After increasing the width, we must also explicitly set the size of the graphics clip. This is all we have to do to allow printing in either orientation.

⑤ The local variable `y` is created to keep track of the current vertical position on the page, and we are now ready to actually start the rendering. We begin with the the table's title. Note that we use the same font as is used in the table application for consistency. We add some white space below the title (by increasing `y`) and then we make preparations for printing our table's

⑥ headers and body. A bold font is used for our table's header. An array, `x[]`, is created which will be used to store the x-coordinate of each column's upper left-hand corner (taking into account that they may be resized and moved). The variable `nColumns` contains the total number of columns in our table.

⑦ Now we actually iterate through the columns and print each column header while filling our `x[]` array. We check each iteration to see if the x-coordinate of the previous column, combined with the width of the column under consideration, will be more than the width of the page. If it will, we set the total number of columns, `nColumns`, to the number that will actually fit on the page, and then we break out of the loop. If it will not, we set the x-coordinate corresponding to the current column, print its title, and continue on to the next iteration.

⑧ Since we've finished printing our table's title and headers, we know how much space is left to print our table's body. We also know the font's height, so we can calculate how many rows can be printed on one page, which is `rowPerPage` (this is calculated as the height of the page minus the current y-offset, all divided by the height of the current font, or 10, whichever is larger). Finally, we calculate the real number of pages, `m_maxNumPage`, by dividing the total row count of our table by the number of rows per page we just calculated as `rowPerPage`. The minimum page count will be 1.

Now we need to actually print the table data. First, we calculate the initial `iniRow` and final `endRow` rows to be printed on this page:

```
TableModel tblModel = m_table.getModel();
int iniRow = pageIndex*rowPerPage;
int endRow = Math.min(m_table.getRowCount(),
    iniRow+rowPerPage);
```

9 Then, in a double `for` loop, iterating through each column of each row in turn, we print the table's contents. This is done by extracting each cell's data as an `Object` (using `getValueAt()`). We store its `toString()` `String` representation in a local variable and check if the object is an instance of our custom inner class, `ColorData` (which was defined in examples in chapter 18). This class is designed to associate a color with a given data object. So if the object is a `ColorData` instance, we grab its color and assign it as the current color of the graphics context. If it isn't, we use black. Finally, we print that object's `toString()` representation and continue on to the remaining cells.

NOTE We are assuming that each object's `toString()` representation is what we want to print. For more complex `TableCellRenderer` implementations, this printing code will need to be customized.

We end by explicitly invoking the garbage collector and returning `PAGE_EXISTS` to indicate a successful print.

22.5.2 Running the code

Figure 22.6 shows a print preview of our table application. Try manipulating the table's contents (choose different dates if you have JDBC and ODBC—see chapter 18) and column orders to see how it affects the table's printout and print preview.

You will notice that in order to fit the whole table on the paper, it must be condensed considerably. It is natural at this point to want to print it with a landscape orientation. Choosing Landscape from the Page Setup dialog modifies the `PageFormat` object that will be sent to our `print()` method when printing begins. However, this will not actually tell the printer to print in landscape mode. In order to do that, we have to explicitly choose landscape mode from the Print dialog as well. Unfortunately, the Page Setup information does not inform the printer, but it is necessary to inform our application.

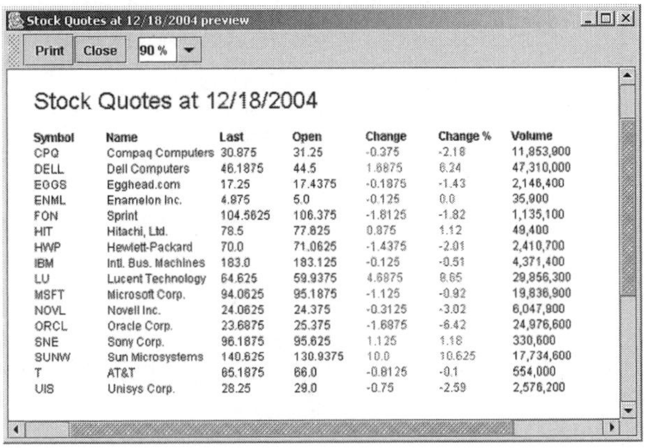

Symbol	Name	Last	Open	Change	Change %	Volume
CPQ	Compaq Computers	30.875	31.25	-0.375	-2.18	11,853,900
DELL	Dell Computers	46.1875	44.5	1.6875	6.24	47,310,000
EGGS	Egghead.com	17.25	17.4375	-0.1875	-1.43	2,146,400
ENML	Enamelon Inc.	4.875	5.0	-0.125	0.0	35,900
FON	Sprint	104.5625	106.375	-1.8125	-1.82	1,135,100
HIT	Hitachi, Ltd.	78.5	77.625	0.875	1.12	49,400
HWP	Hewlett-Packard	70.0	71.0625	-1.4375	-2.01	2,410,700
IBM	Intl. Bus. Machines	183.0	183.125	-0.125	-0.51	4,371,400
LU	Lucent Technology	64.625	59.9375	4.6875	8.65	29,856,300
MSFT	Microsoft Corp.	94.0625	95.1875	-1.125	-0.92	19,836,900
NOVL	Novell Inc.	24.0625	24.375	-0.3125	-3.02	6,047,900
ORCL	Oracle Corp.	23.6875	25.375	-1.6875	-6.42	24,976,600
SNE	Sony Corp.	96.1875	95.625	1.125	1.18	330,600
SUNW	Sun Microsystems	140.625	130.9375	10.0	10.625	17,734,600
T	AT&T	65.1875	66.0	-0.8125	-0.1	554,000
UIS	Unisys Corp.	28.25	29.0	-0.75	-2.59	2,576,200

Figure 22.7
The print preview component modified for landscape orientation

Though our application can print successfully with a landscape orientation, our print preview component is not designed to display anything but portrait-oriented previews. Because of the way our `PrintPreview` component has been constructed, it is quite easy to add the ability to preview landscape-oriented pages. The only necessary modification is the addition of a parameter to its constructor which specifies the orientation to use. This parameter can then be assigned to the `PageFormat` object used in constructing each `PagePreview` object. We will not show the code here, but we have included a modified version of `PrintPreview` and the `StocksTable` application to demonstrate how you can implement this functionality. See **\Chapter22\5**. Figure 22.7 illustrates this.

CHAPTER 23

Constructing an XML editor

There has been tremendous hype over XML, much of which is not unfounded. XML, for those who haven't had exposure to it, is poised to become the next generation of HTML and then some. Where HTML consists of a set of predefined tags, XML allows definition of your own tags. By creating a set of tags to describe data and agree on meaning, two or more entities can communicate in a standardized way. The applications of this language take us far beyond web pages to more complicated uses such as data exchange between businesses, standardized representations of various forms of data, and so forth.

There is a plethora of material about XML freely available on the web and we will not waste space here introducing the basic concepts of elements, attributes, schemas, DTDs, and so on. A good place to start for this is www.xml.org. As of Java 1.4, XML support is now part of the core Java platform. Assuming a basic understanding of XML, we've added this chapter to show how Swing can be used to build a fully functional XML editor application.

23.1 *XML EDITOR, PART I: VIEWING NODES*

This example shows how to display an XML document using a JTree and Java's built-in XML support. Because XML documents are hierarchical, JTree is a natural fit for the task.

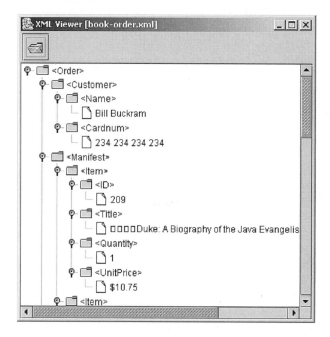

Figure 23.1
JTree displaying
an XML document

Example 23.1

XMLViewer.java

see \Chapter23\1

```
import java.awt.*;
import java.awt.event.*;
import java.io.*;

import javax.swing.*;
import javax.swing.tree.*;

import javax.xml.parsers.*;
import org.w3c.dom.*;

public class XmlViewer extends JFrame {

    public static final String APP_NAME = "XML Viewer";

    protected Document m_doc;

    protected JTree m_tree;
    protected DefaultTreeModel m_model;
```

```
protected JFileChooser m_chooser;
protected File m_currentFile;

public XmlViewer() {
  super(APP_NAME);
  setSize(400, 400);
  getContentPane().setLayout(new BorderLayout());

  JToolBar tb = createToolbar();
  getContentPane().add(tb, BorderLayout.NORTH);

  DefaultMutableTreeNode top =
    new DefaultMutableTreeNode("No XML loaded");
  m_model = new DefaultTreeModel(top);
  m_tree = new JTree(m_model);

  m_tree.getSelectionModel().setSelectionMode(
    TreeSelectionModel.SINGLE_TREE_SELECTION);
  m_tree.setShowsRootHandles(true);
  m_tree.setEditable(false);

  DefaultTreeCellRenderer renderer =
    new DefaultTreeCellRenderer()
  {
    public Component getTreeCellRendererComponent(JTree tree,
      Object value, boolean sel, boolean expanded,
      boolean leaf, int row, boolean hasFocus) {
      Component res = super.getTreeCellRendererComponent(tree,
        value, sel, expanded, leaf, row, hasFocus);
      if (value instanceof XmlViewerNode) {
        Node node = ((XmlViewerNode)value).getXmlNode();
        if (node instanceof Element)
          setIcon(expanded ? openIcon : closedIcon);
        else
          setIcon(leafIcon);
      }

      return res;
    }
  };
  m_tree.setCellRenderer(renderer);

  JScrollPane s = new JScrollPane(m_tree);
  getContentPane().add(s, BorderLayout.CENTER);

  m_chooser = new JFileChooser();
  m_chooser.setFileSelectionMode(JFileChooser.FILES_ONLY);
  m_chooser.setFileFilter(new SimpleFilter("xml",
    "XML Files"));
  try {
    File dir = (new File(".")).getCanonicalFile();
    m_chooser.setCurrentDirectory(dir);
  } catch (IOException ex) {}
}

protected JToolBar createToolbar() {
```

① **Custom tree cell renderer to indicate whether or not a node is an XML document element**

```
      JToolBar tb = new JToolBar();
      tb.setFloatable(false);

      JButton bt = new JButton(new ImageIcon("Open24.gif"));
      bt.setToolTipText("Open XML file");
      ActionListener lst = new ActionListener() {
        public void actionPerformed(ActionEvent e) {
          openDocument();
        }
      };
      bt.addActionListener(lst);
      tb.add(bt);

      return tb;
    }

    public String getDocumentName() {
      return m_currentFile==null ? "Untitled" :
        m_currentFile.getName();
    }

    protected void openDocument() {
      Thread runner = new Thread() {
        public void run() {
          if (m_chooser.showOpenDialog(XmlViewer.this) !=
            JFileChooser.APPROVE_OPTION)
            return;
          File f = m_chooser.getSelectedFile();
          if (f == null || !f.isFile())
            return;

          setCursor(Cursor.getPredefinedCursor(
            Cursor.WAIT_CURSOR));
          try {
            DocumentBuilderFactory docBuilderFactory =
              DocumentBuilderFactory.newInstance();
            DocumentBuilder docBuilder = docBuilderFactory.
              newDocumentBuilder();

            m_doc = docBuilder.parse(f);

            Element root = m_doc.getDocumentElement();
            root.normalize();

            DefaultMutableTreeNode top = createTreeNode(root);

            m_model.setRoot(top);
            m_tree.treeDidChange();
            expandTree(m_tree);
            m_currentFile = f;
            setTitle(APP_NAME+" ["+getDocumentName()+"]");
          }
          catch (Exception ex) {
            showError(ex, "Error reading or parsing XML file");
          }
          finally {
```

2 Uses JFileChooser in separate thread to open an XML file from disk

```
        setCursor(Cursor.getPredefinedCursor(
          Cursor.DEFAULT_CURSOR));
        }
      }
    };
    runner.start();
  }
```

Recursive method to build tree nodes from XML document ❸

```
  protected DefaultMutableTreeNode createTreeNode(Node root) {
    if (!canDisplayNode(root))
      return null;
    XmlViewerNode treeNode = new XmlViewerNode(root);
    NodeList list = root.getChildNodes();
    for (int k=0; k<list.getLength(); k++) {
      Node nd = list.item(k);
      DefaultMutableTreeNode child = createTreeNode(nd);
      if (child != null)
        treeNode.add(child);
    }
    return treeNode;
  }
```

❹ **Returns true if given node is an element node or nonempty text node, and false otherwise**

```
  protected boolean canDisplayNode(Node node) {
    switch (node.getNodeType()) {
    case Node.ELEMENT_NODE:
      return true;
    case Node.TEXT_NODE:
      String text = node.getNodeValue().trim();
      return !(text.equals("") ||
        text.equals("\n") || text.equals("\r\n"));
    }
    return false;
  }

  public void showError(Exception ex, String message) {
    ex.printStackTrace();
    JOptionPane.showMessageDialog(this,
      message, APP_NAME,
      JOptionPane.WARNING_MESSAGE);
  }
```

❺ **Recursive method to expand entire tree**

```
  public static void expandTree(JTree tree) {
    TreeNode root = (TreeNode)tree.getModel().getRoot();
    TreePath path = new TreePath(root);
    for (int k = 0; k<root.getChildCount(); k++) {
      TreeNode child = (TreeNode)root.getChildAt(k);
      expandTree(tree, path, child);
    }
  }
```

❺ **Recursive method to expand given path and path to given node**

```
  public static void expandTree(
    JTree tree, TreePath path, TreeNode node)
  {
    if (path==null || node==null)
```

```
          return;
        tree.expandPath(path);
        TreePath newPath = path.pathByAddingChild(node);
        for (int k = 0; k<node.getChildCount(); k++) {
          TreeNode child = (TreeNode)node.getChildAt(k);
          if (child != null) {
            expandTree(tree, newPath, child);
          }
        }
      }

    public static void main(String argv[]) {
      XmlViewer frame = new XmlViewer();
      frame.setDefaultCloseOperation(JFrame.EXIT_ON_CLOSE);
      frame.setVisible(true);
    }
  }

  class XmlViewerNode extends DefaultMutableTreeNode {
    public XmlViewerNode(Node node) {
      super(node);
    }

    public Node getXmlNode() {
      Object obj = getUserObject();
      if (obj instanceof Node)
        return (Node)obj;
      return null;
    }

    public String toString () {
      Node node = getXmlNode();
      if (node == null)
        return getUserObject().toString();
      StringBuffer sb = new StringBuffer();
      switch (node.getNodeType()) {
      case Node.ELEMENT_NODE:
        sb.append('<');
        sb.append(node.getNodeName());
        sb.append('>');
        break;
      case Node.TEXT_NODE:
        sb.append(node.getNodeValue());
        break;
      }
      return sb.toString();
    }
  }

  // Class SimpleFilter unchanged from chapter 14
```

⑥ Custom tree node representing an XML element or text node

23.1.1 Understanding the code

Class XmlViewer

Two packages we have not yet discussed are imported:

- `javax.xml.parsers`: This package consists of classes used to process XML documents.
- `org.w3c.dom`: This package consists of a set of interfaces that define the DOM (Document Object Model) which is an API that allows dynamic access to the structure and data of XML documents. Examples are `Document`, `Element`, `Node`, `Attr`, and so forth.

`XmlViewer` extends `JFrame` and represents the main application frame for this example. Five instance variables are defined:

- `Document m_doc`: the current XML document (note that this is an instance of `org.w3c.dcom.Document`; not a text document [`javax.swing.text.Document`]).
- `JTree m_tree`: the tree component used to display the current XML file.
- `DefaultTreeModel m_model`: tree model constructed to mimic the XML file.
- `JFileChooser m_chooser`: File chooser used for opening and saving XML files.
- `File m_currentFile`: reference to the current XML file.

The `XmlViewer` constructor creates and installs a toolbar with our `createToolbar()` method, instantiates tree model `m_model` with a top node containing "No XML loaded" as user data, and instantiates tree `m_tree` with `m_model`. Selection is set to `SINGLE_TREE_SELECTION` and the tree is set to noneditable. A custom tree cell renderer is created to display an appropriate icon based on whether or not a node represents an XML document element. This renderer is assigned to our tree and the tree is then placed in a scroll pane which is added to the center of the frame. File chooser `m_chooser` is instantiated and an "xml" file filter is applied to it so only XML files will be displayed.

The `createToolbar()` method creates a `JToolBar` with an Open button that invokes our `openDocument()` method.

The `getDocumentName()` method retrieves the name of the current file referenced with our `m_currentFile` variable.

The `openDocument()` method shows our `JFileChooser` in a separate thread to allow selection of an XML file to open for viewing. `javax.xml.parsers.DocumentBuilderFactory`'s static `newInstance()` is used to create a new instance of `DocumentBuilderFactory` which is used to create an instance of `DocumentBuilder`. `DocumentBuilder` is used to parse the selected XML file with its `parse()` method, storing the resulting `Document` instance in our `m_doc` variable. The root element of this document is retrieved with `Document`'s `getDocumentElement()` method. This element is used as the root node for our tree model, and our custom `createTreeNode()` creates the tree node hierarchy corresponding to the node passed to it. The resulting tree node is then set as the root node of our tree and our custom `expandTree()` method is used to expand all nodes to display the entire XML document.

The `createTreeNode()` method takes a root node (instance of `org.w3c.dom.Node`) as parameter (note that `org.w3c.dom.Element` is a subinterface of `Node`). Our `canDisplayNode()` method is used to find out whether the root node is either an element or a text node. If so, an instance of our custom `XmlViewerNode` is created to represent that node. Then a

NodeList is created representing all child nodes of the root node. For each child node a tree node is created by passing it recursively to createTreeNode().

The canDisplayNode() method checks whether a given Node is of type ELEMENT_NODE or TEXT_NODE. If it isn't one of these types it should not be displayed in our tree.

The showError() method is used to display exceptions in a JOptionPane dialog.

5 The static expandTree() methods are responsible for expanding each parent node so that the entire tree is expanded and visible in the viewer.

6 *Class XmlViewerNode*

This class extends DefaultMutableTreeNode to represent the XML nodes in our viewer. The main customization is in the overriden toString() implementation which returns a textual representation of the node depending on whether it is of type ELEMENT_NODE or TEXT_NODE.

23.1.2   Running the Code

Figure 23.1 shows our XML viewer in action with a sample file open. To open this file use the toolbar buttons to bring up the file chooser and navigate to the \Chapter23\XML-Samples directory where you will find book-order.xml.

23.2   *XML EDITOR, PART II: VIEWING ATTRIBUTES*

In this example we add the ability to view XML attributes in a windows explorer-style combination of JTree and JTable.

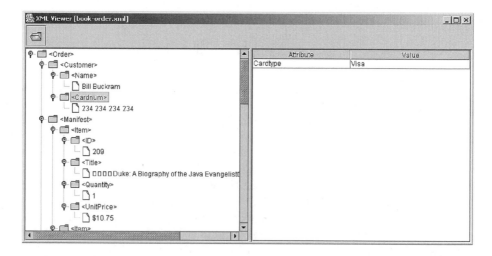

Figure 23.2   JTree and JTable in an explorer-style combination

Example 23.2

see \Chapter23\2

```java
import java.awt.*;
import java.awt.event.*;
import java.io.*;

import javax.swing.*;
import javax.swing.event.*;
import javax.swing.tree.*;
import javax.swing.table.*;

import javax.xml.parsers.*;
import org.w3c.dom.*;

public class XmlViewer extends JFrame {
  public static final String APP_NAME = "XML Viewer";

  protected Document m_doc;

  protected JTree m_tree;
  protected DefaultTreeModel m_model;

  protected JTable m_table;
  protected AttrTableModel m_tableModel;

  protected JFileChooser m_chooser;
  protected File  m_currentFile;

  public XmlViewer() {
    super(APP_NAME);
    setSize(800, 400);
    getContentPane().setLayout(new BorderLayout());

    JToolBar tb = createToolbar();
    getContentPane().add(tb, BorderLayout.NORTH);

    // Unchanged code from example 23.1

    m_tableModel = new AttrTableModel();
    m_table = new JTable(m_tableModel);

    JScrollPane s1 = new JScrollPane(m_tree);
    JScrollPane s2 = new JScrollPane(m_table);
    s2.getViewport().setBackground(m_table.getBackground());
    JSplitPane sp = new JSplitPane(
      JSplitPane.HORIZONTAL_SPLIT, s1, s2);
    sp.setDividerLocation(400);
    sp.setDividerSize(5);
    getContentPane().add(sp, BorderLayout.CENTER);

    TreeSelectionListener lSel = new TreeSelectionListener() {
      public void valueChanged(TreeSelectionEvent e) {
        Node node = getSelectedNode();
        setNodeToTable(node);
```

Listens for tree selection events and displays node properties in JTable **1**

```
    }
  };
  m_tree.addTreeSelectionListener(lSel);

  m_chooser = new JFileChooser();
  m_chooser.setFileSelectionMode(JFileChooser.FILES_ONLY);
  m_chooser.setFileFilter(new SimpleFilter("xml",
    "XML Files"));
  try {
    File dir = (new File(".")).getCanonicalFile();
    m_chooser.setCurrentDirectory(dir);
  } catch (IOException ex) {}
}

// Unchanged code from example 23.1

protected void openDocument() {
  Thread runner = new Thread() {
    public void run() {
      // Unchanged code from example 23.1
      try {
        // Unchanged code from example 23.1

        m_model.setRoot(top);
        m_tree.treeDidChange();
        expandTree(m_tree);
        setNodeToTable(null);
        m_currentFile = f;
        setTitle(APP_NAME+" ["+getDocumentName()+"]");
      }
      catch (Exception ex) {
        showError(ex, "Error reading or parsing XML file");
      }
      finally {
        setCursor(Cursor.getPredefinedCursor(Cursor.DEFAULT_CURSOR));
      }
    }
  };
  runner.start();
}

// Unchanged code from example 23.1

public XmlViewerNode getSelectedTreeNode() {
  TreePath path = m_tree.getSelectionPath();
  if (path == null)
    return null;
  Object obj = path.getLastPathComponent();
  if (!(obj instanceof XmlViewerNode))
    return null;
  return (XmlViewerNode)obj;
}

public Node getSelectedNode() {
  XmlViewerNode treeNode = getSelectedTreeNode();
```

1 Listens for tree selection events and displays node properties in JTable

```
      if (treeNode == null)
        return null;
      return treeNode.getXmlNode();
  }

  public void setNodeToTable(Node node) {              ❷ Refreshes table with attributes
    m_tableModel.setNode(node);                           of given node object
    m_table.tableChanged(new TableModelEvent(m_tableModel));
  }

  // Unchanged code from example 23.1

  public static void main(String argv[]) {
    XmlViewer frame = new XmlViewer();
    frame.setDefaultCloseOperation(JFrame.EXIT_ON_CLOSE);
    frame.setVisible(true);
  }

  class AttrTableModel extends AbstractTableModel {      ❸ Custom table model
    public static final int NAME_COLUMN = 0;                used to display
    public static final int VALUE_COLUMN = 1;               attributes of a
                                                            selected XML tree node
    protected Node m_node;
    protected NamedNodeMap m_attrs;

    public void setNode(Node node) {
      m_node = node;
      m_attrs = node==null ? null : node.getAttributes();
    }

    public Node getNode() {
      return m_node;
    }

    public int getRowCount() {
      if (m_attrs == null)
        return 0;
      return m_attrs.getLength();
    }

    public int getColumnCount() {
      return 2;
    }

    public String getColumnName(int nCol) {
      return nCol==NAME_COLUMN ? "Attribute" : "Value";
    }

    public Object getValueAt(int nRow, int nCol) {
      if (m_attrs == null || nRow < 0 || nRow>=getRowCount())
        return "";
      Attr attr = (Attr)m_attrs.item(nRow);
      if (attr == null)
        return "";
      switch (nCol) {
        case NAME_COLUMN:
          return attr.getName();
```

```
      case VALUE_COLUMN:
        return attr.getValue();
    }
    return "";
  }

  public boolean isCellEditable(int nRow, int nCol) {
    return false;
  }
  }
}
```

// Unchanged code from example 23.1

23.2.1   Understanding the code

Class XmlViewer

Two new instance variables have been added:

- JTable m_table: table component used to display node attributes.
- AttrTableModel m_tableModel: instance of our custom table model used for attributes.

1 The XmlViewer constructor instantiates our instance variables and adds the table to a scroll pane. The table and tree components are now placed in a JSplitPane, and a TreeSelectionListener is added to the tree to respond to tree node selection changes by retrieving the selected node using our custom getSelectedNode() method and passing it to our custom setNodeToTable() method to display that node's attributes in the table component.

The new getSelectedTreeNode() method retrieves the currently selected node and returns it as an instance of XmlViewerNode.

The getSelectedNode() method retrieves the currently selected node by calling getSelectedTreeNode() and, if not null, returns the Node instance by calling XmlViewerNode's getXmlNode() method.

2 The setNodeToTable() method refreshes the table component with the currently selected node's attributes by calling AttrTableModel's setNode() method.

3 ### Class XmlViewer.AttrTableModel

This inner class extends AbstractTableModel and is used to display the attributes of a given node. Two class variables are defined:

- int NAME_COLUMN: index of the column representing attribute name.
- int VALUE_COLUMN: index of the column representing attribute value.

Two instance variables are defined:

- Node m_node: the node instance whose attributes are represented by this model.
- NamedNodeMap m_attrs: collection of nodes that can be accessed by name; this instance represents all attribute nodes (of type ATTRIBUTE_NODE) of the m_node parent.

The setNode() method assigns a given node to the m_node variable and reinitializes the m_attrs collection using Node's getAttributes() method.

The getRowCount() method returns the number of attributes in the m_attrs collection which is equivalent to the number of rows that should be displayed in the table.

The getValueAt() method returns the value of the attribute name or value at a given table cell corresponding to the m_attrs attribute collection.

23.2.2   Running the code

Figure 23.2 shows our XML viewer in action displaying attributes of a selected node in a table component on the right. Try opening the sample document and navigating through the nodes to see how the tree and table component work easily together.

23.3   *XML EDITOR, PART III: EDITING NODES AND ATTRIBUTES*

In this example we add the ability to edit the text of an XML node and its attributes as well as save any changes to the orginal file.

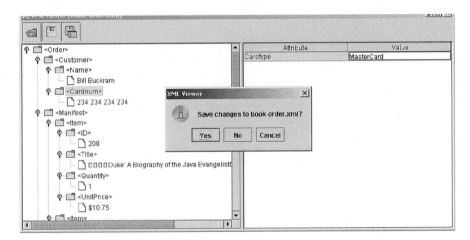

Figure 23.3   Editing an attribute value in our XML editor

Example 23.3

XmlViewer.java

see \Chapter23\3

```
import java.awt.*;
import java.awt.event.*;
import java.io.*;
import java.util.*;

import javax.swing.*;
import javax.swing.event.*;
import javax.swing.tree.*;
import javax.swing.table.*;
```

```java
import javax.xml.parsers.*;
import org.w3c.dom.*;

public class XmlViewer extends JFrame {

  public static final String APP_NAME = "XML Viewer";

  protected Document m_doc;

  protected JTree  m_tree;
  protected DefaultTreeModel m_model;
  protected DefaultTreeCellEditor m_treeEditor;
  protected Node m_editingNode = null;

  protected JTable m_table;
  protected AttrTableModel m_tableModel;

  protected JFileChooser m_chooser;
  protected File  m_currentFile;
  protected boolean m_xmlChanged = false;

  public XmlViewer() {
    super(APP_NAME);
    setSize(800, 400);
    getContentPane().setLayout(new BorderLayout());

    // Unchanged code from example 23.2

    m_treeEditor = new DefaultTreeCellEditor(m_tree, renderer) {
      public boolean isCellEditable(EventObject event) {
        Node node = getSelectedNode();
        if (node != null && node.getNodeType() == Node.TEXT_NODE)
          return super.isCellEditable(event);
        else
          return false;
      }

      public Component getTreeCellEditorComponent(
        JTree tree, Object value,
        boolean isSelected, boolean expanded, boolean leaf, int row)
      {
        if (value instanceof XmlViewerNode)
          m_editingNode = ((XmlViewerNode)value).getXmlNode();
        return super.getTreeCellEditorComponent(tree,
          value, isSelected, expanded, leaf, row);
      }
    };
    m_treeEditor.addCellEditorListener(new XmlEditorListener());
    m_tree.setCellEditor(m_treeEditor);
    m_tree.setEditable(true);
    m_tree.setInvokesStopCellEditing(true);

    m_tableModel = new AttrTableModel();
    m_table = new JTable(m_tableModel);

    // Unchanged code from example 23.2

    WindowListener wndCloser = new WindowAdapter() {
```

Custom tree cell editor to only allow editing of text nodes ❶

```
        public void windowClosing(WindowEvent e) {
          if (!promptToSave())           ❷  Ensures user has a chance
            return;                          to save changes before
          System.exit(0);                    closing application
        }
      };
      addWindowListener(wndCloser);

      // Unchanged code from example 23.2
    }

    protected JToolBar createToolbar() {
      // Unchanged code from example 23.2

      ActionListener lst = new ActionListener() {
        public void actionPerformed(ActionEvent e) {
          if (!promptToSave())           ❸  Prompt to save changes
            return;                          before opening a document
          openDocument();
        }
      };
      bt.addActionListener(lst);
      tb.add(bt);

      bt = new JButton(new ImageIcon("Save24.gif"));
      bt.setToolTipText("Save changes to current file");
      lst = new ActionListener() {
        public void actionPerformed(ActionEvent e) {
          saveFile(false);
        }                                Button to save     ❹
      };                                 current XML file
      bt.addActionListener(lst);
      tb.add(bt);

      bt = new JButton(new ImageIcon("SaveAs24.gif"));
      bt.setToolTipText("Save changes to another file");
      lst = new ActionListener() {
        public void actionPerformed(ActionEvent e) {
          saveFile(true);
        }                                Button to save current  ❹
      };                                 XML file under new name
      bt.addActionListener(lst);         and/or in new location
      tb.add(bt);

      return tb;
    }

    // Unchanged code from example 23.2

    protected boolean saveFile(boolean saveAs) {  ❺  Uses JFileChooser
      if (m_doc == null)                              and FileWriter
        return false;                                 to save current
      if (saveAs || m_currentFile == null) {          XML file to disk
        if (m_chooser.showSaveDialog(XmlViewer.this) !=
          JFileChooser.APPROVE_OPTION)
```

```
      return false;
    File f = m_chooser.getSelectedFile();
    if (f == null)
      return false;
    m_currentFile = f;
    setTitle(APP_NAME+" ["+getDocumentName()+"]");
  }

  setCursor(Cursor.getPredefinedCursor(Cursor.WAIT_CURSOR) );
  try {
    FileWriter out = new FileWriter(m_currentFile);
    XMLRoutines.write(m_doc, out);
    out.close();
  }
  catch (Exception ex) {
    showError(ex, "Error saving XML file");
  }
  finally {
    setCursor(Cursor.getPredefinedCursor(Cursor.DEFAULT_CURSOR));
  }
  m_xmlChanged = false;
  return true;
}

protected boolean promptToSave() {
  if (!m_xmlChanged)
    return true;
  int result = JOptionPane.showConfirmDialog(this,
    "Save changes to "+getDocumentName()+"?",
    APP_NAME, JOptionPane.YES_NO_CANCEL_OPTION,
    JOptionPane.INFORMATION_MESSAGE);
  switch (result) {
  case JOptionPane.YES_OPTION:
    if (!saveFile(false))
      return false;
    return true;
  case JOptionPane.NO_OPTION:
    return true;
  case JOptionPane.CANCEL_OPTION:
    return false;
  }
  return true;
}

// Unchanged code from example 23.2
public static void main(String argv[]) {
  XmlViewer frame = new XmlViewer();
frame.setDefaultCloseOperation(JFrame.DO_NOTHING_ON_CLOSE);
  frame.setVisible(true);
}

class XmlEditorListener implements CellEditorListener {
  public void editingStopped(ChangeEvent e) {
```

6 Prompts user to save changes

Custom cell editor listener responsible for updating value of node in model when changed by a cell editor **7**

```
      String value = m_treeEditor.getCellEditorValue().toString();
      if (m_editingNode != null)
        m_editingNode.setNodeValue(value);
      TreePath path = m_tree.getSelectionPath();
      if (path != null) {
        DefaultMutableTreeNode treeNode =
          (DefaultMutableTreeNode)path.getLastPathComponent();
        treeNode.setUserObject(m_editingNode);
        m_model.nodeStructureChanged(treeNode);
      }
      m_xmlChanged = true;
      m_editingNode = null;
    }

    public void editingCanceled(ChangeEvent e) {
      m_editingNode = null;
    }
  }

// Unchanged code from example 23.2

class AttrTableModel extends AbstractTableModel {    ❽  Updated to allow
    public static final int NAME_COLUMN = 0;             editing of attributes
    public static final int VALUE_COLUMN = 1;

    // Unchanged code from example 23.2

    public boolean isCellEditable(int nRow, int nCol) {
      return (nCol==VALUE_COLUMN);
    }

    public void setValueAt(Object value, int nRow, int nCol) {
      if (nRow < 0 || nRow>=getRowCount())
        return;
      if (!(m_node instanceof Element))
        return;
      String name = getValueAt(nRow, NAME_COLUMN).toString();
      ((Element)m_node).setAttribute(name, value.toString());
      m_xmlChanged = true;
    }
  }
}
                                              ❾  Utility class with methods to write
                                                  current XML document represented
// Unchanged code from example 23.2            by our viewer to a file

class XMLRoutines {
  public static void write(Document doc, Writer out) throws Exception {
    write(doc.getDocumentElement(), out);
  }

  public static void write(Node node, Writer out) throws Exception {
    if (node==null || out==null)
      return;

    int type = node.getNodeType();
    switch (type) {
```

```
case Node.DOCUMENT_NODE:
  write(((Document)node).getDocumentElement(), out);
  out.flush();
  break;

case Node.ELEMENT_NODE:
  out.write('<');
  out.write(node.getNodeName());
  NamedNodeMap attrs = node.getAttributes();
  for (int k = 0; k< attrs.getLength(); k++ ) {
    Node attr = attrs.item(k);
    out.write(' ');
    out.write(attr.getNodeName());
    out.write("=\"");
    out.write(attr.getNodeValue());
    out.write('"');
  }

  out.write('>');
  break;

case Node.ENTITY_REFERENCE_NODE:
  out.write('&');
  out.write(node.getNodeName());
  out.write(';');
  break;

// print cdata sections
case Node.CDATA_SECTION_NODE:
  out.write("<![CDATA[");
  out.write(node.getNodeValue());
  out.write("]]>");
  break;

// print text
case Node.TEXT_NODE:
  out.write(node.getNodeValue());
  break;

// print processing instruction
case Node.PROCESSING_INSTRUCTION_NODE:
  out.write("<?");
  out.write(node.getNodeName());
  String data = node.getNodeValue();
  if ( data != null && data.length() > 0 ) {
    out.write(' ');
    out.write(data);
  }
  out.write("?>");
  break;

default:
  out.write("<TYPE="+type);
  out.write(node.getNodeName());
  out.write("?>");
```

```
      break;
    }

    NodeList children = node.getChildNodes();
    if ( children != null ) {
      for ( int k = 0; k<children.getLength(); k++ ) {
        write(children.item(k), out);
      }
    }

    if (node.getNodeType() == Node.ELEMENT_NODE ) {
      out.write("</");
      out.write(node.getNodeName());
      out.write('>');
    }
    out.flush();
  }
}
```

23.3.1 Understanding the code

Class XmlViewer

Three new instance variables have been added:

- `DefaultTreeCellEditor m_treeEditor`: custom tree cell editor to only allow editing of text nodes.
- `Node m_editingNode`: reference to the current node being edited.
- `boolean m_xmlChanged`: flag specifying whether the XML document has changed since loading.

❶ The `XmlViewer` constructor now creates a custom tree cell editor to allow editing of only Nodes of type `TEXT_NODE`. Also, an instance of our custom `XmlEditorListener` is set to as
❷ a cell editor listener to this customized tree cell editor. A new `WindowListener` is added to the `XmlViewer` frame to invoke our custom `promptToSave()` method before exiting to give the user a chance to save changes made, if any.

❸ The Open toolbar button's `actionPerformed()` code now invokes `promptToSave()` before loading a new file to allow the user to save changes before proceeding. The toolbar also
❹ gets two new buttons: Save and Save As. Both invoke our custom `saveFile()` method to save changes made to the XML document.

❺ The `saveFile()` method is used to write to disk the XML file represented by our tree. First this method shows a file chooser if the parameter is `true` (meaning the Save As button was pressed) or if the `m_currentFile` variable is `null` (meaning the XML document is new). The file chooser is used to specify a name and location for the target file. The document is then written to disk using a `FileWriter` and the static `write()` method of our custom `XMLRoutines` class.

❻ The `promptToSave()` method shows a `JOptionPane` asking the user whether or not to save any changes made to the document before proceeding with a pending action.

❼ *Class XmlViewer.XmlEditorListener*

This class implements `CellEditorListener` and is used to set the value of a `Node` after its corresponding tree node is edited.

❽ *Class XmlViewer.AttrTableModel*

The `isCellEditable()` method is overridden to return `true` for the `VALUE_COLUMN` so that the user can edit attribute values.

The `setValueAt()` method is overridden to perform the actual attribute value modification after the edit occurs in the table.

❾ *Class XMLRoutines*

This class consists of two static methods used to write the XML file represented by our viewer to a file using a `Writer` instance.

23.3.2   Running the code

Figure 23.3 shows our XML viewer after having edited an attribute value and attempted to close the application. A dialog is displayed asking whether or not we want to save the changes. Try opening the sample XML document and modifying both text nodes and attribute values.

23.4   *XML EDITOR, PART IV: ADD, EDIT, REMOVE NODES AND ATTRIBUTES*

In this example we add the ability to add, delete, and edit XML nodes and attributes.

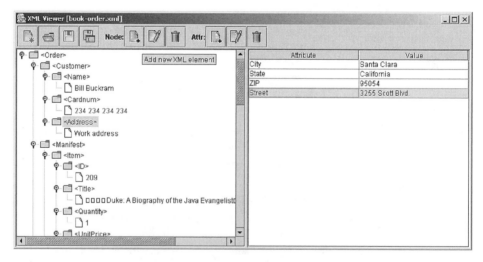

Figure 23.4   XML Editor application with add/edit/delete nodes and attributes functionality

Example 23.4

see \Chapter23\4

```java
import java.awt.*;
import java.awt.event.*;
import java.io.*;
import java.util.*;

import javax.swing.*;
import javax.swing.event.*;
import javax.swing.tree.*;
import javax.swing.table.*;

import javax.xml.parsers.*;
import org.w3c.dom.*;

public class XmlViewer
  extends JFrame {

  public static final String APP_NAME = "XML Viewer";

  // Unchanged code from example 23.3

  protected JButton m_addNodeBtn;
  protected JButton m_editNodeBtn;
  protected JButton m_delNodeBtn;
  protected JButton m_addAttrBtn;
  protected JButton m_editAttrBtn;
  protected JButton m_delAttrBtn;

  public XmlViewer() {
    super(APP_NAME);
    setSize(800, 400);
    getContentPane().setLayout(new BorderLayout());

    // Unchanged code from example 23.3

    TreeSelectionListener lSel = new TreeSelectionListener() {
      public void valueChanged(TreeSelectionEvent e) {
        Node node = getSelectedNode();
        setNodeToTable(node);
        enableNodeButtons();
        enableAttrButtons();
      }
    };
    m_tree.addTreeSelectionListener(lSel);

    ListSelectionListener lTbl = new ListSelectionListener() {
      public void valueChanged(ListSelectionEvent e) {
        enableAttrButtons();
      }
    };
    m_table.getSelectionModel().addListSelectionListener(lTbl);
```

① New add, edit, and delete toolbar buttons for nodes and attributes

② Updates attribute buttons whenever a table selection occurs

```java
    enableNodeButtons();
    enableAttrButtons();

    // Unchanged code from example 23.3
}

protected JToolBar createToolbar() {
    JToolBar tb = new JToolBar();
    tb.setFloatable(false);

    JButton bt = new JButton(new ImageIcon("New24.gif"));
    bt.setToolTipText("New XML document");
    ActionListener lst = new ActionListener() {
        public void actionPerformed(ActionEvent e) {
            if (!promptToSave())
                return;
            newDocument();
        }
    };
    bt.addActionListener(lst);
    tb.add(bt);

    // Unchanged code from example 23.3

    tb.addSeparator();
    tb.add(new JLabel("Node:"));
    m_addNodeBtn = new JButton(new ImageIcon("Add24.gif"));
    m_addNodeBtn.setToolTipText("Add new XML element");
    lst = new ActionListener() {
        public void actionPerformed(ActionEvent e) {
            addNewNode();
        }
    };
    m_addNodeBtn.addActionListener(lst);
    tb.add(m_addNodeBtn);

    m_editNodeBtn = new JButton(new ImageIcon("Edit24.gif"));
    m_editNodeBtn.setToolTipText("Edit XML node");
    lst = new ActionListener() {
        public void actionPerformed(ActionEvent e) {
            editNode();
        }
    };
    m_editNodeBtn.addActionListener(lst);
    tb.add(m_editNodeBtn);

    m_delNodeBtn = new JButton(new ImageIcon("Delete24.gif"));
    m_delNodeBtn.setToolTipText("Delete XML node");
    lst = new ActionListener() {
        public void actionPerformed(ActionEvent e) {
            deleteNode();
        }
    };
    m_delNodeBtn.addActionListener(lst);
    tb.add(m_delNodeBtn);
```

3 Button to create a new XML document

3 Button for adding a new node

3 Button for editing a node

3 Button for deleting a node

```
    tb.addSeparator();
    tb.add(new JLabel("Attr:"));
    m_addAttrBtn = new JButton(new ImageIcon("Add24.gif"));
    m_addAttrBtn.setToolTipText("Add new attribute");
    lst = new ActionListener() {
      public void actionPerformed(ActionEvent e) {
        addNewAttribute();
      }
    };
    m_addAttrBtn.addActionListener(lst);
    tb.add(m_addAttrBtn);

    m_editAttrBtn = new JButton(new ImageIcon("Edit24.gif"));
    m_editAttrBtn.setToolTipText("Edit attribute");
    lst = new ActionListener() {
      public void actionPerformed(ActionEvent e) {
        editAttribute();
      }
    };
    m_editAttrBtn.addActionListener(lst);
    tb.add(m_editAttrBtn);

    m_delAttrBtn = new JButton(new ImageIcon("Delete24.gif"));
    m_delAttrBtn.setToolTipText("Delete attribute");
    lst = new ActionListener() {
      public void actionPerformed(ActionEvent e) {
        deleteAttribute();
      }
    };
    m_delAttrBtn.addActionListener(lst);
    tb.add(m_delAttrBtn);

    return tb;
  }

  public String getDocumentName() {
    return m_currentFile==null ? "Untitled" :
      m_currentFile.getName();
  }

  public void newDocument() {
    String input = (String) JOptionPane.showInputDialog(this,
      "Please enter root node name of the new XML document",
      APP_NAME, JOptionPane.PLAIN_MESSAGE,
      null, null, "");
    if (!isLegalXmlName(input))
      return;

    setCursor(Cursor.getPredefinedCursor(Cursor.WAIT_CURSOR) );
    try {
      DocumentBuilderFactory docBuilderFactory =
        DocumentBuilderFactory.newInstance();
      DocumentBuilder docBuilder = docBuilderFactory.
        newDocumentBuilder();
```

4 Button for adding an attribute

3 Button for editing an attribute

3 Button for deleting an attribute

5 Creates a new XML document and corresponding tree model

```
      m_doc = docBuilder.newDocument();

      Element root = m_doc.createElement(input);
      root.normalize();
      m_doc.appendChild(root);

      DefaultMutableTreeNode top = createTreeNode(root);

      m_model.setRoot(top);
      m_tree.treeDidChange();
      expandTree(m_tree);
      setNodeToTable(null);
      m_currentFile = null;
      setTitle(APP_NAME+" ["+getDocumentName()+"]");
      m_xmlChanged = true;// Will prompt to save
    }
    catch (Exception ex) {
      showError(ex, "Error creating new XML document");
    }
    finally {
      setCursor(Cursor.getPredefinedCursor(Cursor.DEFAULT_CURSOR));
    }
  }

// Unchanged code from example 23.3

  protected void enableNodeButtons() {          ❻  Controls state of node buttons
    boolean b1 = (getSelectedNode() instanceof Element);
    boolean b2 = (getSelectedNode() != null);
    m_addNodeBtn.setEnabled(b1);
    m_editNodeBtn.setEnabled(b2);
    m_delNodeBtn.setEnabled(b2);
  }

  protected void enableAttrButtons() {          ❼  Controls state of attribute buttons
    boolean b1 = (m_tableModel.getNode() instanceof Element);
    boolean b2 = (m_table.getSelectedRowCount() > 0);
    m_addAttrBtn.setEnabled(b1);
    m_editAttrBtn.setEnabled(b2);
    m_delAttrBtn.setEnabled(b2);
  }

  protected void addNewNode() {                 ❽  Adds a new XML node
    if (m_doc == null)
      return;
    XmlViewerNode treeNode = getSelectedTreeNode();
    if (treeNode == null)
      return;
    Node parent = treeNode.getXmlNode();
    if (parent == null)
      return;

    String input = (String)JOptionPane.showInputDialog(this,
      "Please enter name of the new XML node",
      APP_NAME, JOptionPane.PLAIN_MESSAGE,
```

```
      null, null, "");
    if (!isLegalXmlName(input))
      return;

    try {
      Element newElement = m_doc.createElement(input);
      XmlViewerNode nodeElement = new XmlViewerNode(newElement);
      treeNode.addXmlNode(nodeElement);

      m_model.nodeStructureChanged(treeNode);
      TreePath path = m_tree.getSelectionPath();
      if (path != null) {
        path = path.pathByAddingChild(nodeElement);
        m_tree.setSelectionPath(path);
        m_tree.scrollPathToVisible(path);
      }
      m_xmlChanged = true;
    }
    catch (Exception ex) {
      showError(ex, "Error adding new node");
    }
  }

  protected void addNewAttribute() {
    Node node = m_tableModel.getNode();
    if (!(node instanceof Element))
      return;

    String input = (String)JOptionPane.showInputDialog(
      this, "Please enter new attribute name",
      APP_NAME, JOptionPane.PLAIN_MESSAGE,
      null, null, "");
    if (!isLegalXmlName(input))
      return;

    try {
      ((Element)node).setAttribute(input, "");
      setNodeToTable(node);
      for (int k=0; k<m_tableModel.getRowCount(); k++)
        if (m_tableModel.getValueAt(
          k, AttrTableModel.NAME_COLUMN).equals(input))
        {
          m_table.editCellAt(k, AttrTableModel.VALUE_COLUMN);
          break;
        }
      m_xmlChanged = true;
    }
    catch (Exception ex) {
      showError(ex, "Error adding attribute");
    }
  }

  protected void editNode() {
    TreePath path = m_tree.getSelectionPath();
```

8 Adds a new attribute to the currently selected node

8 Edits currently selected node

```
    XmlViewerNode treeNode = getSelectedTreeNode();
    if (treeNode == null)
      return;
    Node node = treeNode.getXmlNode();
    if (node == null)
      return;
    try {
      switch (node.getNodeType()) {
      case Node.ELEMENT_NODE:
        // Find child text node
        for (int k=0; k<treeNode.getChildCount(); k++) {
          XmlViewerNode childNode = (XmlViewerNode)
            treeNode.getChildAt(k);
          Node nd = childNode.getXmlNode();
          if (nd instanceof Text) {
            path = path.pathByAddingChild(childNode);
            m_tree.setSelectionPath(path);
            m_tree.scrollPathToVisible(path);
            m_tree.startEditingAtPath(path);
            return;
          }
        }
        // Not found, so add a new text node
        Text text = m_doc.createTextNode("");
        XmlViewerNode nodeText = new XmlViewerNode(text);
        treeNode.addXmlNode(nodeText);
        m_model.nodeStructureChanged(treeNode);
        path = path.pathByAddingChild(nodeText);
        m_tree.setSelectionPath(path);
        m_tree.scrollPathToVisible(path);
        m_tree.startEditingAtPath(path);
        return;
      case Node.TEXT_NODE:
        m_tree.startEditingAtPath(path);
        return;
      }
    }
    catch (Exception ex) {
      showError(ex, "Error editing node");
    }
  }

  protected void editAttribute() {              ⑧ Edits currently selected attribute
    int row = m_table.getSelectedRow();
    if (row >= 0)
      m_table.editCellAt(row, AttrTableModel.VALUE_COLUMN);
  }

  protected void deleteNode() {                 ⑧ Deletes currently
    TreePath path = m_tree.getSelectionPath();      selected node
    XmlViewerNode treeNode = getSelectedTreeNode();
    if (treeNode == null)
      return;
```

```
        Node node = treeNode.getXmlNode();
        if (node == null)
          return;
        int result = JOptionPane.showConfirmDialog(
          XmlViewer.this, "Delete node "+node.getNodeName()+" ?",
          APP_NAME, JOptionPane.YES_NO_OPTION);
        if (result != JOptionPane.YES_OPTION)
          return;

        try {
          TreeNode treeParent = treeNode.getParent();
          treeNode.remove();
          m_model.nodeStructureChanged(treeParent);
          m_xmlChanged = true;
        }
        catch (Exception ex) {
          showError(ex, "Error deleting node");
        }
      }

      protected void deleteAttribute() {
        int row = m_table.getSelectedRow();
        if (row < 0)
          return;
        Node node = getSelectedNode();
        if (!(node instanceof Element))
          return;

        String name = (String)m_tableModel.getValueAt(row,
          AttrTableModel.NAME_COLUMN);
        int result = JOptionPane.showConfirmDialog(
          XmlViewer.this, "Delete attribute "+name+" ?",
          APP_NAME, JOptionPane.YES_NO_OPTION);
        if (result != JOptionPane.YES_OPTION)
          return;

        try {
          ((Element)node).removeAttribute(name);
          setNodeToTable(node);
          m_xmlChanged = true;
        }
        catch (Exception ex) {
          showError(ex, "Error deletinging attribute");
        }
      }

      // Unchanged code from example 23.3

      public boolean isLegalXmlName(String input) {
        if (input==null || input.length()==0)
          return false;
        if (!(XMLRoutines.isLegalXmlName(input))) {
          JOptionPane.showMessageDialog(this,
            "Invalid XML name", APP_NAME,
```

8 Deletes currently selected attribute

9 Determines whether or not the given string is a legal XML name

```
        JOptionPane.WARNING_MESSAGE);
      return false;
    }
    return true;
  }

  public void showError(Exception ex, String message) {
    ex.printStackTrace();
    JOptionPane.showMessageDialog(this,
      message, APP_NAME,
      JOptionPane.WARNING_MESSAGE);
  }

  // Unchanged code from example 23.3
}

class XmlViewerNode extends DefaultMutableTreeNode {
  public XmlViewerNode(Node node) {
    super(node);
  }
  public Node getXmlNode() {
    Object obj = getUserObject();
    if (obj instanceof Node)
      return (Node)obj;
    return null;
  }

  public void addXmlNode(XmlViewerNode child)
    throws Exception {
    Node node = getXmlNode();
    if (node == null)
      throw new Exception(
        "Corrupted XML node");
    node.appendChild(child.getXmlNode());
    add(child);
  }

  public void remove() throws Exception {
    Node node = getXmlNode();
    if (node == null)
      throw new Exception(
        "Corrupted XML node");
    Node parent = node.getParentNode();
    if (parent == null)
      throw new Exception(
        "Cannot remove root node");
    TreeNode treeParent = getParent();
    if (!(treeParent instanceof DefaultMutableTreeNode))
      throw new Exception(
        "Cannot remove tree node");
    parent.removeChild(node);
    ((DefaultMutableTreeNode)treeParent).remove(this);
  }
```

⑩ Updated to allow addition and removal of child nodes

```
      // Unchanged code from example 23.3
    }

// Unchanged code from example 23.3

class XMLRoutines {
    // Unchanged code from example 23.3
```
⑪ Added method for verifying whether or not a given string is legal XML

```
    public static boolean isLegalXmlName(String input) {
      if (input == null || input.length() == 0)
        return false;
      for (int k=0; k<input.length(); k++) {
        char ch = input.charAt(k);
        if (Character.isLetter(ch) ||
            (ch == '_') || (ch == ':').||
            (k>0 &&
                (Character.isDigit(ch) ||(ch == '.') || (ch == '-'))))
        {
          continue;
        }
        return false;
      }
      return true;
    }
}
```

23.4.1 Understanding the code

Class XmlViewer

❶ This class now has six additional instance variables:

- JButton m_addNodeBtn: toolbar button to add a node.
- JButton m_editNodeBtn: toolbar button to edit a node.
- JButton m_delNodeBtn: toolbar button to delete a node.
- JButton m_addAttrBtn: toolbar button to add an attribute.
- JButton m_editAttrBtn: toolbar button to edit an attribute.
- JButton m_delAttrBtn: toolbar button to delete an attribute.

The custom TreeSelectionListener now invokes our enableNodeButtons() and enableAttrButtons() methods whenever the tree selection changes.

❷ A custom ListSelectionListener is created to invoke enableAttrButtons() whenever the table selection changes. This listener is added to our table model.

❸ The createToolbar() method adds a new button for creating a new XML document which does so by invoking our custom newDocument() method. A new button for adding a new node is added which invokes our custom addNewNode() method. Buttons for editing

❹ and deleting the selected node are added and invoke our custom editNode() and delete-Node() methods respectively. Similarly, buttons for adding, editing, and deleting attributes are added and invoke our custom addNewAttribute(), editAttribute(), and delete-Attribute() methods respectively.

⑤ The `newDocument()` method by uses `JOptionPane` to prompt the user for a root node name, creating a `Document` instance with a root element of that name, creating a `TreeNode` structure using that element, and finally assigning that tree node structure as the tree model.

⑥ The `enableNodeButtons()` method enables the add node button only if the selected node is an instance of `Element`. It enables the edit node and delete node buttons only if the selected node is not `null`.

⑦ The `enableAttrButtons()` method enables the add attribute button only if the selected node is an instance of `Element`. It enables the edit attribute and delete attribute buttons only if there is a table row selected.

⑧ The `addNewNode()`, `editNode()`, `deleteNode()`, `addNewAttribute()`, `editAttribute()`, and `deleteAttribute()` methods perform basic XML and Swing tree and table operations, as well as the use of `JOptionPane`, to update the XML document appropriately.

⑨ The `isLegalXmlName()` method takes a `String` parameter and returns a boolean flag specifying whether or not the `String` is legal according to `XMLRoutine`'s static `isLegalXmlName()` method. If it is not legal a warning message is displayed.

⑩ *Class XmlViewerNode*

The new `addXmlNode()` method is added to enable adding a child node to an existing node.

The `remove()` method is added to allow removal of nodes. Nodes without a parent (such as root nodes) cannot be deleted.

⑪ *Class XMLRoutines*

The new `isLegalXmlName()` method takes a `String` parameter and checks whether the String represents a valid XML element name. The first character can only be a letter character, an "_" (underscore) or a ":" (colon). Remaining characters can be letters, digits, "_"s (underscores), ":"s (colons), "."s (periods) or "-"s (dashes). If the given `String` does not adhere to these rules this method returns `false`.

23.4.2   Running the Code

Figure 23.4 shows our updated XML editor application in action. The figure shows where we've added an Address node with text node Word address. We've also added attributes to the Address node called City, State, ZIP and Street. Try opening the sample XML file and adding, editing, and deleting nodes and attributes.

23.5   *XML EDITOR, PART V: CUSTOM DRAG AND DROP*

This example shows how to implement custom drag and drop behavior to move nodes from one parent node to another. There are several UI features that occur during a custom drag and drop operation in this example:

- The cursor changes based on location indicating whether a drop is or is not available
- The target component changes if a drop is available
- When the drag cursor is hovering over the edge of the scroll pane, scrolling occurs.

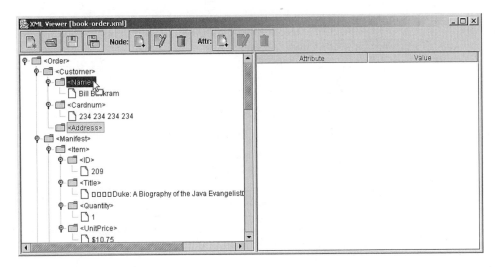

Figure 23.5 XML Editor showing a custom drag and drop in action

NOTE   One good exercise would be to compare this drag and drop behavior to the standard Swing drag and drop behavior covered in chapter 24.

Example 23.5

XmlViewer.java

see \Chapter23\5

```
import java.awt.*;
import java.awt.event.*;
import java.io.*;
import java.util.*;

import javax.swing.*;
import javax.swing.event.*;
import javax.swing.tree.*;
import javax.swing.table.*;

import javax.xml.parsers.*;
import org.w3c.dom.*;

public class XmlViewer
  extends JFrame {

  public static final String APP_NAME = "XML Viewer";

  protected Document m_doc;

  protected JTree  m_tree;
  protected JScrollPane m_treeScrollPane;
```

```java
protected DefaultTreeModel m_model;
protected DefaultTreeCellEditor m_treeEditor;
protected Node m_editingNode = null;

// Unchanged code from example 23.4

protected Cursor m_dragCursor;
protected Cursor m_nodropCursor;
protected XmlViewerNode m_draggingTreeNode;
protected XmlViewerNode m_draggingOverNode;

public XmlViewer() {
  // Unchanged code from example 23.4

  DefaultTreeCellRenderer renderer = new DefaultTreeCellRenderer() {
    Color m_draggingBackground = new Color(0, 0, 128);
    Color m_draggingForeground = Color.white;
    Color m_standardBackground = getBackgroundNonSelectionColor();
    Color m_standardForeground = getTextNonSelectionColor();


    public Component getTreeCellRendererComponent(JTree tree,
      Object value, boolean sel, boolean expanded,
      boolean leaf, int row, boolean hasFocus) {
      if (value.equals(m_draggingOverNode)) {
        setBackgroundNonSelectionColor(m_draggingBackground);
        setTextNonSelectionColor(m_draggingForeground);
        sel = false;
      }
      else {
        setBackgroundNonSelectionColor(m_standardBackground);
        setTextNonSelectionColor(m_standardForeground);
      }

        // Unchanged code from example 23.4
    }
  };
  m_tree.setCellRenderer(renderer);

  // Unchanged code from example 23.4

  m_tableModel = new AttrTableModel();
  m_table = new JTable(m_tableModel);

  m_treeScrollPane = new JScrollPane(m_tree);
  JScrollPane s2 = new JScrollPane(m_table);
  s2.getViewport().setBackground(m_table.getBackground());
  JSplitPane sp = new JSplitPane(JSplitPane.HORIZONTAL_SPLIT,
    m_treeScrollPane, s2);
  sp.setDividerLocation(400);
  sp.setDividerSize(5);
  getContentPane().add(sp, BorderLayout.CENTER);

  // Unchanged code from example 23.4

  enableNodeButtons();
  enableAttrButtons();
```

Custom foreground and background colors to indicate whether a drop is possible **1**

```
      // Load drag-and-drop cursors.
   try {
      ImageIcon icon = new ImageIcon("DragCursor.gif");
      m_dragCursor = Toolkit.getDefaultToolkit().
         createCustomCursor(icon.getImage(),
         new Point(5, 5), "D&D Cursor");
      icon = new ImageIcon("NodropCursor.gif");
      m_nodropCursor = Toolkit.getDefaultToolkit().
         createCustomCursor(icon.getImage(),
         new Point(15, 15), "NoDrop Cursor");
   } catch (Exception ex) {
      System.out.println("Loading cursor: "+ex);
      m_dragCursor = Cursor.getPredefinedCursor(Cursor.HAND_CURSOR);
      m_nodropCursor = m_dragCursor;
   }


   TreeMouseListener dnd = new TreeMouseListener();
   m_tree.addMouseListener(dnd);
   m_tree.addMouseMotionListener(dnd);

   // Unchanged code from example 23.4
}

// Unchanged code from example 23.4

protected boolean dragNodeOverTree(int screenX, int screenY) {
   Point pt = m_treeScrollPane.getLocationOnScreen();
   int x = screenX - pt.x;
   int y = screenY - pt.y;
   if (!m_treeScrollPane.contains(x, y))
   {
      JViewport viewPort = m_treeScrollPane.getViewport();
      int maxHeight =
         viewPort.getView().getHeight()-viewPort.getHeight();
      if (x > 0 && x < m_treeScrollPane.getWidth()
       && y < 0) {
       pt = viewPort.getViewPosition();
       pt.y -= 3;
       pt.y = Math.max(0, pt.y);
       pt.y = Math.min(maxHeight, pt.y);
       viewPort.setViewPosition(pt);
      }
      if (x > 0 && x < m_treeScrollPane.getWidth()
       && y > m_treeScrollPane.getHeight()) {
       pt = viewPort.getViewPosition();
       pt.y += 3;
       pt.y = Math.max(0, pt.y);
       pt.y = Math.min(maxHeight, pt.y);
       viewPort.setViewPosition(pt);
      }
      m_draggingOverNode = null;
      m_tree.repaint();
      return false;
```

Custom foreground and background colors to indicate whether a drop is possible ❷

Determines and repaints target node of drop based coordinates ❸

```
        }

        pt = m_tree.getLocationOnScreen();
        x = screenX - pt.x;
        y = screenY - pt.y;
        TreePath path = m_tree.getPathForLocation(x, y);
        if (path == null) {
          m_draggingOverNode = null;
          m_tree.repaint();
          return false;
        }

        Object obj = path.getLastPathComponent();
        if (obj instanceof XmlViewerNode &&
            ((XmlViewerNode)obj).getXmlNode() instanceof Element) {
          m_draggingOverNode = (XmlViewerNode)obj;
          m_tree.scrollPathToVisible(path);
          m_tree.repaint();
          return true;
        }
        else {
          m_draggingOverNode = null;
          m_tree.repaint();
          return false;
        }
      }

      protected void moveNode(
        XmlViewerNode source, XmlViewerNode target)
      {
        if (source == null || target == null)
          return;
        if (isChildNode(source, target)) {
          JOptionPane.showMessageDialog(this,
            "Cannot move node to it's child node", APP_NAME,
            JOptionPane.WARNING_MESSAGE);
          return;
        }
        try {
          // Remove node from old parent
          TreeNode srcParent = source.getParent();
          source.remove();
          m_model.nodeStructureChanged(srcParent);

          // Add node to new parent
          target.addXmlNode(source);
          m_model.nodeStructureChanged(target);

          TreePath path = getTreePathForNode(source);
          m_tree.setSelectionPath(path);
          m_tree.scrollPathToVisible(path);
          m_xmlChanged = true;
        }
        catch (Exception ex) {
```

❹ **Moves a given node (source) to become the child of target node**

```
        showError(ex, "Error moving node");
    }
  }

  // Unchanged code from example 23.4

  public static TreePath getTreePathForNode(TreeNode node) {
    Vector v = new Vector();
    while (node != null) {
      v.insertElementAt(node, 0);
      node = node.getParent();
    }
    return new TreePath(v.toArray());
  }

  public static boolean isChildNode(TreeNode parent, TreeNode node) {
    if (parent == null || node == null)
      return false;
    if (parent.equals(node))
      return true;
    for (int k=0; k<parent.getChildCount(); k++) {
      TreeNode child = parent.getChildAt(k);
      if (isChildNode(child, node))
        return true;
    }
    return false;
  }

  public static void main(String argv[]) {
    XmlViewer frame = new XmlViewer();
    frame.setDefaultCloseOperation(JFrame.DO_NOTHING_ON_CLOSE);
    frame.setVisible(true);
  }

  // Unchanged code from previous section

  class TreeMouseListener extends MouseInputAdapter {
    private boolean m_isDragging = false;

    public void mousePressed(MouseEvent evt){
      XmlViewerNode treeNode = getSelectedTreeNode();
      if (treeNode != null && treeNode.getXmlNode() instanceof Element)
        m_draggingTreeNode = treeNode;
      m_draggingOverNode = null;
    }

    public void mouseDragged(MouseEvent evt) {
      if (m_draggingTreeNode == null)
        return;
      if (!m_isDragging) {
        // Update cursor only on move, not on click
        m_isDragging = true;
        m_tree.setCursor(m_dragCursor);
      }
      Component src = (Component)evt.getSource();
```

⑤ Custom mouse input adapter providing drag and drop functionality

```
        Point p1 = src.getLocationOnScreen();
        int x = p1.x + evt.getX();
        int y = p1.y + evt.getY();
        if (dragNodeOverTree(x, y))
          m_tree.setCursor(m_dragCursor);
        else
          m_tree.setCursor(m_nodropCursor);
      }

      public void mouseReleased(MouseEvent evt){
        if (m_draggingTreeNode == null)
          return;
        m_tree.setCursor(Cursor.getDefaultCursor());

        moveNode(m_draggingTreeNode, m_draggingOverNode);

        m_isDragging = false;
        m_draggingTreeNode = null;
        m_draggingOverNode = null;
        m_tree.repaint();
      }
    }
  }
}

// Unchanged code from example 23.4
```

23.5.1   Understanding the code

Class XmlViewer

This class has five new instance variables:

- JScrollPane m_treeScrollPane: scroll pane used to hold the tree (this isn't new but we need to reference it from other methods).
- Cursor m_dragCursor: cursor used to indicate a drag and drop will be successful.
- Cursor m_dropCursor: cursor used to indicate a drop would not be successful.
- XmlViewerNode m_draggingTreeNode: reference to the tree node being dragged.
- XmlViewerNode m_draggingOverNode: reference to the tree node the mouse is currently dragging over.

❶ The custom tree cell renderer now uses custom foreground and background colors to indicate when it is the target of a possible drop. In this case it uses a dark blue background color and a white foreground color.

❷ An instance of our custom TreeMouseListener class is added to our tree as a Mouse-Listener and a MouseMotionListener. This is where all the custom drag and drop behavior starts.

❸ The dragNodeOverTree() method takes two int parameters representing coordinates. Given these coordinates the method attempts to locate a node at the given coordinates, set it as the m_draggingOverNode, and repaint the tree so that the target node can be rendered properly by our custom renderer. This method also checks whether the coordinates are beyond the width or height of the visible portion of the tree and scrolls the tree accordingly. This method returns true if the location represents a possible target node.

④ The moveNode() method performs the actual relocation of a node. It takes source and target nodes as parameters, removes the source from its parent, and adds to the target as a child.

The static getTreePathForNode() method returns a TreePath from the root node to the given node passed in as a parameter.

The isChildNode() method takes two nodes as parameters and returns a boolean flag specifying whether or not the second is a child of the first.

⑤ *Class XmlViewer.TreeMouseListener*

This class extends MouseInputAdapter to provide our custom drag and drop behavior. The m_isDragging flag is used to specify whether or not a node drag is currently in progress.

The mousePressed() method retrieves the selected node and sets it as m_draggingTreeNode.

The mouseDragged() method updates the m_isDragging flag if m_draggingTreeNode is not null, and changes the cursor to m_dragCursor. It then uses our custom dragNodeOverTree() to determine how to set the cursor as well as update m_draggingOverNode.

The mouseReleased() method sets the cursor back to its default and invokes our custom moveNode() method to perform an actual node relocation.

Running the code

Figure 23.5 shows our XML editor with a drag and drop in process. The Address node is about to be moved to become a child of the Name node. Note the dark blue background of the name node, and the cursor over it indicating that the drop would be successful if the mouse button is released. Try opening the sample XML file and moving nodes. Note how the cursor changes based on whether or not the target node is a valid new parent for the node being dragged.

C H A P T E R 2 4

Drag and drop

24.1 DRAG AND DROP OVERVIEW

Drag and drop has been supported, in some capacity, since the early days of AWT and Swing. As of Java 1.4, however, these features have been significantly improved and are much easier to work with. Most Swing components now have built-in support for drag and drop operations, and the effort required to implement this behavior has been significantly reduced.

- `JColorChooser`: supports both drag and drop by default
- `JEditorPane`: supports both drag and drop by default
- `JFileChooser`: supports drag by default
- `JFormattedTextField`: supports both drag and drop by default
- `JLabel`: neither supported
- `JList`: supports drag by default
- `JPasswordField`: supports drop by default
- `JTable`: supports drag by default
- `JTextArea`: supports both drag and drop by default
- `JTextField`: supports both drag and drop by default
- `JTextPane`: supports both drag and drop by default
- `JTree`: supports drag by default

Support for dragging is usually disabled by default, but in many cases it can be manually enabled with a setDragEnabled() method. Support for drop is either enabled by default or not supported.

24.1.1 The Transferable interface

interface java.awt.datatransfer. Transferable

The Transferable interface is implemented by classes which can be used in drag and drop operations. An array of java.awt.datatransfer.DataFlavor instances are used to describe the type of format a Transferable's data can appear in. Some flavors include:

- DataFlavor.stringFlavor: supports transfer of a java.lang.String instance.
- DataFlavor.imageFlavor: supports transfer of a java.awt.Image instance.
- DataFlavor.javaFileListFlavor: supports transfer of an instance of java.util.-List where each element is of type java.io.File.
- DataFlavor.javaJVMLocalObjectMimeType: supports transfer of an arbitrary Java object which can be transferred within a JVM session.
- DataFlavor.javaSerializedObjectMimeType: supports transfer of a graph of objects (serialized) that can be transferred between applications and separate JVMs.

To check whether a Transferable object supports a given data flavor we use a Transferable's isDataFlavorSupported() method. The getTransferDataFlavors() method returns an array of DataFlavor objects which shows the various flavors (i.e., formats) the Transferable object's data can be provided in. The getTransferData() method returns the appropriate Object of class type determined by the DataFlavor instance passed as parameter (if it is supported).

24.1.2 Clipboard

class java.awt.datatransfer. Clipboard

This class defines a place to store Transferable objects during a data transfer. The constructor takes a String to use as the clipboard's name which is retrievable using the getName() method. The getContents() method returns the currently stored Transferable object. The setContents() method sets the Transferable object as well as the ClipboardOwner to those specified as parameters. If there is already an existing ClipboardOwner, its lostOwnership() method is invoked before the new ClipboardOwner is assigned.

In every Java session there is a special shared Clipboard instance called the system clipboard. This clipboard interfaces with the clipboard facilities of the native operating system Java is running on. In this way data can be transferred between native programs and Java applications.

24.1.3 The ClipboardOwner interface

interface java.awt.datatransfer. ClipboardOwner

This interface is implemented by classes that need the capability of providing data to a clipboard. It consists of one method: lostOwnership(). This method takes a Clipboard and a Transferable object as parameters. It is intended to notify the object that it is no longer the owner of the contents (the `Transferable` object) of the specified `Clipboard`. Each `Clipboard` instance can have no more than one specified `ClipboardOwner` at any given time.

24.1.4 TransferHandler

class javax.swing.TransferHandler

This class is used as a conduit to transfer `Transferables` to and from Swing components. It handles all interaction with the clipboard to temporarily store the data being transferred. The default implementation's behavior assigns data to a component property by specifying the name of the component property in the constructor. There are three constants used for specifying the kind of transfer operation that can occur through a TransferHandler: `COPY`, `MOVE`, and `COPY_OR_MOVE`.

TransferHandler consists of several methods we are particularly concerned with here:

- `boolean importData()`: causes a transfer of data from a `Transferable` object to a specified `JComponent`. Returns `true` if successful.
- `boolean canImport()`: checks whether a specified `JComponent` can accept a given set of `DataFlavors`.
- `void createTransferable()`: creates a `Transferable` object to use as a conduit for transfering data from the specified `JComponent`.
- `void exportAsDrag()`: initiates a drag operation by transferring the appropriate data from the specified `JComponent` to a `Transferable` object. The `exportDone()` method is called after the transfer completes.
- `void exportDone()`: this method is called after data has been exported. If the operation was of type `MOVE`, this method is intended to be responsible for removing the transferred data from the source component after the transfer has been completed.

The following example shows how to enable drag and drop to transfer text from one text field to another.

Figure 24.1
Drag and drop test application dragging text from first field to second

Example 24.1

DragDropTest.java

see \Chapter24\1

```
import java.awt.*;
import java.awt.datatransfer.*;
import javax.swing.*;

public class DragDropTest extends JFrame {
  public DragDropTest() {
    super("Drag & Drop Test");
```

```
        TransferHandler th = new TransferHandler("text");

        JPanel contentPane = (JPanel) getContentPane();

        JTextField tf1 = new JTextField("DRAG_ME", 10);
        tf1.setTransferHandler(th);
        JTextField tf2 = new JTextField(10);
        tf2.setTransferHandler(th);

        tf1.setDragEnabled(true);

        contentPane.setLayout(new GridLayout(2,2));
        contentPane.add(new JLabel("Text Field (Drag enabled): "));
        contentPane.add(tf1);
        contentPane.add(new JLabel("Text Field (Drag not enabled): "));
        contentPane.add(tf2);

        pack();
    }

    public static void main(String args[]) {
        DragDropTest ddt = new DragDropTest();
        ddt.setDefaultCloseOperation(JFrame.EXIT_ON_CLOSE);
        ddt.show();
    }
}
```

The first text field acts as a drag source and has its dragEnabled property set to true using the setDragEnabled() method. Using a TransferHandler based on the text property, here's what TransferHandler does behind the scenes:

- When a drag is intiated on the first text field the getText() method is used to obtain the text and place it in a Clipboard as a Transferable object.
- When a drop is initiated on the second text field the setText() method is used to set the text to the content of the Transferable object in the clipboard.

Figure 24.1 shows this example in action dragging the text from the first text field and about to drop it in the second.

Customized TransferHandler functionality to support unique drag and drop behavior is easily achievable by overriding a few of the methods described earlier. We'll show how to do this in the fianal example of this chapter.

24.1.5   DropTarget

class java.awt.dnd.DropTarget

A DropTarget is used to enable drops on a component. By passing a Component and a DropTargetListener instance to the constructor, drop events are enabled on the specified component, and the specified DropTargetListener's drop() event is responsible for handling this functionality.

24.1.6 The DropTargetListener interface

interface java.awt.dnd.DropTargetListener

This interface consists of several methods responsible for defining the behavior of various stages of a drop operation. In example 24.3 we'll show how to implement a custom `DropTargetListener` implementation to drop files from the native operating system into a `JDesktopPane`.

NOTE   There are several classes and interfaces in the `java.awt.datatransfer` and `java.awt.dnd` packages we did not discuss here. Because data transfer in Java 1.4 has been simplified considerably, most drag and drop behavior can be implemented without needing to know any more than what we've described. For more complicated, customized implementations you may need to delve deeper into these packages.

24.2 ADDING DRAG AND DROP SUPPORT WITHIN BASIC TEXT EDITOR

This example adds the ability to drag and drop a selected region of text from one internal frame to another in our Basic Text Editor application constructed in chapter 12 (and added to in chapters 14, 16, and 22). Only a few lines of code are necessary.

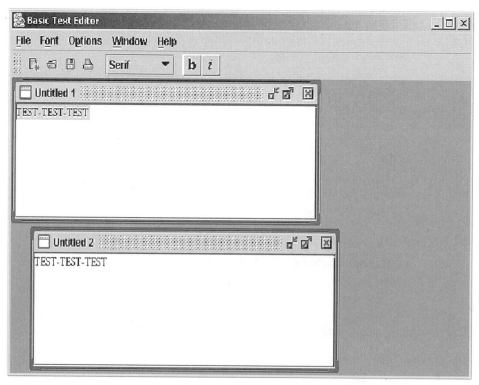

Figure 24.2 `JBasicTextEditor` **with drag and drop between internal frames**

Example 24.2

BasicTextEditor.java

see \Chapter24\2

```java
import java.awt.*;
import java.awt.event.*;
import java.io.*;
import java.util.*;
import java.awt.print.*;

import javax.swing.*;
import javax.swing.border.*;
import javax.swing.event.*;

public class BasicTextEditor extends JFrame {

  public static final String APP_NAME = "Basic Text Editor";

  // Unchanged code from example 22.3

  // Internal frame with editor
  class EditorFrameextends JInternalFrame implements Printable {
    // Unchanged code from example 22.3

    public EditorFrame(File f) {
      super("", true, true, true, true);
      m_currentFile = f;
      setTitle(getDocumentName());
      setDefaultCloseOperation(DO_NOTHING_ON_CLOSE);

      m_editor = new CustomTextArea();
      JScrollPane ps = new JScrollPane(m_editor);
      getContentPane().add(ps, BorderLayout.CENTER);

      // Unchanged code from example 22.3

      m_editor.setDragEnabled(true);
      TransferHandler tr = new TransferHandler("selectedText");
      m_editor.setTransferHandler(tr);
    }

    // Unchanged code from example 22.3
  }

  // Important: this class must be public or invocation will fail
  public class CustomTextArea extends JTextArea {
    public void setSelectedText(String value) {
      replaceSelection(value);
    }
  }
}

// Unchanged code from Chapter 22.3
```

24.2.1 Understanding the code

Class BasicTextEditor.EditorFrame

EditorFrame's text area is now an instance of our custom `CustomTextArea` class. The `drag-Enabled` property is set to `true` on the text area and a `TransferHandler` based on the `selectedText` property is created and assigned to the text area. Note that `JTextComponent` has a `getSelectedText()` method, but there is no `setSelectedText()` method. In order for drag and drop to work with the default `TransferHandler` implementation we are using here, we must implement a `setSelectedText()` method in our `CustomTextArea` class.

Class CustomTextArea

This class is a subclass of `JTextArea` that includes a `setSelectedText()` method which is required for a `TransferHandler` based on the `selectedText` property.

24.2.2 Running the code

Figure 24.2 shows our basic text editor application after having dragged and dropped text from one internal frame into another. Try doing this several times. Note that you first need to select text to drag before a drag will work.

24.3 DRAG AND DROP FILES TO BASIC TEXT EDITOR

This enhancement allows drag and drop of files from other native applications into our Basic Text Editor application. For example, dragging a text file from a Windows desktop into our editor desktop pane, an internal frame is opened containing the contents of that file.

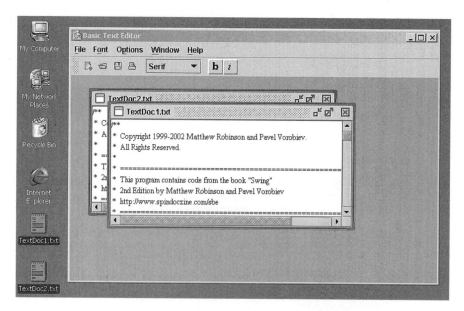

Figure 24.3   Basic Text Editor with native drag and drop file support

Example 24.3

BasicTextEditor.java

see \Chapter24\3

```java
import java.awt.*;
import java.awt.event.*;
import java.io.*;
import java.util.*;
import java.awt.print.*;
import java.awt.dnd.*;
import java.awt.datatransfer.*;

import javax.swing.*;
import javax.swing.border.*;
import javax.swing.event.*;

public class BasicTextEditor extends JFrame {

  public static final String APP_NAME = "Basic Text Editor";

  // Unchanged code from example 24.2

  public BasicTextEditor() {
    super(APP_NAME);
    setSize(600, 400);

    m_fonts = new Font[FONTS.length];
    for (int k=0; k<FONTS.length; k++)
      m_fonts[k] = new Font(FONTS[k], Font.PLAIN, 12);

    m_desktop = new JDesktopPane();
    getContentPane().add(m_desktop, BorderLayout.CENTER);

    new DropTarget(m_desktop, new FileDropper());

    JMenuBar menuBar = createMenuBar();
    setJMenuBar(menuBar);

    // Unchanged code from example 24.2
  }

  // Unchanged code from example 24.2

  public static void main(String argv[]) {
    BasicTextEditor frame = new BasicTextEditor();
    frame.setDefaultCloseOperation(JFrame.DO_NOTHING_ON_CLOSE);
    frame.setVisible(true);
  }

  class FileDropper extends DropTargetAdapter {
    public void drop(DropTargetDropEvent e) {
      try {
        DropTargetContext context = e.getDropTargetContext();
        e.acceptDrop(DnDConstants.ACTION_COPY_OR_MOVE);
        Transferable t  = e.getTransferable();
        Object data = t.getTransferData(DataFlavor.javaFileListFlavor);
```

```
        if (data instanceof java.util.List) {
          java.util.List list = (java.util.List)data;
          for (int k=0; k<list.size(); k++) {
            Object dataLine = list.get(k);
            if (dataLine instanceof File)
              addEditorFrame((File)dataLine);
          }
        }
        context.dropComplete(true);
      }
      catch (Exception ex) {
        ex.printStackTrace();
      }
    }
  }
}

// Unchanged code from example 24.2
```

24.3.1 Understanding the code

Class BasicTextEditor

The only addition to this constructor is the creation of a `DropTarget` instance with the desktop pane as the target component and an instance of our custom `FileDropper` class.

Class BasicTextEditor.FileDropper

This class extends `DropTargetAdapter` (a concrete `DropTargetListener` implementation in the `java.awt.dnd` package) and overrides the `drop()` method. Our new `drop()` method accepts the drop using `DropTargetDropEvent`'s `acceptDrop()` method, and obtains the transferred data which is expected to be an instance of `java.util.List` (which is expected to contain all the selected `File`s). We iterate through the list and for each item that is a `File` instance we send it to our `addEditorFrame()` method which opens that file in an internal frame editor.

24.3.2 Running the code

Figure 24.3 shows our Basic Text Editor application after having dragged two text files from a Windows 2000 desktop into the desktop pane. Try dropping other types of documents such as .java and .html files.

24.4 DRAG AND DROP WITH JAVA OBJECTS

This example shows how to drag and drop Java objects between two lists. The component developed here contains two mutable `JList`s: one containing an initial set of items and the other initially empty. Items can be moved back and forth between both lists using either buttons or drag and drop operations.

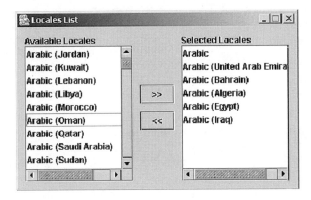

Figure 24.4
Mutable list components
which support drag and drop

Example 24.4

DnDList.java

see \Chapter24\4

```java
import java.awt.*;
import java.awt.event.*;
import java.awt.datatransfer.*;
import java.io.*;
import java.util.*;

import javax.swing.*;
import javax.swing.border.*;
import javax.swing.event.*;

public class DnDList extends JFrame {
  public DnDList() {
    super("Locales List");

    Locale[] allLocales = Locale.getAvailableLocales();
    Locale[] selLocales = new Locale[0];

    TwoListsPanel pp = new TwoListsPanel(
      allLocales, "Available Locales",
      selLocales, "Selected Locales");
    getContentPane().add(pp, BorderLayout.CENTER);

    setResizable(false);
    pack();
  }

  public static void main(String argv[]) {
    DnDList frame = new DnDList();
    frame.setDefaultCloseOperation(JFrame.EXIT_ON_CLOSE);
    frame.setVisible(true);
  }
}
```

1 Array of all
available locales

2 Locale arrays
used to create
an instance
of our custom
TwoListsPanel
component

```
class TwoListsPanel extends JPanel {
  public static final int LIST_WIDTH = 150;
  public static final int LIST_HEIGHT = 200;

  private boolean m_selectionChanged = false;

  private MutableList m_leftList;
  private MutableList m_rightList;

  public TwoListsPanel(Object[] leftData, String leftTitle,
      Object[] rightData, String rightTitle) {
    super(new BorderLayout(10, 10));
    setBorder(new EmptyBorder(10, 10, 10, 10));

    m_leftList = new MutableList(leftData);
    m_leftList.setCellRenderer(new LocaleListRenderer());
    JScrollPane spl = new JScrollPane(m_leftList);
    JPanel p2l = new JPanel(new BorderLayout());
    p2l.setPreferredSize(
      new Dimension(LIST_WIDTH, LIST_HEIGHT));
    p2l.add(spl, BorderLayout.CENTER);
    p2l.add(new JLabel(leftTitle), BorderLayout.NORTH);
    add(p2l, BorderLayout.WEST);

    m_rightList = new MutableList(rightData);
    m_rightList.setCellRenderer(new LocaleListRenderer());
    JScrollPane spr = new JScrollPane(m_rightList);
    JPanel p2r = new JPanel(new BorderLayout());
    p2r.setPreferredSize(
      new Dimension(LIST_WIDTH, LIST_HEIGHT));
    p2r.add(spr, BorderLayout.CENTER);
    p2r.add(new JLabel(rightTitle), BorderLayout.NORTH);
    add(p2r, BorderLayout.EAST);

    JPanel p2c = new JPanel();
    p2c.setLayout(new BoxLayout(p2c, BoxLayout.Y_AXIS));
    p2c.add(Box.createVerticalGlue());

    JButton btnToRight = new JButton(">>");
    btnToRight.setRequestFocusEnabled(false);
    btnToRight.addActionListener(new LeftToRightMover());
    p2c.add(btnToRight);
    p2c.add(Box.createVerticalStrut(10));

    JButton btnToLeft = new JButton("<<");
    btnToLeft.setRequestFocusEnabled(false);
    btnToLeft.addActionListener(new RightToLeftMover());
    p2c.add(btnToLeft);

    p2c.add(Box.createVerticalGlue());
    add(p2c, BorderLayout.CENTER);
  }

  public boolean selectionChanged() {
    return m_selectionChanged;
  }
```

3 Custom component containing two mutable lists with ability to move items between lists with buttons or drag and drop

4 Custom mutable list component and custom renderer assigned to it

4 Custom mutable list component and custom renderer assigned to it

5 Custom ActionListeners to perform movement of item from one list to another

5 Custom ActionListeners to perform movement of item from one list to another

```java
  public void moveFromLeftToRight(Object obj) {
    if (obj == null)
      return;
    m_leftList.removeElement(obj);
    m_rightList.addElement(obj);
  }

  public void moveFromRightToLeft(Object obj) {
    if (obj == null)
      return;
    m_rightList.removeElement(obj);
    m_leftList.addElement(obj);
  }

  class LeftToRightMover implements ActionListener {
    public void actionPerformed(ActionEvent evt) {
      Object[] values = m_leftList.getSelectedValues();
      for (int k=0; k<values.length; k++) {
        m_leftList.removeElement(values[k]);
        m_rightList.addElement(values[k]);
        m_selectionChanged = true;
      }

      m_leftList.repaint();
      m_rightList.repaint();
    }
  }

  class RightToLeftMover implements ActionListener {
    public void actionPerformed(ActionEvent evt) {
      Object[] values = m_rightList.getSelectedValues();
      for (int k=0; k<values.length; k++) {
        m_rightList.removeElement(values[k]);
        m_leftList.addElement(values[k]);
        m_selectionChanged = true;
      }
      m_leftList.repaint();
      m_rightList.repaint();
    }
  }

  class LocaleListRenderer extends DefaultListCellRenderer {
    public Component getListCellRendererComponent(JList list,
      Object value, int index, boolean isSelected,
      boolean cellHasFocus) {

      if (value instanceof Locale)
        value = ((Locale)value).getDisplayName();

      return super.getListCellRendererComponent(list,
        value, index, isSelected, cellHasFocus);
    }
  }
}
```

6 Moves an item from left list to right list

6 Moves an item from right list to left list

7 ActionListener to move items from left list to right list

8 ActionListener to move items from right list to left list

9 Custom renderer for displaying locale objects using their display name

```
class MutableList extends JList {
  private DefaultListModel m_model;

  public MutableList() {
    m_model = new DefaultListModel();
    setModel(m_model);
    installDnD();
  }

  public MutableList(Object[] arr) {
    m_model = new DefaultListModel();
    for (int k=0; k<arr.length; k++)
      m_model.addElement(arr[k]);
    setModel(m_model);
    installDnD();
  }

  public MutableList(Vector v) {
    m_model = new DefaultListModel();
    for (int k=0; k<v.size(); k++)
      m_model.addElement(v.elementAt(k));
    setModel(m_model);
    installDnD();
  }

  public void addElement(Object obj) {
    m_model.addElement(obj);
    repaint();
  }

  public void removeElement(Object obj) {
    m_model.removeElement(obj);
    repaint();
  }

  public Object[] getData() {
    return m_model.toArray();
  }

  protected void installDnD() {
    setDragEnabled(true);
    setTransferHandler(new ListTransferHandler());
    DnDStarter starter = new DnDStarter();
    addMouseListener(starter);
    addMouseMotionListener(starter);
  }

  class DnDStarter extends MouseInputAdapter {
    public void mousePressed(MouseEvent e) {
      TransferHandler th =
        MutableList.this.getTransferHandler();
      th.exportAsDrag(
        MutableList.this, e, TransferHandler.MOVE);
    }
  }
}
```

10 Custom list component with add mutable (add/remove) capabilities

11 Enables drag operations (drop operations enabled by default) and assigns appropriate **TransferHandler**

12 Custom mouse input adapter to invoke a data export when a mouse press occurs

```java
class ArrayTransfer implements Transferable {
  public static DataFlavor FLAVOUR;

  static {
    try {
      FLAVOUR = new DataFlavor(
        DataFlavor.javaJVMLocalObjectMimeType);
    }
    catch (Exception ex) {
      ex.printStackTrace();
    }
  }

  protected JComponent m_source;
  protected Object[] m_arr;

  public ArrayTransfer(JComponent source, Object[] arr) {
    m_source = source;
    m_arr = arr;
  }

  public Object getTransferData(DataFlavor flavor)
      throws UnsupportedFlavorException, IOException {
    if (!isDataFlavorSupported(flavor))
      throw new UnsupportedFlavorException(flavor);
    return this;
  }

  public boolean isDataFlavorSupported(DataFlavor flavor) {
    return FLAVOUR.equals(flavor);
  }

  public DataFlavor[] getTransferDataFlavors() {
    return new DataFlavor[] { FLAVOUR };
  }

  public JComponent getSource() {
    return m_source;
  }

  public Object[] getData() {
    return m_arr;
  }
}

class ListTransferHandler extends TransferHandler {
  public boolean importData(JComponent c, Transferable t) {
    if (!(c instanceof MutableList))
      return false;
    MutableList list = (MutableList)c;
    try {
      Object obj = t.getTransferData(ArrayTransfer.FLAVOUR);
      if (!(obj instanceof ArrayTransfer))
        return false;
      ArrayTransfer at = (ArrayTransfer)obj;

// block transfer to self!
```

13 **Transferable representing an array of objects**

Custom TransferHandler to serve as a conduit for dragging and dropping MutableList data

14

```
        if (c.equals(at.getSource()))
          return false;

        Object[] arr = at.getData();
        for (int k=0; k<arr.length; k++)
          list.addElement(arr[k]);
      }
      catch (Exception ex) {
        ex.printStackTrace();
        return false;
      }
      return true;
    }

    public boolean canImport(JComponent c,
        DataFlavor[] transferFlavors) {
      if (!(c instanceof MutableList))
        return false;
      for (int k=0; k<transferFlavors.length; k++)
        if (transferFlavors[k].equals(ArrayTransfer.FLAVOUR))
          return true;
      return false;
    }

    public int getSourceActions(JComponent c) {
      if (!(c instanceof MutableList))
        return NONE;
      return COPY_OR_MOVE;
    }

    protected Transferable createTransferable(JComponent c) {
      if (!(c instanceof MutableList))
        return null;
      Object[] arr = ((JList)c).getSelectedValues();
      return new ArrayTransfer(c, arr);
    }

    protected void exportDone(
     JComponent source, Transferable t, int action)
    {
      if (!(source instanceof MutableList))
        return;
      MutableList list = (MutableList)source;
      if (!(action == COPY_OR_MOVE || action == MOVE))
        return;
      try {
        Object obj = t.getTransferData(ArrayTransfer.FLAVOUR);
        if (!(obj instanceof ArrayTransfer))
          return;
        ArrayTransfer at = (ArrayTransfer)obj;
        if (!source.equals(at.getSource()))
          return;
        Object[] arr = at.getData();
        for (int k=0; k<arr.length; k++)
```

```
                list.removeElement(arr[k]);
        }
        catch (Exception ex) {
          ex.printStackTrace();
        }
      }
    }
  }
```

24.4.1   Understanding the code

Class DnDList

❶ This class extends `JFrame` to form the main container for the example. The constructor starts
❷ by creating an array of all available `Locale`s, as well as an empty array of `Locale`s. These
arrays are used to create an instance of our custom `TwoListsPanel` component.

❸ *Class TwoListsPanel*

❹ This class represents a component containing two instances of our `MutableList` component
as well as two buttons used to move selected items back and forth between the two `Mutable-
Lists`. An instance of our custom `LocaleListRenderer` (discussed below) is used as the
❺ `ListCellRenderer` for the `MutableLists`. The arrays passed to the `TwoListsPanel`
constructor are sent to the `MutableList` constructors respectively. The two buttons receive
instances of our custom `LeftToRightMover` and `RightToLeftMover` `ActionListeners`
which invoke our `moveFromLeftToRight()` and `moveFromRightToLeft()` methods
respectively.

❻ The `moveFromLeftToRight()` method takes an `Object` as parameter, removes it from the
left `MutableList` and adds it to the right `MutableList`. The `moveFromRightToLeft()`
method does the opposite. These methods are used during drag and drop operations (not by
the buttons).

❼ *Class TwoListsPanel.LeftToRightMover*

This `ActionListener` implementation removes all selected items from the left `MutableL-
ist` and adds them to the right `MutableList`.

❽ *Class TwoListsPanel.RightToLeftMover*

This `ActionListener` implementation removes all selected items from the right `Mutable-
List` and adds them to the left `MutableList`.

❾ *Class TwoListsPanel.LocaleListRenderer*

This custom `ListCellRenderer` uses `Locale`'s `displayName` property for display rather
than the default value provided by `toString()`.

❿ *Class MutableList*

This class extends `JList` to add mutable behavior. Two constructors allow creation by taking
either an array of `Objects` or a `Vector` as a parameter. In either case the collection is iterated
through and each item is added to the model. Then the `installDnd()` method is called to
enable drag and drop operations on the component.

Two methods, `addElement()` and `removeElement()`, are used to provide the mutable behavior to this `JList` subclass by invoking similar methods on the list model.

⑪ The `installDnD()` method sets `MutableList`'s `dragEnabled` property to `true` and assigns it an instance of our custom `ListTransferHandler`. An instance of our custom `DnDStarter` class is also added as a `MouseListener` and `MouseMotionListener` to invoke a data export on a mouse press.

⑫ *Class MutableList.DnDStarter*

This `MouseInputAdapter` subclass invokes a data export on `MutableList`'s `Transfer-Handler` when a mouse press occurs.

⑬ *Class ArrayTransfer*

This implementation of `Transferable` represents an array of `Object`s that can be used in data transfer operations. The constructor takes a source `JComponent` and an `Object` array as parameters.

The `getTransferData()` method returns a reference to this object itself because it represents the data being transferred.

The supported `DataFlavor` is `DataFlavor.javaJVMLocalObjectMimeType` and the `isDataFlavorSupported()` method only returns `true` if the `DataFlavor` parameter matches this type.

The `getSource()` method returns the source `JComponent` and the `getData()` method returns the array of `Object`s.

⑭ *Class ListTransferHandler*

This class extends `TransferHandler` and overrides the `importData()`, `canImport()`, `getSourceActions()`, `createTransferable()`, and `exportDone()` methods to build a custom conduit for dragging and dropping `MutableList` data from one `MutableList` to another.

The `importData()` method is called when a drop is initiated. This implementation returns `false` if the target component passed as parameter is not a `MutableList`. If it is, this method checks first whether the `Transferable` is an instance of `ArrayTransfer` and returns `false` if not. Then the method checks that the target component is not the same as the source component to prevent dropping data to the same list it came from. If all checks out, each `Object` in the `ArrayTransfer`'s `Object` array is added to the target `MutableList` with its `add-Element()` method. If the import occurs successfully this method returns `true`.

The `canImport()` method is called to check whether a given component can import (i.e., accept a drop) of a given array of `DataFlavor`s. This implementation checks whether the target component is an instance of `MutableList` and whether the `DataFlavor`s are of type `DataFlavor.javaJVMLocalObjectMimeType`. If all checks out the method returns `true`.

The `getSourceActions()` method returns the `TransferHandler` action type based on the type of the source component passed in as a parameter. This implementation checks whether the source component is an instance of `MutableList` and if not returns `NONE`. Otherwise it returns `COPY_OR_MOVE`.

The `createTransferable()` method is responsible for creating a `Transferable` instance containing the data from the source component to transfer. This implementation checks whether the source component is an instance of `MutableList` and if not returns `null`.

Otherwise it retrieves the source `MutableList`'s selected items as an array of `Objects` and creates and returns an `ArrayTransfer` instance containing this array.

The `exportDone()` method is called when a drag has been initiated. This implementation checks whether the source component is an instance of `MutableList` and whether the action type is either `MOVE` or `COPY_OR_MOVE`. If so, the `Transferable`'s data is retrieved as an `Object`. If this `Object` is not an instance of `ArrayTransfer` the method returns. Otherwise it checks to ensure that the source component of the export is in fact the same source component the data in the `MutableList` came from. If so, this data is then removed from the source `MutableList`.

24.4.2   Running the code

Figure 24.4 shows our example application after having dragged and dropped the first six locales from the left list into the right list. Try selecting multiple items from either list and dragging and dropping them to the other list. Try moving one item at a time with the buttons. Note that in both cases moved items appear on the bottom of the list they are moved to (rather than occupying their old location). Also note that you cannot drop items in the same list.

APPENDIX A

Java Web Start

Java Web Start technology provides the ability to download and launch Java applications with a single click of an HTML link in the browser. The only prerequisite is that Java Web Start be installed on the client machine (similar to Adobe Acrobat or the Real Audio player). Java Web Start also manages versions of the program automatically and caches the current version, so that only one download of the application is required until a new version is posted.

With Java Web Start the user can run applications locally even while not connected to the Internet (because they are cached). Java Web Start applications are run in their own ìsand-boxî, meaning that they have limited access to local files and resources if they are not from a trusted source.

Underlying Java Web Start is the Java Network Launching Protocol and API (JNLP) which, as of this writing, is currently under development. A new .jnlp file type has been defined to describe how to launch a Java Web Start application.

How to deploy an application with Java Web Start

The Java Web Start Developer's Guide is referenced here several times. To view this online see: http://java.sun.com/products/javawebstart/docs/developersguide.html

1 In order for clients of a Java Web Start application to run the application they must first download Java Web Start. It can be downloaded here: http://java.sun.com/products/javawebstart. A link to this page should be included on the page where the link to your Java Web Start application resides.

2 Package your application into a jar file. For example, if all your application's class files are located in one directory, a command such as the following will create a jar file containing your entire application:

```
jar -cvf HTMLEditor.jar *.class
```
For more information on creating jar files see:

http://java.sun.com/docs/books/tutorial/jar/index.html

3   Your web server needs to know to launch Java Web Start whenever a JNLP file is encountered. This is done by configuring your web server so that files with the `.jnl` extension are set to the `application/x-java-jnlp-file` MIME type (you may need to check your web server's documentation to find out how to accomplish this).

4   To create a JNLP file describing how Java Web Start should launch your application, use the following as a template and modify it for your needs:

```xml
<?xml version="1.0" encoding="utf-8"?>
<!-- JNLP File for HTMLEditor Example -->
<jnlp  spec="1.0+"  codebase="http://www.manning.com/sbe/files/HTMLEdi-
tor/" href="HTMLEditor.jnlp">
  <information>
    <title>HTML Editor Application</title>
    <vendor>Sun Microsystems, Inc.</vendor>
    <homepage href="HTMLEditor.html"/>
    <description>HTMLEditor Example</description>
    <description kind="short">An HTML editor application
      constructed in Chapter 20.</description>
    <icon href="logo.gif"/>
    <offline-allowed/>
  </information>
  <security>
    <all-permissions/>
  </security>
  <resources>
    <j2se version="1.3"/>
    <jar href="HTMLEditor.jar"/>
  </resources>
  <application-desc main-class="HTMLEditor"/>
</jnlp>
```

> **NOTE**   The Java Web Start Developer's Guide details the meaning of the JNLP XML tags and how to use them.

5   The application jar file and the JNLP file must be placed on the web server along with an HTML file containing a link to the JNLP file such as:

```html
<html>
  <head>
    <title>HTMLEditor Java Web Start Example</title>
  </head>
  <body>
    <a href="HTMLEditor.jnlp">Launch HTMLEditor</a>
  </body>
</html>
```

> **NOTE**   The Java Web Start Developer's Guide shows how to use JavaScript to detect whether or not the client has Java Web Start installed, and display an appropriate message if not.

That's it! Assuming you've performed each step without error and your JNLP file is valid, your application should start right up using Java Web Start when you click the link in the HTML file.

For more detailed information regarding security and the use of digital signatures, syntax of the JNLP file format, and using the JNLP API (to control caching, file access, printing, clipboard operations, etc.) see the Developer's Guide.

APPENDIX B

Resources

SWING REFERENCES

1 Andrews, Mark. "Accessibility and the Swing Set." *The Swing Connection*, Sun Microsystems, 1999. http://java.sun.com/products/jfc/tsc/articles/accessibility/index.html

2 Andrews, Mark. "Getting Started with Swing." *The Swing Connection*, Sun Microsystems, 1998. http://java.sun.com/products/jfc/tsc/articles/getting_started/index.html

3 Andrews, Mark. "Introducing Swing Architecture." *The Swing Connection*, Sun Microsystems, 1998. http://java.sun.com/products/jfc/tsc/articles/architecture/index.html

4 Drye, Stephen and William Wake. *Java Foundation Classes: Swing Reference*. Manning Publications, 1999.

5 Eckstein, Robert, Marc Loy and Dave Wood. *Java Swing*. O'Reilly & Associates, 1998.

6 Fowler, Amy. "Mixing Heavy and Light Components." *The Swing Connection,* Sun Microsystems, 1998. http://java.sun.com/products/jfc/tsc/articles/mixing/index.html

7 Fowler, Amy. "Painting in AWT and Swing." *The Swing Connection*, Sun Microsystems, 1998. http://java.sun.com/products/jfc/tsc/articles/painting/index.html

8 Geary, David. *Graphic Java 2, Mastering the JFC: AWT* (Sun Microsystems Press Java Series). Prentice Hall, 1999.

9 Geary, David. *Graphic Java 2, Mastering the JFC: Swing* (Sun Microsystems Press Java Series). Prentice Hall, 1999.

10 Gutz, Steven. *Up to Speed With Swing: User Interfaces With Java Foundation Classes.* Manning Publications, 1998.

11 Joshi, Daniel and Pavel Vorobiev. *JFC: Java Foundation Classes*. IDG Books Worldwide, 1998.

12 Kar, Ralph. "Component Orientation in Swing," *The Swing Connection*, Sun Microsystems, 1999. http://java.sun.com/products/jfc/tsc/articles/bidi/index.html

13 Muller, Hans and Kathy Walrath. "Threads and Swing," *The Swing Connection*. Sun Microsystems, 1998. http://java.sun.com/products/jfc/tsc/articles/threads/threads1.html

14 Muller, Hans and Kathy Walrath. "Using a Swing Worker Thread," *The Swing Connection*. Sun Microsystems, 1998. http://java.sun.com/products/jfc/tsc/articles/threads/threads2.html

15 Prinzing, Tim. "How to Customize a Text Editor," *The Swing Connection*. Sun Microsystems, 1998. http://java.sun.com/products/jfc/tsc/articles/text/editor_kit/index.html

16 Prinzing, Tim. "Using the Swing Text Package," *The Swing Connection*. Sun Microsystems, 1998. http://java.sun.com/products/jfc/tsc/articles/text/overview/

17 Ryan, Chris. "The Java Look and Feel High-Level Specification," *The Swing Connection*. Sun Microsystems, 1998. http://java.sun.com/products/jfc/tsc/articles/jlf/index.html

18 Sun Microsystems. "Coming Swing API Changes for Java 2 SDK, Standard Edition, v. 1.4," *The Swing Connection*. Sun Microsystems, 2001. http://java.sun.com/products/jfc/tsc/articles/merlin/index.html

19 Topley, Kim. *Core Java Foundation Classes* (Core Series). Prentice Hall, 1998.

20 Violet, Scott. "The Element Interface," *The Swing Connection*. Sun Microsystems, 1999. http://java.sun.com/products/jfc/tsc/articles/text/element_interface/

21 Violet, Scott. "How the Swing Text Package Handles Attributes," *The Swing Connection*. Sun Microsystems, 1999. http://java.sun.com/products/jfc/tsc/articles/text/attributes/

22 Violet, Scott. "Tabbing in Text Documents," *The Swing Connection*. Sun Microsystems, 1999. http://java.sun.com/products/jfc/tsc/articles/text/tabs/

23 Violet, Scott. "Understanding the ElementBuffer," *The Swing Connection*. Sun Microsystems, 1999. http://java.sun.com/products/jfc/tsc/articles/text/element_buffer/

24 Wilson, Steve. "The Look and Feel Class Reference," *The Swing Connection*. Sun Microsystems, 1998. http://java.sun.com/products/jfc/tsc/articles/lookandfeel_reference/index.html

Other sources

1 *JavaSoft resources*
   The JFC product site
   http://java.sun.com/products/jfc/

2 *The Swing Connection:*
   http://java.sun.com/products/jfc/tsc/

3 "Creating a GUI with JFC/Sfwing" java Tutorial trail:
   http://java.sun.com/docs/books/tutorial/uiswing/index.html

4 The Java Look and Feel Design Guidelines, 2nd edition:
   http://java.sun.com/products/jlf/ed2/guidelines.html

Examples

1 CodeGuru
http://www.codeguru.com/java/Swing/

2 Global OnLine Japan:
http://www2.gol.com/users/tame/swing/examples/SwingExamples.html

Magazines

1 JavaWorld magazine: http://www.javaworld.com

2 Java Developers Journal: http://www.javadevelopersjournal.com/

3 JavaPro magazine: http://www.devx.com/javapro/

Mailing lists

1 To subscribe to either list, send a message to the corresponding email address with body of the form "subscribe username@domain.com".
to unsubscribe send a message to the appropriate email address with empty body:
swing-unsubscribe@eos.dk
advanced-swing-unsubscribe@eos.dk

2 A request to subscribe or unsubscribe will be followed by an auto generated confirmation email.

3 Simply reply to this email to complete the intended action. Note that most subscribers are subscribed to both lists, so we recommend that any given message be posted to exclusively one or the other.

USER INTERFACE DESIGN REFERENCES

...recommeded and referenced by David Anderson, UI Guidelines author

User Task Analysis and User Centered Design

1 Beyer, Hugh and Karen Holtzblatt. *Contextual Design*. Morgan Kaufmann, 1997.

2 Hackos, JoAnn, and Janice Redish. *User and Task Analysis for Interface Design*. John Wiley, 1998.

3 Robert, Dave, Dick Berry, Scott Isensee, John Mullaly, and Dave Roberts. *Designing for the User with OVID*. MacMillan, 1998.

User Interaction Analysis

1 Anderson, David J. *User Interface Analysis*. White Paper, 1999. http://www.uidesign.net

User Interface Design

1 Arlov, Laura. *GUI Design for Dummies*. IDG, 1997.

2 Cooper, Alan. *About Face: The Essentials of User Interface Design*. IDG, 1995.

3 Norman, Donald. *The Design of Everyday Things*. Doubleday, reissued 1990.

4 Norman, Donald. *The Things that Make Us Smart*. Perseus Press, 1994.

5 Schneiderman, Ben. *Designing the User Interface*, 3rd ed. Addison Wesley, 1997.

Graphic Design

1 Horton, William. *The Icon Book*. Wiley, 1997.

2 Mullet, Keven and Darrell Sano. *Designing Visual Interfaces - Communication Oriented Techniques*. Sunsoft, Prentice Hall, 1995.

3 Tufte, Edward. *The Visual Display of Quantitative Information*. Graphic Press, 1992.

4 Tufte, Edward. *Envisioning Information*. Graphic Press, 1990.

5 Tufte, Edward. *Visual Explanations*. Graphic Press, 1997.

Object-Oriented Analysis and Design

1 Coad, Peter, et al. *Java Modeling in Color with UML: Enterprise Components and Process*. Prentice Hall, 1999.

2 Coad, Peter, et al. *Java Design: Building Better Apps and Applets*, 2nd ed. Prentice Hall, 1998.

index